ABOUT THE AUTHORS

Both David Moore and Philip Williamson have been involved with assessing high quality wine for the best part of 20 years. Both have travelled widely and been exposed to hands-on winemaking from Bordeaux to Australia. During the past 10 years both writers have contributed to a diverse range of wine information media. The authors were influential in the establishment of the Oz Clarke's Wine Guide CD Rom, working in both a consultancy and editing role over several years, and have also contributed to several other Oz Clarke titles. They were also involved with the London based *Vinopolis Wine Experience* in its inception, ensuring its authenticity as a major Wine tourist attraction. In 2000-2001 they collaborated with Oz Clarke as wine judges for *Wine Today Europe* for the *New York Times*.

From 2001 the pair pooled their substantial wine tasting resources to set about creating a wine guide of unprecedented depth and scope. The result, the critically acclaimed *Wine behind the label* (first edition 2003) covers all the world's top wine producers, and their wines, in a truly global context, in a way no other wine book has before. Rejecting a UK-centred approach to wine writing and assessment, Williamson and Moore actively seek out new producers, travelling extensively to visit them at their wineries or meet them at the most important of the world's major wine fairs. Crucially, David and Philip continue to have no commercial links with wine producers in order to maintain their independent stance and unreserved critical analysis.

The 2006 edition of Wine Wizards includes information from *The Top 100 UK Restaurant Wine Lists* by Neville Blech. Neville has had long experience in both the wine and restaurant trades. His particular expertise in matching fine wine and food, and skill in compiling wine lists has been used in conjunction with the wine ratings from *Wine behind the label*.

First published in 2005 by Williamson Moore
13 Rances Way Winchester Hampshire SO22 4PN United Kingdom
Tel/Fax +44 (0)1962 625 539
E-mail: info@williamson-moore.co.uk

A catalogue record for this book is available from the British Library.

ISBN 0-9544097-7-9

Editorial assistance from Bill Evans and Ed Francis

Designed by Davis Wadicci

Printed and bound in Great Britain by Ashford Colour Press Ltd, Fareham, Hants

Wine Wizards

Philip Williamson & David Moore

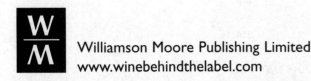

Williamson Moore Publishing Limited
www.winebehindthelabel.com

Contents

Wine Wizards - the concept

Wine Wizards is the new look compact wine guide from Williamson and Moore, an enhanced version of our 2005 pocket guide. It is has been distilled from *Wine behind the label* 2006, the most comprehensive single volume guide and analysis of the world's best wine producers ever produced. The majority of producer profiles are reproduced here in a condensed form together with the most important of the individually rated wines. Fully up-to-date, it is intended to be accessible to the novice and learned alike. The convenient size obviously makes it more usuable when browsing for wine in a shop or even scanning a restaurant wine list but also lightens the load when travelling.

What makes it different?

Wine Wizards we believe is like no other wine guide in this format. It concentrates only on the regions and the producers that produce the world's best and most interesting wines. What's more every wine is rated and price coded. Where possible there are also codes for UK stockists. Even one star wines are of good quality so this guide may be used to explore the ever expanding vinous world with confidence. Contrast the best new wines from France, Italy, Spain, Portugal, Germany or Austria with those from Australia, New Zealand, South Africa or North or South America. Also included is information from *The Top 100 UK Restaurant Wine Lists* to help you avoid having a great dining experience let down by a poor or over-priced wine list.

Winemaking and a wine's origins

We've also tried to provide some insight as to where wine quality and character come from - the most relevant aspects of winemaking (eg oak), viticulture (yield), and vineyard site (as well as vintages) that contribute to what's in your glass. There is also information on the extent of the wine's manipulation such as fining and/or filtration, and whether organic or biodynamic practices are employed. We are also keeping tabs on the biggest premium brands as some famous names have now lost the grape sources which contributed to their early quality and fame.

Tasting, ratings, and assessing producers

Our Quality Rating (see **How to use this guide**) is intended to give a truer assessment of wine quality than a vintage dependent point score. It is nearly always based on scores from a minimum of two recent vintages. Wine shows and competitions encourage the production of wines of flattering first impressions but don't always reward those that show at their best with age. Nor do they address the implications of the vintage characteristics. Rather than a snapshot, consensual tasting mentality we believe in tasting wines again and again (both blind and non-blind) in order to gain a better understanding of a wine's style and when it should be drunk. A rating combined with an understanding of the style is the key to discovering the best wines, and that means those you will most enjoy. Before choosing a bottle for immediate consumption always ask yourself which wine works best now, reflects my mood, personality, or that of my friends or family? What flavours do I want? How much flavour? By buying wine for cellaring it will be possible to contrast different vintages of the same wine. Alternatively from a case of the same wine the gradual development and increasing maturity of a specific vintage can be assessed over a decade or more.

How to use this guide

The main part of each regional section in this guide is an A-Z of the region's best producers. Each profile includes the wine region, website (where possible) and an **UK Stockists Code** (see below). It also includes a selection of that producer's best wines together with a **Quality Rating** and **Price Bracket** (both explained below). Most sections also begin with a map for orientation and a brief introduction or a guide to understanding wine styles. Also, where relevant, vintage information is provided (also see **Vintage Charts**). Under **Author's Choice** are a personal selection of wines that should prove a good starting point to discovering some of a region's best wines and producers, and in particular some of the best value wines to be had.

Symbols: ● red wine ○ white wine ◉ rosé wine

Quality Ratings:

★   a wine of good quality, not just sound but of good fruit and with some character.

★★   a wine with more depth, interest and concentration, usually with some aging potential

★★★   a very good, even fine, wine. In the case of many reds repaying lengthy cellaring.

★★★★   a wine of very high quality, among the very best even in a top appellation or region.

★★★★★   outstanding quality, potentially a classic.

✪✪✪✪✪   super 5 stars, restricted to the true classics, out-and-out world class.

Price Brackets:

All wines have been given a code indicating the price bracket a wine is likely to fall within but is only an estimation of current retail or market value. A standard 75cl bottle size is assumed so wines produced only in 1.5 litre (magnums), 50 cl (half litre) or 37.5 cl (half bottle) formats have been given 75cl price equivalents. A half bottle costing £8.95/$16.00 for instance will have a price code of £D.

£A: less than £5:00 / $9.00   £E: £20 - 30 / $36 - 54

£B: £5 - 10 / $9 - 18   £F: £30 - 50 / $54 - 90

£C: £10 - 15 / $18 - 27   £G: £50 - 75 / $90 - 135

£D: £15 - 20 / $27 - 36   £H: £75/ $135 or more

UK Stockists:

Details of these codes can be found in the UK Stockists section. Those in **bold** indicate an agent or direct importer of the wines. Also provided is general information on buying quality wines. In future editions we plan to provide details of agents and stockists in other countries.

A-Z Order:

The order of the A-Z entries is based on the name they are most commonly referred to and they appear as they are written but with priority to surnames. 'Domaine' is ignored but 'Château', 'Castello', 'Quinta' etc are respected as is the definite article when implicitly part of the name (eg Il Poggione appears under 'I'). The only exception to these principles is in Bordeaux where the name of the château or estate takes precedent.

Vintages Charts:

A section of Vintage Charts is provided at the end of the guide for those regions where vintages have the greatest significance. This is in addition to comments for individual years for the classic wines of Bordeaux, Burgundy, Piedmont, Tuscany and Port (found in the relevant sections). We have given rating between one and five stars for individual years (a split rating encompasses both lower and upper ends of quality). Those coded NYR (not yet rated) are for those years where it isn't possible to provide a balanced judgement on the vintage until nearer the wines' release (eg. Brunello di Montalcino). When to drink the wines of a given vintage is a largely subjective, personal judgement, and can depend as much on mood or context. However the ratings are suffixed A, B, C or D as a general indication of their likely development:

A - wines to Anticipate, not ready for drinking

B - wines that can be Broached, but with much more to give

C - wines to Consume, at or near their best

D - wines likely to be in Decline, past their best

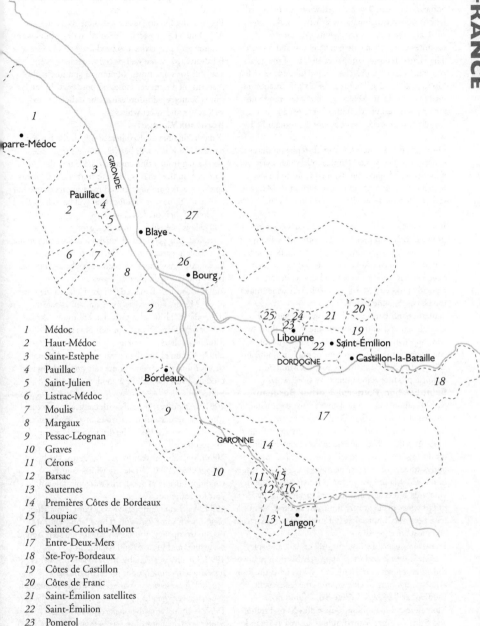

1. Médoc
2. Haut-Médoc
3. Saint-Estèphe
4. Pauillac
5. Saint-Julien
6. Listrac-Médoc
7. Moulis
8. Margaux
9. Pessac-Léognan
10. Graves
11. Cérons
12. Barsac
13. Sauternes
14. Premières Côtes de Bordeaux
15. Loupiac
16. Sainte-Croix-du-Mont
17. Entre-Deux-Mers
18. Ste-Foy-Bordeaux
19. Côtes de Castillon
20. Côtes de Franc
21. Saint-Émilion satellites
22. Saint-Émilion
23. Pomerol
24. Lalande-de-Pomerol
25. Fronsac & Canon-Fronsac
26. Côtes de Bourg
27. Côtes de Blaye / Premières Côtes de Blaye

Médoc, Graves & Sauternes

Some of the world's greatest red wines are produced here as well as benchmark sweet whites and a very small amount of stylish dry white. Médoc AC produces wines which are generally soft and forward. The Haut-Médoc encompasses all four of the great communal appellations close to the Gironde as well as Listrac and Moulis. There can be a wide variation in quality in the Haut-Médoc AC but a few properties are very serious indeed. Both Listrac-Médoc and Moulis also produce the occasiuonal distinguished wine.

Of the great red wine ACs Saint-Estèphe produces the densest, sturdiest wines. Pauillac offers rich styles laden with cassis and spice. Saint-Julien tends to be less opulent than Pauillac, and more perfumed. Margaux can produce the most elegant and refined wines of the Médoc.

Immediately south of Bordeaux, Pessac-Léognan produces rich, complex and ageworthy reds and great whites that can rival those of the Côte de Beaune (see Burgundy). Graves AC is never as good as Pessac-Léognan but some good red and dry whites are regularly produced as well as a few sweet wines under the Graves Supérieures AC

Sauternes and Barsac can both produce wines of truly magnificent concentration and intensity. A third sweet wine appellation, Cérons, does not enjoy the same conditions for the development of noble rot but can along with Cadillac, Sainte-Croix-du-Mont and Loupiac produce some impressive sweet wines.

Saint-Émilion, Pomerol & other Bordeaux

Saint-Émilion and Pomerol are the two great names associated with the Right Bank but there are an increasing number of exciting wines emerging from the other ACs here. With diverse *terroirs* Saint-Émilion is producing some exceptional wines as well as some fairly ordinary ones, particularly in the southern plains of the AC. Major investment in recent years in both vineyards and cellars, has resulted in some highly priced wines made in very limited quantities. Some have been very impressive, but many are over-extracted and most are expensive.

Pomerol, is generally opulent, full of dark and spicy fruit. It is supple and more approachable than many of the other top wines in Bordeaux. Wines of distinction are also beginning to emerge from the lesser Saint-Émilion satellite ACs, Lussac-Saint-Émilion, Montagne-Saint-Émilion, Puisseguin-Saint-Émilion and Saint-Georges-Saint-Émilion, as well as Lalande-de-Pomerol.

The Côtes de Bourg is producing some fine modern reds as are Fronsac and Canon-Fronsac. Good, stylish, well-made dark-fruited styles are also made at Côtes de Castillon and Bordeaux-Côtes de Francs. These are

areas of great potential and the best wines are still well-priced.

Between the Dordogne and Garonne rivers are nine ACs. Entre-Deux-Mers, is devoted to dry whites with a number of properties also producing good AC Bordeaux red. Some well-priced wines have been available for some time. Vibrant red and rosé is also made in the Premières Côtes de Bordeaux. In the far east is Saint-Foy-de-Bordeaux, where there are reds as well as dry and sweet whites.

Bordeaux Vintages

Winemaking has evolved here and with the top reds, particularly, it is worth bearing in mind if you are purchasing from a fine current vintage that the approach in the cellar is different to that of 20 years ago. The wines are suppler and more approachable but it remains to be seen whether they will be as long-lived as some of their predecessors.

2004: This looks like it could be a good to very good year producing good reds throughout the region. On the Left Bank in particular, the wines are powerful and backward. Dry whites look promising wheras Sauternes is likely to be good rather than great.

2003: Good Left Bank reds, in particular to the north of the Médoc. Graves was more uneven as was the Right Bank. Those who picked at optimum ripeness will be very fine. A small amount of very rich Sauternes is likely to emerge.

2002: A good rather than great year for reds more successful in the Médoc. Some very good whites were produced and this will be a good year too for Sauternes.

2001: A good year for reds with classically structured wines. Sauternes and sweet wines in general look to be very impressive indeed. The dry whites were also close to exceptional.

2000: Magnificent year for red Bordeaux, the best vintage since 1990. While dry whites enjoyed conditions nearly as good, this was a disappointing year for Sauternes.

1999: A generally impressive year throughout the region, with some variation. Those who went for maximum ripeness and harvested late did well. Sound dry whites and some splendid Sauternes.

1998: Quality was variable in the Médoc. A better year for earlier-ripening Merlot on the Right Bank producing some supple wines. Dry whites were good, Sauternes very good.

1997: A trying year, the one exception being Sauternes, which produced its best vintage since 1990. Dry whites should now be drunk up.

1996: A year of great wines in the Médoc, particularly in the northern appellations.The Right Bank fared less well, being hit by rain just as the Merlot ripened. Very good dry whites, the best are drinking well now.

Sauternes had its best year since 1990.

1995: A very good year for both Left and Right Bank. The wines are not only classically structured but have rich ripe fruit as well. Some good dry whites and these are now drinking well. However Sauternes was generally disappointing.

1994: Some soft agreeable reds on both Right and Left Banks. Many top wines are now beginning to drink well. Good year for dry whites but dismal in Sauternes.

1993: This was a disappointing vintage throughout the region with a wet harvest. The odd decent result emerged on both Banks and these wines should now be drunk. Sauternes was disastrous.

1992: A very disappointing year in the Médoc, only slightly better on the Right Bank.

1991: Much of France was hit by severe Spring frosts and Bordeaux was no exception. The yield was poor and the resulting wines lacked substance.

1990: The finest red wine vintage since 1982. Also impressively good for dry whites, some of the very best are still drinking well now. It was exceptional for Sauternes. Most reds, apart from the very top growths, are drinking now but will continue to develop.

For older vintages 1989 and the more structured 1988s were both good. 1986 was good on the Left Bank and some fine 1985s emerged throughout the region. Good 1983s with some exceptional Margaux's. 1982 more successful in the Médoc produced the best wines since 1961. Many are excellent now. Great Médocs from 1978 and 1970 are superb, the best will evolve further. A handful of 1975s have turned out very well. 1966 was good in the Médoc. 1964 might be worth a look for top Saint-Émilion or Pomerol. 1961 was a classic and many wines are still excellent. You could also consider 1959, 55, 49, 47, 45 and if you're exceptionally adventurous 35 or 28. Bear in mind that the provenance of the wine is as important as anything if you are acquiring very old vintages.

Wizard's Wishlist

MÉDOC, GRAVES & SAUTERNES
Great cellarworthy Left Bank reds

CH. COS D'ESTOURNEL ● Saint-Estèphe 2ème CC
CH. DUCRU-BEAUCAILLOU ● Saint-Julien 2ème CC
CH. HAUT-BRION ● Pessac-Léognan I er CC
CH. LAFITE-ROTHSCHILD ● Pauillac I er CC
CH. LATOUR ● Pauillac I er CC
CH. LÉOVILLE-LAS-CASES ● Saint-Julien 2ème CC
CH. MARGAUX ● Margaux I er CC
CH. LA MISSION-HAUT-BRION ● Pessac-Léognan CC
H. MOUTON-ROTHSCHILD ● Pauillac I er CC
CH. PICHON-LONGUEVILLE-LALANDE
● Pauillac 2ème CC

The best of Sauternes and Barsac

CH. CLIMENS O Barsac I er CC
CH. COUTET O Barsac I er CC
CH. GUIRAUD O Sauternes I er CC
CH. LAFAURIE-PEYRAGUEY O Sauternes I er CC
CH. RAYMOND-LAFON O Sauternes
CH. RIEUSSEC O Sauternes I er CC
CH. SIGALAS-RABAUD O Sauternes I er CC
CH. SUDUIRAUT O Sauternes I er CC
CH. LA TOUR BLANCHE O Sauternes I er CC
CH. D'YQUEM O Sauternes I er GCC

Classic dry whites

CH. CARBONNIEUX O Pessac-Léognan CC
DOM. DE CHEVALIER O Pessac-Léognan CC
CLOS FLORIDÈNE O Graves
CH. DE FIEUZAL O Pessac-Léognan
CH. HAUT-BRION O Pessac-Léognan
CH. LAVILLE-HAUT-BRION O Pessac-Léognan CC
CH. LA LOUVIÈRE O Pessac-Léognan
CH. PAPE-CLÉMENT O Pessac-Léognan
PAVILLON BLANC DE MARGAUX O Bordeaux
CH. SMITH-HAUT-LAFITTE O Pessac-Léognan

Good values and fine lesser growths

CH. BEYCHEVELLE ● Saint-Julien 4ème CC
CH. BRANAIRE ● Saint-Julien 4ème CC
CH. CLERC-MILON ● Pauillac 5ème CC
CH. D'ISSAN ● Margaux 3ème CC
CH. LÉOVILLE-POYFERRÉ ● Saint-Julien 2ème CC
CH. PONTET CANET ● Pauillac 5ème CC
CH. POTENSAC ● Médoc
CH. DU TERTRE ● Margaux 5ème CC
VIEUX CH. GAUBERT O Graves
CH. BASTOR-LAMONTAGNE O Sauternes

SAINT-ÉMILION, POMEROL & OTHER BORDEAUX
Great cellarworthy Right Bank reds

CH. AUSONE ● Saint-Émilion I er Grand Cru Classé
CH. CHEVAL-BLANC
● Saint-Émilion I er Grand Cru Classé
CH. LA CONSEILLANT ● Pomerol
CH. L'ÉGLISE-CLINET ● Pomerol
CH. LAFLEUR ● Pomerol
CH. PAVIE-DECESSE ● Saint-Émilion Grand Cru Classé
CH. PÉTRUS ● Pomerol
CH. LE PIN ● Pomerol
CH. TERTRE-RÔTEBOEUF ● Saint-Émilion Grand Cru
CH. TROPLONG-MONDOT
● Saint-Émilion Grand Cru Classé
CH. PAVIE ● Saint-Émilion Grand Cru Classé

CH. CANON ● Saint-Émilion Grand Cru Classé
CH. DE VALANDRAUD ● Saint-Émilion Grand Cru
VIEUX CH. CERTAN ● Pomerol
CH. CHAUVIN ● Saint-Émilion Grand Cru Classé

New Right Bank classics
CH. BEAU-SÉJOUR BÉCOT
● Saint-Émilion La Gomerie Grand Cru
CH. BEAUREGARD ● Pomerol
LE DÔME ● Saint-Émilion Grand Cru
CH. FAUGÈRES ● Saint-Émilion Péby-Faugères Grand Cru
LA FLEUR DU BOÙARD ● Lalande-de-Pomerol
CH. FOMBRAUGE
● Saint-Émilion Magrez-Fombrauge Grand Cru
LA MONDOTTE ● Saint-Émilion Grand Cru
CH. MONBOUSQUET ● Saint-Émilion Grand Cru
CH. QUINAULT
● Saint-Émilion Quinault l'Enclos Grand Cru
CH. GAZIN ● Pomerol
CH. FOMBRAUGE
● Saint-Émilion Magrez-Fombrauge Grand Cru
LA MONDOTTE ● Saint-Émilion Grand Cru

Emerging Right Bank reds
DOM. DE L'A ● Côtes de Castillon
CH. D'AIGUIHE ● Côtes de Castillon
LA CROIX DE PEYROLIE ● Lussac-Saint-Émilion

CH. FONTENIL ● Fronsac
CH. MOULIN PEY-LABRIE ● Canon-Fronsac
CLOS PUY ARNAUD ● Côtes de Castillon
CH. PUYGUERAUD ● Bordeaux-Côtes des Francs
CH. DE LA RIVIÈRE ● Fronsac
CH. ROC DE CAMBES ● Côtes de Bourg
CH. LA VIEILLE CURE ● Fronsac
CH. AMPÉLIA ● Côtes de Castillon
CH. CARIGNAN ● 1er Côtes de Bordeaux Prima
ESSENCE DE DOURTHE ● Bordeaux
CH. MOULIN HAUT-LAROQUE ● Fronsac
CH. GRAND CORBIN_DESPAGNE
● Saint-Émilion Grand Cru

Top Right Bank values
CH. BARRABAQUE ● Fronsac
CH. BEL-AIR LA ROYÈRE ● Côtes de Castillon
CH. BONNET ● Bordeaux Réserve
CH. CARSIN O Bordeaux Cuvée Prestige
CH. LA DAUPHINE ● Fronsac
CH. DAUPHINÉ-RONDILLON ● Loupiac La Cuvée d'Or
CH. REIGNAC ● Bordeaux Superieur
CLOS NARDIAN O Bordeaux
CH. CAP DE FAUGÈRES ● Côtes de Castillon
VIEUX CH. GACHET ● Lalande-de-Pomerol
CH. LA MAURIANE ● Puisseguin-Saint-Emilion
CH. REYNON O Bordeaux Vieilles Vignes

Bordeaux A-Z of producers

Médoc, Graves & Sauternes

CH. D'ARMAILHAC Pauillac 5ème CC www.bpdr.com UK stockists: AAA
Good Pauillac in the ripest years like 2001, 00, 99, 98 and 95. When conditions are less favourable the wine struggles a little. Good drinking at six or seven years. (DM)
● Château d'Armailhac Pauillac★★★ £D

CH. BASTOR-LAMONTAGNE Sauternes www.bastorlamontagne.com UK stockists: AAA
Consistently fine operation which has provided the essence of Sauternes at an affordable price for many vintages. As well as Sémillon and Sauvignon, just a small amount of Muscadelle adds aroma. Second wine from young vines is Les Remparts de Bastor. (DM)
● Château Bastor-Lamontagne Sauternes★★★ £E
● Château Bel Air Marquis d'Aligre Margaux★★★ £D

CH. BEYCHEVELLE Saint-Julien 4ème CC www.beychevelle.com UK stockists: AAA
Sizeable property with 90 ha. At its best the wine shows real finesse, splendid purity of fruit and very subtle oak, not full and powerful but more refined and elegant. Avoid lesser years. (DM)
● Château Beychevelle Saint-Julien★★★ £E

CH. BOYD-CANTENAC Margaux 3ème CC www.boyd-cantenac.fr UK stockists: AAA
Very good, elegant Margaux. Increasing use of new oak and no filtration. Fragrant and supple with attractive dark berry fruit and an increasing richness. Rating applies to vintages from 1998 on. (DM)
● Château Boyd-Cantenac Margaux★★★ £E

CH. BRANAIRE Saint-Julien 4ème CC www.branaire.com UK stockists: AAA
Significant cellar investment is undoubtedly paying off. The Cab Sauv component now really shows and the wines

New entries have producer's name underlined

are sturdier and denser with much greater depth and power. Impressive since 1994. (DM)

● **Château Branaire** Saint-Julien★★★ £F

CH. BRANE-CANTENAC Margaux 2ème CC www.lucienlurton.com   *UK stockists:* AAA
Since the late 1990s has shown real evidence of its Second Growth status. It is a classic blend of Cab Sauv, Merlot and Cab Franc with intense, cedary Margaux perfume, subtle oak and sheer class and intensity. Second wine, Baron de Brane, is of decent quality. (DM)

● **Château Branaire** Margaux★★★★ £F   ● **Baron de Brane**★★ £D

CH. BRANON Pessac-Léognan CC   www.château-haut-bergey.com   *UK stockists:* Gen
This boutique winery makes a single red wine from equal parts of Cabernet Sauvignon and Merlot. It is a wine of enormous power and concentration with intensely perfumed fruit. Jean-Luc Thunevin is the consultant winemaker. (NB)

● **Château Branon** Pessac-Léognan★★★★ £G

CH. CALON-SÉGUR Saint-Estèphe 2ème CC   *UK stockists:* AAA
Marked upturn in quality during the late 1990s. An opulent, modern Médoc with weight, concentration and power. It has a much more velvety texture than of old. Very good since 1996 and seemingly improving with the vintages since 2000. (DM)

● **Château Calon-Ségur** Saint-Estèphe★★★★ £F

CH. CAMBON-LA-PELOUSE Haut Médoc   *UK stockists:* Wai
Well-priced and impressively structured Haut-Médoc that has been on much improved form since 1999. The wine tends to be full, fleshy and relatively forward. Nevertheless, it possesses well-honed tannins and an impressive depth and purity. (DM)

● **Château Cambon-La-Pelouse** Haut-Medoc★★★ £C

CH. CANTENAC-BROWN Margaux 5ème CC   *UK stockists:* AAA
Purchased in 1987 by AXA Millésimes. The rating is for its current performance rather than earlier vintages and, given the performance of other châteaux within the AXA group, one would expect things here to continue to improve. (DM)

● **Château Cantenac-Brown** Margaux★★★ £E

CH. CARBONNIEUX Pessac-Léognan CC   *UK stockists:* F&R,N&P,Tur
Good rather than memorable red and white Pessac-Léognans. White is barrel-fermented, around half of which is new, and ageing is on lees. The red doesn't quite reach the same level but has also been consistent over recent vintages. (DM)

● **Château Carbonnieux** Pessac-Léognan★★ £E
● **Château Haut-Vigneau** Pessac-Léognan★ £D
O **Château Carbonnieux** Pessac-Léognan★★★ £E

CH. LES CARMES HAUT-BRION Pessac-Léognan   *UK stockists:*AAA
Tiny property and, like Haut-Brion, located amongst the suburbs of Bordeaux. Plots are fermented separately and malolactic takes place in barrel in one-third new wood. The wine is supple and rich, with firm but nicely rounded tannins. (DM)

● **Château les Carmes Haut-Brion** Pessac-Léognan★★★ £E

CH. DE CHANTEGRIVE Graves www.château-chantegrive.com
Four wines are produced. Good red and white Graves and the limited production barrel-fermented rich, creamy Cuvée Caroline. The sweet Cérons is a full, fat style with good depth and some honeyed complexity. (DM)

● **Château de Chantegrive** Graves★★ £C
O **Château de Chantegrive** Cuvée Caroline★★★ £C Cérons★★ £C

CH. CHARMAIL Haut-Médoc   *UK stockists:* AAA
Consistent performer during the last five or six vintages, located just to the north of Saint-Estèphe. Neither fined nor filtered, it is marked by supple tannin and attractive, dark berry fruit and hints of cassis, not least as a result of a touch of pre-fermentation maceration. (DM)

● **Château Charmail** Haut-Médoc★★★ £D

FRANCE

CH. CHASSE-SPLEEN Moulis www.chasse-spleen.com *UK stockists:* AAA
Along with Poujeaux and Maucaillou, one of the only wines in the Moulis AC really to perform with any consistent class. The 2001, 00 and 99 are noteworthy. Second wine, L'Ermitage de Chasse-Spleen, can be better than most. (DM)
● **Château Chasse-Spleen** Moulis★★★ £E

DOM. DE CHEVALIER Pessac-Léognan CC *UK stockists:* AAA
Important producer, noted particularly for its splendid white. The production of this is very low, with just 4.5 of the 37.5 ha vineyard planted to Sauvignon and Sémillon. The red has been less impressive in recent years. (DM)
● **Domaine de Chevalier** Pessac-Léognan★★★★ £E
O **Domaine de Chevalier** Pessac-Léognan✪✪✪✪✪ £F

CH. CISSAC Haut-Médoc www.château-cissac.com *UK stockists:* AAA
Traditional, firm very fairly priced Médoc. Becomes rounder and suppler than of old with a little age. From the best vintages the wine is undoubtedly complex and harmonious but really needs cellaring for 8 to 10 years. (DM)
● **Château Cissac** Haut-Médoc★★★ £C

CH. CLERC-MILON Pauillac 5ème CC www.bpdr.com *UK stockists:* AAA
Planted to less than 50 per cent Cab Sauv with over a third Merlot, the style is very rounded and surprisingly approachable for Pauillac. While overshadowed by its sister château Mouton-Rothschild, Clerc-Milon is nevertheless an excellent, stylish source of the appellation. (DM)
● **Château Clerc-Milon** Pauillac★★★★ £F

CH. CLIMENS Barsac 1er CC www.château-climens.fr *UK stockists:* AAA
Exceptional sweet wine and the leading property in Barsac. Best to age it for at least five years and it will be better with twice that time in the cellar. Truly great in 2001, 97, 90, and 89. (DM)
● **Château Climens** Barsac✪✪✪✪✪ £G

CLOS FLORIDÈNE Graves www.denisdubourdieu.com *UK stockists:* F&R,Dec
The barrel-fermented white is a particularly impressive example and puts many more exalted Pessac-Léognans to shame. The red is sound and well crafted but lacks the same excitement. Denis Dubourdieu also produces the wines of Château Reynon. (DM)
● **Clos Floridène** Graves★ £C   O **Clos Floridène** Graves★★★ £C

CH. COS D'ESTOURNEL Saint-Estèphe 2ème CC *UK stockists:* AAA
The premier château in Saint-Estèphe. A very powerful and opulent wine which demands a decade or more in the cellar. The second wine Les Pagodes de Cos is regularly been at one to two stars. (DM)
● **Château Cos d'Estournel** Saint-Estèphe✪✪✪✪✪ £G

CH. COUTET Barsac 1er CC *UK stockists:* AAA
Very good property and near neighbour of Climens. In exceptional years a special super-concentrated Cuvée Madame is released. This is certainly of super-five quality. (DM)
O **Château Coutet** Barsac★★★★ £F

CH. DOISY-VÉDRINES Barsac 2ème CC *UK stockists:* AAA
This is the biggest of the three Doisy properties with 27 ha. Tends to produce wine with more overt luscious honeyed fruit than other fine Barsac. Retains an elegant finesse in lighter years when the wine carries less weight. (DM)
● **Château Doisy-Védrines** Sauternes★★★★ £E

CH. DUCRU-BEAUCAILLOU Saint-Julien 2ème CC *UK stockists:* AAA
One of the greatest wines of Saint-Julien. It is a very impressive, classically structured example of the appellation: always elegant, very intense, with subtle cedar and dark fruit underpinned by finely integrated oak. Very good in recent vintages. (DM)
● **Château Ducru-Beaucaillou** Saint-Julien✪✪✪✪✪ £H

CH. DUHART-MILON Pauillac 4ème CC www.lafite.com *UK stockists:* AAA
Intriguingly, this Rothschild property is also part-owned by the Chalone Wine Group from the USA. A

12

New entries have producer's name underlined

modern, supple style 1999, 98 and 96 were all nudging four-star quality. (DM)

● **Château Duhart-Milon** Pauillac★★★ £E

CH. DE FARGUES Sauternes www.château-de-fargues.com *UK stockists:* AAA
A rare wine with a price to match produced from 15 ha owned by the Lur-Saluces family of Yquem. This is one of the finest examples of Sauternes and one of the longest-lasting wines in the AC. (NB)

O **Château de Fargues** Sauternes★★★★★ £F

CH. FERRIÈRE Margaux 3ème CC www.ferriere.com
Dramatically improved property during the 1990s. Now one of the best properties in the Margaux AC. The wine is rich, intense and concentrated with malolactic in barrel. The wine comfortably absorbs the impact of 60 per cent new oak. (DM)

● **Château Ferrière** Margaux★★★★ £E

CH. DE FIEUZAL Pessac-Léognan CC www.fieuzal.com *UK stockists:* THt, AAA
Opulent, richly textured, forward, modern and approachable red, accessible very shortly after release. Rich, forward, honeyed white with a solid dose of new oak. Both are very good value. (DM)

● **Château de Fieuzal** Pessac-Léognan★★★ £E
O **Château de Fieuzal** Pessac-Léognan★★★★ £E

CH. GISCOURS Margaux 2ème CC www.château-giscours.com *UK stockists:* AAA
Investment in the vineyard and cellars with reduced yields and careful vinification has produced some impressive examples. Will add increasing richness with 8 to 10 years' age. (DM)

● **Château Giscours** Margaux★★★★ £E

CH. GRAND-PUY-LACOSTE Pauillac 5ème CC *UK stockists:* AAA
Under the same ownership as Ducru-Beaucaillou, this has been an admirable and classic red Bordeaux for the past three decades. 1990, and more recently 95 and 96, are wines of significant class and 2000 looks very much of the same order. (DM)

● **Château Grand-Puy-Lacoste** Pauillac★★★★ £F

CH. GRUAUD-LAROSE Saint-Julien 2ème CC *UK stockists:* AAA
Formidable and massively structured during the 1980s. Quality generally has remained impressive but not at quite the same level. Second wine, Sarget de Gruaud-Larose is best in better years. (DM)

● **Château Gruaud-Larose** Saint-Julien★★★★ £F

CH. GUIRAUD Sauternes Ier CC www.châteauguiraud.fr *UK stockists:* AAA
Impressive Sauternes in the top vintages of the 1990s. The wines are of sometimes blockbuster proportions, rich, very honeyed and peachy, with spice and vanilla from new oak. It is not to all tastes, and on occasion more refinement would help. (DM)

O **Château Guiraud** Sauternes★★★★ £F

CH. HAUT-BAILLY Pessac-Léognan CC *UK stockists:* RsW, AAA
A supple, elegant and consistently well-crafted red which is both approachable and refined. Consistent throughout the mid- to late 1990s. The wine ages very well indeed. (DM)

● **Château Haut-Bailly** Pessac-Léognan★★★★ £E

CH. HAUT-BRION Pessac-Léognan Ier CC www.haut-brion.com *UK stockists:* AAA
One of the four original properties classified as a First Growth in the 1855 Classification of the red Bordeaux wines. Both red and white have been magnificent through the late 1990s. Very dense and powerful, a minimum of 10 years is needed. (DM)

● **Château Haut-Brion** Pessac-Léognan✪✪✪✪ £H
● **Le Bahans Haut Brion** ★★★ £E
O **Château Haut-Brion** Pessac-Léognan✪✪✪✪ £G

CH. HAUT-MARBUZET Saint-Estèphe *UK stockists:* PBW, Col
Fleshy, powerful, very rich Saint-Estèphe marked by well-integrated spicy new oak. Only surpassed within the appellation by Cos d'Estournel and Montrose. It offers very good value. (DM)

● **Château Haut-Marbuzet** Saint-Estèphe★★★★ £E

CH. D'ISSAN Margaux 3ème CC www.château-issan.com *UK stockists:* AAA
Disappointing in the late 1980s and early 90s. Since 1995 things have been looking much better and the wine
is once more in the elegant, cedary and perfumed style that represents fine Margaux. (DM)
● **Château d'Issan** Margaux★★★ £E

CLOS DU JAUGUEYRON Margaux *UK stockists:* **WTs**
Michel Théron's 0.4-ha estate is in the commune of Cantenac but only entitled to the Haut-Médoc AC. There is
remarkable quality for the price. He also owns a small parcel in the Margaux AC with just 100 cases produced. This
is probably the ultimate *garagiste* property in the Médoc. (NB)
● **Clos du Jaugueyron** Margaux★★★★ £F ● **Clos du Jaugueyron** Haut-Médoc★★★ £D

CH. KIRWAN Margaux 3ème CC www.château-kirwan.com *UK stockists:* AAA
Since the mid-1990s Michel Rolland has provided winemaking guidance and quality has been consistently good
since 1996, if a touch overextracted in 98. (DM)
● **Château Kirwan** Margaux★★★ £E

CH. LAFAURIE-PEYRAGUEY Sauternes 1er CC *UK stockists:* AAA
Combines the intense richness and honeyed concentration of the finest Sauternes with something of the
elegance found in Climens. The wines are very stylish and long-lived. The 1999, 98 and 97 are all
extraordinarily fine super-fives and 2001 may have the potential to be exquisite. (DM)
● **Château Lafaurie-Peyraguey** Sauternes★★★★★ £F

CH. LAFITE-ROTHSCHILD Pauillac 1er CC www.lafite.com *UK stockists:* AAA
A consistent and superlative performer throughout the mid- to late 1990s. The 2000, 98 and 96 are exceptional
wines and 2003 shows similar promise. A minimum of 15 to 20 years is required to achieve a harmony between
the formidable, powerful tannins and the intense and fragrantly rich cedar and cassis fruit. The second wine, Les
Carruades de Lafite-Rothschild, is very impressive for a second label. (DM)
● **Château Lafite-Rothschild** Pauillac✪✪✪✪✪ £H
● **Les Carruades de Lafite-Rothschild**★★★★ £F

CH. LAFON-ROCHET Saint-Estèphe 4ème CC *UK stockists:* AAA
Under the same ownership as Pontet-Canet. Has performed well, sometimes very well throughout the mid- to
late 1990s. A great deal more supple and approachable than it used to be. (DM)
● **Château Lafon-Rochet** Saint-Estèphe★★★ £E

CH. LAGRANGE Saint-Julien 3ème CC www.château-lagrange.com *UK stockists:* Eno,SsG
This wine is rich and concentrated, but in an approachable style, with supple, well-rounded tannin.
Consistently good over the last five or six years, it just needs that extra dimension. (DM)
● **Château Lagrange** Saint-Julien★★★ £F

CH. LANGOA-BARTON Saint-Julien 3ème CC *UK stockists:* AAA
Sister property to Léoville-Barton. Consistent performer, producing elegant Saint-Julien with attractive dark
fruit and some cedary complexity. 2001, 00 and 98 stand out in recent vintages. (DM)
● **Château Langoa-Barton** Saint-Julien★★★ £E

CH. LARRIVET HAUT-BRION Pessac-Léognan *UK stockists:* BBR,F&R,N&P,Sec
Both wines are impressive, with consultancy from Michel Rolland. The property is worthy of being upgraded to
Cru Classé. Both 1998 and 99 are very good and 00 and 01 have great potential. (DM)
● **Château Larrivet Haut-Brion** Pessac-Léognan★★★ £E
O **Château Larrivet Haut-Brion** Pessac-Léognan★★★ £E

CH. LATOUR Pauillac 1er CC www.château-latour.com *UK stockists:* AAA
To many this is the greatest of all the great wines of the Médoc and to some the greatest in the entire region. At
its magnificent best it is massively concentrated and very harmonious and refined. It requires cellaring for one or
preferably two decades. Recent vintages of particular note include 1999, 96, 95 and 90. Les Forts de Latour is a
very impressive second wine. (DM)
● **Château Latour** Pauillac✪✪✪✪✪ £H ● **Les Forts de Latour**★★★★ £F

New entries have producer's name underlined

CH. LA TOUR CARNET Haut-Médoc   *UK stockists:* L&W,BBR,N&P,Tur
A rich, fleshy style of Médoc with Michel Rolland consulting. Around 70 per cent new oak is used and all operations are carried out by gravity. Needs four to five years to harmonise. (DM)
● **Château La Tour Carnet** Haut-Médoc★★★ £C

CH. LATOUR-MARTILLAC Pessac-Léognan CC   *UK stockists:* AAA
Good to very good white and red Pessac from old vines. The red is an approachable, supple wine; the white is rich and honeyed, with a real toasty, creamy character from barrel-fermentation. (DM)
● **Château Latour-Martillac** Pessac-Léognan★★★ £D
O **Château Latour-Martillac** Pessac-Léognan★★★ £D

CH. LAVILLE HAUT-BRION Pessac-Léognan CC   *UK stockists:* F&R,C&R
A blend of Sémillon, Sauvignon and just a hint of Muscadelle, Laville is one of the great Pessac whites, powerfully structured and developing intense honeyed, mineral notes with age. It is barrel-fermented and aged mostly in new oak and requires considerable cellaring to show all its magic. (DM)
O **Château Laville Haut-Brion** Pessac-Léognan✪✪✪✪✪ £G

CH. LÉOVILLE-BARTON Saint-Julien 2ème CC   *UK stockists:* AAA
Consistent red which has long been one of Bordeaux's great-value wines. Vinified at its sister property Langoa-Barton, as there is no winemaking facility at Léoville. No blockbuster but very good and long-lived. Seriously nudging super-five in 1996 and potentially 2000 as well. (DM)
● **Château Léoville-Barton** Saint-Julien★★★★★ £F

CH. LÉOVILLE-LAS-CASES Saint-Julien 2ème CC   *UK stockists:* AAA
Universally regarded as the finest of the super-seconds. High standards ensure that a significant amount of the Grand Vin is declassified as Clos du Marquis, which is one of the very best of the Médoc's second labels. Quality was top-notch throughout the 1990s. (DM)
● **Château Léoville-las-Cases** Saint-Julien✪✪✪✪✪ £H   ● **Clos du Marquis**★★★ £E

CH. LÉOVILLE-POYFERRÉ Saint-Julien 2ème CC   *UK stockists:* AAA
The third among the great Léoville super-seconds. Poyferré, while a serious, dense and powerfully structured wine, is more approachable than the other two. 2000, 96 and 90 were all extremely fine examples of five-star quality. (DM)
● **Château Léoville-Poyferré** Saint-Julien★★★★ £F

CH. LA LOUVIÈRE Pessac-Léognan   www.andrelurton.com   *UK stockists:* AAA
Both wines are approachable and forward in style but will also age well in the medium term. The red is supple and rounded tannin, the white ripe and full of citrus and subtle toasted oak. (DM)
● **Château la Louvière** Pessac-Léognan★★★ £E
O **Château la Louvière** Pessac-Léognan★★★ £E

CH. LYNCH-BAGES Pauillac 5ème CC   www.lynchbages.com   *UK stockists:* AAA
Regarded rightly during the 1980s as one of the great super-seconds despite its lower official classification but during the late 1990s lost just a touch of the sheen. The wine at its best is still very fine, full of dark cassis and ripe stylish tannin Among recent vintages the 2000, 96 and 95 were all very impressive. (DM)
● **Château Lynch-Bages** Pauillac★★★★★ £F
O **Château Lynch-Bages** Bordeaux★★ £D

MAGREZ-TIVOLI Médoc
This wine comes from 40-year-old vines on a tiny 2.5-ha plot planted two-thirds/one-third Cabernet Sauvignon and Merlot. Handled entirely by gravity and aged in oak for 22 months, it is both fleshy and concentrated with a pure cedary undercurrent to the fruit. (DM)
● **Magrez-Tivoli** Médoc★★★★ £F

CH. MALARTIC-LAGRAVIÈRE Pessac-Léognan CC   *UK stockists:* F&R,N&P
Purchased by the Bonnie family in 1997 and since then there has been a dramatic raising of standards. Both red and white will develop well over the medium term. The second label for both red and white, Le Sillage de Malartic, now offers reliable drinking. (DM)

FRANCE

● Château Malartic-Lagravière Pessac-Léognan★★★ £E
O Château Malartic-Lagravière Pessac-Léognan★★★★ £E

CH. MALESCOT-SAINT-EXUPÉRY Margaux 3ème CC *UK stockists:* AAA
Quality has taken a significant step up in recent vintages. The wine is now riper and fuller but not at all extracted, retaining a typically elegant, perfumed Margaux character. (DM)
● Château Malescot-Saint-Exupéry Margaux★★★★ £F

CH. DE MALLE Sauternes 2ème CC *UK stockists:* AAA
Consistently fine and elegant Sauternes since the late 1980s. The wine increasingly shows a rich, opulent character as well as an intense fragrance. It perfectly balances weight and finesse. (DM)
● Château de Malle Sauternes★★★★ £E

CH. MARGAUX Margaux 1er CC www.château-margaux.com *UK stockists:* AAA
Corinne Mentzelopoulos and general manager Paul Pontallier have crafted truly great red Bordeaux now for upwards of two decades. The wine is not only remarkably elegant, with the unmistakably intense perfume of the AC, but also enormously rich. Second label, Pavillon Rouge, is itself regularly very impressive. Among top recent years are 2000, 99, 96, 95 and 90. (DM)
● Château Margaux Margaux❍❍❍❍❍ £H
● Pavillon Rouge de Château Margaux★★★★ £F
O Pavillon Blanc de Château Margaux Bordeaux★★★★★ £F

MAROJALLIA Margaux *UK stockists:* AAA
Tiny 2.5-ha property with an exceptional *terroir* close to du Tertre. Very lush and rich, with a sumptuous texture and impressive depth. Second wine, Clos Margalaine, is more obviously fleshy and forward and very impressive for a second label. (DM)
● Marojallia Margaux★★★★★ £H ● Clos Margalaine Margaux★★★★ £E

CLOS MARSALETTE Pessac-Léognan CC *UK stockists:* AAA
Small, potentially excellent property now with involvement from Stéphan von Neipperg of Canon-La-Gaffelière. The wine is a 50/50 blend of Merlot and Cabernet Sauvignon. Rich and supple in texture it develop very well in the medium term. (DM)
● Clos Marsalette Pessac-Léognan★★★★ £E

MA VÉRITÉ Haut-Médoc
Produced from a tiny 2-ha vineyard with strictly limited yields, this is part of the Terroirs d'Exception range by Bernard Magrez. Clay and limestone soils are planted to a mix of 55 per cent Cabernet Sauvignon, 40 per cent Merlot and the balance Cabernet Franc and Petit Verdot. Richly textured but also elegant cedary with copious quantities of ripe cassis and spicy new oak. It will benefit from five or six years' ageing. (DM)
● Ma Vérité Haut-Médoc★★★★ £F

CH. LA MISSION HAUT-BRION Pessac-Léognan CC *UK stockists:* AAA
La Mission is only surpassed among Graves reds by Haut-Brion. Massive, dense and powerful with dark, mineral and black fruits underpinned by cedar and oak. 2000, 98 and 95 are recent benchmarks. Second wine, La Chapelle de la Mission Haut-Brion, is four-star in the ripest years. (DM)
● Château la Mission Haut-Brion Pessac-Léognan❍❍❍❍❍ £H

CH. MONTROSE Saint-Estèphe 2ème CC *UK stockists:* AAA
The property is second only behind Cos d'Estournel in the AC hierarchy. These are massive, powerful, brooding wines – dense, tannic and long-lived. 1990 and 95 suggest super-five quality and 2000 may well turn out the same. La Dame de Montrose is an impressive second wine. (DM)
● Château Montrose Saint-Estèphe★★★★★ £F La Dame de Montrose★★★ £E

CH. MOUTON-ROTHSCHILD Pauillac 1er CC www.bpdr.com *UK stockists:* AAA
Unique among the First Growths of Bordeaux in that the wine was elevated to its current classification only in 1973. The most opulent and approachable of the top growths. 1996, 98, 99 and 00 have all been very fine. The second wine is Le Petit Mouton and a small amount of a premium white Aile d'Argent is also produced. (DM)
16 ● Château Mouton-Rothschild Pauillac❍❍❍❍❍ £H

CH. NAIRAC Barsac 2ème CC   *UK stockists:* AAA
Small property often outperforming its Second Growth status. Always picked very ripe, it gains real structure from a high proportion of new oak. This can seem overpowering in its youth but given time the wine can show a marvellous balance. Definitely cellar for six or seven years. (DM)
● **Château Nairac** Barsac★★★★ £E

CH. LES ORMES DE PEZ Saint-Estèphe www.ormesdepez.com   *UK stockists:* AAA
One of the most underrated wines in the Médoc, a chunky, dense, plummy wine with lots of upfront fruit. Jean-Michel Cazes and his team have got just about the maximum potential from this property. (NB)
● **Château Les Ormes de Pez** Saint-Estèphe★★★ £C

CH. PALMER Margaux 3ème CC   www.château-palmer.com   *UK stockists:* AAA
This marvellous property is often thought of as a Second Growth. At its best the wine displays not only the perfume of the appellation but ripe, powerful, almost sumptuous dark fruit. 2000, 99, 98, 96 and 95 were of a very high standard. (DM)
● **Château Palmer** Margaux★★★★★ £G

CH. PAPE-CLÉMENT Pessac-Léognan CC   www.pape-clement .com   *UK stockists:* AAA
Both wines are rich and powerful. The tiny production of white has an elegant, intense mineral and citrus streak adding to its complexity and all nicely supported by sufficient creamy new oak. Generally very good throughout the 1990s and particularly after 1995. (DM)
● **Château Pape-Clément** Pessac-Léognan★★★★ £E
O **Château Pape-Clément** Pessac-Léognan★★★★ £E

CH. PEYRABON Haut-Médoc   *UK stockists:* BBR,F&R
Both Haut-Médoc and a limited volume of stylish, cassis-laden Pauillac are produced. Both wines are likely to add further complexity with five or six years' cellaring. (DM)
● **Château Peyrabon** La Fleur Peyrabon Pauillac★★★ £D
● **Château Peyrabon** Haut Médoc★★ £C

CH. PIBRAN Pauillac   *UK stockists:* AAA
From the same stable as Pichon Longueviulle, this Cru Bourgeois continues to improve as the vineyard becomes more mature. The wine is sweet-fruited and richly textured with supple, soft tannins but the cassis character of the appellation still shines through. (DM)
● **Château Pibran** Pauillac★★★ £E

CH. PICHON-LONGUEVILLE Pauillac 2ème CC   *UK stockists:* AAA
Owned by AXA Millésimes. 1989 and 90 were world-class, super-five wines: deep, dark, powerful Pauillac but very finely balanced. Quality since then has not been at quite the same heady heights; although 2001 looks to have great potential. (DM)
● **Château Pichon-Longueville** Pauillac★★★★ £F

CH. PICHON-LONGUEVILLE-LALANDE Pauillac 2ème CC   *UK stockists:* AAA
A property marked by its rich, elegant, almost sumptuous style of wine. Vineyards border Saint-Julien which helps contribute to the wine's intense, fragrant and complex style. Vintages of the late 1990s were strangely disappointing but quality looks to be back in the top division. (DM)
● **Château Pichon-Longueville-Lalande** Pauillac★★★★★ £G
● **Réserve de la Comtesse**★★ £E

CH. PONTET-CANET Pauillac 5ème CC   www.pontet-canet.com   *UK stockists:* AAA
Now producing quintessential Pauillac – big, powerful and dense with supple, well-rounded tannin and an intense fragrance of cassis and cedar. 2000 and 99 clearly rated four stars. (DM)
● **Château Pontet-Canet** Pauillac★★★ £F

CH. POTENSAC Médoc   www.château-potensac.com   *UK stockists:* AAA
Under the same ownership as Léoville-las-Cases and the finest property sold as Médoc AC. Bottled without

FRANCE

filtration it is better with five years' cellaring. Both 2000 and 96 are particularly impressive. (DM)
● **Château Potensac** Médoc★★★ £D

CH. POUJEAUX Moulis www.châteaupoujeaux.com *UK stockists:* AAA
Along with Chasse-Spleen, this is one of the two best wines in the Moulis AC. It has performed with an impressive consistency throughout the last 10 years and more. (DM)
● **Château Poujeaux** Moulis★★★ £E

CH. RABAUD-PROMIS Sauternes 1er CC *UK stockists:* AAA
This is a full, rich and honeyed wine with not only impressive depth, concentration and the structure to age very well but also real balance and harmony. Impressive since 1994. (DM)
O **Château Rabaud-Promis** Sauternes★★★★ £F

CH. RAUZAN-SÉGLA Margaux 2ème CC *UK stockists:* AAA
Margaux with a fine, elegant texture and complex dark fruits and cedar. Also surprising tannin – the wine will improve with at least five or six years' cellaring. Reasonably consistent since 1995. (DM)
● **Château Rauzan-Ségla** Margaux ★★★★ £F

CH. RAYMOND-LAFON Sauternes www.château-raymond-lafon.fr *UK stockists:* AAA
Tiny output, just over 1,600 cases a year from neighbour of Yquem. It has consistently produced wines in the great years of the last two decades which rival all but the absolute best in Sauternes. The wine is barrel-fermented and aged for up to three years in wood. (DM)
O **Château Raymond-Lafon** Sauternes★★★★★ £F

CH. RIEUSSEC Sauternes 1er CC www.lafite.com *UK stockists:* AAA
Under the same ownership as Lafite-Rothschild, this Sauternes is generally regarded as being second only in weight and power to Yquem. It has generally performed at that level since 1995 and particularly during the trio of great Sauternes years from 88 to 90. (DM)
O **Château Rieussec** Sauternes✪✪✪✪ £F

CH. ROLLAN-DE-BY Médoc www.rollandeby.com
This 37-ha property has performed with distinction throughout the past decade and is a shining light for other producers in the outlying areas of the Médoc. Haut-Condissas is a premium label with more Cab Sauv. (DM)
● **Château Rollan-de-By** Médoc★★★ £D ● **Château Haut-Condissas** Médoc★★★★ £E

CH. SÉNÉJAC Haut-Médoc *UK stockists:*AAA
34-ha property noted for its now well-established, densely structured special *cuvée* Karolus which is 100% Cabernet Sauvignon. The regular bottling has been increasingly good across recent vintages and is produced in a lighter style but with impressive cedary complexity and persistence of fruit. (DM)
● **Château Sénéjac** Haut-Médoc★★★ £D Haut-Médoc Karolus★★★★ £F
● **Château Siran** Margaux★★★ £C

CH. SIGALAS-RABAUD Sauternes 1er CC *UK stockists:* AAA
Smaller part of the original Château Rabaud, which was divided nearly a century ago. The wine is very rich and gloriously honeyed and can show very marked botrytis while retaining real elegance. 2001, 99, 98, 97and 96 were all on top form and are nudging five stars. (DM)
O **Château Sigalas-Rabaud** Sauternes★★★★ £F

CH. SMITH HAUT LAFITTE Pessac-Léognan CC *UK stockists:* AAA
The white is dominated by Sauvignon with a sprinkling of Sémillon and more unusually Sauvignon Gris. The red is lighter in style than some of its neighbours but now possesses impressive depth. Neither wine is filtered and both have performed admirably since 1995. (DM)
● **Château Smith Haut Lafitte** Pessac-Léognan★★★★ £F
O **Château Smith Haut Lafitte** Pessac-Léognan★★★★ £F

CH. SOCIANDO-MALLET Haut-Médoc *UK stockists:* AAA
Now undoubtedly the most impressive estate in the Haut-Médoc and quality here since 1995 has been good to very good. The style is of a true *vin de garde*, in part due to the well-drained gravel soils, which produce supple

New entries have producer's name underlined

but youthfully firm, powerful tannins. (DM)
● **Château Sociando-Mallet** Haut-Médoc★★★★ £E

CH. SUDUIRAUT Sauternes 1er CC www.suduiraut.com *UK stockists:* AAA
More care has been taken with harvesting at this property which neighbours Yquem since its purchase by AXA in 1992. As a result the wine has become increasingly full and rich. Very good recently in 95, 96 and 97. 2001 also looks extremely promising. (DM)
○ **Château Suduiraut** Sauternes★★★★★ £F

CH. TALBOT Saint-Julien 2ème CC www.château-talbot.com *UK stockists:* AAA
Talbot is now very international in style and quite different to some of the very firm earlier examples under Cordier ownership. 1998 and 00 were both very good and 01 looks similarly promising. (DM)
● **Château Talbot** Saint-Julien★★★ £F

CH. DU TERTRE Margaux 5ème CC *UK stockists:* AAA
Under Eric Albada Jedgersma this property is beginning to show its true potential as one of the most beguiling and perfumed of all Margaux reds. Six or more years age will add further complexity. (DM)
● **Château du Tertre** Margaux★★★★ £F

CH. LA TOUR BLANCHE Sauternes 1er CC *UK stockists:* Col
This property is run by the Ministry of Agriculture and although this is also an agricultural school very high standards are maintained. The vineyards are particularly well sited and result in a big, full-bodied Sauternes produced with marked botrytis and well-judged new oak.
○ **Château la Tour Blanche** Sauternes★★★★ £F

CH. LA TOUR HAUT-BRION Pessac-Léognan CC *UK stockists:* BBR,N&P,Sec,Tur
Originally the second wine at La Mission Haut-Brion, this property stands alone with its own identity now that the vineyard is ageing. 1995 and 98 were both very impressive and 00 looks to have equal potential. (DM)
● **Château la Tour Haut-Brion** Pessac-Léognan★★★★ £F

VIEUX CHÂTEAU GAUBERT Graves *UK stockists:* BBR,CTy
Good red and white are produced. Red is a 50/50 blend of Cab. Sauv. and Merlot and this is emphasised in its vibrant dark plummy fruit. The white, from a roughly equal blend of Sémillon and Sauvignon, is barrel-fermented in 60 per cent new oak. Both will benefit from two or three years' ageing in bottle. (DM)
● **Vieux Château Gaubert** Graves★★★ £C ○ **Vieux Château Gaubert** Graves★★★ £C

CH. D'YQUEM Sauternes 1er GCC *UK stockists:* AAA
Arguably the greatest sweet wine in the world. Purchased by LVMH in 1999. The vineyards have a superb exposure in the centre of the appellation and enjoy an ideal mix of morning mist and warm sunshine. With a sizeable production it is certain that, while occasional TBAs from Germany or SGNs from Alsace might rival it for sheer depth, dimension and fruit intensity, they never will match the volume of quality wine produced at Yquem. (DM)
○ **Château d'Yquem** Sauternes❍❍❍❍ £H

Other wineries of note
Ch. d'Agassac (Haut-Médoc), Ch. d'Angludet (Margaux), Ch. d'Arche (Sauternes), Ch. Batailley (Pauillac), Ch. Bel Air Marquis d'Aligre (Margaux), Ch. Belgrave (Haut-Médoc), Ch. Brown (Pessac-Léognan), Ch. Caillou (Sauternes), Ch. Camensac (Haut-Médoc), Ch. Cantemerle (Haut-Médoc), Ch. Clarke (Listrac-Médoc), Ch. Clos Haut-Peyraguey (Sauternes), Ch. Cos Labory (Saint-Estèphe), Ch. Couhins-Lurton (Pessac-Léognan), Ch. Doisy-Daene (Sauternes), Ch. Dauzac (Margaux), Ch. Filhot (Sauternes), Ch. de France (Pessac-Léognan), Ch. Gloria (Saint-Julien), Ch. Haut-Batailley (Pauillac), Ch. Haut-Bergey (Pessac-Léognan), Ch. la Lagune (Haut-Médoc), Ch. Lamothe-Guignard (Sauternes), Ch. Lanessan (Haut-Médoc), La Sérénité (Pessac-Léognan), (Ch. Lascombes (Margaux), Ch. Lynch Moussas (Pauillac), Ch. Mayne-Lalande (Listrac-Médoc), Ch. Marquis de Terme (Margaux), Ch. Phélan-Ségur (Saint-Estèphe), Ch. Pontac Monplaisir (Pessac-Léognan), Ch. Preuillac (Médoc), Ch. Prieuré-Lichine (Margaux), Ch. Rayne-Vigneau ((Sauternes), Ch. Saint-Pierre (Saint-Julien), Ch. Siran (Margaux), Ch. Vieux-Robin (Médoc), Ch. Villa Bel Air (Graves)

An in-depth profile of every producer can be found in Wine behind the label 2006

FRANCE

Saint-Emilion, Pomerol & other Bordeaux

DOM. DE L'A Côtes de Castillon   *UK stockists:* N&P
This is the tiny 4-ha home property of winemaking guru Stéphane Derenoncourt. The wine is fermented in wood, aged on lees to add weight and texture and bottled without fining or filtration. (DM)
● **Domaine de l'A** Côtes de Castillon★★★ £E

CH. D'AIGUILHE Côtes de Castillon   www.neipperg.com   *UK stockists:* BBR, N&P, Tur
This very fine Castillon property is under of the same ownership as Canon La Gaffelière and La Mondotte. Lushly textured, concentrated and impressively complex, it has a fine tannic structure, which needs a good five or six years' ageing. (DM)
● **Château d'Aiguilhe** Côtes de Castillon★★★★ £E

CH. AMPÉLIA Côtes de Castillon   *UK stockists:* AAA
An example of why this AC is emerging as one of the most exciting of the Right Bank satellites. The wine is big, full and fleshy but also retains the mineral purity found in top examples. (DM)
● **Château Ampélia** Côtes de Castillon★★★ £C

CH. ANGÉLUS Saint-Emilion 1er GCC   www.angelus.com   *UK stockists:* AAA
Consistently one of the top-performing Saint-Emilion Grands Crus Classés over the last 10 to 15 years. Deeply coloured, concentrated and extracted wines with deep, dark blackcurrant and plum fruit. (DM)
● **Château Angélus** Saint-Emilion Grand Cru Classé★★★★★ £H

CH. AUSONE Saint Émilion 1er GCC   *UK stockists:* AAA
One of the great wines of the Right Bank. Ausone, along with Cheval-Blanc, has always been considered to stand out and the two are classified Premiers Grands Crus Classés A-grade properties. Very fine and complex, it is now increasingly rich and oaky. Absolutely top-flight since 1995. (DM)
● **Château Ausone** Saint Émilion Grand Cru Classé✪✪✪✪✪ £H

CH. BARRABAQUE Fronsac
Small 9-ha property planted to Merlot (70%), Cab Franc (20%) and Cab Sauv (10%). The robust, densely structured, plummy Prestige comes from one of the best-exposed sites in the appellation, which stands on a mix of sandy-clay and chalky-clay soils. (DM)
● **Château Barrabaque** Canon-Fronsac Prestige★★★ £C

CH. BEAU-SÉJOUR BÉCOT Saint-Emilion 1er GCC   *UK stockists:* AAA
The Bécot brothers seek to produce an opulent, rich, heavily oaked red with sumptuous, plummy fruit. They also make a *garagiste*-style *cuvée* called La Gomerie. This Merlot aged in 100 per cent new oak is sourced from a tiny 2.5-ha plot which is itself unclassified. (DM)
● **Château Beau-Séjour Bécot** Saint-Emilion Grand Cru Classé★★★★ £G
● **La Gomerie** Saint-Emilion Grand Cru★★★★★ £H

CH. BEAUREGARD Pomerol   *UK stockists:* AAA
Ripe and forward Pomerol, with attractively brambly fruit and a hint of oak spice, but with less overtly fleshy, plummy Merlot fruit than some. It is approachable and supple at four or five years. (DM)
● **Château Beauregard** Pomerol★★★ £E

CH. BEAUSÉJOUR Saint-Emilion 1er GCC   *UK stockists:* AAA
Medium to full with a marked black fruit opulence but also the structure for real cellaring. Consistent throughout the 90s with 2000 again looking like it will provide that extra dimension. (DM)
● **Château Beauséjour** Saint-Emilion Grand Cru Classé★★★★ £E

CH. BELLEVUE Saint-Emilion GCC   *UK stockists:* BBR, Far
This is now a big, powerful and structured wine with rich, dark fruit, well-judged oak and powerful tannins in its youth. It has impressive depth, purity and impeccable balance. The wine undoubtedly needs 5 or 6 years' cellaring. (DM)
● **Château Bellevue** Saint-Emilion Grand Cru Classé★★★★ £F

20

CH. BELLEVUE-MONDOTTE Saint-Emilion GC   *UK stockists:* AAA
A tiny-production *cuvée* from Gérard Perse, the owner of PAVIE. This is a big, full and formidably extracted wine with lashings of new oak; very good, if just lacking the depth and purity of the truly great Right Bank reds. (DM)
● **Château Bellevue** Saint-Emilion Grand Cru★★★★ £H

CH. LA BIENFAISANCE Saint-Emilion GC   www.labienfaisance.com   *UK stockists:* F&R
Bienfaisance is traditional with fermentation in cement and ageing in a small proportion of new oak. A more opulent garage-style wine, Sanctus, is aged in 100 per cent new oak. Made with consultation from Stéphane Derenoncourt, it is less extracted and better balanced than many of its peers. (DM)
● **Château La Bienfaisance** Saint-Emilion Grand Cru ★★ £D
● **Sanctus** Saint-Emilion Grand Cru ★★★★ £E

CH. LE BON PASTEUR Pomerol   *UK stockists:* AAA
Small Pomerol property of less than 7 ha owned by roving consultant Michel Rolland. Fleshy, rich and characteristic of the Rolland style with malolactic fermentation instigated in barrel. While structured and ageworthy the wine is supple, rounded and approachable with just a few years' cellaring. (DM)
● **Château le Bon Pasteur** Pomerol★★★★ £F

CH. CANON Saint-Emilion 1er GCC   contact@château-canon.com A:AAA
Significantly improved since 1998 after cellar taint problems. Prior to this you should tread with caution. At its best this is a taut, restrained style with finely structured tannin. (DM)
● **Château Canon** Saint-Emilion Grand Cru Classé★★★ £F

CH. CANON-LA-GAFFELIÈRE Saint Émilion GCC   www.neipperg.com   A:AAA
The style here, as with all the von Neipperg wines, is opulent, rich and supple, with finely integrated oak and soft, velvety tannin. Canon-la-Gaffelière is itself surprisingly approachable at three or four years. The *super-cuvée* La Mondotte is also now made here. (DM)
● **Château Canon-la-Gaffelière** Saint Émilion Grand Cru Classé★★★★ £F

CH. CARIGNAN Premières Côtes de Bordeaux   *UK stockists:* C&B
Very good, well-priced Bordeaux from one of the outlying appellations. Roughly one-third of the vineyard is now over 40 years old. The richly textured, dark plum and spice Prima is one of the best examples from the lesser appellations and is aged in 100 per cent new wood for 18 months. (DM)
● **Château Carignan** Premières Côtes de Bordeaux Prima★★★ £C
● **Château Carignan** Premières Côtes de Bordeaux★★ £B

CH. CERTAN-DE-MAY Pomerol   *UK stockists:* AAA
Very good, stylish and elegant Pomerol from a tiny holding of vineyards close to Pétrus. This is more classically structured than many of its peers and is tight and almost austere when young. (DM)
● **Château Certan-de-May** Pomerol★★★★ £H

CH. CHAUVIN Saint-Emilion GCC   www.châteauchauvin.com   *UK stockists:* BBR,F&R,Tur
This property has been a consistent performer through most of the mid- to late 1990s and continues to be so. Consultancy comes from Michel Rolland and the style is full, rich and fleshy. (DM)
● **Château Chauvin Saint-Emilion** Grand Cru Classé★★★★ £E

CH. CHEVAL BLANC Saint-Emilion 1er GCC   *UK stockists:* AAA
One of the two great wines of Saint-Emilion and produced in much greater quantity than Ausone. The style is rich, concentrated and opulent, with intensely complex, dark berry fruit and spice all underpinned by a structured velvety texture. To fully appreciate it, age for 10 years more. (DM)
● **Château Cheval Blanc** Saint-Emilion Grand Cru Classé✪✪✪✪✪ £H

CH. CLINET Pomerol   www.wines-uponatime.com   *UK stockists:* AAA
Consistently ripe to very ripe, full, rich and almost opulent with a supple silky texture, the wine is always bottled unfiltered and aged in new oak. Best with at least five years' ageing. (DM)
● **Château Clinet** Pomerol★★★★ £G

21

FRANCE

CLOS L'ÉGLISE Pomerol   *UK stockists:* **J&B,**AAA
Fine and impressively dense and powerful Pomerol, lent considerable structure by the inclusion of up to 40 per cent Cab Franc. Very rich and fleshy, it is loaded with dark plum and spicy vanilla oak. It was very stylish in 2001, 00, 99 and 98 and will cellar well for up to a decade. (DM)
● **Clos l'Église** Pomerol★★★★ £H

CH. LA CONSEILLANTE Pomerol   *UK stockists:* AAA
One of the great Pomerols. The best years show remarkably complex dark fruits and oriental spices. The wine benefits from six to seven years' ageing at least. 2000 could well be exceptional. (DM)
● **Château La Conseillante** Pomerol★★★★★ £G

CH. LA CROIX-DE-GAY Pomerol   *UK stockists:* AAA
Good middle-ranking Pomerol with an attractive plump, plummy Merlot character after three or fours years of bottle-age but without any great depth. What marks the property out is the quality of a superior selection called la Fleur-de-Gay. (DM)
● **Château La Croix-de-Gay** Pomerol★★ £E
● **La Fleur-de-Gay** Pomerol★★★★ £H

CH. DAUPHINÉ-RONDILLON Loupiac
The Darriet family pursue a number of interests from their base in Loupiac but it is the splendid Dauphiné-Rondillon that really stands out. This is a very fine alternative to lesser Sauternes from vineyards just the other side of the Garonne. They also produce a pair of fine, essentially fruit-driven Graves. (DM)
Château Dauphiné-Rondillon
● **Château Dauphiné-Rondillon** La Cuvée d'Or Loupiac★★★ £D
Château Moutin
● **Château Moutin** Graves★★ £C   ● **Château Moutin** Graves★★ £C

CH. LA DOMINIQUE Saint-Emilion GCC   *UK stockists:* AAA
This property, in very close proximity to Cheval-Blanc, has been a reasonably consistent performer since the late 1980s. It is supple but well-structured and very ageworthy. 1998 was very good and 2000 looks set to be in the same mould. (DM)
● **Château La Dominique** Saint-Emilion Grand Cru Classé★★★★ £G

DOM. DE L'EGLISE Pomerol   *UK stockists:*AAA
The Castéja family are also significant *négociants* and own Trottevieille in Saint-Emilion. A rich and sumptuous example of the AC, this wine has a firm mineral structure that will ensure continued development in bottle, particularly in the classic vintages. (DM)
● **Domaine de L'Église** Pomerol★★★★ £F

CH. L'ÉGLISE-CLINET Pomerol   *UK stockists:* AAA
Magnificent small Pomerol property with very old vines, some nearing 100 years. It is structured, dense and backward when young. Given six or seven years the result is an elegant, velvety and classically proportioned example of the appellation. Very impressive in 2000, 98, 97, 96 and 95. (DM)
● **Château L'Église-Clinet** Pomerol✪✪✪✪✪ £H

ESSENCE DE DOURTHE Bordeaux   *UK stockists:***Dou,** AAA
Flagship red of the Dourthe *négociant* house. It is sourced from 10ha of the best plots of the firm's leading properties, including Belgrave in the Haut-Médoc, La Garde in Pessac-Léognan and Marsau in the Côtes de Francs. It is rich, full and showy and while impressively structured, it just seems to be missing an element that would move it up among the region's great reds. (DM)
● **Essence de Dourthe** Bordeaux★★★★ £F

CH. L'ÉVANGILE Pomerol   www.lafite.com   *UK stockists:* AAA
This is an impressively deep, structured and powerful example of Pomerol with formidably concentrated levels of complex, dark, spicy fruit. There is oak evident here but its very harmoniously integrated. It has been remarkably good in the best years of the last decade. (DM)
● **Château l'Évangile** Pomerol★★★★★ £H

New entries have producer's name underlined

CH. FAUGÈRES Saint-Emilion GC www.château-faugères.com *UK stockists:* AAA

The regular Saint-Emilion is a dense, richly concentrated Grand Cru, aged in new oak. Since 1998 a super-rich special *cuvée*, Château Péby Faugères, has been produced as well as Cap de Faugères, a supple, rounded and forward style produced from vineyards owned in the Côtes de Castillon. (DM)

Château Faugères
● **Château Faugères** Saint-Emilion Grand Cru★★★ £E
● **Péby Faugères** Saint-Emilion Grand Cru★★★★ £G
Château Cap de Faugères
● **Château Cap de Faugères** Côtes de Castillon★★★ £C

CH. FEYTIT-CLINET Pomerol *UK stockists:* AAA

Really characterful and impressive Pomerol is now being made at this well-sited property. The wine offers real style and substance: rich, concentrated dark-berry fruit is underpinned by lots of very well-integrated new oak. A supple and approachable wine, but give it 4 or 5 years for real balance and harmony. (DM)
● **Château Feytit-Clinet** Pomerol★★★★ £F

CH. FIGEAC Saint-Emilion 1er GCC www.château-figeac.com *UK stockists:* AAA

At its best the wine from this property is both refined and very characterful. It has though been variable over the past decade and a half. At its best, powerful and structured. Recent vintages look very good, four stars at least, but 1996 and 97 were disappointing. (DM)
● **Château Figeac** Saint-Emilion Grand Cru Classé★★★ £G

CH. LA FLEUR DE BOÜARD Lalande-de-Pomerol *UK stockists:* AAA

One of the benchmark properties from this AC. The regular label is rich, concentrated and fleshy with opulent, dark, spicy fruit. The brilliantly crafted Le Plus offers layers of flavour and complexity and has a special minerality and fine cedary structure that mark it as one of the region's great reds. (DM)
● **Château La Fleur de Boüard** Lalande-de-Pomerol★★★ £E
● **Le Plus de La Fleur de Boüard** Lalande-de-Pomerol★★★★ £G

CH. LA FLEUR-PÉTRUS Pomerol *UK stockists:* AAA

Like Pétrus itself this property is owned by the Moueix family. Somewhat erratic in the 1980s, the wine been a model of consistency since the mid- to late 90s. (DM)
● **Château la Fleur-Pétrus** Pomerol★★★★ £G

CH. FOMBRAUGE St-Émilion GC www.fombrauge.com *UK stockists:* AAA

Fombrauge is proving as elsewhere that the less-fancied plots in this sizeable appellation can provide impressive wines. A limited-production, rich and powerful highly priced special *cuvée*, Magrez-Fombrauge, has also now been released. (DM)
● **Château Fombrauge** Saint-Emilion Grand Cru★★★ £D
● **Magrez-Fombrauge** Saint-Emilion Grand Cru★★★★★ £G

CH. FONTENIL Fronsac *UK stockists:* THt

Small Fronsac property owned by Michel and Dany Rolland. The wine is lushly textured, rich, supple and full of opulence, with just a hint of cassis adding depth and weight to the bramble and dark berry fruit. A tiny-production *super-cuvée*, Défi de Fontenil, is also now produced. (DM)
● **Château Fontenil** Fronsac★★★★ £D

CH. FOUGAS Côtes de Bourg *UK stockists:* F&R,Sec,N&P,Tur

This is the larger of the two properties of the Béchets, who also own the tiny Saint-Emilion property Riou de Thaillas. The special *cuvée* Maldoror is sourced from the best individual plots on the property and is aged in 100 per cent new oak. Both wines will stand a litle age. (DM)
● **Château Fougas** Côtes de Bourg★★ £B Côtes de Bourg Maldoror★★★ £C

CLOS FOURTET Saint-Emilion 1er GCC www.premiers-saint-emilion.com *UK stockists:* THt

Clos Fourtet is densely extracted and sees a high proportion of new oak. Recent vintages have been refined and classy with great intensity. The 2003 has splendid potential, and may turn out to be worthy of five stars so this

FRANCE

trend is likely to continue. (DM)

● **Clos Fourtet St-Émilion** Grand Cru Classé★★★★ £F

CH. FRANC-MAILLET Pomerol

Vieux Château Gachet is impressively structured and almost restrained in style. Aged in one-third new wood, it is dense and backward. Franc-Maillet is a classically structured Pomerol with subtle cedar as well as dark berry and plum notes. Jean Baptiste comes from an older vine parcel. (DM)

Château Franc-Maillet

● **Château Franc-Maillet** Pomerol★★★★ £D ● **Château Franc-Maillet Jean Baptiste** Pomerol★★★★ £E

Vieux Château Gachet

● **Vieux Château Gachet** Lalande-de-Pomerol★★★ £C

CH. FRANC-MAYNE Saint-Emilion GCC *UK stockists:* N&P,F&R

Relatively tiny Grand Cru Classé property of just 7 ha which has produced increasingly good wine in recent vintages. The wine is richly textured and impressively concentrated with dark spicy fruit and sufficiently supple tannin to drink well with three or four years' ageing. (DM)

● **Château Franc-Mayne** Saint-Emilion Grand Cru Classé★★★ £E

CH. DES FRANCS Bordeaux Côtes des Francs

Hubert de Boüard, owner of La Fleur de Boüard, also part-owns this excellent satellite property. Les Cerisiers is the more serious of the wines, offering rich, plummy varietal Merlot character and a fleshy, densely textured palate with impressive depth. (DM)

● **Château de Francs** Bordeaux Côtes de Francs★★ £B Bordeaux Côtes de Francs Les Cerisiers★★★ £C

CH. GACHON Montagne-Saint-Emilion *UK stockists:* Hal

Gérard Arpin, who also owns Château Franc-Maillet in Pomerol, produces one of the best wines from this Saint-Emilion satellite appellation. It is rich and fleshy in a fruit-driven style with an impressively supple structure and minimal oak influence. (DM)

● **Château Gachon** Montagne-Saint-Emilion★★★ £C

CH. LE GAY Pomerol *UK stockists:* AAA

This 10-ha property is now owned by Catherine Péré-Vergé, whose portfolio of interests also includes another Pomerol property, Montviel, and a share in Argentina's Clos de Los Siete. Le Gay is increasingly impressive an opulent, modern, fleshy style laden with rich berry fruit. (DM)

● **Château Le Gay** Pomerol★★★★ £F

CH. GAZIN Pomerol www.gazin.com *UK stockists:* AAA

This is among Pomerol's larger properties. The trio of vintages 1998, 99 and 00 were particularly good here. The style is rich, forward and opulent with ripe and plummy dark fruit and an increasing amount of new oak used. (DM)

● **Château Gazin** Pomerol★★★★ £G

GRACIA Saint-Emilion GC

Small garage operation with facilities in the centre of Saint-Emilion. Les Angelots is the lighter and more accessible of the two wines; the Gracia label is richer and fleshier with loads of dark blackberry fruit and sweet oak. It offers impressive depth and is supple and well structured. (DM)

● **Gracia** Saint-Emilion Grand Cru★★★★ £F Saint-Emilion Grand Cru Les Angelots de Gracia★★★ £E

CH. GRAND CORBIN-DESPAGNE Saint-Emilion GC *UK stockists:* Col,BBR,F&R,Tur

The Despagne family have been producing good, well-priced examples of the appellation since the 1998 vintage. Rich and fleshy in style, it requires four to five years' cellaring to throw the aggressive character of its youthful tannin. (DM)

● **Château Grand Corbin-Despagne** Saint-Emilion Grand Cru★★★ £E
● **Château Grand Corbin-Despagne** Saint-Emilion Petit Corbin-Despagne★ £C

CH. GRAND-MAYNE Saint-Emilion GCC www.grand-mayne.com *UK stockists:* AAA

Grand-Mayne produces impressively dark, dense and well-structured Saint-Emilions. An increasing use of new

New entries have producer's name underlined

oak is helping to underpin the character of the château. While firmly structured when young, the wine avoids austerity. (DM)

● **Château Grand-Mayne** Saint-Emilion Grand Cru Classé★★★★ £F

CH. GRAND ORMEAU Lalande-de-Pomerol
Two *cuvées* are now made at this property located in the highest part of the AC. The regular bottling is soft and approachable, while the Cabernet elements are quite apparent in the impressively structured, dark and spicy Madeleine. (DM)

● **Château Grand Ormeau** Lalande-de-Pomerol★★ £E

● **Château Grand Ormeau Madeleine** Lalande-de-Pomerol★★★ £E

CH. GREE LAROQUE Bordeaux Supérieur
This tiny-volume wine sourced from 1.6 ha of vineyards to the north of Libourne and Fronsac. Bottled unfiltered, the wine is impressively deep and concentrated with dark, spicy fruit, opulent oak and just a hint of dark pepper in the background. Give it three to four years. (DM)

● **Château Gree Laroque** Bordeaux Supérieur★★★ £D

CH. HAUT-BERTINERIE www.châteaubertinerie.com *UK stockists:* AAA
Top wines here are labelled Haut-Bertinerie. A high Cabernet Sauvignon component is reflected in the firmly structured Haut-Bertinerie red, the white is barrel-fermented with a rich, full texture on the palate and good background acidity. The Bertinerie wines are softer and more approachable. (DM)

● **Château Haut-Bertinerie** Premieres Côtes de Blaye★★ £B Premieres Côtes de Blaye Landreau★★★ £D

O **Château Haut-Bertinerie** Premieres Côtes de Blaye★★ £C

● **Château Bertinerie** Premieres Côtes de Blaye★★ £B O **Château Bertinerie** Premieres Côtes de Blaye★ £C

CH. HAUT-CHAIGNEAU Lalande-de-Pomerol
Haut-Chaigneau is one of the largest properties in this AC from which a parcel of 40-year-old vines are used to produce La Sergue. Haut-Chaigneau is made in a very ripe, sweet style and is supple and approachable. The more structured and backward La Sergue is in the house style with more marked new wood. (DM)

Château Haut-Chaigneau

● **Château Haut-Chaigneau** Lalande-de-Pomerol★★ £C

Château La Sergue

● **Château La Sergue** Lalande-de-Pomerol★★★ £C

CH. HAUT-MAZERIS Canon-Fronsac *UK stockists:*BBR
This 11-ha property offers some of the finest red wine in this small satellite AC. The wines are deep, dark and concentrated. A 2-ha parcel of the oldest vines is retained to produce the richly textured Cuvée Spéciale. (DM)

● **Château Haut-Mazeris** Canon-Fronsac★★★ £C Canon-Fronsac Cuvée Spéciale★★★ £D

CH. HAUT-MAZERIS Fronsac *UK stockists:*BBR
This wine that has greater structure and grip than those from most neighbouring properties, no doubt aided by the high proportion of the Cabernets in the blend. It is rich, dense and fleshy with just a hint of youthful oak. (DM)

● **Château Haut Mazeros** Fronsac★★★ £C

CH. HOSANNA Pomerol *UK stockists:*AAA, Las
Small Pomerol property showing consistently high quality over the last 5 or 6 vintages. This is a rich, supple and very elegant wine with a fine mineral core, no doubt helped by the sizeable proportion of Cabernet Franc. (DM)

● **Château Hosanna** Pomerol★★★★ £F

CH. HOSTENS-PICANT Sainte-Foy Bordeaux *UK stockists:* NYg,TPg
Absolute benchmark property for this lesser AC. Both reds are modern and fleshy; the regular label is more fruit-driven, while the Lucullus is bigger and fuller. A decent white Cuvée des Demoiselles is also produced. (DM)

● **Lucullus** Sainte-Foy Bordeaux★★★ £C ● **Château Hostens-Picant** Sainte-Foy Bordeaux★★ £C

CH. JOANIN BÉCOT Côtes de Castillon *UK stockists:* AAA
This small and very fine Castillon property is owned by the Bécot family of Beau-Séjour-Bécot. There are just over 5ha under vine and production is tiny at a mere 2,500 cases a year. Merlot is the dominant variety but the vineyard

FRANCE

25

also has a fair amount of Cabernet Franc, accounting for a quarter of the plantings. This is a rich, dense Castillon with a hint of new oak, impressive depth and a subtle mineral purity. Give it 3 or 4 years although its opulent character suggests the wine will be very attractive in its relative youth. (DM)
● **Château Joanin Bécot** Côtes de Castillon★★★ £C

LA CROIX DE PEYROLIE Lussac-Saint-Emilion
Tiny property of just 1.3 ha that yields a mere 12.5 hl/ha, so this is very much a garage-style operation. Rich and very concentrated, it will benefit from five or six years' ageing. (DM)
● **La Croix de Peyrolie** Lussac-Saint-Emilion★★★★ £F

CH. LARCIS-DUCASSE Saint-Emilion GC   UK stockists::J&B, Far
This estate is run by Nicolas Thienpont with consultancy input from Stéphane Derenoncourt. The wine is produced in a supple, accessible style with loads of dark, spicy, fleshy fruit underpinned by fairly high-toast oak. (DM)
● **Château Larcis-Ducasse** Saint-Emilion Grand Cru★★★★ £E

CH. LAFLEUR Pomerol   UK stockists: AAA
Exceptional Pomerol property consisting of a mere 4.5 ha of vines, half surprisingly planted to Cab Franc, which provides considerable structure. The wine ages gracefully for two decades and more. Remarkably consistent throughout the 1990s. (DM)
● **Château Lafleur** Pomerol✪✪✪✪✪ £H

CH. LAROZE Saint-Emilion GCC   www.ch-laroze.com
This is another Saint-Emilion property much improved in the late 1990s. The wine is crafted in a lush, fleshy and opulent style with supple tannins and a very appealing youthful character. It is bottled unfiltered. (DM)
● **Château Laroze** Saint-Emilion Grand Cru Classé★★★ £E

LA MONDOTTE Saint-Emilion   www.neipperg.com   UK stockists: AAA
Along with Le Dôme, this is one of the two great garage wines to emerge in the last half decade. Produced at Canon-La-Gaffelière, it offers a truly opulent and exotic array of dark fruits and oriental spices. Ageing is on lees in new oak for a year and a half and bottling is without filtration. (DM)
● **La Mondotte** Saint-Emilion Grand Cru★★★★★ £H

CH. LATOUR-À-POMEROL Pomerol   UK stockists: AAA
Another property under the Moueix family umbrella. These are supple, ripe and at their best richly plummy examples of Pomerol, produced to showcase the more opulent character of the appellation. It develops well with six or seven years' age. (DM)
● **Château Latour-à-Pomerol**★★★ £H

LE DÔME Saint-Emilion   info@teyssier.fr   UK stockists: AAA
Vies with La Mondotte to be first among the garage wines of Saint-Emilion. Modern in style, malolactic is in barrel and then 50 per cent is drawn off and aged in a second series of brand new oak. Deep and very concentrated, with a fine mineral structure. (DM)
● **Le Dôme** Saint-Emilion Grand Cru Classé★★★★★ £G

CH. LUCIE Saint-Emilion GC
Less than 2 ha under vine of very old vines, some over 100 years. The wine is loaded with dense, dark fruit but there is a real purity and depth often missing in other wines made in a similar style. Accessible from a young age, the wine will nevertheless add further complexity with cellaring. (DM)
● **Lucia** Saint-Emilion Grand Cru★★★★ £E

CLOS DES LUNELLES Côtes de Castillon
Very impressive Castillon from the owner of Château Pavie. The old-vine character of the wine really shines through with complex, smoky, dark berry and cocoa spice aromas and considerable depth and concentration. Just a hint more purity and elegance would lift this to a different level. (DM)
● **Clos des Lunelles** Côtes de Castillon★★★ £D

LYNSOLENCE Saint-Emilion GC
Tiny garage-style operation producing barely more than 500 cases a year from 100% Merlot. This is very good, rich,

New entries have producer's name underlined

fleshy and concentrated wine and the oak is very well judged. It is a supple, forward style with a velvety texture.(DW)
● **Lynsolence** Saint-Emilion Grand Cru★★★★ £F

CH. MAGDELAINE   Saint-Emilion 1er GCC   *UK stockists:* AAA
An opulent, richly plummy, Merlot-dominated wine crafted from older vines than is usual for the region. Will be enjoyable with as little as five years' cellaring and will keep for much longer. (DM)
● **Château Magdelaine** Saint-Emilion Grand Cru Classé★★★★ £D

CH. MONBOUSQUET   Saint-Emilion GC   www.château-pavie.com   *UK stockists:* AAA
A typically modern extractive style of winemaking produces a ripe and bold style of Saint-Emilion here. The driving force behind the renaissance of this once-mediocre property is Gérard Perse, who also owns Pavie and Pavie-Decesse. Expect the wines to develop well in the medium term. (DM)
● **Château Monbousquet** Saint-Emilion Grand Cru★★★★ £F

CH. MONTVIEL   Pomerol
Catherine Péré-Vergé, produces a rich and concentrated Pomerol with a typically fleshy Merlot palate but it stands out thanks to a real purity and a mineral quality to the fruit that is often absent in the AC. (DM)
● **Château Montviel** Pomerol★★★★ £E

CH. LE MOULIN   Pomerol
Rich and sumptuous, if pricey, Pomerol. While supple and approachable, it also possesses a depth and persistence so often absent in other examples. (DM)
● **Château le Moulin** Pomerol★★★★ £G

CH. MOULIN PEY-LABRIE   Canon-Fronsac   *UK stockists:* **C&B**
Small property of some 6.5 ha producing modern, stylish and ripe reds with a high proportion of Merlot and increasing use of new oak. The rounded, velvety tannin is assisted by completion of the malolactic fermentation in barrel. (DM)
● **Château Moulin Pey-Labrie** Canon-Fronsac★★★ £D

CH. MOULIN SAINT-GEORGES   Saint-Emilion GC   *UK stockists:* AAA
Located in close proximity to Ausone and in fact owned by the same family. Quality here has been consistently improving in recent vintages, and has rated four stars since 1998. It will be all the better for four or five years' ageing. (DM)
● **Château Moulin Saint-Georges** Saint-Emilion Grand Cru★★★★ £F

CLOS DE L'ORATOIRE   Saint-Emilion GCC   info@neipperg.com   *UK stockists:* AAA
Under the same ownership as Canon-La-Gaffelière. As at Stéphan von Neipperg's other properties, the style here is modern and approachable but the wine is neither overripe nor excessively extracted. Classy and ageworthy. (DM)
● **Clos de l'Oratoire Saint-Emilion** Grand Cru Classé★★★★ £G

CH. PAVIE   Saint-Emilion 1er GCC   www.château-pavie.com   *UK stockists:* AAA
Purchased in 1998 by Gérard Perse. Pavie is increasingly very late-harvested and more akin to a full-blown Napa red than a classical Saint-Emilion of the old school. If you are a fan of rich and concentrated reds with massive extract then this will appeal. (DM)
● **Château Pavie** Saint-Emilion Grand Cru Classé★★★★ £H

CH. PAVIE-DECESSE   Saint-Emilion GCC   www.château-pavie.com   *UK stockists:* AAA
Like Pavie, owned by Gérard Perse and now producing wines of greater density and power than a few years back. The style, as at Pavie, is for rich and opulent reds but there has always been a tighter, leaner edge to Decesse when compared with its larger, more illustrious neighbour. (DM)
● **Château Pavie-Decesse** Saint-Emilion Grand Cru Classé★★★★ £G

CH. PAVIE-MACQUIN   Saint-Emilion GCC   pavie.macquin@wanadoo.fr   *UK stockists:* AAA
Consultancy from Stéphane Derenoncourt at this biodynamically farmed property. The wines are dense, powerful and structured, with seamlessly integrated dark, spicy fruit and oak and great purity. They age very well. (DM)
● **Château Pavie-Macquin** Saint-Emilion Grand Cru Classé★★★★★ £F

FRANCE

CH. PÉTRUS Pomerol *UK stockists:* AAA
One of the most expensive wines in the world and one of Bordeaux's truly great reds. The vineyards sit upon a plateau of remarkably well-drained clay soils and provide a unique *terroir*. It is consistently great and perhaps only struggles very slightly in lesser years, but then so does every other property in the region. (DM)
● **Château Pétrus** Pomerol❂❂❂❂ £H

CH. LE PIN Pomerol *UK stockists:* AAA
Ripe, opulent and approachable wine rather than one that is overstructured and austere and the vinification reflects this approach. Malolactic is carried out in barrel and the wine sees 100 per cent new oak. Undoubtedly a very fine and richly opulent example of Pomerol. (DM)
● **Château le Pin** Pomerol❂❂❂❂ £H

CH. LE PIN BEAUSOLEIL Bordeaux-Supérieur *UK stockists:* Cam,F&R
Small-production, top-quality red from one of the region's humbler appellations. Initially backward and firm in structure, it displays an array of dark, spicy almost exotic flavours. Give it four or five years to round out. (DM)
● **Château Le Pin Beausoleil** Bordeaux Supérieur★★★ £C

CLOS PUY ARNAUD Côtes de Castillon *UK stockists:* F&R
One of a handful of really impressive properties from this now excellent satellite appellation. The vines are also now farmed biodynamically. It is a dense and richly concentrated red with dark berry fruit, spicy oak and a supple, firm structure. Consistently right on the cusp of four stars. (DM)
● **Clos Puy Arnaud** Côtes de Castillon★★★★ £D
● **Château Pervenche Puy Arnaud** Côtes de Castillon★ £B

CH. PUYGUERAUD Bordeaux-Côtes de Francs *UK stockists:* Sec,F&R
Refined and surprisingly structured for this lesser appellation and displays an impressive array of cedar, dark fruit and oriental spices. Will benefit from a few years in the cellar. A special limited production wine, Cuvée Georges, was produced in 2000. (DM)
● **Château Puygueraud** Bordeaux-Côtes de Francs★★★ £C

CH. QUINAULT Saint-Emilion GC *UK stockists:* CTy,BBR,Sec,N&P,F&R
Despite being only a regular Saint-Emilion Grand Cru, this is a serious example from a vineyard with an average age of around 50 years. Rich, supple and opulent, best with 8 to 10 years' age. A limited-production special bottling has been produced in 2003, Oriel l'Absolu. (DM)
● **Château Quinault L'Enclos** Saint-Emilion Grand Cru★★★★ £F
● **Château Quinault L'Enclos** Saint-Emilion Grand Cru Lafleur de Quinault★★ £D

CH. REIGNAC Bordeaux-Supérieur *UK stockists:* CTy,Tur,F&R
One of the best examples of this lesser appellation and it should be a benchmark for others. The wine is dense, dark and structured. It should develop very well in the medium term. There are also two special limited-releases Reignac and Balthus. (DM)
● **Château Reignac** Bordeaux Supérieur★★ £C Bordeaux Supérieur Reignac★★★ £D
● **Balthus** Bordeaux Supérieur★★★★ £E

CH. REYNON Premières Côtes de Bordeaux *UK stockists:* Han
Denis Dubourdieu makes some very good dry white and red, along with a little sweet Cadillac from a total of some 57 ha of vineyards. Both the Vieilles Vignes white and the red will evolve nicely in the short term. (DM)
● **Château Reynon** Premières Côtes de Bordeaux★★ £C O **Bordeaux** Vieilles Vignes★★ £B

CH. RIOU DE THAILLAS Saint-Emilion GC *UK stockists:* Jas
The Béchets also own the impressive Château Fougas in the Côtes de Bourg. This property is smaller and they make just one wine, a dense, powerful and initially tannic Saint-Emilion. Given six or seven years, the wine will offer increasing richness and complexity. (DM)
● **Château Riou de Thaillas** Saint-Emilion Grand Cru★★★★ £F

CH. ROC DE CAMBES Côtes de Bourg *UK stockists:* C&B,Sav
This property is not only a serious benchmark for the Côtes de Bourg but also for all the lesser Right Bank appellations. Always harvested as late as possible and from very low yields. It is long, complex, powerful and

28

ageworthy. 2000, 99 and 98 were all very impressive. (DM)
● **Château Roc de Cambes** Côtes de Bourg★★★★ £F

CH. ROL VALENTIN   Saint-Emilion GC   *UK stockists:* AAA
Small property producing wines from old vines and yields that are much lower than elsewhere in the region. All the modern cellar techniques are in evidence: 100% new oak, malolactic in barrel and ageing on lees with micro-oxygenation. This is opulent, rich and supple. (DM)
● **Château Rol Valentin** Saint-Emilion Grand Cru★★★★ £F

CH. LA ROUSSELLE   Fronsac
One of the emerging lights of Fronsac. Traditionally vinified and aged for around a year in oak, the wine shows marked Merlot character when young as well as impressive purity and depth. Four or five years' ageing will provide yet greater richness and weight. (DM)
● **Château La Rousselle** Fronsac★★★ £C

CLOS SAINT MARTIN   Saint-Emilion GCC
This tiny 1.3-ha property is the smallest Grand Cru Classé in the AC. It produces a full, rich and concentrated red with dark, spicy-plummy fruit and a hint of vanilla and cocoa from 100% new wood. (DM)
● **Clos Saint Martin** Saint-Emilion Grand Cru Classé★★★★ £F

CLOS DE SARPE   Saint-Emilion GC
Barely 1,000 cases are made a year of this massive and densely textured old-style Bordeaux red. The wine is dark when young and marked by an intense, almost overwhelming blackberry fruit character. The second label, Charles de Sarpe, is softer and quite a bit lighter. (DM)
● **Clos de Sarpe** Saint-Emilion Grand Cru★★★★ £G   ● **Charles de Sarpe** Saint-Emilion Grand Cru★★★ £E

CH. TERTRE-RÔTEBOEUF   Saint-Emilion GC   *UK stockists:* AAA
Although this remarkable Saint-Emilion has not been elevated to Grand Cru Classé status, the property enjoys a highly propitious site for producing fine wine. Very complex with a myriad of dark and spicy fruits and stylish oak. It will age gracefully and requires six or seven years' patience. (DM)
● **Château Tertre-Rôteboeuf** Saint-Emilion Grand Cru★★★★★ £H

CH. TEYSSIER   Saint-Emilion GC   *UK stockists:* AAA
Teyssier itself is a soft and attractive, relatively forward, spicy Saint-Emilion sourced from the low-lying vineyards in the south of the AC. The more serious Château Laforge comes from a number of superior Grand Cru sites. Le Dôme is the top red label. The range is completed by a fine barrel-fermented white, Clos Nardian.(DM)
● **Château Teyssier** Saint-Emilion Grand Cru★★★ £D   ● **Château Laforge** Saint-Emilion Grand Cru★★★★ £F
○ **Clos Nardian** Bordeaux★★★★ £F

CH. TOUR DE MIRAMBEAU   Entre-deux-Mers   *UK stockists:* Odd
A decent white takes the Bordeaux AC as does a rosé and there is an Entre-deux-Mers white as well. Cuvée Passion white is good and the red version is one of the best wines of the Bordeaux Supérieur AC. The recently produced super-*cuvée* Girolate only takes the humble Bordeaux AC but is a wine of serious depth and structure. (DM)
Château Tour de Mirambeau
● **Château Tour de Mirambeau** Bordeaux Supérieur Cuvée Passion★★ £C   Bordeaux Supérieur★ £B
○ **Château Tour de Mirambeau** Bordeaux Supérieur Cuvée Passion★★ £C
● **Girolate** Bordeaux★★★★ £E

CH LA TOUR FIGEAC   Saint-Emilion GCC   *UK stockists:* AAA
Biodynamically tended property with consultancy from Christine Derenoncourt, wife of roving Bordeaux guru Stéphane. The wine is produced very much in an opulent, forward and showy style and the oak can be just a bit assertive in its youth, but it will offer good drinking within 4 or 5 years. (DM)
● **Château La Tour Figeac** Saint-Emilion Grand Cru Classé★★★★ £F

CH. TROPLONG-MONDOT   Saint-Emilion GCC   *UK stockists:* AAA
Consistently excellent source of top Saint-Emilion over the past decade. The initial firm tannic structure means the wine needs six or seven years' cellaring. 2000 was of five-star quality. (DM)
● **Château Troplong-Mondot** Saint-Emilion Grand Cru Classé★★★★ £G

29

FRANCE

CH. TROTANOY Pomerol *UK stockists:* AAA
Small Pomerol property of 7 ha. The wine is dense and very seriously structured, with considerable grip and tannin when young. Seven or eight years' cellaring will see the evolution of all sorts of opulent black fruit. On top form since 1997. (DM)
● **Château Trotanoy** Pomerol★★★★★ £H

CH TROTTEVIEILLE Saint-Emilion 1er GCC *UK stockists:* AAA
Since 2000 this property has reclaimed its place in the top rank of Saint-Emilion. The wine is rich and plump with dark, spicy berry fruit and marked new oak, underpinned by a fine mineral purity. (DM)
● **Château Trottevieille** Saint-Emilion 1er Grand Cru Classé★★★★ £F

CH. DE VALANDRAUD Saint-Emilion GC www.thunevin.com *UK stockists:* **Far,**AAA
Original *garagiste* wine, first made in 1991. New plots have been added and two second labels, Clos Badon and Virginie de Valandraud, help in ensuring the integrity of the *grand vin.* Arguably the best Kosher wine is produced her now and a further label Prieuré Lescours has also now been added. Valandraud is neither fined nor filtered and is dense, fleshy and extracted. Impressive grip and structure. (DM)
● **Château de Valandraud** Saint-Emilion Grand Cru★★★★★ £F
● **Château de Valandraud Kosher** Saint-Emilion Grand Cru★★★ £F

CH. LA VIEILLE CURE Fronsac www.expressions-de-fronsac.com *UK stockists:* N&P,F&R
Another outperformer in Bordeaux's lesser appellations.A good medium-term ageing prospect. Good to very good since the late 1990s. Impressive second wine, Sacristie de La Vieille Cure.(DW)
● **Château La Vieille Cure** Fronsac★★★ £D

VIEUX-CHÂTEAU-CERTAN Pomerol www.vieuxchâteaucertan.com *UK stockists:* AAA
Cab Franc and Cab Sauv account for 40 per cent of the vineyard, part of the reason for the surprisingly dense and powerful structure of the wine. Needs a decade to begin to show its true class, when it becomes very refined and harmonious. Excellent from 1998 on – five stars. (DM)
● **Vieux-Château-Certan** Pomerol★★★★★ £H

Other wineries of note
Ch. l'Archange (Saint-Emilion), Ch. Armens (Saint-Emilion), Ch. l'Arrosée (Saint-Emilion), Clos Badon (Saint-Emilion), Ch. Bel-Air la Royère (Blaye), Ch. Berliquet (Saint-Emilion), Ch. de Bois Pertuis (Bordeaux), Ch. Bonalgue (Pomerol), Ch. Bonnet (Entre-deux-Mers), Ch. Bourgneuf-Vayron (Pomerol), Ch. Canon de Brem (Canon-Fronsac), Ch. Carsin (Premières Côtes de Bordeaux), Ch. Clémence (Pomerol), Clos du Clocher (Pomerol), Ch. Clos des Jacobins (Saint-Emilion), Ch La Clotte (Saint-Emilion), Ch. La Commanderie de Mazeyres (Pomerol), Ch. Côte de Baleau (Saint-Emilion), Ch. la Couspaude (Saint-Emilion), Ch. La Croix-Canon (Canon-Fronsac), Ch. La Croix du Casse (Pomerol), Ch. de la Dauphine (Fronsac), Ch. Destieux (Saint-Emilion), Ch. Faizeau (Montagne-Saint-Emilion), Ch. Falfas (Côtes de Bourg), Ch. Fleur-Cardinale (Saint-Emilion), Ch. La Gaffelière (Saint-Emilion), Ch. Grand-Pontet (Saint-Emilion), Ch. Les Grandes Murailles (Saint-Emilion), Ch. Gravières (Saint-Emilion), Ch. Larcis-Ducasse (Saint-Emilion), Ch. de Laussac (Côtes de Castillon), Ch. Lusseau (Saint-Emilion), Ch. Marsau (Bordeaux Côtes des Francs), Ch. La Mauriane (Puisseguin-Saint-Emilion), Ch. Mont Perat (Premières Côtes de Bordeaux), Ch. Moulin Haut-Laroque (Fronsac), Passion du Prieuré Malessan (Premières Côtes de Blaye), Ch. Petit-Village (Pomerol), Ch. Prieuré Lescours (Saint-Emilion), Ch. de la Rivière (Fronsac), Ch. Rouget (Pomerol), Ch. Sansonnet (Saint-Emilion), Ch. Taillefer (Pomerol), Ch. Tertre-Daugay (Saint-Emilion), Ch. Thieuley (Bordeaux), Ch. Les Trois Croix (Fronsac), Ch. Veyry (Côtes de Castillon), Ch. Vieux Maillet (Pomerol), Virginie de Valandraud (Saint-Emilion),

An in-depth profile of every producer can be found in Wine behind the label 2006

30

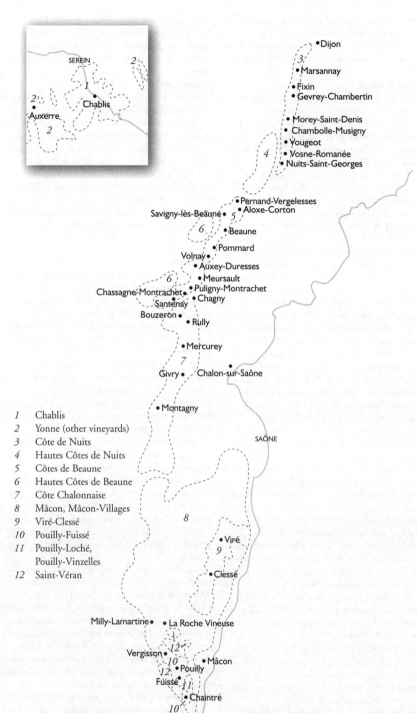

• Dijon
3
• Marsannay

• Fixin
• Gevrey-Chambertin

• Morey-Saint-Denis
• Chambolle-Musigny
• Vougeot
4 • Vosne-Romanée
• Nuits-Saint-Georges

SEREIN
2
1
2 Chablis
Auxerre
2

• Pernand-Vergelesses
Savigny-lès-Beaune • • Aloxe-Corton *5*
6 • Beaune

• Pommard
Volnay • • Auxey-Duresses
6 • Meursault
Chassagne-Montrachet • • Puligny-Montrachet
Santenay • • Chagny
Bouzeron • • Rully

• Mercurey
7
Givry • • Chalon-sur-Saône

• Montagny

SAÔNE

1 Chablis
2 Yonne (other vineyards)
3 Côte de Nuits
4 Hautes Côtes de Nuits
5 Côtes de Beaune
6 Hautes Côtes de Beaune
7 Côte Chalonnaise
8 Mâcon, Mâcon-Villages
9 Viré-Clessé
10 Pouilly-Fuissé
11 Pouilly-Loché,
Pouilly-Vinzelles
12 Saint-Véran

8

• Viré
9
• Clessé

Milly-Lamartine • • La Roche Vineuse
12
Vergisson • *10* • Mâcon
12 • Pouilly
Fuissé • *11*
• Chaintré
10

31

Burgundy Overview

FRANCE

Burgundy can be considered as four distinct entities. In the north lies Chablis, at its heart is the Côte d'Or, next comes the Côte Chalonnaise then, still further south, the Mâconnais. The main appellations for each are given below.

Chablis & Yonne

Chablis and the surrounding vineyards are isolated from the heart of Burgundy, being almost halfway to Paris from the Côte d'Or. All Chablis is produced from the Chardonnay grape and is classified by vineyard site as either **Petit Chablis, Chablis, Chablis Premier Cru** or **Chablis Grand Cru**. Other than Chablis there's Sauvignon under the **Saint-Bris** AC and occasional pure cherryish Pinot Noir from **Irancy** AC. Pinot Noir or Chardonnay from other villages in the Yonne is suffixed **Bourgogne**.

Côte d'Or & Côte Chalonnaise

The CÔTE DE NUITS is Burgundy's most classic red wine district and based primarily on just one grape variety, Pinot Noir. It runs from **Marsannay** and **Fixin** through the leading communes of **Gevrey-Chambertin** (including leading *grands crus* **Chambertin** and **Clos de Bèze**), **Morey-Saint-Denis** (with *grands crus* **Clos de la Roche, Clos Saint-Denis, Clos des Lambrays** and **Clos de Tart**), **Chambolle-Musigny** (with **Bonnes Mares** and **Le Musigny**) and **Vougeot** (for **Clos Vougeot**), **Flagey-Echezeaux** (for **Echezeaux** and **Grands Echezeaux**), **Vosne-Romanée** (*grands crus* **La Romanée, Romanée-Conti, Richebourg, Romanée-Saint-Vivant, La Grande Rue,** and **La Tâche**) to **Nuits-Saint-Georges**. The CÔTE DE BEAUNE is famous for great white Burgundy made from Chardonnay, although more Pinot Noir is planted. Much of both is at least potentially very high quality. In a confusion of appellations in the north, **Aloxe-Corton** with the famous *grands crus* of **Corton** (mostly red) and **Corton-Charlemagne** (white) stands out. **Beaune, Pernand-Vergelesses** and **Savigny-lès-Beaune** produce fine reds but some good whites too, while the celebrated **Pommard** and **Volnay** are restricted to red. **Monthélie,** and **Auxey-Duresses** provide more affordable red and a little white, while **Saint-Romain** and the often excellent **Saint-Aubin** do better with white. The big three white Burgundy appellations are **Meursault, Puligny-Montrachet** (including *grands crus* **Chevalier-Montrachet, Le Montrachet** and part of **Bâtard-Montrachet**) and **Chassagne-Montrachet**. The latter also produces red as do **Santenay** and **Maranges** in the tail of the Côte d'Or.

The CÔTE CHALONNAISE begins close to this tail. Both the wines and the countryside are distinctly different but the village appellations are again classified for wines from Chardonnay and/or Pinot Noir – with the exception the first village, **Bouzeron**, which is classified for Aligoté.

Rully makes more white than red, while **Mercury** and **Givry** produce mostly red. The southernmost appellation, **Montagny**, is for Chardonnay alone. **Crémant de Bourgogne** is for the region's sparkling wine.

Mâconnais

As in the Côte de Beaune here too there is greatness in white wine (from Chardonnay), with a new wave of excellent producers beginning to emerge. Quality wine production is focused on **Pouilly-Fuissé** (with its four communes of Chaintré, Fuissé, Solutré and Vergisson), adjoined at its eastern end by the small **Pouilly-Loché** and **Pouilly-Vinzelles** ACs. Many other vineyards north and south of Pouilly-Fuissé qualify as **Saint-Véran**. There is fine quality too from **Viré-Clessé** and increasingly from several of some 43 villages that can be suffixed to Mâcon (eg **Mâcon-Bussières**).

Chablis

Chablis is one of the great white wines of the world, and partly because the cultivation of the Chardonnay grape in these cool hills is so close to the limit of where obtaining full ripeness is possible. Success rarely comes easily, fraught with an annual battle against frost and rain, demanding constant diligence. The importance of fully ripe fruit cannot be understated. The wines should be vigorous, fresh, suffused with minerality but also with generosity and length of flavour without the greeness, harshness or indeed sulphur that some disciples have been duped into believing was authentic Chablis character.

Chablis Vintages

No two vintages in Chablis are quite alike and even from a good producer the choice of vintage can make a significant difference to the quality in your glass. Given the problems of frost, the not uncommon struggle for ripeness in cooler years, the incidence of mildew and rot in wetter years, and, too often, lack of a rigorous grape selection, short of being able to afford Raveneau from every vintage it is important to choose a vintage carefully especially if the wines are intended for cellaring.

The last five vintages in Chablis have been by no means bad though conditions have been highly variable. **2004★★★/★★★★**: A cool vintage but a large crop. Claims of 'quality and quantity' only likely to be justified where yields were kept down and the healthiest, ripest fruit was used. **2003★★/★★★★**: Extreme heat and a very early harvest (late August!). Much better than further south in Burgundy with good structure from the best names. Much basic Petit Chablis and Chablis is uncharacteristically ripe and drinkable. **2002★★★★/★★★★★**: Much more complete than 2003. Wines are ripe and concentrated, if just

New entries have producer's name underlined

occasionally a little broad and diffuse. Many
outstanding, balanced and ageworthy examples.
2001★★/★★★★: A difficult vintage due to wet and
cold. However where selection was rigorous the wines
can be very good and very expressive of terroir (Fèvre
for instance). **2000★★★/★★★★**: Overall quality was
higher than in 2001 though yields were mostly high
and some wines are evolving quite quickly. The best,
though, are concentrated, structured and balanced.
1999★★★★: Like 2000, 1999 was also fine - some
excellent wines for drinking now but best *grands crus*
should be kept another 5-10 years.
There were several other good vintages in the 1990s but
(1990 apart) all come from the latter half of the decade.
1995, 1996 and **1997** all produced good wines,
particular the latter. **1998** Chablis however is generally
better avoided now as are the vast majority of wines
from 1994, 1993, 1992, and 1991. However for a taste
of how well Chablis can age consider the best from
1990 (an exceptional vintage), 1988 or even 1986.

Wizard's Wishlist

A selection of classic Chablis
BILLAUD-SIMON ○ Chablis Grand Cru Vaudésir
ADHÉMAR & FRANCIS BOUDIN
○ Chablis Premier Cru L'Homme Mort
DOM. DU COLOMBIER ○ Chablis Grand Cru Bougros
DANIEL DAMPT ○ Chablis Premier Cru Côte de Léchet
RENÉ ET VINCENT DAUVISSAT
○ Chablis Grand Cru Preuses
DOM. BERNARD DEFAIX

○ Chablis Premier Cru Côte de Léchet
JEAN-PAUL DROIN
○ Chablis Premier Cru Montée de Tonnerre
JOSEPH DROUHIN ○ Chablis Grand Cru Les Clos
WILLIAM FEVRE ○ Chablis Grand Cru Valmur
JEAN-PIERRE GROSSOT
○ Chablis Premier Cru Mont de Milieu
DOM. LAROCHE
○ Chablis Grand Cru Blanchots Réserve de l'Obédience
DOM. DES MALANDES ○ Chablis Premier Cru
Fourchaume
DOM. LOUIS MICHEL
○ Chablis Premier Cru Montée de Tonnerre
MOREAU-NAUDET
○ Chablis Premier Cru Montée de Tonnerre
DOM. PINSON ○ Chablis Premier Cru Mont de Milieu
DOM. RAVENEAU ○ Chablis Grand Cru Blanchots

Good value Chablis & Yonne whites
BILLAUD-SIMON ○ Chablis Tête d'Or
JEAN-MARC BROCARD
○ Chablis Vieilles Vignes Dom. Sainte-Claire
DOM. DU COLOMBIER ○ Chablis
WILLIAM FEVRE ○ Chablis
GHISLAINE ET JEAN-HUGUES GOISOT
○ Bourgogne Côte d'Auxerre
DOM. DES MALANDES ○ Chablis
DOM. LOUIS MOREAU ○ Chablis Dom. du Cèdre D'oré
DIDIER & PASCAL PICQ ○ Chablis Vieilles Vignes
DENIS RACE ○ Chablis

Chablis & Yonne/A-Z of producers

BILLAUD-SIMON   www.billaud-simon.com   *UK stockists:* BBR, CTy, L&W, WSc, NYg, Sel
Family domaine dating from 1815 making brilliant, predominantly unoaked Chablis. 20 ha include *grands crus*
Les Clos, Preuses and Vaudésir and a tiny bit of Blanchots, as well as significant *premier cru* holdings. These are
delicious, graceful, stylish wines with extra distinction and depth at the *premier cru* level and wonderful
dimension and complexity at the *grand cru* level. (PW)
○ Chablis Grand Cru Preuses★★★★ £E Vaudésir★★★★★ £E Les Clos★★★★★£E
○ Chablis Premier Cru Vaillons★★★★ £C Montée de Tonnerre★★★★ £C

A & F BOUDIN/DOM. DE CHANTEMERLE   *UK stockists:* L&S, Rae, IGH, Maj
Exciting small domaine where low yields, manual harvesting and vinification in inert vats contribute to a
rich, ripe, almost buttery style (yet minerally too) but without any oak influence. Particularly worth seeking
out is L'Homme Mort, bottled separately from the rest of Fourchaume. All the wines can be drunk quite
young but will keep for a decade – even the regular Chablis. (PW)
○ Chablis Premier Cru Fourchaume★★★ £C L'Homme Mort★★★ £D
○ Chablis★★ £B

JEAN-MARC BROCARD   www.domaine-brocard.fr   *UK stockists:* JBa, Adm, BWC, J&B, Odd
Expanding domaine, now with 96 ha, with an emphasis on 'typical' Chablis that is minerally and elegant but
they can be a bit lean and underripe. Better *premiers* and *grands crus* needing 4 years' age. Bourgogne Blancs

33

named after soil types are of good Petit Chablis quality; newer blended Premier Cru Chablis go some way to live up to their names: Minéral, Extrême, Sensuel and Paradoxe. Chablis Domaine de la Boisseneuse is biodynamically produced. More variable from lesser years. (PW)

O **Chablis Grand Cru** Bougros★★ £E Vaudésir★★★ £E
O **Chablis Premier Cru** Montmains Le Manant★★★ £C Vaucoupin★★ £C
O **Chablis**★ £B Vieilles Vignes★ £B   O **Bourgogne Aligoté**★ £B

LA CHABLISIENNE www.chablisienne.com   UK stockists: **SsG, Cib, E&T, Maj, WSc, Wai**
With 1,100 ha of vineyards the La Chablisienne co-op produces a quarter of all Chablis made, much of it going under the labels of supermakets and *négociants*. Basic wines can be lean and dilute, while some of the *premiers crus* and *grands crus* are excessively oaked (even the prized Château Grenouilles). Vaulorent, Montmains and Montée de Tonnerre can be really good and the Vieilles Vignes is typically concentrated with good balance. (PW)

O **Chablis Grand Cru** Blanchots★★★ £E Grenouilles★★★ £E Preuses★★★ £E
O **Chablis Premier Cru** Montmains★★ £D Montée de Tonnerre★★ £D
O **Chablis Premier Cru** Vaulorent★★ £D   O **Chablis** Vieilles Vignes★★ £C

DOM. DU COLOMBIER   UK stockists: **FMV**
All levels of Chablis are produced at this 35-ha estate and all are unwooded. The style is ripe and intense with good minerality and restrained lees influence. *Premier crus* Fourchaume and Vaucoupin are refined as is a richer and more concentrated Bougros. Petit Chablis and Chablis should be drunk fairly young but both *premiers crus* and Bougros with at least 5 years' age. (PW)

O **Chablis Grand Cru** Bougros★★★★ £E
O **Chablis Premier Cru** Fourchaume★★★ £C Vaucoupin★★★ £C
O **Chablis**★★ £B   O **Petit Chablis**★ £B

DANIEL DAMPT www.dampt-defaix.com   UK stockists: **Bal, HHC, NYg**
Very good Chablis vinified in stainless steel, with the emphasis on a ripe fruit and floral character but retaining firm acidity and a minerally influence. A good inexpensive source of wines that drink well with three or four years' age but will keep for longer in the case of the *premiers crus*. (PW)

O **Chablis Premier Cru** Beauroy★★★ £C Vaillons★★ £C Fourchaume★★★ £C
O **Chablis Premier Cru** Côte de Léchet★★★ £C   O **Chablis**★★ £B

RENÉ ET VINCENT DAUVISSAT   UK stockists: **DDr, HHB, J&B, L&S, Tan, IGH, F&M**
Almost all of the 11.5 ha here are either *premier* or *grand cru* with high average vine age and all the grapes are manually picked. Most wines are fermented and aged in used oak and are simply marvellous, characterised by depth, breadth and body, filled with a gently honeyed ripeness and stylish minerality. Even the Petit Chablis is fine. All need ageing – *grands crus* for six or seven years. (PW)

O **Chablis Grand Cru** Preuses★★★★★ £F Les Clos❂❂❂❂❂ £F
O **Chablis Premier Cru** Séchet★★★★ £E Forest★★★★ £E Vaillons★★★★ £E
O **Chablis**★★★ £C   O **Petit Chablis**★★ £B

DOM. BERNARD DEFAIX www.bernard-defaix.com   UK stockists: **HrV, F&R**
This 25-ha estate includes a large chunk of *premier cru* Côte de Lechet for a very distinctive floral, mineral and flinty example with good weight and breadth. Other wines are good too, properly ripe with good body in part from lees enrichment; Les Lys is more floral, Vaillons more mineral. Also Fourchaume and *grand cru* Bougros under the Sylvain & Didier Defaix label. (PW)

O **Chablis Premier Cru** Côte de Lechet★★★ £C Les Lys★★★ £C Vaillons★★★ £C
O **Chablis** Vieille Vigne★★ £C

DANIEL-ÉTIENNE DEFAIX www.chablisdefaix.com   UK stockists: **GFy, BBR, Con, Tan, Han, IGH**
Effectively organic domaine with wines of depth, intensity and complexity. Most can be drunk soon after release but will keep. Les Lys has more mineral, citrus character; Côte de Léchet and Vaillons are more leesy. Also rare old-vine Bourgogne Rouge and a tiny amount of Grand Cru Blanchots. (PW)

O **Chablis Premier Cru** Côte de Léchet★★★ £D Les Lys★★★ £D
O **Chablis Premier Cru** Vaillons★★★ £D   O **Chablis** Vieilles Vignes★★ £C

New entries have producer's name underlined

JEAN-PAUL & BENOIT DROIN   www.jeanpaul-droin.fr   *UK stockists:* **RsW, DDr,** BBR, Bib, UnC
Jean-Paul Droin and his son Benoît have 20 ha in *cru* sites. The range is generally of high quality but basics are variable. Rich, ripe and full *premiers* and *grands crus* see oak but this rarely overwhelms the fruit. Nearly all can be drunk at just three or four years, but will improve for as long again. *Grand cru* Blanchots and *premiers crus* Côte de Lechet and Vaucoupin are also made. (PW)
O **Chablis Grand Cru** Grenouilles★★★★ £E Vaudésir★★★★ £E Les Clos★★★★ £E
O **Chablis Premier Cru** Montmains★★★ £C Montée de Tonnerre★★★★ £C
O **Chablis Premier Cru** Fourchaume★★★ £C Vosgros★★★ £C

JOSEPH DROUHIN (CHABLIS)   www.drouhin.com   *UK stockists:* **DAy,** Add, MCW, WsB
Grapes from more than 40 ha in Chablis are pressed locally then vinified at the Drouhin headquarters in Beaune. Low yields contribute to wines with ripe, concentrated fruit. Oak is used in the top wines but there is usually a good minerally aspect to their character. (PW)
O **Chablis Grand Cru** Preuses★★★ £F Vaudésir★★★★ £F Les Clos★★★★★ £F
O **Chablis Premier Cru** Sécher★★★ £E Vaillons★★★ £E
O **Chablis**★ £B Domaine de Vaudon★★ £C

GÉRARD DUPLESSIS   *UK stockists:* RsW, A&B, Rae, Maj
Excellent small grower with 7 ha, mostly in top *premiers crus*. Wines are vinified in stainless steel and matured in old wood. Classic underlying richness and steely, minerally character can provide wonderful drinking with five years' age; even better with another 5 or 10 in a top vintage. (PW)
O **Chablis Grand Cru** Les Clos★★★★ £E   O **Chablis**★★ £C
O **Chablis Premier Cru** Fourchaume★★★ £D Montée de Tonnerre★★★ £D
O **Chablis Premier Cru** Vaillons★★ £D Montmains★★★ £D

JEAN DURUP ET FILS   www.durup-chablis.com   *UK stockists:* ABy, DDr, THt, HRp, Tan, Hrd
Largest estate in the region and a leading advocate of unoaked Chablis. Well-balanced wines with adequate richness that drink well with two to five years' age; *premiers crus* can age for up to a decade. Main labels are Jean Durup, Domaine de l'Eglantière and Château de Maligny, but wines are also bottled under Domaine de la Paulière and Domaine des Valéry labels. Some *grand cru* Vaudésir and Les Clos have also been made. (PW)
O **Chablis Premier Cru** Montée de Tonnerre★★ £C L'Homme Mort★★★ £C
O **Chablis Premier Cru** Fourchaume★★ £C Vau-de-Vey★★ £C
O **Chablis**★ £B Vieilles Vignes★★ £B Vigne de la Reine★★ £C Carré de César★★ £C

WILLIAM FÈVRE   www.williamfevre.com   *UK stockists:* **JEF, HBJ,** BBR, WSc, F&M, Wai
The leading estate in Chablis, owned by Henriot of Champagne, combining outstanding quality with significant quantity from an unrivalled collection of *premiers* and *grands crus*. Oak, overused in the mid-90s, is in balance since 1998 and harvesting is now by hand. Wines may be seen under the names Domaine de la Maladière, Ancien Domaine Auffray or Jeanne-Paule Filippi. (PW)
O **Chablis Grand Cru** Les Clos✪✪✪✪✪ £F Vaudésir✪✪✪✪✪ £F Preuses★★★★★ £F
O **Chablis Grand Cru** Bougros Côte de Bougerots★★★★★ £F Bougros★★★★ £E
O **Chablis Premier Cru** Fourchaume★★★★ £E Montée de Tonnerre★★★★ £D
O **Chablis Premier Cru** Vaillons★★★★ £D Mont de Milieu★★★★ £D

GHISLAINE ET JEAN-HUGUES GOISOT   Saint-Bris   *UK stockists:* **DDr,** HHB, Rae
Extremely high quality yet good prices thanks to the lowly appellations. The wines are ripe, concentrated and aromatic, with lovely definition and length, and under the Corps de Garde label are worth keeping for two or three years. Also made but not tasted are prestige *cuvées* from Côtes d'Auxerre whites, Biaumont and Gondonne, and an Irancy, Mazelots. (PW)
O **Bourgogne Côtes d'Auxerre**★★ £B Corps de Garde★★★ £C
O **Saint-Bris**★★ £B Corps de Garde Gourmand★★ £B
O **Bourgogne Aligoté**★ £B ● **Bourgogne** Rouge★ £B Corps de Garde★★ £C

JEAN-PIERRE GROSSOT & CORINNE PERCHAUD   *UK stockists:* **L&W, Lib, Eno,** IGH
A great source for Chablis from some excellent *premiers crus*, sold under both the Grossot and Corinne Perchaud labels. If initially a little austere, the wines are intensely fruity, with excellent definition, weight and

35

FRANCE

fine perfumes. Some oak is used but only Fûts de Chênes is obviously oaky. Delicious with three or four years' ageing, but they will keep longer. (PW)

O **Chablis Premier Cru** Fourchaume★★★ £C Mont de Milieu★★★ £C
O **Chablis★** £B Fûts de Chênes★ £B La Part des Anges★★ £C

DOM. LAROCHE www.michellaroche.com *UK stockists:* **Bib**, NYg
Michel Laroche is one of Chablis' major players with 100 ha of vines here and projects in the South of France and Chile. The wines are supple and gently creamy, without the austerity of much young Chablis but still retaining a mineral stamp. *Grands crus* can be very good; a small portion of the Blanchots is set apart for the top wine, Réserve de l'Obédience. Pricey for the quality. (PW)

O **Chablis Grand Cru** Les Clos★★★★ £F Blanchots★★★ £E
O **Chablis Premier Cru** Vaillons V. Vignes★★★ £D Fourchaumes V. Vignes★★★ £D
O **Chablis Premier Cru** Beauroy★★ £D Montmains★★ £D Vau de Vey★★★ £C

LONG-DEPAQUIT *UK stockists:* Bal, BBR
Historic estate now with 65 ha including the famous La Moutonne vineyard. Most wines are vinified and aged in stainless steel for classic, flinty, minerally Chablis style, while the *grands crus* see varying percentages of oak. At best they have intensity, style and finesse; top wines, especially La Moutonne, become honeyed with age. Quality can be a bit uneven and prices are on the high side. (PW)

O **Chablis Grand Cru** Vaudésir★★★ £E Les Clos★★★ £E La Moutonne★★★★ £E
O **Chablis Premier Cru** Vaillons★★ £C Montée de Tonnerre★★★ £D

DOM. DES MALANDES www.domainedesmalandes.com *UK stockists:* **CHk**, Evg, WSc
26-ha estate with a good following for unoaked Chablis from low yields and fully ripe fruit made with a non-interventionist philosophy. Fourchaume and Montmains are the pick of the *premiers crus*; the *grands crus* are very classy. Though all can be drunk fairly young, these are the wines to keep. (PW)

O **Chablis Grand Cru** Vaudésir★★★★★ £E Les Clos★★★★ £E
O **Chablis Premier Cru** Montmains★★★ £C Fourchaume★★★ £C
O **Chablis★★** £B Vieilles Vignes Tour du Roy★★ £C

DOM. LOUIS MICHEL ET FILS *UK stockists:* **OWL, DAy**, BBR, Eno, IGH, Odd, WSc
Much-lauded producer of unoaked Chablis. Fifth-generation Jean-Loup Michel now makes these widely exported wines. Austere but with an underlying minerally fruit richness when young, the *premiers crus* are always better with three to five years' ageing, the *grands crus* with five or more. Fine *terroir* definition at best but buy from the better vintages only. (PW)

O **Chablis Grand Cru** Grenouilles★★★★ £E Vaudésir★★★★ £E Les Clos★★★★★ £E
O **Chablis Premier Cru** Montée de Tonnerre★★★★ £D Vaillons★★★ £C
O **Chablis★★** £B O **Petit Chablis★** £B

MOREAU-NAUDET *UK stockists:* OWL, L&S, SVS, Tan, WSc, Hrd
Stéphane Moreau has been running this 21-ha estate since 1999 and even his basic wines are now ripe and intense with a mineral aspect. Excellent, expressive *premiers crus*. Deep, minerally Valmur is long and classy, an excellent and affordable example of this often pricey *grand cru*. (PW)

O **Chablis Grand Cru** Valmur★★★★ £D O **Chablis★★** £B
O **Chablis Premier Cru** Vaillons★★★ £C Montée de Tonnerre★★★ £C

DIDIER & PASCAL PICQ *UK stockists:* FMV, BBR, NYg
The grapes here are picked as late as possible and both fermentation and ageing are in stainless steel. The wines are crisp and fresh, quite floral and fruity. Vieilles Vignes should be drunk with at least three years' ageing, the *premiers crus* with five or more. The wines are also labelled Gilbert Picq et Fils. (PW)

O **Chablis Premier Cru** Vaucoupin★★★ £C Vosgros★★★ £C
O **Chablis★★** £B Vieilles Vignes★★ £B

DOM. PINSON FRÈRES www.domaine-pinson.com *UK stockists:* A&B, CPp, L&W, NYg
Brothers Laurent and Christophe seem set on a new image for this traditional estate while continuing to make Chablis of real depth and character from top-class vineyards. Ageing in used oak contributes to the excellent texture and breadth but only subtly influences flavour. All the wines are better with five years' ageing or more.

36

Premiers crus Vaillons and Vaugiraut are also made. (PW)

O **Chablis Grand Cru** Les Clos★★★★ £D   O **Chablis**★★ £B
O **Chablis Premier Cru** Mont de Milieu★★★ £C   Montmains★★★ £C

DENIS POMMIER   www.denis-pommier.com   *UK stockists:* L&S, Han

Denis Pommier is forging a reputation as a *vigneron* of talent. The style is evolving and oak is deployed with sensitivity. The wines show concentrated ripe fruit with the mineral and citrus intensity set against a spicy oak character and a gently buttery texture in the Côte de Léchet. The small production quickly sells out. (PW)

O **Chablis Premier Cru** Côte de Léchet★★★ £C   Beauroy★★ £C
O **Chablis**★★ £B   Croix aux Moines★★ £B   Vieilles Vignes★★ £B

DENIS RACE   www.chablisrace.com   *UK stockists:* **FMV**, All, BBR, Mar, PWa

Exponent of unoaked Chablis. Grapes are machine-harvested but carefully prepared beforehand. Montmains Vieilles Vignes is from 65-year-old vines, giving notable depth and concentration. All the wines show good *terroir* definition. A steely, minerally Mont de Milieu contrasts with a softer, more elegant Vaillon. A little *grand cru* Blanchots is also made. (PW)

O **Chablis Premier Cru** Montmains Vieilles Vignes★★★ £D   Montmains★★ £C
O **Chablis Premier Cru** Mont de Milieu★★ £C   Vaillon★★   O **Chablis**★ £B

DOM. RAVENEAU   *UK stockists:* JAr, HHC, Sec, Blx

Superb Chablis from just 7.5 ha of *premier* and *grand cru* sites. Outstanding use of oak: the wines have fabulous structure yet never taste as if they have seen the inside of a barrel. They build in richness and complexity over a decade or longer. (PW)

O **Chablis Grand Cru** Blanchots★★★★★ £E   Valmur★★★★★ £E   Les Clos✪✪✪✪✪ £E
O **Chablis Premier Cru** Vaillons★★★★ £E   Montée de Tonnerre★★★★ £E

GÉRARD TREMBLAY   www.chablis-tremblay.com   *UK stockists:* Anl, Eno, Cav

Well-established family domaine with a good record for classic minerally Chablis. Oak is used but rarely obvious and the wines have impressive structure. They open out with four to five years' age from a good vintage. (PW)

O **Chablis Grand Cru** Vaudésir★★★★ £E
O **Chablis Premier Cru** Fourchaume★★★ £C   Montmains★★★ £C
O **Chablis Premier Cru** Côte de Léchet★★★ £C   O **Chablis**★★ £B

DOM. VOCORET   www.vocoret.com   *UK stockists:* **HHB**, IGH, Maj

Family domaine of 40 ha. Much of the fruit is mechanically harvested, but wines are generally ripe and concentrated. Vinification is in stainless steel but the *crus* are aged in large used oak. Quality is generally very good with an intense, vibrant fruit character and reasonable depth. (PW)

O **Chablis Grand Cru** Blanchot★★★ £D   Les Clos★★★ £D
O **Chablis Premier Cru** Côte de Léchet★★ £C   La Forêt★★ £C   Montmains★★ £C
O **Chablis Premier Cru** Montée de Tonnerre★★ £C   Vaillons★★ £C   O **Chablis**★ £B

Also see the following Burgundy *négociants* with an entry in the section *Côte D'Or & Côte Chalonnaise:*
OLIVIER LEFLAIVE FRÈRES, VERGET

Other wineries of note
Jean-Claude Bessin, Dom. de Bois d'Yver, Anita et Jean-Pierre Colinot (Irancy), Bernard Legland/Dom. des Marronniers, Dom. Louis Moreau

An in-depth profile of every producer can be found in Wine behind the label 2006

FRANCE

Côte d'Or & Côte Chalonnaise

What a difference a new generation and a responsive market can make. Younger, highly-trained and talented winemakers have played their part in transforming quality in this the most complex and magical of France's wine regions. No stronger argument can be made for the validity of terroir than in Burgundy, where subtle differences of climate, soil composition and aspect identified over the course of centuries and expressed in individual climats make this region so complex and fascinating. Red Burgundy should enthrall with its perfume, complexity, finesse and textural qualities rather than power, oak and out-and-out concentration. White Burgundy should express complexity in both aroma and flavour, be it more minerally or buttery and nutty, and have a depth, structure and balance proportionate to its origins. Both should be more than just the most noble expression of two grapes, now familiar the world over, Pinot Noir and Chardonnay.

Côte d'Or & Côte Chalonnaise Vintages

In general terms red Burgundy doesn't offer the same potential longevity as do Bordeaux or other great Cabernet-based wines. Exceptional wines can, however, be very long-lived, and it is not unusual for the top whites to outlast the best reds. Ageing potential depends both on origin and the style favoured by individual producers - comments here need to be considered together with those in producer profiles. While the very best estates now produce consistently high quality, in most instances vintage choice remains crucial, especially given the struggle for ripeness in Burgundy's more marginal vineyard sites.

2004: In complete contrast to 03, it was cool, wet and grey. Worse it was hit by hail and oidium (mildew which attacks the grapes). Yields are high and whites look to be better than reds. The latter are likely to be very producer-dependent, particularly in the Côte de Beaune.

2003: An extraordinarily hot year but resulting in generally high quality reds, especially successful from cooler sites. Whites have an immediate exotic fruit appeal but in many cases not much else and even those from top sites will need to be drunk early.

2002: An exciting red wine vintage with intense, ripe and ageworthy wines from low yields. The best whites are concentrated, structured with perfectly ripe fruit and good balance.

2001: Demanding vintage but good fruit from best-managed vineyards. Wines have improved in the bottle and show good terroir expression. Variable in whites; some concentrated but others lack ripeness.

2000: Reds better in Côte de Nuits than Côte de Beaune. Rain affected, best wines from near the top of hierarchy. Very good for whites if slightly less consistent than 99. Decent in Côte Chalonnaise.

1999: Excellent large vintage for reds with remarkable colour, good acidity and ripe tannins. Plentiful whites too, with outstanding examples from top estates. Excellent in Côte Chalonnaise in both colours.

1998: Vintage with more potential in red than 97 thanks to better acidity and more stuffing. Much more irregular at a lower level, with some coarse tannins. Variable for whites, some evolving quickly but the best are good.

1997: Forward, attractive reds that has already given much pleasure. Lowish acidities in whites too though best have richness and intensity. Most wines for drinking, not keeping.

1996: One of the finest of 1990s for reds with excellent fruit intensity, generally ripe tannins and good acidity, although in some cases the tannins have proved hard. The best require further keeping. Exceptional Côte Chalonnaise reds or whites might still be drinking.

1995: Reds of only moderate richness but are ripe and structured. Will still keep at the top level. Excellent for whites, the best will still improve.

1994: Weak red wine vintage if a better bet in the Côte de Nuits than the Côte de Beaune. Most reds and whites now best left for the unwary.

1993: Very fine reds with great vigour, structure and intensity - the best will still improve. Much weaker in white though some will provide rich, mature drinking.

1992: Large red harvest, some wines full and charming but lack intensity and definition. Whites showed some delicious fruit but few still enjoyable.

1991: Many rich, concentrated and structured reds, the best still drinking well. Whites mostly ordinary at best.

1990: A superlative vintage for red and very good vintage for whites too. Many fine bottles, including those from some of the lesser *climats*, and will continue to keep.

1989: A warm, plentiful vintage still good at top level. Good structure in whites that have proved more long-lived than 88, 90 or 92.

1988: Firm, austere vintage with high acidity and tannins in reds. Best are now revealing the underlying refinement. Less good whites.

Earlier Years

At the top level 1985 can still provide good drinking, but more for white than the once rich, ripe reds. A few structured 83 reds can still be vigorous where rot was avoided. Still older vintages should only be considered for an outstanding *cru* from an impeccable source. Vintages from the 1970s include 78, 76 and 71 while the more successful 1960s include 69, 66, 64, 62 and 61. Buy only with advice from a trusted merchant or friend or consult Michael Broadbent's *Vintage Wine*.

FRANCE

Wizard's Wishlist

Classic red Burgundies
MARQUIS D'ANGERVILLE
● **Volnay** 1er Cru Clos des Ducs
COMTE ARMAND
● **Pommard** 1er Cru Clos des Epeneaux
DOM. ROBERT ARNOUX
● **Vosne-Romanée** 1er Cru Les Suchots
GHISLAINE BARTHOD
● **Chambolle-Musigny** 1er Cru Les Charmes
BOUCHARD PÈRE ET FILS ● **Pommard** 1er Cru Rugiens
SYLVAIN CATHIARD ● **Romanée-Saint-Vivant**
ROBERT CHEVILLON
● **Nuits-Saint-Georges** 1er Cru Les Saint-Georges
BRUNO CLAIR
● **Gevrey-Chambertin** 1er Cru Les Cazetiers
CLOS DE TART ● **Clos de Tart**
DOM. DE COURCEL
● **Pommard** 1er Cru Grand Clos des Epenots
DOM. DUJAC ● **Clos de la Roche**
DOM. RENÉ ENGEL ● **Clos de Vougeot**
DOM. FAIVELEY ● **Chambertin Clos-de-Bèze**
GEANTET-PANSIOT ● **Charmes-Chambertin**
DOM. HENRI GOUGES
● **Nuits-Saint-Georges** 1er Cru Les Vaucrains
DOM. JEAN GRIVOT
● **Vosne-Romanée** 1er Cru Les Beaux Monts
ANNE GROS ● **Richebourg**
LOUIS JADOT
● **Gevrey-Chambertin** 1er Cru Clos Saint-Jacques
MICHEL LAFARGE ● **Volnay** 1er Cru Clos des Chênes
DOM. DES LAMBRAYS ● **Clos des Lambrays**
MÉO-CAMUZET
● **Vosne-Romanée** 1er Cru Cros Parentoux
HUBERT DE MONTILLE ● **Volnay** 1er Cru Taillepieds
DENIS MORTET
● **Gevrey-Chambertin** 1er Cru Lavaux Saint-Jacques
JACQUES-FRÉDÉRIC MUGNIER ● **Musigny**
DOM. PONSOT ● **Griotte-Chambertin**
DOM. ROUMIER ● **Bonnes Mares**
DOM. ARMAND ROUSSEAU ● **Chambertin**
DOM. TRAPET PÈRE ET FILS
● **Gevrey-Chambertin** 1er Cru Petite Chapelle
DOM. COMTES GEORGES DE VOGÜÉ
● **Musigny** Vieilles Vignes

Consistently fine Côte de Beaune whites
DOM. GUY AMIOT ET FILS
○ **Chassagne-Montrachet** 1er Cru Les Caillerets
ROGER BELLAND
○ **Chassagne-Montrachet** 1er Cru Morgeot Clos Pitois
DOM. BONNEAU DU MARTRAY ○ **Corton-Charlemagne**
MICHEL BOUZEREAU ET FILS

○ **Meursault** 1er Cru Genevrières
LOUIS CARILLON
○ **Puligny-Montrachet** 1er Cru Perrières
GÉRARD CHAVY ET FILS
○ **Puligny-Montrachet** 1er Cru Folatières
JEAN-FRANÇOIS COCHE-DURY
○ **Meursault** 1er Cru Perrières
MICHEL COLIN-DELÉGER ET FILS
○ **Puligny-Montrachet** 1er Cru Les Demoiselles
JEAN-PHILIPPE FICHET ○ **Meursault** Tessons
VINCENT GIRARDIN
○ **Chassagne-Montrachet** 1er Cru Morgeot
PATRICK JAVILLIER ○ **Meursault** Les Tillets
DOM. DES COMTES LAFON
○ **Meursault** 1er Cru Charmes
DOM. LEFLAIVE
○ **Puligny-Montrachet** 1er Cru Les Pucelles
DOM. MARC MOREY
○ **Chassagne-Montrachet** 1er Cru Les Vergers
DOM. ROULOT ○ **Meursault** 1er Cru Perrières

Value for money red Burgundy
DENIS BACHELET ● **Côtes de Nuits-Villages**
GHISLAINE BARTHOD ● **Chambolle-Musigny**
ROGER BELLAND ● **Santenay** 1er Cru Beauregard
DOM. CARRÉ-COURBIN ● **Volnay** Vieilles Vignes
SYLVAIN CATHIARD ● **Bourgogne Rouge**
JEAN-JACQUES CONFURON
● **Côtes de Nuits-Villages** Les Vignottes
DOM. DES COMTES LAFON
● **Monthelie** 1er Cru Les Duresses
JEAN-MARC PAVELOT
● **Savigny-lès-Beaune** 1er Cru La Dominode
FRANÇOIS RAQUILLET ● **Mercurey** 1er Cru Les Naugues
MICHELE & PATRICE RION
● **Bourgogne Rouge** Bons Bâtons
A & P DE VILLAINE
● **Bourgogne Côte Chalonnaise** Digoine

Value for money white Burgundy
ROGER BELLAND ○ **Santenay** 1er Cru Beauregard
BOUCHARD PERE ET FILS
○ **Beaune** 1er Cru Clos Saint-Landry
MICHEL COLIN-DELÉGER ○ **Chassagne-Montrachet**
VINCENT DUREUIL-JANTHIAL
○ **Rully** 1er Cru Les Margotés
JEAN-JACQUES GIRARD
○ **Pernand-Vergelesses** Les Belles Filles
HENRI ET PAUL JACQUESON ○ **Rully** 1er Cru La Pucelle
PATRICK JAVILLIER ○ **Bourgogne** Cuvée Oligocène
HUBERT LAMY ○ **Bourgogne Blanc**
OLIVIER LEFLAIVE ○ **Rully** 1er Cru Vauvry
FRANÇOIS LUMPP ○ **Givry** 1er Cru Petite Marole

39

Côte d'Or & Côte Chalonnaise/A-Z of producers

STÉPHANE ALADAME Montagny *UK stockists:* **Goe, Lib**, ACh

One of the few independent estates in Montagny worth investigating. The 2002s are particularly good, combining ripe fruit with weight on the palate and structure so that only now are the wines beginning to open out fully. Prices are comparable to other good Chalonnaise whites. (PW)

○ **Montagny** 1er Cru★★ £C 1er Cru Cuvée Selection★★★ £C

○ **Montagny** 1er Cru Les Coères★★★ £C

BERTRAND AMBROISE Nuits-Saint-Georges *UK stockists:* CTy, Jas, Bal, BBR, Win

Red Burgundies of unmatched colour and strength. The biggest are bold, oaky and tannic but something of the wine's origin and a certain finesse come with age. Whites are rich and not excessively oaky, often with a real succulence that encourages early drinking. Lesser wines are coarser but don't lack for fruit or flavour. 2002 Nuits-Saint-Georges *premiers crus* are over-extracted but 2003s much better. (PW)

● **Corton Le Rognet**★★★★ £F ● **Clos de Vougeot**★★★★ £F

● **Nuits-Saint-Georges** 1er Cru Clos des Argillières★★★ £E 1er Cru Vaucrains★★★ £E

○ **Chassagne-Montrachet** 1er Cru Maltroie★★★ £E ○ **Corton-Charlemagne**★★★★ £F

DOM. GUY AMIOT ET FILS Chassagne-Montrachet *UK stockists:* Bal, Bib, Gen, HRp, L&S

Guy Amiot and son Thierry make a string of white Chassagne-Montrachet *crus*, of increasing refinement and complexity in recent vintages. Interesting reds have very good richness for the southern Côte de Beaune, with added length and style in Clos Saint-Jean. Most whites deserve 3-4 years' age. (PW)

○ **Chassagne-Montrachet** 1er Cru Baudines★★★ £E 1er Cru Macharelles★★★★ £E

○ **Puligny-Montrachet** 1er Cru Demoiselles★★★★★ £E

● **Chassagne-Montrachet** 1er Cru Clos Saint-Jean★★★ £E 1er Cru Maltroie★★★ £E

AMIOT-SERVELLE Chambolle-Musigny *UK stockists:* **CTy**, Add, Jas

Christian and Elizabeth Amiot farm almost 7 ha. The wines are sturdy, and can at times be a little too structured to let the fruit sing through, although they always offer more with age. Concentrated Chambolle-Musigny *crus* include little-known Derrière la Grange. 2001 and 02 recommended. Also Bourgogne Rouge, Aligoté and Chardonnay. (PW)

● **Clos de Vougeot**★★★★ £F

● **Chambolle-Musigny** 1er Cru Amoureuses★★★★★ £F 1er Cru Charmes★★★★ £F

● **Chambolle-Musigny**★★★ £D 1er Cru Derrière la Grange★★★★ £E

MARQUIS D'ANGERVILLE Volnay *UK stockists:* C&B, CTy, JAr, OWL, , Maj

Marvellous expressions of Volnay from the estate of the late Jacques d'Angerville's are taut and structured when young but classy and refined with concentrated, intense fruit underneath. Includes prized *monopole* Clos des Ducs which reveals excellent structure, superb length and class while Taillepieds combines great refinement and fullness. Currently no Caillerets but all deserve minimum 5-6 years'. Powerful Meursault-Santenots white has lots of substance and fruit richness. (PW)

● **Volnay** 1er Cru Clos des Ducs✪✪✪✪✪ £F 1er Cru Taillepieds★★★★★ £F

● **Volnay** 1er Cru Frémiets★★★★ £E 1er Cru Champans★★★★ £E

○ **Meursault-Santenots** 1er Cru★★★★ £E

COMTE ARMAND *UK stockists:* HRp, GFy, L&S, L&W, FMV, Gau

The famous Pommard Clos des Epeneaux, once the only wine, comes from a 5-ha plot in the *premier cru* Les Grands Epenots. Others have been added since 1995. Yields are low and certified biodynamic since 2001. Reds are notable for their colour, structure and depth; the Clos is always full-bodied and powerful but balanced and complex. Very good 2001s, even better 02s. (PW)

● **Pommard**★★★ £E 1er Cru Clos des Epeneaux★★★★★ £F

● **Volnay** Frémiets★★★★ £E ● **Auxey Duresses** 1er Cru★★★ £D

○ **Auxey-Duresses**★★ £C

DOM. ROBERT ARNOUX Vosne-Romanée *UK stockists:* A&B, BWC, Eno, CTy, HRp, JAr, Gau

Pascal Lachaux has been making better and better wines here over the past decade. The top wines receive 100%

new oak treatment but rarely is this obvious. The wines are sturdy and structured with at times almost overwhelming intensity and power. (PW)

- **Romanée-Saint-Vivant**✪✪✪✪✪ £H • **Clos de Vougeot**★★★★★ £F
- **Vosne-Romanée**★★★ £D 1er Cru Reignots★★★★ £F 1er Cru Suchots★★★★ £F
- **Nuits-Saint-Georges**★★★ £D 1er Cru Corvées Pagets★★★★ £E

FRANCE

DENIS BACHELET Gevrey-Chambertin *UK stockists:* HRp, FMV

Denis Bachelet's wines have great finesse and class with lovely fruit intensity and harmony. If rich, intense Premier Cru Les Corbeaux and complex and classy *grand cru* Charmes-Chambertin are hard to find, the village Gevrey-Chambertin Vieilles Vignes is a super example; all three are made from old vines. Côte de Nuits-Villages and Bourgogne Rouge are delicious and affordable. (PW)

- **Charmes-Chambertin**★★★★★ £F
- **Gevrey-Chambertin** Vieilles Vignes★★★★ £D 1er Cru Corbeaux★★★★ £E
- **Côte de Nuits-Villages**★★ £C • **Bourgogne Rouge**★★ £B

GHISLAINE BARTHOD Chambolle-Musigny *UK stockists:* RsW, FMV, BBR, Rae, Tan, L&W

Small family domaine with seven tiny plots of Chambolle *premiers crus*. Ghislaine Barthod's wines have grace, finesse and succulence; there is nothing brash or harsh yet they have very good structure and personality. Cras and Charmes are the top two wines though the Véroilles is also consistently fine. Excellent village Chambolle-Musigny and attractive, fruity and delicious Bourgogne Rouge. (PW)

- **Chambolle-Musigny** 1er Cru Cras★★★★★ £E 1er Cru Charmes★★★★★ £E
- **Chambolle-Musigny** 1er Cru Chatelots★★★★ £E 1er Cru Véroilles★★★★ £E
- **Chambolle-Musigny**★★★ £D 1er Cru Fuées★★★★ £E • **Bourgogne Rouge**★★ £B

ROGER BELLAND Santenay *UK stockists:* Lib, BBR, BSh, B&T

Excellent source of top white Burgundy. Belland goes to great lengths to maximise the quality of the fruit. Whites see new oak – 100 per cent for the *grand cru* Criots – but the intensity and depth of the fruit are only enhanced by it. Red Santenay *premiers crus* are full of ripe berry fruits with good structure and length. Great value too. (PW)

- O **Criots-Bâtard-Montrachet**✪✪✪✪ £H
- O **Santenay**★★ £C 1er Cru Beauregard★★★ £C
- **Pommard** Cras★★★ £E • **Volnay** 1er Cru Santenots★★★ £E
- **Santenay** 1er Cru Commes★★★ £C 1er Cru Beauregard★★★ £C
- **Santenay** 1er Cru Gravières★★★ £C

DOM. BERTAGNA Vougeot www.domainebertagna.com *UK stockists:* **FMV**, BBR

30-ha estate with a wide spread of vineyards. producing vigorous, rich and structured reds. *Terroir* is emphasised rather than suppressed, especially as the wines age. All the best *premiers crus* and *grands crus* need 8–10 years. Clos de la Perrière is a *monopole*. Also classy and structured whites, if needing a little more definition. (PW)

- **Clos Saint-Denis**★★★★★ £G • **Clos de Vougeot**★★★★ £G
- **Vougeot** 1er Cru Petits Vougeots★★★ £
- **Vougeot** 1er Cru Les Cras★★★ £F 1er Cru Clos de la Perrière★★★★ £F
- **Vosne-Romanée** 1er Cru Beaux-Monts★★★★ £F

DOM. SIMON BIZE ET FILS Savigny-les-Beaune *UK stockists:* ABy, Gen, HRp, JAr, L&W, OWL

A leading exponent of red Savigny, greatly improved since 1999, in a bold, sturdy style. Top wines improve beyond five years, with good weight and richness in Marconnets and real intensity in Aux Vergelesses. Whites have plenty of fruit and good structure. Red and white Bourgogne as good as 'lesser' Savignys. Also a little Latricières-Chambertin. (PW)

- **Savigny-lès-Beaune** 1er Cru Vergelesses★★★ £D 1er Cru Marconnets★★★ £D
- **Savigny-lès-Beaune** 1er Cru Serpentières★★★ £D 1er Cru Guettes★★★ £D
- O **Corton-Charlemagne**★★★ £F O **Savigny-lès-Beaune**★★ £C Vergelesses★★★ £D

BLAIN-GAGNARD Chassagne-Montrachet *UK stockists:* JAr, HHC, Maj, F&R

Wines of good richness and structure that are true to their origins. Ripe, minerally and well-structured regular Chassagne; *premiers crus* add more depth and richness with 4 or 5 years. Bâtard-Montrachet has terrific dimension and becomes marvellously complex. Also Criots-Bâtard-Montrachet and tiny amount of Le

Montrachet. Reasonably elegant red; Clos Saint-Jean adds a little depth. Some Jacques Gagnard wines under the Gagnard-Delagrange label (PW)

O **Bâtard-Montrachet**★★★★★ £F   O **Puligny-Montrachet**★★★ £E
O **Chassagne-Montrachet** 1er Cru Caillerets★★★★ £E   1er Cru Morgeots★★★★ £E
O **Chassagne-Montrachet** 1er Cru Clos Saint-Jean★★★ £E   1er Cru Boudriotte★★★ £E

JEAN-MARC BOILLOT   Pommard   *UK stockists:* RsW, BBR, DDr, L&S, Rae, F&R

Wines with a fruit richness and depth to marry with the oak input. Reds range from a full Beaune to more structured Pommards (superb rich Rugiens and Volnay-like Jarolières) to stylish, perfumed Volnays. Even village examples are very good. Whites are even better, with intense pure fruit and great class, best in Combettes. Also makes wine in the Coteaux du Languedoc. (PW)

● **Pommard**★★★ £D   1er Cru Jarolières★★★ £E   1er Cru Rugiens★★★★ £F
● **Volnay**★★★ £E   1er Cru Carelle-sous-Chapelle★★★ £E   1er Cru Pitures★★★ £E
O **Puligny-Montrachet** 1er Cru Champ Canet★★★★ £F   1er Cru Combettes★★★★ £F

DOM. BONNEAU DU MARTRAY   *UK stockists:* HHC, BBR, L&W, HRp, L&S, JAr, F&R, C&R, Las

Outstanding domaine producing just two wines. Long-lived white Corton-Charlemagne (from 9.5 ha of best-sited part of the famous vineyard) has tremendous richness, great depth and character. Since 95 the red (from 1.5 ha at base of Corton hill) has taken on greater flesh and extract without sacrificing finesse. (PW)

O **Corton-Charlemagne** ✪✪✪✪✪ £F   ● **Corton**★★★★ £F

BOUCHARD PÈRE ET FILS   Beaune   www.bouchard-pereetfils.com   *UK stockists:* JEF, AAA

One of the best-known merchant names in Burgundy, dramatically improved since purchase by Henriot (see Champagne) in 1995. Reds show greater richness, better structure and recently more expression and individuality. The best whites show superb fruit combined with excellent structure and concentration and are particularly fine in 2000. Excellent style and consistency in 2002. Good 2003 reds too. Just a few wines are listed here. (PW)

● **Le Corton**★★★★ £G   ● **Beaune** 1er Cru Grèves Vigne de L'Enfant Jésus★★★ £E
● **Beaune** 1er Cru★★ £D   1er Cru Clos de la Mousse★★ £E   1er Cru Teurons★★★ £E
● **Volnay** 1er Cru★★ £D   1er Cru Caillerets★★★★ £E
O **Corton-Charlemagne**★★★★★ £F   O **Chevalier-Montrachet**★★★★★ £H
O **Meursault** 1er Cru Genevrières★★★★★ £F   1er Cru Perrières★★★★★ £F
O **Beaune** 1er Cru Clos Saint-Landry★★★ £C   1er Cru Sur Les Grèves★★ £C

RENÉ BOUVIER   Gevrey-Chambertin   *UK stockists:* THt, DDr, UnC

Increasingly fine domaine for Marsannay and other Côtes de Nuits *crus*. Working in part in a *négociant* role Bernard Bouvier is expanding on his father's achievements. Beyond good Gevrey-Chambertin there is fine Chambolle-Musigny, Vosne-Romanée and even Echezeaux and Clos de Vougeot. 2001 and 02 recommended. Some of the best value is at the lower levels. (PW)

● **Marsannay** Longeroies★★ £C   Clos du Roy★★ £C   Champs Salomon★★ £C
● **Gevrey-Chambertin** Jeunes Rois★★★ £D   1er Cru Petite Chapelle★★★★ £F
● **Chambolle-Musigny** 1er Cru Les Noirots★★★ £F   ● **Clos de Vougeot**★★★★ £G

MICHEL BOUZEREAU ET FILS   Meursault   *UK stockists:* FMV, BBR, CTy, L&W, F&R

A good bet for ripe, full yet elegant Meursault. Stylish and pure whites show good definition with subtle differences between *crus*: outstanding Meursault-Charmes, austere but deep and minerally Meursault-Blagny, Genevrières very suggestive of this *cru*. Caillerets is much the better of the two Pulignys. Reasonably priced reds and good Aligoté and Bourgogne Chardonnay. (PW)

O **Meursault** 1er Cru Blagny★★★★ £E   1er Cru Genevrières★★★★ £E
O **Meursault** Grands Charrons★★★ £D   Limouzin★★★ £D   Les Tessons★★★ £D
O **Bourgogne Aligoté**★ £B   O **Bourgogne Chardonnay**★★ £B

LOUIS CARILLON ET FILS   Puligny-Montrachet   *UK stockists:* BBR, CTy, L&W, Las, JNi, Maj

Whites have great vibrancy and expressive fruit. Champ Canet is the most elegant and approachable when quite young; Combettes is seductive and more immediate than the bigger, more structured Perrières; the citrusy, minerally Referts fattens up with age. The *grand cru* Bienvenues is the most complex and refined of all. (PW)

O **Bienvenues-Bâtard-Montrachet**✪✪✪✪ £H

New entries have producer's name underlined

O **Puligny-Montrachet** 1er Cru Perrières★★★★ £F   1er Cru Referts★★★★ £E
O **Puligny-Montrachet**★★★ £E   1er Cru Combettes★★★★ £F

DOM. CARRÉ-COURBIN   Volnay   *UK stockists:* **FMV**, BBR, P&S
After a steady improvement they really hit jackpot here in 2002, making superb, ripe concentrated Volnay with great depth and fine structure. Similarly fine 2003s confirm that this estate has really arrived. Drink village Volnay and Pommard with 5 years' age or more, Volnay *premiers crus* with 6–10 and Grands Épenots with 10 or more. (PW)
● **Volnay** 1er Cru Clos de la Cave des Ducs★★★★ £E
● **Volnay** 1er Cru Les Lurets★★★★ £E   1er Cru Taillepieds★★★★★ £F
● **Volnay**★★★ £D Vieilles Vignes★★★★ £E   1er Cru Robardelle★★★★ £E
● **Pommard**★★★ £D 1er Cru Grands Epenots★★★★ £F

SYLVAIN CATHIARD   Vosne-Romanée   *UK stockists:* OWL, L&W, FMV, BBR, HHC, SVS
Very refined, subtle but harmonious wines. All the Vosne-Romanées have plenty of substance and are ripe with increasing intensity and length of flavour, culminating in an inspired *grand cru* Romanée-Saint-Vivant. A sophisticated Bourgogne Rouge and elegant Chambolle-Musigny apart, all deserve to be kept for at least five or six years. Recent vintages have been outstanding with superb 2002s. (PW)
● **Vosne-Romanée** 1er Cru Malconsorts★★★★★ £F   1er Cru En Orveaux★★★★ £F
● **Chambolle-Musigny** Clos de L'Orme★★★★ £E
● **Nuits-Saint-Georges** 1er Cru Murgers★★★★ £E ● **Bourgogne Rouge**★★ £C

MAISON CHAMPY   Beaune   www.champy.com   *UK stockists:* HHC, Sav, Pol, ThP, F&R
Old *négociant* house revived by the Meurgey family. Individual *terroirs* shine through. Among the reds, Vosne-Romanée Les Suchots stands out with fine fruit, class and great length. The 2000 and 02 whites are the best yet and reasonably priced, particularly regular Savigny-lès-Beaune and Pernand-Vergelesses. An increasingly good, reliable source of Burgundy. (PW)
● **Vosne-Romanée** 1er Cru Les Beaumonts★★★ £F   1er Cru Les Suchots★★★★ £F
● **Aloxe-Corton** 1er Cru Les Vercots★★ £D ● **Volnay** 1er Cru Les Caillerets★★★ £E
● **Savigny-lès-Beaune** 1er Cru Les Peuillets★★ £C   1er Cru Les Vergelesses★★ £C
O **Pernand-Vergelesses**★★ £C O **Savigny-lès-Beaune**★★ £C

CHANDON DE BRIAILLES   Savigny-lès-Beaune   *UK stockists:* HHC, L&S, L&W, Tan, F&M
A popular and fine domaine favouring elegance over power. Corton Clos du Roi is structured and profound top red. The Pernand-Vergelesses are medium-bodied, the slender but intense Île des Vergelesses adds a little weight with age. Tight minerally whites become richer with age. Corton becomes fuller and broader than a deeper, more minerally Corton-Charlemagne. (PW)
● **Corton** Bressandes★★★★ £E ● **Pernand-Vergelesses** 1er Cru Île Vergelesses★★★ £D
● **Savigny-lès-Beaune** 1er Cru Fourneaux★★ £C   1er Cru Lavières★★ £D
O **Pernand-Vergelesses** 1er Cru Île des Vergelesses★★★ £D

CHANSON PÈRE ET FILS   www.vins-chanson.com   *UK stockists:* **Cha**, Men, F&R
Hugely improved historic Beaune *maison* (dating from 1750) under Champagne Bollinger ownership since 1999. Richer, better structured wines have been produced from lower yields, re-emphasising differences of *terroir* across some of Beaune's finest *premiers crus*. (PW)
● **Beaune** 1er Cru Grèves★★★ £E   1er Cru Champs Pimonts★★★★ £E
● **Beaune** 1er Cru Bressandes★★★ £E   1er Cru Clos des Mouches★★★★ £F
● **Beaune** 1er Cru Clos des Fèves★★★★ £F ● **Côte de Beaune-Villages**★★ £C
O **Beaune** 1er Cru Clos des Mouches★★★★ £F
O **Meursault** 1er Cru Perrières★★★★ £F

PHILIPPE CHARLOPIN   Gevrey-Chambertin   *UK stockists:* IVV
Late harvesting, rigorous selection and quite liberal helpings of new oak result in richly textured, chewy, sometimes tannic wines, yet still reflecting the general style of their appellations. Village wines have plenty of immediate appeal; top wines will keep for at least a decade. Bonnes Mares, Clos de Vougeot and Echezeaux are the newest of a burgeoning range of *grands crus*. (PW)
● **Chambertin**★★★★ £G ● **Charmes-Chambertin**★★★★ £F

43

● **Clos Saint-Denis**★★★★ £F ● **Bonnes Mares**★★★★ £G
● **Gevrey-Chambertin** Justice★★ £D V. Vignes★★★ £E ● **Morey-Saint-Denis**★★ £D

GÉRARD CHAVY ET FILS Puligny-Montrachet   *UK stockists:* BBR, CTy, Eno, HRp, FMV, CPp
Emerging star with Puligny of some substance and style. Premiers crus are forging the reputation, including a very minerally, full Perrières and an elegant Clavoillons that contrasts with the firmer, more structured Folatières. An intense, weighty Champs-Gain first made in 2002 shows real promise. Good prices. (PW)
○ **Puligny-Montrachet** 1er Cru Perrières★★★★ £E   1er Cru Clavoillons★★★★ £E
○ **Puligny-Montrachet**★★ £D   Charmes★★★ £D   1er Cru Folatières★★★★ £E
○ **Saint-Aubin** 1er Cru En Remilly★★ £C   ○ **Bourgogne Blanc**★ £B

ROBERT CHEVILLON Nuits-Saint-Georges   *UK stockists:* J&B, Gen, WTs, F&M, Sec, Las, F&R, Maj
One of the celebrated names of this appellation with 8 *premiers crus* with a high average vine age. Wines are full-bodied and tannic but with the flesh, depth and fruit intensity to be very rich and satisfying with 8-10 years. Fullest and most structured are Les Saint-Georges and Vaucrains, followed by Les Cailles. Also a little white Nuits and Bourgogne Rouge. (PW)
● **Nuits-Saint-Georges** 1er Cru Les Vaucrains★★★★ £E   1er Cru Les Saint-Georges★★★★ £E
● **Nuits-Saint-Georges** 1er Cru Les Roncières★★★ £E   1er Cru Les Chaignots★★★ £E
● **Nuits-Saint-Georges** Vieilles Vignes★★ £D   1er Cru Les Cailles★★★ £E

CH. DE LA MALTROYE Chassagne-Montrachet   *UK stockists:* Anl, OWL, HRp,
Jean-Pierre Cornut now makes some of the best whites in the appellation: ripe, concentrated and with terrific fruit intensity and excellent balance. Impressive as the 2002s taste young, they'll only really open out with 6 years' age or more. A significant amount of red is produced too, including that from part of the 2.5-ha Clos du Château de la Maltroye monopole. (PW)
○ **Chassagne-Montrachet** 1er Cru Dent de Chien★★★★★ £F
○ **Chassagne-Montrachet** 1er Cru Grandes Ruchottes★★★★ £F
○ **Chassagne-Montrachet** 1er Cru Clos du Château de Maltroye★★★ £E
○ **Santenay** 1er Cru Comme★★★ £D   ● **Santenay** 1er Cru Comme★★ £C
● **Chassagne-Montrachet** 1er Cru Clos du Château de Maltroye★★★ £E

BRUNO CLAIR Marsannay   *UK stockists:* J&B, Col, Tan, WSc, F&R
Reds of great balance, harmony and elegance from the northern Nuits. Classic Gevrey *premiers crus* Clos Saint-Jacques and Cazetiers and *grand cru* Chambertin Clos de Bèze have great purity and exceptional length. Best value from Marsannay. All reds need at least 3 or 4 years' age; 7 or 8 for top examples. Also rare Morey-Saint-Denis white. (PW)
● **Chambertin Clos de Bèze**★★★★★ £G   ● **Vosne-Romanée** Champs-Perdrix★★★ £E
● **Gevrey-Chambertin** 1er Cru Clos Saint-Jacques★★★★ £G   1er Cru Cazetiers★★★★ £F
● **Savigny-lès-Beaune** 1er Cru La Dominode★★★ £E
● **Marsannay** Grasses Têtes★★ £C   Longeroies★★★ £C   Vaudenelles★★ £C

FRANÇOISE ET DENIS CLAIR Santenay   *UK stockists:* HHC
Denis and his son Jean-Baptiste produce some of the best examples of red Santenay but their 14ha of vineyards also includes fine Saint-Aubin whites. Santenays range from a deep and intense village-level Clos Genet to fine *premiers crus* including rich and structured Clos de Tavannes and classy Clos de la Comme. Reds are particularly good in the best vintages (recently 2003, 02, 01 and 99). (PW)
● **Santenay** Clos Genet★★ £C   1er Cru Beaurepaire★★★ £D
● **Santenay** 1er Cru Clos Tavannes★★★ £D   1er Cru Clos des Mouches★★★ £D
● **Santenay** 1er Cru Clos de la Comme★★★ £E

BRUNO CLAVELIER Vosne-Romanée   *UK stockists:* Dec, HRp, OWL, , Sav
Newish star, now fully biodynamic, showing increasing refinement, richness and expression. Old vines give wines with delicious fruit, ample concentration and a real sense of *terroir*. Vosne-Romanée Beaux-Monts has the greater structure, Aux Brulées a touch more refinement. Chambolle-Musigny combines grace with richness. Old-vine Aligoté is just about as good as it gets. (PW)
● **Vosne-Romanée** 1er Cru Les Beaux Monts★★★★ £F   1er Cru Aux Brulées★★★★ £F

New entries have producer's name underlined

● **Chambolle-Musigny** 1er Cru Combe d'Orveau★★★★★ £F
● **Nuits-Saint-Georges** 1er Cru Aux Cras★★★★ £E

CLOS DE TART   Clos de Tart   *UK stockists:* Cas, BBR, HRp, WSc, F&R
Winemaker Sylvain Pitiot has made this 7.53-ha *grand cru monopole* between Bonnes Mares and Clos des
Lambrays great again. Succulence combines with power and spice and red and black cherries are the
predominant flavours when young but wait 10 years from a top vintage. Buy 1996 or later. (PW)
● Clos de Tart❂❂❂❂❂ £G

JEAN-FRANÇOIS COCHE-DURY   Meursault   *UK stockists:* BBR, Far, Hrd, Sec, Las, F&R
Outstanding domaine for whites with grace, subtlety and purity allied to remarkable complexity. Floral, fruit and
mineral components, as well as a fine grilled nuts character with age, give extra finesse. Nearly all whites deserve
5 years' age and will keep for 10 or more. Also fine Volnay Premier Cru and a little Auxey-Duresses and
Monthelie.. (PW)
○ Corton-Charlemagne❂❂❂❂❂ £H ○ Meursault 1er Cru Perrières❂❂❂❂❂ £H
○ Meursault Narvaux★★★★ £F Caillerets★★★★ £G Chevalières★★★★ £F
● Volnay 1er Cru★★★ £F ● Bourgogne Pinot Noir★ £C

DOM. MARC COLIN ET FILS   Saint-Aubin   *UK stockists:* CCC, RsW, F&R
Renowned for its finest whites: rich, ripe wines with good complexity and a distinct and attractive minerality.
Chassagne-Montrachet is led by an intense, minerally Caillerets. Really fine Saint-Aubin comes in both colours;
best whites are minerally, stylish En Remilly, structured La Chatenière, classy Les Charmes and rich Sentier du
Clou. Also some *négociant* wines. (PW)
○ Montrachet★★★★ £H ○ Chassagne-Montrachet 1er Cru Caillerets★★★ £F
○ Saint-Aubin 1er Cru La Chatenière★★★ £D 1er Cru En Remilly★★★ £D
○ Saint-Aubin 1er Cru En Montceau★★ £D ● Santenay Vieilles Vignes★★★ £D

MICHEL COLIN-DELÉGER ET FILS   *UK stockists:* BWC, BBR, MCW, HRp, L&W, F&R
Intense, concentrated, beautifully balanced wines from low-yielding vines. En Remilly heads a raft of fine
Chassagne-Montrachet *premiers crus*. Reds, once a little tough, are now richer with riper tannins (2002
recommended); Santenay Gravières and Chassagne-Montrachet Morgeots stand out. Also attractive *négociant*
whites. (PW)
○ Chassagne-Montrachet 1er Cru Morgeots★★★★ £F 1er Cru En Remilly★★★★£F
○ Chassagne-Montrachet 1er Cru Les Chaumées★★★★ £F 1er Cru Vergers★★★★ £F
● Chassagne-Montrachet Morgeots★★★ £D ● Santenay 1er Cru Gravières★★★ £C

DOM. JEAN-JACQUES CONFURON   Nuits-Saint-Georges   *UK stockists:* Bal, OWL, Eno, BBR
Increasingly good wines from 7 ha of organic, low-yielding vines. Quite dense and concentrated with plenty of
oak; fruit unfurls with 5-10 years' age. The results can be a little uneven but there's great intensity and length
of flavour. (PW)
● Romanée-Saint-Vivant★★★★★ £G ● Clos Vougeot★★★★ £G
● Nuits-Saint-Georges Fleurières★★★ £D Chaboeufs★★★ £E 1er Cru Boudots★★★★ £E
● Côte de Nuits-Villages Les Vignottes★★ £C

DOM. CONFURON-COTÉTIDOT   Vosne-Romanée   *UK stockists:* Gen, L&S, OWL
These are intense, deep and at times tannic Burgundies, but with more refinement of late. Wines need time and
should be cellared and revisited over a period of years (2001 and 02 recommended). A tiny amount of Mazis-
Chambertin and Clos de Vougeot are also made. (PW)
● Charmes-Chambertin★★★★ £F ● Echezeaux★★★★ £F
● Vosne-Romanée★★★ £E 1er Cru Suchots★★★★ £F
● Chambolle-Musigny★★★ £E ● Nuits-Saint-Georges★★★ £E 1er Cru★★★ £F

DOM. DE COURCEL   Pommard   *UK stockists:* HRp, Gen, OWL, L&S, P&S, C&C
Wines made by Yves Confuron of Confuron-Cotétidot. At the heart of the estate is 5 ha of Grand Epenots.
Recent vintages have been vigorous, sturdy, concentrated, more oaky than previously and capable of ageing for a
decade; the Grand Clos des Epenots and the Rugiens need almost that long just to open up. Consistently
excellent Bourgogne Rouge. (PW)

● **Pommard** 1er Cru Rugiens★★★★ £F 1er Cru Grand Clos des Epenots★★★★ £F
● **Pommard** Croix Noires★★★ £E Les Valmuriers★★★ £E 1er Cru Fremiers★★★ £E

JEAN-YVES DEVEVEY/DOM. DU BOIS-GUILLAUME Hautes-Côtes de Beaune *UK stockists:* **FMV**
An excellent source of inexpensive red and white Burgundy. Hautes-Côtes de Beaune whites are both fermented and aged in oak: Les Champs Perdrix is atypically full and concentrated, Les Chagnots is more overtly oak-enriched but has lots of promise and is better than many a basic village Meursault. Also very appealing, expressive red Beaune Pertuisots and stylish white Chassagne-Montrachet. (PW)
O **Hautes-Côtes de Beaune** Les Champs Perdrix★★ £B
O **Hautes-Côtes de Beaune** Les Chagnots XVIII lunes★★★ £C
O **Chassagne-Montrachet**★★★ £E O **Bourgogne Aligoté**★ £B
● **Beaune** 1er Cru Pertuisots★★★ £E

JOSEPH DROUHIN Beaune www.drouhin.com *UK stockists:* **DAy**, OWL, L&W, Sav, C&R, Wai, Las
Excellent high-profile domaine (owning over 72 ha) and négociant that combines integrity and know-how to deliver good quality at every level. Generally the wines are expressive, subtle and elegant, but they need some age to fill out. Celebrated red Beaune Clos des Mouches can be surpassed by a Grèves bottling, but white can be superb, with its delicate spice complexity, and elegance. Drouhin also makes Marquis de Laguiche wines. Also see Joseph Drouhin Chablis and Domaine Drouhin (Oregon). (PW)
● **Musigny**✪✪✪✪ £H ● **Grands-Echezeaux**★★★★★ £G ● **Griotte-Chambertin**★★★★ £G
● **Chambolle-Musigny**★★ £E 1er Cru★★★ £E 1er Cru Amoureuses★★★★ £F
● **Beaune** 1er Cru Clos des Mouches★★★ £E 1er Cru Grèves★★★ £E
● **Côte de Beaune**★★ £D ● **Chorey-lès-Beaune**★★ £C
O **Montrachet** Marquis de Laguiche✪✪✪✪ £H
O **Corton-Charlemagne**★★★★ £G O **Beaune** 1er Cru Clos des Mouches★★★★ £F
O **Chassagne-Montrachet** Marquis de Laguiche★★★ £F

CLAUDE DUGAT Gevrey-Chambertin *UK stockists:* Eno, HRp, Hrd, Sec, Las, F&R
Cousin of Bernard Dugat (Dugat-Py) with similarly rich, concentrated wines swaddled in, but not swamped by, new oak. The wines balance fine ripe tannins and good acidities, some with old-vine succulence, and deserve 6-10 years' ageing. Very good if no longer inexpensive village-level Gevrey and Bourgogne Rouge. A tiny amount of Chapelle-Chambertin is also made. (PW)
● **Charmes-Chambertin**✪✪✪✪✪ £H ● **Griottes-Chambertin**✪✪✪✪✪ £H
● **Gevrey-Chambertin** 1er Cru Lavaux-Saint-Jacques★★★★★ £G
● **Gevrey-Chambertin**★★★★ £F 1er Cru★★★★ £G ● **Bourgogne Rouge**★★ £D

BERNARD DUGAT-PY www.dugat-py.com *UK stockists:* THt, BBR, Blx, Sec, JNi, F&R
Big, dense wines but in the best sense: the concentration and richness of fruit, lush oak, silky textures and fine tannins make them irresistible. The Lavaux-Saint-Jacques and the tiny amounts of *grands crus* from very old vines have extra class and dimension as well as concentration; Chambertin has very, very concentrated black fruit. Vieilles Vignes Vosne-Romanée is from 70-year-old vines. (PW)
● **Chambertin**✪✪✪✪✪ £H ● **Mazis-Chambertin**✪✪✪✪✪ £H
● **Charmes-Chambertin**✪✪✪✪✪ £H ● **Vosne-Romanée** Vieilles-Vignes★★★★ £F
● **Gevrey-Chambertin** 1er Cru★★★★ £G 1er Cru Lavaux-Saint-Jacques★★★★★ £G

DOM. DUJAC Morey-Saint-Denis www.dujac.com *UK stockists:* OWL, FMV, L&W, HRp, Las, WSc
Jacques Seysses is one of the most respected winemakers in Burgundy, now joined by his son Jeremy. Wines are intense, clean, elegant and perfumed and gain in richness and harmony with age, becoming ever more expressive of their *terroir*. Of five *grands crus*, the Bonnes Mares is arguably the best, with remarkable breadth, power and flavour profile. Also a little white Morey-Saint-Denis and some very good Dujac Fils et Père wines from bought-in grapes. (PW)
Domaine Dujac:
● **Bonnes Mares**✪✪✪✪✪ £H ● **Clos de la Roche**★★★★★ £H ● **Echezeaux**★★★★ £H
● **Clos Saint-Denis**★★★★★ £G ● **Charmes-Chambertin**★★★★ £G
● **Gevrey-Chambertin** 1er Cru Aux Combottes★★★★ £G
● **Morey-Saint-Denis**★★★ £E 1er Cru★★★★ £F O **Morey-Saint-Denis**★ £E

DOM. V DUREUIL-JANTHIAL Rully   *UK stockists:* THt, CdP, OWL, Rae, Gau, CPp, Sel
Whites are among the best locally, especially *premiers crus* from low-yielding old vines. New oak is apparent but they have a depth and fullish fruit character as well as decent acidity to drink well at two or three years. Bourgogne Rouge is good in 2002. (PW)
O Rully★★ £C   1er Cru Margotés★★★ £C   1er Cru Le Meix Cadot★★★ £C
● Rully★★ £C   Maizières★★★ £C   ● Mercurey★★ £C   ● Bourgogne Rouge★ £B
● Nuits-Saint-Georges   1er Cru Clos des Argillières★★★ £E

MAURICE ÉCARD ET FILS   Savigny-lès-Beaune   *UK stockists:* Las, Win, Dec
Source of good-quality, full and concentrated red Burgundy at reasonable prices from leading Savigny-lès-Beaune *premiers crus.* Serpentières is the most floral, Peuillet more solid if less expressive and Narbantons has the richness and depth typical of this *cru.* Best is Jarrons (50-year-old vines) with still more concentration and depth and deserving of least 5–6 years' age. A little white Savigny is also made. (PW)
● Savigny-lès-Beaune★★ £C   1er Cru Narbantons★★★ £D
● Savigny-lès-Beaune   1er Cru Jarrons★★★ £D
● Savigny-lès-Beaune   1er Cru Serpentières★★★ £D   1er Cru Peuillets★★★ £D

DOM. RENÉ ENGEL   www.domaine-engel.com   *UK stockists:* FMV, Con, Gau, Gen, HRp, F&M
For more than 2 decades prior to his untimely death in May 2005, Philippe Engel made a fabulous range of wines of power, structure and richness, typically deep coloured and full with dark fruit and impressive depth and length. Vosne-Romanée Les Brulées from very old vines shows tremendous fruit quality and arguably represents the best value. All the wines become ever richer and more luscious with age – up 10 years for the *crus.* Great 2002s and 2003s. (PW)
● Grands-Echezeaux✪✪✪✪ £G   ● Clos de Vougeot★★★★★ £F   ● Echezeaux★★★★ £F
● Vosne-Romanée★★★ £E   1er Cru Les Brulées★★★★★ £F

ARNAUD ENTE   Meursault   *UK stockists:* FMV, Sec, Hrd
A young grower whose wines are ripe, concentrated but not overdone with fine structures and good flavour intensity and depth. Meursault Goutte d'Or has a floral, exotic character in contrast to a citrusy but very concentrated Vieilles Vignes. The Puligny has a spicy intensity but less depth. Decent Bourgogne Blanc and Bourgogne Aligoté usually show good fruit too. (PW)
O Puligny-Montrachet   1er Cru Les Referts★★★ £F
O Meursault★★★ £E   Vieilles Vignes★★★★ £F   1er Cru Goutte d'Or★★★ £F
O Bourgogne Chardonnay★★ £C

FRÉDÉRIC ESMONIN   Gevrey-Chambertin   *UK stockists:* JAr, HRp, Hrd
Small estate and *négociant* operation. The Estournelles does justice to the *cru*'s cachet and other estate wines show fine fruit and depth too, including intense, meaty Ruchottes-Chambertin and very powerful, black-fruited and classy Mazis-Chambertin. *Négociant* wines of a high standard include Clos de Vougeot, Chambertin and Chambertin Clos-de-Bèze. Prices are very reasonable. (PW)
● Chambertin★★★★★ £F   ● Chambertin Clos-de-Béze★★★★★ £F
● Ruchottes-Chambertin★★★★ £F   ● Charmes-Chambertin★★★★ £F
● Gevrey-Chambertin   1er Cru Estournelles Saint-Jacques★★★★ £E

SYLVIE ESMONIN   Gevrey-Chambertin   *UK stockists:* FMV, HHB, C&R
7-ha domaine, previously called Domaine Michel Esmonin et Fille. Highly trained Sylvie Esmonin has worked with her father for more than a decade and made a major impact. Extra vigour and concentration in the most recent vintages has been added whilst retaining the wines' silky elegance. The wines can be drunk reasonably young but the 1999s, in particular, need more time. (PW)
● Gevrey-Chambertin★★ £E   V.Vignes★★★ £E   1er Cru Clos Saint-Jacques★★★★ £F
● Volnay   Santenots★★★ £E   ● Côte de Nuits-Villages★★ £C

DOM. FAIVELEY   www.bourgognes-faiveley.com   *UK stockists:* MMD, BBR, HHC, HRp, JAr, L&W
Faiveley commands more than 120 ha in the Côte d'Or and Côte Chalonnaise and nearly all the wines in the high-quality range come from their own vineyards. Wines typically show fine perfumes combined with lots of depth and dimension and are proven keepers at every level. The character varies enormously from appellation to

47

appellation, from intense, raspberryish Mercureys to burly, meaty Nuits. Superb in the best years such as 99 and 02. (PW)

● **Chambertin Clos-de-Bèze**✪✪✪✪✪ £H ● **Corton** Clos des Cortons✪✪✪✪✪ £G
● **Mazis-Chambertin**★★★★★ £G ● **Latricières-Chambertin**★★★★ £G
● **Nuits-Saint-Georges** 1er Cru Porets Saint-Georges★★ £E 1er Cru Damodes★★★ £E
● **Mercurey** Clos des Myglands★★ £C Clos du Roy★★ £C La Framboisière★★ £C
O **Corton-Charlemagne**★★★★ £H O **Mercurey** Les Mauvarennes★ £C Clos Rochette★ £C

JEAN-PHILIPPE FICHET Meursault UK stockists: FMV, Bal, HHB, Goe, WSc
Ever better white wines from a range of *climats* in the Côte de Beaune. Individual Meursault *lieux-dits* show definite stylistic differences, from a ripe, typical Gruyaches through minerally Chevalières to a structured, classy Tessons that needs the greatest amount of time. All contrast with a Puligny of real vigour and intensity. Reasonable prices. A little red wine is also made. (PW)

O **Meursault** Meix sous le Château★★★ £E Chevalières★★★ £E Tessons★★★★ £E
O **Meursault**★★★ £D Criots★★★ £E O **Puligny-Montrachet** 1er Cru Referts★★★★ £F
O **Bourgogne Blanc**★★ £B O **Auxey-Duresses**★★ £B

RICHARD FONTAINE-GAGNARD Chassagne-Montrachet UK stockists: JAr, Dec, Maj
Richard Fontaine married one of Jacques Gagnard's daughters, Jean-Marc Blain the other (see Blain-Gagnard). These are full and ripe, with lots of fruit, good breadth and balanced acidities, not heavy or overoaked. *Premiers crus* show fine citrus and mineral intensity when young but generally drink best between 4 and 8 years. *Grands crus* add more weight, breadth and class. (PW)

O **Bâtard-Montrachet**★★★★★ £G O **Criots-Bâtard-Montrachet**★★★★★ £G
O **Chassagne-Montrachet** 1er Cru Caillerets★★★★ £F 1er Cru La Maltroie★★★★ £E
● **Volnay** 1er Cru Clos des Chênes★★★ £E

DOM. FOURRIER Gevrey-Chambertin UK stockists: THt, JAr, Ben, Gau, Goe, HRp, Hrd, Sel
Since assuming control from his father in the mid-1990s, Jean-Marie Fourrier has determinedly pursued quality, aiming for finer structures that allow the fruit to shine. He certainly has a good smattering of *crus* from which subtle differences of *terroir* may be unearthed. All the wines are deep and ripe, with increasing concentration and complexity in the top wines. (PW)

● **Griotte-Chambertin**★★★★★ £G
● **Gevrey-Chambertin** 1er Cru Clos Saint-Jacques★★★★★ £F
● **Gevrey-Chambertin** 1er Cru Cherbaudes★★★★ £E 1er Cru Champeaux★★★ £E

JEAN-NOËL GAGNARD Chassagne-Montrachet UK stockists: GBa, JAr, Far, J&B, WSc
Caroline Lestimé has taken over this leading domaine from her father and the wines have gained in both richness and finesse. *Premiers crus* range from elegant and more forward Chevenottes through fuller Champgains to rich, concentrated Blanchot-Dessus and Caillerets that need at least five or six years. The Bâtard-Montrachet adds more again. Reds can be attractive but lack richness and depth. (PW)

O **Bâtard-Montrachet**★★★★★ £H O **Chassagne-Montrachet** 1er Cru Caillerets★★★★★ £F
O **Chassagne-Montrachet** 1er Cru Champgains★★★★ £F 1er Cru Chevenottes★★★★ £E
O **Chassagne-Montrachet** 1er Cru Blanchots-Dessus★★★★ £F

GEANTET-PANSIOT www.geantet-pansiot.com UK stockists: DDr, HRp, EoR, F&R, C&R
Fine source for intense, concentrated and well-balanced northern Côte de Nuits reds with new cellars. Very high average vine age shows in the wines, adding a succulence and intensity to the fruit. The Charmes-Chambertin is a really fine example of how good this *grand cru* can be. New Gevrey-Chambertins En Champ from extremely old vines since 2000. Consistent and good value. (PW)

● **Charmes-Chambertin**★★★★★ £F ● **Marsannay** Champ-Perdrix★★ £C
● **Gevrey-Chambertin** Vieilles Vignes★★★★ £D 1er Cru Le Poissenot★★★★ £E
● **Chambolle-Musigny** Vieilles Vignes★★★ £E 1er Cru★★★★ £E

DOM. HENRI GERMAIN ET FILS Meursault UK stockists: DDr, L&S, Tan, Adm, HRp
Small estate with a habit of making fine wines. Even the village Meursault is of good quality: attractive fairly young, with pronounced citrus, spice and floral aspects, but built to last. Reds show fine, complex, sappy but ripe cherry, berry aromas and real intensity and breadth. The wines develop slowly in a cold cellar and are bottled late;

New entries have producer's name underlined

all deserve six years or so. Some red Chassagne-Montrachet is also made. (PW)
O **Meursault**★★★ £D   Chevalières★★★ £E   1er Cru Charmes★★★★ £E
O **Chassagne-Montrachet** 1er Cru Morgeot★★★★ £E   O **Bourgogne Blanc**★★ £B
● **Beaune** 1er Cru Bressandes★★★ £D

VINCENT GIRARDIN   Santenay   *UK stockists:* THt, CTy, OWL, BWC, HRp, Tan, JNi, Sel, WSc, Las
Dynamic Santenay-based grower and *négociant*. Brilliant affordable red and white domaine Santenay – modern,
fruit-rich and clean with a healthy dose of new oak. There is an energy and zip about most of the wines and real
consistency too. Most are made in relatively small quantities. (PW)
O **Bienvenue-Bâtard-Montrachet**★★★★★ £H   O **Corton-Charlemagne**★★★★ £F
O **Chassagne-Montrachet** 1er Cru Le Cailleret★★★ £E   1er Cru Morgeots★★★★ £E
O **Santenay** 1er Cru Beaurepaire★★ £C   1er Cru Clos du Beauregard★★ £C
●**Charmes-Chambertin**★★★★★ £G   ● **Clos de la Roche**★★★★ £G   ●**Echezeaux**★★★★ £G
●**Volnay** 1er Cru Santenots★★★★ £F   ●**Santenay** 1er Cru Gravières Vieilles Vignes★★★ £C

DOM. HENRI GOUGES   www.gouges.com   *UK stockists:* OWL, Gen, CTy, HBJ, NYg, Sec, HRp, Las
Famous estate, essentially organic, with a full hand of some of Nuits' best *crus*, including the 3.5-ha *monopole* of
Clos des Porrets-Saint-Georges. Powerful, structured wines with excellent definition but most of all with
exceptional intensity and fruit quality (particularly in Vaucrains and Les Saint-Georges). All need 6-8 years'
ageing. The white is a spicy, minerally, exotic treat. (PW)
●**Nuits-Saint-Georges** 1er Cru Les Vaucrains★★★★★ £E   1er Cru Les Saint-Georges★★★★★ £F
● **Nuits-Saint-Georges**★★★ £D   1er Cru Clos des Porrets-Saint-Georges★★★★ £E
O **Nuits-Saint-Georges** 1er Cru La Perrière★★★ £E

DOM. JEAN GRIVOT   Vosne-Romanée   www.grivot.com   *UK stockists:* RsW, Bal, BBR, HRp
Étienne Grivot's wines are marvellous and much sought after, combining great richness and concentration and
despite their size avoid any heaviness, with an excellent balance. They all need at least five years and will be better
with 10 or more. Top Vosnes and *grands crus* are an excellent cellaring prospect. (PW)
● **Richebourg**✪✪✪✪✪ £H   ● **Echezeaux**✪✪✪✪✪ £G   ● **Clos de Vougeot**★★★★ £F
● **Vosne-Romanée** 1er Cru Beaux Monts✪✪✪✪✪ £F   1er Cru Suchots✪✪✪✪✪ £F
● **Nuits-Saint-Georges** 1er Cru Boudots★★★★ £F   1er Cru Pruliers★★★★ £F
● **Nuits-Saint-Georges** Lavières★★★ £E   1er Cru Roncières★★★★ £E
● **Chambolle-Musigny** Combe d'Orveaux★★★ £E

ROBERT GROFFIER   Morey-Saint-Denis   *UK stockists:* A&B, JAr, F&M, F&R, Blx, Las
Since the late 1990s the wines are rich and concentrated, adding to their already intense and classy character.
Stunning *grands crus*; also just over 1 ha of excellent Chambolle-Musigny Les Amoureuses. Only rarely is new
oak excessive, with real charm and style in the Hauts Doix and Les Sentiers. The wines can be drunk fairly
young but bring further rewards with 8 years. (PW)
● **Chambertin Clos-de-Bèze**✪✪✪✪✪ £H   ● **Bonnes Mares**✪✪✪✪✪ £G
● **Chambolle-Musigny** 1er Cru Les Amoureuses★★★★★ £G
● **Chambolle-Musigny** 1er Cru Hauts Doix★★★★ £F   1er Cru Sentiers★★★★ £F

A F GROS & FRANÇOIS PARENT   Beaune   *UK stockists:* BSh, Dec, HHC,
Anne-Françoise Gros is one of many family members involved in wine. The wines are made by her husband,
François Parent. Wines can be somewhat indistinguishable but with very good depth and breadth. However, since
1999 there has been more finesse and flair. The Vosne-Romanée *lieux-dits* are reasonably priced, the Echezeaux
rich and concentrated and the Richebourg really profound, intense and very powerful and long. Fine solid
Beaune and Pommard under François Parent's own label. (PW)
A.F Gros:
● **Richebourg**✪✪✪✪✪ £H   ● **Echezeaux**★★★★★ £F
● **Vosne-Romanée** Clos de la Fontaine★★★ £D   Aux Maizières★★★ £D
● **Chambolle-Musigny**★★★ £D   ● **Savigny-lès-Beaune** 1er Cru Clos des Guettes★★★ £D

F Parent:
● **Beaune** 1er Cru Boucherottes★★★ £D   ● **Pommard** 1er Cru Arvelets★★★★ E

49

FRANCE

ANNE GROS Vosne-Romanée www.anne-gros.fr UK stockists: Adm, Lay, L&W, HRp, JAr, Las
Smallest of the various Gros estates but the wines are the most complete and refined of all, with a harmony and fruit quality that set them apart. Village-level Chambolle-Musigny and Vosne-Romanée are lovely. Clos de Vougeot and Richebourg absorb plentiful new oak and have a wonderful, silky texture that belies excellent structure. Older wines are labelled Domaine Anne et François Gros. (PW)
● **Richebourg**✪✪✪✪✪ £H ● **Clos de Vougeot** Grand Maupertuis★★★★★ £G
● **Vosne-Romanée** Barreaux★★★ £E ● **Chambolle-Musigny** Combe d'Orveau★★★ £E
O **Bougogne Blanc**★★ £C O **Bourgogne Hautes-Côtes de Nuits**★★ £C

MICHEL GROS www.domaine-michel-gros.com UK stockists: THt, JNi, ABy, Tan,
Michel has nearly 18 ha but only a little in the top sites. The real exception is the 2.12-ha *monopole* Clos des Réas, a Vosne-Romanée *premier cru*. Quite a lot of new oak is used. These are intense, elegant, very stylish wines, structured but not big or overpowering. Morey-Saint-Denis En La Rue de Vergy is from young vines. Hautes-Côtes de Nuits is consistently good. (PW)
● **Vosne-Romanée** 1er Cru Aux Brulées★★★★ £F 1er Cru Clos des Réas★★★★★ £F
● **Nuits-Saint-Georges** Chaliots★★★ £E 1er Cru★★★ £F ● **Chambolle-Musigny**★★★ £E
● **Bourgogne Hautes-Côtes de Nuits**★★ £C ● **Bourgogne Rouge**★★ £C

HENRI ET PAUL JACQUESON Rully UK stockists: THt, BWC, L&S, JNi, HHB
Superb Rully in both colours, natural, pure and expressive, with delicious fruit. Pucelle white is full and stylish, slightly floral and exotic; Grésigny is more structured and minerally. Enticing red Chaponnières; extra weight and class in Les Cloux. Also white Rully Raclot and decent Bourgogne Passetoutgrains. (PW)
O **Rully** 1er Cru Grésigny★★ £C 1er Cru Pucelle★★★ £C O **Bourgogne** Aligoté★ £B
● **Rully** Chaponnières★★ £C 1er Cru Les Cloux★★ £C
● **Mercurey** 1er Cru Les Naugues★★ £C

LOUIS JADOT Beaune www.louisjadot.com UK stockists: HMA, AAA
Burgundy of the highest order under master winemaker Jacques Lardière from one of the region's giants. Around half of the 144 ha is in the Côte d'Or, the rest in Beaujolais (see Château des Jacques). Most top wines come from owned vineyards, comprising 5 separate domaines. New oak is used sparingly and the winemaking approach is responsive but generally non-interventionist. Reds nearly always have good colour, excellent breadth and depth and plenty of structure but also marvellous concentration, complexity and class in the top wines. (PW)
● **Bonnes Mares**✪✪✪✪✪ £H ● **Chambertin Clos de Bèze**✪✪✪✪✪ £H
● **Gevrey-Chambertin** 1er Cru Clos Saint-Jacques✪✪✪✪✪£F
● **Beaune** 1er Cru Clos de Couchereaux★★★ £E 1er Cru Clos des Ursules★★★ £E
● **Savigny-lès-Beaune** 1er Cru La Dominode★★★ £D ● **Beaune** 1er Cru Teurons★★★ £E
O **Chevalier-Montrachet** Les Demoiselles✪✪✪✪✪ £H **Corton-Charlemagne**✪✪✪✪✪ £G
Duc de Magenta:
O **Puligny-Montrachet** 1er Cru Clos de la Garenne★★★★ £G
O **Chassagne-Montrachet** Morgeots Clos de la Chapelle★★★★ £G

PATRICK JAVILLIER Meursault UK stockists: FMV, BBR, L&W, OWL, Sel, N&P
Fine Meursault *lieux-dits*; the best taste like *premiers crus*, rich and ripe, with surprising class and depth. Les Clous, Les Tillets and Les Narvaux always show a little more verve and racy minerality. Tête de Murgers is the richest, deepest and most complex. Puligny-Montrachet has less character but finesse and delineation. Bourgogne Blanc Oligocène is effectively Meursault. (PW)
O **Corton-Charlemagne**★★★★★ £G
O **Meursault** Tête de Murgers★★★★ £F Clos du Cromin★★★ £E Les Tillets★★★★ £E
O **Bourgogne Blanc** Cuvée des Forgets★★ £C Cuvée Oligocène★★★ £C

FRANÇOIS JOBARD Meursault UK stockists: RsW, A&B, Rae, Hrd, Sec
François Jobard makes somewhat tighter, more traditional wines than his nephew, Rémi Jobard. They are meant to be aged, when a deep, ripe, leesy nuttiness and flavour complexity develop. Blagny is usually deep and minerally, Poruzots is also minerally but peachier, Genevrières more honeyed, and Charmes the most refined. A little Puligny-Montrachet and some red Blagny are also made. (PW)

50

O **Meursault** 1er Cru Genevrières★★★★ £F   1er Cru Poruzots★★★★ £F
O Meursault En la Barre★★★ £E   1er Cru Blagny★★★ £F   O **Bourgogne Blanc**★★ £C

FRANCE

DOM. JOBLOT   Givry   *UK stockists:* **Hal**, F&R
One of Givry's most important estates. Yields are low, reflected in reds with intense, concentrated fruit and plenty of acidity. Powerful oak-enhanced structures ensure they are approachable young but capable of at least 5–6 years' age. Now is the time to be opening the 99s. Also very successful 01, 02 and 03 vintages here. Whites with good intensity and precision too. (PW)
● **Givry** Pied de Chaume★★ £C   1er Cru Clos Grand Marole★★★ £C
● **Givry** Cellier aux Moines★★★ £C   1er Cru Clos de la Servoisine★★★ £D
O **Givry** Pied de Chaume★★ £C   O **Givry** 1er Cru Clos de la Servoisine★★★ £C

DOM. MICHEL JUILLOT   Mercurey   www.domaine-michel-juillot.fr   *UK stockists:* DDr, HHB
Laurent Juillot makes very attractive whites and excellent reds. Clos des Barraults is the most forbidding and structured red but all reveal good depth and richness with three years' age or more. Some Combins and highly regarded Clos du Roi (both *premiers crus*) are also made and, outside Mercurey, a little Corton Perrières (red), Corton-Charlemagne and village-level Aloxe-Corton. (PW)
● **Mercurey** 1er Cru Clos des Barraults★★ £D   1er Cru Champs-Martin★★ £D
● **Mercurey** 1er Cru Clos Tonnerre★★ £C
O **Mercurey** 1er Cru Clos des Barraults★★ £D   1er Cru Champs-Martin★★ £D

MICHEL LAFARGE   Volnay   *UK stockists:* BBR GFy, Gau, HRp, Sec
Michel and and his son Frédéric have an excellent and deserved reputation for Volnay from their biodynamic domaine with relatively old vines. Wines are elegant and sophisticated, with magical aromas and superb fruit - always a lovely expression of their appellation. They really start to open out after 5 years; a minimum for Clos des Chênes. Fine Bourgogne Rouge. (PW)
● Volnay 1er Cru Clos du Château des Ducs★★★★ £F   1er Cru Clos des Chênes★★★★★ £F
● Volnay Vendange Sélectionée★★★ £E   1er Cru★★★★ £F   1er Cru Caillerets★★★★ £F
● **Beaune** 1er Cru Grèves★★★ £F   ● **Côte de Beaune-Villages**★★ £C

DOM. DES COMTES LAFON   Meursault   *UK stockists:* Adm, FMV, BBR, JAr, Far, F&M, Las
Meursault's finest and one of the very best in Côte d'Or, now biodynamic. In Meursault *premiers crus* the fruit is intense, rich and pure with a precise but seamless structure. Opulent Gouttes d'Or, expressive Charmes and profound Genevrières are surpassed by peerless Perrières. Fine Volnays are crowned by a rich Santenots du Milieu. Most expensive is a tiny-production Montrachet. Also very good Mâconnais from Domaine des Heritiers Comtes Lafon. (PW)
O **Meursault** 1er Cru Perrières✪✪✪✪✪ £G   1er Cru Charmes★★★★★ £G
O **Meursault** 1er Cru Goutte d'Or★★★★ £G   1er Cru Genevrières★★★★★ £G
O **Meursault** Clos de la Barre★★★ £F   ● **Monthelie** 1er Cru Duresses★★★ £D
● **Volnay** 1er Cru Champans★★★★ £E   1er Cru Santenots du Milieu★★★★★ £F

DOM. FRANÇOIS LAMARCHE   www.domaine-lamarche.com   *UK stockists:* Col, Rae, RsW ,Sec
Recently improved estate with all 1.65 ha of *grand cru* La Grande Rue (between La Tâche and La Romanée-Conti). Wines are more concentrated and classy but still start out quite tight and tannic and demand patience. La Grande Rue is very fine indeed but only the most recent vintages should be bought for cellaring. (PW)
● **La Grande Rue**✪✪✪✪✪ £G   ● **Echezeaux**★★★★ £F   ● **Clos de Vougeot**★★★★ £F
● **Vosne-Romanée** 1er Cru Croix Rameau★★★★ £E   1er Cru Malconsorts★★★★ £F
● **Vosne-Romanée**★★ £E   1er Cru Chaumes★★★ £E   1er Cru Suchots★★★★ £E

DOM. DES LAMBRAYS   Morey-Saint-Denis   *UK stockists:* OWL, HRp, BBR, HHC, Sel
Gunter Freund owns almost all of the 8.8-ha Clos des Lambrays, fully on form since 1996. The wine is seductively plump and silky with terrific class and complexity, softer than adjoining Clos de Tart. The Moreys, especially Les Loups, share the delicious fruit and superfine tannins. Very exciting Puligny Clos du Caillerets and Les Folatières. (PW)
● **Clos des Lambrays**★★★★★ £F   ● **Morey-Saint-Denis** 1er Cru Loups★★★★ £E
O **Puligny-Montrachet** 1er Cru Clos du Cailleret★★★★★ £F

FRANCE

HUBERT LAMY Saint-Aubin *UK stockists:* BBR, DDr, Gen, L&S, L&W

A new generation has honed the Saint-Aubin whites into ripe, rich and stylish examples. Reds are increasingly ripe and concentrated too. Puligny Les Tremblots could pass for a *premier cru* wine. A very small amount of Criots-Bâtard-Montrachet is also made. Good-value source of Burgundy. (PW)

O **Saint-Aubin** 1er Cru En Remilly★★★ £D 1er Cru Murgers Dents de Chien★★★ £D
O **Saint-Aubin** 1er Cru Les Frionnes★★★ £C 1er Cru Clos de la Chatenière★★★ £D
● **Saint-Aubin** 1er Cru Les Castets ★★ £C 1er Cru Derrière Chez Edouard★★★ £C

LOUIS LATOUR www.louislatour.com *UK stockists:* **LLt**, Hay, BBR, C&R, MCW, F&M

With an annual production of 5.5 million bottles from all over Burgundy and beyond, this historic house (and domaine of 50 ha) is widely seen outside of France. Reds, controversially made with flash-pasteurisation, can be lacking. White grapes are harvested late, yields are low and plenty of new oak is used and some of the top *crus* can be astonishingly good, with great concentration, complexity and power. (PW)

O **Bâtard-Montrachet**★★★★ £H O **Chevalier-Montrachet** Demoiselles★★★★ £H
O **Corton-Charlemagne**★★★★ £G
O **Meursault** 1er Cru Château de Blagny★★★ £E 1er Cru Goutte d'Or★★★ £E

LATOUR-GIRAUD Meursault *UK stockists:* Bib, THt

Previously underperforming domaine now living up to its impressive holdings, including elegant and intense Genevrières. This and minerally Perrières will slowly unfurl with up to 10 years' ageing. Fine Charmes (also two other *premiers crus*, Bouchères and Poruzots). Village wines give classic Meursault style at a more affordable price. Some red is made, mostly from Maranges. (PW)

O **Meursault** 1er Cru Genevrières★★★★★ £F 1er Cru Perrières★★★★★ £F
O **Meursault** 1er Cru Charmes★★★★ £F Charles Maxime★★★ £E Le Limozin★★★ £E
O **Puligny-Montrachet** Champs Canet★★★★ £F

DOMINIQUE LAURENT Nuits-Saint-Georges *UK stockists:* Far, HBJ, N&P, HRp, Hrd

Ex-pastry chef Dominique Laurent buys only the best small lots of young red wine made from old low-yielding vines, ages them himself, then sells the many individual cuvées for very high prices. The wines are typically big, powerful and very concentrated, with lots of extract and tannin. Oak, once excessive, now enriches and enhances the fruit richness, resulting in a succulent creaminess. See also Tardieu-Laurent in the Rhône. (PW)

OLIVIER LEFLAIVE Puligny-Montrachet A: C&B, HHC, L&W,WSc

Consistent merchant house producing three-quarters of a million bottles, mostly from bought-in grapes. All 6 Côte de Beaune *grands crus* are made, including very fine Criots-Bâtard-Montrachet and Le Montrachet. Leading *premiers crus* from Puligny-Montrachet, Chassagne-Montrachet and Meursault can be good if a little variable. Lower level wines can be a little dull, even dilute. A increasing amount of fine Chablis. Structured, oaky reds from Pommard and Volnay are very satisfying with five years' age or more. (PW)

O **Puligny-Montrachet** 1er Cru Champ Canet★★★ £F 1er Cru Pucelles★★★★ £F
O **Meursault** Narvaux★★ £E 1er Cru Poruzots★★★ £F 1er Cru Perrières★★★★ £F
O **Chablis Premier Cru** Fourchaumes★★★ £D Montée de Tonnerre★★★ £D Vaillons★★★ £D
● **Volnay** 1er Cru Champans★★★ £E 1er Cru Santenots★★★ £E
● **Pommard**★★ £D 1er Cru Charmots★★★ £E 1er Cru Rugiens★★★ £E

DOM. LEFLAIVE Puligny-Montrachet *UK stockists:* JAr, BBR, Goe, L&W, HRp,Tan, Hrd

Under the direction of Anne-Claude Leflaive, an unsurpassed holding of prime white Burgundy vineyard (biodynamic since 1998). Of the 23.5 ha, 11.5 ha are of *premiers crus*, 5 ha of *grands crus*, including nearly 2 ha each of Chevalier-Montrachet and Bâtard-Montrachet. The wines, made by Pierre Morey, have endless flavour nuances with wonderful purity and clarity, great concentration and intensity but almost perfect precision and poise. Compelling *grands crus*. Very expensive. (PW)

O **Le Montrachet**✪✪✪✪✪ £H O **Chevalier-Montrachet**✪✪✪✪✪£H
O **Bienvenues-Bâtard-Montrachet**✪✪✪✪✪ £H O **Bâtard-Montrachet**✪✪✪✪✪ £H
O **Puligny-Montrachet** 1er Cru Pucelles★★★★★ £G 1er Cru Combottes★★★★★ £G

DOM. LEROY www.domaineleroy.com *UK stockists:* JAr, BBR, C&R, Far, HRp, Sec, F&R, Las

22 ha of some of the finest *crus* are run by the formidable and dynamic Madame Lalou Bize-Leroy, a champion of biodynamic viticulture. Reds have quite staggering concentration and richness, sometimes overwhelming

52

extract and structure, as well as great intensity, depth and length. All need up to 10 years and usually keep much longer. Generally the *grands crus* are five stars, leading *premiers crus* four or five stars, and others at least three stars. Also white Corton-Charlemagne. Bize-Leroy's own domaine is Domaine d'Auvenay, while Leroy SA is the *négociant* and distribution operation. (PW)

DOM. LORENZON Mercury *UK stockists:* **FMV**
Bruno Lorenzon gets fully ripe fruit and the wines have shown lots of intensity and extract in recent vintages; 2002 and 03 promise much with 5 years' age. Cuvée Carline is especially fine – suggestive of good village-level Vosne-Romanée. A small amount of vibrant, intense white is also made. (PW)
● **Mercurey★★** £C 1er Cru Champs-Martin★★ £C
● **Mercurey** 1er Cru Champs-Martin Cuvée Carline £D
O **Mercurey** 1er Cru Croichots★★ £C 1er Cru Champs Martin★★★ £C

FRANÇOIS LUMPP Givry *UK stockists:* **THt, L&S, N&P, JNi, Hrd**
One of the best Givry producers, making supple, harmonious and balanced reds, especially with a couple of years' bottle-age. The Crausot is particularly impressive. Fine whites are ripe but not overripe, with good intensity and balance and an elegant minerality in the Petite Marole. (PW)
O **Givry** 1er Cru Petit Marole★★★ £C Clos des Vignes Rondes★★ £C
● **Givry** 1er Cru Clos Jus★★ £C 1er Cru Crausot★★★ £C
● **Givry** Pied du Clou★★ £C 1er Cru Petite Marole★★ £C

DOM. MICHEL MAGNIEN ET FILS Morey-Saint-Denis *UK stockists:* JAr
Frédéric Magnien works with his father on the family domaine but also has his own *négociant* label. The style is for richness and extract combined with lots of new oak. The wines are succulent, fleshy and richly fruity, with fine ripe tannins in the best years. Top reds will keep but give hedonistic pleasure with just 5 or 6 years' age. (PW)
Domaine Michel Magnien et Fils:
● **Clos de la Roche★★★** £F ● **Clos Saint-Denis★★★★** £G
● **Gevrey-Chambertin** Aux Echezeaux★★★ £E 1er Cru Les Cazetiers★★★ £F
● **Morey-Saint-Denis** Mont Luisants★★★ £E 1er Cru Les Chaffots★★★★ £E

DOM. MATROT Meursault *UK stockists:* C&B, BBR, Gau, GFy, Con, T&W
Devoted *vigneron* Thierry Matrot produces rich, powerful and structured whites, sometimes sulphury when young. They can seem a little awkward at first and all the *premiers crus* should have a minimum of five years' age. Amongst the reds, both Volnay Santenots and Blagny are ripe, long and quite classy. May now be labelled Pierre Matrot or Thierry Matrot. (PW)
O **Meursault** 1er Cru Perrières★★★★★ £F 1er Cru Blagny★★★★ £E
O **Puligny-Montrachet** 1er Cru Chalumeaux★★★★ £F 1er Cru Combettes★★★★ £F
● **Blagny** 1er Cru Pièce sous le Bois★★★ £E ● **Volnay** 1er Cru Santenots★★★★ £E

MÉO-CAMUZET www.meo-camuzet.com *UK stockists:* BBR, Fie, RsW, N&P, F&M, Las, F&R
Jean-Nicolas Méo continues the tradition of one of Burgundy's great 20th-century winemakers, Henri Jayer, at this fine estate. 100 per cent new oak is nearly always in evidence but the wines are polished and complete. At a lower level there is not the purity or intensity of others, but the Cros Parentoux and Richebourg and increasingly the Corton and Echezeaux are very classy, very exciting wines. Expensive. (PW)
● **Richebourg✪✪✪✪✪** £H ● **Clos de Vougeot★★★★** £H ● **Echezeaux★★★★** £H
● **Corton★★★★** £H ● **Vosne-Romanée** 1er Cru Cros Parentoux★★★★★ £H
● **Vosne-Romanée★★★** £F 1er Cru Chaumes★★★ £G 1er Cru Brulées★★★★★ £H

FRANÇOIS MIKULSKI Meursault *UK stockists:* Eno, GFy, Han, N&P, Sec, Blx
One of the newest stars of the Côte de Beaune, with attention-grabbing Meursault. All the wines are ripe and full-bodied and develop a creamy, honeyed richness with a little age. Genevrières has the structure to match the concentration. More affordable ripe, fruity Bourgogne Blanc and Aligoté don't lack for flavour or character. Reds Meursault and Volnay don't as yet show the flair of the whites. (PW)
O **Meursault★★★** £E 1er Cru Genevrières★★★★ £F 1er Cru Poruzots★★★★ £F
O **Bourgogne Blanc★★** £B O **Bourgogne Aligoté★** £B

FRANCE

HUBERT DE MONTILLE Volnay *UK stockists:* Gen, OWL, HRp, CTy, GFy, Sel
The wines of Hubert de Montille (star of film Mondovino) always showed great dimension and depth but with a lot of extract and tannin, only opening out after 10 years. Vintages since 1998 made by his son Étienne are less formidable yet retain elegance and individuality. Now also biodynamic. Full and stylish Pommard; Rugiens is the most intense and classy. Volnay can be a little lighter; Taillepieds reveals great length and finesse. (PW)
● **Pommard** 1er Cru Rugiens★★★★★ £F 1er Cru Pézerolles★★★★ £F
● **Volnay** 1er Cru Mitans★★★★ £F 1er Cru Taillepieds★★★★★ £F
O **Puligny-Montrachet** 1er Cru Cailleret★★★★★ £F

DOM. MARC MOREY Chassagne-Montrachet *UK stockists:* HHC, JAr, Gau, Las
Bernard Mollard and his son Jerôme make outstanding whites. An excellent, minerally Chassagne has good citrus intensity. Of the classy *premiers crus* Les Vergers is tight and minerally, Virondot more forward and fatter, while Cailleret and Morgeot are both rich and concentrated. Powerful, classy and complex Bâtard-Montrachet. (PW)
O **Bâtard-Montrachet**✪✪✪✪ £G
O **Chassagne-Montrachet** 1er Cru En Virondot★★★ £E 1er Cru Les Vergers★★★★ £E
O **Chassagne-Montrachet**★★★ £E 1er Cru Les Chenevottes★★★ £E

PIERRE MOREY/MOREY BLANC Meursault *UK stockists:* HRp, L&W, MCW, Tan
One of Burgundy's most highly regarded makers of white wine (see also Domaine Leflaive). The wines build great richness and opulence with age, becoming nutty, buttery and peachy. Meursault Perrières has intense minerally depth; Bâtard-Montrachet is classy and complex. Give them 5-6 years. Reds include good Pommard Epenots. Morey Blanc is the high-class *négociant* label. (PW)
Pierre Morey:
O **Bâtard-Montrachet**✪✪✪✪ £H
O **Meursault**★★★ £E Tessons★★★★ £F 1er Cru Perrières★★★★★ £F
O **Bourgogne Blanc**★★ £B ● **Pommard** Grands Epenots★★★ £E
Morey Blanc:
O **Meursault**★★★ £E Navaux★★★ £E 1er Cru Genevrières★★★ £E
O **Saint-Aubin** 1er Cru★★ £C

DOM. MOREY-COFFINET Chassagne-Montrachet *UK stockists:* RsW, BBR, L&W, A&B, UnC, SVS
Michel Morey makes fine Chassagne-Montrachet *premier cru* whites with impressive intensity, concentration and good structure. All deserve to be drunk with at least 5–6 years' age. Also excellent Puligny-Montrachet Les Pucelles with the sheer style of this *cru*, and Bâtard-Montrachet with typical richness and breadth. (PW)
O **Chassagne-Montrachet**★★ £E 1er Cru Caillerets★★★★ £F
O **Chassagne-Montrachet** 1er Cru En Remilly★★★★ £F
O **Chassagne-Montrachet** 1er Cru Romanée★★★★ £F
O **Puligny-Montrachet** 1er Cru Les Pucelles★★★★ £F

DENIS MORTET www.denismortet.com *UK stockists:* BBR, DDr, Sec, WSc, HHB, Las
One of the truly outstanding Gevrey estates, with 11 ha of fine *premiers crus* and some of the best village *lieux-dits*. These are marvellously complete wines, full, ripe and rich and with everything in balance. Recent vintages show still greater refinement and harmony. Drink with 5 years' ageing or more. (PW)
● **Chambertin**✪✪✪✪ £H ● **Clos de Vougeot**★★★★ £G
● **Gevrey-Chambertin** 1er Cru Lavaux Saint-Jacques★★★★★ £F
● **Gevrey-Chambertin** Au Vellé★★★ £E En Champs★★★ £E En Motrot★★★ £E

MUGNERET-GIBOURG/DR GEORGES MUGNERET *UK stockists:* BWC, HRp, L&S, OWL
Consistently refined wines from this 8.8-ha estate. The original vineyards of the property are sold under the Mugneret-Gibourg label, those acquired by the late Dr Georges Mugneret, are sold under his name. All the wines show a measure of oak but have pure ripe Pinot fruit within a firm structure and real definition. Village wines and the elegant, seductive Chambolle-Musigny need 5 years, the complex, refined Chaignots and the *grands crus* need more. (PW)
● **Clos de Vougeot**★★★★ £F ● **Ruchottes-Chambertin**★★★★★ £F
● **Echezeaux**★★★★ £F ● **Vosne-Romanée**★★★ £D
● **Nuits-Saint-Georges**★★★ £D 1er Cru Les Chaignots★★★★ £E

54

JACQUES-FRÉDÉRIC MUGNIER www.mugnier.fr   UK stockists: HHB, HRp, FMV, Sec, Las
The early 18th-century Château de Chambolle-Musigny pales beside the elegance, finesse even grandeur of these, at times, sublime wines from just 4 ha. No blockbusters here; these are beautiful wines true to their appellations that gain with age. The regular Chambolle-Musigny can sometimes be a little slight but there's a hint of nobility even here. (PW)
● Musigny✪✪✪✪✪ £H   ● Bonnes Mares★★★★★ £G
● Chambolle-Musigny 1er Cru Fuées★★★★ £F 1er Cru Amoureuses★★★★★ £G

MICHEL NIELLON Chassagne-Montrachet   UK stockists: OWL, BBR, RRi, F&R, C&R, Sec
Much praised small domaine. The wines are tight and intense when young with restrained oak. The very expensive *grands crus* are usually brilliant but the *premiers crus*, while often very good, do not approach the same level. At their best there is depth, fine fruit concentration and good style. All the wines deserve at least five to six years' age. (PW)
○ Chevalier-Montrachet✪✪✪✪✪ £H   ○ Bâtard-Montrachet✪✪✪✪✪ £H
○ Chassagne-Montrachet 1er Cru Les Chaumées★★★★ £F
○ Chassagne-Montrachet★★ £E 1er Cru Champs Gain★★★ £F

JEAN-MARC PAVELOT Savigny-lès-Beaune   UK stockists: DDr, L&W,
Superior Savigny domaine where the wines have a grace and charm that sets them apart from the fruity but unrefined norm. Vigorous Guettes and a seductive Aux Gravains reveal are delicious and stylish with a little age; Narbantons and Peuillets are fuller and meatier. La Dominode from very old vines is the richest and most complete. Regular red and white Savigny are great drinking with a little bottle-age. (PW)
● Savigny-lès-Beaune 1er Cru La Dominode★★★★ £D
● Savigny-lès-Beaune★★ £C 1er Cru Peuillets★★ £D 1er Cru Guettes★★★ £D
● Pernand-Vergelesses 1er Cru Les Vergelesses★★ £C ○ Savigny-lès-Beaune★★ £C

DOM. PAUL PERNOT ET FILS Puligny-Montrachet   UK stockists: JAr, Bal, L&S, HRp, Las
Concentrated, powerful whites that become increasingly rich and honeyed with age yet retain wonderful proportion and balance. Reds have good intensity if not that much refinement. The village Puligny-Montrachet is remarkably good value. (PW)
○ Bâtard-Montrachet✪✪✪✪✪ £G   ○ Bienvenues-Bâtard-Montrachet✪✪✪✪✪ £G
○ Puligny-Montrachet★★★ £E 1er Cru Folatières★★★★ £F
● Pommard Noizons★★ £D   ● Volnay 1er Cru Carelles★★★ £D

PERROT-MINOT Morey-Saint-Denis   UK stockists: BWC, Bal, Blx, F&R, HHB
Christophe Perrot and his father produce wines with impressive power and intensity that reveal great style and individuality with age. Chambolle-Musigny Combe d'Orveau is the most classy and complex. Good Bourgogne Rouge. Exciting new wines of the same stamp include old-vine Nuits-Saint-Georges La Richemone, Vosne-Romanée Les Beaux-Monts and Gevrey-Chambertin Les Cazetiers. (PW)
● Chambertin★★★★ £G   ● Charmes-Chambertin★★★★ £G
● Morey-Saint-Denis En la Rue de Vergy★★★ £E 1er Cru La Riotte V.Vignes★★★ £F
● Chambolle-Musigny 1er Cru La Combe d'Orveau★★★★ £F
● Chambolle-Musigny Vieilles Vignes★★★ £E 1er Cru Les Fuées★★★★ £F

FERNAND ET LAURENT PILLOT Chassagne-Montrachet   UK stockists: THt, L&S
Quality used to be a little uneven here with lesser reds struggling for ripeness and richness in cooler years. Current releases, however, are very good: 2003 whites are ripe and concentrated if relatively forward while the 02s have structure, intensity and complexity. The pick of the reds are the Pommard *premiers crus* although the village-level Tavannes shouldn't be overlooked. (PW)
○ Chassagne-Montrachet 1er Cru Vide Bourse★★★★ £E
○ Chassagne-Montrachet 1er Cru Grandes Ruchottes★★★★ £E
○ Chassagne-Montrachet 1er Cru Vergers★★★ £E 1er Cru Morgeots★★★★ £E
○ Meursault 1er Cru Caillerets★★★★ £E   ● Pommard 1er Cru Rugiens★★★★ £F

JEAN PILLOT ET FILS Chassagne-Montrachet   UK stockists: C&C, Eno, BBR, CTy, JNi
Family domaine reputed for whites and an increasingly good source of red Chassagne. The whites are more

FRANCE

consistent and richer, riper and oakier under Jean-Marc Pillot, with marvellous concentration, breadth and depth in the top *premiers crus*. The reds show proper ripeness and richness too. Very fine Puligny-Montrachet Premier Cru Les Caillerets and Chevalier-Montrachet from bought-in wine. Good Saint-Romain white, red Santenay and Bourgogne red and white are made in most vintages too. (PW)

○ **Chassagne-Montrachet** Ier Cru Morgeots★★★★ £E Ier Cru Vergers★★★★ £E
○ **Chassagne-Montrachet**★★★ £D Ier Cru Macherelles★★★ £E
● **Chassagne-Montrachet** Ier Cru Macherelles★★ £D Ier Cru Morgeots★★★ £D

DOM. PONSOT www.domaine-ponsot.com UK stockists: BBR, Bal, Goe, L&W, F&R, Sec, Las
Very serious traditional estate that places huge importance on *terroir*. No two wines are quite alike but there is a strength underpinning the truly marvellous expression and fine, silky textures that can be spellbinding. The Morey-Saint-Denis white is mostly Aligoté but very full, ripe and structured. Village Gevrey and Morey can be superb value. (PW)

● **Clos de la Roche** V.Vignes✪✪✪✪✪ £H ● **Clos Saint-Denis** V.Vignes✪✪✪✪✪ £H
● **Griotte-Chambertin**✪✪✪✪✪ £G ● **Chapelle-Chambertin**★★★★ £G
● **Morey-Saint-Denis** Cuvée des Grives★★★ £E Ier Cru Alouettes★★★★ £E

NICOLAS POTEL Nuits-Saint-Georges UK stockists: GFy, Bib, BBR, L&W, Tan, Gau, JNi
Nicolas Potel, formerly of Domaine de la Pousse d'Or, now works with an extensive range of bought-in wines. Already well-established are some stylish, fragrant Volnays, concentrated Pommards and full, quite classy Nuits-Saint-Georges. Clos de Vougeot is a fine example. (PW)

● **Clos de Vougeot**★★★★ £F ● **Grands Echezeaux**★★★★★ £G
● **Nuits-Saint-Georges** Ier Cru Les Saint-Georges★★★ £E Ier Cru Roncières★★★ £E
● **Volnay** V.Vignes★★ £D Ier Cru Champans★★★ £E Ier Cru Pitures★★★★ £E
● **Pommard** Ier Cru Epenots★★★ £E Ier Cru Rugiens★★★ £E

DOM. DE LA POUSSE D'OR Volnay www.lapoussedor.fr UK stockists: DLW, HRp
Famous estate gradually revitalised since 1997. 15ha include the *premier cru* Volnay *monopoles* of La Bousse d'Or (2.14ha) and celebrated 2.4-ha Clos des 60 Ouvrées. New owner Patrick Landanger has further reduced yields, extended maceration times and used an increased percentage of new oak. 2002s of both Volnays are impressively complex and meaty with lots of depth and style. Also new Corton reds. (PW)

● **Volnay** Ier Cru Clos de la Bousse d'Or★★★★ £F
● **Volnay** Ier Cru Clos des 60 Ouvrées★★★★ £F
● **Santenay** Ier Cru Clos Tavannes★★★ £D

DOM. JACQUES PRIEUR UK stockists: BBR, L&S, Blx, F&R, Las
Prestigious estate with previously flagging reputation recently revived by Rodet's winemaker, Nadine Gublin. Whites are rich, ripe and powerful, if sometimes at the expense of expression and finesse, and include *grands crus* Le Montrachet, Chevalier-Montrachet and Corton-Charlemagne, and *premiers crus* Meursault Perrières and Puligny-Montrachet Les Combettes. Reds, more consistently improved than whites, include *grands crus* Musigny, Echezeaux, Chambertin, Clos de Vougeot and Corton Bressandes; and *premiers crus* from Volnay and Beaune. (PW)

● **Corton Bressandes**★★★★ £G ● **Clos de Vougeot**★★★★★ £G
● **Volnay** Ier Cru Clos des Santenots★★★ £F
● **Beaune** Ier Cru Champs Pimont★★★ £F
● **Beaune** Ier Cru Clos de la Féguine★★★ £F Ier Cru Grèves★★★★ £F
○ **Corton-Charlemagne**★★★★ £G

RAMONET Chassagne-Montrachet UK stockists: C&B, Far, OWL, HRp, Sel
One of the great white Burgundy estates. Noël Ramonet makes the fantastic array of wines in a somewhat intuitive fashion. They usually have an explosive concentration and breadth within a powerful structure but are variable so do some research before cellaring. (PW)

○ **Bâtard-Montrachet**✪✪✪✪✪ £H ○ **Bienvenues-Bâtard-Montrachet**★★★★★ £H
○ **Chassagne-Montrachet** Ier Cru Grandes Ruchottes★★★★★ £F
○ **Chassagne-Montrachet** Ier Cru Boudriottes★★★★ £F Ier Cru Morgeots★★★★ £F
● **Chassagne-Montrachet** Ier Cru Clos de la Boudriotte★★★ £E

56

FRANÇOIS RAQUILLET Mercurey   *UK stockists:* THt, FMV, NYg, P&S, F&M, Sel
Young vigneron who is turning his family's 11 ha into some of the most prized in Mercurey. *Premier cru* reds see
new oak and retain fruit purity without unwanted firmness. Naugues is the most sophisticated. Also *premier cru*
Clos l'Eveque. Promising 2002s. (PW)
- **Mercurey** Vieilles Vignes★★ £C   1er Cru Vasées★★ £C   1er Cru Veleys★★ £C
- **Mercurey** 1er Cru Puillets★★ £C   1er Cru Naugues★★★ £C

MICHÈLE & PATRICE RION Nuits-Saint-Georges   *UK stockists:* FMV, NYg, UnC
Patrice Rion built a good track record while at the family domaine (Daniel Rion et Fils). Now with his own
estate wines and promising *négociant* range (from 2000) under the Patrice Rion. (PW)
Dom. Michèle & Patrice Rion:
- **Chambolle-Musigny** Les Cras★★★ £E   1er Cru Les Charmes★★★★ £F
- **Nuits-Saint-Georges** 1er Cru Clos des Argillières★★★★ £F
- **Bourgogne Rouge** Bons Batons★★ £C
Patrice Rion:
- **Nuits-Saint-Georges** Vieilles Vignes★★★ £E   • **Gevrey-Chambertin** Clos Prieur★★★★ £E

DOM. DANIEL RION ET FILS Nuits-Saint-Georges   *UK stockists:* CTy, N&P, JNi, WSc
Christophe and Olivier make the wines here after the departure of their brother Patrice (Michèle & Patrice
Rion) following the 2000 vintage. Wines have strength and firmness allied to depth and intensity, recently
with finer tannins and more immediate richness. Particularly successful in top years. Reds can be transformed
with a little extra bottle age. Rich, creamy white Nuits from Pinot Blanc. (PW)
- **Clos de Vougeot**★★★★★ £F
- **Vosne-Romanée**★★ £D   1er Cru Chaumes★★★★ £E   1er Cru Beaux-Monts★★★★★ £E
- **Nuits-Saint-Georges** 1er Cru Vignes Rondes★★★ £E   Vieilles Vignes★★★ £E
- **Côte de Nuits-Villages**★★ £C   O Nuits-Saint-Georges 1er Cru Terres Blanches★★★ £E

ANTONIN RODET Mercurey   www.rodet.com   *UK stockists:* BBR, C&R, MCW, Las, N&P
Négociant house with substantial holdings in both the Côte d'Or and Côte Chalonnaise. Estates owned, partly
owned or made and distributed by Rodet include the Meursault-based Domaine Jacques Prieur, gradually
restoring its reputation under Rodet's winemaker, Nadine Gublin. The best Antonin Rodet-labelled wines are
consistently very good, at times quite oaky but rich and ripe, with great depth and complexity. Also owns
Domaine de l'Aigle in Limoux, Languedoc-Roussillon. (PW)
Antonin Rodet:
- **Charmes-Chambertin**★★★★ £G   • **Clos de Vougeot**★★★★ £G
- **Gevrey-Chambertin** 1er Cru Estournelles★★★★ £F
- **Nuits-Saint-Georges** 1er Cru Les Saint-Georges★★★ £F   1er Cru Porêts-Saint-Georges★★★★ £F
Domaine des Perdrix:
- **Echezeaux**★★★★ £G   • **Vosne-Romanée**★★★ £E
- **Nuits-Saint-Georges**★★★ £E   1er Cru Aux Perdrix★★★★★ £F
Château de Chamirey:
- O **Mercurey**★ £C   1er Cru La Mission★★ £D   • **Mercurey**★★ £C   1er Cru Les Ruelles★★★ £D

DOM. DE LA ROMANÉE-CONTI Vosne-Romanée   *UK stockists:* **C&B**, BBR, F&M, Hrd, Las, F&R
DRC is considered by many to be Burgundy's greatest domaine but seriously challenged by part-owner Lalou
Bize-Leroy's own estate, Domaine Leroy. Now essentially biodynamic with lower yields and older vines than
previously. All the wines see 100 per cent new oak. When on form all wines rate five stars. The holdings are
monopoles La Romanée Conti (1.81 ha) and La Tâche (6.06 ha), Richebourg (3.51 ha), Romanée-Saint-Vivant
(5.28 ha), Echezeaux (4.67 ha), Grands-Echezeaux (3.53 ha) and the solitary white, Le Montrachet (0.68 ha).
All the wines are £H. A second selection, Cuvée Duvault-Blochet, sold as Vosne Romanée Premier Cru, was
produced in 1999 and 2002. (PW)

DOM. ROULOT Meursault   *UK stockists:* DDr, HHC, HRp, JAr, BWC
Highly respected domaine with a hatful of Meursault *crus*. The wines show something of a leesy character and
and some new oak influence but neither dominate. Perrières is easily the most complex and complete. Les

Tessons and Les Tillets offer relatively good value for Meursault. The intense, vibrant, minerally Monthelie adds richness with two or three years' age. (PW)

O **Meursault** 1er Cru Charmes★★★★ £F 1er Cru Perrières★★★★★ £F
O **Meursault** Meix Chavaux★★★ £D Les Tillets★★★★ £D Les Tessons★★★★ £D
O **Meursault** Les Vireuils★★★ £D O **Monthelie** 1er Cru Champs Fulliot★★ £C

DOM. ROUMIER www.roumier.com UK stockists: JAr, HHC, DDr, HRp, FMV, Tan, Las
A fabulous domaine whose wines express the essence of Chambolle-Musigny in each vintage with fragrant and elegant wines. Impressive structure, dimension and depth without a trace of hardness, allied to harmony and persistence. Powerful, elegant Le Musigny contrasts with muscular, intense Bonnes Mares. Firmer, tighter Morey-Saint-Denis (a *monopole*) can be very good value. (PW)

● **Le Musigny**✪✪✪✪✪ £H ● **Bonnes Mares**✪✪✪✪✪ £H
● **Chambolle-Musigny**★★★ £D 1er Cru Les Cras★★★★★ £F
● **Morey-Saint-Denis** 1er Cru Clos de la Bussière★★★★ £E

DOM. A ROUSSEAU www.domaine-rousseau.com UK stockists: HRp, BBR, HBJ, OWL, F&M, Las
Famous Gevrey-Chambertin domaine with a remarkable 8 ha of the 14 ha planted in *grands crus*. All wines have vigour and intensity and impressive texture. Chambertin and Chambertin Clos-de-Bèze show all the class and breed of great *grand cru* Burgundy. Charmes and Mazy emphasise finesse and elegance. All need 5 years, the top wines 10 or more. The 2002s are superlative. (PW)

● **Chambertin**✪✪✪✪✪ £H ● **Chambertin Clos-de-Bèze**✪✪✪✪✪ £H
● **Ruchottes-Chambertin** Clos des Ruchottes✪✪✪✪✪ £G
● **Charmes-Chambertin**★★★★ £F ● **Clos de la Roche**★★★★★ £F
● **Gevrey-Chambertin** 1er Cru Clos Saint-Jacques✪✪✪✪✪ £F

ETIENNE SAUZET www.etienne-sauzet.com UK stockists: HHC, L&W, OWL, BBR, Hrd, Tan, Las
This estate has a fabulous reputation and highly respected winemaker in Gérard Boudot. However it is now significantly smaller than it once was. There are 8 ha (but much boosted by bought-in grapes) with small amounts of four *grands crus* and more significant amounts of some of Puligny's best *premiers crus*. Form in the 1990s was irregular – invest with some caution. 1999 and 02 are best recent vintages. (PW)

O **Le Montrachet**★★★★★ £H O **Chevalier-Montrachet**★★★★★ £H
O **Puligny-Montrachet** 1er Cru Champ-Canet★★★★ £F 1er Cru Perrières★★★★ £F
O **Puligny-Montrachet** 1er Cru Combettes★★★★ £F 1er Cru Referts★★★★ £F
O **Puligny-Montrachet**★★★ £E 1er Cru Folatières★★★ £F 1er Cru Garenne★★★ £F

COMTE SENARD Aloxe-Corton UK stockists: Anl, F&R
Stylish and aromatic red Burgundies with cool, pure, vibrant fruit intensity. The Cortons add breadth, length and elegance: Bressandes and Clos du Roi show lots of intensity and depth, En Charlemagne classy fruit and good dimension. Age at least 5 years. Good white Aloxe-Corton from old-vine Pinot Gris; Corton Blanc is gaining in richness and complexity. (PW)

● **Corton** Clos du Roi★★★ £F ● **Corton** Clos de Meix★★★ £F
● **Aloxe-Corton**★★ £D 1er Cru Les Valozières★★ £E O **Corton** Blanc★★★ £F

CHRISTIAN SÉRAFIN Gevrey-Chambertin UK stockists: Eno, Goe, BBR F&R
Christian Sérafin embellish Gevrey power with plenty of oak and spice to produce wines that are lush and fruit-rich, with lots of obvious appeal. The top *crus* add more class and breadth. The Vieilles Vignes is meaty and full of ripe fruit, with plenty of depth. All show very well with just 5 years' age. (PW)

● **Gevrey-Chambertin** 1er Cru Cazetiers★★★★★ £F 1er Cru Corbeaux★★★★ £F
● **Gevrey-Chambertin**★★★ £E V. Vignes★★★★ £E 1er Cru Fontenys★★★★ £F
● **Chambolle-Musigny** 1er Cru Les Baudes★★★★ £F

DOM. TRAPET PÈRE ET FILS UK stockists: C&B, C&C, Hrd, F&R
Jean-Louis Trapet has revived the venerable vineyards, which include nearly 2 ha of Chambertin and decent segments of Chapelle-Chambertin and Latricières-Chambertin. The accent is on the quality of the fruit and producing wines of finesse and real class. Given time these wines are some of the very best from Gevrey and are reasonably priced in that context. (PW)

58

FRANCE

● Chambertin★★★★★ £G   ● Latricières-Chambertin★★★★★ £G
● Gevrey-Chambertin★★★ £D   1er Cru Petite Chapelle★★★★ £F

VERGET   www.verget-sa.com   *UK stockists:* Far, L&S, L&W, BBR, Odd, F&R, C&R, Las
Jean-Marie Guffens' merchant house, built around the less hallowed vineyards of the Mâconnais (see Guffens-Heynen in Mâconnais section) and increasingly Chablis. The wines from the Côte d'Or are true to the Verget style of great extract, concentration and richness. The Chablis are also deep and concentrated but a little tighter, cooler and more minerally (if ripe and full by Chablis standards). Almost all of the wines can be broached fairly young but should keep for a decade. (PW)
O Bâtard-Montrachet★★★★ £H   O Corton-Charlemagne★★★★ £E
O Meursault Tillets★★★★ £E   Rougeots★★★ £E
O Puligny-Montrachet Enseignières★★★ £F   1er Cru Sous le Puits★★★ £F
O Chablis Premier Cru Forêts★★★ £D   Montée de Tonnerre★★★ £E   Vaillons★★★★ £D

AUBERT ET PAMÉLA DE VILLAINE   Bouzeron   *UK stockists:* **C&B,** ACh
The co-director of the Côte d'Or's most prestigious estate (Domaine de la Romanée-Conti) also makes a fine, characterful Aligoté along with some red Mercurey and white Rully. The wines are elegant and harmonious with real depth and intensity in the Mercurey Montots. All are better with 2 or 3 years' age. (PW)
● Mercurey Montots★★ £C   ● Bourgogne Côte Chalonnaise La Digoine★★ £C
O Rully Saint-Jacques★★ £C   O Bouzeron Aligoté★★ £B
O Bourgogne Côte Chalonnaise Les Cloux★★ £C

DOM. COMTE GEORGES DE VOGÜÉ   *UK stockists:* Men, DWS, JAr, BBR, F&M, Far, Sec, Las, Hrd
Estate is known for its Musigny, one of the single greatest red Burgundies made. The domaine owns 7.2 ha of the 10.7 ha *grand cru.* Since 1990 the wine has extraordinary aromatics, with preserved fruits and floral notes, silky texture, wonderful definition and mouthfilling dimension that becomes increasingly opulent with age. Remarkable longevity from top vintages. Amoureuses has wonderful class, intensity and concentration and there's a rich, sturdy, darker fruit density to the Bonnes Mares. (PW)
● Musigny Vieilles Vignes❂❂❂❂❂ £H   ● Bonnes Mares★★★★★ £H
● Chambolle-Musigny★★★ £F   1er Cru Les Amoureuses★★★★★ £H

DOM. DE LA VOUGERAIE   *UK stockists:* Hay, FMV, L&W, BWC, Wai
New venture from Boisset (Burgundy's single biggest producer) pooling all of its owned vineyards, predominantly in the Côte de Nuits. Directed by highly regarded Pascal Marchand (Comte Armand), 37 ha (certified organic) now treated biodynamically. Nearly all the wines are very good examples of their respective appellations, with richness, depth and class. (PW)
● Clos de Vougeot★★★★ £F   ● Charmes-Chambertin★★★★ £F
● Vougeot 1er Cru Les Cras★★★ £F   ● Vougeot Clos du Prieuré★★★ £E
● Chambolle-Musigny★★★ £E   ● Pommard Les Petit Noizons★★★ £E
O Vougeot 1er Cru Clos Blanc de Vougeot★★★★ £F   O Corton-Charlemagne★★★★ £G

Other wineries of note
Dom. de l'Arlot (Nuits-Saint-Georges), Dom. d'Auvenay (Saint-Romain), Dom. Jean Boillot et Fils (Volnay), Louis Boillot, Lucien Boillot et Fils (Gevrey-Chambertin), Boyer-Martenot (Meursault), Dom. Brintet (Mercurey), Alain Burguet (Gevrey-Chambertin), Dom. du Ch. de Chorey (Chorey-lès-Beaune), Ch. de Puligny-Montrachet, Clos Salomon (Givry), Dom. Pierre Damoy (Gevrey-Chambertin), Darviot-Perrin (Monthelie), Jean-Michel Gaunoux (Meursault), Génot-Boulanger (Meursault), Dom. Antonin Guyon (Savigny-lès-Beaune), Heresztyn (Gevrey-Chambertin), Hudelot-Noëllat (Chambolle-Musigny), Rémi Jobard (Meursault), Vincent & François Jouard (Chassagne-Montrachet), Vicomte Liger-Belair (Vosne-Romanée), Hubert Lignier (Morey-Saint-Denis), Prince de Mérode (Ladoix), Alain Michelot (Nuits-Saint-Georges), Deux Montille, Bernard Morey (Chassagne-Montrachet), Dom. Albert Morot (Beaune), Dom. Rapet Père et Fils (Pernand-Vergelesses), Rossignol-Trapet (Gevrey-Chambertin), Emmanuel Rouget (Vosne-Romanée), Tollot-Beaut (Chorey-lès-Beaune), Dom. Tortochot (Gevrey-Chambertin)

59

An in-depth profile of every producer can be found in Wine behind the label 2006

FRANCE

Mâconnais background

The Mâconnais is Burgundy's frontier region where the full potential of the Chardonnay grape is only just beginning to be realised. Thanks in part to a new wave of producers Pouilly-Fuissé is now at an unprecedented level of quality, increasingly expressed in individual climats that make this region so complex and fascinating. Not only is the trend swinging away from overblown high-octane examples but a handful of growers are also revitalising the soils of vineyard plots scattered wide across the Mâconnais.

Mâconnais Vintages

The ageing potential of the finest white Burgundy from the Mâconnais varies greatly, even within Pouilly-Fuissé. Most regular examples will only improve for 2 or 3 years' from the vintage date. Vineyard-designated or special *cuvées* on the other hand might improve for 5 to 10 years. However, not only does quality vary from producer to producer but so does style and the structure, and consequently it is difficult to generalize about ageing potential. The 2004 vintage looks very promsing, the first wines are fresh with good intensity and purity of fruit. Of other recent vintages, 2002 is the star. Despite changeable weather conditions healthy grapes were harvested with excellent balance between ripeness and acidity. There are many good wines, vibrant with marvellous fruit and style. By contrast the extreme heat of 2003 mean't producers had to battle to produce balanced, harmonious wines. Too many are overblown and will be short-lived. Conditions in 2001 were also much more difficult with an unsettled growing season and a struggle to achieve ripeness and avoid rot due to damp, warm conditions. Despite this the best 2001s, if sometimes leaner, can show good minerality and ripe fruit. There's plenty of excellent wine from 2000 due to a favourable growing season and harvest.

Wizard's Wishlist

Great Mâcon whites

DANIEL ET MARTINE BARRAUD
O **Pouilly-Fuissé** En Buland Vieilles Vignes
DOM. GEORGES BURRIER O **Pouilly-Fuissé** Les Champs
CH. DES RONTETS O **Pouilly-Fuissé** Les Birbettes
DOM. CORDIER PÈRE ET FILS
O **Pouilly-Fuissé** Vignes Blanches
HÉRITIERS DU COMTE LAFON
O **Mâcon Milly Lamartine** Clos du Four
DOM. DES DEUX ROCHES O **Saint-Véran** Cras
DOM. J A FERRET
O **Pouilly-Fuissé** Ménétrières Hors Classé
DOM. GUFFENS-HEYNEN O **Pouilly-Fuissé**
OLIVIER MERLIN O **Pouilly-Fuissé** Terroir de Vergisson
DOM. RIJCKAERT O **Viré-Clessé** En Thurissey Vieilles Vignes
DOM. ROBERT-DENOGENT
O **Pouilly-Fuissé** Cuvée Claude Denogent
DOM. LA SOUFRANDIÈRE
O **Pouilly-Vinzelles** Les Quarts Millerandée
DOM. LA SOUFRANDISE/MELIN
O **Pouilly-Fuissé** Vieilles Vignes
JEAN THÉVENET
O **Mâcon-Villages** Quintaine Domaine Emilian Gillet
DOM. VALETTE
O **Pouilly-Fuissé** Clos de M Noly Vieilles Vignes Réserve

Value for money Mâcon whites

AUVIGUE O **Mâcon-Fuissé** Moulin du Pont
DOM. DE LA CROIX SENAILLET O **Saint-Véran**
DOM. DES GERBEAUX O **Saint-Véran**
NICOLAS MAILLET O **Mâcon-Verzé**
OLIVIER MERLIN
O **Mâcon-La Roche Vineuse** Vieilles Vignes
ALAIN NORMAND O **Mâcon-La Roche Vineuse**
DOM. RIJCKAERT O **Saint-Véran** En Faux Vieilles Vignes
DOM. ROBERT-DENOGENT
O **Pouilly-Fuissé** La Croix Vieilles Vignes
VERGET O **Mâcon-Charnay** Clos Saint-Pierre

Mâconnais/A-Z of producers

FRANCE

AUVIGUE   Pouilly-Fuissé   *UK stockists:* **WSS**, P&S
Small quantities but a wide range of Mâcon whites. Top wines show particularly good structure. *Cru* Pouilly-Fuissé Vieilles Vignes has depth and intensity and calls for at least four or five years' age. The Hors Classé is a late-picked, rich, blockbuster style, balanced by excellent strucure. (PW)
O **Pouilly-Fuissé** Les Chailloux★★ £C V.Vignes★★★ £D Hors Classé★★★★ £D
O **Pouilly-Fuissé** La Frairie★★ £C O **Mâcon-Fuissé** Moulin du Pont★★ £B
O **Saint-Véran** Moulin du Pont★★ £B Les Chênes★★ £B

DANIEL ET MARTINE BARRAUD   Pouilly-Fuissé   *UK stockists:* **L&S**, NYg
Leaders in differentiating and better defining the various *terroirs* of Pouilly-Fuissé. New oak is usually well-judged. Vieilles Vignes wines are from vineyards with an average vine age in excess of 40 years; En Buland is the richest, most full-bodied. Reasonable prices for the quality. (PW)
O **Pouilly-Fuissé** La Roche★★★ £C En Bulands V.Vignes★★★★ £D
O **Pouilly-Fuissé** Les Crays V.Vignes★★★ £D La Verchère V.Vignes★★ £C
O **Saint-Véran** En Crèches★★ £B Les Pommards★★ £C

CH. DE BEAUREGARD/JOSEPH BURRIER   Pouilly-Fuissé   *UK stockists:* DDr
Frédéric-Marc Burrier is increasingly realising the potential of some of Pouilly-Fuissé's finest *climats*. The oak-fermented and aged Beauregard wines show good structure, fruit and depth if not quite the extra intensity and precision of the region's best. Very good wines from the 4-ha estate of Georges Burrier made here in 2003 were atypically well-defined in the vintage. (PW)

Ch. de Beauregard:
O **Pouilly-Fuissé**★★ £C Les Châtaigniers★★ £D Les Grands Champs★★★ £D
O **Pouilly-Fuissé** Les Cras★★★★ £D

Dom. Georges Burrier:
O **Pouilly-Fuissé**★★ £C La Côte★★★ £D Les Champs★★★★ £D

CH. DE FUISSÉ   Pouilly-Fuissé   www.château-fuisse.fr   *UK stockists:* **ABy, OWL**, BBR, Hrd
Jean-Jacques Vincent's estate is arguably Pouilly-Fuissé's most famous, if no longer one of the very best. A number of different *cuvées* are vinified in oak followed by nine months in barrel. Vieilles Vignes is easily the most convincing wine; others have lost intensity. The top wines usually come into their own with at least five years' age. A second range is made under the Vincent label. (PW)

Château-Fuissé:
O **Pouilly-Fuissé**★★★ £D V.Vignes★★★ £E Les Brûles★★★ £E
O **Pouilly-Fuissé** Les Combettes★★ £D Le Clos★★ £E O **Saint-Véran**★ £C

CH. DES RONTETS   Pouilly-Fuissé   *UK stockists:* VTr, C&R
Claire Gazeau and her Italian husband, Fabio Montrasi, have transformed the wines here since the mid-1990s, taking advantage of high average vine age. Les Birbettes has really superb fruit which easily takes up the new oak (30 per cent) and is one of the most stylish examples of Pouilly-Fuissé. (PW)
O **Pouilly-Fuissé** Clos Varambon★★ £C Pierrefolle★★★ £D Les Birbettes★★★ £D

DOM. CORDIER PÈRE ET FILS   Pouilly-Fuissé   *UK stockists:* Gen, L&S, Maj, WSc
Powerful wines, many of them high in alcohol, but still remarkably well-balanced. An intense minerality complements a preserved citrus character and oak-derived spiciness in many. Can be drunk young but Vers Cras and Vers Pouilly will be better with four or five years' age. Prices are high. (PW)
O **Pouilly-Fuissé** Vignes Blanches★★★★ £E Vers Cras★★★★ £E Vers Pouilly★★★★ £E
O **Pouilly-Fuissé**★★★ £C V.Vignes★★★ £D La Vigne de Mr Marguin★★★★ £E
O **Saint-Véran** Clos à la Côte★★★ £C En Faux★★★ £C Les Crais★★★★ £D

DOM. DE LA CROIX SENAILLET   Saint-Véran   *UK stockists:* OWL, CTy, B&T,Goe, P&S, CeB
The Martins' regular Saint-Véran is an excellent example, ripe and intense with a refined floral and mineral character. Les Rochats shows more depth and a touch of class but needs three to four years' age. Rich, ripe

61

FRANCE

Pouilly Fuissé comes from old-vines in the *lieu-dit* En Pommard. (PW)
O **Pouilly-Fuissé★★★** £C   O **Saint-Véran★★** £B   Les Rochats★★★ £C
O **Mâcon Blanc★** £B

DOM. DES DEUX ROCHES   Saint-Véran   *UK stockists:* **BBR,** ThP
This 35-ha estate has long shown that high quality is possible in Saint-Véran. Attractive, fruity regular *cuvées*; some new oak is used for top wines. Generally there is good ripeness as well as a mineral aspect. Also a little Pouilly-Fuissé La Roche. Christian Collovray and Jean-Luc Terrier also own Domaine d'Antugnac in the Limoux AC in the Languedoc-Roussillon. (PW)
O **Saint-Véran★** £B   V.Vignes★★ £C   Terres Noires★★ £C   Cras★★★ £D
O **Mâcon-Villages★** £B

DOM. J A FERRET   Pouilly-Fuissé   *UK stockists:* Bal, JAr, Lay, Rae
Colette Ferret's Pouilly-Fuissés have been compared to *grand cru* Côte de Beaune whites. The wines are barrel-fermented and aged with extended lees-contact. Rich and honeyed, they also display fine floral, mineral aspects as well as a classic grilled nuts character. The Hors Classé designation applies only to a selection of old vines in the best years. (PW)
O **Pouilly-Fuissé** Ménétrières Hors Classé★★★★ £D
O **Pouilly-Fuissé** Tournant de Pouilly Hors Classé★★★★ £D
O **Pouilly-Fuissé** Le Clos Tête de Cru★★★ £D   Perrières Tête de Cru★★★ £D

DOM. DES GERBEAUX   Pouilly-Fuissé   *UK stockists:* **WTs,** BBR
Beatrice and Jean-Michel Drouin's wines are very reasonably priced and sell out fast. All show excellent intensity, texture and structure and have balanced alcohol and attractive minerality. (PW)
O **Pouilly-Fuissé** Terroir de Solutré Vieilles Vignes★★★ £C
O **Saint-Véran★★** £B   O **Mâcon-Solutré** Le Clos★★ £B   O **Mâcon-Chaintré★★** £B

DOM. GUFFENS-HEYNEN   www.verget-sa.com   *UK stockists:* L&W, L&S, Far, C&R, Odd
Private estate of larger-than-life Jean-Marie Guffens, the man behind important *négociant* Verget. Very ripe grapes are pressed very slowly in an old-fashioned vertical press. A mix of oak is used and the wines have fantastic richness, depth and substance as well as finesse and elegance. Some inconsistency but top vintages will provide memorable drinking for up to a decade. (PW)
Guffens-Heynen:
O **Pouilly-Fuissé★★★★** £E
O **Mâcon-Pierreclos★★★** £C   En Chavigne★★★★ £D
Verget:
O **Pouilly-Fuissé** Terroir de Vergisson★★★ £D   O **Pouilly-Vinzelles** Les Quarts★★ £B
O **Saint-Véran** Terroirs de Davayé★★ £C   Vignes de Saint-Claude★★★ £C
O **Mâcon-Vergisson** La Roche★★★ £B   O **Mâcon-Charnay** Clos Saint-Pierre★★ £B

HÉRITIERS DU COMTE LAFON   Macon-Villages   *UK stockists:* **FMV,** BBR, P&S
Leading Meursault producer Dominique Lafon (see Domaine des Comtes Lafon) is now showing the quality that is possible in the Mâcon. Mâcon-Bussières Le Monsard has real intensity of ripe citrus with a stony aspect, best with four or five years' age from a fine vintage. New vineyards from the villages of Chardonnay and Uchizy will augment production from 2003. (PW)
O **Mâcon Milly Lamartine★★★** £C   Clos du Four★★★ £D
O **Mâcon-Bussières** Le Monsard★★★ £D   O **Mâcon Villages★★** £C

DOM. ROGER LASSARAT   Pouilly-Fuissé   *UK stockists:* THt, Mar, Sel
Manual picking of carefully maintained, low-yielding old vines ensures quality. Ripe and richly textured wines are part barrel-fermented with prolonged lees-enrichment in barrel. Recent vintages are best yet. The range has very recently been expanded to single out more individual *climats*. (PW)
O **Pouilly-Fuissé** Clos de France★★ £C   Cuvée Prestige★★★ £D
O **Saint-Véran** Fournaise★★ £C   Cuvée Prestige★★★ £C
O **Mâcon-Vergisson** La Roche★★ £B

62

NICOLAS MAILLET Pouilly-Fuissé www.vins-nicolas-maillet.com *UK stockists:* TPg
Nicolas Maillet makes excellent, inexpensive wines without any oak. Whites have super fruit and purity, with fine
minerality in Mâcon-Verzé, and more structure, depth and intensity in a Le Chemin Blanc version. Also a stylish
Bourgogne Rouge with pure cherry and cassis fruit, a subtle minerality and fine tannins. (PW)
O **Mâcon-Verzé★★** £B Le Chemin Blanc★★★ £B O **Bourgogne Aligoté★** £B
O **Crémant de Bourgogne★** £B ● **Bourgogne Rouge★★** £B

OLIVIER MERLIN Mâcon-Villages *UK stockists:* FMV, P&S, Hrd, WSc
One of Mâcon's most reliable as well as exciting producers. Rich, full-bodied Mâcon whites show deep ripe fruit
and a certain finesse and complexity, particularly in the very complete, old-vine Les Cras. Pouilly-Fuissé has
good structure; Fuissé is the most classic, creamy Chaintré quite Meursault-like. Sophisticated Moulin-à-Vent
too. (PW)
O **Mâcon-La Roche Vineuse★★** £B V.Vignes★★★ £C Les Cras★★★ £C
O **Pouilly-Fuissé** Terroir de Chaintré★★★ £D Terroir de Vergisson★★★ £D
O **Pouilly-Fuissé** Terroir de Fuissé★★★ £D O **Saint-Véran** Grand Bussière★★★ £C

CAVE PRISSÉ Pouilly-Fuissé *UK stockists:* CTy, Maj, Wai
Prissé-Sologny-Verzé is a grouping of 3 co-operatives, with some 500 growers and 1,000ha of vineyards. The large
production runs from Bourgogne Aligoté through sparkling Crémant, Mâcon-Villages and Saint-Véran to Pouilly-
Fuissé. Those tasted have been consistently well-made and offer reasonable value. (PW)
O **Pouilly-Fuissé★★★** £C O **Saint-Véran** Les Pierres Blanches★★ £B
O **Mâcon Milly Lamartine★★** £B O **Mâcon Prissé** Les Clochettes★ £B

DOM. RIJCKAERT Viré-Clessé *UK stockists:* JAr, Far, BBR, Odd
Jean Rijckaert helped mould the Verget style and is one of the Mâconnais' most exciting new producers, with
precise, aromatic, minerally, concentrated wines. Rijckaert also believes passionately in restoring life to the soils
and the importance of promoting deep roots in the vines. He makes more than two dozen individual *cuvées*,
mostly from old vines, both from his own 4 ha of vineyards (green label) and for other small growers (brown
label). Also a number of excellent Jura whites. (PW)
O **Pouilly-Fuissé** Vers Chânes V.Vignes★★★ £C
O **Saint-Véran** En Avonne★★ £C L'Epinet★★ £C En Faux V.Vignes★★★ £C
O **Viré-Clessé** Les Vercherres V.Vignes★★ £C En Thurissey V.Vignes★★★ £C

DOM. ROBERT-DENOGENT Pouilly-Fuissé *UK stockists:* Bib, Gau
Jean-Jacques Robert draws on a tremendous resource of old vines and yields are further reduced through
careful pruning. Though new oak is used, all the wines show lovely fruit intensity and fine structures with
pronounced *terroir* character. Les Carrons comes from an exceptional old site with a higher clay content.
The top wines benefit from at least three to four years' ageing. (PW)
O **Pouilly-Fuissé** Reisses★★ £C Claude Denogent★★★ £D Les Carrons★★★★ £E
O **Pouilly-Fuissé** La Croix★★ £C O **Mâcon-Solutré** Clos Bertillonnes★★ £C

SAUMAIZE-MICHELIN Pouilly-Fuissé *UK stockists:* Eno, CTy, Rae, SVS
Impressive consistency resulting from utmost attention to detail and hygiene. These wines show that Vergisson
has the potential to equal the highly regarded commune of Fuissé. Wines can be quite firm and steely when very
young but have good definition and added richness with age. Ampelopsis is a remarkably concentrated and
proportioned old-vine *cuvée*. (PW)
O **Pouilly-Fuissé** Ampelopsis★★★ £D Ronchevats★★★ £C
O **Pouilly-Fuissé** Vigne Blanche★★ £C Clos sur la Roche★★★ £C
O **Saint-Véran** Crêches★★ £B V.Vignes★★ £B O **Mâcon-Villages** Sertaux★★ £B

DOM. DE LA SOUFRANDIÈRE Pouilly-Vinzelles *UK stockists:* FMV, BBR, F&M, WSc
The young Bret brothers have made the finest wines ever under the small Pouilly-Vinzelles AC. All the grapes
are picked by hand and the wines are ripe and concentrated. Millerandée show tremendous richness, coming
from very small (*millerandé*) grapes from 70-year-old vines. It deserves to be drunk with five years' age. Wines
under the Bret Brothers label are made from bought-in grapes. (PW)

FRANCE

Dom. de la Soufrandière:
O **Pouilly-Vinzelles**★★ £B Les Quarts★★★ £D Les Quarts Millerandée★★★ £E
Bret Brothers:
O **Pouilly-Vinzelles** Les Remparts★★★ £D

JEAN THÉVENET Macon-Villages *UK stockists:* L&S, GBa, Adm, HHB, JNi, T&W
Jean Thévenet's wines are like no one else's – atypically rich, very ripe and honeyed but with great structure and vibrancy. Residual sugar denies them the Viré-Clessé AC despite their evident quality. Cuvée Spéciale Botrytis is made when exceptional conditions permit (such as 2000 and 1995), a wine of exceptional richness but with excellent acidity and the ability to keep for more than a decade. (PW)
O **Mâcon-Villages** Tradition Sélection EJ Thévenet Dom. de la Bongran★★★ £D
O **Mâcon-Villages** Quintaine Domaine Emilian Gillet★★★ £C

DOM. THIBERT Pouilly-Fuissé *UK stockists:* **ABy**, Dec, CRs, Wai
These wines show more finesse and less upfront richness than some but combine a minerally intensity with good concentration in the best years. Subtle oak enhances the structure and the wines have excellent ageing potential, especially the top *cuvées*. (PW)
O **Pouilly-Fuissé**★★ £C V. Vignes★★★ £C Vignes Blanches★★★ £D
O **Mâcon-Fuissé**★ £B O **Mâcon-Prissé** En Chailloux★ £B

DOM. VALETTE Pouilly-Fuissé *UK stockists:* FMV, WSc
Gérard Valette and son Philippe run an effectively organic 17-ha estate. Réserve Pouilly-Fuissés are powerful, very ripe-fruited, oaky blockbusters, although usually with the balance to provide heady, complex drinking soon after their (delayed) release and for another five years or more. (PW)
O **Pouilly-Fuissé** Tradition★★★ £D Clos Reyssie Réserve★★★★ £E
O **Pouilly-Fuissé** Clos de Monsieur Noly V. Vignes Réserve★★★★ £F
O **Mâcon-Chaintré** V. Vignes★★ £B

DOM. VESSIGAUD Pouilly-Fuissé www.domainevessigaud.com *UK stockists:* **Anl, DLW,** Odd
A new star in the southern Mâconnais. High-quality fruit is transformed into deep, expressive and well-defined whites, especially individual-*climat* wines which could easily pass for fine *premier cru* Côte de Beaune wines. Rich 2003s have far better structures than is typical in this vintage while 04 promises elegance, purity and more mineral intensity. (PW)
O **Pouilly-Fuissé** Vieilles Vignes★★★ £C Vers Pouilly★★★★ £D
O **Mâcon-Fuissé**★★ £B Les Taches★★★ £B

Also see the following Burgundy producers with an entry in the section *Côte D'Or & Côte Chalonnaise:*
BOUCHARD PERE ET FILS

as well as Beaujolais producers with an entry in the *Beaujolais* section:
GEORGES DUBOEUF

Other wineries of note
André Bonhomme (Viré-Clessé), **Corsin** (Pouilly-Fuissé), **Corinne & Thierry Drouin** (Pouilly-Fuissé)

An in-depth profile of every producer can be found in Wine behind the label 2006

Beaujolais background

Now that the cheap trick that was Beaujolais Nouveau seems pretty much played out the world over, more seems set to be made of the region's real strengths. Its crus, the Gamay grape, the old vines, its granite, schist and sandy soils, its many small estates and some dedicated vignerons are the fundamentals. Add improved vinification, breathe life back into the soils and promote a willingness to explore different interpretations of just what Beaujolais can be (both a quaffer and something more serious) and more wine lovers might just add it to their shopping lists.

Beaujolais by village

The best Beaujolais comes from the Haut-Beaujolais and is sold as **Beaujolais-Villages** or as one of 10 recognised *crus*. They begin at the bottom of Mâconnais with the generally unexciting **Saint-Amour**. In contrast, **Juliénas** provides wines with better depth and intensity than most. Lighter **Chénas** occupies higher ground than the adjoining **Moulin-à-Vent** and it is the latter that has the most strength, structure and longevity of all the *crus*. Its prices are matched only by **Fleurie**, the best examples of which are perfumed but also often unequalled for their density of fruit and lush texture. From elevated **Chiroubles** the best wines are light but as refined as they get. At the heart of **Morgon** is the Côte de Py which can give dense and intensely cherryish wines. **Regnié** is rarely exciting while only a handful of wines from the large **Brouilly** *cru* have attractive fruit. Marginally better is **Côte de Brouilly** from the slopes of the hill of Mont Brouilly.

Beaujolais Vintages

Do vintages in Beaujolais matter with most of the wines being drunk so young? As some of the better quality *cru* Beaujolais need at least 2 or 3 years' to open out, for these choosing one vintage over another can make a big difference to what's in your glass. Take 2003 and 2002. The latter was spoilt by late rains and many a supposedly better cru is marred by poor quality fruit. It has been recently shown that in some instances this was due to contamination of the grapes by Geosmin. Although harmless, it gives a distinctive unpleasant musty/vegetal character to the wine. However, even those wines produced from healthy ripe fruit tend to be a little dull and uninspiring. By contrast the hot dry 2003 vintage ensured healthy grapes and there are some super wines with thrilling vibrant fruit, in many instances without the low acidities (and the consequent need for acidification) that might have been expected. While some are over-ripe and others show green tannins, look out for some real gems. 2004 seems mostly free of the Geosmin taint and the best wines are intense, pure and elegant. Of older vintages, although 2001 has turned out better than first expected, some 2000s (those Geosmin free) and most 1999s are superior.

Wizard's Wishlist

Some favourite Beaujolais

DOM. CALOT ● **Morgon** Tête de Cuvée

NICOLE CHANRION/LA VOUTE DES CROZES
● **Côte de Brouilly**

CH. DE BEAUREGARD ● **Moulin-à-Vent** Clos des Pérelles

CH. DES JACQUES ● **Moulin-à-Vent**

MICHEL CHIGNARD ● **Fleurie** Les Moriers

CLOS DE LA ROILETTE/COUDERT
● **Fleurie** Clos de la Roilette

DOM. DE COLONAT
● **Morgon** Les Charmes Cuvée Marguerite Montchanay

GEORGES DUBOEUF ● **Moulin-à-Vent** Prestige

DOM. PAUL ET ERIC JANIN
● **Moulin-à-Vent** Clos du Tremblay

DOM. DE LA MADONE ● **Fleurie** Vieilles Vignes

MICHEL TETE/DOM. CLOS DU FIEF ● **Saint-Amour**

DOM. DU VISSOUX ● **Fleurie** Les Garants

Beaujolais/A-Z of producers

DOM. F ET J CALOT Morgon www.domaine-calot.com *UK stockists:* **HHB**, BBR, SVS
Excellent source of ripe, concentrated and characterful Morgon, from a supple, fruity regular Cuvée Tradition to a deep, intense Vieilles Vignes that needs three years or so to soften. Vinification is traditional, not the semi-carbonic maceration favoured by most, and both small and large oak are used for ageing. Very reasonable prices. (PW)
● **Morgon** Tradition★★ £B Vieilles Vignes★★ £B
● **Morgon** Tête de Cuvée★★ £B Cuvée Jeanne★★★ £B

NICOLE CHANRION/LA VOÛTE DES CROZES Côte de Brouilly *UK stockists:* **THt**, L&W
Small estate producing one of the best Côte de Brouilly from 6ha of well-established vines. It is consistently expressive and fruit-rich with a profusion of mineral, raspberry and cherry framed by good acidity and soft tannins. Drink young or with 3–5 years' age. (PW)
● **Côte de Brouilly**★★★ £B

FRANCE

CH. DE BEAUREGARD/JOSEPH BURRIER Beaujolais   *UK stockists:* DDr
Pouilly-Fuissé-based Château de Beauregard (see Mâconnais section) has 10ha in Beaujolais for full, supple examples
– with real density and flesh in Moulin-à-Vent. Oak-aged Clos de Pérelles has rich, mineral-imbued fruit, depth and
breadth, needing 4–5 years' age. Also Moulin-à-Vent La Salomine and Fleurie Les Colonies de Rochgrès. (PW)
● **Moulin-à-Vent**★★★ £C Clos de Pérelles★★★ £D ● **Fleurie**★★ £B

CH. DES JACQUES Moulin-à-Vent www.louis-jadot.com   *UK stockists:* HMA, Wai
Leading Beaujolais estate, now Jadot-owned. A singular approach to vinification includes destemming and
fermentation in open tanks, resulting in full, rich wines. Wines from five separate sites are aged in new oak
and show a previously unseen sumptuous, velvety quality. Chardonnay is also grown for whites. In 2001 Jadot
added Château Bellevue, one of Morgon's most prized estates - look out for new *crus* under the Château des
Lumières label. (PW)
Château des Jacques:
● **Moulin-à-Vent** Clos du Grand Carquelin★★★ £C Champ de Cour★★★ £C
● **Moulin-à-Vent**★★ £C Grand Clos des Rochegrès★★ £C
O **Beaujolais-Villages** Chardonnay★★ £B O **Bourgogne Blanc** Clos de Loyse★★ £B
Château des Lumières:
● **Morgon**★★ £C

MICHEL CHIGNARD Fleurie   *UK stockists:* FMV
There probably isn't any better Fleurie than that from Michel Chignard. His wines manage to be ripe, full and
intense with rich textures that offer some immediate gratification but have the structure and substance to improve
for at least 3–5 years. (PW)
● **Fleurie** Les Moriers★★★ £B Spéciale Vieilles Vignes★★★ £C

CLOS DE LA ROILETTE/COUDERT Fleurie   *UK stockists:* DDr, L&W, Sav, L&S
The Couderts possess very old vines in the best part of La Roilette, the finest Fleurie *climat*, giving more body,
depth and complexity than is typical. Grapes are harvested very ripe and the wines are sleek and supple, with a
black fruit character and a subtle mineral streak. (PW)
● **Fleurie** Cuvée Christal★★ £B
● **Fleurie** Clos de la Roilette★★★ £B Cuvée Tardive★★★ £C

DOM. DE COLONAT Morgon
The Collonges 12ha of vines include the prized Les Charmes in Morgon. The wines are traditional in structure,
needing at least 3–4 years to unfurl. *Barrique*-aged Cuvée Marguerite Montchanay is from 50-year-old vines and
develops a Pinot-like complexity with 5 years' age. (PW)
● **Morgon** Les Charmes★★ £B Cuvée Marguerite Montchanay★★★ £B

DOM. LOUIS-CLAUDE DESVIGNES Morgon   *UK stockists:* Sav, BBR
One of the first Beaujolais estates to produce separate *cuvées* from the best parcels. Two rich, vibrant, aromatic
and distinctly different Morgons benefit from low yields and a cold pre-fermentation maceration. Wines to
drink with at least three or four years' age; unrivalled at the price. (PW)
● **Morgon** La Voûte Saint-Vincent★★ £B Javernières★★ £B Côte de Py★★ £B

GEORGES DUBOEUF Beaujolais www.duboeuf.com   *UK stockists:* BWC, JNi, Maj
Ubiquitous and admirably consistent institution; production is now 30 million bottles and includes examples of
all Beaujolais *crus*. Individual *cuvées* (most from single domaines) are nearly always worth the small premium,
particularly those from Moulin-à-Vent and Fleurie. (PW)
● **Moulin-à-Vent** Domaine des Rosiers★★ £B Tour de Bief★★★ £B Prestige★★★ £B
● **Fleurie** Domaine des Quatre Vents★★ £B La Madone★★ £B
● **Morgon** Domaine Jean Descombes★★ £B O **Pouilly-Fuissé** Prestige★★ £B

HENRY FESSY Beaujolais www.vins-henry-fessy.com   *UK stockists:* Cib, For, Frw
With both a domaine of 12 ha and a *négociant* business, Henry and Serges Fessy make a number of ripe,
vigorous, perfumed Beaujolais. Brouilly wines are particularly good for this *cru*, with both intensity and length
of flavour. (PW)
● **Brouilly** Cuvée Georges Fessy★★ £B Plateau de Bel Air★★ £B Pur Sang★★ £B

New entries have producer's name underlined

● **Morgon** Cuvée Luquet★★ £B   ● **Fleurie** Mauriers ★★ £B

JEAN FOILLARD Morgon   *UK stockists:* **HHB**
Beaujolais fashioned in an altogether different way from the modern standard: low yields of very ripe grapes receive a long cool vinification, practically zero sulphur and minimal or no filtration. Intense, spice- and mineral-rich Côte du Py (Morgon's best site) needs age but achieves real harmony in top years. (PW)
● **Morgon** Première★★ £B   Côte du Py★★★ £C

DOM. PAUL ET ERIC JANIN Moulin-à-Vent   *UK stockists:* **DDr, L&S, CPp, Rae, SVS**
Eric Janin makes excellent Moulin-à-Vent to a biodynamic recipe. 10 ha of old vines are carefully nurtured by father and son and the resulting wines have a marvellous fruit quality and good concentration and depth. Tannins can be a little firm but the Clos du Tremblay (which is a selection of the very best old vines) in particular benefits from a couple of years' age. Prices are very reasonable. (PW)
● **Moulin-à-Vent** Clos du Tremblay★★★ £C   Vignes du Tremblay★★ £B
● **Beaujolais-Villages** Domaine des Vignes du Jumeaux★ £B

JACKY JANODET/DOM. LES FINE GRAVES   *UK stockists:* **THt, BBR, Tan, UnC, Sel**
One of the best-known growers based in Moulin-à-Vent. The wine is classically powerful with good depth, its concentration, structure and texture owed in part to ageing in small barrels. Best with three to four years' age. Some Chénas, Beaujolais-Villages and a tiny amount of white are also made. (PW)
● **Moulin-à-Vent** Vieilles Vignes★★★ £B

HUBERT LAPIERRE Chénas   www.domaine-lapierre.com   *UK stockists:* **L&W**
Chénas with good weight and ripe raspberryish fruit in both Vieilles Vignes and *barrique*-aged versions. The 7.5ha of vineyards also includes more ample, riper, darker-fruited Moulin-à-Vent with good acidity – a Vieilles Vignes version will keep 5–6 years. Very good 2003s. (PW)
● **Chénas** Fût de Chêne★★ £B   Vieilles Vignes★★ £B
● **Moulin-à-Vent** Tradition★★ £B   Vieilles Vignes★★★ £B

DOM. DE LA MADONE Fleurie   *UK stockists:* **OWL, THt, Gen, Ear, RHW, NDb**
Benchmark Fleurie from almost 9 ha of vines on south-west facing slopes. The regular *cuvée* is supple and smooth with raspberry, cherry and refined floral characters. Vieilles Vignes offers more complexity and refinement. Grille Midi from old vines in a particularly warm site can be more fleshy, more structured but with fine minerality. Also made are a little Juliénas, an oak-aged Fleurie and some Beaujolais-Villages. (PW)
● **Fleurie**★★ £B   Vieilles Vignes★★★ £C   Grille Midi Vieilles Vignes★★★ £C

MICHEL TÊTE/DOM. CLOS DU FIEF Juliénas   *UK stockists:* **L&W**
A rare good example of Saint-Amour is silky, refined and harmonious particularly in warm vintages. Regular Juliénas is full and chewy with good structure while Prestige version from lower-yielding old vines is oak-aged. The latter can be kept at least 4–5 years, becoming more seductive and complex. (PW)
● **Juliénas**★★ £B   Cuvée Prestige★★★ £C   ● **Beaujolais-Villages**★ £B
● **Saint-Amour**★★★ £B

DOM. DU VISSOUX Beaujolais   *UK stockists:* **Eno, Vne, Hrd**
Improving 30-ha estate with excellent Fleurie and Moulin-à-Vent. Fleurie has lovely style and intensity, the Garants showing the lusher texture of the two bottlings. From Moulin-à-Vent, both Rochegrès and slightly superior Rochelle show more spice, mineral and greater breadth but are less consistent. The regular Beaujolais Traditionelle, sourced from the southern Beaujolais, is not of the same ilk. (PW)
● **Fleurie** Poncié★★ £B   Les Garants★★★ £C
● **Moulin-à-Vent** Rochegrès★★ £C   Rochelle★★★ £C

Other wineries of note
Dom. de la Chanaise (Morgon), Dom. de la Chaponne (Morgon), Ch. Thivin (Côte de Brouilly), Bernard Métrat (Fleurie), Dom. des Terres Dorées (Beaujolais)

An in-depth profile of every producer can be found in Wine behind the label 2006

Alsace

Introduction

Alsace is a narrow stretch of vineyards running north-south at the base of and nestled into the eastern foothills of the Vosges mountains. These, along with the Rhine just to the east of the *vignoble*, provide the region with an impressively favourable climate for such a northerly latitude. Southern stretches are known as the **Haut Rhin**; the northern part is the **Bas Rhin**. The generic appellation of the region is simply **Alsace AC** with the vast majority of wine is labelled by grape variety. Generic blends are labelled either Edelzwicker or Gentil. 50 *grands crus* vineyards are entitled to the **Alsace Grand Cru AC (GC)**. Late-harvested wines are classified as *Vendange Tardive* (VT) and *Sélection de Grains Nobles* (SGN), botrytis often featuring in the latter and VTs often surprisingly dry. Traditional method sparkling wine is released as **Crémant d'Alsace AC**.

Alsace Vintages

The lesser whites should be drunk young and certainly by the time they have had four or five years' ageing. Riesling is better in slightly cooler years, Gewürztraminer and Tokay Pinot Gris add dimension in warmer years. See Vintage Charts to provide a reliable guide as to what you should expect. Great early years to consider are 1983, 1976 and for very top wines 1971 and 1967.

Wizard's Wishlist

15 Alsace values

JEAN-BAPTISTE ADAM **O Tokay Pinot Gris** Letzenberg
DOM. BOTT-GEYL **O Muscat** Riquewihr
ERNEST BURN **O Pinot Blanc**
DIRLER-CADE **O Riesling** Saering Grand Cru
MARC KREYDENWEISS **O Klevner** Kritt
DOM. ALBERT MANN
O Pinot Blanc/Auxerrois Vieilles Vignes
JOSMEYER **O Pinot Auxerrois** H Vieilles Vignes
OSTERTAG **O Sylvaner** Vieilles Vignes
DOM. SCHOFFIT **O Riesling** Harth Cuvée Alexandre
ANDRE KIENTZLER **O Gewürztraminer**
DOM. WEINBACH **O Riesling** Cuvée Theo
ZIND-HUMBRECHT **O Tokay Pinot Gris** Vieilles Vignes
PIERRE FRICK **O Pinot Blanc** Précieuse
BRUNO SORG **O Gewürztraminer** Vieilles Vignes
CAVE DE TURKHEIM **O Tokay Pinot Gris** Réserve

20 striking dry whites

DOM. PAUL BLANCK
O Gewürztraminer Grand Cru Furstentum Vieilles Vignes
DOM. BOTT-GEYL **O Riesling** Mandelburg Grand Cru

ERNEST BURN
O Tokay Pinot Gris Goldert Grand Cru Cuvée de la Chapelle
MARCEL DEISS **O Altenberg Grand Cru**
MARC KREYDENWEISS **O Le Clos du Val d'Eléon**
DOM. ALBERT MANN
O Pinot Blanc/Auxerrois Vieilles Vignes
RENÉ MURÉ
O Riesling Clos Saint Landelin Vorbourg Grand Cru
SEPPI LANDMANN
O Gewürztraminer Zinnkoepfle Grand Cru
DOM. SCHOFFIT
O Gewürztraminer Harth Cuvée Alexandre Vieilles Vignes
TRIMBACH **O Riesling** Clos Sainte-Hune
DOM. WEINBACH **O Muscat** Réserve Personelle
JEAN BECKER **O Riesling** Froehn Grand Cru
DIRLER-CADE **O Gewürztraminer** Kessler Grand Cru
A & R GRESSER **O Riesling** Kastelberg Grand Cru
DOM. SCHLUMBERGER
O Gewürztraminer Grand Cru Kitterelé
BRUNO SORG **O Tokay Pinot Gris** Grand Cru Florimont
DOM. RIEFLÉ **O Tokay Pinot Gris** Grand Cru Steinert
GÉRARD NEUMAYER
O Tokay Pinot Gris Grand Cru Bruderthal
FRANCOIS LICHTLÉ **O Tokay Pinot Gris** Cuvée Leo
ZIND-HUMBRECHT **O Riesling** Brand Grand Cru

An exciting selection of late harvest whites

DOM. JEAN BECKER
O Gewürztraminer Schoenenbourg Grand Cru SGN
DOM. LÉON BEYER **O Tokay Pinot Gris** SGN
DOM. BOTT-GEYL
O Tokay Pinot Gris Sonnenglanz Grand Cru SGN
HUGEL ET FILS **O Riesling** SGN
ANDRÉ KIENTZLER **O Gewürztraminer** Vendange Tardive
DOM. ALBERT MANN
O Tokay Pinot Gris Hengst Grand Cru SGN
OSTERTAG **O Gewürztraminer** Fronholz Vendange Tardive
ROLLY-GASSMANN
O Muscat Moenchreben Vendange Tardive
DOM. SCHOFFIT
O Riesling Clos Saint Théobald Rangen Grand Cru Vendange Tardive
DOM. WEINBACH
O Gewürztraminer Cuvée d'Or Quintessence SGN
DOM. SCHLUMBERGER
O Gewürztraminer Christine Vendanges Tardives
KUENTZ-BAS **O Riesling** Caroline Vendange Tardive
CAVE DE TURKHEIM
O Tokay Pinot Gris Vendange Tardive
DOM. RIEFLÉ **O Tokay Pinot Gris** SGN
FRANCOIS LICHTLÉ **O Riesling** SGN

New entries have producer's name underlined

Alsace/A-Z of producers

DOM. JEAN-BAPTISTE ADAM Ammerschwihr *UK stockists:* **All**
Established in 1614. Just 15 ha but output is a sizeable 80,000 cases. Decent Sélection and Réserve wines; better Jean-Baptiste labels. The heart of the estate are *lieux-dits* Letzenberg and Kaefferkopf plus Riesling from GC Winneck-Schlossberg. Occasional VT and SGN; sound Crémant d'Alsace. (DM)
O **Gewürztraminer** Kaefferkopf Jean-Baptiste★★★ £C VT★★★£D
O **Riesling** GC Winneck-Schlossberg★★★ £C   O **Pinot Gris** Letzenberg★★★ £C

DOM. JEAN BECKER Zellenberg vinsbecker@aol.com
Of 18 ha of vineyards, 4 ha are *grands cru*. Traditional, elegant, structured Riesling, Pinot Gris, Muscat, Gewürz and some fine late-harvest wines from Sonnenglanz, Schoenenbourg and Froehn. Pinot Gris and Gewürz often produced as VT and occasionally SGN, from Rimelsberg. Fruit-driven organic Pinot Blanc and Pinot Gris. Top *crus* have a fine mineral complexity and will age well. (DM)
O **Gewürztraminer** VT★★★★ £D GC Schoenenbourg SGN★★★★ £E
O **Riesling** GC Froehn★★★ £C   O **Pinot Gris** GC Froehn★★★ £C

LÉON BEYER Eguisheim www.leonbeyer.fr *UK stockists:* **Hal, BBR**
There are 20 ha of vineyards as well as bought-in grapes for *négociant* wines. Holdings include GCs Eichberg and Pfersigberg but wines are not released as such. Dry, almost austere generics develop well in bottle. Better are rich, concentrated Grandes Cuvées Comtes d'Eguisheim. Gewürz VT good; very impressive Gewurz and particularly Pinot Gris SGN. Structured, rich and very ageworthy. (DM)
O **Gewürztraminer** Comtes d'Eguisheim★★ £D VT★★★ £E SGN★★★★ £F
O **Riesling** Comtes d'Eguisheim★★ £D   O **Pinot Gris** SGN✪✪✪✪ £F

DOM. PAUL BLANCK Kaysersberg www.blanck.com *UK stockists:* **Lay**
Medium-sized family producer with good to very good rich, opulent wines with quite marked residual sugar. Sound generics include very good old-vine Sylvaner. Extensive range of vieilles vignes, GCs (from Furstentum, Sommerberg and Schlossberg), VT and SGN. Almost all GC bottles at least three stars. Top wines are very ageworthy. (DM)
O **Gewürztraminer** Furstentum GC VV★★★★ £E Furstentum GC VT★★★★★ £E
O **Riesling** Schlossberg GC★★★★ £D   O **Pinot Gris** SGN✪✪✪✪ £G

DOM. BOTT-GEYL Beblenheim bottgeyl@libertysurf.fr *UK stockists:* **CTy**
Explosively rich wines with marked residual sugar. Great-value generic Pinot Auxerrois, Gewürz Beblenheim and Muscat Riquewihr. Gewürz and Pinot Gris from GCs Furstentum and Sonnenglanz and *lieu-dit* Schlosselreben always three stars. Riesling comes from Mandelberg (the fullest), Schoenenbourg and Grafenreben. Gewürz VT is tight and restrained; Pinot Gris SGN from Sonnenglanz is rich and sumptuous. Top wines will age extraordinarily well. (DM)
O **Gewürztraminer** Sonnenglanz GC VV★★★★ £D Sonnenglanz GC VT★★★★★ £E
O **Pinot Gris** Furstentum GC★★★★ £C Sonnenglanz GC SGN✪✪✪✪ £F

ALBERT BOXLER Niedermorschwihr albert.boxler@9online.fr *UK stockists:* **Gau**
Dry, almost austere minerally wines. Good generics including Riesling and Pinot Blanc. Top Gewürz and Pinot Gris comes from Brand; Riesling from Brand and Sommerberg stands out with formidable structure and depth. Riesling and Pinot Gris VT and SGN can be up to super-five stars. (DM)
O **Gewürztraminer** Brand GC★★★ £D   O **Riesling** Sommerberg GC★★★★ £D
O **Pinot Blanc**★★ £B   O **Pinot Gris**★ £B Brand GC★★★ £C

ERNEST BURN www.domaine-burn.fr *UK stockists:* **Has, HHB, NYg, Gau**
Monopole Clos Saint Imer is part of the GC Goldert and accounts for over half the vineyard holdings. Fine Pinot Blanc and well-crafted, rich and stylish Muscat, Pinot Gris, Gewürz and Riesling. GC wines are rich, structured and very late-harvested. Riesling at its best in cooler years. Some very fine, sumptuous and honeyed VT from Gewürz and Pinot Gris. (DM)
O **Gewürztraminer** Goldert GC Cuvée de la Chapelle★★★★ £E
O **Pinot Gris** Goldert GC Cuvée de la Chapelle★★★★ £D   O **Pinot Blanc**★★ £B

Alsace

MARCEL DEISS Bergheim www.marceldeiss.com *UK stockists:* Bal, L&S
One of the best producers in the region, run on biodynamic lines. An exemplary range comes from holdings that include GCs Altenberg, Mambourg and Schoenenbourg. Unusual, very rich field blends of the noble varieties from GCs. Occasional super-rich VT and SGN. (DM)

O **Altenberg** GC✪✪✪✪✪ £F   O **Gewürztraminer** Bergheim★★★★ £D
O **Riesling** Altenberg GC✪✪✪✪✪ £F   O **Pinot Gris** Bergheim★★★★ £E

DOM. DIRLER-CADÉ Bergholz jbdirler@terre-net.fr
Biodynamic since 1998. Over 40 per cent of the family holding is GC with vines planted at Saering, Spiegel, Kessler and Kitterlé. Traditional dry and tightly structured wines. Very striking Muscat; the GC Spiegel is one of the finest in the AC. Some truly excellent GC Riesling and Gewürz are produced as well as rich and pure VT and exquisite Gewürz Spiegel SGN. (DM)

O **Gewürztraminer** GC Kessler★★★★ £C   GC Spiegel SGN★★★★★ £F
O **Riesling** GC Saering★★★★ £C   O **Muscat** GC Spiegel★★★★ £C

DOM. PIERRE FRICK Pfaffenheim pierre.frick@wanadoo.fr *UK stockists:* Vcs
Biodynamically farmed 12-ha property. The wines often have some residual sugar but are rich, opulent and always balanced. Good generic Cuvées Classiques but better single-vineyard, GC and special Précieuse selections. Holdings in *lieux-dits* Bergweingarten, Bihl, Rot Murle and Strangenberg as well as GCs Steinert, Vorbourg and Eichberg. Both VT and SGN are released in best vintages. (DM)

O **Pinot Blanc** Précieuse★★★ £C   O **Gewürztraminer** GC Steinert★★★★ £C
O **Riesling** Précieuse★★★ £C   VT★★★★ £C   ● **Pinot Noir** Rot Murle★★★ £C

DOM. ANDRÉ ET RÉMY GRESSER Andlau *UK stockists:* SVS
There are 10 ha, producing a total of 5,000 cases a year. Andlau is in the centre of the Bas-Rhin, so is cool and favours the production of tight, minerally, pure Riesling of classic structure and dimension from GCs Kastelberg and Moenchberg. In warmer years wines are often of VT ripeness. (DM)

O **Gewürztraminer** Duttenberg VV★★★ £C   O **Riesling** Kastelberg VV★★★★ £C
O **Pinot Gris** Brandhof VV★★★★ £C

HUGEL ET FILS Riquewihr www.hugel.fr *UK stockists:* Day,OWL,BBR,PFx,WSc,Har
With Trimbach one of the two best-known names in the region. There are extensive vineyard holdings – some 127 ha. Top Jubilee wines here are excellent, structured examples of the region, towards the drier end of the spectrum, but there are disappointing generics. Both Pinot Gris and Riesling SGN have remarkable richness, depth and complexity. (DM)

O **Gewürztraminer** Tradition★★ £B   Jubilee★★★ £F   VT★★★★ £F
O **Riesling** Jubilee★★★ £C   Vendange Tardive★★★★ £F   SGN✪✪✪✪ £H
O **Pinot Gris** Jubilee★★★ £F   VT★★★★ £F   SGN✪✪✪✪ £H

JOSMEYER Wintzenheim www.josmeyer.com *UK stockists:* Pol,May,Vts
Small merchant house with 31 ha of vineyard. The Classic labels are straightforward, the Artist Label series a step up. Prestige selections include Pinot Gris Foundation 1854, opulent Gewürz Archenets and intense Pinot Blanc Les Lutins. *Grand cru* holdings include plots on Brand and Hengst. VT is produced from Pinot Gris and Riesling, SGN from Pinot Gris and Gewürz. Very rare late-harvest Pinot Blanc Derrière La Chapelle is probably the best example in the region. (DM)

O **Gewürztraminer** GC Hengst★★★★ £E   O **Riesling** GC Hengst★★★★ £E
O **Pinot Gris** Foundation 1854★★★★ £E   O **Pinot Blanc** Les Lutins★★★ £C

ANDRÉ KIENTZLER Ribeauvillé *UK stockists:* JAr, HHB
6,500 cases produced across an impressive range marked by purity of fruit and elegant structure at all levels. Profound Riesling from the GCs Geisberg (occasionally VT and SGN) and Osterberg; very good Muscat and Pinot Gris from Kirchberg. No GC Gewürz but occasional VT and SGN. Even the lesser Pinot Blanc, Auxerrois and Chasselas offer excellent quality and value. (DM)

O **Gewürztraminer** VT★★★★ £E   O **Riesling** Geisberg GC★★★★ £D
O **Pinot Gris**★★ £B   Kirchberg GC★★★★ £E

New entries have producer's name underlined

MARC KREYDENWEISS Andlau *UK stockists:* C&C, Har
12-ha domaine in the Bas Rhin. Kreydenweiss also owns Costières de Nîmes property Domaine des Perrières.
The wines are marked by intense fruit purity. Unusual is a blend of mainly Riesling and some Pinot Gris
labelled Le Clos du Val d'Eléon, technically an Edelzwicker, as well as Klevner from Kritt. Very stylish VT and
SGN Gewürz and VT Riesling from Kastelberg. (DM)

O **Le Clos du Val d'Eléon**★★★ £D   O **Gewürztraminer** Kritt★★★ £C
O **Pinot Gris** Moenchberg GC★★★★ £E   O **Riesling** Kastelberg GC★★★★ £E

DOM. SEPPI LANDMANN Soultzmatt www.seppi-landmann.fr *UK stockists:* **Tra**
Bewildering array of wines of exemplary quality from the lesser as well as noble varieties. Regular wines are
labelled Vallée Noble and these range from good to very fine in the case of the Gewürz VT. Gewürz, Riesling
and Pinot Gris (and Sylvaner Z) come from Zinnekoepflé with occasional VT and SGN. (DM)

O **Gewürztraminer** GC Zinnekoepflé★★★ £E   GC Zinnekoepflé VT★★★★★ £E
O **Pinot Gris** GC Zinnekoepflé★★★ £C   O **Riesling** GC Zinnekoepflé★★★ £C

DOM. FRANÇOIS LICHTLÉ hlichtle@aol.com
The 6 ha here includes Sylvaner, Pinot Blanc, Gewürz and Pinot N from the *lieu-dit* of Horain. Riesling comes
from Pfersigberg as well as a little Chardonnay used in the Crémant d'Alsace. Pinot Gris Leo is rich and
pungent, in contrast to the minerally, steely Riesling Pfersigberg. Good to very good examples of both VT and
SGN from Gewürz and Pinot Gris plus a fine, elegant and intense Riesling SGN. (DM)

O **Gewürztraminer** VV★★★ £C   O **Riesling** SGN★★★★ £E
O **Pinot Gris** Réserve★★ £C   Cuvée Leo★★★★ £D

DOM. ALBERT MANN Wettolsheim vins@mann-albert.com *UK stockists:* NYg
Very fine producer with a bewildering array of labels from just under 19 ha of organic vineyards. The wines are
ripe, full-bodied and traditional. Generics can be very good: Pinot Blanc/Auxerrois is one of the best in the
region. The style throughout is rich, opulent, almost extracted and the wines can be approached quite young,
though the top examples age very well indeed. (DM)

O **Pinot Gris** Hengst GC SGN❂❂❂❂❂ £E   Furstentum GC SGN❂❂❂❂❂ £E
O **Gewürztraminer** Furstentum GC VV★★★★ £D

RENÉ MURÉ Rouffach www.mure.com *UK stockists:* BWC, Gau
There are two elements to this operation. Domaine wines are labelled Clos Saint-Landelin and produced from 20
ha of estate vineyards at the GC Vorbourg, including the *monopole* Clos Saint-Landelin. The quality is
substantially above that of the *négoçiant* wines under the René Muré label, of which superior bottlings go under
the Côte de Rouffach label. The Domaine wines are steely, structured and ageworthy, Muscat and Gewürz more
opulent. VT and SGN are both regularly produced. (DM)

O **Pinot Gris** Clos Saint Landelin Vorbourg GC★★★ £D
O **Riesling** Clos Saint Landelin Vorbourg GC★★★★ £E   O **Sylvaner** Oscar★★ £B

OSTERTAG Epfig *UK stockists:* FMV, Har, BBR
Radical biodynamic domain producing *barrique*-aged Pinot Blanc, Pinot Gris and Pinot Noir. Generic wines
are labelled as *vins du fruit*, the *lieux-dits* and GCs as *vins du terroir*. Late-harvest bottlings are *vins du temps*.
Most oak-handled wines work well. Also very good Riesling with no recourse to wood, particularly GC
Muenchberg, and some very fine Gewürz. Sylvaner from very old vines is arguably the best example in the
region. (DM)

O **Gewürztraminer** d'Epfig★★★ £C   O **Riesling** Muenchberg GC★★★★ £E
O **Pinot Gris** Barriques★★ £C   Zellberg★★★ £E   Muenchberg GC★★★★ £E

CAVE DE RIBEAUVILLÉ Ribeauvillé www.cave-ribeauville.com
Founded in 1895, the oldest wine co-op in France. As well as a good range of generic varietals there is a series of
exciting Martin Zahn biodynamic wines. An extensive range of well-priced GC wines is also produced: Gewürz
comes from Gloekelberg and Osterberg, Pinot Gris from Gloekelberg and Riesling from Altenberg de
Bergheim, Kirchberg, Osterberg and Rosacker. (DM)

O **Gewürztraminer** Weingarten Collection d'Artistes★★ £B
O **Riesling** Martin Zahn★★★ £B   O **Pinot Gris** Martin Zahn★★★ £B

ROLLY-GASSMANN   Rorschwihr   *UK stockists:* RsW, Bib, Rae, WSc
Extensive range of very good, traditionally produced wines emerges from a family domaine. No GC vineyards but a number of excellent *lieux-dits*. Also some particularly fine VT and SGN bottlings. The top wines need some cellaring. (DM)
O **Muscat** Moenchreben VT★★★★ £E   O **Gewürztraminer** SGN★★★★ £F
O **Pinot Gris** Réserve★★★ £C   O **Riesling** Kappelweg★★★ £C

DOM. SCHOFFIT   Colmar   *UK stockists:* HBJ, BBR, Gau, Har
Brilliant 16-ha domaine. Regular bottlings are all very good. Pinot Blanc and particularly Chasselas from ancient vines really stand out. A significant part of the Schoffits' vineyard holding is in lesser sites but quality is still admirable. The focal point is the Clos Saint-Théobald in the GC Rangen with its fine volcanic soils. The wines are structured but with a remarkable array of exotic fruit aromas and always a pure mineral undercurrent. (DM)
O **Gewürztraminer** Rangen GC★★★★ £E   Rangen GC VT★★★★★ £F
O **Riesling** Rangen GC VT✪✪✪✪✪ £F   O **Pinot Gris** Rangen GC★★★★★ £E
O **Pinot Gris** Rangen GC SGN✪✪✪✪✪ £F

DOM. BRUNO SORG   Eguisheim   *UK stockists:* THt, BBR
Based just south of Colmar with 10 ha of well-sited vineyards including holdings in the GCs Eichberg, Florimont and Pfersigberg. Muscat is musky and complex; Pfersigberg is a benchmark. Riesling is steely and minerally, Pinot Gris and Gewürz are richly textured and opulent, the latter full of concentrated lychee and tropical spices. Top wines are ageworthy. (DM)
O **Gewürztraminer** VV★★★ £C   O **Riesling** GC Pfersigberg VV★★★★ £D
O **Pinot Gris** GC Florimont★★★★ £D   O **Muscat** GC Pfersigberg★★★ £C

TRIMBACH   Ribeauvillé   www.maison-trimbach.fr   *UK stockists:* Par, BBR, WSc, Sel, Har
Merchant house producing close to 100,000 cases a year. As at Hugel, the top wines are very impressive, particularly remarkable Riesling Clos Sainte-Hune, the greatest dry example in the region. All the wines are dry, steely and restrained. Very good VT and SGN just a little way short of the very best. The generics are less exciting and prices for these are quite steep. (DM)
O **Gewürztraminer** Seigneurs de Ribeaupierre★★★ £E   VT★★★★ £F
O **Riesling** Cuvée Frédéric Émile★★★★ £E   Clos Sainte-Hune✪✪✪✪ £G
O **Pinot Gris** Réserve Personnelle★★★ £C   SGN★★★★ £G

DOMAINE WEINBACH   Kaysersberg   *UK stockists:* J&B, Tan, NYg
One of the great names of Alsace. run biodynamically since 1998. The wines are rich, powerful and complex, particularly concentrated and impressive in the top *cuvées*. The most important holdings are the 5-ha walled Clos des Capucins and 10 ha in the GC Schlossberg, but outstanding wines are also made from *lieu-dit* Altenbourg. VT and SGN styles add more sweetness to the usual Weinbach concentration and depth whilst retaining good balance. (PW)
O **Riesling** Schlossberg GC Sainte-Catherine l'Inédit★★★★ £F   VT★★★★★ £F
O **Pinot Gris** Sainte-Catherine Fut II★★★★ £E
O **Gewürztraminer** Cuvée d'Or Quintessence SGN✪✪✪✪✪ £G

ZIND-HUMBRECHT   Turckheim   *UK stockists:* ABy, BBR, Har, Wai
Olivier Humbrecht runs perhaps the greatest domaine in the AC. From 40 ha of vineyards more than 30 wines are produced in every vintage. Some *crus* are also produced in late-harvested VT and SGN styles. Top wines come from a bewildering range of vineyards bur always offer exquisite fruit, weight and opulence. Regular bottlings should have at least two or three years' ageing; most *lieu-dits* or GCs deserve at least five or six years. (PW)
O **Riesling** Rangen GC Clos Saint-Urbain★★★★ £F   Brand GC✪✪✪✪✪ £F
O **Pinot Gris** Rangen GC Clos Saint-Urbain★★★★★ £F   Clos Windsbuhl★★★★★ £F
O **Gewürztraminer** Clos Windsbuhl★★★★ £E   O **Muscat** Goldert GC★★★★ £D

Other wineries of note
Dom. Lucien Albrecht, Dom. Cécile Bernhard-Riebel, Cave de Cleebourg, Fernand Engel, Dom. Paul Ginglinger, Kuentz-Bas, Dom. Gerard Neumeyer, Dom. Rieflé, Dom. Schlumberger, Cave de Turkheim

An in-depth profile of every producer can be found in Wine behind the label 2006

New entries have producer's name underlined

The Region

The appellation falls into five main districts. **Montagne de Reims** is just to the south of that city and Pinot Noir and Pinot Meunier produce rich, full-bodied Champagnes. **Vallée de la Marne** is to the north-west of the Montagne de Reims and red grapes predominant. The **Côte des Blancs** is virtually all Chardonnay. In the far south-west of the main Champagne area, north of Troyes, is the **Côte de Sézanne** mainly Chardonnay is planted. Way to the south of Troyes and away from the main Champagne appellation boundaries is the **Aube**. which at present is largely planted to Pinot Noir. Within the appellation the communes are also classified as Grand Cru, Premier Cru or Deuxième Cru.

The Styles

Sparkling white and rosé along with the still red wines which use the **Coteaux Champenois** AC are produced. Most common are the regular **non-vintage** blends with a huge variation in quality. Vintage *cuvées* are a significant step up. **Blanc de Blancs** is produced solely from Chardonnay while **Blanc de Noirs** is produced from Pinot Noir and/or Pinot Meunier.. **Rosé** can be made either by blending in a little red wine (the only AC where this is permitted) or, and generally with better results, by the normal manner of a short maceration on skins. The most expensive Champagnes are the deluxe bottlings.

Wizard's Wishlist

Good value Champagnes

AGRAPART ○ Brut Grand Cru Vintage
EDMOND BARNAUT ○ Brut Sélection-Extra Non-Vintage
BEAUMONT DE CRAYERES ○ Fleur de Prestige Vintage
RAYMOND BOULARD ○ Brut Millésimé Vintage
DEUTZ ○ Brut Classic Non-Vintage

DOQUET_JEANMAIRE
○ Blanc de Blancs Premier Cru Coeur de Terroir Vintage
SERGE MATHIEU ○ Brut Millésime Vintage
PIERRE MONCUIT ○ Blanc de Blancs Grand Cru Vintage
FRANÇOIS SECONDÉ ○ Brut Clavier Non-Vintage
JOSEPH PERRIER ○ Cuvée Royale Brut Non-Vintage

A selection of lesser known Champagnes

PAUL BARA ○ Brut Grand Cru Vintage
PHILIPONAT ○ Clos des Goisses Vintage
EGLY-OURIET ○ Brut Tradition Non-Vintage
PIERRE GIMONNET ET FILS
○ Blanc de Blancs Cuis Premier Cru Non-Vintage
ALFRED GRATIEN ○ Paradis Non-Vintage
LARMANDIER-BERNIER
○ Extra Brut Vieille Vignes de Cramant Vintage
SERGE MATHIEU ○ Brut Millésime Vintage
GOSSET ○ Celebris Vintage
BRUNO PAILLARD ○ Nec Plus Ultra Vintage
JACQUES SELOSSE
○ Blanc de Blancs Tradition Non-Vintage

Pick of the luxury cuvée's

BILLECART-SALMON
○ Brut Cuvée Nicolas-François Billecart Vintage
BOLLINGER ○ RD Vintage
CHARLES HEIDSIECK ○ Charlie Vintage
KRUG ○ Clos du Mesnil Vintage
LAURENT-PERRIER ○ Grand Siécle Vintage
MOËT ET CHANDON ○ Dom Pérignon Vintage
POL ROGER ○ Sir Winston Churchill Vintage
LOUIS ROEDERER ○ Cristal Vintage
SALON ○ Salon Vintage
VEUVE CLICQUOT ○ La Grande Dame Vintage

Champagne/A-Z of producers

AGRAPART www.champagne-agrapart.com
The Agraparts' holding is exclusively Chardonnay, the oldest parcels over 55 years. Brut Reserve gets four years on its lees, Brut Millésime six. Marvellously intense, citrus and mineral-laden L'Avizoise comes from the oldest vines. Wines of great intensity and purity. (DM)
○ Brut Réserve Grand Cru NV★★ £C   ○ Brut Grand Cru Vintage★★★ £D
○ L'Avizoise Brut Grand Cru Vintage★★★★ £E

AYALA www.champagne-ayala.fr   *UK stockists:* **Men**
Recent releases here have been showing greater richness, weight and concentration than a decade ago. These are very ripe, almost rustic styles of Champagne. The Blanc de Blancs is rich and weighty for the style. A light, fruit-driven rosé and also a special prestige bottling Grand Cuvée are made. (DM)
○ Brut NV★★ £D   ○ Brut Vintage★★★ £E
○ Brut Blanc de Blancs Vintage★★★ £E   ◉ Brut NV★ £D

FRANCE

PAUL BARA   *UK stockists:* OWL
Very good small and traditional producer with vineyard holdings in the *grand cru* village of Bouzy. The wines have a high level of Pinot Noir in the blend and this tends to show through with weight and substance. The wines are all good value. (DM)
O **Brut GC Comtesse Marie de France** Vintage★★★★ £E
O **GC Vintage Club** Vintage★★★★ £E   ◉ **Brut GC Grand** Rosé de Bouzy★★★ £D

EDMOND BARNAUT   www.champagne-barnaut.com   *UK stockists:* L&S, GFy
The Barnaut vineyards contain a high proportion of Chardonnay. This gives an added finesse and grip although the wines are of an impressively weighty, substantial style. There are also a limited-production special Cuvée Edmond Brut, a Cuvée Douceur Sec and a fruity Bouzy Rouge. (DM)
O **Brut Sélection-Extra** NV★★★ £D   O **Grand Réserve** NV★★★ £D
O **Blanc de Noirs** NV★★★ £D   ◉ **Brut Authentique** NV★★ £D

BEAUMONT DES CRAYERES   www.champagne-beaumont.com   *UK stockists:* Tan
Small, quality-concious co-op. Grande Réserve is a soft, forward and fruity. Grand Prestige is subtler and more elegant. Fleur de Prestige is particularly good value, Chardonnay adding intensity and elegance. The top *cuvée*, Nostalgie, is rich and softly structured. (DM)
O **Brut Grande Réserve** NV★ £C   O **Brut Grand Prestige** NV★★ £C
O **Fleur de Prestige** Vintage★★★ £D   O **Nostalgie** Vintage★★★ £E

BILLECART-SALMON   www.champagne-billecart.fr   *UK stockists:* **B-S**, AAA
Founded in 1818. The Brut Réserve NV is classy stuff at this level and the top wines are very intense and marvellously refined. A sizeable proportion of Chardonnay is used and this helps the wines' structure. Super Cuvée Nicolas-François Billecart is a very complex and elegant. (DM)
O **Brut Réserve** NV★★★ £E   O **Blancs de Blancs GC** NV★★★★ £F
O **Brut Cuvée Nicolas-François Billecart** Vintage★★★★★ £F

BOLLINGER   www.champagne-bollinger.fr   *UK stockists:* **Men**, AAA
One of the greatest names in sparkling wine production. Special Cuvée is always full and rich in style. The vintage Grande Année can almost take on a hint of Burgundian gaminess with age, as can the remarkable RD which is kept on lees for up to 10 years. (DM)
O **Brut Spécial Cuvée** NV★★★ £E   O **Brut Grande Année** Vintage★★★★★ £G
O **RD**✪✪✪✪✪ £H   ◉ **Brut Grande Année** Rosé Vintage★★★ £G

RAYMOND BOULARD   www.champagne-boulard.com   *UK stockists:* IdG
Small grower with impressively aged vineyards averaging around 30 years. and a holding spread across 7 villages. Red dominates the plantings with Pinot Meunier accounting for nearly half the vignoble. The wines are striking nonetheless, wines of depth and real persistence throughout the small range. (DM)
O **Blanc de Blancs Brut** Non-Vintage★★★ £D
O **Brut Réserve** Non-Vintage★★ £C   O **Brut Millésimé** Vintage★★★ £D
O **Petraea Brut** Vintage★★★★ £E

DEUTZ   www.champagne-deutz.com   *UK stockists:* BWC, Lay
Owned by Roederer, quality is now very good indeed and the wines are well priced, perhaps with the exception of the luxury *cuvées* William Deutz and Blanc de Blancs Amour de Deutz. (DM)
O **Brut Classic** NV★★★ £E   O **Brut** Vintage★★★★ £F
O **William Deutz** Vintage★★★★★ £G   O **Blanc de Blancs** Vintage★★★★ £F

EGLY-OURIET
Quality is high, with vines over 30 years old. Wonderfully pure, full-bodied wines of great character. A very good example of Coteaux Champenois is also produced but available only in very limited quantities. (DM)
O **Brut Tradition** NV★★★ £D   O **GC** Vintage★★★★★ £E
O **Blanc de Noirs Vieilles Vignes** NV★★★★ £E   ◉ **Brut** Rosé NV★★★ £D

PIERRE GIMONNET ET FILS   www.champagne-gimmonet.com
Based on the the Côte des Blancs part of the vineyard is *premier cru* and part *grand cru*. Style varies from the fresh, taut and lightly toasty Cuis Premier Cru to the weightier and richer Fleuron and Club Premier Cru

New entries have producer's name underlined

FRANCE

labels. (DM)
○ **Blanc de Blancs Puis** PC NV★★ £D ○ **Brut Fleuron** PC Vintage★★★ £E
○ **Brut Club** PC Vintage★★★ £E ○ **Extra-Brut Oenophile** Vintage★★★ £E

GOSSET www.champagne-gosset.com *UK stockists:* **McK**
Non-vintage Excellence is better than it has been. The Grande Réserve and Grand Rosé, both non-vintage, and the vintage offerings are a step up. The style is one of weight and a rich toastiness in the top wines. Celebris is clearly a cut above the rest. (DM)
○ **Brut Excellence** NV★★ £D ○ **Grande Réserve** NV★★★ £F
○ **Grande Millésime** Vintage★★★ £F ○ **Celebris** Vintage★★★★ £G

ALFRED GRATIEN www.alfredgratien.com *UK stockists:* **Wit, WSc**
Very good, traditional house which produces barely 15,000 cases a year. The base wines are vinified in wood. Malolactic fermentation is blocked and this provides the taut, structured style. The wines, even the non-vintage, are ageworthy. (DM)
○ **Brut** Réserve NV★★★ £E ○ **Paradis** NV★★★★ £F
○ **Brut** Vintage★★★★★ £F ◉ **Brut Rosé Paradis** NV★★★ £F

CHARLES HEIDSIECK www.charlesheidsieck.com *UK stockists:* **Max**
Quality at this house over the past 15 years has been very impressive. The non-vintaged Brut Réserve Mis-en-Cave is arguably the best of its style in the appellation. Two first-class vintage reserves: elegant Blanc des Millénaires, made from Chardonnay, and Pinot-dominated Charlie. (DM)
○ **Brut Réserve Mis-en-Cave** NV★★★★ £E ○ **Charlie** Vintage★★★★★ £G
○ **Blanc des Millénaires** Vintage★★★★★ £G ◉ **Brut** Rosé Vintage★★★★ £G

HENRIOT contact@champagne-henriot.com *UK stockists:* **JEF**
Medium-sized producer. All including the straightforward Brut Souverain non-vintage are weighty enough but The Cuvée des Enchanteleurs is a marked step up in both elegance and depth. (DM)
○ **Brut Souverain** NV★★★ £E ○ **Brut** Vintage★★★ £E
○ **Cuvée des Enchanteleurs**★★★★ £F ◉ **Brut** Rosé Vintage★★★★ £E

JACQUESSON champagne.jacquesson@wanadoo.fr *UK stockists:* **May**
Family-run operation. Barrel-fermentation is used for the base wine and the resulting Champagnes are characterful and refined. Vintage bottlings are serious and structured. A complex and very pricey Dégorgement Tardif is now being produced, which is given extended ageing on lees. (DM)
○ **Brut Perfection** NV★★ £E ○ **Grand Vin Signature** Vintage★★★★ £G
○ **Blanc de Blancs** Vintage★★★★ £G ◉ **Grand Vin Signature** Vintage★★★ £E

KRUG krug@krug.fr *UK stockists:* **Par**, AAA
Arguably the most prestigious of all the great Champagne houses. Quite remarkably impressive and structured wines. Tight and very restrained, they demand cellaring. The range is completed by the tiny-production and undoubtedly very fine non-vintage Rosé. (DM)
○ **Grande Cuvée** NV★★★★★ £H ○ **Clos du Mesnil** Vintage✪✪✪✪✪ £H
○ **Vintage**✪✪✪✪✪ £H

LARMANDIER-BERNIER larmandier@terre-net.fr *UK stockists:* VTr
Small, top-class grower based in the Côte des Blancs. Very structured, minerally, intense Champagnes that have been given weight and depth through cask-ageing prior to bottling and further cellaring prior to release. They will reward ageing. (DM)
○ **Brut Tradition** NV★★★ £D ○ **Blanc de Blancs** NV★★★ £D
○ **Extra Brut Vieille Vignes de Cramant** Vintage★★★★★ £E

LAURENT-PERRIER www.laurent-perrier.co.uk *UK stockists:* **L-P**, AAA
Non-vintage is straightforward. Top wines are the Grand Siècle labels. The two whites have a rich, powerful, bready character underpinned by a pure mineral structure. The rosé is very complex with a remarkable array of berry fruit aromas. (DM)
○ **Brut LP** NV★ £E ○ **Vintage**★★ £F ○ **Ultra Brut** NV★★★ £F
○ **Grand Siècle La Cuvée** NV★★★★ £G Vintage★★★★★ £H

FRANCE

A.R. LENOBLE www.champagne-lenoble.com *UK stockists:* **EoR**
Small house with some fine Gtand Cru holdings. Both Chardonnay and Pinot Noir feature stoingly. The non-vintage gets around 25% reserve wine, the vintage is tighter with a purer mineral structure and impressive depth. Particularly striking is the luxury cuvée Les Aventures which comes from the terroir of the same name. (DM)
O **Brut Réserve** Non-Vintage★ £C O **Blanc de Blancs Grand Cru** Non-Vintage★★ £D Vintage★★★ £E
O **Blancs de Noirs Premier Cru** Vintage★★ £D
O **Cuvée Les Aventure Grand Cru Blanc de Blancs** Vintage★★★★ £F ◉ **Brut Millésimé Rosé** Vintage★★ £D

SERGE MATHIEU www.champagne-serge-mathieu.fr *UK stockists:* SVS
Small but very good property based in the Aube. Pinot Noir is the key component here and the wines certainly display a real weight and concentration. However, what marks them out is their elegance and refinement. (DM)
O **Brut Tradition** NV★★ £C O **Brut Prestige** NV★★ £D ◉ **Brut Rosé** NV★★ £D
O **Brut Millésime** Vintage★★★ £E O **Tête de Cuvée** NV★★★ £E

MOËT ET CHANDON www.moet.com *UK stockists:* **MHn,** AAA
The consumer favourite among the big Champagne houses. Brut Impérial can be a lot more impressive than it is often given credit for. White Star, marketed in the US, contains a higher *dosage*. Like the house itself, Dom Pérignon is the most established of the region's luxury *cuvées*. (DM)
O **Brut Impérial** NV★★ £E O **Brut White Star** NV★ £E
O **Brut Impérial** Vintage★★★ £E O **Dom Pérignon** Vintage★★★★★ £E

PIERRE MONCUIT *UK stockists:* **HHB,** SVS
The Moncuits produce two very fine Blanc de Blancs. The Grand Cru vintage bottling is superbly crafted, intense and refined with a rich, biscuity approachability. The Vieilles Vignes is intense, refined and very ageworthy. Sadly very little is made. (DM)
O **Blanc de Blancs** GC Vintage★★★ £D O **Nicole Moncuit VV** Vintage★★★★ £E

MONTAUDON *UK stockists:* **GPW,** ACh
Small house producing producing wines in a showy and opulent style. Elegant Classe M is the houses luxury cuvée and offers real breadth as well as persistence with very complex candied, citrus and toasted aromas opening out on the palate. (DM)
O **Réserve Première** Non-Vintage★★ £E ◉ **Millésimé** Vintage★★★ £E
O **Classe M** Non-Vintage★★★★ £F

BRUNO PAILLARD www.champagnebrunopaillard.com *UK stockists:* **Bib**
The style is relatively austere but these are wines, particularly the vintage *cuvées*, that should develop well in bottle. The prestige NPU (Nec Plus Ultra) is undoubtedly a serious step up from the rest of the range but is also very pricey. (DM)
O **Brut Première Cuvée** NV★ £E O **Brut Millésime** Vintage★★★ £F
O **Chardonnay** Réserve Privée★★ £E O **Nec Plus Ultra** Vintage★★★★ £H

JOSEPH PERRIER www.josephperrier.com *UK stockists:* CHk, SsG, GWW
Noted for traditional, medium- to full-bodied wines. The Brut Royale non-vintage is a full, fruity style. The vintage is more complex. Joséphine vintage is of a different order and will cellar well. (DM)
O **Brut Royale** NV★★ £E O **Brut Royale** Vintage★★★ £F
O **Joséphine** Vintage★★★★ £G ◉ **Brut Royale** NV★★ £E

PHILIPPONNAT www.champagnephilipponnat.com *UK stockists:* Eur, Las
Small *négociant-manipulant*. Until its acquisition by Bruno Paillard, the range was decidedly ordinary – with the exception of the great prestige *cuvée* Brut Clos des Goisses, a wine of super-five quality in extravagant vintages. Things now appear to be taking a turn for the better. (DM)
O **Brut Royale Réserve** NV★ £E O **Brut Réserve Spécial** Vintage★★ £F
O **Grand Blanc** Vintage★★★ £F O **Clos des Goisses** Vintage★★★★★ £H

POL ROGER www.polroger.co.uk *UK stockists:* **Pol,** AAA
Sizeable and consistently fine house. The non-vintage White Foil shows real depth and a refined biscuity character. Very good and intense vintage as well as impeccably balanced Blanc de Blancs. The Sir Winston Churchill prestige *cuvée* demands to be cellared. (DM)
O **Brut White Foil** NV★★★ £E O **Brut** Vintage★★★★ £F ◉ **Brut** Vintage★★★ £F

New entries have producer's name underlined

FRANCE

○ **Brut Chardonnay** Vintage★★★ £F   ○ **Sir Winston Churchill** Vintage★★★★★ £H

LOUIS ROEDERER   www.champagne-roederer.com   *UK stockists:* **MMD,**AAA
long established as one of the great Champagne houses. The style here is weighty and rich with a considerable
Pinot Noir influence. Blanc de Blancs is the most obviously restrained style. Cristal prestige *cuvée* is one of the
greatest and most refined sparkling wines in the world. It needs time. (DM)
○ **Brut Premier** NV★★★ £E   ○ **Brut** Vintage★★★★ £F   ◉ **Brut** Vintage★★★ £F
○ **Blanc de Blancs** Vintage★★★ £F   ○ **Cristal** Vintage✪✪✪✪ £H

RUINART   www.ruinart.com   *UK stockists:* **Rui**
Among the big houses Ruinart has maintained a relatively low profile in recent years. The wines, though, are
sound to excellent, with the prestige *cuvées* (both Blanc de Blancs Dom Ruinart and the Rosé) worthy of a
super-five rating on occasion. (DM)
○ **Brut R de Ruinart** NV★★★ £E   ○ **Brut R de Ruinart** Vintage★★★★ £F
○ **Dom Ruinart** Vintage★★★★★ £H   ◉ **Dom Ruinart** Vintage★★★★★ £H

SALON   *UK stockists:* **C&B,** Las
Now owned by Laurent-Perrier. Just one exceptional wine is produced here: a Blanc de Blancs, in fact the first
created, sourced entirely from selected vineyard plots in the village of Le Mesnil. Only bottled in the very best
vintage years. (DM)
○ **Salon** Vintage✪✪✪✪ £H

FRANÇOIS SECONDÉ
Very well-priced and finely structured Champagne from just 5 ha. Despite a high proportion of Pinot Noir the
wines are tight and restrained, they need a little time after release to show at their best. (DM)
○ **Brut** NV★★★ £C   ○ **Brut Clavier** NV★★★ £D   ◉ **Brut Rosé** NV★★ £C

JACQUES SELOSSE
Remarkable small biodynamic producer. New and old oak are used to barrel-ferment the base wine. Extensively
aged prior to release, these are massive and powerful wines for Champagne but no less impressive for that. Some
of the most exciting and original wines of the appellation. (DM)
○ **Blanc de Blancs Tradition** NV★★★ £E   ○ **Originale** Extra-Brut NV★★★★ £E
○ **GC Substance** NV★★★★ £E   ○ **Blanc de Noirs Contraste** NV★★★★ £E

TAITTINGER   www.taittinger.com   *UK stockists:* **HMA,**AAA
Large house producing generally reliable if rather unexciting non-vintage Brut Réserve. Better are some really
very fine vintage wines and an exceptional Blanc de Blancs prestige *cuvée* Comtes de Champagne, matched by
an equally exquisite and very rare rosé. (DM)
○ **Brut Réserve** NV★ £E   ○ **Brut Millésime** Vintage★★★ £F
○ **Blanc de Blancs Comtes de Champagne** Vintage✪✪✪✪ £H

VEUVE CLICQUOT   www.veuve-clicquot.fr   *UK stockists:* **Par,**AAA
Second to Moët et Chandon in the LVMH hierarchy in terms of volume but most certainly ahead in terms of
quality. Throughout the last five or six years the quality here has always been good, even for the regular Carte
Jaune (Yellow Label). (DM)
○ **Brut Carte Jaune** NV★★★ £E   ○ **Vintage Réserve**★★★ £F
○ **Rich Réserve** Vintage★★★ £F   ○ **La Grande Dame** Vintage✪✪✪✪ £H

Other wineries of note
Doquet-Jeanmaire, Lanson, G H Mumm, Perrier Jouët, Piper-Heidsieck, Pommery

An in-depth profile of every producer can be found in Wine behind the label 2006

Loire Valley

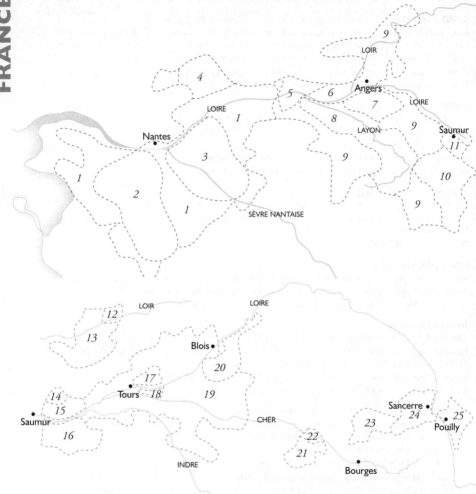

1	Muscadet	14	Saint-Nicolas-de-Bourgueil
2	Muscadet Côtes de Grand Lieu	15	Bourgueil
3	Muscadet de Sèvre-et-Maine	16	Chinon
4	Muscadet des Coteaux de la Loire	17	Vouvray
5	Anjou Coteaux de la Loire	18	Montlouis
6	Savennières	19	Touraine
7	Coteaux de l'Aubance	20	Cheverny, Cour Cheverny
8	Coteaux du Layon	21	Reuilly
9	Anjou	22	Quincy
10	Saumur	23	Menetou-Salon
11	Saumur-Champigny	24	Sancerre
12	Jasnières	25	Pouilly-Fumé
13	Coteaux du Loir		

The Regions

The **Pays Nantais** generally means just one wine: Muscadet. The best examples come from **Muscadet de Sèvre-et-Maine**, **Muscadet-Coteaux de la Loire** and **Muscadet Côtes de Grandlieu** with the best wines bottled *sur lie*. A few decent wine are also emerging from **Fiefs Vendéens VDQS**.
At **Anjou** and **Saumur** some good red and white are released as **Anjou AC** as well as red from **Anjou-Villages**. Key sweet wines to look out for are **Coteaux de l'Aubance**, **Coteaux du Layon**, **Bonnezeaux** and **Quarts de Chaume**. All are made from Chenin Blanc as are a small number from the **Coteaux de Saumur**. Top class dry whites emerge from **Savennières** and fine reds as well as white from **Saumur**. **Saumur-Champigny** is solely for reds, as elsewhere from Cab Sauv and Cab Franc. Sparkling wines are made in many ACs and there is a catch all appellation **Crémant de Loire**.
The catch-all **Touraine AC** encompasses most of the region. Sauvignon is as important for whites here as Chenin. In the far west of the region are the red wine appellations of **Bourgueil**, **Saint-Nicolas-de-Bourgueil** and **Chinon**. At **Vouvray** amd **Mountlois** dry, *demi-sec* and *moelleux* styles are all made. To the north of Tours are the ACs of the **Coteaux du Loir** and its sub-region of **Jasnières**. A handful of very good wines are made.
To the east the main wines of consequence are the Sauvignons from **Quincy**, **Reuilly**, **Menetou-Salon**, **Sancerre** and **Poully-Fumé**. Good Pinot Noir is also made at Sancerre and to a lesser extent at Menetou-Salon.

Loire Valley Vintages

The best red and white wines will age very well. Reds are more marked by their acidity than their tannin. The great dry whites of Savennières and top demi-secs from Vouvray and Montlouis are capable of being held in your cellar for well over three decades. Top Sancerre and Pouilly-Fumé, particularly those wines that are barrel-fermented, are surprisingly ageworthy. Most recent vintages are rated in the Vintage appendix to the guide. 2004 looks promising and 2003 in particular produced some exceptional sweet whites and 2002 was also very good. Of the great earlier years Savennières was particularly impressive in 1985, 1983, 1982, 1978 and 1976. The great sweet wine vintages to consider were 1985, 1983, 1982, 1976, 1971, 1959, 1949, 1947 and 1921. Top reds were made in 1986, 1985, 1983, 1982, 1978 and 1976.

Wizard's Wishlist

A diverse selection of sweet whites

PATRICK BAUDOUIN O **Coteaux du Layon** Aprés Minuit
DOM. DES BAUMARD O **Quarts de Chaume**
CH. DE FESLES O Bonnezeaux
DOM. DU CLOS NAUDIN O **Vouvray** Moelleux
PHILIPPE DELESVAUX
O **Coteaux du Layon** Grains Nobles
OLIVIER DELÉTANG
O **Montlouis** Les Petits Boulay Garde Réserve
JOËL GIGOU O **Jasnières** Sélection de Grains Nobles
HUET L'ECHANSONNE O **Vouvray** Haut-Lieu Moelleux
YVES SOULEZ O **Coteaux du Layon** Les Tetuères
TAILLE AUX LOUPS O **Montlouis** Cuvée Romulus
DOM. DES FORGES O **Quarts de Chaume**
CH. LA VARIÈRE O **Quarts de Chaume** Les Querches
RENÉ MOSSÉ
O **Coteaux du Layon-Saint-Lambert** Bonnes Blanches
JO PITHON O **Quarts de Chaume** Les Varennes
DOM. FRANÇOIS CHIDAINE O **Montlouis** Le Lys

A choice of individual dry whites

DOM. HENRI BOURGEOIS O **Sancerre** La Bourgeoise
CH. D'EPIRÉ O **Savennières** Cuveé Spéciale
CH. DE VILLENEUVE O **Saumur** Cormiers
JEAN-CLAUDE CHATELAINE O **Pouilly Fumé** Prestige
CLOS DE LA COULÉE DE SERRANT
O **Savennières** Coulée de Serrant
PASCAL COTAT O **Sancerre** Monts Damnés
DIDIER DAGUENEAU O **Pouilly Fumé** Silex
HENRY PELLÉ O **Menetou-Salon** Clos des Blanchais
DOM. DE LA SANSONNIÈRE O **Anjou** La Lune
SILICES DE QUINCY O **Quincy**
DOM. DE BELLIVIÈRE
O **Coteaux du Loir** Eparses Vieilles Vignes
DOM. SAINT-NICOLAS
O **Fiefs Vendéens** Le Haut des Clous

The best of the reds

PHILIPPE ALLIET ● **Chinon** Vieilles-Vignes
YANNICK AMIRAULT
● **Saint-Nicolas-de-Bourgueil** Malgagnes
BERNARD BAUDRY ● **Chinon** Croix Boisée
CH. DU HUREAU ● **Saumur-Champigny** Lisgathe
CLOS ROUGEARD ● **Saumur-Champigny** Poyeux
PIERRE-JACQUES DRUET ● **Bourgueil** Vaumoreau
DOM. OGEREAU ● **Anjou-Villages** Côte de la Houssaye
DOM. DES OUCHES ● **Bourgueil** Grande Réserve
DOM. DES ROCHES NEUVES
● **Saumur-Champigny** Marginale
DOM. DE LA COTELLERAIE
● **Saint-Nicolas-de-Bourgueil** L'Envol
CH. DE COULAINE ● **Chinon** Les Picasses
DOM. FRÉDÉRIC MABILEAU
● **Saint-Nicolas-de-Bourgueil** Éclipse

A selection of great Loire values

AMPELIDAE O **Vin de Pays de la Vienne** Le C

79

Loire Valley

AUBERT LA CHAPELLE O Jasnières
DOM. DE LA BUTTE ● Bourgueil Perrières
ALAIN CAILBOURDIN O Pouilly Fumé Les Cris
CH. DE VILLENEUVE O Saumur
DOM. FRANÇOIS CHIDAINE
O Montlouis Clos des Breuil
DOM. LAURENT CHATENAY O Montlouis La Vallée
DOM. DU CLOS NAUDIN O Vouvray Sec
DOM. DU CLOSEL O Savennières Clos du Papillon

DOM DE L'ECU
O Muscadet Sèvre-et-Maine Expression de Granit
DOM. GUIBERTEAU O Saumur Le Clos
DOM. LA TOUR SAINT MARTIN
O Menetou-Salon Morogues
DOM. RENÉ-NOEL LEGRAND ● Saumur La Chaintre
ALEX MATHUR O Touraine Cuvée des Pruides
DOM. GÉRARD MORIN O Sancerre PMG

Loire Valley/A-Z of producers

PHILIPPE ALLIET   Chinon   *UK stockists:* **Lay**
One of the very best producers in Chinon with 9 ha of Cab Franc planted on the *coteaux* at Cravant. The wines offer pure blackcurrant and cedar fruit all underpinned by supple, velvety tannins. New oak is avoided as are fining and filtration. (DM)
● **Chinon**★★ £B   Coteau de Noiré★★★★ £C   Vieilles Vignes★★★★ £C

YANNICK AMIRAULT   Bourgueil   *UK stockists:* **L&S, SVS, THt**
17 ha spread throughout Bourgueil and Saint-Nicolas-de-Bourgueil. The wines are among the best in either AC. The Bourgueils are marginally deeper, more brawny wines, the Saint-Nicolas a touch more elegant and tightly structured. (DM)
● **Bourgueil** Quartiers★★★ £B   La Petite Cave★★★ £C
● **Saint Nicolas-de-Bourgueil** Graviers★★★ £B   Malgagnes★★★★ £C

AMPELIDÆ   Haut-Poitou
Domaine located south of the Loire towards Poitiers with a fairly extensive range of wines. Basic fruit-driven reds and whites come under the Marigny label but the striking *vins de pays* varietals marketed under the Ampelida label really stand out. (DM)
● **Vin de Pays de la Vienne** PN 1328★★★ £C   Le K★★ £C
● **Vin de Table** Le Y★★ £C
O **Vin de Pays de la Vienne** Le C★★★ £C   Le S★★ £C

DOM. DES AUBUISIÈRES   Vouvray   www.vouvrayfouquet.com   *UK stockists:* **C&R**
22-ha domaine making bone dry to lusciously sweet Vouvray. Silex is dry, almost austere and very pure, while the stylish Marigny Sec is barrel-fermented. Girardières is sweet, citrusy and minerally. Magnificent Moelleux Cuvée Alexandre is made when conditions are favourable. (DM)
O **Vouvray** Brut★★ £C   Silex Sec★★ £B   Marigny Sec★★★ £C
O **Vouvray** Girardières Demi-Sec★★★ £B

PATRICK BAUDOUIN   Coteaux du Layon   *UK stockists:* **WTs**
One of the Layon's "sugar hunters", Baudouin also produces two good reds. The Anjou is solely Cab Franc; the Anjou-Villages is more structured, a blend of both Cabs, part oak-aged. Neither is filtered. Top sweet wine Aprés Minuit, made in tiny quantities, is selected berry by berry, very concentrated and complex. (DM)
O **Coteaux du Layon** Les Bruandières★★★ £D   Grains Nobles★★★★ £F
O **Coteaux du Layon** Maria Juby★★★★★ £F   Aprés Minuit❂❂❂❂❂ £G

BERNARD BAUDRY   Chinon   www.bernard-baudry@chinon.com   *UK stockists:* **L&S**
25 ha under vine with a tiny amount of Chenin, producing impressive white Chinon Croix Boisée. Good regular red Chinon is marked by approachable leafy, berry fruit and a hint of spiciness. Les Granges is soft, vibrant and forward. The three top *cuvées* stand out. (DM)
● **Chinon** Les Granges★★ £B   Clos Guillot★★★ £C   Grézeaux★★★ £C
● **Chinon** Croix Boisée★★★★ £C

DOM. DES BAUMARD   Anjou-Saumur   www.baumard.fr
Top dry and sweet wines. Anjou red and white, Rosé de Loire, Cabernet d'Anjou rosé and Crémant de Loire

80

New entries have producer's name underlined

all produced. Gems here are the Layon sweet wines and the various *cuvées* of steely, structured Savennières. Quarts de Chaumes – a restrained and extraordinarly subtle sweet wine – is a super-five in great years. (DM)

O **Savennières** Clos du Papillon★★★★ £C   O **Quarts de Chaume**★★★★★ £E
O **Coteaux du Layon** Carte d'Or★★ £B   Clos Sainte-Catherine★★★★ £D

DOM. DE BELLIVIÈRE   Coteaux du Loir   www.belliviere.com   *UK stockists:* **RsW**

Brilliantly styled, mineral whites are made at this 11-ha domaine. Reds from the Coteaux du Loir are also worth looking at. Eparses from 50–80-year-old vines is a wine of marvellous depth and persistence. (DM)

O **Jasnières** Les Rosiers★★★★ £D   O **Coteaux du Loir** L'Effraie★★★ £C   Eparses Vieilles Vignes★★★★ £D
● **Coteaux du Loir** e Rouge-Gorge★★★ £C

DOM. HENRI BOURGEOIS   Sancerre   www.bourgeois-sancerre.com   *UK stockists:* WSS

Substantial Sancerre producer and *négociant*. The Bonnes Bouches and Grande Réserve are the regular *cuvées* of Sancerre, while the MD de Bourgeois and Bourgeoise are a level up. D'Antan comes from 65-year-old vines, while Jadis is intense and minerally. Top wine is the very intense Étienne Henri, vinified in oak for 12 months on fine lees. (DM)

O **Sancerre** Bonne Bouches★★ £B   La Côte des Monts Damnés★★★ £C
O **Sancerre** Bourgeoise★★★ £C   Jadis★★★★ £D   d'Antan★★★★ £E

DOM. DE LA BUTTE   Bourgueil   www.jackyblot.com   *UK stockists:* J&B,JAr,Far

As well as making some brilliant Montlouis and, more recently, Vouvray bottlings at Taille aux Loups, Jacky Blot now owns this fine 14-ha Bourgueil property from which he is producing some of the best reds of the AC. Wines are 100% Cabernet Franc with a firm, elegant leafiness. (DM)

● **Bourgueil** Le Pied de la Butte★ £B   Perrieres★★ £C   Le Haut de la Butte★★★ £C   Mi-Pente★★★★ £D

ALAIN CAILBOURDIN   Pouilly-Fumé   *UK stockists:* THt

16 ha Pouilly Fumé domaine producing tight, minerally whites. The vineyards are up to 65 years old and planted in limestone and flint soils. The Cuvée de Boisfleury is light and floral; Les Cris is fuller and more structured; Les Cornets is the sturdiest. All will evolve well over five years or more.

O **Pouilly Fumé** Les Cris★★★ £C   Cuvée de Boisfleury★★★ £C
O **Pouilly Fumé** Les Cornets★★★ £C

LAURENT CHATENAY   Montlouis   www.laurentchatenay.com

Very old vines (40 to 80 years) are behind some of the finest Mountlouis. Les Maisonnettes is tight, steely dry style; La Vallée is demi-sec but the piercing fruit and high acidity mask the sweetness. 2001 and 02 yielded a moelleux La Vallée aux Prêtres; liquoreux Clos Michet was made in 01 and 03. (DM)

O **Montlouis** Les Maisonnettes★★ £B   La Vallée★★★ £B

JEAN-CLAUDE CHATELAIN   Pouilly-Fumé   *UK stockists:* CTy,Wai

20 ha domaine and small-scale *négociant* with sound Sancerre and Pouilly. Les Charmes is richer and 10 per cent barrel-fermented; old-vines *cuvée* Prestige is tight and structured and very classy. (DM)

O **Pouilly Fumé**★★ £B   Les Charmes★★★ £C   Préstige★★★★ £D
O **Sancerre**★★ £B

CH. DE COULAINE   Chinon

The Bonnaventure family have 14ha, just 0.5ha of which is Chenin Blanc for white Chinon. They also have a few parcels in Bourgueil from which they produce a single *cuvée* Bonnaventure which, like the Chinon reds, is marked by its elegant, stylish fruit and well-defined supple tannic structure. (DM)

● **Chinon** Clos de Turpenay★★★ £C   La Diablesse★★★ £D   Les Picasses★★★ £D
● **Chinon**★★ £C   Bonnaventure★★★ £C   ● **Bourgueil** Bonnaventure★★★ £C

CH. DE FESLES   Bonnezeaux   www.vgas.com   *UK stockists:*Bsh, BBR, WTs

Owned by Bordeaux proprietor Bernard Germain. The Bonnezeaux is once more truly great. One other property also acquired by Germain, the Château de la Roulerie, is also turning out impressive Coteaux du Layon and some classy reds from Anjou. (DM)

Château de Fesles
● **Anjou** VV★★ £B   ● **Anjou-Villages**★★★ £C   O **Bonnezeaux**★★★★★ £F

Château de la Roulerie
● Anjou★ £B   ○ Coteaux du Layon Chaume Aunis★★★★ £E

CH. DE FOSSE-SÈCHE   Saumur   www.châteaudefosseseche.com
Reds and whites of impressive depth come from 30–50-year-old vines picked as ripe as possible. Tris de La Chapelle
is sourced from very late-harvested fruit, often picked as late as November, and is vinified in small oak, a proportion
of which is new. The top red, the Réserve de Pigeonnier, is one of the best examples in the region. The wines are
bottled unfined and unfiltered. (DM)
● Saumur★★ £B La Clef de Voûte★★★ £D Réserve de Pigeonnier★★★ £E
○ Saumur★★★ £C Les Tris de La Chapelle★★★★ £D

CH. DU HUREAU   Saumur-Champigny   www.domaine-hureau.fr   *UK stockists:* **GWW**
Good Saumur Blanc and sumptuous and supple Saumur-Champigny. 21 ha
planted in tufa/limestone soils, particularly suitable for producing first-rate Cab Franc. Sourced from old vines,
Cuvée des Fevettes gets new wood treatment, whereas the Lisgathe is aged in old barrels. Approachable but
ageworthy wines. (DM)
● Saumur-Champigny Grande Cuvée★★ £B Fevettes★★★ £C Lisgathe★★★★£C
○ Saumur★★★£B

CH. PIERRE-BISE   Coteaux du Layon   *UK stockists:* L&S
Claude Papin has 53 ha of vines spread across the Anjou-Villages, Coteaux du Layon and Savennières ACs. The
wines are well-crafted and offer great value for money. The reds are aged in a small proportion of new oak. The
Coteaux du Layon *cuvées* are full of peach, honey and nutmeg; the Quarts de Chaume is richer still, with
formidable depth. (DM)
● Anjou-Villages Sur Spilite★★★ £B   ○ Anjou Haut de la Garde★★ £B
○ Coteaux du Layon Rouannières★★★★£D   ○ Quarts de Chaume★★★★★ £F

CH. LA VARIERE   Anjou   *UK stockists:* L&S, Wai
Good-quality Anjou, both red and white, is made at this 90-ha property. The really striking wines are the late-
harvest whites which are some of the best of the region, particularly in great vintages like 2003. (DM)
● Anjou-Villages Brissac La Grande Chevalerie★★★ £C   ○ Anjou Clos Division★★ £B
○ Bonnezeaux Melleresses★★★★£E   ○ Quarts de Chaume Les Querches★★★★★ £F

CH. DE VILLENEUVE   Saumur-Champigny   *UK stockists:* THt
Organic property producing excellent reds and whites. The white Cormiers is subtly oaked and barrel-fermented
with a period on lees. The reds are concentrated, dark and spicy examples of the very best Loire Cab Franc. All
will improve in bottle. (DM)
● Saumur-Champigny★★ £B Vieille Vignes★★★ £C
○ Saumur★★★ £B Cormiers★★★ £C

DOM. FRANÇOIS CHIDAINE   Montlouis
During recent vintages this domaine has emerged as one of the very finest in the AC, producing wines of real class
and finesse. There are currently 20ha in Montlouis and a further 10ha in Vouvray. An extensive range includes a
number of single-plot wines as well as *cuvées* at different sweetness levels and in 2003 exceptional wines were made
across the board. (DM)
○ Montlouis Les Tuffeaux★★★★ £C Moelleux★★★★ £C Le Lys★★★★★ £F
○ Montlouis Clos des Breuil★★★ £B Clos Habert★★★ £C
○ Vovray Argiles★★ £B Clos Baudoin★★★ £B Moelleux★★★ £C Le Bouchet★★★★ £C

CLOS DE LA COULÉE DE SERRANT   Savennières   *UK stockists:* Yap
Outspoken proponent of biodynamic farming, producing some of the finest expressions of dry Chenin in the
world. The supremely structured and refined Coulée de Serrant is loaded with subtle citrus, mineral and flint,
very ageworthy. When vintage conditions allow, there is a small amount of Moelleux. (DM)
○ Savennières★★★ £D   ○ Savennières Coulée de Serrant❋❋❋❋❋ £F
○ Savennières Roches aux Moines Clos de la Bergerie★★★★ £E

DOM. DU CLOS NAUDIN   Vouvray   *UK stockists:* Gau, SVS
Marvellous producer of the some of the greatest Vouvrays made in recent decades. *Sec* and *demi-sec* are tight,
New entries have producer's name underlined

very minerally and superbly structured. Very good sparkling Méthode Traditionelle Réserve and very occasional great sweet wines. (DM)
O **Vouvray** Sec★★★ £B Demi-Sec★★★ £B Méthode Traditionelle Réserve★★★ £C

CLOS ROUGEARD Saumur-Champigny *UK stockists:* HHB
Classic Cab Franc reds and a very scarce Saumur Blanc Brezé. The two top *cuvées*, Bourg and Poyeux, are equally velvety in texture but with greater depth and power than the regular label. (DM)
● **Saumur-Champigny**★★★ £B Bourg★★★★ £C Poyeux★★★★ £C

DOM. DU CLOSEL Savennières www.savennieres-closel.com *UK stockists:* Yap, BBR
Producer of impressive, rich, and mineral-laden Savennières. Top wine Clos du Papillon is very impressive indeed; intense and minerally but with a remarkable depth of citrus and rich honeyed aromas emerging with age. All are cellarworthy, particularly the Clos du Papillon. (DM)
● **Savennières** Les Vaults★★ £B Caillardières★★★ £C Clos du Papillon★★★★ £C

PASCAL COTAT Sancerre *UK stockists:* Bal, Gau, Rae, SVS
These are among the very finest Sancerres. Superb naturally low-yielding sites and neither fining nor filtration are keys. Rich, explosive Sauvignon Blancs which need at least a year or two to show at their best. Remarkable Cuvée Spéciale produced in the greatest years for both wines. (DM)
O **Sancerre** Grande Côte★★★★ £C Monts Damnés★★★★ £D

DOM. DE LA COTELLERIE Saint-Nicolas-de-Bourgueil
This fine Saint-Nicolas property now has 25ha of vineyards producing an impressive small range of reds. Le Vau Jaumier is aged in used oak. The L'Envol is rich, full and very intense and offers real grip and structure. (DM)
● **Saint-Nicolas-de-Bourgueil** Cuvée Domaine★★★ £C L'Envol★★★ £C
● **Saint-Nicolas-de-Bourgueil** Les Perruches★★ £B Le Vau Jaumier★★★ £C

LUCIEN CROCHET Sancerre lcrochet@terres-net.fr *UK stockists:* BSh, EoR
Producer and *négociant*. Inevitably the best wines here are from their own vineyards. As well as the white Sancerre, the reds are also noteworthy. Cuvée Prestige white and red are both old-vine bottlings. The white Le Chêne Marchand is lighter but very intense. (DM)
O **Sancerre** Le Chêne Marchand★★★ £C Cuvée Prestige★★★ £D
● **Sancerre** Le Croix du Roy★★ £C Cuvée Prestige★★★ £D

DIDIER DAGUENEAU Pouilly-Fumé silex@wanadoo.fr *UK stockists:* HHB, Tan, BBR
The finest producer of complex, ageworthy Sauvignon Blanc in Pouilly Fumé. Buisson Renard, Pur-Sang and the magnificent Silex are all barrel-fermented. Superbly structured, wines that demand cellaring for half a dozen years or more. (DM)
O **Pouilly-Fumé** En Chailloux★★★★ £E Buisson Renard★★★★★ £E
O **Pouilly-Fumé** Pur-Sang★★★★★ £E Silex❂❂❂❂ £F

PHILIPPE DELESVAUX Coteaux du Layon *UK stockists:* Gau
Top Coteaux du Layon grower. Anjou reds are deeper and better structured than most. Anjou Blanc is barrel-fermented as are the richly textured sweet Layons. In exceptional vintages two remarkable special *cuvées*, Anthologie and Carbonifera, are produced, both comfortably five-star wines. (DM)
● **Anjou**★★ £B ● **Anjou-Villages**★★ £B O **Anjou** Feuille d'Or★★★ £B
O **Coteaux du Layon** Clos de la Guiberderie★★★★ £D Grains Nobles★★★★ £E

PIERRE-JACQUES DRUET Bourgueil *UK stockists:* J&B, Bal, HHB, ABy, Har
Brilliant source of top Cab Franc. There are three *cuvées* of Bourgueil as well as the marvellously elegant and pure Chinon Clos de Danzay, aged in *demi-muids*. The top red, Vaumoreau, comes from nearly 100-year-old vines – an unfiltered, dense, very powerful and concentrated red, full of ripe intense cassis and cedar. (DM)
● **Bourgueil** Cent Boiselées★★ £B Grand Mont★★★ £C Vaumoreau★★★★ £E
● **Chinon** Clos de Danzay★★★ £C

DOM. DES FORGES Coteaux du Layon *UK stockists:* FMV, Tan, SVS, BBR, Wai
Underrated property with a wide range of Anjou wines. Best of all are the impressive sweet Coteaux du Layon and Quarts de Chaume. The top wines are the Quarts de Chaume and Coteaux du Layon-Chaume. There is

FRANCE

also a good, well-crafted Savennières which is tight and flinty. (DM)

○ **Coteaux du Layon**★★ £C ○ **Coteaux du Layon-Saint-Aubin**★★★ £C
○ **Coteaux du Layon-Chaume**★★★★ £D Les Onnis★★★★ £E

JOËL GIGOU/DOM. DE LA CHARRIÈRE Jasnières *UK stockists:* Yap

Very structured wines with a piercing minerality. The Clos Saint-Jacques takes on a rich citrus and honeyed character with age. The SGN is far removed from a Bonnezeaux or a Quarts de Chaume. Tightly structured, lightly honeyed but very long and intense, it is extraordinarily long-lived. (DM)

○ **Jasnières** Cuvée Trois Clos★★ £B Clos Saint-Jacques Vieilles-Vignes★★★ £C
○ **Jasnières** Sélection de Grains Nobles★★★★ £D

VIGNOBLES GITTON Sancerre www.gitton.fr *UK stockists:* Wai

Pascal Gitton's family-owned domaine covers some 27ha with vineyard parcels spread across various sites. All the wines are from separate vineyards and display the characteristics of their individual *terroirs*. The top wines here should develop very well in bottle for 4 or 5 years. (DM)

○ **Sancerre** Galinot★★★ £D Vigne du Larrey★★★ £D Herses d'Or★★★ £C
○ **Sancerre** Les Romains★★ £B Les Belles Dames★★ £B L'Amiral★★ £C Herses★★ £C
○ **Sancerre** Les Montachins★★ £B ○ **Pouilly Fume** Clos Joanne d'Orion★★ £D

DOM. GUIBERTEAU Saumur *UK stockists:* **Sav**

Impressive new Saumur property with 8.5 ha. Low-yielding organic vineyards produce top-quality fruit. Good regular red Saumur; Motelles and especially Arboises both have an extra dimension. Whites are barrel-fermented,Le Clos is a *cru*. (DM)

● **Saumur**★★ £B Motelles★★★ £C Les Arboises★★★ £D
○ **Saumur**★★ £B Le Clos★★★ £C

HUET L'ECHANSONNE Vouvray *UK stockists:* RsW,WSc,Sel,Har,Wai

Superb biodynamically farmed domaine which is the standard-bearer for all Vouvray. Fruit comes from three sites; Clos du Bourg, Haut-Lieu and Le Mont. The wines are made as *sec, demi-sec* and when conditions allow *moelleux,* including the extraordinary Cuvée Constance. Dry wines are very backward when young but all evolve into complex, honeyed masterpieces with time. (DM)

○ **Vouvray** Clos du Bourg Sec★★★ £B Demi-Sec★★★ £C Moelleux★★★★★ £E
○ **Vouvray** Haut-Lieu Sec★★★ £B Demi-Sec★★★★ £C Moelleux★★★★★ £E
○ **Vouvray** Le Mont Sec★★★ £B Demi-Sec★★★ £C Moelleux★★★★★ £E

DOM. CHARLES JOGUET Chinon *UK stockists:* FMV,SVS,OWL,BBR,Wai

Among the great names for Loire reds. Seven to eight different *cuvées* are made each year based on both vine age and soil type. The are marked by their traditional style. Even the lesser *cuvées* can seem angular and awkward when young. Chenin was planted in the early to mid-1990s and now makes a Touraine white Clos de la Plante Martin. (DM)

● **Chinon** Clos du Chêne Vert★★★ £C Clos de la Dioterie★★★ £C
● **Chinon** Terroir★★ £B Clos de la Cure★★ £B Varennes du Grand Clos★★★ £C

DOM. DE JUCHEPIE Coteaux du Layon www.juchepie.com

Eddy Oosterlinck is making some increasingly good dry and late-harvested whites. The vineyard faces south to south-west and the oldest vines are close to 100 years. The sweet Layons are harvested in 6–8 tries and yields are low at 30 hl/ha for the dry Anjou and just 10hl/ha for the Layons. (DM)

○ **Coteaux du Layon** Les Quarts de Juchepie★★★ £D La Quintessence de Juchepie★★★★ £E
○ **Anjou** Le Sec de Juchepie★★ £B

LA TOUR SAINT MARTIN Menetou-Salon

Fast emerging as one of the very leading lights in Menetou-Salon. The wines are modern, stylish, vibrant and essentially fruit-driven. Honorine is aged on fine lees with *bâttonage* and offers greater depth and intensity than the Morogues. (DM)

● **Menetou-Salon** Morogues★★ £B Celestin★★ £C
○ **Menetou-Salon** Morogues★★ £B Honorine★★★ £C

84

DOM. FRÉDÉRIC MABILEAU Saint-Nicolas-de-Bourgueil *UK stockists:* Cam
9 ha domaine with three structured, well-crafted Saint-Nicolas-de-Bourgueil reds as well as a softly fruity Cab Sauv
Anjou made from younger vines and a Bourgueil, Les Racines. Wines of elegance and finesse rather than weight.
The brilliant, piercingly intense top wine, Éclipse, is aged with malolactic in barrel. All are ageworthy. (DM)
● **Saint-Nicolas-de-Bourgueil** Les Coutures★★★ £C Éclipse★★★★ £C
● **Saint-Nicolas-de-Bourgueil** Rouillères★★ £B

DOM. HENRI MARIONNET Touraine
Substantial operation long regarded as a benchmark for Touraine AC wines, although now rivalled by some smaller
domaines. The key varieties are Gamay and Sauvignon and there is also a little Cot, Chenin Blanc and Romorantin.
Vinifera bottlings come from ungrafted vines. (DM)
● **Touraine** Gamay★ £C I ère Vendange★★ £B Gamay Cépages Oubliés★★ £B
● **Touraine** Gamay Vinifera★★ £B Cot Vinifera★★★ £C
○ **Touraine** Sauvignon★ £B Sauvignon Vinifera★★★ £C

ALEX MATHUR/DOM. LEVASSEUR Montlouis
This excellent 10-ha domaine makes a small range of Montlouis as well as a little Touraine Sauvignon, Cabernet and some
Crémant de Loire. The Montlouis Chenins really stand out and represent extraordinarily good value for money. (DM)
○ **Montlouis** Rive Gauche★★★★ £D Dionysus★★★★ £B Lumen★★★ £B Les Perruches★★ £C
○ **Touraine** Cuvée des Pruides★★★★ £D

ALPHONSE MELLOT Sancerre mellot@sifiedi.fr *UK stockists:* **Hal**, GVF
Négociant and better domaine wines produced. Top *cuvées*, white Edmond and Génération XIX, made from
very old vines and vinified in oak, are wines of real dimension. Pinot Noir is increasingly impressive, particularly
the subtly oaked Génération XIX. (DM)
○ **Sancerre** La Moussière★★★ £C Edmond★★★★ £E Génération XIX★★★★ £E
● **Sancerre** Génération XIX★★★★ £F

MOLLET-MAUDRY Sancerre *UK stockists:* **WTs**
Regular Sancerre and Pouilly-Fumé are good, rather than spectacular. A clear level up are the Pouilly-Fumé Les
Sables and Sancerre Roc de l'Abbaye from older vines. L'Antique is the top label, the Pouilly-Fumé is fuller and more
opulent in style than the tighter, more intense and minerally Sancerre. (DM)
○ **Sancerre**★★ £C Roc de l'Abbaye★★★ £C Futs de Chene★★★ £D L'Antique★★★ £D
○ **Pouilly Fume**★★ £C Les Sables★★ £C L'Antique★★★ £D

DOM. RENÉ MOSSE Anjou www.domaine-mosse.com
A good red Anjou, aged in oak for 12 months with malolactic in barrel, is joined by Anjou dry whites which are
vinified and aged in oak for a year. The top wine is the Coteaux du Layon Bonnes Blanches, made in the best
vintages and strikingly impressive in 2003. (DM)
● **Anjou** Le Gros★★ £C ○ **Anjou**★★ £C Les Bonnes Blanches★★★ £C Rouchefer★★★ £C
○ **Coteaux du Layon-Saint-Lambert** Les Bonnes Blanches★★★★ £E

HENRY PELLÉ Menetou-Salon www.henry-pelle.com *UK stockists:* PBW,HHB,GVF,Sel,Wai
Leading estate, now run organically. Menetou-Salon and Sancerre white and red come from a mix of estate and
bought-in grapes. Clos de Ratier is from a single parcel as is Clos des Blanchais, also from the domaine's oldest
vines. Reds can be insubstantial. (DM)
○ **Menetou-Salon** Clos de Ratier★★ £B Clos des Blanchais★★★ £C
○ **Sancerre** La Croix au Garde★★ £C ○ **Menetou-Salon** Morogues★★ £B

VINCENT PINARD Sancerre *UK stockists:* GWW, HHB, Han
Model Sancerre domaine. Regular red is good and fruity, Charlouise is denser, richer. Of the whites the two top
whites are fuller and more complex and vinified in wood. Harmonie needs time. (DM)
● **Sancerre**★★ £C Charlouise★★★ £D
○ **Sancerre** Cuvée Florés★★£D Nuance★★★ £C Harmonie★★★ £D

DOM. JO PITHON Coteaux du Layon *UK stockists:*BBR
Jo, like his bother Olivier Pithon in the Côtes du Roussillon, makes wine without compromise and with a dedication
solely to high quality. Very good dry barrel-fermented Anjou whites and now Savennières are very striking. Both the

FRANCE

Coteaux du Layon and the Quarts de Chaume come from 100% botrytised fruit and see plenty of new oak. (DM)
O **Anjou** Pépinières★★★ £C Bergères★★★ £C Bonnes Blanches★★★★ £D
O **Savennieres** La Croix Picot★★ £C O **Quarts de Chaume** Les Varennes★★★★ £F
O **Coteaux du Layon** 4 Villages★★★★ £E O **Coteaux du Layon-Saint-Lambert** Bonnes Blanches★★★★ £E

DOM. DES ROCHES NEUVES Saumur-Champigny www.rochesneuves.com
Opulent, powerful, ripely extracted oaky reds from Cab Franc. Also very good
barrel-fermented, citrusy white Saumur. Marginale is marked by new oak in its youth and needs time. (DM)
● **Saumur-Champigny**★★ £B Terres Chaudes★★★ £C Marginale★★★ £C
O **Saumur** Insolite★★★ £C

DOM. SAINT NICOLAS Fiefs Vendéens www.domaine-saint-nocolas..com
This biodynamically run property is a real benchmark for this unheralded region on the Atlantic coast south of
Nantes. Chenin, Le Haut de Clous and Soleil de Chine are 100% Chenin. Cuvée Jacques is Pinot Noir while the
fascinating Le Poiré is produced solely from a small holding of Negrette. (DM)
● **Fiefs Vendeens** Reflets★★ £B Cuvée Jacques★★★ £D Le Poiré★★★ £D
O **Fiefs Vendeens** Les Clous★★ £B Le Haut des Clous★★★ £D
O **Cuvée Soleil de Chine** Vin de Table★★★ £D ◉ **Fiefs Vendeens** Reflets★ £B

DOM. DE LA SANSONNIÈRE Anjou UK stockists: Har
7 ha farmed biodynamically. Very fine complex examples of Anjou AC. Tiny amounts (from less than a hectare)
of Bonnezeaux are released as Les Blanderies and Le Coteau du Houet. The largest volume is the Anjou La Lune.
Les Fouchardes and Les Vieilles Vignes des Blanderies are produced in tiny quantities. The range is completed by
a Cab Sauv, Les Gelinettes, and a Rosé d'Anjou, Coteau du Houet. (DM)
O **Anjou** La Lune★★★★ £E

SILICES DE QUINCY Quincy UK stockists: Gau,Har,THT
This is the benchmark for the AC; biodynamically farmed, with very old vines. The top wine will develop
surprisingly well over at least four or five years. Second label is Silicette. (DM)
O **Quincy**★★★ £C

YVES SOULEZ/CH. DE LA GENAISERIE Coteaux du Layon UK stockists: GVF
Stylish and refined Coteaux du Layon-Chaume in a more restrained style than most. Les Tetuères is the fullest
and most obviously honeyed of the three and generally has more marked botrytis character. Also good Anjou
reds from Gamay and Cab Franc and a fruity, fresh, medium-sweet Cabernet d'Anjou. (DM)
● **Anjou**★ £B O **Coteaux du Layon**★★★ £C Les Simonelles★★★★ £D
O **Coteaux du Layon** La Roche★★★★ £D Les Tetuères★★★★ £D

TAILLE AUX LOUPS Montlouis UK stockists: FMV
A varying range of *sec, demi-sec* and sweet wines. The Montlouis Remus *sec* is barrel-fermented. *Moelleux*
Cuvée des Loups and particularly Montlouis Cuvée Romulus can be explosively rich. Vouvray is now
produced from Clos de Venise as well as some fine bottlings of Bourgueil. (DM)
O **Montlouis** Brut Tradition★★ £B Pétillant★★ £B Sec★★ £B Demi-Sec★★★ £C
O **Montlouis** Moelleux★★★ £D Cuvée des Loups★★★★ £E O **Vouvray** Clos de Venise Sec★★★ £C

DOM. VACHERON Sancerre UK stockists: E&T, SsG, TWS
One of a handful of growers in Sancerre to make impressive red wines. Good rosé is also produced. The white
Sancerre has fine grass and mineral notes and the Romains impressive depth with nutty, oak-derived notes. Top
wines have the structure to develop well with five years' cellaring. (DM)
● **Sancerre**★★ £C Belle Dame★★★ £C O **Sancerre**★★ £C Romains★★★ £D

Other wineries of note
**Aubert La Chapelle (Jasnieres), Dom. Bourillon-Dorléans (Vouvray), D. Champalou (Vouvray), Ch. d'Epiré
(Savennières), Ch. de Tracy (Pouilly-Fumé), O. Delétang (Montlouis), Dom. de l'Ecu (Muscadet Sèvre-et-
Maine), R-N Legrand (Saumur-Champigny), Gérard Morin (Sancerre), Henry Natter (Sancerre), Dom.
Ogereau (Anjou), Dom des Ouches (Bourgueil)**

An in-depth profile of every producer can be found in Wine behind the label 2006

New entries have producer's name underlined

FRANCE

Côte du Jura AC reds and rosés are produced from Poulsard, Trousseau and Pinot Noir. Among the whites, Chardonnay is good better are the Savagnin-based wines. Speciality of the region is *vin jaune* which can also be found at Arbois, Château Chalon and L'Étoile. The rare *vin de paille* is a late-harvested sweet white with a hint of nutty oxidation. Sparkling wine is made by the traditional method and labelled Crémant de Jura. The high alpine Savoie vineyard area is located just to the south-west of Geneva. The regional AC is Vin de Savoie.

Jura & Savoie Vintages
In general most red and white from Jura and Savoie should be drunk young. However, in the Jura, *vin jaune* is remarkably long-lived; it is typically released with 10 years age. Other Savagnin-based white also develops well for a decade or so.

Wizard's Wishlist

A dozen good value reds and whites
DOM. PAUL BENOIT ● Arbois-Pupillin Ploussard
DOM. BERTHET-BONDET O Côtes du Jura Alliance
CH. D'ARLAY O Côtes du Jura Chardonnay a la Reine
DOM. GANEVAT O Côtes du Jura Cuvée Florine Ganevat
DOM. ROLET O Arbois Chardonnay
ANDRE & MIREILLE TISSOT O Arbois Sélection
JACQUES TISSOT O Arbois Chardonnay
DOM. RIJCKAERT O Bandol Tradition

DOM. BELLUARD ● Vin de Savoie Mondeuse
ANDRÉ & MICHEL QUÉNARD O Roussette de Savoie
DOM. RAYMOND QUÉNARD
O Vin de Savoie Chignin-Bergeron Les Terrasses
DOM. J-P & J-F QUÉNARD O Vin de Savoie Chignin

A selection of classics from the Jura
DOM. BERTHET-BONDET O Château-Chalon
CH. D'ARLAY O Côtes du Jura Tradition
DOM. GANEVAT ● Côtes de Jura Julienne Ganevat
DOM. PAUL BENOIT ● Arbois-Pupillin La Loge
DOM. ROLET O Arbois Tradition
DOM. ROLET O Arbois Vin Jaune
ANDRE & MIREILLE TISSOT O Arbois Savagnin
ANDRE & MIREILLE TISSOT O Spirale Von de Pays
JACQUES TISSOT O Arbois Savagnin
JACQUES PUFFENEY O Arbois Chardonnay

Some of the best of Savoie
DOM. BELLUARD O Vin de Savoie Gringet
G & G BOUVET ● Vin de Savoie Amariva
BRUNO LUPIN O Roussette de Savoie Frangy
MICHEL GRISARD O Roussette de Savoie
ANDRÉ & MICHEL QUÉNARD
O Vin de Savoie Chignin-Bergeron Les Terrasses
DOM. J-P & J-F QUÉNARD
● Vin de Savoie Mondeuse Cuvée Sélection de Terroir
DOM. RAYMOND QUÉNARD ● Vin de Savoie Mondeuse
DOM. LOUIS MAGNIN
● Vin de Savoie Mondeuse Vieilles Vignes

Jura

DOM. PAUL BENOIT Arbois-Pupillin www.paulbenoitetfils-pupillin.com
Among the very best of the small producers based in the sleepy little village of Pupillin to the south of Arbois. Paul Benoit has a number of very well-sited vineyard holdings in some of the best *terroirs* in the AC and makes a full range of reds and whites as well as some intriguing Macvin, both white and, more unusually, rosé. (DM)
● Arbois-Pupillin Ploussard★★ £B Pinot Noir★★ £C La Grande Chenevrière★★ £C
● Arbois Trousseau★★ £C O Arbois-Pupillin La Loge★★★ £E Vin de Paille★★★★ £E
O Arbois-Pupillin Chardonnay★★ £B Savagnin★★★ £C Vin Jaune★★★★ £E

DOM. BERTHET-BONDET Château-Chalon
Great traditional Jura Alliance is produced from Chardonnay, the more complex and structured salty, citrusy Tradition from a blend of Savagnin and Chardonnay. Château-Chalon, a *vin jaune*, has piercing acidity, lending the structure for very long ageing. All wines require three or four years. (DM)
O Côtes du Jura Alliance★★★ £B Tradition★★★★ £C O Ch.-Chalon★★★★ £E

DOM. GANEVAT Côtes du Jura UK stockists: CdP
Good white and red are made here. As well as a lightly citrusy and nutty Chardonnay there is a fine old-vine bottling and a dry Savagnin. Red Poulsard is light but exuberant; Trousseau is big, firm and structured; and Pinot Noir of subtle but piercing depth is found in the Cuvée Julien Ganevat. (DM)
● Côtes du Jura Poulsard Vieilles Vignes★★ £C Trousseau Sous La Roche★★★ £D
● Côtes du Jura Cuvée Julienne Ganevat★★★ £C O Côtes du Jura Cuvée Florine Ganevat★★ £C

FRANCE

DOM. ROLET Arbois   www.rolet-arbois.com   *UK stockists:* SVS
Sizeable producer for the region but also one of the very best in all styles, especiall *vin jaune* and *vin de paille,* which is rich and intense although not as sweet as some. Top red, Memorial, is a very impressive blend of Trousseau and Pinot Noir. Côtes du Jura and Arbois Tradition whites are both Chardonnay and Savagnin. (DM)

● **Arbois** Poulsard Vieilles Vignes★★ £B Pinot Noir★★ £C Trousseau★★★ £C Memorial★★★ £C
○ **Arbois** Chardonnay★★ £B ○ **Côtes du Jura** Chardonnay★★ £B ○ **Côtes du Jura** Chardonnay★★ £B
○ **Côtes du Jura**★★★ £C ○ **Arbois** Tradition★★★ £C Vin Jaune★★★★★ £E Vin de Paille★★★★★ £F

DOM. ANDRÉ & MIREILLE TISSOT Arbois   *UK stockists:* SVS
Some of the most outstanding wines in the region in a very pure, fruit-driven style quite unlike many of their neighbours. Extraordinary Spirale *vin de paille* is from fruit genuinely aged on straw mats. The 2002 achieved just 8% alcohol with 300 grams of residual sugar and as a result it is classified as *vin de pays.* (DM)

● **Arbois** Poulsard Vieilles Vignes★★ £B Trousseau★★★ £C ● **Côtes du Jura** Pinot Noir En Barberan★★★ £C
○ **Arbois** Chardonnay la Mailloche★★★ £C Chardonnay les Bruyeres★★★ £C
○ **Arbois** Chardonnay les Graviers★★★ £C
○ **Arbois** Sélection★★★ £B Savagnin★★★★ £C Vin Jaune★★★★ £E ○ **Spirale** Vin de Pays★★★★★ £B

DOM. JACQUES TISSOT Arbois
Jacques Tissot produces fine reds particularly the Grande Resrve bottlings, an elegant Pinot Noir and firmly structured Trousseau. Excellent Arbois whites include a traditional Savagnin and marvellously intense *vin jaune.*(DM)

● **Arbois** Trousseau Grande Reserve★★★ £C ● **Côtes du Jura** Pinot Noir Grande Reserve★★★ £C
● **Arbois-Pupillin** Poulsard La Ronde★★ £B ● **Arbois** Tradition★★ £B
○ **Arbois** Chardonnay★★ £B Naturé★★ £C Blanc-Typé★★★ £C Savagnin★★★ £C
○ **Côtes du Jura** Vin Jaune★★★★ £E ○ **Arbois** Vin Jaune★★★★ £E

Savoie

DOM. ANDRÉ & MICHEL QUÉNARD Vin de Savoie
Perhaps the best known of the various branches of the Quénards in Chignin with 21ha of vineyards. Whites are the main focus and a fine old-vine Chignin is also made. Among reds from the small holding of Gamay, Mondeuse and Pinot Noir the Chignin Mondeuse Vieilles Vignes is particularly striking. (DM)

● **Vin de Savoie** Mondeuse Vieilles Vignes★★★ £C ○ **Vin de Savoie** Chignin-Bergeron Les Terrasses★★★ £B
○ **Roussette de Savoie**★★ £B ○ **Vin de Savoie** Chignin★ £B

DOM. JEAN-PIERRE & JEAN-FRANÇOIS QUÉNARD Vin de Savoie
Good Mondeuse is the focus of the reds here. The Sélection de Terroir is a vineyard selection aged in used oak. Whites should be drunk young with the exception of the old-vine bottling, Tradition, which is aged in used small oak. (DM)

● **Vin de Savoie** Gamay★ £B Mondeuse★★★ £C Mondeuse Cuvée Séléction de Terroir★★★ £C
○ **Vin de Savoie** Chignin★★ £B Anne de la Biguerne★★ £B ○ **Vin de Savoie** Cepage Tradition★★★ £C
○ **Vin de Savoie** Chignin-Bergeron Les Demoiselles★★ £C

DOM. RAYMOND QUÉNARD Vin de Savoie
Raymond Quénard makes a small range of good to very good red and white from his 4ha in Chignin. Structured but sufficiently supple Mondeuse is impressively serious. Cépage Jacquère is from very old vines. The Chignin-Bergeron (100% Roussanne) is fuller and more opulent in style with a touch of oak. (DM)

● **Vin de Savoie** Gamay★ £B Mondeuse★★★ £C
○ **Vin de Savoie** Chignin Cepage Jacquere Vieilles Vignes★★★ £C
○ **Vin de Savoie** Chignin-Bergeron★★★ £C

Other wineries of note
G & G Bouvet (Vin de Savoie, Ch. d'Arlay (Côtes du Jura), Dom. Belluard (Vin de Savoie), Dom. Rijckaert (Côtes du Jura)

An in-depth profile of every producer can be found in Wine behind the label 2006

FRANCE

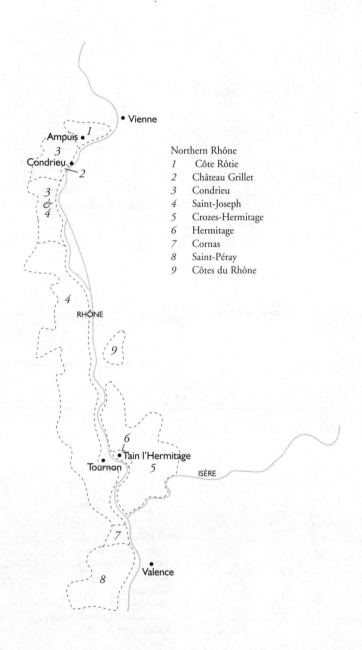

• Vienne

Ampuis •   *1*

3

Condrieu •

2

3
&
4

Northern Rhône
1   Côte Rôtie
2   Château Grillet
3   Condrieu
4   Saint-Joseph
5   Crozes-Hermitage
6   Hermitage
7   Cornas
8   Saint-Péray
9   Côtes du Rhône

4

RHÔNE

9

6

• Tain l'Hermitage
Tournon •   *5*
                    ISÈRE

7

8   • Valence

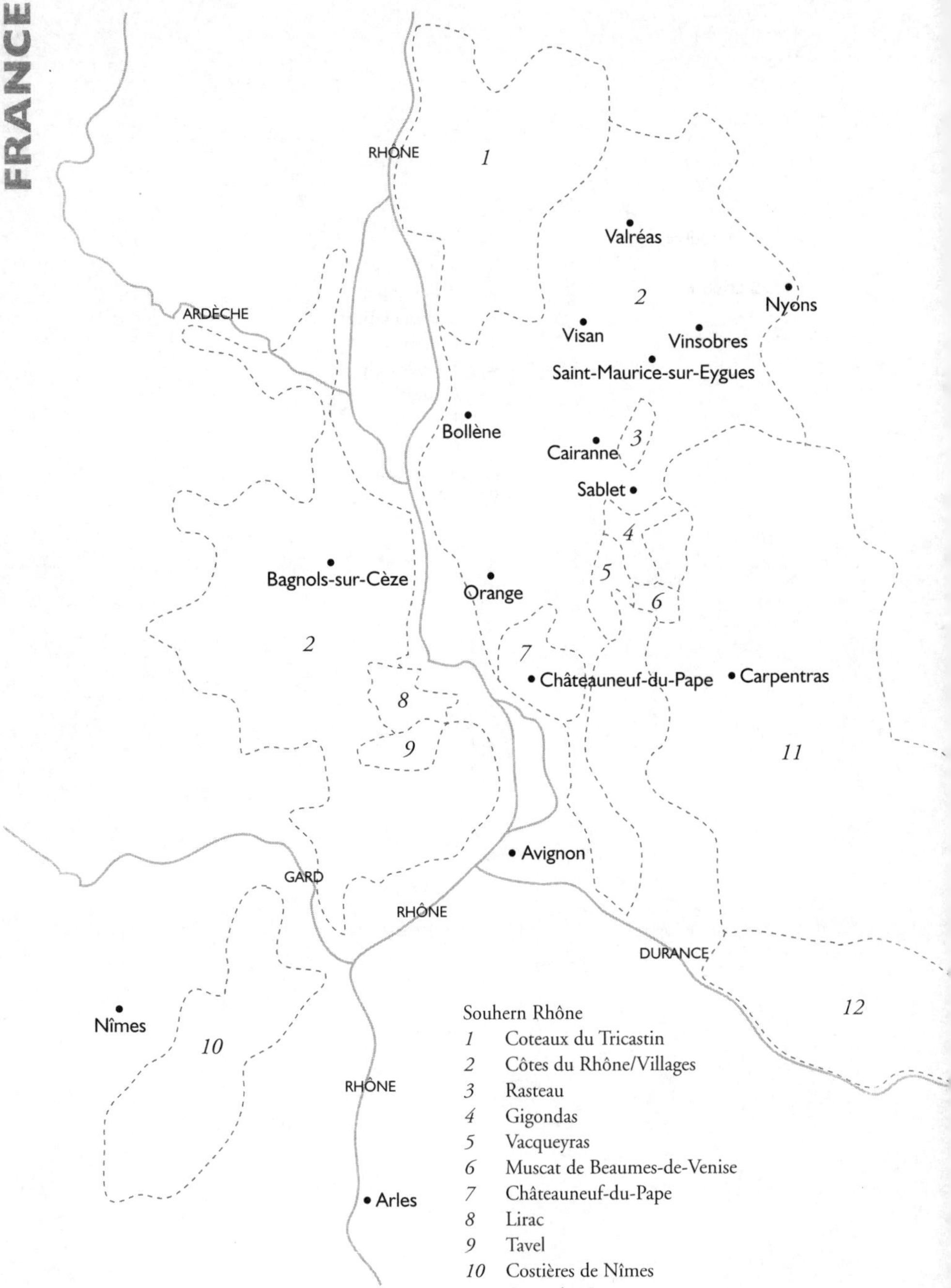

FRANCE

RHÔNE

1

Valréas

2

Nyons

Visan

Vinsobres

Saint-Maurice-sur-Eygues

ARDÈCHE

Bollène

Cairanne

3

Sablet

4

5

Bagnols-sur-Cèze

Orange

6

2

7

8

Châteauneuf-du-Pape

Carpentras

9

11

Avignon

GARD

RHÔNE

DURANCE

12

Nîmes

10

RHÔNE

Arles

Souhern Rhône

1   Coteaux du Tricastin
2   Côtes du Rhône/Villages
3   Rasteau
4   Gigondas
5   Vacqueyras
6   Muscat de Beaumes-de-Venise
7   Châteauneuf-du-Pape
8   Lirac
9   Tavel
10 Costières de Nîmes
11 Côtes du Ventoux
12 Côtes du Luberon

FRANCE

The Northern Rhône

Côte-Rôtie with vineyards planted on steep, precipitous terraces produces often sublime reds from Syrah and occasionally a little Viognier. **Condrieu** produces aromatic wines from Viognier. The most extensive AC in the north is **Saint-Joseph**. Reds are produced from Syrah, while the whites are a blend of Marsanne and Roussanne. The best wines come from the gravel-based soils close to the river. **Hermitage** produces exquisite red Syrah and long-lived whites based on Marsanne and Roussanne. Surrounding the hill of Hermitage is **Crozes-Hermitage**. The same grapes are used but the vineyard area is much larger. The better wines are made on isolated outcrops of granite. To the south **Cornas,** which borders southern Saint-Joseph, produces dense and muscular Syrah. Many of the Cornas growers also make the still and sparkling wines of **Saint-Péray**; the still having greater potential. They are blended from Marsanne and Roussanne.

The Southern Rhône

The most important quality AC is **Châteauneuf-du-Pape**.with some Grenache-based rich, heady, reds and floral and nutty whites. **Côtes du Rhône-Villages** and the separate ACs of **Gigondas** and **Vacqueyras**. also offer some very exciting reds with an increasing amount of Syrah planted. There are 16 villages which can append their names to the Côtes du Rhône-Villages AC. Among these are **Cairanne**, **Rasteau**, **Sablet** and **Beaumes-de-Venise** to the south and **Valréas**, **Vinsobres** and **Saint-Maurice** further north. A number of very good wines under both this AC and the humble **Côtes du Rhône** label are now being produced. **Muscat de Beaumes de Venise** is a floral, grapey fortified Muscat. **Rasteau** is a fortified red *vin doux naturel* produced from Grenache. **Tavel**. produces only rosé, **Lirac** produces some very good Grenache-based reds. Other lesser ACs include the **Côtes du Vivarais** and the **Coteaux du Tricastin**. To the south in the Vaucluse are the vineyards of the **Côtes du Ventoux**, and on the borders of Provence, is the **Côtes du Lubéron**. To the far east towards the Alps some good reds and whites are also emerging from the **Coteaux de Pierrevert**. Just to the west of the Rhône is the emerging region of the **Costières de Nîmes** producing Grenache-based reds with an increasing amount of Mourvèdre. Many of these properties also make rich, stylish blends of Cab Sauv and Syrah, generally labelled as **Vin de Pays du Gard**.

Rhône Valley Vintages

Top wines throughout the region will keep very well, 10 even 20 years in the best examples. The lesser wines from good recent years will last comfortably for five years or more.

2004: A much easier year for growers in both the north and south of the region. than 2003. The best reds look like they have good depth with deep colours and form and in the main well ripened tannins. Likely to be of a similar level to 2001 in the north and 1999 in the south.

2003: The super warm summer of may result in some superb wines from this vintage in the north. Potentially great in the south, some wines will be very alcoholic though and achieving balance with Grenache will be the key.

2002: After the previous four bountiful vintages this was a major disappointment. The wines are for early drinking, some growers sold in bulk rather than release under their own labels.

2001: Very good throughout the valley, if not quite hitting the heights of 1999 for the northern ACs or 2000 for the south. White Hermitage is very ageworthy.

2000: A generally very good year, particularly in the south with some very rich, profound and complex wines. Not quite the same quality in the north, but ageworthy wines were produced.

1999: Very good in the north, with well-structured, opulent wines being produced in all the major ACs. The south was good to very good but lacked the sheer quality of 1998 and 2000.

1998: The northern appellations fared well. In the south the vintage was spectacularly good. The wines are both ripe and exotic with great balance and structure.

1997: A moderate year in the south almost all should be drunk now. The north fared better. Saint-Joseph and Crozes-Hermitage are at their peak.

1996: Moderate year with the best results in the north. Some good wines were produced in a relatively austere style. The south produced soft, forward reds which should now be drunk.

1995: The best year since 1990 for reds with the exception of the magnificent 1991 Côte-Rôties. Whites were somewhat less impressive and will be surprisingly short-lived. All but the best white Hermitage should now be drunk.

1994: Neither north nor south produced wines with the density or structure of the 1995s. Many are drinking well now, lesser wines should be drunk up.

1991: This was a good to very good year in the northern Rhône and in Côte-Rôtie in particular. Some producers were more successful than others, particularly in Cornas and Hermitage. The south was disappointing and the wines should by now have been drunk.

1990: Superb year for great long-lived Hermitage. These will need more time to achieve their full potential. Côte-Rôtie did not quite match the superb 91s. and with Cornas are drinking well now. Excellent Châteauneuf-du-Pape red is also very fine now. **Earlier Years:** 1989 was good for reds throughout the region. 1998 produced classic Northern reds. 1985 was good in both north and south. 1983 produced some excellent long-lived Hermitage. Châteauneuf-du-Pape in 1981 is worth considering from very top producers. A few good 1979s from both north and south are still drinking well. 1978 was a truly great year in the north, with some very fine Châteauneuf too. Other very good earlier years for the north were 1971, 1970, 1969, 1966, 1964 and 1961.

Wizard's Wishlist

10 of the Northern Rhône's most distinguished reds

THIERRY ALLEMAND ● Cornas Reynard

M CHAPOUTIER ● Hermitage Le Pavillon

CH. D' AMPUIS ● Côte-Rôtie La Turque

JEAN-LOUIS CHAVE

● Hermitage Ermitage Cuvée Cathelin

AUGUSTE CLAPE ● Cornas

CLUSEL ROCH ● Côte-Rôtie Les Grandes Places

PAUL JABOULET AINÉ ● Hermitage La Chapelle

DOM. JAMET ● Côte-Rôtie

RENÉ ROSTAING ● Côte-Rôtie Côte Blonde

MARC SORREL ● Hermitage Le Gréal

A choice of opulent dry whites

M CHAPOUTIER ○ Hermitage Cuveé de l'Orée

JEAN-LOUIS CHAVE ○ Hermitage

DOM. DU CHENE ○ Condrieu

YVES CUILLERON ○ Condrieu Chaillets Vieilles Vignes

DOM. YVES GANGLOFF ○ Condrieu

DOM. DU MURINAIS

○ Crozes Hermitage Vieilles Vignes

ANDRÉ PERRET ○ Condrieu Coteaux du Chéry

GEORGES VERNAY ○ Condrieu Les Chaillées de L'Enfer

FRANÇOIS VILLARD ○ Saint-Joseph Côtes de Mairlant

ALAIN VOGE ○ Saint-Péray Cuvée Fleur du Crussol

A selection of up and coming reds and whites

ALBERT BELLE ● Crozes-Hermitage Cuvée Louis Belle

M CHAPOUTIER ● Saint-Joseph Les Granits

YANN CHAVE ● Crozes-Hermitage Tête de Cuvée

JEAN-LUC COLOMBO ○ Hermitage Le Louet

DOM. COMBIER ○ Crozes-Hermitage Clos des Grives

YVES CUILLERON ○ Saint-Joseph Le Lombard

DELAS FRÈRES ● Crozes-Hermitage Le Clos

PIERRE GAILLARD ○ Côtes du Rhône Viognier

DOM. MICHEL OGIER

● Vin de Pays des Collines Rhodaniennes La Rosine

DOM. DU TUNNEL ○ Saint-Peray Prestige

12 benchmark Châteauneuf-du-Papes

DOM. DE BEAURENARD

● Châteauneuf du Pape Boisrenard

M CHAPOUTIER ● Châteauneuf du Pape Barbe Rac

CH. DE BEAUCASTEL

● Châteauneuf du Pape Hommage à Jacques`Perrin

CH. LA NERTHE

● Châteauneuf du Pape Cuvée des Cadettes

CH. RAYAS ● Châteauneuf du Pape

CLOS DES CAILLOU ● Châteauneuf du Pape Réserve

CLOS DES PAPES ● Châteauneuf du Pape

DOM DE LA JANASSE

● Châteauneuf du Pape Vieilles Vignes

DOM. DE MARCOUX

● Châteauneuf du Pape Vieilles Vignes

DOM. DE LA MORDORÉE

● Châteauneuf du Pape Reine des Bois

DOM. DE LA VIEILLE-JULIENNE

● Châteauneuf du Pape Vieilles Vignes Réservé

DOM. DU VIEUX TÉLÉGRAPHE ● Châteauneuf du Pape

A diverse selection of emerging reds

DANIEL ET DENIS ALARY

● Côtes du Rhône-Villages Cairanne La Font d'Estevenas

DOM. BRUSSET ● Gigondas   Les Hauts de Montmirail

CLOS DES CAZAUX ● Vacqueyras Grénat Noble

CLOS PETITE BELLANE

● Côtes du Rhône Valréas Vieilles Vignes

DOM. DE DEURRE ● Côtes du Rhône Les Rabasses

GOURT DE MAUTENS

● Côtes du Rhône-Villages Rasteau

DOM. LA SOUMADE

● Côtes du Rhône-Villages Rasteau Fleur de Confiance

DOM. LES APHILLANTHES

● Côtes du Rhône-Villages Vieilles Vignes

DOM. DE L'ORATOIRE SAINT-MARTIN

● Côtes du Rhône-Villages Cairanne Haut Coustias

DOM. DE PIAUGIER

● Côtes du Rhône-Villages Sablet Réserve Alphonse Vautour

MARCEL RICHAUD

● Côtes du Rhône-Villages Cairanne Les Estrambords

DOM. SANTA-DUC ● Gigondas Les Hautes Garrigues

A selection of good value reds and whites

CH. SAINT-COSME ● Côtes du Rhône Les Deux Albions
DOM. CHAUME-ARNAUD
O Côtes du Rhône-Villages Vinsobres
CROS DE LA MÛRE ● Côtes du Rhône-Villages
DOM. DE FONDRÈCHE
● Côtes du Ventoux Cuvée Persia
FONT DE MICHELLE
O Côtes du Rhône F de Font de Michelle

DOM. LA GARRIGUE ● Vacqueyras
DOM. GRAMENON O Côtes du Rhône Vie on y est
DOM. GRAPILLON D'OR ● Gigondas
DOM. RABASSE-CHARAVIN
● Côtes du Rhône-Villages Cairanne Estevenas
DOM. DE RÉMÉJEANNE
● Côtes du Rhône Les Génevriers
SANG DES CAILLOUX ● Vacqueyras Classique
DOM. SAINTE-ANNE O Côtes du Rhône Viognier

Rhône Valley/A-Z of producers

Northern Rhône

THIERRY ALLEMAND Cornas   UK stockists:RsW,Sec,Rae
Small Cornas domaine with just over 3 ha. Vinification is traditional and the wines are impressive, concentrated and very elegant. Both are bottled unfiltered. Reynard, made from vines that are over 80 years old, is very ageworthy. (DM).
● Cornas Chaillot★★★★ £E Reynard★★★★★ £F

GILLES BARGE Côte-Rôtie   UK stockists: C&B,Bib,Tan,SVS,Rae,Sec
Very good if not top-flight Côte-Rôtie, which is still vinified with stems but the tannins are ripe and supple. Bottled unfiltered. Cuvée du Plessy is the lighter of the two *cuvées*. Both will age well. Enjoy his peachy Condrieu and spicy, berry-fruited Saint-Joseph young. (DM)
● Côte-Rôtie Cuvée du Plessy★★★ £E Côte Brune★★★★ £F

DOM. BONNEFOND Côte-Rôtie   UK stockists:Goe,GWWSVS,Odd,N&P,WAe
Very good Condrieu and modern, fleshy, lightly oaky Côte-Rôties. The regular Côte-Rôtie is a little light in comparison to Côte Rozier and Les Rochains, which is rich and firmly structured, needing five or six years' ageing. Condrieu is opulent, peachy and immediately accessible. (DM)
● Côte-Rôtie★★★ £E Côte Rozier★★★★ £E Les Rochains★★★★★ £F
O Condrieu★★★ £D

BERNARD BURGAUD Côte-Rôtie   UK stockists: J&B,BBR,Yap, SVS
Just one wine is produced here but it is among the better examples in the appellation. Sourced from different sites that are always vinified separately, it is concentrated and full of character and needs four to five years' ageing. (DM)
● Côte-Rôtie★★★★ £E

M CHAPOUTIER Hermitage www.chapoutier.com   UK stockists: Men,Tan, Sel,BBR,F&M,Wai, Las
One of the most important *négociants* in the northern Rhône. The gems here are the top *cuvées* from Hermitage, Côte-Rôtie, Saint-Joseph and Crozes-Hermitage. Lesser bottles are less impressive. Good Châteauneuf-du-Pape too. Interests now in the Midi and M Chapoutier Australia in South Australia. Top Hermitage wines are labelled with the traditional spelling, Ermitage. (DM)
● Hermitage Pavillon✪✪✪✪✪ £H ● Côte-Rôtie Mordorée✪✪✪✪✪ £H
O Hermitage de l'Orée✪✪✪✪✪ £H ● Crozes-Hermitage Varonniers★★★★ £E
● St-Joseph Les Granits★★★★ £E ● Châteauneuf-du-Pâpe Barbe Rac★★★★★ £G

CH. D'AMPUIS Côte-Rôtie www.guigal.com   UK stockists: JEF,BBR,C&B
The label for the top Guigal wines. The three top Côte-Rôties are benchmarks and sell for stratospheric prices. The vinification of each is quite unique but all are very oaky young. Standard Côte-Rôtie and Condrieu La Doriane are very good but not of the same order. Also now owns the domaine of Jean-Louis Grippat. The Vignes de l'Hospice red remains particularly striking. (DM)
● Côte-Rôtie Ch. d'Ampuis★★★★ £E Mouline✪✪✪✪✪ £H
● Côte-Rôtie La Landonne✪✪✪✪✪ £H La Turque✪✪✪✪✪ £H
O Condrieu La Doriane★★★★★ £F

93

FRANCE

DOM. YANN CHAVE Hermitage   *UK stockists:* **GrD**,HHB,L&W,SVS,Gau
Fine, improving small domaine with 16 ha of Syrah and a tiny amount of Marsanne and Roussanne producing increasingly impressive supple and structured red wines. Crozes-Hermitage Tête de Cuvée and Hermitage will improve in bottle for up to 10 years. (DM)
● **Hermitage**★★★★ £E ● **Crozes-Hermitage**★★ £B Tête de Cuvée★★★ £C
○ **Crozes-Hermitage**★★ £B Le Rouvre★★★ £C

JEAN-LOUIS CHAVE Hermitage   *UK stockists:* Yap,Adm,BBR,WSc,C&BTan,Sel,F&M, Las
Utterly splendid ancient domaine, perhaps the finest in the northern Rhône with plots in all seven *lieux-dits* on the Hermitage hill. The wines have marvellous complexity and finesse. Cuvée Cathelin is a special selection which sees more new wood. All will improve for many years. (DM)
● **Hermitage**✪✪✪✪✪ £F Ermitage Cuvée Cathelin✪✪✪✪✪ £H
○ **Hermitage**✪✪✪✪✪ £F ● **Saint-Joseph**★★★ £C

DOM. DU CHÊNE Côte-Rôtie   *UK stockists:* Rev,F&M
Good red and white Saint-Joseph, as well as a striking and intensely peachy, honeyed Condrieu. There is a much deeper special Cuvée Anais, best with three or four years' age. (DM)
○ **Condrieu**★★★★ £E ○ **Saint-Joseph**★★ £C
● **Saint-Joseph**★★ £C Cuvée Anais★★★ £D

DOM. LOUIS CHÈZE Condrieu   *UK stockists:***C&C**,N&P
Condrieu from mainly young vines but well-crafted with nicely integrated oak. The Coteau de Brèze in particular is very fine. The white Saint-Joseph emphasises Marsanne's broad, nutty character. Top reds are supple and structured. (DM)
○ **Condrieu**★★★ £D Coteau de Brèze★★★★ £E ○ **Saint-Joseph** Ro-Rée★★ £C
● **Saint-Joseph** Ro-Rée★★ £C Cuvée des Anges★★★ £C Caroline★★★ £C

AUGUSTE CLAPE Cornas   *UK stockists:***Yap**,Sel,F&M, Las
Fiercely traditional domaine: no new wood and destemming is rare but the wines are always supple and harmonious. Cuvée Renaissance is a second wine, made to help maintain the quality of the Cornas. Both the spicy Côtes du Rhône red and Saint-Péray offer good value. (DM)
● **Cornas**★★★★★ £D Cuvée Renaissance★★ £C ● **Côtes du Rhône**★★ £B
○ **Saint-Péray**★★ £B

CLUSEL ROCH Côte-Rôtie   *UK stockists:* L&S,VTr
Among the leading handful of small domaines in Côte-Rôtie making powerful and structured wines, particularly Les Grandes Places, made from 65- to 70-year-old vines. The Condrieu is good, with attractive peachy Viognier fruit, but lacks the intensity and depth of the reds. (DM)
● **Côte-Rôtie**★★★★ £D Les Grandes Places★★★★★ £F ○ **Condrieu**★★★ £D

DOM. DU COLOMBIER Hermitage   *UK stockists:* Bib, Gau, J&B,Tan,HHB,BBR, **Bal,SVS**
The Viale family own some very old vines on the Hermitage hill. The cool-fermented white Crozes-Hermitage is vinified with a touch of oak. The Crozes-Hermitage Cuvée Gaby and in particular the Hermitage are powerful, structured reds that benefit from five or six years' cellaring. (DM)
● **Crozes-Hermitage**★★★ £B Cuvée Gaby★★★ £C ● **Hermitage**★★★★ £D
○ **Crozes-Hermitage**★★ £B

JEAN-LUC COLOMBO Cornas   *UK stockists:* **L&W**, HHB,N&P
Domaine Jean-Luc Colombo produces wines from vineyards in and around Cornas and Saint-Péray, whereas the Jean-Luc Colombo label applies to an extensive range of *négociant* wines from the Rhône and Provence. There are also two domaines in the Midi. Domaine de Salente in the Languedoc, and Domaine de Saint-Luc in the Roussillon. The *négociant* wines range from ordinary to very good. Top Cornas *cuvées* Les Ruchets and La Louvée, aged in new oak, are very impressive. (DM)
Domaine Jean-Luc Colombo
● **Cornas** Terres Brûlées★★★ £E Les Ruchets★★★★ £F La Louvée★★★★★ £F
Jean-Luc Colombo

94

FRANCE

● **Hermitage** Le Louet★★★ £E   ○ **Hermitage** Le Louet★★★ £E
○ **Condrieu**★★★ £E   ● **Châteauneuf-du-Pape** Les Bartavelles★★★★ £D

DOM. COMBIER   Crozes-Hermitage   *UK stockists:* **Eno**
Good regular red and white Crozes-Hermitage; Clos des Grives are a solid step up. The red is dense and muscular, aged in new oak and requires a little patience. Both whites are mainly Roussanne, barrel-fermented and kept on their lees with *bâtonnage*. (DM)
● **Crozes-Hermitage**★★ £B   Clos des Grives★★★ £C   ● **Saint-Joseph**★★ £C
○ **Crozes-Hermitage**★★ £B   Clos des Grives★★★ £C

DOM. DE COULET   Cornas   *UK stockists:* J&B
Newly emerging 4.5-ha biodynamic domaine with 2 wines. Les Belles des Serre is the softer and more accessible; Les Belles Nom deeper and more structured, a wine of tremendous potential from higher-altitude vineyards and 70–90-year-old vines. (DM)
● **Cornas** Les Belles des Serre★★★★ £E   Les Belles Nom★★★★ £E

DOM. COURBIS   Saint-Joseph   *UK stockists:* Ege,HHB,SVS
Saint-Joseph from young vines is quite light; Cornas is of a different order. Les Eygats and La Sabarotte are wines of dense, muscular power,the latter from old vines, that will improve for up to a decade. (DM)
● **Saint-Joseph**★★ £B   Domaine Les Royes★★★ £C   ○ **Saint-Joseph**★★ £B
● **Cornas** Champelrose★★★ £C   Les Eygats★★★★ £E   La Sabarotte★★★★ £E

DOM. PIERRE COURSODON   Saint-Joseph   *UK stockists:* Win,WSc,BRW
Jérôme Coursodon has now taken over the winemaking and the results in the late 90s have been impressive, particularly with the top red *cuvées*, which are better balanced than of old. The very fine La Sensonne is produced in association with Patrick Lesec. (DM)
● **Saint-Joseph**★★ £B   L'Olivaie★★★ £C   La Sensonne★★★★ £D
○ **Saint-Joseph**★ £B   Le Paradis St-Pierre★★ £C

YVES CUILLERON   Condrieu   *UK stockists:* Eno,A&B,BBR,Swg,P&S,Las,But
New superstar of the northern Rhône. Exceptional range of barrel-fermented Condrieus. Fleur d'Automne is a distinctive botrytised sweet example. Also a small range of first-class Saint-Joseph. Cuilleron also works with François Villard and Pierre Gaillard at Les Vins de Vienne. (DM)
● **Côte-Rôtie** Terres Sombres★★★★★ £F   ● **Saint-Joseph** L'Amarybelle★★★ £C
○ **Condrieu** Les Ayguets❁❁❁❁❁ £F   Fleur d'Automne❁❁❁❁❁ £G
○ **Saint-Joseph** Le Lombard★★★★ £C   Lyseras★★★ £C

DELAS FRÈRES   Hermitage   *UK stockists:* **BWC**, BBR, Las
Emerged in the late 1990s as a top Rhône négociant after being purchased by Louis Roederer. The range is comprehensive and even the humbler wines are now well crafted. Top cuvées, both red and white, are densely textured and explosively rich and concentrated. (DM)
● **Côte-Rôtie** La Landonne★★★★★ £G   ● **Hermitage** Les Bessards❁❁❁❁❁ £H
● **Crozes-Hermitage** Le Clos★★★★ £E   ● **Saint-Joseph** Sainte-Épine★★★ £D

DOM. DE FAUTERIE   Cornas   *UK stockists:* FMV, BBR,Yap
Recently established Sylvain Bernard trained with Jean-Louis Chave and makes good traditional wines. Leased Cornas vines are around 100 years old, producing a wine with considerable depth, complexity and some power. Recent vintages are particularly impressive. (DM)
● **Cornas**★★★★ £D   ● **Saint-Joseph**★★★ £C   Les Combaud★★★ £C
○ **Saint-Péray** Les Hauts de Fauterie★★ £B

PIERRE GAILLARD   Saint-Joseph   *UK stockists:* HHB,Cav,J&B,L&S,Sel
Small but expanding domaine with scattered holdings in Saint-Joseph, Côte-Rôtie and Condrieu. The wines are modern and stylish and more will come as the vines age. New oak is not overdone in the best reds. Gaillard is also the inspiration and one of the partners at Les Vins de Vienne. (DM)
● **Côte-Rôtie**★★★ £D   Rose Pourpre★★★★ £E   ○ **Condrieu**★★★★ £E
● **Saint-Joseph** Clos du Cuminaille★★★★ £C   ○ **Saint-Joseph**★★★ £C

FRANCE

DOM. YVES GANGLOFF   Condrieu   *UK stockists:* **Rae**,FMV,F&M
Small 3.5 ha property producing rich, opulent Condrieu which unusually will age for four or five years. Of two Côte-Rôties, Barbarine from young vines, is blended with a little Viognier. The sturdier Sereine Noir is partly aged in new wood and needs cellaring. (DM)
● **Côte-Rôtie** Barbarine★★★★ £D   Sereine Noir★★★★★ £E
O **Condrieu**★★★★ £E

JEAN-MICHEL GERIN   Côte-Rôtie   *UK stockists:* **C&C**,IVV,Blx,Las
These are rich and modern Côte-Rôties and new oak is not used sparingly. La Landonne and Les Grandes Places, from 80-year-old vines, are very good indeed. These top *cuvées* need five years at a minimum and will keep much longer. (DM)
● **Côte-Rôtie** Champin Junior★★ £C   Champin Le Seigneur★★★ £E
● **Côte-Rôtie** Les Grandes Places★★★★★ £F   La Landonne★★★★★ £F

ALAIN GRAILLOT   Crozes-Hermitage   *UK stockists:* Yap, L&W,ABy,Sel
Probably the benchmark for red Crozes-Hermitage. Graillot has been the inspiration for an appellation that for too long represented mediocrity. White is vinified in wood and *inox* and kept on lees. The special *cuvée* La Guiraude is a very impressive barrel selection. (DM)
● **Crozes-Hermitage**★★★ £B   La Guiraude★★★★ £C   O **Crozes-Hermitage**★★ £B
● **Hermitage**★★★ £D   ● **Saint-Joseph**★★★ £C

DOM. BERNARD GRIPA   Saint-Joseph   *UK stockists:* VTR, Las, F&R
A real benchmark for characterful white Saint-Peray. Fine Saint-Joseph, both red and white, is also produced from a total of 12ha. Densely textured Les Figuières is the best wine here – long, persistent and ageworthy. (DM)
● **Saint-Joseph**★★ £C   Les Berceau★★★ £C   O **Saint-Joseph**★★ £C   Les Berceau★★★ £C
O **Saint-Peray**★★★ £B   Les Figuières★★★ £C

E GUIGAL   Côte-Rôtie   www.guigal.com   *UK stockists:* **JEF**,AAA
The E. Guigal label covers an extensive range produced from the length and breadth of the Rhône Valley. The vibrant red Côtes du Rhône, if not quite of the quality of a decade ago, remains a model of consistency. The Côte-Rôtie Brune et Blonde, which is sourced mainly from bought-in fruit, is good rather than great. More impressive is the Hermitage. The southern Rhône wines in general lack the quality and refinement of their northern counterparts. (DM)
● **Côte-Rôtie** Brune et Blonde★★★ £D   O **Condrieu**★★★ £D
● **Hermitage**★★★★ £D   O **Hermitage**★★★ £D   ● **Côtes du Rhône**★ £B

PAUL JABOULET AINÉ   Hermitage   *UK stockists:* **DAy**,Tan,BBR,WSc,F&M,Wai, Las
Large *négociant* operation with 100 ha of vineyards. Quality is variable but the best are impressive. Focal point of the range is the very ageworthy *cuvée* of red Hermitage, La Chapelle. Recent vintages have not been quite so good, although 2000 looks to be back on fine form. Other wines of note are the Thalabert, Domaine de Saint-Pierre Cornas and the Châteauneuf-du-Pape Les Cèdres. Top wines are ageworthy but lesser appellations should be approached young. (DM)
● **Hermitage** La Chapelle❂❂❂❂❂ £G   O **Hermitage** Sterimberg★★★★ £E
● **Crozes-Hermitage** Raymond Roure★★★ £C   Thalabert★★★ £C
● **Cornas** St Pierre★★★ £D   O **Muscat de Beaumes-de-Venise**★★★ £C

DOM. JAMET   Côte-Rôtie   *UK stockists:* **Bib**,C&B,IVV,Las
Brothers Jean-Luc and Jean-Paul Jamet own 6.5 ha of Syrah and a tiny amount of Viognier. They make a sumptuous, almost opulent unfiltered Côte-Rôtie which has marvellous balance and poise. (DM)
● **Côte-Rôtie**★★★★★ £E

DOM. JASMIN   Côte-Rôtie   *UK stockists:* Yap,F&M
Patrick Jasmin makes traditional and elegant Côte-Rôtie. He now destems which helps in lesser years, and the wine is aged for around two years in mainly old wood. Never blockbusters, the wines always have great purity of fruit and impressive intensity and depth. (DM)
● **Côte-Rôtie**★★★★ £E

96

New entries have producer's name underlined

DOM. DU MONTEILLET Condrieu   *UK stockists:* Cdp,Goe,GWW,Gau,SVS
7 ha in Condrieu, Côte-Rôtie and Saint-Joseph. Vinification is modern and plenty of new oak is used in the top *cuvées*. Condrieu will stand a little age. A late-harvest label, Tries Grains de Folie, is also produced when conditions permit. The red Cuvée Papy and Côte-Rôtie are wines of considerable dimension. (DM)
● **Côte-Rôtie** Fortis★★★★ £E   ● **Saint-Joseph** Fortior★★★ £C Papy★★★ £C
O **Condrieu**★★★★ £D Grands Chaillees★★★★★ £E   O **Saint-Joseph**★★ £C

DOM. NIERO-PINCHON Condrieu   *UK stockists:*FMV,SVS,PWa
Robert Niero has been in charge of this fine domaine since the 1980s. Les Ravines is part vinified in *inox* and part in old wood. The Coteau de Chéry, from old vines, is fuller and more opulent with greater weight and concentration. Côte-Rôtie is lighter than other examples but very elegant. (DM)
● **Côte-Rôtie**★★★★ £E
O **Condrieu** Les Ravines★★★ £E Coteau de Chéry★★★★ £E

DOM. MICHEL OGIER Côte-Rôtie   *UK stockists:* CTy, BBR,N&P,Las
Some exceptional modern Côte-Rôtie is made at this 3.5 ha property as well as very good *vin de pays* La Rosine. There are a number of pricey limited-release special bottlings, Belle Hélène, Les Embruns and Lancement. The wines are supple and velvety, with a real dimension to the fruit. (DM)
● **Côte-Rôtie** Embruns★★★★★ £F Belle Hélène✪✪✪✪ £H
● **Côte-Rôtie**★★★★ £E Lancement★★★★★ £F
● **Vin de Pays des Collines Rhodaniennes** La Rosine★★★ £C

DOM. ALAIN PARET Saint-Joseph
Structured Condrieu, particularly Lys de Volan, and very good Saint-Joseph red. Also red and white *vins de pays* and unusual late-harvest *vin de table*, Cuvée Marie-Josée (Syrah/Grenache/Viognier). Occasional late-harvest Sortilèges d'Automne. (DM)
● **Saint-Joseph** Domaine Bertrand★★ £C Larmes du Père★★★ £C 420 Nuits★★★ £D
O **Condrieu** Ceps du Nebadon★★★ £E Lys de Volan★★★★ £E
O **Saint-Joseph** Larmes du Père★★ £C

DOM. ANDRÉ PERRET Côte-Rôtie   *UK stockists:*VTr,L&W,CTy,WTs,FMV
Some of the finest Condrieu made, vinified like the white Saint-Joseph in a combination of *inox* and oak. Some good modern-style red Saint-Joseph, particularly the ageworthy Les Grissières. Syrah and Marsanne vins de pays offer attractive early drinking. (DM)
O **Condrieu**★★★ £D Clos Chanson★★★★ £E Coteau du Chéry★★★★★ £F
● **Saint-Joseph**★★ £B Les Grissières★★★ £C   O **Saint-Joseph**★★ £B

DOM. ÉTIENNE POCHON Crozes-Hermitage   *UK stockists:*J&B,GBa,L&W,WSc,Las
Decent red and white Crozes-Hermitage. Château de Curson wines are vinified with more oak and are a significant step up in quality. Curson white is mainly Roussanne and is enticingly floral and spicy. The red Curson is weighty but supple and needs two or three years' ageing. (DM)
● **Crozes-Hermitage**★★ £B Cuvée Château de Curson★★★ £C
O **Crozes-Hermitage**★ £B Cuvée Château de Curson★★★ £C

DOM. DES REMIZIÈRES Crozes-Hermitage   *UK stockists:* Bib, SVS
Much improved property in recent years. The red Hermitage Émilie is powerful and structured with loads of old-vine complexity. The Cuvée Christophe red is ripe and full of dark fruit. The whites display all the nutty, pure character of Marsanne at its best. (DM)
● **Hermitage** Émilie★★★★ £E   O **Hermitage** Émilie★★★★ £E
● **Saint-Joseph**★★ £C   ● **Crozes-Hermitage** Christophe★★★ £C

DOM. GILLES ROBIN Crozes-Hermitage   *UK stockists:*:L&S
Gilles Robin's wines have a depth and purity of Syrah fruit rarely found among his neighbours. The Albéric Bouchet shows real depth, structure and character and both wines will develop well. Also red Saint-Joseph, Andre Péalat.(DM)
● **Crozes-Hermitage** Papillon★★ £C Albéric Bouchet★★★ £C

RENÉ ROSTAING Côte-Rôtie   *UK stockists:* **Mis**, BBR, J&B, HHB, GBa,SVS,Las
One of the best producers of great unfiltered Côte-Rôtie. Rostaing has tremendous vineyards to draw upon, La

FRANCE

Landonne is dense, massive in its youth, while the Côte Blonde is lighter and typically more elegant. A peachy Condrieu should be drunk young. (DM)

● **Côte-Rôtie**★★★ £D   Classique★★★ £E   La Viallières★★★★ £E
● **Côte-Rôtie** La Landonne★★★★★ £F   Côte Blonde✪✪✪✪✪ £G

MARC SORREL   Hermitage   marc.sorrel@wanadoo.fr   *UK stockists:* CTy,Gau,NYg,Las
The regular bottlings here are a touch disappointing but Le Gréal is powerful, dense and complex with a backward structure. Les Rocoules is an equally fine, and equally backward example of great Marsanne. Honeyed, nutty and complex with age. Both need at least ten years. (DM)

● **Hermitage**★★★ £D   Le Gréal★★★★★ £F   O **Hermitage** Rocoules★★★★★ £F
● **Crozes-Hermitage**★★ £B   O **Crozes-Hermitage**★ £B

DOM. DU TUNNEL   Saint-Péray   *UK stockists:*HHB,Gau,Lib,FCA
Regular Saint-Péray is fresh and forward; the Prestige is denser and altogether more concentrated. The two Cornas are both splendid wines. Prestige comes from a parcel of 80-year-old vines. (DM)

● **Cornas**★★★ £D   Prestige★★★★ £E   ● **Saint-Joseph**★★★ £C
O **Saint-Péray**★★ £B   Prestige★★★ £C

DOM. GEORGES VERNAY   Condrieu   *UK stockists:* Yap,Win, Cco
Daughter Christine now runs this domaine. Increasingly impressive is the Côte-Rôtie, an appellation Vernay used to struggle with. *Vin de pays* Viognier is made from the youngest vines but Condrieu is the main focus. The top two are part barrel-fermented and of serious depth and concentration. (DM)

● **Côte-Rôtie** Blonde du Seigneur★★★ £E   Cuvée Maison Rouge★★★★ £E
O **Condrieu** Les Chaillées de L'Enfer★★★★ £E Coteau du Vernon★★★★ £E

FRANÇOIS VILLARD   Condrieu   *UK stockists:* HHB,
Three excellent Condrieus are vinified in new oak on their lees with bâtonnage, they have considerable depth and structure for Viognier and age uncharacteristically well. Sweet Quintessence is also made as are very good Côte-Rôtie and red and white Saint-Joseph. François is a partner in Les Vins de Vienne. (DM)

● **Côte-Rôtie** la Brocarde★★★★★ £E   ● **Saint-Joseph** Reflet★★★★ £D
O **Condrieu** Quintessence✪✪✪✪✪ £G   Coteaux de Poncin★★★★★ £E
O **Saint-Joseph** Côtes de Mairlant★★★★ £C

LES VINS DE VIENNE   Côte-Rôtie   *UK stockists:* Goe,C&B,BBR,Lay
Part domaine and part *négociant*. Vineyards are held in the Côteaux du Seyssuel to the west of Vienne from which red Sotanum, a wine of real potential, and a partially barrel-aged Viognier, Taburnum, are produced. The *négociant* wines range from good to exciting. Côte-Rôtie Les Essartailles and Condrieu La Chambée particularly stand out. (DM)

● **Vin de Pays** Sotanum★★★★ £C   O **Vin de Pays** Taburnum★★★ £C
● **Côte-Rôtie** Essartailles★★★★★ £E   O **Condrieu** Chambée★★★★ £E

ALAIN VOGE   Cornas   *UK stockists:* GWW,VTr, SVS
Great Cornas and some of the best Saint-Péray, both dry and sparkling. His Cornas vineyards are increasingly ancient and this is showing through in wines which are complex and smoky. A very small amount of new oak is used in barrel-ageing, The wines should be cellared for five years or more. (DM)

● **Cornas**★★★ £D   Vieilles Vignes★★★★ £E   Vieilles Fontaines★★★★★ £E
O **Saint-Péray** Cuvée Fleur du Crussol★★★ £B   Cuvée Boisée★★★ £B

Other wineries of note

Dom. Balthazar (Cornas), Albert Belle (Crozes-Hermitage), Dom de Bonserine (Côte-Rôtie), Dom. de Champal (Saint-Joseph), Ch. Grillet (Ch Grillet), Pierre Dumazet (Condrieu), Eric et Joël Durand (Cornas), Dom des Entrefaux (Crozes-Hermitage), Bernard Faurie (Hermitage), Dom. Pierre Gonon (Saint-Joseph), Dom. du Murinais (Crozes-Hermitage), Cave de Tain l'Hermitage (Hermitage)

An in-depth profile of every producer can be found in Wine behind the label 2006

98

Southern Rhône

DANIEL ET DENIS ALARY   Cairanne   *UK stockists:* HHB,Sel
Nearly 90 per cent of the Alary vineyard is planted to red varieties, with some very old vines. The Font
d'Estevenas white is a rich, nutty blend of Roussanne and Viognier. Of the unfiltered reds the Font d'Estevenas
and Jean de Verde are among the best expressions of old-vine Grenache outside Châteauneuf-du-Pape. (DM)
● **Cairanne** Réserve du Vigneron★★★ £B La Jean de Verde★★★ £C
● **Cairanne** La Font d'Estevenas★★★★ £C   O Côtes du Rhône La Chevre d'Or★★ £B
O **Cairanne** La Font d'Estevenas★★★ £C

DOM. DES AMOURIERS   Vacqueyras   *UK stockists:* EoR, HHB
34 ha all planted to reds, half Grenache with the balance a mix of Mourvèdre, Syrah and Carignan. The
Vacqueyras are wines of depth and rich savoury fruit and considerable structure, with new oak playing a large
part in the style. (DM)
● **Vacqueyras** Les Hautes Terrasses★★★ £C Les Genestes★★★ £C
● **Vacqueyras**★★ £B Signature★★ £B   ● **Côtes du Rhône**★ £B

DOM. PAUL AUTARD   Châteauneuf-du-Pape   *UK stockists:* **Las**
Good, sound, forward Côtes du Rhône and more serious red Châteauneuf-du-Papes. Traditionelle blends
Grenache with Syrah, Counoise and Mourvèdre. Côte Ronde is richer with a firmer structure and demands five
years' ageing. White Châteauneuf-du-Pape is barrel-fermented. Je ne Souvione is a late-harvest Viognier. (DM)
● **Châteauneuf du Pape** Traditionelle★★★ £D La Côte Ronde★★★★ £E
O **Châteauneuf du Pape**★★★ £D   O **Vin de Pays** Je ne Souvione★★★ £D

DOM. DE BEAURENARD   Châteauneuf-du-Pape   www.beaurenard.fr   *UK stockists:* BWC,Las
Impressive range of stylish reds and whites in modern, well-equipped cellars. The Boisrenard is a dense,
powerful wine produced from very low yields of 15 to 20 hl/ha that requires six or seven years' ageing. A
fortified Rasteau is one of the better examples. (DM)
● **Châteauneuf du Pape**★★★ £D Boisrenard★★★★★ £F   ● **Côtes du Rhône**★ £A
● **Côtes du Rhône-Villages** Rasteau★★ £B   O **Châteauneuf du Pape**★★★ £C

DOM. BERTHET-RAYNE   Châteauneuf-du-Pape
Small range of good middle-grade Châteauneuf-du-Pape and sound red and white Côtes du Rhônes. Vieilli en
Fûts de Chêne, added in 2000, will only be released in similarly good vintages. Cadiac is the most structured
and dense of the wines, rich and impressively concentrated. (DM)
● **Châteauneuf du Pape** Vieilli en Fûts de Chêne★★★★ £E Cadiac★★★★ £F
● **Côtes du Rhône**★ £B   O **Châteauneuf du Pape**★★ £C

BOIS DE BOURSAN   Châteauneuf-du-Pape   *UK stockists:* Tur
The reds here are dense, powerful wines needing time to soften. Both are bottled without filtration. The exotic
Cuvée Felix is aged in part in smaller oak. Both are ageworthy. (DM)
● **Châteauneuf du Pape**★★★★ £D Cuvée des Felix★★★★★ £E

HENRI BONNEAU   Châteauneuf-du-Pape   *UK stockists:* HHB, BBR, Sec,Las
Controversial producer; M. Bonneau is one of Châteauneufs more interesting characters. The two special *cuvées*,
which are produced from a high proportion of Grenache, are generally only bottled if the vintage justifies it. (DM)
● **Châteauneuf du Pape** Marie Beurrier★★★★★ £F
● **Châteauneuf du Pape** Réserve des Célestins✪✪✪✪ £G

BOSQUETS DES PAPES   Châteauneuf-du-Pape   *UK stockists:* Cty, HHB, SVS, OWL,Las
Traditional and potentially great reds, particularly the old-vine Cuvée Chantemerle. Bottling is carried out
according to demand, so beware, there can be considerable variation. Buy as close to the vintage as possible. (DM)
● **Châteauneuf -du-Pape**★★★ £C Cuvée Grenache★★★★ £E
● **Châteauneuf -du-Pape**★★★ £C Cuvée Chantemerle★★★★★ £F

DOM. BRESSY-MASSON   Rasteau
First class Rasteau-based property producing classic Côtes du Rhône Rasteau. Cuvée Paul Emile includes some 80-
year-old Grenache, A La Gloire de Mon Père 45-year-old Syrah and Mourvèdre. Also traditional *rancio* Rasteau.(DM)

● **Côtes du Rhône-Villages Rasteau**★★ £B Cuvée Paul Emile★★★ £C A La Gloire de Mon Père★★★ £C

DOM. BRUSSET Cairanne www.domaine brusset.fr *UK stockists:* Eno, NYg,Sel,Las
The Brusset family make an excellent range of modern wines with pre-fermentation maceration, ageing on lees
and no filtration. Les Hauts de Montmirail is a magnificent, complex old-vine *cuvée* mainly from Grenache. By
contrast lesser *cuvées* exhibit vibrant juicy fruit and are great youthful gluggers. (DM)
● **Gigondas** Grand Montmirail★★★ £C Hauts de Montmirail★★★★ £D
● **Cairanne** Travers★★ £B Hommage à André Brusset★★★★ £D

DOM. DE CASSAN Beaunes-de-Venise *UK stockists:* **SVS**
Fine Beaumes-de-Venise property equally known for sturdy, classic Gigondas, a dark, structured wine of great depth
and persistence at a very reasonable price. Beaumes-de-Venise is no less impressive. (DM)
● **Côtes du Rhône-Villages Beaumes-de-Venise**★★ £B Cuvée Saint-Christophe★★★ £C
● **Gigondas**★★★ £C O **Côtes du Rhône-Villages Beaumes de Venise**★★ £B

DOM. DU CAYRON Gigondas *UK stockists:* JAr
Just one wine is made at this traditional estate. A blend of Grenache (70 per cent) and equal amounts of
Cinsault and Syrah. With vines close to 50 years old and very well-drained stony soils producing fruit of
exceptional quality, this is one of the best estates in the appellation. (DM)
● **Gigondas**★★★ £C

DOM. DE LA CHARBONNIÈRE Châteauneuf-du-Pape *UK stockists:* GVVW,VVs, BBR
Generally good, if not in the top division. The wines are unfiltered. The impressively concentrated Haut
Brusquières (blending a proportion of Syrah with Grenache) and Vieilles Vignes bottlings stand out. The
Vacqueyras is a good chunky, earthy example and good-value. (DM)
● **Châteauneuf-du-Pape**★★£C Mourre des Perdrix★★★ £D
● **Châteauneuf-du-Pape** Haut Brusquières★★★★ £E Vieilles Vignes★★★★ £E
● **Vacqueyras**★★ £B

GÉRARD CHARVIN Châteauneuf-du-Pape *UK stockists::* Las,VTR
Both the Côtes du Rhône and the Châteauneuf-du-Pape offer quality and value. The latter is a blend of
Grenache with a little Syrah, Mourvèdre and Vaccarese adding both definition and a firm youthful structure. (DM)
● **Côtes du Rhône**★★ £B ● **Châteauneuf-du-Pape**★★★★ £D

CH. DE BEAUCASTEL Châteauneuf-du-Pape *UK stockists:* Mis,Far,Tan,Rae,F&M
One of the great Châteauneuf-du-Pape estates. Notable for organic farming and a process called *vinification à
chaud*, which extracts colour and fruit and guards against bacteria and oxidation. Reds are dominated by
Mourvèdre and Syrah and both reds and whites are long-lived. There is a decent second label Coudoulet de
Beaucastel. The Perrins also have a *négociant* operation and a partnership in the Californian Paso Robles winery
Tablas Creek. (DM)
● **Châteauneuf-du-Pape**★★★★★ £E Homage à Jacques Perrin❁❁❁❁ £H
O **Châteauneuf-du-Pape**★★★★ £E Vieilles Vignes❁❁❁❁ £G

CH. DE FONSALETTE Côtes du Rhône *UK stockists:* Sec, Blx, Las
Owned by the Reynaud family of Château Rayas. Emmanuel Reynaud now also undertakes vinification here as
well as at Rayas and his own Vacqueyras property, Château des Tours. The regular bottling is a blend of
Grenache with a sizeable dollop of Cinsault. (DM)
● **Côtes du Rhône**★★★ £C Syrah★★★★ £D O **Côtes du Rhône**★★★ £C

CH. DE FONTSÉGUGNE Côtes du Rhône
Small Côtes du Rhône property with its first vintage in 2000. All wines show impressive depth and purity of fruit.
Santo Estello comes from 30-year-old vines; Li Felibre is aged in small used oak. (DM)
● **Côtes du Rhône** Tradition★★ £B Santo Estello★★★ £B Li Felibre★★★ £C

CH. LA GARDINE Châteauneuf-du-Pape www.gardine.com *UK stockists:* T&W
Modern, dense and deeply coloured red Châteauneuf. Initially firm, it requires several years' ageing.
Temperature control is used to produce fruity, gloriously nutty whites, with new oak in abundance in the top
cuvées. Purchased the Lirac property Domaine Saint-Roch in 1998 and has started to bring about

New entries have producer's name underlined

improvements. (DM)

● **Châteauneuf-du-Pape** Tradition★★★★ £D Gaston Philippe★★★★★ £F
O **Châteauneuf-du-Pape** Tradition★★★ £D Marie-Léoncie★★★★ £E

CH. LA NERTHE Châteauneuf-du-Pape *UK stockists:* BBR, C&C
Large (for Châteauneuf) property with an output of around 25,000 cases. Cadettes, a sturdy blend of 100-year-old Grenache and Mourvèdre, is right on the edge of five stars. Modern, stylish barrel-handled whites. (DM)

● **Châteauneuf-du-Pape★★★★** £D Cuvée des Cadettes★★★★ £E
O **Châteauneuf-du-Pape★★★** £C Clos de Beauvenir★★★★ £D

CH. MAS NEUF Costières de Nîmes www.châteaumasneuf.com
Decent white Compostelle Blanc blends Grenache Blanc and Roussanne; *vin de pays* Chardonnay/ Viognier is leaner, more aromatic. Compostelle Rouge, from Syrah, Grenache and Mourvèdre and two vin de pays varietal reds are impressively structured. New is a red super-cuvée, Armonio. (DM)

● **Costières de Nîmes** Compostelle★★★ £C ● **Vin de Pays** Merlot★★★ £C
● **Vin de Pays** Syrah★★★ £CO **Costières de Nîmes** Compostelle★★ £B

CH. MONT-REDON Châteauneuf-du-Pape *UK stockists:* PFx,Sel
Large property producing good to very good rather than exceptional wines. Vinification is modern, using a mix of *inox* and *barriques* for the Châteauneuf bottlings. A Lirac property, Château Cantegril, has recently been purchased and these wines are now labelled Mont-Redon. (DM)

● **Côtes du Rhône★★** £B ● **Châteauneuf-du-Pape★★★** £D ● **Lirac★★** £B
O **Châteauneuf-du-Pape★★★** £C O **Côtes du Rhône★** £B Viognier★ £B

CH. MOURGUES DU GRÈS Costières de Nîmes
20,000 cases of red, white and rosé are now made here each year. Galets is the label for the basic range. The second tier Terre d'Argence wines are more serious. The best red, Capitelles des Mourgues, spends a year in barrel. Top reds will improve with short ageing. (DM)

● **Costières de Nîmes** Terre d'Argence★★★ £B Capitelles des Mourgues★★★ £C
O **Costières de Nîmes** Terre d'Argence★★ £B

CH. PESQUIÉ Côtes du Ventoux *UK stockists:* VWs, OWL
Terrasses labels are simple and straightforward and there is a characterful rosé, Perle de Roses. The real stars though, are Syrah/Grenache blends Prestige and Quintessence, both aged in small barrels, around 30 to 35 per cent new. (DM)

● **Côtes du Ventoux** Terre Précieuse★ £B Prestige★★★ £B Quintessence★★★ £B
◉ **Côtes du Ventoux** Perle de Roses★ £A

CH. RAYAS Châteauneuf-du-Pape *UK stockists:* OWL, BBR, Las
Legendary estate with 14 ha of old vines planted on sand and clay/limestone soils, rather than on *galets roulés*. Second label, Pignan, is also very impressive and comes from a separate plot rather than a selection. Red is made solely from Grenache while the very ageworthy white is 50/50 Clairette and Grenache Blanc. Very fine in the late 1990s but not of the sublime quality of earlier years. (DM)

● **Châteauneuf-du-Pape✪✪✪✪** £F Pignan★★★★★ £E
O **Châteauneuf-du-Pape★★★★★** £E

CH. REDORTIER Gigondas *UK stockists:* BRW
Good reds from young vines around 25 years, so there should be more to come. Gigondas is dominated by Grenache but there is a hefty dollop of Syrah as well. Firm and more structured than some of its neighbours. Beaumes-de-Venise Cuvée Prestige is an undoubted star of that village. (DM)

● **Côtes du Rhône-Villages Beaumes-de-Venise★★** £B Cuvée Prestige★★ £C
● **Gigondas★★★** £C

CH. SAINT-COSME Gigondas *UK stockists:* Dec, NYg, Han
Louis Barruol owns vines only in Gigondas but in recent years he has made an excellent small range of négociant wines as well. The Gigondas Cuvée Valbelle, Châteauneuf-du-Pape and Côte-Rôtie are all impressively concentrated and ageworthy. (DM)

● **Côtes du Rhône** Deux Albions★★ £B ● **Gigondas★★** £C Valbelle★★★ £D

● Châteauneuf-du-Pape★★★ £E ● Côte-Rôtie★★★ £E ○ Condrieu★★ £E

CH. DES TOURS Vacqueyras *UK stockists:* Yap, Bib, Rae
Emmanuel Reynaud, the nephew of the late Jacques Reynaud, is now vinifying the wines at Château Rayas and Château de Fonsalette. His Vacqueyras has long been a yardstick example for the AC and is produced mainly from Grenache from very low-yielding old vines. (DM)
● Côtes du Rhône★★ £B ● Vacqueyras★★★ £C ○ Côtes du Rhône★ £B

DOM. DE LA CITADELLE Côtes du Lubéron *UK stockists:* HHB, Vnf
Top-flight traditional Lubéron, *vin de pays* Viognier and a fairly leafy Cabernet Sauvignon. Le Gouverneur is an impressively dense and concentrated dark, spicy red. 2 tiny-volume *cuvées* from single parcels of old vines can be obtained from the winery: Noé comes from Syrah, Paul from Mourvèdre. (DM)
● Côtes du Luberon Les Artèmes★★★ £B Le Gouverneur Saint-Auban★★★ £C
● Côtes du Luberon La Châtaignier★★ £B ● Vin de Pays Cabernet Sauvignon★ £B
○ Côtes du Luberon Les Artèmes★★ £B ○ Vin de Pays Viognier★ £B

CLOS DU CAILLOU Châteauneuf-du-Pape *UK stockists:* HHB, BBR, NYg, Las
Quality at this domaine has gone from strength to strength. Careful vineyard management, modern vinification with some malolactic in cask and a tight control of yields are producing excellent results. The top two *cuvées* will age very well. (DM)
● Côtes du Rhône Bouquet des Garrigues★ £B ● Châteauneuf-du-Pape★★★ £D
● Châteauneuf-du-Pape Les Quartz★★★★ £E Réserve Clos du Caillou★★★★★ £F

CLOS DES CAZAUX Vacqueyras *UK stockists:* CBg, Lay, VWs, Tan
Fascinating, diverse range of wines from holdings in Vacqueyras and Gigondas. Some good whites including a very small amount of a 100 per cent Grenache Blanc Quintessence. Reds stand out and Templiers is unusually dominated by Syrah. Very rare and generally successful is a late-harvest Vacqueyras produced from Grenache infected by noble rot, Grenat Noble. (DM)
● Vacqueyras Templiers★★★ £B Réserve★★★ £C Grénat Noble★★★★ £C
● Gigondas La Tour Sarrazine★★★ £C ○ Vacqueyras Blanc Barrique★★ £B

CLOS DES PAPES Châteauneuf-du-Pape *UK stockists:* RsW, Rae, SVS, BBR
Benchmark names in Châteauneuf-du-Pape, producing just one white and one splendid red which is a very structured, ageworthy example of the AC. It is always destemmed and the different varieties are fermented together. Both will age well. (DM)
● Châteauneuf-du-Pape★★★★★ £E ○ Châteauneuf-du-Pape★★★★ £D

CLOS PETITE BELLANE Valréas *UK stockists:* Odd
Modern, stylish wines, although some Grenache vines are up to 65 years old. Whites are all given a period of *macération pelliculaire*. Les Echalas is 100 per cent Roussanne. Red Côtes du Rhône is ripe and forward, the Valréas bottlings fuller and more concentrated. The top two reds have real depth and concentration. (DM)
● Côtes du Rhône Valréas★★ £B Les Echalas★★★ £D Vieilles Vignes★★★★ £D
● Côtes du Rhône★★ £B ○ Côtes du Rhône Valréas Les Echalas★★★ £D

DOM. DE CRISTIA Châteauneuf-du-Pape *UK stockists:* Las
Fine modern Côtes du Rhône and Châteauneuf-du-Pape made in an accessible style. The top wine, Cuvée Renaissance, comes from 100-year-old Grenache, with a hint of Syrah and Mourvèdre. (DM)
● Châteauneuf du Pape★★★ £D Cuvée Renaissance★★★★★ £E
● Côtes du Rhône★ £B ● Côtes du Rhône-Villages★★ £B

CROS DE LA MÛRE Côtes du Rhône *UK stockists:* JAr, CBg
Small estate making stylish, elegant Côtes du Rhône, Côtes du Rhône-Villages and denser, fuller Gigondas. Not blockbusters but wines with very good classic *garrigue*-scented red berry fruit. (DM)
● Côtes du Rhône★ £B ● Côtes du Rhône-Villages★★★ £B
● Gigondas★★★ £B

CUVÉE DU VATICAN Châteauneuf-du-Pape *UK stockists:* BBR, Far, Las
Domaine de Bres-Casenove offers much more than most red *vin de pays*, while the regular red Châteauneuf is more

New entries have producer's name underlined

powerful and structured than most *classique* bottlings. Dark and smoky Reserve Sixteen is one of the great wines of the appellation – old Grenache, Syrah and Mourvèdre aged in a mix of small oak and *foudres*. (DM)

● **Châteauneuf-du-Pape**★★★★ £D Reserve Sixteen★★★★★ £D
● **Vin de Pays** Domaine de Bres-Casenove★★★★ £D O **Châteauneuf-du-Pape**★★ £D

DOM. DE DEURRE Vinsobres *UK stockists:* MtC, SVS
New but promising domaine where the wines show increasing potential. There are two fine Côtes du Rhônes. Les Oliviers is 100 per cent Syrah, the brilliant Les Rabasses 100 per cent Grenache. Newly added Cuvée J M Valayer resembles a very good Châteauneuf-du-Pape. (DM)

● **Côtes du Rhône** Les Oliviers★★★ £C Les Rabasses★★★ £C
● **Côtes du Rhône-Villages Vinsobres**★★ £B Cuvée JM Valayer★★★★ £C

DOM. DURBAN Beaumes-de-Venise *UK stockists:* Yap, BBR
Decent red Beaumes-de-Venise Vieilles Vignes. However, it is the fortified Muscat de Beaumes-de-Venise that marks out this estate. In the style of the appellation, drink young and fresh. (DM)

● **Côtes du Rhône-Villages Beaumes-de-Venise** Vieille Vignes★★ £B
O **Muscat de Beaumes-de-Venise**★★★ £C

DOM. DES ESPIERS Vacqueyras *UK stockists:* Bal
Solid Côtes du Rhône and fine Gigondas. Cuvée des Blâches, from 35-year-old vines, is wonderfully dense and gamey with attractive herbal *garrigue* notes. Gigondas and Sablet benefit from some age. (DM)

● **Côtes du Rhône**★ £B ● **Côtes du Rhône-Villages Sablet**★★ £B
● **Gigondas**★★★ £B Cuvée des Blâches★★★★ £C

DOM. FOND CROZE Côtes du Rhône-Villages www.domainefondcroze.com
Much-improved 65-ha property. White Cuvée Analys is Viognier from very low-yielding, late-harvested vines. Top reds come under the Côtes du Rhône umbrella: Saint-Romanaise is solely Grenache; Fond Croze is dominated by Syrah, as is new Shyros. (DM)

● **Côtes du Rhône-Villages** Cuvée Vincent de Catari★★ £B
● **Côtes du Rhône** Cuvée Fond Croze★★★ £C Cuvée Shyros★★★ £C
● **Côtes du Rhône**★★ £B Cuvée Saint-Romanaise★★★ £B
O **Côtes du Rhône** Cuvée Analys★★ £B

DOM. DE FONDRÈCHE Côtes du Ventoux *UK stockists:* N&P
Benchmark wines for the appellation, well worth seeking out and very good value. Varietal reds have also been made in recent vintages. Roussanne is an important component of the two whites. (DM)

● **Côtes du Ventoux**★ £A Cuvée Fayard★★ £B Cuvée Persia★★★ £B
● **Côtes du Ventoux** Cuvée Carles Nadal★★★ £B
O **Côtes du Ventoux**★ £A Cuvée Persia★★ £B

FONT DE MICHELLE Châteauneuf-du-Pape *UK stockists:* JAr, Yng, Tan, WSS
Good Côtes du Rhône and Rhône-Villages as well as cool-fermented Viognier. Châteauneuf red benefits from some very old Grenache: 50-year-old vines go into the regular wine and 90-year-olds into the *barrique*-aged (part new) Etienne Gonnet. (DM)

● **Châteauneuf-du-Pape**★★★ £D Etienne Gonnet★★★★★ £F
O **Châteauneuf-du-Pape**★★ £C Etienne Gonnet★★★★ £E

DOM. DE FONT SANE Gigondas *UK stockists:* Bib, GBa
Good Gigondas and Côtes du Ventoux. The Ventoux is among the better examples in that AC and excellent value for money. Oak-aged barrel selection Cuvée Futée is dense, powerful and very ageworthy. It is generally made from the oldest vines on the property. (DM)

● **Côtes du Ventoux**★ £A ● **Gigondas**★★★ £C Futée★★★★ £C

DOM. LA GARRIGUE Vacqueyras
Good traditional domaine with 65 ha of vineyard spread across Vacqueyras and Gigondas and additional holdings simply classified as Côtes du Rhône. The main focus of the property is on red Vacqueyras and Gigondas. Vinification is traditional with no destemming, fining or filtration. (DM)

● **Vacqueyras**★★★ £B Cuvée de Hostellerie★★★ £C ● **Gigondas**★★★ £C

GOURT DE MAUTENS Rasteau *UK stockists:* Rae, SVS

Very impressive producer. The red, from 80-year-old vines, has recently matched top Châteauneuf. The white, a blend of Bourboulenc and Grenache Blanc, doesn't quite hit the same stellar heights but is still among the most interesting and structured examples of the region.(DM)

● **Côtes du Rhône-Villages Rasteau**★★★★ £D

O **Côtes du Rhône-Villages Rasteau**★★★★ £D

DOM. GRAMENON Côtes du Rhône *UK stockists:* BRW, HHB, Rae, SVS

Long established as one of the great producers in the Côtes du Rhône. The vineyard is planted to Grenache and Syrah with a little Cinsault and Carignan for the reds and a little Clairette and Viognier for the whites. The Ceps Centenaires Cuvée Mémé, produced from very old vines, is as fine as the very best from the southern Rhône. (DM)

● **Côtes du Rhône** La Sagesse★★★ £B Ceps Centenaires Mémé★★★★ £C

● **Côtes du Rhône-Villages** Les Hauts de Gramenon★★★ £C

DOM. DE LA JANASSE Châteauneuf-du-Pape *UK stockists:* Eno, N&P, NYg, WSc, Las

Splendid, medium-sized domaine producing good to excellent wines across the board. Châteauneuf vines are planted on ideal, free-draining stony soils and this, together with a vine age averaging over 60 years, results in lovely supple, dense and powerful wines. (DM)

● **Châteauneuf-du-Pape**★★★★ £D Chaupin★★★★★ £E Vieilles-Vignes★★★★★ £F

O **Châteauneuf-du-Pape** Tradition★★★ £C Prestige★★★★ £F

DOM. LAFOND-ROC-EPINE Tavel www.lafond.roc-epine.com *UK stockists:*CTy, BBR

Excellent-value domaine. Lirac and Châteauneuf-du-Pape will evolve well in the medium term. Also one of the better Tavels, which shows some vibrant fresh fruit. (DM)

● **Lirac**★★ £B La Ferme Romaine★★★ £C _● **Châteauneuf-du-Pape**★★★ £D

● **Côtes du Rhône**★★ £B O **Lirac**★ £B

DOM. LA GUINTRANDY Visan

One of the new stars of the southern Rhône. Old vines and low yields are key to quality. The Visan Vieilles Vignes is a blend of mainly 50-year-old Grenache with a little Carignan and Syrah. The Cuvée Les Devès and top Cuvée Louise Amelie are both aged in oak. (DM)

● **Côtes du Rhône-Villages Visan** Les Devès★★★ £B Louise Amelie★★★ £C

● **Côtes du Rhône**★★ £B ● **Côtes du Rhône-Villages Visan** VV★★★ £C

DOM. LA ROQUETTE Châteauneuf-du-Pape *UK stockists:*L&W, BBR

Owned by the Bruniers of Vieux-Télégraph. Produced from vineyard parcels spread throughout the appellation, these are unfiltered modern wines of some class and finesse. (DM)

● **Châteauneuf-du-Pape**★★★ £D O **Châteauneuf-du-Pape**★★★ £D

DOM. LA SOUMADE Rasteau *UK stockists:* BBR, HHB, NYg, Hal

A great range of wines, especially the impressive red Côtes du Rhône, Rasteau and Gigondas. These are vinified as true vins de garde. André Romero also produces fine vins doux naturels under the Rasteau AC. (DM)

● **Côtes du Rhône-Villages Rasteau** Prestige★★★ £C Confiance★★★★ £D

● **Côtes du Rhône-Villages Rasteau** Fleur de Confiance★★★★★ £E

DOM. LE MURMURIUM Côtes du Ventoux

Emerging Ventoux star with organical viticulture and yields restricted to 15–25 hl/ha. White, rosé and 4 red *cuvées* are produced including limited-production Florence. All the reds are bottled unfined and unfiltered. (DM)

● **Côtes du Ventoux**★★★ £B Opéra★★★★ £C Carpe Diem★★★★ £D

O **Côtes du Ventoux**★★ £B ◉ **Côtes du Ventoux**★ £B

DOM. LES APHILLANTHES Travaillan *UK stockists:*Sec, Las

One of the rising stars of the southern Rhône, producing brilliant fleshy, forward reds. Opulent and accesible alternatives to more traditional Châteauneuf and Gigondas. Bottled with neither fining nor filtration, all the wines show real depth and impressive concentration. (DM)

● **Côtes du Rhône-Villages** Cuvée du Cros★★★★ £C Vieilles Vignes★★★★ £C

● **Côtes du Rhône-Villages** Galets★★★ £C Trois Cépages★★★ £C R & R★★ £B

New entries have producer's name underlined

LES CAILLOUX Châteauneuf-du-Pape *UK stockists:* Hal, SVS, Las
Traditional producer of Côtes du Rhône and Châteauneuf-du-Pape. The Côtes du Rhônes are produced at the Brunel family property Domaine de l'Enclos. The profound Cuvée Centenaire produced from 100-year-old vines is one of the great wines of the appellation. (DM)

● **Côtes du Rhône**★★ £C Sommelongue★★★ £B
● **Châteauneuf-du-Pape**★★★★ £C Centenaire✪✪✪✪✪ £E

PATRICK LESEC SELECTIONS *UK stockists:* **Gau,**NYg
Brilliant *négociant* with an extraordinary range of wines produced in collaboration with some of the best winemakers in both the Rhône and the Midi. Lesec endeavours to ensure wines of both depth and purity, perhaps best expressed by a number of marvellous Châteauneuf-du-Papes. (DM)

● **Hermitage** Émilie★★★★★ £E ● **Saint-Joseph** La Sensonne★★★★ £C
● **Cornas** Le Vignon★★★★ £E ● **Châteauneuf-du-Pape** Galets Ronds★★★★★ £F

DOM. LES GRANDS BOIS Côtes du Rhône-Villages *UK stockists:*Gau
The Besnardeau family have mature vineyards in a number of villages, among them Rasteau and Cairanne. The oldest vines are now over 70 years. A range of splendid red Villages wines includes 3 Cairanne *cuvées,* the Maximilien perhaps the most exciting. (DM)

● **Côtes du Rhône-Villages Cairanne** Maximilien★★★ £C Eloise★★★ £C Mireille★★★ £C
● **Côtes du Rhône-Villages** Gabrielle★★ £C Philippine★★ £C
◉ **Côtes du Rhône** Les Trois Soeurs★ £B Les Trois Soeurs★★ £B O **Malorie** Vin de Table★★ £B

LES PALLIÈRES Gigondas www.vignoblesbrunier.fr *UK stockists:* THt,F&M
The great traditional domaine of Gigondas now owned as a joint venture between the Bruniers of Vieux-Télégraph and US wine merchant Kermit Lynch. At last the potential of the *terroir* is beginning to be fully explored. (DM)

● **Gigondas**★★★ £C

DOM. DE MARCOUX Châteauneuf-du-Pape *UK stockists:* HHB, CCC, Alo, Las
Model 24-ha property run on biodynamic lines since 1990. Vieilles Vignes has for a decade been one of the benchmark wines of the appellation: very ageworthy and extraordinarily complex. (DM)

● **Châteauneuf-du-Pape**★★★★ £E Vieilles Vignes✪✪✪✪✪ £F
O **Châteauneuf-du-Pape**★★★ £D

DOM. MATHIEU Châteauneuf-du-Pape
Good, small, family-run domaine with 22ha in 50 separate plots. Marquis Anselme Mathieu comes from some of the oldest Grenache on the property, from a vineyard originally planted in 1890. (DM)

● **Châteauneuf-du-Pape**★★★ £D Vin de Felibre★★★ £E Marquis Anselme Mathieu★★★★ £E
O **Châteauneuf-du-Pape**★★ £D

DOM. LA MILLIERE Châteauneuf-du-Pape *UK stockists:* RsW
Fine Châteauneuf-du-Pape as well as Côtes du Rhône from vineyards up to 100 years of age. Tremendous raw material, organic farming and a general minimalist approach result in some excellent wines. (DM)

● **Châteauneuf-du-Pape**★★★ £D Vieilles-Vignes★★★★ £E
● **Côtes du Rhône-Villages**★★ £B ● **Côtes du Rhône**★ £B Vieilles Vignes★★★ £B

DOM. DE LA MONARDIÈRE Vacqueyras
A fine small range is made at this well-established Vacqueyras property. The Vieilles Vignes, dense and imposingly structured, is a wine of real depth and intensity. Both the top reds will benefit from four or five years' patience. (DM)

● **Vacqueyras** Calades★★ £B Réserve des Deux Monardes★★ £C VV★★★ £C
O **Vacqueyras**★★ £C

DOM. MONTIRIUS Vacqueyras
Biodynamic property with 50 ha of vineyard of which 35 ha are in Vacqueyras. Powerful Gigondas and two good red Vacqueyras. The Clos Montirius comes from an 8.5-ha sector of the Vacqueyras vineyard with a very localised drier mesoclimate. (DM)

FRANCE

FRANCE

● Vacqueyras★★ £B Clos Montirius★★★ £C ● Gigondas★★★ £C
● Côtes du Rhône★★ £B O Vacqueyras★ £B

DOM. DE MONTPERTUIS Châteauneuf-du-Pape *UK stockists:* L&W, SVS
Impressively deep and concentrated red Châteauneuf-du-Pape, as well as some fine Côtes du Ventoux from Château de Valcombe. Winemaker Gilles Basq also makes a dense, richly concentrated Côtes du Rhône under his own label, Domaine La Manarine. (DM)
Domaine de Montpertuis
● Châteauneuf-du-Pape★★★ £D ● Vin de Pays du Gard Counoise★ £B
O Châteauneuf-du-Pape★★ £C O Côtes du Rhône★ £B

DOM. DE LA MORDORÉE Tavel *UK stockists:* L&S, Bal, Box, Rae, HHB, Las
Benchmark Tavel from a biodynamic domaine, arguably the best of the appellation, with an extensive and impressive range of wines. The various Reine des Bois *cuvées* are refined and characterful and will improve in bottle for 5 to 10 years, the Châteauneuf almost certainly longer. (DM)
● Lirac★★★ £C Reine des Bois★★★★ £C O Lirac Reine des Bois★★★ £C
● Châteauneuf-du-Pape★★★★ £D Reine des Bois★★★★★ £F

MOULIN DE LA GARDETTE Gigondas *UK stockists:* A&B
Powerful, traditionally slightly rustic Gigondas. The vines are over 50 years old and the wines are neither fined nor filtered. Fine and very intense, they drink very well over the medium term. (DM)
● Gigondas★★ £C Cuvée Ventabren★★★ £C

DOM. DE MOURCHON Seguret www.domainedemourchon.com *UK stockists:* L&W
Purchased by Walter McKinlay in 1998 and quality is moving forward very impressively. From 24ha he now produces benchmark Séguret reds. Tradition, aged in *cuve*, is vibrant, dark and spicy while Grande Réserve is powerful and concentrated with a marvellous old-vine purity. (DM)
● Côtes du Rhône-Villages Seguret Tradition★★★ £B Grande Reserve★★★ £C
◉ Côtes du Rhône Pié Loubié★ £B

DOM. DE L'ORATOIRE SAINT-MARTIN Cairanne *UK stockists:* Car
Top property in this outperforming Rhône village. All the Cairanne bottlings are very impressive. Haut Coustias red can hold its own against top-quality Châteauneuf-du-Pape. (DM)
● Cairanne Haut Coustias★★★★ £C Prestige★★★ £B Seigneurs★★★ £C
O Cairanne Haut Coustias★★★ £C

DOM. DU PEGAÜ Châteauneuf-du-Pape www.pegau.com *UK stockists:* Gau, GrD, Las
Very fine traditional domaine producing powerful, formidably structured reds and a rich, nutty white. *Vin de table* Plan Pegaü is good, if a little light, but in the traditional style of the property. Cuvée da Capo has emerged as one of the Rhône Valley's great reds. (DM)
● Vin de Table Plan Pegau★★ £B O Châteauneuf-du-Pape Réservée★★★ £D
● Châteauneuf-du-Pape Réservée★★★★★ £E Cuvée da Capo✪✪✪✪✪ £G

DOM. DES PERRIÈRES Costières de Nîmes
Marc Kreydenweiss is best known for his stylish Alsace wines. His reds here are refined, more elegant than powerful. Domaine de Grimaud is forward and supple; Domaine des Perrières, from older vines, has more depth and a firmer structure. (DM)
● Costières de Nîmes Perrières★★★ £C Domaine de Grimaud★★ £B

DOM. DE PIAUGIER Sablet piaugier@wanadoo.fr *UK stockists:* GVF
Good Gigondas and a number of splendid Sablet bottles. Vinification is traditional and the fruit is not destemmed. The result, though, is never rustic. A slight green hint can creep into the lesser wines in cooler years. Top Sablet reds and the Gigondas improve with three or four years' ageing. (DM)
● Côtes du Rhône-Sablet Briquières★★★★ £C Alphonse Vautour★★★★ £D
● Côtes du Rhône-Sablet Réserve de Maude★★★★ £D ● Gigondas★★ £C

DOM. RABASSE-CHARAVIN Cairanne *UK stockists:* THt
Very fine property with an output almost exclusively of reds. Average vine age is now over 50 years, helping

New entries have producer's name underlined

quality. Cuvée Estevenas has impressive depth and firm tannin in its youth. (DM)

● **Cairanne★★** £B   Estevenas★★★ £B   O **Cairanne★** £B
● **Côtes du Rhône-Villages Rasteau★★** £B

DOM. DES RELAGNES   Châteauneuf-du-Pape

Very rich and concentrated red Châteauneuf from vines averaging 60 years. Cuvée Vigneronne is unusually a blend of 6 varieties; Petits Pieds d'Armande comes mainly from a century-old plot of Grenache. (DM)

● **Châteauneuf-du-Pape** Tradition★★★ £D   Cuvée Vigneronne★★★★ £E   Les Petits Pieds d'Armand★★★★ £E
● **Côtes du Rhône★** £B
● **Côtes du Rhône-Villages★★★** £B   Garances★★ £B

DOM. RÉMÉJEANNE   Côtes du Rhône-Villages   *UK stockists:* CTy

Benchmark Côtes du Rhône property. Les Arbousiers red is vibrant and spicy, the white subtly nutty. Les Chevrefeuilles adds Carignan and Counoise from old vines to Syrah and Grenache. The top two *cuvées* are the concentrated Les Églantiers (100 per cent Syrah) and Les Génevriers, a blend of Grenache, Syrah and Mourvèdre. (DM)

● **Côtes du Rhône** Arbousiers★★ £B   Chèvrefeuilles★★★ £B   Églantiers★★★★ £C
O **Côtes du Rhône** Arbousiers★ £B   ● **Côtes du Rhône-Villages** Génevriers★★★ £B

MARCEL RICHAUD   Cairanne   *UK stockists:* Lib

Marcel Richaud's reds all have impressive, spicy berry fruit. The top two *cuvées* are impressively structured, putting many a Châteauneuf to shame. The Estrambords is aged in *barriques*. (DM)

● **Côtes du Rhône★** £B   Terres d'Aigues★★ £B   Les Garrigues★★★ £B
● **Cairanne★★★** £B   L'Ebrescade★★★★ £C   Les Estrambords★★★★ £C

DOM. ROCHE-AUDRAN   Côtes du Rhône   *UK stockists:* Gau

Some extraordinary and very complex Côtes du Rhône red is now made at this small domaine. Very good red and white Côtes du Rhône, Visan as well as 3 brilliant Côtes du Rhône special *cuvées*. These latter wines are sourced from a range of *terroirs*, some with vines older than 100 years. (DM)

● **Côtes du Rhône★★** £B   Père Mayeaux★★★ £C   Cesar★★★★ £C   Le Caillou★★★★ £C
● **Côtes du Rhône-Villages Visan★★★** £B   O **Côtes du Rhône★★★** £B

DOM. ROUGE GARANCE   Côtes du Rhône-Villages

Fine producer of classic, sturdy Rhône red, Saintpierre is a low-yielding special cuvée. Garances and Feuille de Garance are softer and more approachable and both ensure the integrity of the top two wines. (DM)

● **Côtes du Rhône-Villages** Les Saintpierre★★★★ £C   Rouge Garance★★★ £C
● **Côtes du Rhône-Villages** Garances★★ £B   ● **Côtes du Rhône** Feuille de Garance★ £B
O **Côtes du Rhône** Blanc de Garance★ £B

DOM. JEAN ROYER   Châteauneuf-du-Pape   *UK stockists:* Idg

Very good, traditionally made Châteauneuf. The wines all get a lengthy vatting and are in a dense, full-bodied style. The Prestige is a selection of older vines; the top wine, made onlyz in great vintages, is the Hommage à Mon Père. (DM)

● **Châteauneuf-du-Pape** Tradition★★★ £D   Prestige★★★★ £E   Hommage à Mon Père★★★★ £E

ROGER SABON   Châteauneuf-du-Pape   *UK stockists:* Gau, Rae, BBR, Bal,Sel

Decent Lirac and Châteauneuf-du-Pape and two marvellous old-vine Cuvée Prestige and Le Secret de Sabon that show real intensity and sheer class. The wines are all bottled without filtration. (DM)

● **Châteauneuf-du-Pape** Prestige★★★★ £E   Le Secret de Sabon★★★★★ £F
● **Châteauneuf-du-Pape** Les Olivets★★ £D   Réservée★★★ £D   ● **Lirac★★** £B

DOM. SAINT DAMIEN   Gigondas

Joel Saurel produces very full, rich and concentrated Gigondas from vines which are in some cases over 100 years old. Even the vines for the subtle, berry-scented Classique are on average over 70 years old. No new oak is used and the wines are all bottled without fining or filtration. (DM)

● **Gigondas★★★** £C   Les Souteyrades★★★★ £D   La Louisiane★★★★ £D

SAINT JEAN DU BARROUX   Côtes du Ventoux
This small property has the potential to become one of the shining lights in Ventoux. The rich and nutty white is Grenache Blanc/Clairette/Bourboulenc. The dense and very concentrated red is Grenache/Syrah/Carignan/Cinsault vinified in *cuve*. (DM)
● **Côtes du Ventoux**★★★ £C   O **Côtes du Ventoux**★★★ £B

DOM. SAINTE-ANNE   Côtes du Rhône   *UK stockists:* OWL, Tan, SVS, BBR
Syrah and Mourvèdre as well as Grenache are important in shaping the style of these reds. Dense and full-bodied, the top two *cuvées* in particular will benefit from medium-term ageing. Viognier is one of the better southern Rhône examples. (DM)
● **Côtes du Rhône-Villages** St Gervais★★★ £B   Notre-Dame des Celettes★★★ £B
O **Côtes du Rhône** Viognier★★ £C

SANG DES CAILLOUX   Vacqueyras   *UK stockists:* CPp
Top-flight Vacqueyras producer with two excellent-value reds. Classique has been variously named Doucinello, Azalais and Floureto over recent vintages, blended from Grenache, Syrah, Mourvèdre and Cinsault. Cuvée Lopy is produced from the oldest Grenache (75 years) and Syrah. (DM)
● **Vacqueyras** Classique★★★ £B   Cuvée Lopy Vieilles Vignes★★★★ £C

DOM. SANTA DUC   Gigondas   *UK stockists:* Bib, Rae, HHB, F&M
Benchmark, modern, fleshy reds from one of the finest names in Gigondas. Côtes du Rhône is lighter than some but has good intensity. In Gigondas the domaine wines stand out over *négociant* wine, La Garancières. A small range of other *négociant* wines is labelled Santa Duc Selections. (DM)
● **Vin de Pays de la Principauté d'Orange**★ £B   ● **Côtes du Rhône**★★ £B
● **Gigondas**★★★ £C   La Garancières★★ £B   Les Hautes Garrigues★★★★ £D

DOM. DE LA SOLITUDE   Châteauneuf-du-Pape   *UK stockists:* Las
Decent red and white Côtes du Rhône as well as some impressive Châteauneuf-du-Pape are made at this ancient estate. Remarkably complex, richly textured Réserve Secret is aged in 80% new oak. This is only made in the best years and is sourced from the best plots. (DM)
● **Châteauneuf-du-Pape** Tradition★★★ £D   Cuvée Barbarini★★★★ £F   Réserve Secret★★★★★ £G
O **Châteauneuf-du-Pape** Tradition★★ £D   Cuvée Barbarini★★★★ £F
● **Côtes du Rhône**★★ £B   O **Côtes du Rhône**★ £B

TARDIEU-LAURENT   *UK stockists:* HBJ, GCW, Rae, BBR, LAS
Exceptional range of wines from throughout the Rhône Valley. Along with wines from the Rhône there are selected bottlings from the Costières de Nîmes, Provence and the Languedoc. Almost everything is of at least two- to three-star quality. (DM)
● **Côtes du Rhône** Guy Louis★★★ £C   ● **Saint-Joseph** VV★★★ £D
● **Côtes du Rhône-Villages** Rasteau VV★★★ £C   ● **Costieres de Nimes**★★★ £B

DOM. DE LA TOURADE   Gigondas
This 15-ha property is now responsible for some of the most exciting Gigondas of all. Also produced is a little spicy, forward Côtes du Rhône and 2 Vacqueyras, of which the old-vine Cuvée de l'Euse is much the more serious. (DM)
● **Gigondas** Traditionelle★★★ £B   Font des Aieux★★★★ £C   Cuvée Morgan★★★★ £C
● **Vacqueyras**★ £B   Cuvée de l'Euse★★★ £C

DOM. DU TRAPADIS   Rasteau   *UK stockists:* GrD, VTr, SVS
Les Adrès is a classic, Grenache-based southern Rhône blend, while Harys is pure Syrah. Traditional vinification (no destemming) produces wines which are both rich and structured. Even the Côtes du Rhône will benefit from short cellaring. (DM)
● **Côtes du Rhône-Villages Rasteau**★★★ £B   Adrès★★★ £C   Harys★★★ £C
● **Côtes du Rhône**★★ £B

PIERRE USSEGLIO   Châteauneuf-du-Pape   *UK stockists:* Gau, BBR, Las
Very good regular red Châteauneuf as well as the super-dense and rich old-vine Mon Aïeul and an exceptional Cuvée Cinquantenaire which was produced in 1999. Expensive Réserve des Deux-Frères replaces the

Cinquantenaire as the top label from 2000. (DM)

● **Châteauneuf-du-Pape** Tradition★★★ £C Mon Aïeul★★★★ £E
○ **Châteauneuf-du-Pape** Tradition★★ £C

RAYMOND USSEGLIO Châteauneuf-du-Pape *UK stockists:* F&R
The reds here are sturdy and traditional. The Tradition is firmly structured in its youth while the Impériale, sourced from a plot planted in 1902, understandably offers greater depth and complexity and is a wine of real substance and power. The reds are bottled unfiltered and offer great value. (DM)

● **Châteauneuf-du-Pape** Tradition★★★ £D Cuvée Impériale★★★★ £E
○ **Châteauneuf-du-Pape** Tradition★★★ £D

DOM. DE LA VIEILLE-JULIENNE Châteauneuf-du-Pape *UK stockists:*SVS, OWL,Sel
Côtes du Rhône and Châteauneuf-du-Pape are all produced from old vines, the key to the good to exceptional wines here. The top two *cuvées* are remarkable. Vieilles Vignes Réservé is extraordinary – 95per cent Grenache, heady and super-rich. (DM)

● **Châteauneuf-du-Pape**★★★ £C VV★★★★★ £F VV Réservé✪✪✪✪✪ £H
● **Côtes du Rhône**★★ £B VV★★★ £B

DOM. DU VIEUX-TÉLÉGRAPHE Châteauneuf-du-Pape *UK stockists:*J&B,BBR,THt,Sel,Tan,Las
The Bruniers have been benchmark producers here for two decades. The Grenache-dominated red is one of the great wines of the AC. Fine white comes from Clairette, Grenache Blanc, Bourboulenc and Roussanne. Vieux Mas des Papes is a very impressive second wine. (DM)

● **Châteauneuf-du-Pape**✪✪✪✪✪ £E Le Vieux Mas des Papes★★★ £C
○ **Châteauneuf-du-Pape**★★★★ £E ● **Vin de Pays de Vaucluse** Le Pigeoulet★★ £B

DOM. VIRET Côtes du Rhône-Villages
Very impressive 30-ha organic domaine. The reds are particularly striking: all come from low yields, are vinified without recourse to sulphur and are bottled without filtration. (DM)

● **Côtes du Rhône-Villages Saint-Maurice** Les Colonnades★★★ £C Emergence★★★★ £C
● **Côtes du Rhône-Villages Saint-Maurice** Renaissance★★★ £B
○ **Côtes du Rhône** La Coudée d'Or★★ £C

Other wineries of note

Dom. des Amadieu (Cairanne), Dom. Amido (Tavel), Dom Lucien Barrot (Châteauneuf-du-Pape), Dom. de Cabasse (Séguret), Cave de Cairanne (Cairanne), Ch. du Campuget (Costières de Nimes), Ch. d'Or et de Gueules (Costières de Nimes), Ch. Saint-Estève d'Uchaux (Côtes du Rhône-Villages), Ch. Saint-Roche (Lirac), Ch. de Valcombe (Côtes du Ventoux), Dom. Chaume-Arnaud (Vinsobres), Clos de Caveau (Vacqueyras), Clos du Mont Olivet (Châteauneuf-du-Pape), Dom. Coste-Chaude (Visan), Dom. Coteaux des Travers (Rasteau), Feraud-Brunel (Châteauneuf-du-Pape), Dom. de Grand Tinel (Châteauneuf-du-Pape), Dom. Grapillon d'Or (Gigondas), Dom. La Blaque (Coteaux de Pierrevert), Dom. La Boussière (Gigondas), Dom. La Manarine (Côtes du Rhône), Dom. Lea (Vins de Pays de Gard), Dom. Le Bérane (Côtes du Ventoux), Dom. Les Goubert (Gigondas), Mas de Boislauzon (Châteauneuf-du-Pape), Dom. Perrin (Côtes du Rhône), Dom. Raspail-Ay (Gigondas), Dom. de Renjarde (Côtes du Rhône), Dom. Saint-Benoit, Dom. de Villeneuve (Châteauneuf-du-Pape)

An in-depth profile of every producer can be found in Wine behind the label 2006

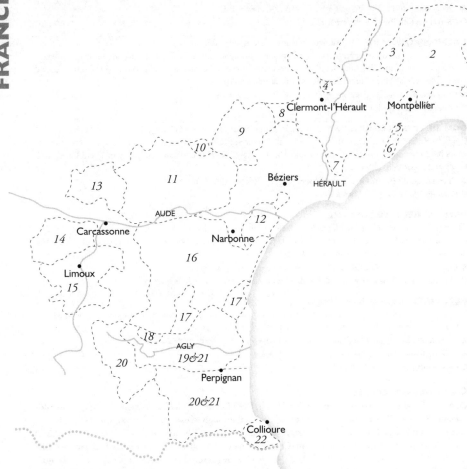

FRANCE

Clermont-l'Hérault

Montpellier

Béziers

HÉRAULT

AUDE

Carcassonne

Narbonne

Limoux

AGLY

Perpignan

Collioure

ESPAÑA

1	Muscat de Lunel	11	Minervois
2	Coteaux du Languedoc	12	Coteaux du Languedoc
3	Coteaux du Languedoc Pic		La Clape
	Saint-Loup	13	Cabardès
4	Coteaux du Languedoc	14	Côtes de la Malepère
	Montpeyroux	15	Limoux
5	Muscat de Mireval	16	Corbières
6	Muscat de Frontignan	17	Fitou
7	Coteaux du Languedoc	18	Maury
	Picpoul de Pinet	19	Côtes du Roussillon-Villages
8	Faugères	20	Côtes du Roussillon
9	Saint-Chinian	21	Rivesaltes, Muscat de Rivesaltes
10	Muscat de Saint-Jean de	22	Banyuls, Collioure
	Minervois		

FRANCE

Languedoc

The key *vins de pays* are **Vins de Pays d'Oc** and **Vin de Pays de l'Hérault**. **Coteaux du Languedoc** includes twelve communes which can add their village names as *crus*. These include **La Clape, Picpoul de Pinet, Cabrières, Montpeyroux, Pic-Saint-Loup** and **Saint-Drézéry**. Reds feature Syrah, Grenache and Mourvèdre, whites Roussanne, Grenache Blanc and Clairette. Fine reds are also emerging from **Faugères** and **Saint-Chinian**. There are a number of Muscat-based *vins doux naturels* including **Muscat de Frontignan, Muscat de Mireval** and **Muscat de Lunel**. South of Narbonne are **Minervois, Corbières** and **Fitou**, where old-vine Carignan plays a key role with some increasingly old Syrah, Grenache and Mourvèdre. **Cabardès** also has real potential with the Bordeaux varieties Cab Sauv, Merlot and Cab Franc. At **Limoux**, cool hillside vineyards are planted to Chardonnay and Mauzac and now red varieties too. Good sparkling wine is made here.

Roussillon

Exciting wines are being made throughout the **Côtes du Roussillon** and the **Côtes du Roussillon-Villages** ACs. As well as Grenache, the other Rhône varieties are important too. **Collioure** AC shares the same vineyard area as **Banyuls**. Syrah, Carignan, Mourvèdre and Cinsault are all cultivated. The **Vin de Pays des Côtes Catalanes** produces red blends based on Cab Sauv and Merlot. A new and very exciting region that covers much of the physical area shared by Maury AC is the newly established **Vin de Pays des Coteaux de Fenouillèdes** in the Agly Valley. The great traditional wines of the Roussillon are the fortified **Maury, Rivesaltes, Banyuls** and **Muscat de Rivesaltes**

Languedoc & Roussillon Vintages

Much of the development in the region in recent years makes a longer term assessment of the wines more erratic than other regions. However, there have been significant changes in vintage conditions from one year to another. These variations are more pronounced as you move further inland. Vineyards nearer the coast benefit from a benign maritime climate and are more consistent. (see also: Vintage Charts)

Wizard's Wishlist

New wave Languedoc whites

DOM. LES AURELLES ○ Coteaux du Languedoc Aurel
STRICTO SENSO ○ Vin de Pays d'Oc Chardonnay
DOM. JEAN-LOUIS DENOIS
○ Vin de Pays d'Oc Sainte Marie
DOM. VIRGILE JOLY ○ Vin de Pays de l'Hérault
DOM. LACOSTE ○ Muscat de Lunel Clos Bellevue
DOM. LE CONTE DE FLORIS

○ Vin de Pays de Cassan Lune Blanche
MAS PLAN DE L'OM
○ Coteaux du Languedoc Feuillage
DOM. DE L'HORTUS
○ Vin de Pays Val de Montferrand Grande Cuvée
MAS JULLIEN ○ Vin de Pay de l'Hérault
MAS DE DAUMAS GASSAC ○ Vin de Pays de l'Hérault
PRIEURÉ DE SAINT-JEAN-DE-BÉBIAN
○ Coteaux du Languedoc
DOM. DE LA GARANCE
○ Vin de Pays des l'Hérault Les Claviers

15 top Languedoc reds

DOM. CANET-VALETTE ● Saint-Chinian Le Vin Maghani
CH. GRÈS SAINT-.PAUL ● Coteaux du Languedoc Syrhus
CH. DES ESTANILLES ● Faugères Cuvée Syrah
MAS DE l'ECRITURE ● Coteaux du Languedoc l'Ecriture
DOM. CLAVEL ● Coteaux du Languedoc Copa Santa
DOM. ALAIN CHABANON
● Coteaux du Languedoc Montpeyroux L'Esprit de Font Caude
DOM. DE LA GRANGE DES PÈRES
● Vin de Pays de l'Hérault
CH. DE LA NÉGLY
● Coteaux du Languedoc Clos du Truffière
MAS CHAMPART ● Saint-Chinian Clos de La Simonette
MAS DE DAUMAS GASSAC ● Vin de Pays de l'Hérault
PRIEURÉ DE SAINT-JEAN-DE-BÉBIAN
● Coteaux du Languedoc
DOM. RIMBERT ● Carignator
DOM. TERRE INCONNUE ● Sylvie
BORIE DE MAUREL ● Minervois Cuvée Sylla
CH. DE CAZENEUVE
● Coteaux du Languedoc Le Sang du Calvaire

Great Languedoc values

DOM. BORIE LA VITARELLE ● Saint-Chinian Les Cres
CH. DES ESTANILLES ● Faugères Prestige
CH. DE JONQUIERES ● Coteaux du Languedoc
CH. CAPITOUL ○ Coteaux du Languedoc Les Rocailles
CLOS BAGATELLE ● Saint-Chinian La Gloire de Mon Pere
MAS PLAN DE L'OM ● Coteaux du Languedoc Roucan
CH. CAZAL VIEL ● Saint-Chinian Cuvée des Fées
CH. LA BARONNE
● Corbières Montagne d'Alaric Unfiltered
GUY MOULINIER ● Saint-Chinian Les Terasses Grillées
CH. SAINT-JACQUES D'ALBAS
● Minervois Château Saint-Jacques d'Albas
CLOS DES CAMUZEILLES
● Vin de Pays de l'Aude Carignan
DOM. LA MAURERIE ● Saint-Chinian Esprit du Terroir
LA REGALONA ● Cabardès La Regalona
MAS DE FOURNEL ● Coteaux du Languedoc Pierre

Languedoc

A selection of fortifieds
CELLIER DES TEMPLIERS
● **Banyuls Grand Cru** Henri Vidal
DOM. CAZES ● **Rivesaltes** Ambré
COUME DEL MAS ● **Banyuls** Quintessence
LES CLOS DE PAULILLES
● **Banyuls** Rimage Mise Tardive
DOM. FONTANEL ● **Rivesaltes**
DOM. LA TOUR VIEILLE ● **Banyuls** Cuvée Francis Cantié
MAS AMIEL ● **Maury** Charles Dupuy
DOM. DU MAS BLANC ● **Banyuls** La Coume
DOM. DES SCHISTES O **Muscat de Rivesaltes**

Classic Rousillon reds
DOM. CALVET-THUNEVIN
● **Côtes du Roussillon-Villages** Hugo
DOM. DE CASENOVE
● **Côtes du Roussillon** Commandant François Jaubert
CLOS DEL REY
● **Côtes du Roussillon-Villages** Clos del Rey
DOM. DU CLOS DES FÉES
● **Côtes du Roussillon-Villages** La Petite Sibérie
DOM. FONTANEL ● **Côtes du Roussillon-Villages** Prieuré
DOM. GARDIES ● **Côtes du Roussillon-Villages** La Torre
DOM. GAUBY
O **Vin de Pays de Côtes Catalanes** Coume Gineste
DOM. LA TOUR VIEILLE ● **Collioure** Puig Oriol
CLOT DE L'OUM
● **Côtes du Roussillon-Villages** Numero Uno
DOM. DEPEYRE

● **Côtes du Roussillon-Villages** Sainte-Colombe
DOM. DE LA RECTORIE ● **Collioure** La Coume Pascole
DOM. LE SOULA
● **Vin de Pays des Côteaux des Fenouillèdes** Le Soula
DOM. MATASSA ● **Vin de Table** Matassa
MAS DE LA DEVEZE ● **Côtes du Roussillon-Villages**
DOM. POUDEROUX
● **Côtes du Roussillon-Villages** Mouriane

A value for money selection
CH. DE CALADROY
● **Côtes du Roussillon-Villages** La Cour Carrée
DOM. DE CASENOVE ● **Côtes du Roussillon** Garrigue
CLOS DEL REY ● **Vin de Pays d'Oc** Mas del Tey
CH. DE JAU ● **Côtes du Roussillon-Villages** Talon Rouge
DOM. FONTANEL ● **Côtes du Roussillon-Villages** Cistes
LES CLOS DE PAULILLES ● **Cóllioure**
DOM. JOREL ● **Vin de Pays d'Oc** Grenache Pesquies
DOM. LA TOUR VIEILLE ● **Collioure** Puig Oriol
DOM. LAGUERRE ● **Côtes du Roussillon** Le Ciste
MAS DES BAUX
● **Vin de Pays des Côtes Catalanes** Rouge Gorge
DOM. PIETRI-GERAUD ● **Collioure**
MAS KAROLINA ● **Vin de Pays des Côtes Catalanes**

Languedoc & Roussillon/A-Z of producers

Languedoc

JEAN-MICHEL ALQUIER Faugères *UK stockists:* Rae
Top quality Faugères and some fine white vins de pays. Reds are dominated by Syrah along with some very old Carignan adding real depth and character. Both whites are blends of Roussanne and Marsanne, the Domaine Jean-Michel Alquier gloriously nutty and complex. (DM)
● **Faugères** Les Premières★★ £B Réserve La Maison Jaune★★★ £C Bastides★★★ £C
O **Vin de Pays de l'Hérault** Roussanne/Marsanne★ £B Jean-Michel Alquier★★★ £C

DOM. L'AIGUELIÈRE Coteaux du Languedoc Montpeyroux *UK stockists:* GVF, N&P
Viognier and Sauvignon Blanc are blended for the fresh, fruit driven white Sarments. Good Tradition red, however the real excitement are the two top reds. Both are 100% Syrah *cuvées*, dense and powerful, with an underlying elegance and refinement often missing in the region. Both will benefit from five years' ageing. (DM)
● **Coteeaux du Languedoc** Côte Dorée★★★★ £B Côte Rousse★★★★★ £B
● **Coteeaux du Languedoc** Tradition★★ £B O **Vin de Pays d'Oc** Sarments★★ £B

DOM. DES AIRES HAUTES Minervois *UK stockists:* Gau, Maj, Gar
As well as the regular forward, fruit-driven Minervois Tradition there is a spicy Vin de Pays d'Oc Malbec and a little Chardonnay. The top two reds are from the sub-appellation of La Livinière and both are blended from Syrah, Grenache and Carignan. (DM)
● **Minervois** La Livinière★★ £B Clos de l'Escandil★★★ £C
● **Minervois** Tradition★ £B

New entries have producer's name underlined

FRANCE

DOM. LES AURELLES Coteaux du Languedoc   *UK stockists:Bal, Han*
Characterful unfiltered wines are made from vines of up to 70 years old. Deella is soft, forward and fruit-driven.
Solen and Aurel are more seriously structured. Solen is 65% Carignan 35% Grenache. Aurel is a blend of
Grenache, Mourvedre and Syrah. Aurel Blanc is 100% barrel-fermented Roussanne. (DM)
● **Coteaux du Languedoc** Déella★★ £B   Solen★★★ £C   Aurel★★★★ £D
O **Coteaux du Languedoc** Aurel★★★★ £D

DOM. LEON BARRAL Faugères   *UK stockists: WTr, A&B, P&S*
Small Faugères domaine producing wines with all the raw, spicy, meaty character of the appellation. Barral's top
red Valinière is outside appellation regulations and is simply labelled, *vin de table*. A heady, rich, ripe and
powerful blend of 80% Mourvedre plus Syrah. The wines are structured and ageworthy. (DM)
● **Faugères**★★ £C   Cuvée Jadis★★★ £D   ● **Valinière** Vin de Table★★★★ £F

DOM. BORIE DE MAUREL Minervois   *UK stockists: Odd, CdP*
Sizeable Minervois property producing some of the best reds in the region. A white, Aude, is broad and fat with
rich nutty fruit. Belle de Nuit is solely Grenache. The more seriously structured La Féline is 70% Syrah, Cuvée
Léopold 100% Cab Sauv. Maxim is 100% Mourvèdre, Sylla 100% Syrah. Both will develop well with four or
five years in bottle. (DM)
● **Minervois** Belle de Nuit★★ £C   Cuvée Maxim★★★ £C   Cuvée Sylla★★★★ £D
● **Minervois La Liviniere** La Féline★★★ £B   ● **Vin de Pays** Cuvée Léopold★★★ £C

DOM. BORIE LA VITARÈLE Saint-Chinian   *UK stockists: GVF, Por*
Most of the vineyard area is in Saint-Chinian and extends into the Coteaux du Languedoc. Powerful, dense and
muscular reds are the order of the day. Of the two Saint-Chinians, Les Schistes, is mainly Grenache with Syrah
and a touch of Carignan. Les Crès, blends Syrah, Grenache and Mourvèdre from vines yielding less than 20
hl/ha. These will age well. (DM)
● **Saint-Chinian** Les Schistes★★★ £C   Les Crès★★★★ £C
● **Coteaux du Languedoc** Les Terres Blanches★★ £B

DOM. CANET-VALETTE Saint-Chinian   *UK stockists: C&C, SVS*
A benchmark for Saint-Chinian, the top red here, Le Vin Maghani, is arguably the finest in the AC. Minimal
handling in the cellar with neither fining nor filtration helps to achieve this. No new oak is used and the
character of the impressively intense fruit really shines through in the wines. (DM)
● **Saint-Chinian** Une et Mille Nuits★★ £B   Le Vin Maghani★★★★ £D

DOM. ALAIN CHABANON Coteaux du Languedoc Montpeyroux   *UK stockists:N&P,Ter*
From his small Montpeyroux property, formerly known as Domaine Font Caude, Alain Chabanon produces three
very good reds and a tiny amount of a white labelled Trelans, which is classified as *vin de table*. The reds are vinified
with long macerations, often over a month, and are aged in wood, not all new. (DM)
● **Coteaux du Languedoc** L'Esprit de Font Caude★★★★ £E Les Boissieres★★★★ £E
● **Vin de Pays d'Oc** Merle aux Alouettes★★★ £E

CH. CAPITOUL Coteaux du Languedoc La Clape   *UK stockists: BFs*
Organically farmed property producing two excellent Les Rocailles labels. The white is a barrel-aged blend of
Roussanne and Viognier. The richly concentrated red is 40% Grenache, 40% Mourvèdre with 20% Carignan
adding some peppery spice. (DM)
● **Coteaux du Languedoc Pic Saint-Loup** Les Lavandines★ £B   Les Rocailles★★★ £C
O **Coteaux du Languedoc** Les Rocailles★★ £B

CH. DE CAZENEUVE Coteaux du Languedoc Pic Saint-Loup   *UK stockists:CBg,Bal,Lay,BBR*
The reds here come in a number of guises. Syrah features strongly in the blend of Les Calcaires and the oak-
aged Le Roc des Mates. Le Sang du Calcaire, now the top red, is an individual selection of the best the harvest
has to offer. The white is a nutty barrel-fermented blend of Roussanne, Grenache Blanc and Viognier. (DM)
● **Coteaux du Languedoc** le Roc des Mates★★★ £C Le Sang du Calvaire★★★ £D
● **Coteaux du Languedoc** Calcaires★★ £B   O **Coteaux du Languedoc**★★ £B

CH. CAZAL VIEL Saint-Chinian   *UK stockists: HWC, Wai*
Large Saint-Chinian domaine producing sturdily traditional reds under the Château Cazal Viel label and a range

FRANCE

of mainly varietal Vin de Pays d'Oc under the Laurent Miquel label, as well as a fine, rich, fleshy and spicy Saint-Chinian, Bardou, sourced from a single block of the finest Syrah on the Cazal Viel estate. (DM)

Château Cazal Viel
- **Saint-Chinian** Cuvée des Fées★★ £B l'Antenne★★ £C Larmes des Fées★★★ £E

Laurent Miquel
- **Saint-Chinian** Bardou★★★ £E

CH. COUPE-ROSES Minervois *UK stockists:*RsW

A quite extensive range is made at this fine Minervois producer. Good whites include a varietal Roussanne Minervois aged in small oak. The impressively concentrated Orience is 90% Syrah with a little Grenache; smoky, herb/spice-edged Granaxa is largely old-vine Grenache. (DM)
- **Minervois** Les Plots★★ £C Cuvée Orience★★★ £C Granaxa★★★ £C
- **Minervois** La Bastide★★ £B ● **Rancio** Vin de Table★★★ £B ○ **Vin de Pays d'Oc** Viognier★★ £B
○ **Minervois**★★ £B ◉ **Minervois**★ £B

CH. DES ESTANILLES Faugères *UK stockists:* THt, Ter,C&R

Syrah is the key variety and is notably successful here. Grenache and Mourvèdre are also important among the reds and the white is a blend of Marsanne, Roussanne and Viognier. The Préstige and Syrah *cuvées*, the latter seeing around a year in oak, will both stand some age.(DM)
- **Faugères** Tradition★ £B Préstige★★★ £B Cuvée Syrah★★★ £C
○ **Coteaux du Languedoc**★★ £B ◉ **Faugères**★ £B

CH. L'EUZIÈRE Coteaux du Languedoc Pic Saint-Loup *UK stockists:* Lib,Gar,But

The nutty, lightly floral white, Grains de Lune, is an unusual blend of Roussanne, Vermentino, Rolle and Grenache Blanc. Of the three reds, Cuvée Tourmaline is a blend of Syrah and Grenache, whereas the more serious and structured Cuvées l'Almandin and Les Escarboucles are neither fined nor filtered and have a small dollop of Mourvèdre. (DM)
- **Coteaux du Languedoc** l'Almandin★★★ £B Escarboucles★★★ £C Tourmaline★★ £B
○ **Coteaux du Languedoc** Grains de Lune★★ £B

CH. GRÈS SAINT-PAUL Coteaux du Languedoc *UK stockists:* FCA,Gar,Idg

An extensive range of wines is produced including some straightforward well-priced, fruit-driven *vin de pays* Chardonnay, Sauvignon and Merlot. The red Coteaux du Languedoc wines are most important though from a quality point of view. There are also two decent sweet Muscats. (DM)
- **Coteaux du Languedoc** Sirius★★★★ £D Antonin★★★ £C
- **Coteaux du Languedoc** Romanis★★ £B La Grange Phlippe★★ £B

CH. DE JONQUIÈRES Coteaux du Languedoc *UK stockists:*Vne,Vnf

The small range includes a good straightforward white, which is barrel-fermented and aged with *bâtonnage*. Its red partner is a juicy, soft, easygoing Vin de Pays de l'Hérault red. More serious are the red Coteaux du Languedoc which blends Mourvèdre with lesser amounts of Syrah, Carignan and Grenache and a Syrah-dominated label Renaissance. (DM)
- **Vin de Pays de l'Hérault** Domaine de Jonquières★★ £B
- **Coteaux du Languedoc**★★★ £C ○ **Coteaux du Languedoc**★ £B

CH. LA LIQUIÈRE Coteaux du Languedoc *UK stockists:*SVS

Sizeable domaine with 55ha of red varieties and 7ha of whites producing good Coteaux du Languedoc and Faugères. Vineyards are largely at altitude in the schistous soils of the best *terroirs* of Faugères. (DM)
- **Faugères** Vieilles Vignes★★ £B Cistus★★★ £C ○ **Coteaux du Languedoc** Schistes★★★ £B

CH. LE THOU Coteaux du Languedoc *UK stockists:* A&B

Significant improvements have been seen in the wines here since the 2000 vintage, particularly the top *cuvée* Georges et Clem. Blended from Syrah(70%) with the balance Grenache, Mourvèdre and a little spicy Carignan, the wine is rich and fleshy. (DM)
- **Coteaux du Languedoc**★★ £B Georges et Clem★★★ £C

CH. MANSENOBLE Corbières mansenoble@wanadoo.fr *UK stockists:*RMe

Fine, modern Corbières property with 20 ha planted to Carignan, Grenache, Syrah and a small amount of

New entries have producer's name underlined

Mourvèdre. Three red Corbières are produced. A small amount of a special limited *cuvée* Marie-Annick is also produced. (DM)
● **Corbières** Montagne d'Alaric★★ £B   Réserve★★★£C

CH. DE MONTPEZAT   Coteaux du Languedoc   UK stockists:Vnf
The Domaine de Montpezat-labelled *vin de pays* bottles are as striking as their Coteaux du Languedoc stablemates. Les Enclos is Merlot with some Cab Sauv, the Cuvée Prestige (Cab Sauv and Syrah) is bigger, more concentrated. Palombieres is ripe and forward, Pharaonne is firmer and impressively structured. (DM)
● **Coteaux du Languedoc** Les Palombières★★ £B   La Pharaonne★★★ £C
● **Vin de Pays d'Oc** Les Enclos★★ £B   Cuvée Prestige★★★ £C

CH. DE LA NÉGLY   Coteaux du Languedoc La Clape   UK stockists: THt
Consistently excellent Languedoc domaine producing sound quality at all price levels. As well as the Mourvedre dominated L'Ancely and splendid Porte au Ciel Syrah, the *super-cuvée* Clos du Truffière, comes from a small plot of exceptional Syrah near Pezenas, which is part owned by Bordeaux wine merchant Jeffrey Davies. These are very ageworthy. (DM)
● **Coteaux du Languedoc** Porte au Ciel★★★★★ £G   Clos du Truffière★★★★★ £G
● **Coteaux du Languedoc** La Falaise★★★ £C   L'Ancely★★★★ £F
● **Coteaux du Languedoc** La Côte★★ £B   Domaine de Boède Le Grès★★★ £C

CH. SAINT-JACQUES D'ALBAS   Minervois   UK stockists:Han,Goe
Two impressive minervois are produced here. The Domaine wine is a blend of Syrah with older vine Grenache and Carignan. The Château label has a higher proportion of Syrah, it is deeper and more firmly structured. (DM)
● **Minervois** Domaine Saint-Jacques d'Albas★★ £B   Ch. Saint-Jacques d'Albas★★★ £C

CHEVALIER VINS   Minervois   www.chevaliervins.fr
Brigitte Chevalier has initially sourced 3 properties where she can select the best parcels and vinify and age the wines in their cellars. A maximum of 500 cases of each wine are produced. Single-varietal entry-level wines under the Stricto Senso label are astonishingly good value for the quality. (NB)
Chevalier Vins
● **Minervois** Laure Saint★★★ £B   ● **Minervois** Concertino★★★ £B
● **Minervois La Liviniere** Clos du Causse★★★ £B   ● **Saint Chinian** Château La Bousquette★★★ £C
Stricto Senso
● **Vin de Pays d'Oc** Cinsault★★★ £B   Grenache★★ £B   Syrah★★ £B
O **Vin de Pays d'Oc** Chardonnay★★★ £B

DOM. CLAVEL   Coteaux du Languedoc   UK stockists: CBg,N&P, Odd,Tan,Adm,NYg
This property is situated just beyond the suburbs of the city of Montpellier. There is a lightly herb-scented, nutty, fruit-driven white as well as three fine reds. The old-vine Copa Santa, regularly on the cusp of four stars, is a splendid ageworthy blend of Syrah, Grenache and Mourvèdre. (DM)
● **Coteaux du Languedoc** Le Mas★★ £B   Les Garrigues★★ £B   Copa Santa★★★★£C

CLOS DE L'ANHEL   Corbières   www.anhel.fr   UK stockists: L&W,SVS
Small 7-ha property making some of the very best wine in Corbières. Les Terrassettes blends 60-year-old Carignan with Grenache, Syrah and Cinsault, Les Dimanches is a more serious and backward blend of just Carignan and Grenache. (DM)
● **Corbières** Les Terrassettes★★ £B   Les Dimanches★★★£C

CLOS BAGATELLE   Saint-Chinian   UK stockists: Han,ACH,Ter
One of the larger Saint-Chinian growers and one of the best. The lesser bottlings all show ripe and dark spicy fruit and there is an attractively fruity characterful rosé. The Veillée d'Automne and premium *cuvée* La Gloire de Mon Père are more seriously structured and ageworthy examples, blends of Mourvèdre, Syrah and Grenache. (DM)
● **Saint-Chinian** Veillée d'Automne★★★ £B   La Gloire de Mon Père★★★★ £D
● **Saint-Chinian** Donnadieu Mathieu et Marie★★ £B

CLOS DES CAMUZEILLES   Fitou   UK stockists:SVS
For Fitou, Laurent Tibes' Clos des Camuzeilles is a real gem producing 2 very fine reds and a Muscat de Rivesaltes as well. A very fine varietal Carignan shows great intensity of fruit while La Grangette Fitou is dominated by 80-year-

FRANCE

old Carignan with a touch of 35-year-old Grenache. (DM)

● **Vin de Pays de l'Aude** Carignan★★★ £B ● **Fitou** La Grangette★★★★ £D

CLOS MARIE Coteaux du Languedoc Pic Saint-Loup

Some of the best and priciest wines in the Coteaux du Languedoc are now emerging from this 17 ha property. Grenache Blanc, Roussanne and Clairette which is used to produce a fine nutty white Manon. The four reds take pride of place and all are serious, dense and powerful examples. L'Olivette will drink well young, the other *cuvées*, should be given five years or so. (DM)

● **Coteaux du Languedoc** Métairie du Clos★★★★ £E Glorieuses★★★★£F
● **Coteaux du Languedoc** L'Olivette★★★ £C Simon★★★£D

DOM. DE LA CROIX-BELLE Vin de Pays des Côtes de Thongue *UK stockists:*Gar,L&S

Extensive range of wines all offering good value. The straightforward varietal wines are soft and fruity. The Champs, No 7 and Cascaillou wines that stand out here. Top of the range Cascaillou, is an elegant blend of Grenache, Syrah and Mourvèdre. (DM)

● **Vin de Pays des Côtes de Thongue** no 7★★ £B Cascaillou★★★ £C Calades★ £B
○ **Vin de Pays des Côtes de Thongue** Les Champ des Lys★ £B no 7★★ £B

DOM. JEAN-LOUIS DENOIS Vin de Pays d'Oc *UK stockists:* BBR, Gar

Excellent small range of reds and whites from the Limoux area including a good barrel-fermented sparkling Tradition Brut. Southern varieties are planted with those from Bordeaux for the reds. *Cuvée* Chloé, is a Merlot and Cabernet Sauvignon. La Rivière is a taut mineral-scented Chenin, Sainte-Marie an elegant and finely structured Chardonnay. (DM)

● **Vin de Pays d'Oc** Grande Cuvée★★ £B Chloé★★★ £C ○ **Tradition Brut**★★ £B
○ **Vin de Pays d'Oc** Sainte Marie★★★ £C ○ **Limoux** La Rivière★★★ £C

DOM. DE LA GARANCE Vin de Pays de l'Hérault *UK stockists:*Ind,GCW

Source of a number of fine, very traditional wines. Key here are some very old plantings of Carignan as well as the lowly Ugni Blanc allied to very low yields of around 15–20 hl/ha, not to mention an excellent *terroir* just to the north of Pézenas. Bruixas is a fascinating pruney and figgy late-harvest red. (DM)

● **Vin de Pays de l'Hérault** Les Armières★★★ £C ● **Bruixas** Vin de Liqueur★★★ £D
○ **Vin de Pays des l'Hérault** Les Claviers ★★ £C
● **Corbières** Réserve★★ £B Cuvée de Quarante★★ £B ◉ **Corbières** ★ £B

DOM. DE LA GRANGE DES PÈRES Vin de Pays de l'Hérault *UK stockists:*Gun

One of the Languedoc's top reds produced from Mourvèdre, Syrah and Cabernet Sauvignon farmed to almost organic standards. Approachable in its youth the wine has all the density, velvety tannin and class to age gracefully. There is a tiny amount of a very fine Roussanne-based white with equally deftly handled oak. (DM)

● **Vin de Pays de l'Hérault**★★★★★ £F

DOM. DE L'HORTUS Coteaux du Languedoc Pic Saint-Loup *UK stockists:* CdP, L&S,

Now one of the benchmark producers for Pic Saint-Loup. The tight and restrained red Grande Cuvée, blended mainly from Syrah and Mourvèdre, is aged in two-thirds new wood. Grande Cuvée white is ripe, almost tropical and produced from barrel-fermented and aged Viognier and Chardonnay. (DM)

● **Coteaux du Languedoc Pic Saint-Loup** Grande Cuvée★★★ £C
○ **Vin de Pays Val de Montferrand** Grande Cuvée★★★ £C

DOM. VIRGILE JOLY Coteaux du Languedoc *UK stockists:* GCW

Very recently established domaine, with an excellent *terroir* producing two fine and pure minerally reds dominated by Carignan, Grenache and Syrah. The barrel-fermented white *vin de pays* bottling is 100% Grenache Blanc. (DM)

● **Coteaux du Languedoc** Saturne★★★ £C Virgile★★★ £D
○ **Vin de Pays de l'Hérault**★★★ £C

DOM. DES JOUGLA Saint-Chinian *UK stockists:*THt,BBR,But

Good earthy examples of Saint-Chinian. Classique is the soft and approachable regular bottling, a blend of Grenache, Syrah, Mourvèdre, Carignan and Cinsault. Tradition is Grenache, Mourvèdre and Syrah. Best of all is the oak aged Cuvée Signée which has a rich and concentrated old-vine character. It is produced from Grenache, Syrah and Carignan. (DM)

116

New entries have producer's name underlined

FRANCE

● **Saint-Chinian** Classique★★ £B Les Tradition★★★ £B Cuvée Signée★★★ £B

DOM. LACOSTE Muscat de Lunel
Very unusual in being planted solely to Muscat à Petits Grains. Sweet and late-harvest wines are the speciality here although a dry Vin de Pays d'Oc Muscat is made. Lacoste is forward and richly grapey, Clos Bellevue is very intense with great poise and refinement. (DM)
○ **Muscat de Lunel** Lacoste★★ £B Clos Bellevue★★★£B

LA GRANGE DE QUATRE SOUS Vin de Pays d'Oc
Well established largely organic property. As well as the oak-aged Jeu du Mail (Viognier and Marsanne), a little Chardonnay is also made. Les Serrottes is a southern-style blend of Syrah and Malbec, whereas the Lo Molin is a fine and elegant Bordeaux blend of Cab Sauv and Cab Franc. (DM)
● **Vin de Pays d'Oc** Lo Molin★★★ £C Les Serrottes★★★£C
○ **Vin de Pays d'Oc** Jeu du Mail★★ £B

LA REGALONA Cabardès
Tiny new operation producing potentially great red. Low yields and modern winemaking including a pre-fermentation cold maceration and malolactic in barrel contribute to a wine of beguiling depth. (DM)
● **Cabardès** La Regalona★★★ £C

DOM. LA TOUR BOISÉE Minervois *UK stockists:* The,HKW,Wat
Among the very best estates in Minervois, producing wines of density and real class. The top wine Jardin Secret is an opulently rich Grenache aged in new oak. Expect all the top reds to develop well with short to mid-term ageing. (DM)
● **Minervois** Marielle et Frédérique★★★ £B Jardin Secret★★★★ £D
● **Minervois**★★ £B Marie-Claude★★★ £B ○ **Minervois** Marie-Claude★★ £B

DOM. LE CONTE DE FLORIS Coteaux du Languedoc *UK stockists:* Idg
Tiny domaine with 4.9ha of red varieties and a mere 1.1ha of white under vine. There are 3 red *cuvées*: La Lena, Villafranchien and the top wine Carbonifère. The white Lune Blanche is a fascinating blend of old-vine Carignan Blanc and Grenache Blanc with Roussanne lending a real floral quality. (DM)
● **Coteaux du Languedoc** Villafranchien★★★ £C ○ **Vin de Pays de Cassan** Lune Blanche★★★ £C

DOM. LES CREISSES Vin de Pays de l'Hérault
Just two reds are produced here. The regular Les Creisses bottling is a blend of Syrah, Grenache and Cab Sauv that will gain flesh with two to three years' age. Les Brunes is a considerable step up in quality and has a price tag to match. A dense, rich, cedary blend of Cabernet Sauv and Syrah. (DM)
● **Vin de Pays d'Oc** Les Creisses★★ £B Les Brunes★★★★ £D

DOM. DE LA MARFÉE Coteaux du Languedoc *UK stockists:* Han
Two sturdy, powerful, initially tannic wines are produced. Les Champs Murmurés is a southern Rhône-style blend with some Cab Sauv thrown in, while Les Vignes qu'on Abat is dominated by old-vine Carignan. There is the potential here for these to be very classy wines indeed. (DM)
● **Coteaux du Languedoc** Champs Murmurés★★★ £E Vignes qu'on Abat★★★ £D

MAS BRUGUIÈRE Coteaux du Languedoc Pic Saint-Loup *UK stockists:* HHB
One of the best producers in the Pic Saint-Loup sub-region. Les Muriers is a nutty, floral, medium-weight spicy white. Cuvée Calcadiz is well-priced but can be a touch raw, L'Arbouse is rounder, suppler and fuller while the flagship La Grenadière is a blockbuster red: spicy and dense, with a solid chunk of vanilla oak. (DM)
● **Coteaux du Languedoc** Calcadiz★ £B L'Arbouse★★ £B Grenadière★★★ £C
○ **Coteaux du Languedoc** Les Muriers★★ £B

MAS CAL DEMOURA Coteaux du Languedoc *UK stockists:* GVF
A vibrant, berry-fruited rosé is joined by the *cuvée* L'Infidèle, a blend of Syrah, Mourvèdre, Grenache, Cinsault and Carignan. The wine is full, rich and quite extracted, part oak aged. The 1999 and 2001 were particularly good. (DM)
● **Coteaux du Languedoc** L'Infidèle★★★ £D

MAS CHAMPART   Saint-Chinian   *UK stockists:*Rs W, SVS, Ter
Top class property producing a fruity rosé and a rich, lightly oaked white as well as four good to very good reds from classic southern varieties. The Vin de Pays d'Oc is an unusual blend of 80% Cab Franc with the balance Syrah. The top two reds will develop well for a decade at least. (DM)
● **Saint-Chinian** Causse de Bousque★★★ £B   Clos de La Simonette★★★★ £C
● **Saint-Chinian** Côte d'Arbo★★ £B   ● **Vin de Pays d'Oc**★ £B

MAS DE DAUMAS GASSAC   Vin de Pays de l'Hérault   *UK stockists:* Adm
Undoubtedly the most famous property in the Midi and the inspiration for the many high-quality winemakers now spread throughout Languedoc and Roussillon. The red dominated by Cab Sauv (80%) and the intense nutty complex white are true benchmarks. Aimé Guibert also produces a range of straightforward wines under the Moulin de Gassac label. (DM)
● **Vin de Pays de l'Hérault** Mas de Daumas Gassac★★★★★ £F
● **Vin de Pays de l'Hérault** Moulin de Gassac Elise★★★ £C
O **Vin de Pays de l'Hérault** Mas de Daumas Gassac★★★★★ £F

MAS D'ESPANET   Vin de Pays d'Oc
The white Eolienne is a part barrel-fermented blend of Sauvignon, Grenache Blanc and Viognier. Les Lens, Cinsault, Grenache and Syrah, displays a pure strawberry, forward character. Top red, Bois du Roi, is a Syrah-based oak-aged red. (DM)
● **Vin de Pays d'Oc** Les Lens★★ £B   Bois du Roi★★★ £C
O **Vin de Pays d'Oc** Eolienne★★ £B

MAS DE L'ECRITURE   Coteaux du Languedoc   *UK stockists:*Han, Ter
Producer of some of the finest red wines in the appellation. Les Pensées is the more approachable and forward of the two. L'Ecriture is a denser, firmer blend of mainly Syrah with some Grenache and Mourvèdre. Both wines are given a lengthy vatting and aged in new and one-year-old oak. Neither is fined nor filtered. (DM)
● **Coteaux du Languedoc** Les Pensées★★★ £D L'Ecriture★★★★ £E

MAS FOULAQUIER   Coteaux du Languedoc Pic Saint Loup   *UK stockists:*THt,BBR
Top-quality small Languedoc producer making richly concentrated reds of great fruit definition and purity. Le Rollier is a roughly equal blend of Syrah and Grenache. Les Calades is mainly Syrah with a touch of oak ageing, it is the most firmly structured of the trio. Handling is kept to a minimum and filtration avoided. (DM)
● **Coteaux du Languedoc** L'Orphée★★★ £B   Rollier★★★ £C   Les Calades★★★★ £C

MAS DE FOURNEL   Coteaux du Languedoc Pic Saint Loup   *UK stockists:*, Han
The regular red here is 70% Syrah and 30% Grenache, ripe and supple with richly concentrated dark berry, mint, herb and spice-scented fruit. Cuvée Pierre is a post-fermentation vat selection aged in small oak, a proportion of it new, and adds some rich creamy vanilla notes to the excellent fruit of the regular bottling. (DM)
● **Coteaux du Languedoc**★★ £B   Pierre★★★ £B

MAS HAUT BUIS   Coteaux du Languedoc
This is one of the better producers in the appellation. Costa Caoude is a blend of Syrah, Grenache and Cab Sauv, of which 70% is aged in barrique. Deep, dense and powerful, a balanced and surprisingly refined wine. (DM)
● **Coteaux du Languedoc** Costa Caoude★★★ £D

MAS JULLIEN   Coteaux du Languedoc   *UK stockists:* Ter,Gun,Han
One of the most established properties in the Coteaux du Languedoc. now farmed biodynamically. Two reds and a floral white Vin de Pays de l'Hérault are produced and the approach is one of restraint, in quite marked contrast to some of the extracted wines of the region. (DM)
● **Coteaux du Languedoc**★★★ £D   États d' Âme★★★£C
O **Vin de Pay de l'Hérault**★★ £C

MAS LUMEN   Coteaux du Languedoc
Tiny and newly established domaine. The organically handled *terroir* appears to be potentially exceptional. The wines are rich, concentrated and very pure. Although possessing immediate appeal, the exceptional La Sylve is firm, supple and will develop greater complexity with age. (DM)

New entries have producer's name underlined

FRANCE

● Coteaux du Languedoc★★★ £B La Sylve★★★★ £C

MAS DE MORTIÈS Coteaux du Languedoc Pic Saint Loup *UK stockists:* HHB, SVS
Fine property in the southern sector of the Pic Saint-Loup sub-region. Good white as well as vibrant dark and chunky Coteaux du Languedoc are produced and Syrah Que Sera Sera is first class. The wines here are very reasonably priced. (DM)
● Coteaux du Languedoc Que Sera Sera★★★ £B

MAS PLAN DE L'OM Coteaux du Languedoc
Another fine emerging Languedoc domaine producing three reds and a white of impressive class and style. The white Feuillage, blending Roussanne with Grenache Blanc. Œillade has immediate forward blackberry and bramble fruit. The top two reds both require a little patience. (DM)
● Coteaux du Languedoc Œillade★★ £B Miéjour★★★ £C Roucan★★★ £D
O Coteaux du Languedoc Feuillage★★★ £B

DOM. DU MÉTEORE Faugères *UK stockists:*SVS
Fine Faugères white as well as red is produced at this small domaine, and a good-quality Viognier is made here too. Two red *cuvées* are produced. The Tradition is unoaked; Les Orionides is more obviously modern and fleshy in style but offers great depth of fruit and perfectly judged spicy, smoky oak. (DM)
● Faugères Tradition★★ £B Les Orionides★★★ £B O Faugères Tradition★★ £B

DOM. DE MONTCALMES Coteaux du Languedoc *UK stockists:* THt
Very impressive new Languedoc red, a dense, fleshy modern blend of Syrah, Grenache and Mourvèdre. Deep and concentrated dark berry fruit is subtly underpinned by a grip of creamy new wood and supple, well-rounded tannins. (DM)
● Coteaux du Languedoc★★★★ £D

DOM. GUY MOULINIER Saint-Chinian
Well established, the Moulinier family continue to produce some of the better wines in this AC. Tradition, a blend of Grenache, Syrah and Mourvèdre is the most accessible of the wines. Les Sigillaires, Mourvèdre and Syrah; and oak-aged Les Terrasses Grillées, 95% Syrah with Grenache and Mourvèdre, are serious and structured. (DM)
● Saint-Chinian Tradition★★ £B Sigillaires★★★ £B Terrasses Grillées★★★ £B

DOM. THIERRY NAVARRE Saint-Chinian *UK stockists:*SVS
Thierry Navarre has 12ha of biodynamically farmed vines from which he produces 2 fine Saint-Chinians and a straightforward third wine, a *vin de table* called Œillades. His *terroir* is excellent with deep, very well-drained schist soils. The Saint-Chinians are among the more striking wines of the appellation. (DM)
● Saint-Chinian Le Laouzil★★ £B Olivier★★★ £C

DOM. DE PEYRE ROSE Coteaux du Languedoc *UK stockists:*Ter
Two of the most renowned reds in the Languedoc are made here. Clos des Cistes with a hint of Grenache is the more forward. Clos Syrah Léone is more structured, denser, darker and on occasion shows real animal aromas. A nutty white is also produced from Rolle, Roussanne and Viognier. (DM)
● Coteaux du Languedoc Clos de Cistes★★★ £E Clos Syrah Léone★★★★ £E

PRIEURÉ DE SAINT-JEAN-DE-BÉBIAN www.bebian.com *UK stockists:*RsW,Ter
One of the esteemed names of the Languedoc. The current vintages of both red from Syrah, Grenache and Mourvèdre and white from mainly Roussanne are very rich and stylish, especially the white. (DM)
● Coteaux du Languedoc★★★ £D O Coteaux du Languedoc★★★★ £D

DOM. DES RAVANES Vin de Pays des Coteaux de Murviel *UK stockists:*GCW
The focus here is on the Bordeaux varieties and the *terroir* supports this with a mix of argile-calcareous and gravel soils. Top red is the splendid Le Prime Verd, a pure Petit Verdot of great intensity. There are 2 unusual late-harvest wines. Cinq Seaux d'Oeillade is solely Cinsault. Cuvée de l'Ille is a very sweet, richly textured Ugni Blanc with marked botrytis. (DM)
● Vin de Pays Le Prime Verd★★★★ £E Les Gravieres du Taurou★★★★ £D
● Vin de Pays Merlot/Cabernet Sauvignon★★ £B Cuvée Diogène★★★ £C
● Vin de Pays Cinq Seaux d'Oeillade★★★ £E O Vin de Pays L'Ille★★★★ £E

119

FRANCE

DOM. RIMBERT   Saint-Chinian   *UK stockists:*FWW,Gar,SVS,Ter
Jean-Marie Rimbert's domaine is the source of good Saint-Chinian as well as two very fine pure Carignan wines simply labelled as *vin de table*, Le Chant de Marjolaine and the extraordinary Carignator, blended from two vintages, sourced from 50- to 70-year-old vines and fermented in *barriques*. Heady and exotic it is one of the most characterful wines of the region. (DM)
- Carignator★★★★ £D ● Le Chant de Marjolaine★★★ £C
- Saint Chinian Les Travers de Marceau★★ £B

ROC D'ANGLADE   Coteaux du Languedoc   *UK stockists:*RsW, GCW
One of the finest reds in the Languedoc is produced at this small domaine owned by Remy Pedreno and René Rostaing from Côte-Rôtie. Pedreno also owns a tiny 0.3-ha vineyard in the Costières de Nîmes from which he produces a very low-yielding Syrah labelled Clos de la Belle. (DM)
- Coteaux du Languedoc★★★★ £E

DOM. DE TABATAU   Saint-Chinian
The Gracia brothers have a small holding of just over 7ha of vineyards, the majority of which are planted to Syrah, Grenache and Carignan with a little Mourvèdre. There is also around 1ha of Chardonnay, Roussanne and Clairette. At present 2 red Saint-Chinians, a rosé and a *vin de pays* Cuvée Geneviève from the white holdings are produced. Bottling is without filtration.(DM)
- Saint-Chinian Élevé en Fûts de Chêne★★ £B Élevé en Fûts de Chêne★★★ £B

DOM. TERRE INCONNUE   Gard
These garage-style wines are simply labelled as *vin de table*. Léonie is an astonishingly heady and rich 100% Carignan, Sylvie is dominated by Syrah with a little Grenache and Carignan, more opulent than the wines of the northern Rhône and loaded with super-ripe fruit. Los Abuelos is 100% Grenache. (DM)
- Los Abuelos★★★★ £E ● Léonie★★★★★ £E ● Sylvie★★★★★ £E

Other wineries of note
Dom. d'Antugnac (Limoux), Baron 'Arques (Limoux), Ch. des Cres Ricards (Coteaux du Languedoc), Ch. l'Engarran (Coteaux du Languedoc), Ch. La Baronne (Corbières), Ch. La Dournie (Saint-Chinian), Ch. de Lascaux (Coteaux du Languedoc), Ch. La Voulte Gasparets (Corbières), Ch. Massamier La Mignarde (Minervois), Clos Centeilles (Minervois), Dom. Grand Arc (Corbières), Dom. Lacroix-Vinel (Coteaux du Languedoc), Dom. La Maurerie (Saint-Chinian), Mas des Brousses (Coteaux du Languedoc), Mas Mouries (Coteaux du Languedoc), Moulin de Ciffre (Saint-Chinian), Dom de Nizas (Coteaux du Languedoc), Sieur d'Arques (Limoux), Val d'Orbieu (Narbonne)

An in-depth profile of every producer can be found in Wine behind the label 2006

Roussillon

DOM. CALVET-THUNEVIN   Maury
One of a number of newly emerging domaines from the Agly Valley producing very fine wines from vineyards more traditionally used for fortifieds. You are struck by the mineral character of the wines rather than their fruit. The Vin de Pays d'Oc bottling has more Carignan and both have a high proportion of Grenache. They will age well. (DM)
- Côtes du Roussillon-Villages★★★★ £E ● Vin de Pays d'Oc★★★★ £D

DOM. DE CASENOVE   Côtes du Roussillon
Impressive modern fruit-driven wines are now being made at this fine property. The Commandant François Jaubert, produced from mainly Syrah and partly aged in new oak, is powerful, dense and smoky. Newly added is a very limited production *super-cuvée* Domaine Saint-Luc Pla del Rei, which is extremely expensive. (DM)
- Côtes du Roussillon Garrigue★★ £B Commandant François Jaubert★★★★ £E

CH. DE CALADROY   Côtes du Roussillon-Villages
Sizeable well established Roussillon property with a fine range of dry reds, a Muscat de Rivesaltes, a relatively light red Rivesaltes and a barrel-fermented white dominated by Chardonnay. Pride of place though are the excellent, characterful and well priced reds. (DM)

New entries have producer's name underlined

● **Côtes du Roussillon-Villages** La Cour Carrée★★★ £B Les Grenats★★★ £B
● **Côtes du Roussillon-Villages** La Juliane★★★ £C ● **Rivesaltes** Tuilé★★ £B

DOM. DU CLOS DES FÉES Côtes du Roussillon-Villages *UK stockists:* Odd
Very impressive newly established domaine producing good to stunning red Roussillons, even the entry level
Les Sorcières is full of dark, spicy bramble and herbs. A tiny amount of a remarkable 100% Grenache, La
Petite Sibérie, is as notable for its astronomical price as for its exceptional quality. (DM)
● **Côtes du Roussillon-Villages** Les Sorcières★★ £B Vieilles Vignes★★★★ £E
● **Côtes du Roussillon-Villages** Clos des Fées★★★★ £F La Petite Sibérie★★★★★ £H

CLOS DE PAULILLES Banyuls & Collioure *UK stockists:*GVF, P&S
Like Château de Jau this domaine is owned by the Dauré family. Collioure is much improved in recent vintages
and there are some striking Banyuls bottlings. Mas Cristine Rivesaltes comes from a separate property, it is rich,
full of dark honeyed aromas and impressively complex on release. (DM)
Clos des Paulilles
● **Collioure**★★★ £C ● **Banyuls** Rimage Mise Tardive★★★ £E Cap Bear★★★ £E
Mas Christine
● **Rivesaltes**★★★ £E

CLOS DEL REY Maury *UK stockists:* GCW
Consistently exciting quality from one of the finest producers in the Roussillon. Mas del Rey is 50/50 Grenache and
Carignan. More edgy, nervy and intense in style is the brilliant Clos del Rey from 100% Carignan. (DM)
● **Côtes du Roussillon-Villages** Clos del Rey★★★★ £E
● **Vin de Pays d'Oc** Mas del Tey★★★★ £D

CLOT DE L'OUM Côtes du Roussillon-Villages
Among the new wave of exciting new arrivals in the Agly Valley. Three very good reds are made here from
vineyards planted at 200 and 500 metres on a mix of granite, gneiss and schistous soils. All the wines have the
structure and refinement to evolve very well in bottle. (DM)
● **Côtes du Roussillon-Villages** Saint-Bart VV★★★★ £C Numero Uno★★★★ £D
● **Côtes du Roussillon-Villages** Las Compagnie des Papillons★★★ £C

COUME DEL MAS Banyuls & Collioure *UK stockists:* GCW, FWW
Now one of the leading lights of both the Banyuls and Collioure ACs. The majority of the vineyard holding is in the
site of Coume del Mas, with south-facing slopes and deep, well-drained clay soils. A number of *cuvées* are produced
from both appellations. (DM)
● **Banyuls** Galateo★★★ £C Quintessence★★★★ £E
● **Collioure** Schistes★★ £B Quadratur★★★ £C O **Collioure** Folio★★★ £C

DOM. DEPEYRE Côtes du Roussillon *UK stockists:* SVS
Small emerging Roussillon property producing a fine barrel-fermented white *vin de pays* from Grenache Gris
and Blanc as well as Muscat. The regular Roussillon red is dominated by Carignan, whereas the Sainte-
Colombe is mainly Grenache and aged in a combination of *cuve* and small oak. (DM)
● **Côtes du Roussillon-Villages**★★★ £B Sainte-Colombe★★★★ £C
O **Vin de Pays Côtes Catalanes** Eleve en Futs de Chene★★ £B

DOM. FONTANEL Côtes du Roussillon-Villages *UK stockists:* SVS
Rich and heady fortifieds are fine examples and good value for money, as are the three Roussillon reds, the
regular bottling is soft, forward and juicy, while Cistes is rich and opulent with upfront, spicy fruit. The Prieuré
is denser, more powerful, a real medium-term cellaring prospect. (DM)
● **Côtes du Roussillon-Villages**★★ £B Cistes★★★ £B Prieuré★★★★ £C
● **Rivesaltes** ★★★ £C O **Muscat de Rivesaltes**★★★ £B

DOM. GARDIES Côtes du Roussillon-Villages *UK stockists:* GVF, Bal, Jer
A really first-class property in this exciting AC. Some good Muscat de Rivesaltes and two whites are produced. It
is the reds though that are particularly noteworthy. La Torre is a massive and dense dark, brooding mix of
Mourvèdre and Carignan. The most expensive wine, La Falaises is an extremely ageworthy and powerful
expression of Syrah. (DM)

● Côtes du Roussillon-Villages VV★★★ £C   La Torre★★★★ £E   Falaises★★★★★ £E
● Côtes du Roussillon-Villages Millères★★★ £B   O Côtes du Roussillon VV★★★ £C

DOM. GAUBY   Côtes du Roussillon-Villages   *UK stockists:* A&B, F&R, Rae
Gérard Gauby is perhaps the most significant producer of modern reds and whites from the Roussillon. He is also involved in producing the thrilling wines of DomaineLe Soula in the high-altitude vineyards of the Agly Valley. The top red, Muntada, a superbly crafted Syrah, is very rich, concentrated and powerful. (DM)
● Côtes du Roussillon-Villages Vieilles Vignes★★★★ £D   Muntada★★★★★ £F
O Vin de Pays de Côtes Catalanes Vieille Vignes★★★ £C   Coume Gineste★★★★ £E

DOM. LAGUERRE   Côtes du Roussillon   *UK stockists:*RSW
Eric Laguerre, the former head of the Saint-Martin de Fenouillet co-op, is also involved with Gérard Gauby at Domaine le Soula but has his own small 15-ha domaine with high-altitude biodynamically farmed vineyards where he produces excellent red and white Côtes du Roussillon. (DM)
O Côtes du Roussillon Le Ciste★★★ £B

LA PASSION D'UNE VIE   Côtes du Roussillon-Villages
First class Roussillon property owned by Henri Despeaux and Bernard Magrez in Bordeaux, the owner of Pape-Clement. This is a rich, opulent, fruit-driven red but of impressive grip and structure. Expect to be able to age the wine for five or more years and gain additional complexity. (DM)
● Côtes du Roussillon-Villages★★★★ £D

DOM. LE SOULA   Vin de Pays des Côteaux des Fenouillèdes   *UK stockists:*RSW,BBR
The white and the red here are labelled under the new Vin de Pays des Fenouilledes in the Agly Valley. The wines are excellent and are indicative of the long-term potential of these biodynamically farmed high-altitude vineyards. Both are benchmark Roussillons. (DM)
● Vin de Pays des Côteaux des Fenouillèdes Le Soula★★★★★ £E
O Vin de Pays des Côteaux des Fenouillèdes Le Soula★★★★ £E

DOM. LA TOUR VIEILLE   Banyuls & Collioure   *UK stockists:* Yap
Well-established producer of both Collioure and Banyuls, the quality of which is consistently good. La Pinède is a full, dense, spicy black-fruit style, while the Puig Oriol is more fragrant with a marvellous *garrigue* scent to its deep berry fruit. (DM)
● Collioure La Pinède★★ £B Puig Oriol★★★ £C   ● Banyuls Francis Cantié★★★ £C
O Vin de Pays de la Côte Vermeille Les Canadells★★★ £C

MAS AMIEL   Maury   A: L&S,HHB
While there are good red and white Roussillons, it is the remarkable range of fortified Maury which stand out. They range from young minimally aged current vintages through to old vintage bottles. The top *cuvées* are Réserve, Privilège and the immensely rich Charles Dupuy. The top wines are extraordinarily intense. (DM)
● Côtes du Roussillon-Villages Carrerades★★★ £C   ● Maury Privilège★★★★ £E
● Maury 15 Ans d'Age★★★★ £E   Charles Dupuy★★★★★ £E

MAS DES BAUX   Côtes du Roussillon
Small Roussillon property producing a comprehensive range of *vin de pays* red, white and rosé as well as a fine, pure and complex Côtes du Roussillon red. The top *vin de pays* Rouge Baux is a rich and opulent blend which adds Cab Sauv to Rhône red varietals and gets 12 months in new oak. The Côtes du Roussillon Soleil Rouge is tighter, more restrained and elegant. (DM)
● Côtes du Roussillon Soleil★★★ £C   ● Vin de Pays Rouge Gorge★★★ £B
● Vin de Pays Rouge Baux★★★ £C   O Vin de Pays Baux Blond★★ £B

DOM. DU MAS BLANC   Banyuls & Collioure   *UK stockists:* VTr, C&R
Splendid 21-ha Banyuls and Collioure property developed by the late Dr André Parcé and now run by his son Jean-Michel. As well as the excellent Collioures, some of the very best Banyuls are also created here, including aged bottles that are both rare and pricey. (DM)
● Collioure La Llose★★ £B   Cosprons Levant★★★ £C   Les Junquets★★★★ £D
● Banyuls Rimage★★★★ £E   La Coume★★★★ £F

FRANCE *(vertical, right margin)*

MAS DE LA DEVÈZE   Côtes du Roussillon-Villages   **A: L&S**
This is a recently established property in the Roussillon village of Tautavel producing both red and white. A premium red Le Mas will be available in 2005. The 66 is a soft, forward brambly red dominated by Grenache. Characterful, barrel-fermented nutty Mas white blends Maccabeu and Grenache Gris in equal amounts. These are well priced wines to watch. (DM)

● **Côtes du Roussillon-Villages** 66★★ £B
○ **Vin de Pays des Pyrénées Orientales★★★** £B

MAS KAROLINA   Côtes du Roussillon-Villages
New domaine adding further evidence of the splendid potential of the Agly Valley. Vinification is modern with a pre-fermentation cold soak for the reds, vatting of 3–4 weeks and malolactic in new oak for the Syrah components. The white is fermented cool and both reds and whites are aged on fine lees. (DM)

● **Côtes du Roussillon-Villages★★★** £D   ● **Vin de Pays des Côtes Catalanes★★★** £C

DOM. MATASSA   Vin de Pays des Côtes Catalanes   *UK stockists:* Adm
Just over 300 cases a year at this excellent high altitude property. The barrel-fermented white is dominated by Grenache Gris, the red, classified as vin de table because of the bureaucracy of the area, is dominated by highly characterful very old vine Carignan, full of dark pepper and herbal spices. (DM)

● **Vin de Table** Matassa★★★★ £E
○ **Vin de Pays des Côtes Catalanes** Matassa★★★ £D

DOM. PIÉTRI-GÉRAUD   Banyuls & Collioure   *UK stockists:* FMV, BBR
This is a very fine mother-and-daughter domaine producing benchmark Collioure and Banyuls. As well as an excellent Collioure, one of the best in the appellation, a white Banyuls and dense Cuvée Joseph Geraud are produced. (DM)

● **Collioure★★★** £C

OLIVIER PITHON   Côtes du Roussillon-Villages   *UK stockists:*CdP
The Pithons have 9ha of organically tended vineyards from which they produce 2 reds and 2 whites of impressive style and intensity. Whites are vinified and aged in a mix of new and used oak; reds get a long 25–30 day maceration and and are aged in a mix of small oak and *foudres*. (DM)

● **Côtes du Roussillon** La Coulée★★★ £B   Les Vignes de Saturne★★★ £B
○ **Côtes du Roussillon** Cuvée Lais★★★ £B   Cuvée D18★★★★ £B

DOM. POUDEROUX   Maury   *UK stockists:* THt, Wai
Splendid producer, with a range of not only excellent Côtes du Roussillon reds but some very fine fortified wines as well. Although among the finest of the new wave of red wine producers in the Roussillon, the Poudereaux domaine is no flash in the pan. The family have been involved in Maury viticulture since 1826. (DM)

● **Côtes du Roussillon-Villages** Terre Brune★★★ £C   Mouriane★★★★ £E
● **Maury** Mise Tardive★★★ £C   Hors d'Age★★★★ £D   Grande Reserve★★★★ £E

DOM. PUIG-PARAHŸ   Côtes du Roussillon
The Puig family have been involved in Roussillon viticulture since the phylloxera crisis in France in 1878 and as a result own some remarkable old-vine holdings. Grenache is up to 80 years old, Carignan as much as 130. This contributes to the fine quality of the reds here. A range of exciting fortifieds is also available. (DM)

● **Côtes du Roussillon** Fort St-Pierre★★★ £C   Ballides★★★ £D   Georges★★★ £B
○ **Vin de Pays d'Oc** Sant Lluc★★ £B   Miserys★★ £B

DOM. DE LA RECTORIE   Banyuls & Collioure   *UK stockists:* A&B, Bal, Cam
One of the finest producers of Collioure and Banyuls. There are three *cuvées* of red Collioure and a presentable rosé. The sturdiest of the three Collioures, Le Seris is produced from very old Carignan and Grenache vines. Very good Banyuls includes two regular *cuvées* – the best is Cuvée Léon Parcé. (DM)

● **Collioure** Col de Bast★★ £B   La Coume Pascole★★★ £D   Le Seris★★★ £C
● **Banyuls** Léon Parcé★★★ £C   ○ **Vin de Pays de la Côte Vermeille** L'Argile★★★ £C

DOM. DES SCHISTES   Côtes du Roussillon-Villages   *UK stockists:*FMV,P&S,ACh
A small, first-class range of both table and fortified wines. The reds are characterised by the old-vine quality of the fruit, which adds an extra dimension. La Coumeille, the top red, is 100% Syrah, aged in oak, the wine is very fine with a spicy, dark, intense fruit quality. (DM)

123

Roussillon

FRANCE

● **Côtes du Roussillon-Villages** Tradition★★ £B Terrasses★★★ £C Coumeille★★★ £C
● **Maury** Cerisaie★★★ £C O **Muscat de Rivesaltes**★★★ £B

DOM. SEGUELA Côtes du Roussillon-Villages   *UK stockists:* GVF, May
Dedicated small Roussillon grower, producing first class, characterful reds with an impressive depth and purity of fruit. Soft, spicy, brambly Condalies is mainly Carignan with some Syrah and Grenache. Jean-Julien is a dense old-vine blend of Syrah and Carignan while Planète-Seguela, very low yielding Carignan, Syrah, Grenache and Cinsault, is rich and well-structured. (DM)
● **Côtes du Roussillon-Villages** Jean-Julien★★★ £C Planète-Seguela★★★★ £E
● **Côtes du Roussillon-Villages** Les Condalies★★★£B

DOM. DE LA SERRE Maury
With vines ranging from 25 to 120 years of age the complex old-vine character of the Grenache and Carignan at Maury is reflected in the wines. Rich, structured with a mineral, fiery character running through them expect these wines to develop well in bottle over at least five to seven years. (DM)
● **Côtes du Roussillon-Villages** Serre Longue★★★★ £C Hypogee★★★★ £D

DOM. SERRELONGUE Maury
Tiny domaine producing exquisite wines from 20 to 120 year old vineyards planted to a combination of Mourvèdre, Syrah, Carignan and Grenache. Do not expect fruit bombs, the overriding character here is minerality, with subtle deeply spicy black fruits and an intensity rarely found in the Midi. These are beguiling wines, full-bodied and rampantly alcoholic but balanced too. (DM)
● **Côtes du Roussillon-Villages** Extrait de Passion★★★★ £D Esprit de Vin★★★★★ £E

DOM. DES SOULANES Vin de Pays des Côtes Catalanes
Based at Tautavel in the heart of Côtes du Roussillon, two of the the wines here take the Vin de Pays des Côtes Catalanes classification. Côtes du Roussillon-Villages and Maury fortifieds are also to be produced. The Grenache dominated Cuvée Bastoul-Laffite is firmly structured and will develop well in bottle. A domaine to watch.(DM)
● **Vin de Pays des Côtes Catalanes** Jean Pull★★★ £B Bastoul-Laffite★★★★ £C

DOM. DU TRAGINER Banyuls & Collioure
A fine range of Banyuls and improving Collioures, a real step up in the 2001 vintage, produced at this small organic property. Top Banyuls are particularly fine, the Grand Cru Hors d'Age is aged for at least 10 years in *demi-muid*. It is rich and toffeed with real depth and intensity. Traginer is one of the few remaining producers of a Banyuls Blanc. (DM)
● **Collioure** Al Riberal★★ £B Octobre★★★ £C Cuvée de Capitas★★★ £C
● **Banyuls** Mise Tardive★★★ £C Rimage★★★ £C Grand Cru Hors d'Age★★★ £E

DOM. VAQUER Vin de Pays des Côtes Catalanes   *UK stockists:* GCW
Long-established domaine with some fine traditional wines, often radically different from many of the region's new wave, including outstanding Rivesaltes. Vinification is traditional and the red wines are aged in *cuve* with no use of new oak. A Vieux Rivesaltes is also produced in very limited quantities. (DM)
● **Vin de Pays** Exigence★★★ £C L'Expression★★★ £D L'Exception★★★ £D
● **Vin de Pays** Bernard Vaquer★★ £B O **Vin de Pays** L'Exception★★★ £C Esquisse★★ £B
● **Rivesaltes** L'Extrait★★ £C Tuilé Post Scriptum★★★ £C O **Muscat de Rivesaltes**★★ £C

Other wineries of note
Dom. Cazes (Rivesaltes), Celliers des Templiers (Banyuls & Collioure), Ch. de Jau (Côtes du Roussillon-Villages), Dom. des Chenes (Côtes du Roussillon-Villages), Dom. Jorel (Vin de Pays d'Oc)

An in-depth profile of every producer can be found in Wine behind the label 2006

124

New entries have producer's name underlined

1 Les Baux de Provence
2 Coteaux d'Aix en Provence
3 Palette
4 Côtes de Provence
5 Coteaux Varois
6 Cassis
7 Bandol
8 Bellet

Provence and Corsica

Inland of Nice the tiny appellation of **Bellet**, offers well-structured reds and lightly floral nutty whites and fruity rosés. Key ACs **Côtes de Provence, Coteaux Varois, Coteaux d'Aix en Provence,Les Baux de Provence** are a source of fine reds and some decent whites and rosés. Tiny **Palette** offers fine red and white. The coastal ACs of **Cassis** and **Bandol** are sources of red, white and rosé. The Mourvèdre based reds from Bandol are particularly striking. There are three main Corsican appellations; **Vin de Corse, Patrimonio** and **Ajaccio**. as well as a number of *crus* within the Vin de Corse AC: **Calvi, Sartène, Figari, Porto-Vecchio** and **Coteaux du Cap Corse**. Both Coteaux du Cap Corse and Patrimonio are also entitled to the Muscat du Cap Corse AC

Provence & Corsica Vintages

The more established Provençal red ACs have consistently produced wines that develop well with age (see also Vintage Charts). Top older years for premium Provençal reds (mainly Bandol) are 1989, 1988, 1985, 1982, 1978, 1975 and 1970.

Wizard's Wishlist

15 Emerging classics from Provence

DOM. DES BÉATES
● Coteaux d'Aix-en-Provence Terra d'Or
CH. DE PIBARNON ● Bandol

CH. PRADEAUX ● Bandol
CH. ROUTAS ○ Vin de Pays du Var Cuvée Coquelicot
CH. SIMONE ○ Palette
DOM. DE LA TOUR DU BON ● Bandol
DOM. DU GROS NORÉ ● Bandol
DOM. LAFRAN-VEYROLLES ● Bandol Tradition
DOM. RABIEGA ● Côtes de Provence Clos Dière I
DOM. RICHEAUME
● Côtes de Provence Cuvée Columelle
DOM. TEMPIER ● Bandol Cabassou
DOM. DE TREVALLON
● Vin de Pays des Bouches-du-Rhône
CH. DE ROQUEFORT
● Côtes de Provence Rubrum Obscurum
DOM. HAUVETTE ● Les Baux de Provence
DOM. DE LAUZIERES ● Sine Nomine

Some great value choices

CH. VIGNELAURE ● Coteaux d'Aix-en-Provence
DUPERE-BARRERA ● Bandol India
DOM. DES BÉATES ● Coteaux d'Aix-en-Provence Béates
DOM. SORIN ● Bandol
DOM. RIMAURESQ ● Côtes de Provence
DOM. DE LA COURTADE ● Côtes de Provence
CH. BAS ● Coteaux d'Aix-en-Provence Cuvée du Temple
CH. DU ROUET ● Côtes de Provence Réservée
DOM. DU GRAND CROS ● Côtes de Provence Nectar

A-Z of producers

Provence

DOM. DES BÉATES Coteaux d'Aix-en-Provence   *UK stockists:* Men
Biodynamic operation formerly part owned by Michel Chapoutier. Les Béatines wines are drink-me-now styles, Domaine des Béates and Terra d'Or labels are blends of Cab Sauv, Syrah and Grenache. Terra d'Or is vinified and aged in new oak. (DM)
● **Coteaux d'Aix-en-Provence** Béates★★★ £C Terra d'Or★★★★ £E
● **Coteaux d'Aix-en-Provence** Les Béatines★ £B

DOM. DE LA BÉGUDE Bandol domainestari@wanadoo.fr   *UK stockists:* GCW
This dramatically improving Bandol domaine is now producing some of the more exciting wines in the appellation. It is ideally situated at the highest point of the AC at 430m. 30-year-old vines and low yields are also important. The red is bottled unfiltered. (DM)
● Bandol★★★★ £D ○ Bandol★★★ £C ◉ Bandol★★ £C

DOMAINES BUNAN Bandol www.bunan.com   *UK stockists:* Yap
The Bunan family have three Bandol estates and a Côtes de Provence property, Domaine Belouve, producing solid red, white and rosé. The top wine, Cuvée Charriage, is the richest and lushest of the range. Structured and supple, it should be very fine with 8 to 10 years' cellaring. (DM)
Château de La Rouvière
● Bandol★★★★ £D
Moulin des Costes
● Bandol★★★ £C Cuvée Charriage★★★★ £E
Mas de la Rouvière
● Bandol★★★ £C

CH. BAS Coteaux d'Aix-en-Provence
Sizeable property with 72 ha of vines. Top Cuvée du Temple wines particularly stand out. Rosé is part barrel-fermented; the red is a blend of Syrah, Cab Sauv and Grenache with impressive depth. The standout wine is the barrel-fermented white from Sauvignon, Rolle and Grenache Blanc. (DM)
● **Coteaux d'Aix-en-Provence** Pierre du Sud★ £B Cuvée du Temple★★★ £B
○ **Coteaux d'Aix-en-Provence** Pierre du Sud★ £B Cuvée du Temple★★★ £B
◉ **Coteaux d'Aix-en-Provence** Cuvée du Temple★★ £B

CH. DE BELLET Bellet châteaudebellet@aol.com
High-altitude vineyards enable Chardonnay to ripen successfully as well as the local Rolle that completes the white blend. The red and rosé are produced from Folle Noire, Bracquet, Cinsault and Grenache. The red is perfumed, supple and approachable, the white lightly floral and aromatic. (DM)
● Bellet★★★ £D ○ Bellet★★ £D ◉ Bellet★ £C

CH. LES VALENTINES Côtes de Provence gilles@lesvalentines.com
Biodynamic estate, producing very good Côtes de Provence. Les Valentines Blanc is vinified from a combination of early- and late-picked fruit. The small-production Cuvée Bagnard red is sourced from the best parcels of Syrah, Mourvèdre and Cab Sauv. (DM)
● **Côtes de Provence**★★ £B Bagnard★★★★ £D ◉ **Côtes de Provence**★★ £B

CH. DE PIBARNON Bandol pibarnon@wanadoo.fr   *UK stockists:* Bal, ABy, N&P, P&S
One of the best properties in Bandol with a powerful, structured, brambly red from mostly Mourvèdre that needs up to a decade to develop fully. White and rosé are a touch less exciting. (DM)
● Bandol★★★★ £D ○ Bandol★★ £C ◉ Bandol★ £C

CH. PRADEAUX Bandol   *UK stockists:* HHB, Lay
From 20 ha of prime Bandol vineyard one red is produced from Mourvèdre and a little Grenache. Traditionally vinified and aged in large wooden *foudres* for over three years. Very ageworthy. (DM)
126 ● Bandol★★★★ £D

CH. REVELETTE   Coteaux d'Aix-en-Provence   *UK stockists:*N&P
This 25-ha domaine produces a very good *vin de pays* Chardonnay, Le Grand Blanc, as well as one of the very best reds in the region from very high-altitude vineyards. Red Grand Rouge is Syrah and Cab Sauv. (DM)
● **Coteaux d'Aix-en-Provence** Le Grand Rouge★★★★ £E

CH. ROMANIN   Coteaux d'Aix-en-Provence   www.romanin.com
Sizeable, biodynamic property with 58 ha under vine. Decent white from Rolle, Ugni Blanc and Bourboulenc but better reds. The top wine, the Coeur Tertius is sourced from the best plots of Syrah, Mourvèdre, Cab Sauv and Grenache. (DM)
● **Les Baux-de-Provence**★★ £C   Coeur Tertius★★★ £E
○ **Les Baux-de-Provence**★★ £B

CH. DE ROQUEFORT   Côtes de Provence   *UK stockists:*Vex
Excellent biodynamic producer with good whites and some exceptional reds. Dense, powerful Rubrum Obscurum blends Grenache, Mourvèdre and Carignan. In exceptional years also produces a stunning Syrah/Carignan, La Pourpre. (DM)
● **Côtes de Provence** Corail★ £B   Mûres★★★ £B   Rubrum Obscurum★★★★ £E
○ **Côtes de Provence** Genêts★★ £B

CH. ROUTAS   Coteaux Varois   www.routas.com   *UK stockists:* **Col**,BBR
A comprehensive range from a state-of-the-art winery. Coquelicot is a nutty, subtly oaked blend of Viognier and Chardonnay. Otherwise the best wines are red. Le Trou de Infernet blends Grenache, Syrah and Cab Sauv; Agrippa d'Aubigne is Syrah/Cab Sauv; Cyrano is a spicy varietal Syrah. (DM)
● **Coteaux Varois** Le Trou de Infernet★★★ £C   Agrippa d'Aubigne★★★ £C
● **Vin de Pays du Var** Cyrano★★★ £C   ○ **Vin de Pays du Var** Coquelicot★★★ £C

CH. SIMONE   Palette   *UK stockists:***Yap**
The benchmark property in this tiny AC. Good, slightly rustic red from Grenache, Mourvèdre and Syrah. Better still is the old fashioned, honeyed white which is mainly Clairette. A small amount of decent but pricy rosé is also made. (DM)
● **Palette**★★★ £E   ○ **Palette**★★★★ £E

CH. VANNIÈRES   Bandol   www.châteauvannieres.com   *UK stockists:* C&O
Top Bandol estate with a powerful, stylish red. Good floral white Bandol is also produced along with a decent rosé and recently a red Côtes de Provence, an increasingly impressive junior version of the *grand vin*.
● **Bandol**★★★★ £E

DOM. DE LA COURTADE   Côtes de Provence   *UK stockists:*GBa
30 ha on the Ile-de-Porquerolles producing nutty, tropical, lightly oaked white from Rolle. The *grand vin* is a rich, brambly, spicy blend of Mourvèdre, Grenache and Syrah. (DM)
● **Côtes de Provence**★★★ £D   Alycastre★★ £B   ○ **Côtes de Provence**★★ £D

DUPÉRÉ BARRERA   Côtes de Provence   vinsduperebarrera@hotmil.com
This small operation is part *micro-négociant*, part producer. Red and a tiny amount of white Côtes de Provence come from the Barreras' own Domaine du Clos de la Procure vineyard. Their most established label, and one of the most opulent and stylish of the AC, is the Bandol India. The wines are bottled unfined and unfiltered. (DM)
● **Côtes de Provence**★★★★ £E   ● **Bandol** India★★★★ £D

DOM. DU GRAND CROS   Côtes de Provence   www.grandcros.fr
Family owned 22-ha property with extensive range of red, white and rosé, both *vin de pays* and AC. Regular Côtes de Provence wines are labelled L'Esprit de Provence. Of two top Nectar labels, the white is a barrel-fermented Chardonnay, the ageworthy red Cab Sauv and a touch of Syrah and Grenache. (DM)
● **Côtes de Provence** L'Esprit de Provence★★ £B   Nectar★★★ £C
● **Vin de Pays** Carignan★★ £B   ○ **Vin de Pays** Chardonnay★★ £B

DOM. DU GROS NORÉ   Bandol   www.gros-nore.com   *UK stockists:***Han**
White is typically fat with broad, warm, nutty fruit. The red Bandol is a big, brooding, unfiltered, complex

127

FRANCE

blend of Mourvèdre, Grenache and Cinsault. Will develop for a decade or more. (DM)
● Bandol★★★★ £C   O Bandol★★ £C

DOM. HAUVETTE Les Baux   *UK stockists:*CdP
First-class 13-ha property with a fine, nutty, citrus-infused barrel-fermented white from Marsanne, Roussanne and Clairette. Red Amethyste is based around Cinsault. Cornaline is bigger, a blend of Carignan (60 per cent) with Cinsault and Grenache. Seriously structured Domaine Hauvette blends Grenache, Syrah and Cab Sauv. (DM)
● Coteaux d'Aix-en-Provence Améthyste★★★ £D Cornaline★★★ £D
● Les Baux-de-Provence★★★★ £D   O Vin de Pays Blanc de Blancs★★★ £D

DOM. LA BASTIDE BLANCHE Bandol   bastide.blanche@libertysurf.fr   *UK stockists:*BRW
Three fine reds stand out. Sturdy Longue Garde is mainly Grenache. Fontanieu and Estagnol are Mourvèdre. All will develop for four to five years.(DM)
● Bandol Longue Garde★★★ £C Fontanieu★★★★£D Estagnol★★★★ £D

DOM. DE LA LAIDIÈRE Bandol
Good-value red, white and rosé Bandol. Mourvèdre-dominated red is firmly structured in its youth with a savoury, almost meaty character. It will gain an extra dimension with five years' age. (DM)
● Bandol★★★ £C

DOM. LAFRAN VEYROLLES Bandol   *UK stockists:* PBW
Very impressive red Bandol is now being made at this 10-ha property. White is also one of the better examples in the AC. Both reds are dense, powerful and finely structured, developing in bottle for five to six years. (DM)
● Bandol Tradition★★★★ £D Spéciale★★★★ £D ◉ Bandol ★£C

DOM. LA SUFFRENE Bandol
Emerging Bandol estate of real class. Spicy, citrusy white blends Clairette with Ugni Blanc. Sturdy regular Bandol blends Mourvèdre, Grenache, Cinsault and Carignan. Superbly supple, concentrated top wine, Cuvée des Lauves, is dominated by Mourvèdre. (DM)
● Bandol★★★ £C Cuvée des Lauves★★★★★ £E   O Bandol★★ £C

DOM. DE LAUZIÈRES Les Baux
Fine estate founded in 1992. Two reds are produced as Baux-de-Provence: lighter Equinoxe and denser, structured Solstice. Top wines are labelled as *vin de table*. The white Astérie is a superbly intense barrel-fermented Grenache Blanc. Muscular Sine Nomine unusually blends Petit Verdot with Grenache. (DM)
● Les Baux-de-Provence Solstice★★ £C Sine Nomine Vin de Table★★★★ £E
O Astérie Vin de Table★★★★ £D

MAS DE LA DAME Les Baux   www.masdeladame.com   *UK stockists:* L&W, HHB, AVn
Good-quality Baux-de-Provence estate producing great olive oils as well as wine. Fine red and white with consultancy provided by Jean-Luc Colombo. Top Coin Caché red is a supple, smoky old-vine blend of Grenache and Syrah. (DM)
● Les Baux-de-Provence Réserve★★ £B la Stèle★★★ £C Coin Caché★★★ £D
O Les Baux-de-Provence Coin Caché★★★ £D

DOM. RABIEGA Côtes de Provence   www.rabiega.com   *UK stockists:* L&S
Swedish-owned property producing good to very good red and white under both Domaine Rabiega and Rabiega Vin labels. Top white Clos d'Ière Blanc is a blend of Sauvignon, Chardonnay and Viognier; red Clos d'Ière I is a rich, oak-aged Syrah which develops for five to six years. (DM)
● Côtes de Provence Carbase★★ £C Mourbase★★ £C Clos d'Ière I★★★★ £E
O Vin de Pays Clos d'Ière★★★ £E   O Côtes de Provence Rouxanne★★ £C

DOM. RICHEAUME Côtes de Provence   *UK stockists:* BGL
25-ha estate producing consistently excellent reds. Tradition is Cab Sauv, Syrah, Grenache and Merlot. Cuvée Columelle is one of the best reds in Provence. Decent Viognier too. (DM)
● Côtes de Provence Tradition★★★ £C Cuvée Columelle★★★★ £E

New entries have producer's name underlined

FRANCE

DOM. RIMAURESQ Côtes de Provence www.rimauresq.fr *UK stockists:*May
36-ha Scottish-owned property. Good rosé and red, the top wines labelled R. Two whites are Ugni Blanc/Rolle
blends; the red R is Syrah and Cab Sauv – firm, structured and needing ageing. The Cuvée R rosé comes from
older plantings of Cinsault, Grenache and Mourvèdre. (DM)

● **Côtes de Provence**★★ £B Cuvée R★★★ £D
◉ **Côtes de Provence**★ £B Cuvée R★★ £C

DOM. SAINT-ANDRÉ DE FIGUIÈRE Côtes de Provence
Maritime-influenced 19-ha property. Some decent *vin de pays* as well as top AC wines. Intense Vieilles Vignes
rosé is Mourvèdre, Cinsault and Grenache, the top white barrel-fermented Rolle. Vieilles Vignes red is
Mourvèdre, 100-year-old Carignan and Syrah. The Reserve is mainly Mourvèdre with Syrah. Both are rich and
ageworthy. (DM)

● **Côtes de Provence** VV★★★ £C Grande Cuvée VV Réserve★★★ £D
O **Côtes de Provence**Delphine Réserve★★★ £D ◉ **Côtes de Provence** VV★★ £D

DOM. SORIN Bandol luc.sorin@wanadoo.fr
Luc Sorin has plots in the Côtes de Provence AC as well as Bandol and produces red wines of impressive density and
depth. As well as the Tradition *rouge* a limited Côtes de Provence Cuvée Privée is also produced which has 50%
Syrah. There is also a white Côtes de Provence Cuvée Sergine. (DM)

● **Bandol** Longue Garde★★★ £D ● **Côtes de Provence** Tradition★★ £C
◉ **Côtes de Provence** Terra Amata★ £D

DOM. TEMPIER Bandol *UK stockists:* Sav,SVS
One of the great Bandol producers. Wines are characterised by elegance rather than sheer power. Regular *cuvée*
is light compared to the others. Cuvée Spéciale is denser and richer. Three single-vineyard wines, La Tourtine,
Migoua and Cabassou, stand out. All will age well over a decade. (DM)

● **Bandol** Classique★★ £C Spéciale★★★ £D La Tourtine★★★★ £E
● **Bandol** Migoua★★★★ £E Cabassou★★★★★ £E ◉ **Bandol**★★ £C

DOM. DE TERREBRUNE Bandol
Massive, muscular and brooding red Bandol. This is a true *vin de garde*: a dense smoky, spicy Mourvèdre
requiring seven or eight years. The small amount of rosé and white produced is of a reasonable quality, the latter
capable of some age. (DM)

● **Bandol**★★★★ £D ◉ **Bandol**★★ £C O **Bandol**★★ £C

DOM. DE LA TOUR DU BON Bandol
Small 12-ha property producing very good red Bandol. Saint-Ferréol is finely structured, refined and very long-
lived. Rosé and white are decent enough but lack the interest of the reds. (DM)

● **Bandol**★★★ £D Saint-Ferréol★★★★ £E O **Bandol**★★ £C

DOM. DE TREVALLON Les Baux-de-Provence www.trevallon.fr *UK stockists:* Yap,Har
One of the great estates of Provence that ludicrously can only label the wines *vin de pays*. The red is a
marvellously intense and balanced blend of Cab Sauv and Syrah. The tiny amount of exquisite white is a
barrel-fermented blend of Marsanne, Roussanne and Chardonnay. (DM)

● **Vin de Pays des Bouches-du-Rhône**★★★★★ £F
O **Vin de Pays des Bouches-du-Rhône**★★★★★ £G

Other wineries of note
Ch. de Rouet (Côtes du Provence), (Ch. Vignelaure (Coteaux d'Aix-en-Provence), Dom. du Clos Alari (Côtes
du Provence), Mas de Cadenet (Côtes du Provence)

An in-depth profile of every producer can be found in Wine behind the label 2006

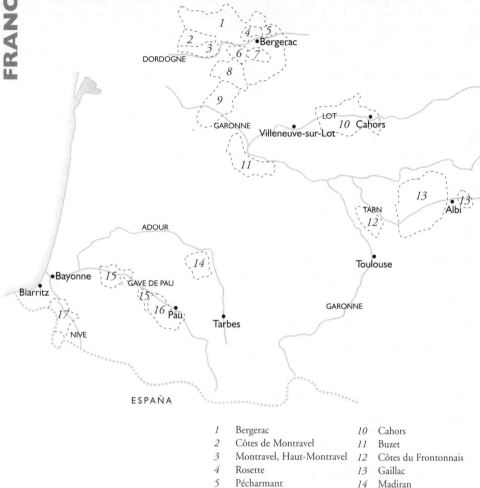

1	Bergerac	10	Cahors
2	Côtes de Montravel	11	Buzet
3	Montravel, Haut-Montravel	12	Côtes du Frontonnais
4	Rosette	13	Gaillac
5	Pécharmant	14	Madiran
6	Saussignac	15	Béarn
7	Monbazillac	16	Jurançon
8	Côtes de Duras	17	Irouléguy
9	Côtes du Marmandais		

The Regions

Bergerac AC encompasses a number of sub-regions. Red, white and rosé are produced from the Bordeaux varieties. **Côtes de Bergerac** is a source of some good reds and sweet whites (labelled as Côtes de Bergerac Moelleux) and **Pécharmant** reds. To the south of the river are the sweet-white ACs of **Monbazillac** and **Saussignac**. Some good red and dry white is also made at **Montravel**. Cahors offers some of the finest red wines of the south-west, based on Malbec. The **Côtes du Frontonnais** AC produces a number of interesting reds based on the Negrette. **Gaillac** AC is a source of some unusual and diverse styles; Mauzac is the key white variety, although Muscadelle is also important.

To the south are the great red and white wines of Gascony. **Madiran** and **Pacherenc du Vic-Bilh** ACs share the same geographical area and many growers produce both. Pacherenc can be dry or sweet, red Madiran produces powerful, dense and ageworthy reds based on Tannat. **Jurançon** is without doubt the finest white-wine appellation of the south-west. Gros and Petit Manseng as well as Petit Courbu are planted.

South-West France Vintages

In general most red and white should be drunk young and only a few appellations provide wines with the substance for real ageing. Top Cahors, Madiran and Jurançon will all develop well. Throughout the south-west 2003, 2002, 2001, 2000, 1999, 1998, 1996 and 1995 were good.

Wizard's Wishlist

A dozen values from the South West

DOM. BERTHOUMIEU ● Madiran Tradition
ALAIN BRUMONT ● Madiran Torus
CAMIN LARREDYA ○ Jurançon Sec
DOM. CAUHAPÉ ○ Jurançon Chant des Vignes
CH. D'AYDIE ○ Pacherenc de Vic-Bilh Frédéric Laplace
CHAPELLE LENCLOS ● Madiran Domaine Mouréou
CH. DU CÈDRE ● Cahors Prestige
CH. JONC BLANC ● Bergerac Cuvée Autumnale
CH. TOUR DES GENDRES ○ Bergerac Cuvée des Conti
CH. VIELLA ● Madiran
CLOS UROULAT ○ Jurançon Cuvée Marie
ROBERT PLAGEOLES ○ Gaillac Ondenc

Cellarworthy South West reds

DOM. BERTHOUMIEU ● Madiran Charles de Batz
ALAIN BRUMONT
● Madiran Château Montus Cuvée Prestige
CHAPELLE LENCLOS ● Madiran la Chapelle Lenclos
CH. D'AYDIE ● Madiran Château d'Aydie

CH. BARREJAT ● Madiran Vieux ceps
CH. BEAULIEU ● Côtes du Marmandais L'Oratoire
CH. DU CÈDRE ● Cahors Le Cèdre
CH. LAGREZETTE ● Cahors Pigeonnier
CH. TOUR DES GENDRES ● Bergerac Moulin des Dames
CH. VIELLA ● Madiran Cuvée Prestige
CLOS TRIGUEDINA ● Cahors Prince Probus
PRIMO PALATUM ● Cahors Mythologia

Diverse regional whites

ROBERT PLAGEOLES ○ Jurançon Noblesse du Temps
CH. TIRECUL-LA-GRAVIÈRE
○ Monbazillac Cuvée Madame
CH. TOUR DES GENDRES ○ Bergerac Cuvée Anthologia
CH. VIELLA ○ Pacherenc du Vic-Bilh Moelleux
CLOS UROULAT ○ Jurançon Clos Uroulat
CH. LAFFITTE-TESTON ○ Pacherenc du Vic-Bilh Ericka
DOM. CAUHAPÉ ○ Jurançon Noblesse du Temps
CAMIN LARREDYA ○ Jurançon Cuvée Simon
CH. BELLEVUE SUR VALLEE
○ Bergerac Le Vin du Bob Sauvignon
PRIMO PALATUM ○ Jurançon Mythologia
DOM. ROTIER ○ Gaillac Renaissance Doux
CH. LAFFITTE-TESTON
○ Pacherenc du Vic-Bilh Moelleux

South-West France/A-Z of producers

DOM. BERTHOUMIEU Madiran barre.didier@wanadoo.fr *UK stockists:* CdP, AVn
The main focus here is Madiran. Tradition is spicy, dense and structured. Old-vine Charles de Batz is richer and sees a large portion of new oak. Pacherenc Sec is crisp and fresh; the sweet Symphonie d'Automne is weighty, rich and more aromatic. (DM)
● Madiran Tradition★★ £B Charles de Batz★★★★ £C
○ Pacherenc de Vic-Bilh Sec★ £B Cuvée Symphonie d'Automne Doux★★ £C

ALAIN BRUMONT Madiran www.montus-madiran.com *UK stockists:* THt, CdP, HHB, N&P
Top Madiran and sound, well-crafted Pacherenc de Vic-Bilh come from Alain Brumont's two properties, Montus and Bouscassé. Production is close to 70,000 cases. Three special Madiran *cuvées* have now been introduced, Argile, Les Menhirs and La Tyre. All offer real weight, power and structure. (DM)
Alain Brumont
● Madiran Torus★★ £B
Château Montus
● Madiran★★★ £C Cuvée Prestige★★★★ £F La Tyre★★★★★ £G
○ Pacherenc de Vic-Bilh★★★ £C
Château Bouscassé
● Madiran★★ £B Vieilles Vignes★★★★ £D Argile★★★★ £D
○ Pacherenc de Vic-Bilh★★ £B

FRANCE

DOM. CAUHAPÉ Jurançon domainecauhape@wanadoo.fr *UK stockists:* SsG, FMV
Henri Ramonteu is arguably the finest producer of the AC. He makes an extensive range with two dry and four sweet wines from very low-yielding vineyards. The sweet wines, with a high proportion of Petit Manseng, are classified according to harvest dates. Structured and very ageworthy. (DM)
O Jurançon Chant des Vignes★★ £B   Sève d'Automne★★★ £C
O Jurançon Ballet d'Octobre★★★ £C Symphonie de Novembre★★★★ £C
O Jurançon Noblesse du Temps★★★★ £E

CHAPELLE LENCLOS Madiran   *UK stockists:* THt, CdP
Patrick Ducournau produces decent, lightly honeyed and intense Pacherenc de Vic-Bilh, occasionally as a *moelleux*. Domaine Mouréou is supple and surprisingly approachable for the AC. Chapelle Lenclos is denser and more structured; it will be better with four or five years' ageing. (DM)
● **Madiran** Domaine Mouréou★★ £B la Chapelle Lenclos★★★ £C
O **Pacherenc de Vic-Bilh** Moelleux★★ £B

CH. D'AYDIE Madiran   *UK stockists:* GBa, AVn
Sizeable property with a small, fine range of Madiran and Pacherenc de Vic-Bilh. Top wine Château d'Aydie is rich and dense, full of dark fruit, well-judged oak and firm tannin in its youth. It is kept on its lees in barrel with micro-oxygenation. Five or six years' ageing is needed. (DM)
● **Madiran** Odé d'Aydie★★ £B Château d'Aydie★★★ £C
O **Pacherenc de Vic-Bilh** Frédéric Laplace★★ £B

CH. BARRÉJAT Madiran
Good to very good structured old-vine Madiran. Remarkable top label Vieux Ceps from vines up to 200 years is rich and very complex. The top two wines will benefit from at leasts five years' ageing. (DM)
● **Madiran** Tradition★★ £B Séduction★★★ £C Vieux Ceps★★★★ £C

CH. BEAULIEU Côtes du Marmandais
Robert Schulte is among a small handful of producers independently striving for fine quality in this lesser-known appellation. Three reds are made here and the style is traditional, particularly for the Côtes du Marmandais and top Cuvée de l'Oratoire. They need at least four or five years. (DM).
● **Côtes du Marmandais**★★ £B l'Oratoire★★★ £C Galapian de Beaulieu★ £B

CH. DU CÈDRE Cahors châteauducedre@wanadoo.fr *UK stockists:* CdP, GWW
The Verhaegue family produce three good to very good reds. The Prestige *cuvée* is both dense and sturdy. The top wine, Le Cèdre, is produced entirely from old Malbec vines and aged in 100 per cent new oak: powerful, structured and very ageworthy. (DM)
● **Cahors**★ £B Prestige★★ £C Le Cèdre★★★★ £E

CH. LAFFITTE-TESTON Madiran   *UK stockists:* CdP, GWW
Jean-Marc Laffitte produces not only good Madiran but also some of the most striking examples of Pacherenc du Vic-Bilh. Ericka is barrel-fermented; Moelleux is opulent and richly textured. Madiran Vieilles Vignes is altogether rounder and fuller than the somewhat angular Tradition. (DM)
● **Madiran** Tradition★★ £B Vieilles Vignes★★★ £C
O **Pacherenc du Vic-Bilh** Ericka★★★ £B Moelleux★★★ £C

CH. LAGREZETTE Cahors www.château-lagrezette.tm.fr *UK stockists:* CCC
No expense is spared at this 65-ha property. Some good regular Cahors is joined by two excellent special *cuvées*, Dame Honneur and the very pricey Pigeonnier, which is 100 per cent Malbec sourced from the property's oldest vines with yields of barely more than 15 hl/ha. (DM)
● **Cahors**★★★ £C Dame Honneur★★★★ £E Pigeonnier★★★★★ £G

CH. TIRECUL-LA-GRAVIÈRE Monbazillac   *UK stockists:* L&S
Arguably the top property for sweet Monbazillac. The Billancinis produce intensely honeyed wines full of rich fruit, quince, toast and very marked botrytis. They achieve this by controlling yields and conducting a succession of *tris* as extensive as any top Sauternes property. (DM)
● **Monbazillac**★★★★ £E Cuvée Madame★★★★★ £F

132

FRANCE

CH. TOUR DES GENDRES Bergerac   *UK stockists:*CdP,GWW,HHB
Very impressive Bergerac property with a range of reds and whites produced as Bergerac as well as a red Côtes de Bergerac, the stylish and concentrated Gloire de Mon Père. Top *cuvées* have real dimension and class. The Anthologia bottlings are as impressive as anything yet produced from the region. (DM)
● Bergerac★ £B Moulin des Dames★★★ £D Cuvée Anthologia★★★★ £E
● Côtes de Bergerac Gloire de Mon Père★★★ £B
O Bergerac Moulin des Dames★★★ £C Cuvée Anthologia★★★★ £E

CH. VIELLA Madiran   *UK stockists:* Ben
Good dry Pacherenc du Vic-Bilh and a very fine late-harvest example which is 100 per cent Petit Manseng, luscious but very finely structured. Regular Madiran is aged in *cuve;* the superior Cuvée Prestige is 100 per cent Tannat aged in new wood and is rich, dense and powerfully structured. (DM)
● Madiran★★ £B Cuvée Prestige★★★ £C
O Pacherenc du Vic-Bilh★★ £B Moelleux★★★ £C

CLOS LAPEYRE Jurançon jean-bernard.larrieu@wanadoo.fr   *UK stockists:* HHB, CdP
Regular Jurançon Sec is fermented in *inox* and kept on lees for added depth. The Vitatge Vielh is barrel-fermented, gaining extra weight. Regular Moelleux is full and spicy, the barrel-fermented Sélection richer and more intensely citrusy. A top late-harvested wine, Vent Balaguer, is produced only in exceptional years. (DM)
O Jurançon Vitatge Vielh★★ £B Moelleux★★ £B Sélection Petit Manseng★★★ £C

CLOS TRIGUEDINA Cahors www.clos-triguedina.com   *UK stockists:* CdP, HHB
The Baldés family have been in the region for nearly two centuries and in the Prince Probus *cuvée* they established one of the benchmark wines of the AC. To this they have added a massive, dark new *cuvée*, New Black Wine, named after the fabled Cahors of old. (DM)
● Cahors★★ £C Prince Probus★★★ £D New Black Wine★★★★ £E

ROBERT PLAGEOLES Gaillac   *UK stockists:* CdP
The Plageoles produce some of the most striking and original of all Gaillac. Reds are in a traditional style and no oak is used. Dry whites Ondenc and Mauzac are very pure and intense The great wine here and surely the finest white in Gaillac is the superbly rich and concentrated late-harvest Vin d'Autan. (DM)
● Gaillac Braucol★★ £B Mauzac Noir★★ £B Syrah★★ £B
O Gaillac Mauzac Vert★★ £B Mauzac Nature★ £B Ondenc★★★ £B
O Gaillac Doux Mauzac Doux★★★ £C Vin d'Autan★★★★★ £F

PRIMO PALATUM Vin de Pays d'Oc xavier.copel@primo-palatum.fr   *UK stockists:* N&P
Xavier Copel has now established himself as a very successful small-scale *négociant*, specialising in limited-production bottlings from important South-West appellations as well as as in the Midi. Regular or lesser bottlings are labelled Classica and the top *cuvées* within an AC Mythologia. (DM)
● Vin de Pays d'Oc Classica★★ £C Mythologia★★★ £C
● Cahors Classica★★★ £C Mythologia★★★★ £D O Limoux Anthologie★★★ £D
O Jurançon Classica★★★ £D Mythologia★★★★ £E

DOM. ROTIER Gaillac   *UK stockists:* GWW
Good-quality small Gaillac grower. The top wines are labelled Renaissance and the reds in particular stand out. The sweet white Renaissance Doux shows good, rich peachy fruit with a fine, piercing citrus structure. Sweet white and the red will develop in the medium term. (DM)
● Gaillac Gravels★★ £B Renaissance★★★ £B
O Gaillac Gravels★ £B Renaissance★★ £B Renaissance Doux★★★ £C

Other wineries of note
Camin Larredya (Jurançon), Ch. Bellevue sur Vallée (Bergerac), Ch Jonc Blanc (Montravel), Ch. Lamartine (Cahors), Clos La Coutale (Cahors), Clos Uroulat (Jurançon)

An in-depth profile of every producer can be found in Wine behind the label 2006

Italy Overview

In order to give some coherence to Italy's wine regions we have divided it into five major sections: Piedmont & North-West Italy, North-East Italy, Tuscany, Central Italy, and Southern Italy & Islands. As an aid to orientation, all of Italy's 20 regions are included below and all of the most important DOCs and DOCGs are summarised.

Piedmont & North-West Italy

The wines of North-West Italy are numerous and diverse. Most of the top reds are produced in small quantities.

Valle d'Aosta

A wide range of wines from diverse (mostly French) grape varieties come from a handful of good producers, most if not all under the **Valle d'Aosta** DOC. The wines are little seen beyond the borders of this mountain enclave.

Piedmont (Piemonte)

Noble Nebbiolo provides majestic **Barolo** and **Barbaresco** but also fine reds in **Roero** and, rarely, in **Ghemme** and **Gattinara**. All are DOCG, including Roero from 2004. Numerous fine examples of Barbera – albeit in diverse styles – emanate from the DOCs of **Barbera d'Alba** and **Barbera d'Asti**. Blended Barbera and Nebbiolo appear as **Langhe** or **Monferrato** DOC sometimes blended with a proportion of French varieties. Intense Dolcetto appears under the DOCs of **Dolcetto di Dogliani** and **Dolcetto di Diano d'Alba**, and of more varied style and in greater quantities in **Dolcetto d'Alba** DOC. Among the many other wines, Arneis appears as dry white **Roero Arneis**, **Gavi** is another dry white, made from the Cortese grape, and **Moscato d'Asti** is a fine sweet Muscat.

Lombardy (Lombardia)

While there's no fine wine to be had from anywhere close to Milan there is fine sparkling DOCG **Franciacorta** from the edge of Lake Iseo. Elegant reds based on Chiavennasca (Nebbiolo) come from close to Switzerland in the Alps as DOCG **Valtellina Superiore**. An intense, powerful version produced from dried grapes, **Valtellina Sforzato**, is also DOCG. In the south of Lombardy in an extension to the Colli Piacentini (see Emilia-Romagna) diverse everyday reds and whites are produced under the **Oltrepò Pavese** and **Valcalepio** DOCs. (For Lugana whites see Veneto)

Liguria

Liguria is known for some occasionally well-made if not widely exported wines, mostly lighter-style reds and whites. DOCs include **Cinqueterre** (white only), **Colli di Luni**, **Riviera Ligure di Ponente** and **Rossese di Dolceaqua** (red only).

North-East Italy

This region is at last beginning to receive greater international recognition for both quality and diversity in both colours and from native grapes as well as international varieties.

Trentino-Alto Adige

The few excellent producers in Trentino make both varietal and blended reds and whites from international varieties, some as **Trentino** DOC, others IGT. Native varieties include the white Nosiola and the potentially exciting smoky, black-fruited red, Teroldego (as **Teroldego Rotaliano**). Decent sparkling wine appears as **Trento**. Much of the quality from the German-speaking South Tirol takes the form of familiar varietals under the **Alto Adige** DOC, including Chardonnay, Sauvignon, Gewürztraminer, Pinot Bianco, Pinot Grigio, Pinot Nero, Cabernet Sauvignon and Merlot, but the recent blaze of quality comes from the native Lagrein.

Veneto

Valpolicella and Amarone/Recioto di Valpolicella are the stars of the Veneto, with very good examples now proliferating. **Soave** (now DOCG for Superiore) from a top producer is of a different order too, whether dry or sweet (**Recioto di Soave** DOCG). If **Bardolino** was always overrated (despite being DOCG for Superiore) there are outcrops of good quality, red and white, in **Breganze**, **Colli Berici** and **Colli Euganei** DOCs as well as some attractive fizz in **Prosecco**. White **Lugana** and decent red and white **Garda** DOC wines come from vineyards close by Lake Garda.

Friuli-Venezia Giulia

More of Italy's fine whites come from Friuli than anywhere else but there are increasing amounts of fine reds too. Whether varietal or blended most quality wines will bear one of three DOCs: **Collio**, **Colli Orientali del Friuli** or **Friuli Isonzo**. Of the international varieties, Chardonnay, Sauvignon, Pinot Grigio, Pinot Bianco, Cabernet Sauvignon and Merlot predominate. Native whites, Tocai Friulano, Ribolla Gialla, Malvasia can be very good while the best native reds, Schioppettino and Pignolo, must be tasted. Wines from the DOCs of **Friuli Grave**, **Friuli Latisana** or **Friuli Aquileia** are typically more everyday.

Tuscany (Toscana)

The sheer volume of fine wine from Tuscany is remarkable. Much of it derives from Sangiovese, though the extent of its Tuscan character can sometimes be enhanced by the inclusion of other natives such as Canaiolo or Colorino or (in some instances only) compromised by Merlot, Cabernet Sauvignon, Syrah and other interlopers. These international varieties are very successful in their own right, often as varietal examples. The classic appellations (all DOCG) include **Carmignano**, **Chianti** (often appended with a sub-zone name such as **Colli Fiorentini** or **Colli Senesi** – the best being

Rufina), Chianti Classico (Tuscany's heart), Brunello di Montalcino (for the biggest, most powerful pure Sangiovese) and Vino Nobile di Montepulciano. The best-known white appellation is Vernaccia di San Gimignano. DOCs or sub-zones close to the Tuscan coast and southern Maremma include Montecarlo, Colline Lucchesi, Colline Pisane, Montescudaio, Bolgheri, Val di Cornia and Morellino di Scansano but here, as in the classic appellations, many fine wines are sold as simply IGT Toscana.

Central Italy

Too often ignored by the wine drinker only familiar with Tuscany and Piedmont. Shame! because there's a mushrooming number of good producers and some real originals.

Emilia-Romagna

Viticulturally, there are two halves to this region too. By far the best reds are Romagna's Sangiovese di Romagna DOC – a very serious alternative to Sangiovese from Tuscany – or IGT equivalents from the best producers. To be sure, Emilia has fabulous ham, cheese and other food products but generally only adequate whites and reds from hillside slopes (*colli*), most notably in the Colli Piacentini and Colli Bolognesi DOCs.

Marche

Marche is for dry white Verdicchio (either Verdicchio dei Castelli di Jesi or Verdicchio di Matelica DOCs), some of it very good, but also for other more everyday dry whites such as Falerio dei Colli Ascolani DOC. The best reds are based on Montepulciano, especially Rosso Conero DOC. From a good producer, Rosso Piceno DOC as well as IGT reds based on Sangiovese or imported varieties can offer both quality and value.

Umbria

There are lots of interesting reds and whites to be found in Umbria. Good Montefalco Rosso should be tried as should the more demanding Montefalco Sagrantino DOCG. A raft of other excellent reds, sold as IGT Umbria, are usually based on Cabernet Sauvignon, Merlot or Sangiovese. Orvieto (a DOC which also covers part of Lazio) when made by a good producer offers personality without heaviness.

Lazio

Lazio has football and Frascati. I'd argue that more of the latter is now clean and characterful. Some other good dry whites are made too as are much-improved reds, even if most come from Merlot, Cabernet or Syrah.

Abruzzo & Molise

Source of many of the best examples of the Montepulciano grape, especially as Montepulciano d'Abruzzo DOC (DOCG in the Colline Teramane). The best are powerful, fleshy, flavoursome and ageworthy. The main white appellation is Trebbiano d'Abruzzo DOC even if most examples from the Trebbiano grape are unexciting. Some adequate examples of Chardonnay are produced as IGTs.

Southern Italy & Islands

Increasingly a cornucopia of vinous delights, especially for reds and whites but also for sweet and fortified wines.

Campania

Aglianico is the star, as Taurasi DOCG but also in Aglianico del Taburno, Falerno del Massico, Sannio DOCs and various IGTs. Excellent, mostly dry whites come from native grapes Greco, Fiano and Falanghina as Greco di Tufo, Fiano di Avellino (both DOCG) and Sannio and Taburno DOCs for Falanghina.

Basilicata and Calabria

Basilicata has more fine Aglianico, nearly all of it labelled Aglianico del Vulture DOC. Calabria has a few exciting reds; most derive much of their character and quality from the native Galioppo grape.

Puglia

Negroamaro and Primitivo provide many of the best Puglian reds, many of them sold as IGTs but Salice Salentino, Brindisi and Primitivo di Manduria are leading DOCs. Further reds come from Montepulciano and Uva di Troia, some under Castel del Monte DOC, and there's some unexpectedly good Chardonnay, again much is sold as IGT.

Sicily (Sicilia)

Ever-burgeoning quantities of quality reds and whites are nearly all sold as IGT Sicilia, as there are few DOCs of note. Leading native varieties Nero d'Avola and Nerello Mascalese compete with imports such as Cabernet Sauvignon, Merlot and Syrah. Most significant of the DOCs are Cerasuolo di Vittoria and Etna for reds, and Moscato di Pantelleria and Passito di Pantelleria for often delicious sweet Muscat.

Sardinia (Sardegna)

The true potential of Sardinia remains largely untapped but there are already good dry whites from Vermentino, as Vermentino di Sardegna DOC and Vermentino di Gallura DOCG. Increasingly fine reds are from Cannonau or Carignano, as Cannonau di Sardegna and Carignano del Sulcis DOCs respectively or from several IGTs.

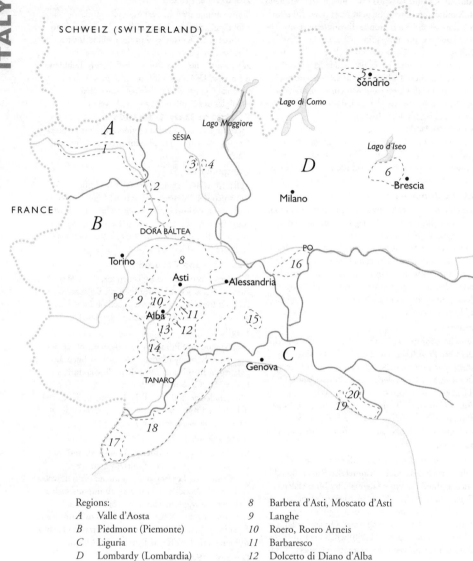

Regions:
A Valle d'Aosta
B Piedmont (Piemonte)
C Liguria
D Lombardy (Lombardia)

Appellations:
1 Valle d'Aosta
2 Carema
3 Gattinara
4 Ghemme
5 Valtellina Superiore
6 Franciacorta
7 Erbaluce di Caluso, Caluso Passito
8 Barbera d'Asti, Moscato d'Asti
9 Langhe
10 Roero, Roero Arneis
11 Barbaresco
12 Dolcetto di Diano d'Alba
13 Barolo
14 Dolcetto di Dogliani
15 Gavi
16 Oltrepò Pavese
17 Rossese di Dolceaqua
18 Riviera Ligure di Ponente
19 Cinqueterre
20 Colli di Luni

Background

Piedmont has made progress like almost no other wine region over the past 20 years. There is both outstanding quality and considerable diversity. What is really wonderful about Piedmont is man's connection with the land and the importance of the link between fine wine, the physical environment and the human endeavour therein. It is illustrated as well here as in any wine region in the world.

Leading Barolo crus

La Morra: Arborina, Brunate, Cerequio, Conca di Annunziata, Fossati, Gattera, Giachini, La Serra, Rocche di Annunziata

Barolo: Brunate, Cerequio, Fossati (all three are shared with La Morra) Bricco Viole, Cannubi, Cannubi Boschis, Le Coste, Sarmassa

Castiglione Falletto: Bricco Boschis, Fiasco, Monprivato, Villero, Rocche

Monforte d'Alba: Bussia Soprana, Bricco Cicala, Colonello, Gavarini, Ginestra, Mosconi, Pianpolvere

Serralunga d'Alba: Cerretta, Falletto, Francia, Lazzarito, Marenca-Rivette, Parafada, Prapò, Vigna Rionda

Leading Barbaresco crus

Barbaresco: Asili, Martinenga, Montefico, Montestefano, Ovello, Pajé, Pora, Rabajà, Rio Sordo, Roncagliette, Secondine

Neive: Bricco, Gallina, Marcorino, Messoirano, Santo Stefano, Serraboella and Starderi

Treiso: Pajoré, Valeirano

Piedmont Vintages

There's never been a better time to add a selection of the best Piedmont wines to a wine cellar. Not just great Barolo and Barbaresco for the medium- and long-term (8 to 30 years) but much excellent Langhe and Barbera for the short- and medium-term (4 to 12 years). When to drink depends on a producer's own style but also on your own preference, whether for the fruit intensity and boldness of youth or the more mellow complexity that comes with age.

2004: Cool nights, and a dry and late finish to the season (end October) saw a return to a more classic vintage. Bright, perfumed whites and pure, ripe and well-structured reds perhaps without the richness of some recent years. Quantities are good too.

2003: After too much rain in 2002, it was too hot and dry with some vines suffering heat stress. Very promising Dolcetto, and some top Barbera, but much more difficult for Nebbiolo.

2002: Cool, wet weather ruined this vintage - worst for Dolcetto and Barbera, in some cases better Nebbiolo thanks to late Autumn sunshine.

2001: Last of long string of fine vintages though intermittent rain and hail in September had a negative effect on quality for some.

2000: Exceptional quality Barolo and Barbaresco from a select few but others show over-ripe fruit and under-ripe tannins. Generally better in Serralunga than La Morra.

1999: This vintage seems to combine the fruit richness and ripeness of 97 with more of the structure of 96. Good for Barbera, Dolcetto and Nebbiolo, with many ageworthy exciting wines.

1998: Smallish crop and Nebbiolo-based wines with more evolved colours but many are full, ripe and balanced. Another very fine vintage for medium- to long-term cellaring.

1997: Hot and dry. Wines have a sweet, lush (sometimes over-ripe) fruit character and relatively low acidities. Many excellent wines but some lack fully ripe tannins and won't repay cellaring.

1996: Cool and classic. Grapes were picked late for fully ripe but powerfully structured wines. Pretty consistent too and one to cellar for at least 10 to 15 years.

1995: Attractive, well-structured if slightly leaner Barolo and Barbaresco now showing well.

1994: Generally weak - go for a specific recommendation or expect to be disappointed.

1993: The best between 90 and 95. Some are too firm for the fruit levels so try from a top grower.

1992: Wet, depressing – the poorest vintage of the 90s - yet there were rare successes.

1991: Generally poorly balanced wines emerged from a wet vintage.

1990: Rich, ripe wines - a good vintage to see how great Barolo/Barbaresco begins to evolve.

1989: A classic year with powerful, structured wines - those from the best growers will still keep.

1988: Dense sturdy wines that have aged well.

Earlier years: Few **1987s★★** ever achieved real harmony but **1986★★★** provided some very attractive Barolo and Barbaresco – but stick with the top wines now, others are past it. **1985★★★** and **1982 ★★★★** were excellent vintages but there were nothing like the number of top examples now being made. Beware of many of the *négociant* labels; seek out a classic from a small grower instead. **1979★★★** provided some refined wines but most of the rare remaining bottles are past their best. Though long-lived, both **1978★★★** and **1974★★★** can be rather tough and old-fashioned – taste before buying any quantity and be sure of its provenance. Well-stored examples from **1971** can still be classic while **1970**, **67**, **64** and **61** might tempt the intrepid.

ITALY

Wizard's Wishlist

Outstanding Barolo
ENZO BOGLIETTI ● Barolo Brunate
DOMENICO CLERICO
● Barolo Ciabot Mentin Ginestra
ALDO CONTERNO ● Barolo Colonello
GIACOMO CONTERNO ● Barolo Riserva Monfortino
CONTERNO-FANTINO ● Barolo Sorì Ginestra
LUIGI EINAUDI ● Barolo Nei Cannubi
ELIO GRASSO ● Barolo Ginestra Casa Matè
GIUSEPPE MASCARELLO & FIGLO
● Barolo Monprivato
ARMANDO PARUSSO ● Barolo Bussia Vigne Rocche
E PIRA & FIGLI ● Barolo Cannubi
LUIGI PIRA ● Barolo Margheria
LUCIANO SANDRONE ● Barolo Le Vigne
PAOLO SCAVINO ● Barolo Bric del Fiasc
VIGNA RIONDA - MASSOLINO ● Barolo Parafada
ROBERTO VOERZIO ● Barolo Brunate

Exciting Barbaresco
PRODUTTORI DEL BARBARESCO
● Barbaresco Riserva Montefico
CERETTO ● Barbaresco Bricco Asili
GAJA ● Barbaresco
BRUNO GIACOSA ● Barbaresco Santo Stefano di Neive
LA SPINETTA ● Barbaresco Vigneto Starderi
MARCHESI DI GRESY
● Barbaresco Martinenga Camp Gros
PAITIN ● Barbaresco Sorì Paitin
PELISSERO ● Barbaresco Vanotu
ALBINO ROCCA ● Barbaresco Brich Ronchi
BRUNO ROCCA ● Barbaresco Rabajà

Other special North-West reds
ANTICHI VIGNETI DI CANTALUPO
● Ghemme Signore di Bayard
MATTEO CORREGGIA
● Nebbiolo d'Alba La Val di Preti
ELIO ALTARE ● Insieme

CA' DEL BOSCO ● Maurizio Zanella
LA SPINETTA ● Monferrato Rosso Pin
NINO NEGRI ● Valtellina Sfursat 5 Stelle
ALDO RAINOLDI
● Valtellina Sfursat Fruttaio Ca' Rizzieri

Super Barbera
BERTELLI ● Barbera d'Asti San Antonio Vieilles Vignes
BRAIDA ● Barbera d'Asti Ai Suma
LUIGI COPPO & FIGLI ● Barbera d'Asti Pomorosso
HASTAE (see Braida) ● Barbera d'Asti Quorum
LA SPINETTA ● Barbera d'Asti Superiore
FRANCO M MARTINETTI
● Barbera d'Asti Superiore Montruc
FERDINANDO PRINCIPIANO
● Barbera d'Alba La Romualda
ROBERTO VOERZIO
● Barbera d'Alba Riserva Vigneto Pozzo dell'Annunziata

Diverse Dolcetto
ANNA MARIA ABBONA ● Dolcetto di Dogliani Maioli
CLAUDIO ALARIO
● Dolcetto di Diano d'Alba Costa Fiore
ENZO BOGLIETTI ● Dolcetto d'Alba Tiglineri
BROVIA ● Dolcetto d'Alba Solatio
G D VAJRA ● Dolcetto d'Alba Coste & Fossati

Piedmont Value
ARALDICA ● Barolo Revello
ASCHERI ● Dolcetto d'Alba Nirane
PRODUTTORI DEL BARBARESCO
● Barbaresco Riserva Rabajà
ENZO BOGLIETTI ● Langhe Nebbiolo
LUIGI BAUDANA ● Langhe Lorenso
CAUDRINA O Moscato d'Asti La Caudrina
CORINO ● Dolcetto d'Alba
ICARDI ● Barbera d'Asti Tabarin
MALVIRA O Roero Arneis Renesio
ANDREA OBERTO ● Barbera d'Alba
SAN ROMANO ● Dolcetto di Doglianii

Piedmont & North-West Italy/A-Z of producers

ANNA MARIA ABBONA Dolcetto di Dogliani *UK stockists:* **Mgi,** L&W
One of the best of a zone dedicated to Dolcetto. Maioli from old vines is rich, almost velvety with lovely fruit, but powerful too with a refined structure. Equally good is an oak-aged Superiore. Attractive fleshy Barbera, Cadò 10 per cent Dolcetto. (PW)
● **Dolcetto di Dogliani** Sorì dij But★★ £B Maioli★★★ £C Superiore★★★ £C
● **Langhe** Cadò★★ £D ● **Langhe** Dolcetto★ £B

CLAUDIO ALARIO Dolcetto di Diano d'Alba *UK stockists:* **WTs,** Bib, Sav, Hrd
Notable for Nebbiolo as well as Dolcetto that is perfumed, balanced and ageworthy. Barolo Riva has excellent texture, breadth and length. Costa Fiore is the more concentrated but backward Dolcetto. Also a well-priced

New entries have producer's name underlined

source of Barbera d'Alba and Nebbiolo d'Alba. (PW)
- **Dolcetto di Diano d'Alba** Costa Fiore★★★ £B Montegrillo★★ £B
- **Barbera d'Alba** Valletta★★ £C ● **Barolo** Riva★★★ £E

GIANFRANCO ALESSANDRIA Barolo   *UK stockists:* **Win, Fal, F&R**
An inspired young grower with a range of ripe, full and stylish reds with restrained oak. Intense Barbera
Vittoria from 65-year-old vines, and beautifully balanced Barolo San Giovanni but all wines show good
fruit in modern accessible style including top version of Insieme (see Altare). (PW)
- **Barolo**★★★ £E San Giovanni★★★★ £F ● **Insieme**★★★★ £F
- **Barbera d'Alba**★★ £B Vittoria★★★★ £C ● **Dolcetto d'Alba**★ £B

ELIO ALTARE Barolo   *UK stockists:* J&B, Fal, F&R
Elio Altare is Barolo's great moderniser and mentor to other small growers. Radically low yields, short
maceration times and new oak are key giving wines of terrific concentration and depth that includes Super-
Langhes Arborina (Nebbiolo), Larigi (Barbera) and La Villa (Nebbiolo/Barbera). Also behind Insieme - 7
producers share resources and expertise to produce concentrated modern oak-aged blends (from Nebbiolo,
Barbera, Cabernet and/or Merlot). Altare's 1997 Barolos and 98 Langhe reds were withheld due to cork
contimination problems. (PW)
- **Barolo**★★★ £E Arborina★★★★ £F Brunate★★★★ £F ● **Insieme**★★★★£F
- **Langhe** Arborina★★★ £F Larigi★★★★ £F La Villa★★★★ £F

ARALDICA VINI PIEMONTESI www.araldicavini.com   *UK stockists:* **Mer,AAA**
Large co-op with 300 members and 900 ha of vineyard. Widely seen are the Alasia varietals which include
bright, clean fruity Barbera, Dolcetto, Chardonnay and Cortese. Promising are Barbaresco (Corsini) and Barolo
(Revello). Superior Poderi Alasia wines are vineyard specific - good Monferrato blend, Luce Monaca combines
Barbera with Merlot and Cab Sauv. (PW)
Araldica:
- **Barolo** Revello★★★ £C ● **Barbaresco** Corsini★★ £C
- **Barbera d'Asti** Ceppi Storici★ £B Vigneti Croja★★ £B O **Gavi** Madonnina★ £B
Poderi Alasia:
- **Barbera d'Asti** Rive★★ £C ● **Monferrato** Luce Monaca★★ £D
- O **Roero Arneis** Podere Alasia Sorilaria★★ £C O **Monferrato** Camillona★★ £C

ASCHERI Barolo www.ascherivini.it   *UK stockists:* **Eno, Bat, Swg**
Matteo Ascheri maintains realistic prices and good quality with naturally made wines of bright, pure varietal
character. Of two *cru* Barolos, Sorano comes from Serralunga and has more depth, grip and class. Since 1999,
a Coste & Bricco selection offers yet more style and expression. (PW)
- **Barolo** Vigna dei Pola★★★ £E Sorano★★★ £E Sorano Coste & Bricco★★★★ £F
- **Barbera d'Alba** Fontanelle★★ £C ● **Montalupa Syrah**★★ £D O **Viognier**★★ £D

AZELIA Barolo   *UK stockists:* J&B
Fine Barolo from favourably positioned Fiasco vineyard but both *crus* Bricco Fiasco and San Rocco (subject to
50% new oak) have good weight, depth and dimension and definite class especially in top vintages since 95.
Both need at least 6-8 years' age, spicy, deep-fruited Barbera d'Alba 3-4. (PW)
- **Barolo**★★★ £E Bricco Fiasco★★★★ £F San Rocco★★★★ £F
- **Barbera d'Alba** Vigneto Punta★★★ £D ● **Dolcetto d'Alba** Bricco dell'Oriolo★ £C

PRODUTTORI DEL BARBARESCO www.produttori-barbaresco.it   *UK stockists:* **V&C**
This super co-op manages around a sixth (100 ha) of Barbaresco vineyard area. Lengthy maceration and ageing
in large *botti* provides wines of marvellous perfume, grace and charm in a top vintage. A splendid expression of
very reasonably priced Riservas can be had from 1997 or 99. (PW)
- **Barbaresco Riserva** Asili★★★★ £E Moccagatta★★★★ £E Montefico★★★★ £E
- **Barbaresco Riserva** Montestefano★★★★ £E Rabajà★★★★ £E Ovello★★★ £E

LUIGI BAUDANA Barolo   *UK stockists:* THt
Full ripeness and a particular intensity from just 5 ha of vineyards. Barolo Cerretta Piani has the extract and
power of Serralunga but also a certain elegance that vintages such as 96 or 99 seem certain to accentuate with a

ITALY

decade's age. Also promsising Baudana *cru* from 99. Lorenso Rosso is oak-influenced Nebbiolo/Barbera/Merlot blend. (PW)

- Barolo★★★ £E Cerretta Piani★★★★ £E ● Langhe Lorenso★★★ £C
- Barbera d'Alba Donatella★★ £C ● Dolcetto d'Alba Sorì Baudana★★ £B

BAVA Barbera d'Asti www.bava.com *UK stockists:* **FMV**, BBR
High profile producer whose best wines come from Barbera. Ageworthy Pianalto and Stradivario are the best of several good examples. Other wines, including Moscato d'Asti are typically sound, safe bets, including sweet, fragrant, *frizzante* red Malvasia di Castelnuovo Don Bosco. (PW)

- Barbera d'Asti Superiore Pianalto★★ £D Superiore Stradivario★★ £D
- Barbera d'Asti Libera★★ £C Arbest★★ £C

BELLAVISTA Franciacorta www.bellavistasrl.it *UK stockists:* **Alv**
Brilliant, refined yet full-flavoured sparkling wines: Chardonnay dominated Gran Cuvée Brut is a step up from Brut Cuvée while Rosé is a sheer delight and Satèn soft, creamy and delicately sparkling. Pas Operé has no dosage while Riserva has extended lees ageing. Rich, complex Chardonnay/Pinot Bianco blend, Convento della Santissima Annunciata is best of still wines. Powerful Cabernet/Merlot blend, Solesine can show well with age. (PW)

- ○ Franciacorta Brut Cuvée★★ £D Gran Cuvée Brut★★★ £E
- ○ Franciacorta Gran Cuvée Pas Operé★★★ £E Gran Cuvée Satèn★★★ £E
- ○ Terre di Franciacorta Santissima Annunciata★★★ £E ● Solesine★★ £E

ENZO BOGLIETTI Barolo *UK stockists:* **L&W**
A modest patchwork of vines but souce of fruit-filled, oak-enriched modern style wines. Old-vine Barbera Vigna dei Romani (from Fossati) can impress almost as much as the Barolos of which classy Brunate is the most expressive and stylish. Also ripe, potent Dolcetto Tiglineri and stylish Buio (Nebbiolo/Barbera - 80/20). (PW)

- Barolo Brunate★★★★ £F Case Nere★★★★ £F Fossati★★★★ £F
- Barbera d'Alba★★ £B Vigna dei Romani★★★ £E Roscaleto★★★ £E
- Dolcetto d'Alba Tiglineri★★★ £C ● Langhe Buio★★★ £D

BONGIOVANNI Barolo *UK stockists:* **CeB, F&R**
Source of good moderately priced reds that result from a flexible winemaking approach. In Barolo Pernanno the extract, weight and richness evident on the palate is reinforced by ageing in (60 per cent) new barriques. Micro-oxygenation is employed for the two fruity Dolcettos while Faletto (Cabernet, Merlot and Barbera) is fruit-rich and oaky. (PW)

- Barolo★★★ £E Pernanno★★★★ £E ● Langhe Faletto★★★ £D
- Barbera d'Alba★★ £C ● Dolcetto di Diano d'Alba★★ £B

BRAIDA Barbera d'Asti www.braida.it *UK stockists:* **GFy, Bal**, Gau, L&W, BBR, N&P
Giacomo Bologna was the king of Barbera and Bricco dell'Uccellone the original oak-aged Barbera of outsized proportions. Ai Suma can be even richer and more powerful but all three top Barberas are often best after 6-8 years. Il Bacialé adds Pinot Nero to Barbera while Barbera La Monella, Brachetto and Moscato (Senza Nome) are great examples of their effervescent type. Working with Berta, Chiarlo, Coppo, Prunotto and Vietti, Hastae is an Asti/Alba axis to promote Barbera resulting in a single lush, flattering wine, Quorum. (PW)
Braida:

- Barbera d'Asti Bricco della Bigotta★★★ £E Bricco dell' Uccellone★★★ £E
- Barbera d'Asti Ai Suma★★★★ £F ● Monferrato Rosso Il Bacialé★★ £C

Hastae:

- Barbera d'Asti Quorum★★★★ £G

BRICCO MAIOLICA Dolcetto di Diano d'Alba www.briccomaiolica.it *UK stockists:* **L&S**
One of the few estates producing fine Nebbiolo (as well as Barbera and Dolcetto) from outside top zones. Vigna Vigia Barbera sees 50 per cent new oak and both Dolcettos show splendid fruit. Langhe white is from Chardonnay and Sauvignon, Langhe Lorié is decent Piedmont Pinot. Also Merlot, Filius from 2001. (PW)

- Nebbiolo d'Alba Il Cumot★★★ £D ● Barbera d'Alba Vigna Vigia★★★ £D
- Dolcetto di Diano d'Alba Sorì Bricco Maiolica★★ £C ● Langhe Lorié★★ £D

140

ITALY

BROVIA   Barolo   www.brovia.net   *UK stockists:* **VDu**, Gau, Bat
Sisters Elena and Cristina Brovia produce full, muscular but ageworthy Barolo that is aged in large oak.
Elegance of Rocche (di Castiglione) contrasts with intensity of Villero and build of Ca' Mia. Late-harvested and
oak-aged Dolcetto, Solatio is deep, smooth and well-balanced. Barberas are good too. (PW)
● **Barolo** Ca' Mia★★★★ £F   Rocche dei Brovia★★★★ £F   Villero★★★★ £F
● **Barbera d'Alba** Brea★★★ £E   ● **Dolcetto d'Alba** Solatio★★★ £E

PIERO BUSSO   Barbaresco   *UK stockists:* **Goe**
Piero Busso believes in a natural expression of each variety and the importance of place (or *tipicità*). All the
wines have classic perfumes and structure typical to their variety and add richness and complexity with age
although Dolcetto and Barbera can struggle for full ripeness - needing a year or two to soften. Langhe white is
from Chardonnay and Sauvignon. (PW)
● **Barbaresco** Bricco Mondino★★ £E   Vigna Borgese★★★ £E
● **Barbera d'Alba** Vigna Majano★★ £C   ● **Dolcetto d'Alba** Vigna Majano★ £B

CA' DEL BOSCO   Franciacorta   www.cadelbosco.com   *UK stockists:* **Eno**, N&P
Italian quality wine pioneer still directed by Maurizio Zanella. Still wines even better than sparkling. Pinèro
(Pinot Nero), Maurizio Zanella (a Bordeaux blend) and Chardonnay are all still among best Italian examples.
Carmenero is a varietal Carmenère. Sparklers include very fine Satèn but this is surpassed by rich, complex,
Cuvée Annamaria Clementi. Prices have always been high. (PW)
○ **Franciacorta** Brut Non-Vintage★★ £D   Brut Vintage★★ £E   Satèn★★★ £F
○ **Franciacorta** Cuvée Annamaria Clementi★★★★ £F   ● **Maurizio Zanella★★★★** £F
○ **Chardonnay★★★★** £F   ● **Carmenero★★★** £F   ● **Pinero★★★** £F

CAPPELLANO   Barolo   *UK stockists:* **RsW**, F&R
One of the great traditionalists of Barolo. From 3ha of Gabutti in Serralunga are produced Piè Rupestris (from 60-
year-old vines) and Franco (from entirely ungrafted vines). Both are powerful, structured Barolos that are complex
and harmonious even when relatively young but can age impressively. Also produced are stylish Nebbiolo d'Alba and
Barbera d'Alba that sees 4 years in large oak. (PW)

CASCINA MORASSINO   Barbaresco   *UK stockists:* **Vim**
Recently much improved, Barbarescos Morassino and Ovello are soft, round and seductive, in a modern style. There
is richer texture, better breadth and lots of extract in Ovello, in part due to *barrique*-ageing, but the oak is not
intrusive. More overtly oaky is spicy, soft, red- and black-fruited Langhe Rosso which lacks a little depth. Very small
amounts of Barbera d'Alba (Vignot) are also made. (PW)
● **Barbaresco** Morassino★★★ £E   Ovello★★★★ £F
● **Langhe Rosso** Vigna del Merlo★★ £D   ● **Dolcetto d'Alba★★** £C

CASCINA VAL DEL PRETE   Roero
Mario Roagna has a small fine range of wines. Delightful fruit-driven, unoaked regular Barbera contrasts with
oaked Carolina which has fabulous style and smoke and plum richness. Also Roero since 1998 but better
Nebbiolo expression in Vigna di Lino. Arneis has more weight and structure than most. (PW)
● **Barbera d'Alba★★** £B   Superiore Carolina★★★ £C   ● **Roero★★** £C
● **Nebbiolo d'Alba** Vigna di Lino★★★ £C   ○ **Roero Arneis** Luèt★★ £B

CASTELLARI BERGAGLIO   Gavi   www.castellaribergaglio.it   *UK stockists:* **Mgi**
Really decent Gavi: perfumed with lots of fruit intensity and good balance, underpinned by good acidity. Rolona,
from older vines, has more depth and intensity than the floral, herbal Fornaci. Rovereto can be richer and more
minerally. Unusual is *barriqued* Pilin produced from dried grapes which adds breadth and texture. All will keep for at
least 3–4 years. (PW)
○ **Gavi del Comune di Tassarolo** Fornaci★★ £C   ○ **Gavi** Pilin★★★ £D
○ **Gavi del Comune di Gavi** Rolona★★★ £C   Rovereto Vigna Vecchia★★★ £C

CASTELLO DI CALOSSO   Barbera d'Asti   www.castellodicalosso.it   *UK stockists:* **Orb**
The 10 growers of the Castello di Calosso all have a small parcel of old-vine Barbera but share the same label
under which they promote their own bottlings. While one or two struggle for balance nearly all are
concentrated with a measure of oak and have a rich, ripe fruit intensity as well as impressive breadth and length

Piedmont & North-West Italy

(6 of 10 are listed). (PW)
- **Barbera d'Asti** Musiano Roberto Paschina★★★ £E Sant' Anna Mauro Grasso★★★ £E
- **Barbera d'Asti** Camp Maìna Renzo Grasso★★★ £E Rodotiglia Due Colline★★★ £E
- **Barbera d'Asti** Belletta La Badia★★★ £E La Cascinetta Giorgio Fogliati★★★★ £E

CAUDRINA Moscato d'Asti www.caudrina.it
Producer of some of the finest Moscato d'Asti for over 20 years. Wonderfully fragrant with apple, citrus, grape and musk scents, the intense, tangy La Galeisa is exquisite when drunk with just a few months' bottle-age. Barbera d'Asti is increasingly good too while oaked Chardonnay and a very good fully sparkling Asti are also made. (PW)
- **Barbera d'Asti** La Solista★ £C Superiore Montevenere★★★ £D
- O **Moscato d'Asti** La Caudrina★★★ £B La Galeisa★★★ £C O **Asti** La Selvatica★★ £C

CAVALLOTTO Barolo www.cavallotto.com   UK stockists: **Goe, HHC**
The 23ha Bricco Boschis estate is being revitalised by a younger generation. Barolo are are aged in large Slavonian oak casks and renewed investment in the vineyard (which includes the 2.5 ha solely owned Vigna San Giuseppe) and winery has paid dividends, especially since 1997. (PW)
- **Barolo** Bricco Boschis★★★ £E Riserva Vignolo★★★ £F
- **Barolo** Riserva Bricco Boschis Vigna San Giuseppe★★★★ £F

CERETTO Barolo www.ceretto.com   UK stockists: **Bib, F&R**
Owning most of its grape sources, Ceretto boast many fabulous sites, including famous Bricco Asili *cru*. Even better are Barolo *crus* Bricco Rocche, Prapò and Brunate. Also made are Riesling (Arbarei), Cabernet, Merlot and Pinot Nero (combined with Nebbiolo in Monsordo Rosso). New oak is used in all the top wines, which when on form are supple, intense and characterful. Best recent vintages of Barolo are 97, 99, 2000 and 01. (PW)
- **Barolo** Brunate★★★★ £F Prapò★★★★ £F Bricco Rocche★★★★ £H
- **Barbaresco** Asij★★ £G Bernadot★★ £G Fasèt★★ £F Bricco Asili★★★ £H

MICHELE CHIARLO Barolo www.chiarlo.it   UK stockists: **Hal, Odd**
Important vineyard owner. Barberas (esp. La Court) and Monferrato reds impress as much as the Barbaresco and Barolos. Of recent releases Barolo Cerequio shows the most purity and style while Barbaresco Asili is deceptive in its accessibility - all need time for the tannic backbone to soften. Seductive Countacc! is Cab Sauv, Nebbiolo and Barbera while moderately priced Airone is Barbera, Cabernet and Shiraz. (PW)
- **Barolo** Cannubi★★★ £F Brunate★★★ £F Cerequio★★★★ £F
- **Barbaresco** Asili★★★ £F ● **Barbera d'Asti Nizza** Superiore La Court★★★ £D
- **Barbera d'Asti** Sup. Cipressi della Court★★ £B ● **Monferrato** Countacc!★★★ £D

FRATELLI CIGLIUTI Barbaresco   UK stockists: **FMV,** BBR, PWa, The, P&S
Dedicated grower with part of *cru* of Serraboella. Oak-influenced concentrated Barbaresco is powerful with ripe tannic structure to improve for a decade or more. Dolcetto, Barbera and Briccoserra (Barbera/Nebbiolo) rarely disappoint. Also Barbera Campass (since 2000) and Barbaresco, Vigna Erte (since 99). Cellar both Barbarescos from 2001. (PW)
- **Barbaresco** Serraboella★★★★ £E Vigne Erte★★★ £E
- **Barbera d'Alba** Serraboella★★ £C Campass★★★ £C
- **Langhe** Briccoserra★★★ £E

DOMENICO CLERICO Barolo   UK stockists: **J&B,** P&S, NYg, F&R, Las
Consistent Barolo superstar since 1980s. Modern-styled but the wines don't lack for stuffing or structure. Three fabulous Barolos include classy Ciabot Mentin Ginestra, more international Pajana and rich, fleshy Per Cristina. Also very worthy are Barbera, Dolcetto and Nebbiolo-based Arte. (PW)
- **Barolo** Ciabot Mentin Ginestra★★★★★ £F Pajana★★★★★ £F
- **Barolo** Riserva Per Cristina★★★★★ £F ● **Langhe** Arte★★★ £E

ELVIO COGNO Barolo www.elviocogno.com   UK stockists: **PaV**
Walter Fissore, makes robustly flavoured wines with an extra fruit intensity. Barolo Ravera assumes an earthy, truffly, savoury complexity with even a little age. Rich, powerful Barolo Vigna Elena comes solely from the Rosé

142

New entries have producer's name underlined

clone of Nebbiolo. Montegrilli is a barrique-aged Nebbiolo/Barbera blend. (PW)
- ● **Barolo** Ravera★★★ £E Vigna Elena★★★★ £E
- ● **Barbera d'Alba** Bricco dei Merli★★ £C ● **Langhe** Montegrilli★★ £D

ALDO CONTERNO www.poderialdoconterno.com   *UK stockists:* Lib, ACh, Maj, Vne, V&C
A house of formidable reputation (and inspiration) - part traditional, part modern. All Barolo, but particularly Cicala, Colonello and Granbussia (a Riserva selection of all plots), show lovely style and dimension with an ensuing complexity and nuance most other miss. Barriques are used for Barbera, Chardonnay Bussiador and Langhe blends Il Favot (Nebbiolo) and Quartetto (Nebbiolo, Barbera, Cabernet and Merlot). Printanié (a second Chardonnay) and Dolcetto are unoaked. (PW)
- ● **Barolo** Bussia★★★★ £F Cicala✪✪✪✪ £G Riserva Granbussia✪✪✪✪ £H
- ● **Barolo** Colonello✪✪✪✪ £G ● **Langhe** Il Favot★★★ £E Quartetto★★★ £E
- ● **Barbera d'Alba** Conca Tre Pile★★★ £D ○ **Langhe** Bussiador★★★ £D

GIACOMO CONTERNO Barolo   *UK stockists:* JAr
Giovanni Conterno's signature was the legendary Monfortino Barolo Riserva. Roberto continues his father's 'traditional' (if recently slightly moderated) winemaking style giving Barolo of sometimes unequalled intensity, power and longevity. Gutsy Dolcetto and Barbera are true to the house style. (PW)
- ● **Barolo** Cascina Francia★★★★★ £G Riserva Monfortino✪✪✪✪ £H
- ● **Barbera d'Alba**★★ £D ● **Dolcetto d'Alba**★★ £C

CONTERNO-FANTINO Barolo www.conternofantino.it   *UK stockists:* Eno, NYg
A partnership producing flawless, modern-style Barolos. Rich and complete Sorì Ginestra is complemented by Vigna del Gris which can show a more floral, exquisite perfume. Parussi only since 1997. Good Langhe blend Monprà (Nebbiolo/Barbera/Cabernet) and one of the best Piedmont Chardonnays. (PW)
- ● **Barolo** Sorì Ginestra★★★★★ £F Vigna del Gris★★★★ £F Vigna Parussi★★★ £E
- ● **Langhe** Monprà★★★ £E ○ **Langhe Chardonnay** Bastia★★★ £D

LUIGI COPPO & FIGLI Barbera d'Asti www.coppo.it   *UK stockists:* L&S
Brilliant Barberas here especially deep, rich and complex Pomorosso. Also increasingly rich Alterego (Cabernet/Barbera) from late 90s vintages while Mondaccione is rare good dry Freisa. Monteriolo is one of best Piedmont Chardonnay. Barbera and Chardonnay are also produced in (pricey) Riserva della Famiglia versions. (PW)
- ● **Barbera d'Asti** Pomorosso★★★★ £E Camp du Rouss★★ £E
- ○ **Piemonte Chardonnay** Monteriolo★★★ £D ● **Monferrato** Alterego★★★ £D

CORDERO DI MONTEZEMOLO Barolo   *UK stockists:* Eur
Well-directed estate centred on the spur of Monfalletto in Annunziata. Impressive modern style wines since 1995. Classy Barolo Enrico VI is from Villero *cru* while Bricco Gattera is from Monfalletto *cru*. Also very good barrique-aged Barbera Funtanì. New is a Barolo Riserva Gorette. (PW)
- ● **Barolo** Monfalletto★★★ £E Bricco Gattera★★★★ £F Enrico VI★★★★ £F
- ● **Barbera d'Alba**★ £C Superiore Funtanì★★★ £D

GIOVANNI CORINO Barolo   *UK stockists:* J&B, Las, F&R
Modern-styled, fruit-rich Barolo from 3.5-ha Giachini *cru* as well as several others made in small quantities including deep, powerful and potentially very ageworthy Vecchie Vigne (a superior selection made since 1997). Excellent Barbera too as is version of Insieme (see Altare). (PW)
- ● **Barolo** Arborina★★★ £F Giachini★★★ £F Rocche★★★★ £F V.Vigne★★★★ £H
- ● **Barbera d'Alba** Pozzo★★★ £E ● **Dolcetto d'Alba**★ £B ● **Insieme**★★★ £F

MATTEO CORREGGIA Roero www.matteocorreggia.com   *UK stockists:* J&B, Sav
The work of Roero's most inspirational grower is now continued by his wife, Ornella. Nebbiolo and Barbera show a density and quality to the fruit in wines of real character, structure and aroma. New Langhe blend, Le Marne Grigie (Nebbiolo, Barbera, Cabernets and Merlot) from 2000 vintage. (PW)
- ● **Roero**★ £B Ròche d'Ampsèj★★★ £E ○ **Roero Arneis**★ £B
- ● **Nebbiolo d'Alba** La Val di Preti★★★ £D ● **Barbera d'Alba** Marun★★★ £D

ITALY

LUIGI EINAUDI Dolcetto di Dogliani www.poderieinaudi.com *UK stockists:* **L&S**, Bal
Dogliani-based estate but also with vineyards for top-flight Barolo. Very complete and harmonious Costa
Grimaldi from 1997, 98 or 99 is a match for that from the recently acquired Cannubi vines. Both show real
class and have excellent cellaring potential. Dense, intense Dolcetto *crus* are amongst the best of the zone. Fruit-
rich, oak-aged Langhe Luigi Einaudi is from Cabernet, Nebbiolo, Barbera and Merlot. (PW)
● **Barolo**★★★ £E Costa Grimaldi★★★★ £E Nei Cannubi★★★★ £F
● **Langhe** Luigi Einaudi★★★ £E ● **Piemonte Barbera**★★★ £C
● **Dolcetto di Dogliani**★ £B I Filari★★★ £C Vigna Tecc★★★ £C

FONTANAFREDDA Barolo www.fontanafredda.it *UK stockists:* **Eno**, JNi, NYg, V&C,
Serralunga-based Barolo heavyweight drawing on own vineyards and bought-in grapes. Past poor showings
surplanted by new quality regime. Barolos from 1997, 98 and 99 stylistically different, much more modern and
expressive: perfumed La Villa, deeper La Rosa and more structured Lazzarito (combined with La Delizia from
99). Best value are Barbera Papagena, Dolcetto di Diano d'Alba and Barolo Serralunga. *Metodo classico* sparklers
much better than the ubiquitous Asti. Also very good new Moscato d'Asti. (PW)
● **Barolo** Serralunga d'Alba★★★ £D La Villa★★★ £F La Rosa★★★★ £F
● **Barolo** La Delizia★★★ £F Lazzarito★★★★ £F ● **Barbaresco** Coste Rubin★★★ £D
● **Dolcetto di Diano d'Alba** La Lepre★★ £B ○ **Moscato d'Asti** Moncucco★★ £B

GAJA Barbaresco *UK stockists:* **L&W**, JAr, Maj, P&S, NYg, V&C, Hrd, F&M, Las
Piedmont's *numero uno*, a veritable phenomenon in the pursuit of quality and the promotion of his native
region. As well as outstanding Barbaresco, celebrated, often stupendous single-vineyard wines Sorì San Lorenzo,
Sorì Tildin (often the richest and deepest), and Costa Russi (all from Barbaresco vineyards) and Sperss and
Conteisa (from Barolo). Also rich and expressive Gaia e Rey Chardonnay and very good if not great Darmagi
(Cab Sauv), Sito Rey (Barbera) and Sito Moresco (Nebbiolo, Merlot and Barbera). Also see Pieve Santa
Restituta for Brunello and Ca' Marcanda for Bolgheri reds. (PW)
● **Barbaresco**❁❁❁❁❁ £H ● **Langhe** Sperss❁❁❁❁❁ £H Conteisa★★★★★ £H
● **Langhe** Costa Russi★★★★★ £H San Lorenzo❁❁❁❁❁ £H S.Tildin❁❁❁❁❁ £H
○ **Langhe Chardonnay** Gaia e Rey★★★★ £G Sito Moresco★★★ £D

ETTORE GERMANO Barolo www.germanoettore.com *UK stockists:* **Ast**, P&S
Sergio Germano is one of emerging small growers in Serralunga with dense but well-structured Barolos - added
refinement in Prapò and greater power and complexity in barrique-aged Cerretta. Also intense Barbera, Vigne
della Madre, and Langhe Balau (mostly Dolcetto with Barbera). Binel, is unusual blend of Chardonnay and
Riesling. Both Prapò and Cerretta need 8 to 10 years' age. (PW)
● **Barolo**★★★ £E Prapò★★★ £F Cerretta★★★★ £F ● **Langhe** Balau★★ £D
● **Barbera d'Alba** Vigna della Madre★★★ £D ● **Dolcetto d'Alba** Pra di Pò★★ £C

ATTILIO GHISOLFI Barolo *UK stockists:* **Ock**
Gian Marco Ghisolfi's Barolo vines are in the lesser known Visette *cru* (a sub-*cru* of Bussia) that gives a wine of
lovely weight and richness with deep, intense fruit. A rich, expansive Alta Bussia is 80% Barbera, 20%
Nebbiolo, while a very individual, if firm, Carlin adds Freisa to Nebbiolo. Old vine Barbera Vigna Lisi is sleek
and stylish with 3-4 years' age. (PW)
● **Barolo** Bricco Visette★★★★ £E ● **Barbera d'Alba**★ £B Vigna Lisi★★★ £C
● **Langhe Rosso** Alta Bussia★★★ £E Carlin★★ £C

BRUNO GIACOSA Barbaresco www.brunogiacosa.it *UK stockists:* **JAr**, Sel, N&P, F&R, Las
Bruno Giacosa supremely complex and harmonious renditions of Nebbiolo have gradually narrowed to
vineyards of his own including top sites Asili in Barbaresco and Falletto in Serralunga. (Red label) Riservas also
made but keep all the *cru* Barbaresco and Barolo for a decade from the vintage date. Prices reflect their sought-
after status. (PW)
● **Barbaresco** Rabajà★★★★ £G Asili★★★★ £G Santo Stefano di Neive★★★★★ £G
● **Barolo** Rocche del Falletto di Serralunga❁❁❁❁❁ £H
● **Barbera d'Alba** Falletto di Serralunga★★★ £C

New entries have producer's name underlined

ITALY

ELIO GRASSO Barolo www.eliograsso.it *UK stockists:* **Mgi,** L&W, Fal, F&R
Elio Grasso and son Gianluca have steep prized vineyards for refined, scented Barolos including recently
replanted Runcot, a superior plot within Gavarini. The wines have an inherent richness and structure from the
fruit to marry with the oak. Very good Barbera and Dolcetto too. (PW)
● **Barolo** Runcot★★★★ £E Ginestra Casa Matè★★★★★ £E
● **Barbera d'Alba** Vigna Martina★★★ £C ● **Dolcetto d'Alba** Vigna dei Grassi★★ £B

SILVIO GRASSO Barolo *UK stockists:* Fal, N&P, F&R
Reliable 10-ha estate for modern well-made Barolos. Both established *cru* bottlings show full, ripe fruit, excellent
balance and well-integrated oak - best with 5-10 years' age. Federico Grasso's Insieme (see Altare) from Nebbiolo
with Barbera, Cabernet and Merlot, is aged in new oak. New Barolo *crus* (Giachini and Pì Vigne) since 99.(PW)
● **Barolo**★★★ £E Bricco Luciani★★★★ £F Ciabot Manzoni★★★★ £F
● **Barbera d'Alba**★ £B Vigna Fontanile★★ £C ● **Insieme**★★★ £F

ICARDI Barbera d'Asti *UK stockists:* **Ast,** Odd, But, VKg
A sizeable 65-ha estate making an extraordinary plethora of pleasurable wines that combine remarkable
drinkability and a succulent fruit richness. Barolo Parej shows increasing depth and structure and new
Barbaresco Montubert (from 2000) is a fine fruit-rich expression of Nebbiolo as is Langhe Pafoj. Bricco del Sole
combines Barbera, Nebbiolo and Cabernet. Langhe Nej is Pinot Nero. (PW)
● **Barolo** Parej★★★★ £F ● **Barbera d'Alba** Surì di Mù★★ £C
● **Barbera d'Asti** Tabarin★★ £B Nuj Suj★★★ £D ● **Dolcetto d'Alba** Rousori★★ £B
● **Langhe** Nej★★ £D Pafoj★★★ £E ● **Monferrato** Cascina Bricco del Sole★★★ £E

LA GIUSTINIANA Gavi *UK stockists:* Lib, Vne
One of a few top Gavi producers making consistently full, concentrated unwooded examples. Lugarara is the
mainstay; slightly minerally, appley Montessora has more intensity and persistence. Just, a partially barriqued
special selection is full, creamy and better again. A red equivalent is mostly from Barbera. 'IL' is new lees-
enriched Gavi. called 'IL'. (PW)
○ **Gavi del Comune di Gavi** Lugarara★★ £C Montessora★★★ £C ○ Just★★★ £E
● **Monferrato** Rosso Just★★ £D

LA SPINETTA Barbaresco *UK stockists:* Eno, WTs, Wtr, Bal, , JNi, NYg, UnC, P&S, Han, Hrd
Giorgio Rivetti has rocketed to fame. The wines are unequivocally modern, nearly all are barrique-aged yet
profound with super fruit. Of the Barbarescos, Starderi is the most structured, Valeirano perhaps most
concentrated, Gallina a touch softer and more expressive. Also smoky, old-vine Barbera d'Asti Superiore and
consistently brilliant Pin. Langhe white is Sauvignon and new sweet Moscato from dried grapes (La Spinetta
Oro) complements fine 3 star Moscato d'Asti. Also extremely promising new Barolo Campe' (from 2000
vintage). (PW)
● **Barbaresco** Gallina★★★★★ £G Starderi★★★★★ £G Valeirano★★★★★ £G
● **Barbera d'Asti** Ca' di Pian★★★ £D Superiore★★★★ £E
● **Barbera d'Alba** Vigneto Gallina★★★★ £E ● **Monferrato** Pin★★★★ £E

TENUTA LA TENAGLIA Barbera d'Asti www.latenaglia.com
Champion of very good Barbera from the Monferrato hills especially the sumptuous, complex barrique-aged
Emozioni from 70-year-old vines. Giorgio Tenaglia version is leaner but stylish. Paradiso is peppery and black-
fruited Syrah while Chardonnay (Oltre) is not unlike a good Pouilly-Fuissé. (PW)
● **Barbera d'Asti** Giorgio Tenaglia★★ £C Emozioni★★★ £D ● **Paradiso**★★ £D
● **Barbera del Monferrato** Superiore Tenaglia è★★ £C

MALVIRÀ Roero www.malvira.com *UK stockists:* **Tri,** V&C
Excellent producer of characterful Arneis - unwooed Renesio, partially oaked Trinità and oak-fermented and
aged Saglietto. Also very good reds: both Roero Superiore combine intensity with real elegance and are best 5
years' age. San Gugliemo is an unwooded, perfumed Barbera/Nebbiolo while oak-aged white Treuve combines
Sauvignon, Chardonnay and Arneis. (PW)
● **Roero Superiore** Mombeltramo★★★ £D Trinità★★★ £D
○ **Roero Arneis** Renesio★★ £B Trinità★★ £B Saglietto★★ £C

ITALY

MARCARINI Barolo www.marcarini.it   *UK stockists:* **RsW**, Rae, BBR, UnC, F&R
The Barolo here is traditionally styled, with no new oak and often ages impressively but forbiddingly structured when young. Also rich Boschi di Berri Dolcetto from 100 years old vines grown on their own roots giving a distinctive almondy, slightly earthy streak to intense berry fruit flavours. (PW)
● **Barolo** Brunate★★★★ £E   ● **Barbera d'Alba** Ciabot Camerano★★ £C
● **Dolcetto d'Alba** Fontanazza★ £B   Boschi di Berri★★★ £C

MARCHESI DI GRÉSY Barbaresco www.marchesidigresy.com   *UK stockists:* **Mer**, Amp,
Famed for the Martinenga *cru*, it is the individual plots of Camp Gros and Gaiun which usually provide splendid graceful and complex wines after a decade or more. Barriques are primarily used for Virtus (Barbera/Cabernet) and Villa Martis (Nebbiolo/Barbera). Also one of Piedmont's best Sauvignons. (PW)
● **Barbaresco** Martinenga★★ £F   Camp Gros★★★★ £F   Gaiun★★★★ £F
● **Langhe** Virtus★★ £E   Villa Martis★★ £E   **O Langhe Sauvignon**★★ £C

FRANCO M MARTINETTI Barbera d'Asti   *UK stockists:* **VDu**, F&R
Martinetti makes excellent Barbera (Montruc) and Barbera/Cabernet (Sul Bric) - powerful, concentrated reds with breadth, refinement and seamless tannins. Also modern and seductive Barolo Marasco from a blend of sites since 1997. Concentrated, sophisticated whites too, both Gavi Minaia and exotic Martin, from obscure local variety Timorasso. (PW)
● **Barbera d'Asti** Superiore Montruc★★★★ £E   ● **Monferrato** Sulbric★★★★ £E
● **Barolo** Marasco★★★ £F   **O Gavi** Minaia★★★ £D

BARTOLO MASCARELLO Barolo   *UK stockists:* Fal
Classic traditionally styled Barolo, made without concession to the modernists. Not for wimps, these are always powerful, broad and firmly tannic yet usually harmonious and superbly expressive with 15 years' age or more. Also sturdy *terroir*-derived Barbera and Dolcetto. (PW)
● **Barolo**★★★★ £F   ● **Barbera d'Alba** Vigna San Lorenzo★★ £C
● **Dolcetto d'Alba** Monrobiolo e Rué★★ £C

GIUSEPPE MASCARELLO & FIGLIO www.mascarello1881.com   *UK stockists:* **Wtr**, BBR
Monprivato is one of the great Barolo *crus*. The wines in the best years combine superb fruit quality with an effortless structure and balance. Riserva Ca' d' Morissio since 1993. Also very small amounts of other Barolo, and Barbera and Dolcetto of great character. Langhe Status is Nebbiolo with a little Barbera and Freisa. Excellent varietal Freisa too. (PW)
● **Barolo** Monprivato★★★★★ £F   Riserva Ca' d' Morissio★★★★★ £F
● **Barbera d'Alba** Scudetto★★★ £D   Codana★★★ £D
● **Dolcetto d'Alba** Bricco★★ £C   ● **Langhe Freisa** Toetto★★ £C

MOCCAGATTA Barbaresco
Reliable source for ripe, intense Barbaresco with a certain style and elegance too. There is little to choose between them but all deserve 5-10 years. Basarin Barbera adds a breadth and lushness over a perfumed regular version while barriqued Chardonnay is increasingly good. (PW)
● **Barbaresco** Basarin★★★ £E   Bric Balin★★★ £E   Cole★★★ £E
● **Barbera d'Alba**★ £C   Basarin★★ £D   **O Langhe Chardonnay** Buschet★★ £D

MAURO MOLINO Barolo   *UK stockists:* F&R
La Morra-based Altare disciple Mauro Molino goes for short maceration times and barrique-ageing for Barolo but from fine quality fruit. Gancia shows a firmer tannic structure than Conca but both show real weight and complexity. Insieme is a fairly typical blend, while Accanzio is mostly Barbera and Nebbiolo. (PW)
● **Barolo**★★★ £E   Vigna Conca★★★★ £F   Gancia★★★★ £F
● **Barbera d'Alba**★ £B   Gattere★★★ £D   ● **Langhe** Accanzio★★ £D

NINO NEGRI Valtellina Superiore www.giv.it   *UK stockists:* **Eno**, , Sel, NYg
Leading producer of Valtellina Superiore from each of its sub-zones: Grumello, Inferno, Sassella and Valgella. Light to medium-bodied, at their best they are intense, perfumed and elegant. Much better is enticingly perfumed 5 Stelle, a Sfursat/Sforzato semi-dried grapes version with sweet, intense fruit, evident tannin and acidity. Oak-aged, perfumed white Ca' Brione is Nebbiolo-based. (PW)

146

● **Valtellina Sfursat**★★★ £E 5 Stelle★★★★ £F O **Ca' Brione**★★ £C
● **Valtellina Superiore** Sassella Le Tense★★ £C Vigneto Fracia★★★ £E

ANGELO NEGRO & FIGLI Roero www.negroangelo.it *UK stockists:* **GWW**
Roero estate with a reputation built around Barbera and Nebbiolo. Top wine, Sudisfà, is deep and powerful with ripe, smooth tannins. Also good Arneis especially fuller more characterful single-vineyard examples. New is Bric Millon (Croatina with some Barbera and Cab Sauv). (PW)
● **Roero**★★ £B Prachiosso★★ £C Sudisfà★★★ £D
● **Barbera d'Alba** Bric Bertu★★★ £C O **Roero Arneis** Perdaudin★★ £C

ANDREA OBERTO Barolo *UK stockists:* **Alv,** V&C
Father and son team make excellent examples of Barbera, Dolcetto and Barolo from new cellars. Very rich, ripe barrique-aged Giada from old vines but also good value regular version. New oak is used for all the Barolos as well as the Nebbiolo/Barbera blend, Fabio. Rocche is a lovely example of the *cru*, with its unique perfumed, floral character around a deep fruit core. Also delicious *cru* Dolcetto. (PW)
● **Barolo**★★★ £E Vigneto Albarella★★★★ £F Rocche★★★★ £F
● **Langhe** Rosso Fabio★★★ £D ● **Barbera d'Alba**★★ £B Giada★★★ £D

PAITIN Barbaresco www.paitin.it *UK stockists:* **HSA,** Win, BBR
The Pasquero-Elia control part of the *cru* of Serraboella producing a dense but increasingly accessible version of real style and complexity with 8-10 years' age. Also high standards in sleek barrique-aged Langhe red, Paitin (Barbera and Nebbiolo with Cabernet and Syrah), Barbera (especially Campolive) and Dolcetto with a touch of class. (PW)
● **Barbaresco** Sorì Paitin★★★ £E ● **Langhe** Paitin★★★ £D
● **Barbera d'Alba** Campolive★★★ £C Serra Boella★★ £C

PARUSSO Barolo www.parusso.com *UK stockists:* **Eno,** NYg, N&P, Las
High-quality range of wines that continue to improve. Modern Barolo with weight and depth to go with evident style, complexity and length in the top *crus*. Also excellent Barberas (Superiore is from old vines) and Langhe Bricco Rovella (Nebbiolo, Barbera and Cabernet). Langhe Nebbiolo is one of best going. Decent Sauvignon too (as Langhe Bianco), richer Bricco Rovella is barrique-aged. (PW)
● **Barolo** Bussia Vigne Rocche★★★★★ £F Bussia Vigne Munie★★★★ £F
● **Barbera d'Alba** Ornati★★★ £C ● **Barbera d'Alba** Superiore★★★★ £E
● **Langhe** Bricco Rovella★★ £D O **Langhe Bianco**★★ £C Bricco Rovella★★ £D

PECCHENINO Dolcetto di Dogliani www.pecchenino.com *UK stockists:* Gen, Odd
Source of dense, succulent Dolcetto with increasingly fine textures and less obtrusive structures thanks in part to micro-oxygenation: unoaked San Luigi, classy partly-oaked Sirì d'Jermu and Bricco Botti (half aged in new oak) Langhe red, La Castella is Barbera with 30% Nebbiolo. New from 2001 are Quass, a lush, fleshy Barbera, and Langhe Nebbiolo, Vigna Botti. (PW)
● **Dolcetto di Dogliani** San Luigi★★ £B Superiore Bricco Botti★★★ £D
● **Dolcetto di Dogliani** Siri d'Jermu★★★ £C ● **Langhe** La Castella★★★ £D

PELISSERO Barbaresco www.pelissero.com *UK stockists:* **Alv,** Odd, Sel
Much improved 20-ha estate with increasingly complex and stylish Barbaresco - especially Vanotu which is aged in mostly new oak. Slightly better 99s than 2000s. There's plenty of fruit in Dolcetto too, especially vibrant, perfumed Augenta. Also good Barbera and Nebbiolo including blend of the two (Long Now). (PW)
● **Barbaresco**★★★ £E Vanotu★★★★ £F ● **Langhe** Long Now★★★ £D
● **Dolcetto d'Alba** Munfrina★★ £B Augenta★★ £C ● **Barbera d'Alba** Piani★★ £C

E PIRA & FIGLI Barolo *UK stockists:* **Eno,** JNi, N&P, F&R, Las
Chiara Boschis efforts centre on 2.5 ha of Cannubi. Recent vintages display tremendous class, elegance, purity and complexity, and will add richness and depth with age. Also smaller volumes of (very good) Barolo Via Nuova and a Barbera of increasing style and purity since 2001. (PW)
● **Barolo** Cannubi★★★★★ £F Via Nuova★★★★ £F ● **Barbera d'Alba**★★ £C

LUIGI PIRA Barolo *UK stockists:* **Bal,** JNi, N&P, F&R, Las
Giampaolo Pira and his family have underlined the potential of Serralunga with excellent wines from the Marenca,

ITALY

Margheria and (since 1997) Vigna Rionda *crus*. Dense, structured Barolos that are concentrated and powerful with great cellaring potential. Also good unoaked Dolcetto and a tiny amount of fine Langhe Nebbiolo. (PW)
● **Barolo**★★★ £E Marenca★★★★ £F Margheria★★★★ £F Vigna Rionda★★★★★ £G
● **Nebbiolo d'Alba** Le Ombre★★★ £F   ● **Dolcetto d'Alba**★★ £C

FERDINANDO PRINCIPIANO Barolo www.ferdinandoprincipiano.it   *UK stockists:* **HSA**
From 10 ha of mostly old vines in SE corner of the Barolo zone is produced Boscareto, a wine of great character, complexity (including woodsmoke and truffles) and structure. The same *cru* also provides half the Barbera for La Romualda which is rich, ripe and lush with old-vine blackberry fruit. Another Barolo, Le Coste shows good balance and intensity. (PW)
● **Barolo** Boscareto★★★★ £E Le Coste★★★ £E
● **Barbera d'Alba** La Romualda★★★ £D   ● **Dolcetto d'Alba** Sant'Anna★ £B

PRUNOTTO Barolo www.prunotto.it   *UK stockists:* **BWC**, Vts, FWC, Cam, Sel, N&P, F&R
Antinori owned with a consistent and not excessively priced range of wine led by the *cru* Barolo Bussia. Something of this wine's harmony and balance, if not concentration or size can be seen in nearly all the wines. Noted Barbera d'Alba Pian Romualdo has recently been surpassed by the super Barbera d'Asti Costamiole. (PW)
● **Barolo**★★★ £E Bussia★★★★ £F   ● **Barbaresco**★★ £E Bric Turot★★★ £F
● **Nebbiolo d'Alba** Occhetti★★ £B   ● **Barbera d'Alba**★ £B Pian Romualdo★★★ £C
● **Barbera d'Asti** Fiulot★★ £B Costamiole★★★★ £E

ALDO RAINOLDI Valtellina Superiore www.rainoldi.com   *UK stockists:* **VDu**, May
Much improved and modernised wines with striking length and flavour intensity in the top wines. Sfursat/Sforzato shows the most power and concentration especially barrique-aged Fruttaio Ca' Rizzieri which is dense and powerful with excellent depth and intensity. Also very attractive white, Ghibellino from Nebbiolo (vinified as a white) and 30% Sauvignon.(PW)
● **Valtellina Superiore** Inferno Riserva Barrique★★★ £D Sassella Riserva★★★ £C
● **Vatellina Sforzato**★★ £D Fruttaio Ca' Rizzieri★★★★ £E   **O Ghibellino**★★ £C

RENATO RATTI Barolo www.renatoratti.com   *UK stockists:* **ViV**
Receiving a renewed boost to quality under the direction of Pietro Ratti. Vineyards in Asti and Monferrato hills as well as 'Marcenasco' vineyards in La Morra. Barolos can lack a little weight and richness but have charm and personality. Villa Pattono, (Barbera, Cabernet and Merlot) is much more showy while Barbera shows good intense fruit and sound structure. (PW)
● **Barolo** Marcenasco★★ £E Conca Marcenasco★★★ £F Rocche Marcenasco★★★ £F
● **Monferrato** Villa Pattono★★★ £D   ● **Barbera d'Alba** Torriglione★★ £C

FRATELLI REVELLO Barolo www.revellofratelli.com   *UK stockists:* Fal, NYg, F&R
Very modern, upfront fruit-filled Barolos without the structure or depth of the very best. However many drinkers are seduced by their lush immediacy. Also small quantities of an explosively fruity barrique-aged Barbera d'Alba Ciabot du Re and a version of Insieme (see Altare) which includes a little Petit Verdot. Another Barolo *cru*, Gattera since 99. (PW)
● **Barolo**★★ £E Vigna Conca★★★ £F Vigna Giachini★★★ £F Rocche★★★ £F
● **Barbera d'Alba**★ £C Ciabot du Re★★★ £D   ● **Insieme**★★★ £F

GIUSEPPE RINALDI Barolo
Giuseppe Rinaldi maintains a staunchly traditional approach. The wines are not in the least bit immediate or fruit-rich but develop splendid complexity with at least 15 years' age. There is also superb texture, dimension and class, especially in the more widely seen Brunate-Le Coste (an equal blend of 2 sites). The second Barolo can be more austere but has similar ageing potential. (PW)
● **Barolo** Brunate-Le Coste★★★★★ £F Cannubi San Lorenzo-Ravera★★★★ £F

ALBINO ROCCA Barbaresco www.roccaalbino.com   *UK stockists:* **J&B**, NYg, F&R
Albino Rocca and his son Angelo make two contrasting and very good Barbarescos: richer, more structured barrique-aged Brich Ronchi and purer, more elegant Loreto. Also first class Barbera with better depth and balance than most. White Langhe, La Rocca is barrique-aged Cortese and better than most Gavi. (PW)
● **Barbaresco** Vigneto Brich Ronchi★★★★ £E Vigneto Loreto★★★★ £E
● **Barbera d'Alba** Gèpin★★★ £D   **O Langhe** La Rocca★★ £C

New entries have producer's name underlined

BRUNO ROCCA   Barbaresco   www.brunorocca.it   *UK stockists:* **Lib, HHB, N&P, C&R**
Rabajà is one of Barbaresco's leading *crus* from which Bruno Rocca makes an excellent modern interpretation.
Also good Coparossa Barbaresco (made since 95) from Fausoni and Pajorè *crus*. Both very good in 99 and 2000.
More fruit-driven Langhe red Rabajolo (Cabernet, Barbera and Nebbiolo) and other wines of good standard. (PW)
● **Barbaresco** Coparossa★★★★ £F   Rabajà★★★★★ £F   ● **Barbera d'Alba**★★★ £C
● **Langhe** Rabajolo★★★ £E   O **Langhe Chardonnay** Cadet★★ £C

ROCCHE DEI MANZONI   Barolo   www.rocchedeimanzoni.it   *UK stockists:* **Alv**
Modern, bold and oaky wines from more than 40 ha. Of expanding range of Barolos, Cappella di Santo Stefano
(made since 1996) has most class and depth. Relatively forward Bricco Manzoni is Nebbiolo/Barbera while
complex, supple Quatr Nas (Nebbiolo, Cab Sauv, Merlot and Pinot Nero) has good substance. Pinònero is pure
Pinot Nero, also oaky Chardonnay and toasty sparkling wine. (PW)
● **Barolo** Vigna Big★★★ £F   Vigna d'la Roul★★★ £F   Pianpolvere Soprano★★★ £F
● **Barolo** Cappella di S. Stefano★★★★ £F   ● **Barbera d'Alba** Sorito Mosconi★★ £C
● **Langhe** Bricco Manzoni★★ £E   Quatr Nas★★★ £E   Pinònero★ £E

SAN FEREOLO   Dolcetto di Dogliani   www.sanfereolo.com
Consistently deep, dense Dolcetto, the Superiore San Fereolo is among the best of the zone. Also a little of '1593'
which see 50% new oak - an attempt at producing a long-lived style. Rich, intense Barbera, aged partly in new
oak, is sold as Brumaio. A new Langhe white (Gewürz/Riesling) since 2001. (PW)
● **Dolcetto di Dogliani** Valdibà★★ £C   Superiore San Fereolo★★★ £C
● **Langhe** Brumaio★★★ £C

SAN ROMANO   Dolcetto di Dogliani   www.sanromano.com   *UK stockists:* **Nov**
Bruno Chionetti makes excellent Dolcetto di Dogliani by concentrating on low yields and top-quality fruit. Vigna
del Pilone is soft but deep with plenty of extract, needing a further 2 or 3 years' bottle-age. Oak-aged Dolianum, a
special selection, is less classic but fuller in texture than typical of Dogliani. Ciancé, (Barbera, Dolcetto, Pinot Nero)
is oaky and black-fruited. (PW)
● **Dolcetto di Dogliani**★★ £B   Vigna del Pilone★★★ £C
● **Dolcetto di Dogliani** Superiore Dolianum★★★ £D
● **Langhe Rosso** Ciancé★★ £C

SANDRONE   www.sandroneluciano.com   *UK stockists:* **RsW, WTs, P&S, UnC, Rae, BBR, NYg, Las**
Luciano Sandrone continues to bring out greatness of both place and grape. Barolos are always super with
splendid complexity and terrific breadth on the palate but also balanced and harmonious. Also good fruit-rich
expressions of Barbera, Dolcetto and Nebbiolo d'Alba. Langhe Pe Mol (Barbera, Nebbiolo) made since 99. (PW)
● **Barolo** Cannubi Boschis❂❂❂❂❂ £H   Le Vigne★★★★★ £G
● **Langhe** Pe Mol★★ £E   ● **Barbera d'Alba**★★★ £D

PAOLO SCAVINO   Barolo   *UK stockists:* **J&B, N&P, F&R, Las**
Premium prices reflect the continued demand for the wines of Enrico Scavino who makes arguably the
definitive example of Barolo Rocche dell'Annunziata, adding power and breadth to the *cru's* classic perfume.
Also often superb, Cannubi and Bric del Fiasc show a little more of the structure indicative of their origins. Oak
plays an important part in all wines including cellar worthy Barbera and Corale (Nebbiolo, Barbera and a little
Cab Sauv). (PW)
● **Barolo**★★★ £F   Carobric★★★★ £G   Cannubi★★★★ £G   Bric del Fiasc★★★★★ £G
● **Barolo Riserva** Rocche dell'Annunziata★★★★★ £G   ● **Langhe** Corale★★★ £E
● **Barbera d'Alba** Affinato in Carati★★★ £E   ● **Dolcetto d'Alba**★ £B

ALDO & RICCARDO SEGHESIO   Barolo   *UK stockists:* **Fal, N&P, F&R**
Seductive, showy and and oak-influenced Barolo in the modern style. Oaky but rich, deep Barbera works better
and is similarly very accessible. Bouquet (Nebbiolo, Cabernet and Merlot) in the same mould while ripe, fruity
unoaked Barbera and Dolcetto are also made. (PW)
● **Barolo** La Villa★★★ £E   ● **Barbera d'Alba**★★ £C   Vigneto della Chiesa★★★ £D
● **Langhe** Bouquet★★ £D   ● **Dolcetto d'Alba** Vigneto della Chiesa★★ £B

G D VAJRA   Barolo   *UK stockists:* **Lib, ACh, Vne, P&S, V&C, Hrd**
Aldo Vaira's vines are at an altitude atypically high for Barolo. but protected, south-facing Bricco delle Viole

149

ripens Nebbiolo with a distinctive floral, plum and cherry fruit character and equally a *superiore* Barbera of great vigour and intensity. Also magnificent spicy, earthy Dolcetto with intense black plum fruit, and Kyé, a wonderfully expressive powerful dry Freisa. All should be given time. Fine Langhe Bianco (Riesling) and well-made regular Dolcetto, Barbera and Nebbiolo. (PW)

● **Barolo**★★★ £E Bricco delle Viole★★★★ £F ● **Barbera d'Alba Sup.**★★★ £D
● **Dolcetto d'Alba**★ £B Coste & Fossati★★★★ £C ● **Langhe Freisa** Kyé★★★ £C

MAURO VEGLIO Barolo www.mauroveglio.com *UK stockists:* Gen, Fal, N&P, F&R
Neighbour to Altare, and one of the closest in style. Barolos Castelletto and Arborina are made in the greatest quantities but all have been impressive over the recent string of good vintages and should have 6-10 years' ageing. Also barrique-aged Cascina Nuova Barbera needing 3-4 years' age. Insieme is from Nebbiolo, Barbera and Cabernet. (PW)

● **Barolo** Arborina★★★ £F Castelletto★★★ £E Gattera★★★ £E Rocche★★★ £E
● **Barbera d'Alba**★ £B Cascina Nuova★★ £D ● **Insieme**★★★ £F

VIETTI Barolo www.vietti.com *UK stockists:* **Vim,** N&P, F&R
Long-established leading Barolo producer with single-vineyard Barolos from estate vineyards. Traditionally vinified but barrique-aged, they add real weight and richness with cellaring. Rocche is often the most classic but all deserve cellaring as does superb, Barbera d'Alba Scarrone Vigna Vecchia. Barbera d'Asti La Crena is a notable single-vineyard example. (PW)

● **Barolo** Castiglione★★ £E Brunate★★★ £F Lazzarito★★★★ £F Rocche★★★★ £F
● **Barbaresco** Masseria★★ £E ● **Barbera d'Asti** Tre Vigne★ £C La Crena★★★ £E
● **Barbera d'Alba** Scarrone★★ £D Scarrone Vigna Vecchia★★★ £E

VIGNA RIONDA - MASSOLINO Barolo *UK stockists:* Lib, Vne, F&M
Mostly traditional-styled Barolos with an intense core that builds with age to give fullness and a marvellous complexity after a decade or so. Intense, tannic yet elegant Margheria and more modern-style Parafada are surpassed by Vigna Rionda Riserva with still more fullness, depth and complexity. Also good Barbera (especially Gisep), Chardonnay and Langhe Piria (Barbera/Nebbiolo). (PW)

● **Barolo**★★★★ £E Margheria★★★★★ £F Parafada★★★★★ £F
● **Barolo Riserva** Vigna Rionda✪✪✪✪✪ £F ● **Barbera d'Alba** Gisep★★★ £D

GIANNI VOERZIO Barolo *UK stockists:* JAr, P&S, PWa, F&R
Gianni Voerzio makes very fine, even elegant wines with great vigour, deep fruit and good balance. Barolo La Serra is dense and intriguing when young but best with 8-10 years'. Barbera and the Nebbiolo/Barbera blend, Serrapiù, show most marked oak but this melts into rich pure fruit with a little age. Arneis and Dolcetto are excellent examples. (PW)

● **Barolo** La Serra★★★★★ £G ● **Langhe** Serrapiù★★★ £E
● **Barbera d'Alba** Ciabot della Luna★★★ £D ● **Dolcetto d'Alba** Rochettevino★★★ £C
● **Langhe Freisa** Sotto I Bastioni★★ £C O **Roero Arneis** Bricco Cappellina★★ £C

ROBERTO VOERZIO Barolo *UK stockists:* **Eno, WTs,** JNi, Hrd, N&P, F&R
Relentless and uncompromising in pusuit of low yields and very concentrated fruit and in use of new oak - now achieves harmony in all wines. Newish are outstanding Riserva, Vecchie Viti dei Capalot e delle Brunate and Sarmassa (since 98). Voerzio's mega-Barbera is the most powerful and concentrated made anywhere. Vignaserra (Nebbiolo, Cab Sauv and/or Barbera) was last made in 2000. (PW)

● **Barolo** Brunate✪✪✪✪✪ £H Cerequio✪✪✪✪✪ £H La Serra★★★★★ £H
● **Barbera d'Alba Riserva** Vigneto Pozzo dell Annunziata✪✪✪✪✪ £F

Other wineries of note
M & E Abbona (Dolcetto di Dogliani), Orlando Abrigo (Barbaresco), Antichi Vigneti di Cantalupo (Ghemme), Bertelli (Barbera d'Asti), Bussia Soprana (Barolo), Ca' Viola (Dolcetto d'Alba), Cascina Chicco (Roero), Quinto Chionetti (Dolcetto di Dogliani), Contratto (Asti), Damilano (Barolo), Forteto della Luja (Loazzolo), Filippo Gallino (Roero), La Barbatella (Barbera d'Asti), La Scolca (Gavi), Giovanni Manzone (Barolo), Monti (Barolo), Fiorenzo Nada (Barbaresco), Fratelli Oddero (Barolo), Orsolani (Erbaluce di Caluso), Pio Cesare (Barolo), Saracco (Moscato d'Asti), Sottimano (Barbaresco), Triacca (Valtellina Superiore), Vignaioli Elvio Pertinace (Barbaresco)

An in-depth profile of every producer can be found in Wine behind the label 2006

New entries have producer's name underlined

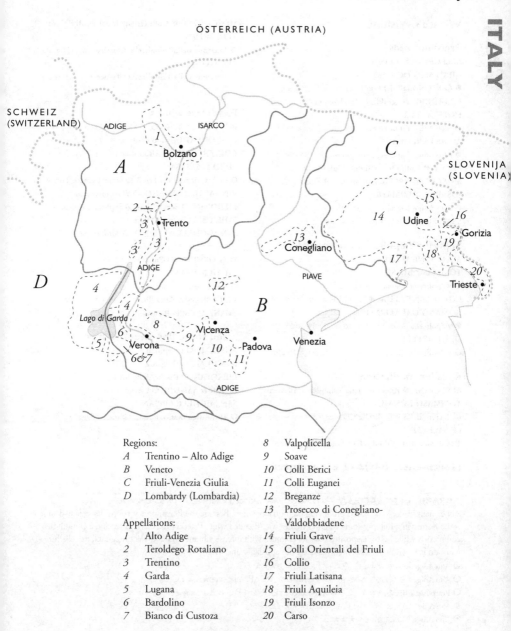

Regions:

A	Trentino – Alto Adige
B	Veneto
C	Friuli-Venezia Giulia
D	Lombardy (Lombardia)

Appellations:

1	Alto Adige	8	Valpolicella
2	Teroldego Rotaliano	9	Soave
3	Trentino	10	Colli Berici
4	Garda	11	Colli Euganei
5	Lugana	12	Breganze
6	Bardolino	13	Prosecco di Conegliano-Valdobbiadene
7	Bianco di Custoza	14	Friuli Grave
		15	Colli Orientali del Friuli
		16	Collio
		17	Friuli Latisana
		18	Friuli Aquileia
		19	Friuli Isonzo
		20	Carso

Background

In North-East Italy fine, elegant whites are produced in the Alto Adige and fuller, more concentrated examples in Friuli-Venezia-Giulia, from a mix of both local and international varieties. Some of Italy's finest sweet wines also come from the North-East as do some high-quality reds - either from Cabernet Sauvignon or Merlot, or more original reds from native grapes Corvina, Lagrein, Teroldego, Pignolo and Schiopettino.

ITALY

Wizard's Wishlist

Premium reds
ALLEGRINI ● La Poja
GIROLAMO DORIGO
● Colli Orientali del Friuli Rosso Montscalapade
FORADORI ● Teroldego Rotaliano Granato
HOFSTÄTTER
● Alto Adige Pinot Nero Barthenau Vigna Sant'Urbano
ALOIS LAGEDER
● Alto Adige Cabernet Sauvignon Cor Römigberg
MIANI ● Colli Orientali del Friuli Merlot
MOSCHIONI ● Colli Orientali del Friuli Celtico Rosso
JOSEF NIEDERMAYR
● Alto Adige Lagrein Aus Gries Riserva
SAN LEONARDO ● San Leonardo

Superior Valpolicella (or equivalent)
ALLEGRINI ● La Grola
TOMMASO BUSSOLA
● Valpolicella Classico Superiore TB
CORTE SANT'ALDA ● Valpolicella Superiore Mithas
ROMANO DAL FORNO
● Valpolicella Superiore Vigneto di Monte Lodoletta
QUINTARELLI
● Valpolicella Classico Superiore Monte Ca' Paletta

Reds for meditation
ALLEGRINI ● Amarone della Valpolicella Classico
TOMMASO BUSSOLA
● Recioto della Valpolicella Classico TB
LE SALETTE
● Amarone della Valpolicella Classico Pergole Vece

MOSCHIONI ● Colli Orientali del Friuli Pignolo
TEDESCHI
● Amarone della Valpolicella Classico Capitel Monte Olmi
ZENATO
● Amarone della Valpolicella Classico Riserva Sergio Zenato

First class whites
BORGO DEL TIGLIO ○ Collio Bianco Studio di Bianco
CESCONI ○ Trentino Chardonnay
COLTERENZIO ○ Alto Adige Chardonnay Cornell
LIVIO FELLUGA
○ Colli Orientali del Fruili Rosazzo Bianco Terre Alte
VINNAIOLI JERMANN ○ Vintage Tunina
PIEROPAN ○ Soave Classico Superiore La Rocca
POJER & SANDRI ○ Faye
SAN MICHELE APPIANO ○ Alto Adige Gewürztraminer Sanct Valentin
SCHIOPETTO ○ Collio Pinot Bianco Amrità
VIE DI ROMANS
○ Friuli Isonzo Chardonnay Vie di Romans
VILLA RUSSIZ ○ Collio Sauvignon de la Tour
ZUANI ○ Collio Bianco

...and some fine sweet whites
ANSELMI ○ I Capitelli
MACULAN ○ Breganze Torcolato
PIEROPAN ○ Passito della Rocca
POJER & SANDRI ○ Essenzia
SAN MICHELE APPIANO
○ Alto Adige Bianco Passito Comtess' Sanct Valentin

North-East Italy/A-Z of producers

ABBAZIA DI NOVACELLA Alto Adige www.abbazianovacella.it *UK stockists:* **Ast**
Abbey high in the Valle Isarco producing high-quality wines. Best are the Praepositus versions. Especially distinctive is the Kerner in a full, pronounced and intense style. Blended white Praepositus has elegance and a Burgundian complexity, while both Praepositus reds are complex with intense vibrant fruit and well-integrated oak. Perfumed Moscato Rosa (Rosenmuskateller) has exceptional balance and length. (PW)
○ Alto Adige Kerner★★ £B Kerner Praepositus★★★ £C
○ Alto Adige Gewürztraminer★ £B Gewürztraminer Praepositus★★★ £C
○ Praepositus Bianco★★★ £C ● Alto Adige Pinot Nero Praepositus★★ £E
◕ Alto Adige Lagrein Riserva Praepositus★★★ £E
◉ Alto Adige Moscato Rosa★★★ £E

STEFANO ACCORDINI Veneto www.accordinistefano.it *UK stockists:* **GFy, Tan**
Small family estate with rich but elegant and expressive Valpolicella, Recioto and Amarone. Valpolicella Acinatico is an intense, very ripe, berryish *ripasso* version. 2000 and 99 were notable for Amarone, 02 and 00 for Recioto. Unusual is Passo, from dried grapes, but adding Cab Sauv and Merlot (together 25%) to the more usual Corvina and Rondinella.(PW)
● Amarone della Valpolicella Classico Acinatico★★★★ £E
● Valpolicella Classico Superiore Acinatico★★ £C
● Recioto della Valpolicela Classico Acinatico★★★ £E

New entries have producer's name underlined

North-East Italy

ITALY

ALLEGRINI   Veneto   www.allegrini.it   *UK stockists:* **Lib,**ACh,Vne, UnC, Con, BBR, F&M
Producer of oak-influenced modern-style reds with excellent fruit, depth and intensity, developing velvety textures with age. Single-vineyard reds based on Corvina - La Grola includes a little Syrah and Sangiovese, Palazzo della Torre is enriched by dried grapes. Amarone is rich and concentrated while La Poja (pure Corvina), from late-harvested grapes, has striking intensity and depth. Also fine Recioto and very ripe Villa Giona (Cab Sauv, Merlot, Syrah). (PW)
● **Amarone Classico**★★★★★ £F   ● **La Poja**★★★★★ £F
● **La Grola**★★★ £D   ● **Palazzo della Torre**★★★ £D
● **Recioto della Valpolicella Classico** Giovanni Allegrini★★★ £F

ANSELMI   Veneto   *UK stockists:* **Eno,** NYg, N&P, FWC, Sel,V&C
Soave-based producer of fine IGT whites. Capitel Foscarino offers a lovely pure citrus and yellow plum fruit, in contrast to oak-influenced Capitel Croce. Star wine is wonderfully elegant, pure-fruited and classy sweet wine, I Capitelli. Realda (Cab Sauv) shows concentrated blackcurrant fruit and a leafy influence. (PW)
○ **San Vicenzo**★ £B   ○ **Capitel Foscarino**★★★ £C   ○ **Capitel Croce**★★ £C
○ **I Capitelli**★★★★ £D   ● **Cabernet Sauvignon Realda**★★ £C

BORGO DEL TIGLIO   Friuli-Venezia Giulia   *UK stockists:* **Ast,** P&S, F&M, UnC, But
Fine source of intense, ripe and ageworthy whites especially in superior versions - oak-influenced, structured Tocai Ronco della Chiesa, and Chardonnay Selezione with more depth, complexity and richness than regular example. Studio di Bianco (Tocai, Sauvignon, Riesling) is stylish and intense. Reds, Rosso della Centa (Merlot) and Collio Rosso Riserva (Merlot, Cab Sauv), more variable but plummy, berryish in warm vintages. (PW)
○ **Collio** Chardonnay Selezione★★★ £E   Tocai Ronco della Chiesa★★★ £E
○ **Collio** Malvasia Selezione★★ £C   ○ **Collio Bianco** Studio di Bianco★★★ £E
● **Collio** Rosso della Centa★★ £E   ● **Collio Rosso** Riserva★★ £E

TOMMASO BUSSOLA   Veneto   *UK stockists:* **Bal,** L&W,The, P&S,Vts, NYg, Hrd
Brilliant and dedicated young grower, one of the stars of Valpolicella. Regular BG range show fine fruit and intensity, and better than many big volume examples. Very small production premium TB wines are from finest fruit aged in new oak - wonderfully perfumed with ever more depth and concentration in the most recent releases. Best wines since 1997. (PW)
● **Amarone Classico** BG★★★ £E   TB★★★★★ £G   TB Vigneto Alto★★★★★ £G
● **Valpolicella Classico** BG★★ £B   Superiore TB★★★ £C
● **Recioto della Valpolicella Classico** BG★★★ £E   TB★★★★★ £F

CA' DEI FRATI   Lombardia   www.cadeifrati.it   *UK stockists:* **Lib,**Con,Vne,P&S, F&M,Sel NYg
Ca' dei Frati set standard for Lugana from consistently stylish Lugana I Frati through elegant, textured Brolettino to lush, exotic and long Pratto (Lugana, Chardonnay, Sauvignon). Sweet Tre Filer from same varieties as Pratto but from dried grapes. Also small amount of concentrated Grande Annata Brolettino. (PW)
○ **Lugana** I Frati★★ £B   Brolettino★★★ £C   Brolettino Grande Annata★★★ £D
○ **Pratto**★★★ £D   ○ **Tre Filer**★★ £E

CANTINA DEL CASTELLO   Veneto   www.cantinacastello.it   *UK stockists:* **Eno**
Consistently characterful and well-made Soave. The basic is very fresh, citrusy and pure when young. Of 2 *crus* Carniga is more minerally and salty as well as fuller and more concentrated. Also rich, lush Acini Soavi from late-harvested grapes and very small amounts of sweet Recioto di Soave Cortepittora and Acini Dolci. (PW)
○ **Soave Classico** Castello★ £B   Pressoni★★ £C   Carniga★★★ £C
○ **Soave Classico** Acini Soavi★★★ £D   ○ **Recioto di Soave** Cortepittora★★★ £E

CESCONI   Trentino   *UK stockists:* **Lib,** Gau,Vne, SVS
Cesconi brothers produce wines of atypical ripeness and richness for region. Oak is employed with restraint in aromatic Sauvignon, weighty Chardonnay and full, creamy Pinot Grigio. Equally good unoaked Traminer. Olivar (Pinot Bianco, Pinot Grigio, Chardonnay) can be most complete and complex. Cool-fruited Merlot (since 98) while Pivier, effectively Riserva Merlot, is oakier with more depth and richness. (PW)
○ **Olivar**★★★ £D   ○ **Trentino** Chardonnay★★★ £C   ○ **Trentino** Sauvignon★★ £C
○ **Trentino** Pinot Grigio★★ £C   ○ **Trentino** Traminer Aromatico★★★ £C
● **Trentino** Merlot★★ £C   ● **Pivier**★★★ £D

153

ITALY

COLTERENZIO Alto Adige www.colterenzio.com   *UK stockists:* **Eno**
Leading co-op of 28 grape growers. Sound quality at 'classic' level, better are 'vineyard series' Praedium, and premium Cornell label. Consistently deep, concentrated Chardonnay Cornell and intense, complex (if a touch overdone) partly oaked Sauvignon Lafoa. Impressive top reds, Cornelius (Cabernet/Merlot) and powerful but less harmonious Cab Sauv Lafoa. Most character in Lagrein especially Cornell with smoky, earthy, roasted qualities. Pinot Nero (Schwarzhaus), Merlot (Riserva Siebeneich) and Moscato Rosa also made. (PW)
O **Alto Adige** Chardonnay Cornell★★★ £E Gewürztraminer Cornell★★ £D
O **Alto Adige** Sauvignon Prail★★ £C Pinot Bianco Weisshaus★★ £C
● **Alto Adige** Lagrein Cornell★★★ £E Cabernet Sauvignon Lafoa★★★ £F

CORTE SANT'ALDA Veneto www.cortesantalda.it   *UK stockists:* **Wtr**, CdP, DWS, BBR, F&M
Excellent committed Valpolicella/Amarone producer. Sleek, elegant wines of indisputably good quality, with excellent expression, intensity and concentration - even regular Valpolicella, Ca' Fiui is good. Also minute quantities of Amarone Mithas (97), dry white, Retratto, (Sauvignon, Chardonnay, Garganega) and a little Soave (Partenio). (PW)
● **Amarone**★★★★ £E ● **Recioto della Valpolicella**★★★★ £E
● **Valpolicella** Superiore Mithas★★★ £C ● **Valpolicella** Superiore Ripasso★★★ £C
● **Valpolicella** Ca' Fiui★★ £B

ROMANO DAL FORNO Veneto   *UK stockists:* **JAr**, Far, BBR, Fal
Valpolicella's most sought-after producer with low trained high density vineyards. Stunning Valpolicella shows extract and concentration missing in most Amarone; fruit-rich, deep and structured, with remarkable character and complexity. Extraordinary Amarone and Recioto of unprecedented breadth and depth set the standard for others to emulate. (PW)
● **Amarone** Vigneto di Monte Lodoletta✪✪✪✪ £H
● **Recioto della Valpolicella** Vigneto di Monte Lodoletta✪✪✪✪ £H
● **Valpolicella Superiore** Vigneto di Monte Lodoletta★★★★ £F

MAURO DRIUS Friuli-Venezia Giulia   *UK stockists:* **HSA**
Intense, elegant Pinot Grigio is amongst the best from Friuli, while Sauvignon has classic herb and mineral complexity. The 2 Tocais are also very impressive; pure, well-defined 2004s contrast with fuller, riper 03s. Blended white Vignis di Sìris has a fine spice and ripe citrus character. The stylish reds do best in riper vintages. (PW)
O **Collio** Sauvignon★★ £C Tocai Friulano★★ £C
O **Friuli Isonzo** Tocai Friulano★★ £C Pinot Bianco★★ £C Pinot Grigio★★★ £C
O **Friuli Isonzo** Malvasia★ £C Vignis di Sìris★★★ £C
● **Friuli Isonzo** Cabernet★★★ £C Merlot★★★ £C

LIVIO FELLUGA Friuli-Venezia Giulia www.liviofelluga.it   *UK stockists:* **Lib**, Vne, P&S, F&M, Hrd
Grand Friuli estate being taken to new heights. Terre Alte (Tocai, Pinot Bianco, Sauvignon) elegant and balanced if less good in 01, 00. Otherwise stylish and intense oak-aged Illivio (Pinot Bianco) needs more restraint. Also aromatic, characterful Shàrjs (Chardonnay, Ribolla Gialla) and unoaked varietals. Fine medium-sweet Picolit and reds Refosco, Vertigo (Merlot, Cab Sauv), and Sossò - deep, polished, lushly berry-fruited Merlot. (PW)
O **COF** Rosazzo Bianco Terre Alte★★ £C O **Sharjs**★★ £C
O **COF** Pinot Bianco Illivio★★★ £C Picolit Riserva★★★★ £G ● **Vertigo**★★ £C
● **COF** Merlot Riserva Sossò★★★ £F Refosco dal Peduncolo Rosso★★★ £F

FORADORI Trentino www.elisabettaforadori.com   *UK stockists:* **JAr**, N&P
Top Italian estate despite little known Teroldego Rotaliano. Smoky, brambly regular version of real poise and persistence while in Granato, a wine of great style and class, are added tobacco, spice and cedar. Also well-defined floral, fruity white Myrto (Chardonnay, Sauvignon, Pinot Bianco) and small amounts of Ailanpa (very good Syrah) and Karanar (Cab Sauv, Syrah, Petit Verdot and Merlot). (PW)
● **Teroldego Rotaliano**★★ £C Granato★★★★ £E
● **Ailanpa**★★★ £E ● **Karanar**★★★ £E O **Myrto**★★ £C

GINI Veneto www.ginivini.com   *UK stockists:* **J&B**
The Gini family have owned vines here for around 300 years. Soave is excellent with real character and

New entries have producer's name underlined

concentration in 2 fine *crus*, La Froscà (50-year-old vines) and Contrada Salvarenza (80-year-old vines). Recioto Col Foscarin has a preserved citrus fruits intensity. Also small volumes of Sauvignon, Chardonnay and Pinot Nero. (PW)

O **Soave Classico** Superiore★★ £B La Froscà★★★ £B
O **Soave Classico** Contrada Salvarenza Vecchie Vigne★★★ £C
O **Recioto di Soave** Col Foscarin★★★ £E

FRANZ HAAS Alto Adige www.franz-haas.it *UK stockists:* **Lib**, Vne, P&S, F&M, V&C
One of most consistent in Alto Adige with noted fruit quality and harmony. Superior versions labelled Schweizer or Cru. Usually excellent intense, vibrant Manna (Riesling, Chardonnay, Gewürz, Sauvignon) and deep, flavoursome white varietals. Distinctive, ripe Istante (Cab Franc, Cab Sauv, Merlot), concentrated, complex Pinot Nero Schweizer, and delicious, perfumed, moderately sweet Moscato Rosa. (PW)

O **Alto Adige** Traminer Aromatico★★ £C O **Manna** Schweizer★★★ £D
◉ **Alto Adige** Moscato Rosa★★★ £F ● **Istante**★★★ £D
● **Alto Adige** Merlot Schweizer★★ £D Pinot Nero Schweizer★★ £D

HOFSTÄTTER Alto Adige www.hofstatter.com *UK stockists:* **Mgi**, N&P
Best Pinot Noir and one of best Gewürz in Italy. Vigna Sant'Urbano Pinot has atypical depth and texture. Also concentrated, expressive site-specific Yngram (Cab Sauv, Petit Verdot, Syrah - 70/25/5 in fine 2000), and barrique-aged Lagrein, Steinraffler. Kolbenhof Gewürz has uncommon depth and richness for Adige while partly barrique-aged Bianco Vigna San Michele (Pinot Bianco, Chardonnay, Riesling) shows similar weight and style. New is late-harvested Gewürz, Joseph. (PW)

● **Alto Adige Pinot Nero** Riserva★ £C Barthenau Vigna Sant'Urbano★★★ £E
● **Alto Adige** Lagrein Steinraffler★★★ £E ● **Yngram**★★★ £E
O **Alto Adige** Gewürztraminer★★ £C Kolbenhof Söll★★★ £D

INAMA Veneto www.inamaaziendaagricola.it *UK stockists:* **Wtr**, JAr, Gen, Rae, F&M, UnC, F&R
Quality Soave-based producer. Two fine barrique-fermented single-vineyard Soaves and very good unoaked regular (Vin Soave) version. Controversial for championing of Chardonnay and Sauvignon (produced in oaked and unoaked versions). Also increasingly fine and ageworthy Bradisismo (Cab Sauv, Carmenère) from Colli Berici with intense wild plum and bramble fruit. New Oracolo (Cab Sauv) in 2000. Vulcaia Après is late-harvested Sauvignon. (PW)

O **Soave Classico Superiore** Vigneti di Foscarino★★★ £C Vigneto du Lot★★★ £D
O **Vulcaia Sauvignon**★★ £C O **Vulcaia Fumé**★★ £D
O **Chardonnay**★★ £C Campo dei Tovi★★ £D
O **Vulcaia Après**★★★ £E ● **Bradisismo**★★★★ £E

VINNAIOLI JERMANN www.jermannvinnaioli.it *UK stockists:* **Eno**, Vne, Sel, Hrd, UnC, V&C
Long-time champion of Friuli. Vinnae (Ribolla Gialla, Malvasia, Riesling) is balanced and characterful. Capo Martino (mostly Pinot Bianco, Tocai) adds a lot more richness while top wine Vintage Tunina (Sauvignon, Chardonnay, Ribolla Gialla, Malvasia and Picolit), shows intense stylish fruit, and refinement. Dreams (Chardonnay) has Burgundian precision and harmony. Also reds: intense Red Angel on the Moonlight (Pinot Nero), seductive if extracted Pignacolusse (Pignolo) and new Blau & Blau (Pinot Nero, Blaufrankisch). (PW)

O **Vintage Tunina**★★★★ £E O **Dreams**★★★★ £E O **Capo Martino**★★★ £E
O **Vinnae**★★ £C O **Pinot Bianco**★★ £C O **Pinot Grigio**★★★ £C
● **Pignacolusse**★★★ £E ● **Red Angel on the Moonlight**★★ £C

ALOIS LAGEDER Alto Adige www.lageder.com *UK stockists:* **Bib**, Hrd, NYg
Alto Adige's leading private estate with fine single-vineyard wines whites. Top red Cor Römingberg (mostly Cab Sauv) is rich, ripe and classy. Bordeaux blend Löwengang rather pales beside it. Also rich, deep Löwengang Chardonnay and promising Pinot Noir (Krafuss), Lagrein (Lindenburg) and Tannhammer (Chardonnay, Sauvignon). Casòn Hirschprunn estate Reserves Contest (Pinot Grigio, Chardonnay, Sauvignon, Viognier and others) and Casòn (Merlot, Cabernets, Lagrein and others), show lovely fruit and composure. Etelle and Corolle are similar blends. (PW)

Alois Lageder:
O **Alto Adige** Sauvignon Lehenhof★★★ £C Chardonnay Löwengang★★★ £D
O **Alto Adige** Pinot Grigio Benefizium Porer★★★ £C Gewürz Am Sand★★ £C

ITALY

● **Alto Adige** Lagrein Lindenburg★★ £D   Cabernet Cor Römigberg★★★★ £E
Casòn Hirschprunn:
● **Corolle**★ £C   ● **Casòn**★★★ £D   O **Etelle**★★ £C   O **Contest**★★★ £D

LE SALETTE   Veneto   www.lesalette.it   *UK stockists:* **Ast**
Consistent, stylish and very drinkable Valpolicella and Amarone. Ca' Carnocchio from dried grapes with texture of Valpolicella but flavour depth of Amarone. Intense but only moderately concentrated La Marega Amarone is partly aged in barriques; deeper, more complex Pergole Vece entirely so. (PW)
● **Amarone Classico** La Marega★★★ £E   Pergole Vece★★★★ £F
● **Valpolicella Classico Superiore** I Progni★★ £C   Ca' Carnocchio★★★ £C
● **Recioto della Valpolicella Classico** Le Traversagne★★ £E   Pergole Vece★★★ £F

LIS NERIS   Friuli-Venezia Giulia   www.lisneris.it   *UK stockists:* **FMV**, BBR
Leading Friulian estates with 40ha of vineyard. Ripe, varietal unoaked Pinot Grigio, Tocai Friulano (Fiore di Campo) and Sauvignon. Partly barrel-fermented Sauvignon (Picol), Pinot Grigio (Gris) and Chardonnay show good restraint and elegance. Also 2 fine blended whites: full and Burgundian Lis and late-harvested Alsace-like Confini. Even better is Tal Lùc, a *passito*-style sweet white from Verduzzo grapes. Spicy, berry-fruited estate red, Lis Neris (mostly Merlot). (PW)
O **Friuli Isonzo** Sauvignon★★★ £C   Picol Sauvignon★★★ £C
O **Friuli Isonzo** Gris Pinot Grigio★★★ £C   O **Fiore di Campo**★★ £C
O **Friuli Isonzo** Jurosa Chardonnay★★★ £C   O **Lis**★★★ £D   O **Confini**★★★ £E
O **Tal Lùc**★★★★ £G   ● **Friuli Isonzo** Lis Neris★★★ £E

MACULAN   Veneto   www.maculan.net   *UK stockists:* **BWC**, Odd, Vts, Sel
Famed for some of Italy's finest sweet wines: grapy, aromatic Dindarella (Moscato Fior d'Arancio), impressive Torcolato (from dried Vespaiola, Garganega, Tocai) and rich Acininobili (botrytis-affected grapes) which is aged in new French oak. Also good reds, premium Fratta (Cab Sauv, Merlot), fruity Brentino (Merlot/Cabernet) and Crosara (Merlot). Improving dry whites: Ferrata (Chardonnay, Sauvignon) and unoaked Pino & Toi (Pinot Bianco, Pinot Grigio, Tocai). (PW)
● **Fratta**★★★ £F   ● **Breganze** Cabernet Sauvignon Palazzotto★★ £C
O **Ferrata**★★ £D   O **Breganze Bianco** Breganze di Breganze★ £B
O **Acininobili**★★★★ £G   O **Breganze** Torcolato★★★★ £E   O **Dindarello**★★★ £D

MARION   Veneto   www.marionvini.it   *UK stockists:* **RsW**
Own-label production only began here in the late 90s. All wines are subject, at least in part, to some drying of the grapes, resulting in ripe, concentrated and vigorous reds with good ageing potential. The ripe, spicy, earthy Teroldego is a rare example from outside Trentino. Amarone has classic raisin, plum and black cherry fruit. (PW)
● **Valpolicella Superiore**★★★ £D   ● **Amarone della Valpolicella**★★★ £F
● **Caberent Sauvignon**★★★ £D   ● **Teroldego**★★★ £D

MASI   Veneto   www.masi.it   *UK stockists:* **BWC**, Odd, Vts, Sel
Large producer of moderate to good quality synonymous with Valpolicella. Leaders in experimentation and enrichment using dried grapes for Brolo di Campofiorin. Also wines from 'rescued' varieties: Osar (80% Oseleta). Newish are Grandarella (primarily dried Refosco grapes) from Friuli, and very modest Serègo Alighieri Possessioni red and white. Argentinian wines Corbec Appassimento and Passo Doble are from dried or semi-dried Malbec and Corvina grapes. (PW)
Masi:
● **Amarone** Campolongo di Torbe★★ £E   Costasera★★★ £E   Mazzano★★★ £F
● **Brolo di Campofiorin**★★ £C   ● **Toar**★★ £B   ● **Osar**★★★ £E
● **Grandarella**★★★ £D   O **Soave Classico** Colbaraca★★ £B
Serègo Alighieri:
● **Amarone** Vaio Armaron★★★ £E   ● **Recioto** Casal dei Ronchi★★ £E

MIANI   Friuli-Venezia Giulia   *UK stockists:* **Ast**, BBR, UnC
Some of the most-sought after wines in northern Italy. Beautifully crafted, expressive, detailed wines from very low yields include fine, complex barrel-femented Sauvignon and a concentrated Tocai Friulano that captures essence of grape. Also fine pure Merlot with too rarely seen enticing berry and plum expression. Also made are

156

Ribolla Gialla, Chardonnay and a few bottles of exceptional Refosco (Calvari). (PW)
O **COF** Tocai Friulano★★★ £E   Sauvignon★★★ £E   ● **COF** Merlot★★★★ £E

MOSCHIONI   Friuli-Venezia Giulia
Exceptional, uncompromising wines - top examples are late-harvested and see 100 per cent new oak. Celtico Rosso (Cab Sauv/Merlot) has terrific intensity, concentration and extract. Also contrast pure, seductive elegance of the Schiopettino with the wild, black-fruited muscularity of Pignolo (which needs 8-10 years). 2001s are most expressive yet. Also brambly, wild plum Refosco and basic Rosso (mostly young-vine Merlot and Cabernet). (PW)
● **COF** Schioppettino★★★★ £E   Pignolo★★★★★ £F   Refosco dal PR★★★ £D
● **COF** Celtico Rosso★★★★ £E   Rosso Moschioni★★ £C

PIEROPAN   Veneto   www.pieropan.it   *UK stockists:* **Lib**,Vne, BBR,ACh, P&S, Hrd,
Soaves made from ever better-quality grapes with reliably good Classico and unoaked single-vineyard Calvarino. Richer La Rocca (pure Garganega) is fermented and aged in oak. Also fine Recioto Le Colombare and intense, exotic, honeyed Passito della Rocca (mostly Sauvignon, Riesling). (PW)
O **Soave Classico** Superiore★★ £B   Calvarino★★★ £C   La Rocca★★★ £D
O **Recioto di Soave** Le Colombare★★★ £E   O **Passito della Rocca**★★★ £F

POJER & SANDRI   Trentino   www.pojeresandri.it   *UK stockists:* **Ast**
Refined whites culminate in elegant, classy Faye (Chardonnay with 10% Pinot Bianco) that builds in texture and complexity with age. Red version is very stylish, beautifully textured wine from Cabernet Sauvignon, Cabernet Franc, Merlot and Lagrein. Also promising barrique-aged white from Maso Besler estate and often exquisite blended sweet wine, Essenzia. (PW)
Pojer & Sandri:
O **Chardonnay**★★ £B   O **Faye**★★★★ £D   O **Trentino** Traminer Aromatico★★ £C
O **Sauvignon**★★ £C   O **Essenzia**★★★ £E   ● **Rosso Faye**★★★ £D
Maso Besler:
O **Besler Bianck**★★★ £D

QUINTARELLI   Veneto   *UK stockists:* **Wtr**, Fal
Valpolicella's greatest advocate of artisanal winemaking. Wines of great power and extract needing long barrel-ageing to evolve into something complex yet demanding. If now surpassed by those showing greater winemaking sophistication wines still impress for sheer intensity. Alzero is from partially dried Cabernet Franc grapes. (PW)
● **Amarone Classico** Monte Ca' Paletta★★★★ £H
● **Recioto della Valpolicella Classico** Monte Ca' Paletta★★★ £H
● **Valpolicella Classico** Superiore Monte Ca' Paletta★★★ £E   ● **Alzero**★★★ £H

ROCCOLO GRASSI   Veneto   *UK stockists:* **Nov**
Rising star focussed on quality in the vineyard. Wines are clean, modern and very fruit-driven yet with classic flavours and ripe tannins. Sheer impact of the fruit masks wines elegance when young. Rich, almost overwhelming Amarone. Also Vigneto La Broia for Soave and Recioto di Soave, the latter almost decadent in its ripe/overripe exotic fruit character. (PW)
● **Amarone**★★★ £E   ● **Recioto della Valpolicella**★★★ £E
● **Valpolicella** Superiore Roccolo Grassi★★★ £C
O **Soave** Superiore La Broia★ £B   O **Recioto di Soave** La Broia★★★ £E

RONCHI DI MANZANO   Friuli-Venezia Giulia   www.roncodimanzano.com   *UK stockists:* **Vim**
Impressive varietal whites are vigorous, expressive and fruit-centred. Ronc di Rosazzo (Sauvignon, Chardonnay, Tocai, Picolit) is ripe, stylish, vibrant and harmonious. Best red is opulent, pure fruited Ronc di Subule from high density vineyard but also lush, fruit intense Le Zuccule (Cab Sauv, Merlot) and Ronc di Rosazzo (adds in Refosco). Characterful robust varietal Refosco and fine sweet Verduzzo and Picolit too. (PW)
O **COF Rosazzo Bianco** Ronc di Rosazzo★★★ £C
O **COF Rosazzo** Picolit Ronc di Rosazzo★★★ £E   Verduzzo★★★ £E
● **COF** Merlot Ronc di Subule★★★ £D   ● **COF Rosazzo** Ronc di Rosazzo★★ £C

157

RONCO DEL GNEMIZ   Friuli-Venezia Giulia   *UK stockists:* **Ast**
Under young Andrea Pittana Sauvignon is now better defined and Pinot Grigio shows better purity and intensity.
Chardonnay is rich, ripe and flavoursome with good structure. Rosso del Gnemiz (from Merlot, Cabernets and
Schioppettino) is complex and intense with real style in 01. Also small volumes of special-selection Merlot Sol and
Sauvignon Sol. (PW)

○ **COF** Pinot Grigio★★ £C   Sauvignon★★ £C   Tocai Friulano★★ £C
○ **COF** Bianco★★ £B   ○ **COF** Chardonnay★★★ £E
● **COF** Rosso★★ £C   ● **COF** Rosso del Gnemiz★★★ £E

RUSSIZ SUPERIORE   Friuli-Venezia Giulia   www.marcofelluga.it   *UK stockists:* **BWC**
Leading red of Russiz Superiore is rich and structured Riserva degli Orzoni (Cab Sauv, Cab Franc, Merlot)
while best white is Russiz Disôre (Pinot Bianco, Tocai, Sauvignon and Ribolla Gialla). From Marco Felluga
estate come stylish, plummy Carantan (Cab Franc, Cab Sauv, Merlot) and Molamotta (Pinot Bianco, Tocai,
Ribolla Gialla) and more good varietals. (PW)

Russiz Superiore:
○ **Collio** Sauvignon★★ £C   ○ **Collio Bianco** Russiz Disôre★★★ £D
● **Collio** Cabernet Franc★★ £D   ● **Collio Rosso** Riserva degli Orzoni★★★ £E

Marco Felluga:
● **Carantan★★★** £E   ● **Refosco★★** £C   ○ **Collio Bianco** Molamotta★★ £C
○ **Collio** Tocai★★ £C   Sauvignon★★ £C   Chardonnay★★ £C

RUSSOLO   Friuli-Venezia Giulia   www.russolo.it   *UK stockists:* **Ast**
Russolo shows what is possible from the flat alluvial soils of Friuli Grave with wines that are bright, open and fruity
with plenty of varietal character. Malvasia Istriana and Müller-Thurgau are atypically refined; attractive *barrique*-aged
Pinot Nero is another surprise while Merlot-based Borgo di Peuma can develop a savoury complexity with 5 years'
age. Doi Raps is a sweet late-harvested white with exotic and ripe stone fruits. (PW)

○ **Malvasia Istriana★★** £B   ○ **Müller-Thurgau** Musignaz★★ £B
○ **Pinot Grigio** Ronco Calaj★★ £B   ○ **Tocai Friulano** Ronco Calaj★★ £B
● **Pinot Nero** Grifo Nero★★ £C   ● **Borgo di Peuma★★** £C
○ **Doi Raps★★★** £C

SAN LEONARDO   Trentino   www.sanleonardo.it   *UK stockists:* **JAr, P&S**
Famed for estate red wine: a complex, refined yet rich, full bend (Cab Sauv, Cab Franc, Merlot - 60/30/10) best
with 6-8 years' age. Occasionally disappointing, but generally of very high standard. Lighter varietal Merlot is
effectively a second wine but also well-made. (PW)
● **San Leonardo★★★★** £E   ● **Merlot di San Leonardo★★** £C

SAN MICHELE APPIANO   Alto Adige   www.stmichael.it   *UK stockists:* **Eur, Hrd, Wai**
Wines made by celebrated Hans Terzer. Best are Sanct Valentin with extra precision and greater aromatic
complexity. Gewürz and Sauvignon are particularly stylish but quality of all varietals is exemplary. Also exquisite
sweet white, Passito Comtess' (Gewürz, Riesling, Sauvignon, Pinot Bianco) and reds (including Pinot Nero)
with good expression and supple textures with a little age, especially Sanct Valentin Lagrein (since 2000) (PW)
○ **Alto Adige** Chardonnay Sanct Valentin★★★ £D   Sauvignon Sanct Valentin★★★ £D
○ **Alto Adige** Pinot Grigio Sanct Valentin★★ £D   Gewürztraminer St Valentin★★★ £D
● **Alto Adige** Cabernet Sanct Valentin★★ £E   Lagrein Sanct Valentin★★★ £E

SCHIOPETTO   Friuli-Venezia Giulia   www.schiopetto.it   *UK stockists:* **L&S, Hrd, NYg, N&P**
Some of Friuli's best unoaked white varietals with intense clear-fruited expression. Also richer, fuller, ageworthy
oak-fermented and aged Amrità (Pinot Bianco), Pardes (Tocai) and Tarsia (Sauvignon). Unoaked Blanc des
Rosis (Pinot Bianco, Tocai, Sauvignon, Malvasia) also impressive while red Rivarossa is blend of Merlot, Cab
Sauv, Cab Franc. New is refined, concentrated Mario Schiopetto (Chardonnay, Tocai). (PW)
○ **Collio** Pinot Bianco★★★ £C   Pinot Bianco Amrità★★★ £E
○ **Collio** Tocai Friulano Pardes★★★ £E   ○ **Collio** Sauvignon Tarsia★★★ £E
○ **Collio** Pinot Grigio★★ £C   ○ **Blanc des Rosis★★★** £E   ● **Rivarossa★★** £C

SERAFINI & VIDOTTO Veneto *UK stockists:* **Ast,**AoW
Fine reds from off the beaten track. Top wine, Rosso dell'Abbazia (mostly Cabernets with some Merlot, Pinot
Nero) is cool but intense, ripe and complex. Enchanting aromatic Pinot Nero if not of the same texture or
breadth as fine Burgundy. Cheaper is medium-bodied slightly herbaceous, flavoursome Phigaia After the Red
(Cab Franc, Merlot). (PW)
● **Rosso dell' Abazia**★★★★ £E ● **Pinot Nero**★★★ £E
● **Phigaia After The Red**★★ £C

SUAVIA Veneto www.suavia.it *UK stockists:* **Bib**
Refined, classy Soave. The regular example is flavoursome and characterful. Of 2 superior bottlings (both 100%
Garganega) Monte Carbonare (in steel) offers refined spiced fruits in contrast with the richer textured and complex,
minerally Le Rive. Both improve for 3–4 years. Recioto Acinatum is medium-bodied, pure and intense. Excellent
olive oil has a spicy, herbaceous intensity. (PW)
O **Soave Classico**★★ £B Monte Carbonare★★★ £C Superiore Le Rive★★★ £D
O **Recioto di Soave Classico** Acinatum★★★ £F

TEDESCHI Veneto www.tedeschiwines.com *UK stockists:* **Hal,** Maj, N&P, Sel,V&C
Premium Amarone and Recioto which show classic vigour, flavour intensity and power. Modern, oak-aged
Rosso La Fabriseria adds a little Cab Sauv to Corvina, Corvinone, Rondinella and Dindarella. Also sweet Vin de
la Fabriseria (Garganega, Soarin), *ripasso* red, Capitel San Rocco, of variable quality, and basic generics of
Valpolicella, Bardolino, Soave, etc. (PW)
● **Amarone Classico**★★ £D Capitel Monte Olmi★★★★ £E La Fabriseria★★★★ £E
● **Recioto della Valpolicella Classico** Capitel Monte Fontana★★★ £E
● **Valpolicella Classico** Capitel dei Nicolò★★ £C ● **Rosso La Fabriseria**★★★ £D

CANTINA TERLANO Alto Adige *UK stockists:* **Ast,** CdP, But, P&S, F&M
One of Alto Adige's most dynamic co-ops. Bold and flavoursome style favoured with occasionally intrusive oak
in top *cuvées*, but sometimes exceptional ageing potential too. Terlano Classico and premium Nova Domus
achieve good harmony between Pinot Bianco, Sauvignon and Chardonnay. Best reds from Lagrein need at least
3-5 years age, especially Porphyr (from 70 year old vines). Also Merlot (Riserva Siebeneich), Pinot Nero (Riserva
Montigl), Cabernet (Riserva Siemegg). (PW)
O **Alto Adige** Pinot Bianco Vorberg★★ £C Sauvignon Quarz★★★ £D
O **Alto Adige Terlano** Classico★★ £B Nova Domus★★★ £D
● **Alto Adige** Lagrein Riserva Gries★★ £C Lagrein Riserva Porphyr★★★ £D

VIE DI ROMANS Friuli-Venezia Giulia www.viediromans.it *UK stockists:* **Lib,**Vne, Hrd
Exceptional examples of Friuli Sauvignon and Chardonnay with superior richness, intensity, breadth and
structure. Tangy, pure unoaked Chardonnay Ciampagnis Vieris contrasts with richer, more complex Vie di
Romans. Piere is unoaked Sauvignon. Flavoursome Flor di Uis from Malvasia, Tocai, Riesling and Chardonnay.
Pinot Grigio Dessimis is oak-aged/fermented while Merlot-based Voos dai Ciamps gains almost velvety texture
with age. (PW)
O **Friuli Isonzo Chardonnay** Ciampagnis Vieris★★★ £D Vie di Romans★★★★ £E
O **Friuli Isonzo Sauvignon** Piere★★★ £E Vieris★★★ £E
O **Friuli Isonzo** Flor di Uis★★★ £E ● **Friuli Isonzo Rosso** Voos dai Ciamps★★★ £E

VILLA RUSSIZ Friuli-Venezia Giulia www.villarussiz.it *UK stockists:* **Bib,** NYg
Run for charitable institute with focus on unoaked varietal whites with excellent intensity and expression,
particularly Sauvignon. Extra depth, structure in de la Tour Sauvignon from lees enrichment. Small volumes
of Gräfin de la Tour (barrique-aged) Chardonnay and red Graf de la Tour Merlot - richer and riper than
other reds. (PW)
O **Collio** Tocai Friulano★★ £C Pinot Bianco★★ £C Pinot Grigio★★ £C
O **Collio** Sauvignon★★ £C Sauvignon de la Tour★★★ £D
O **Collio** Gräfin de la Tour★★★ £D ● **Collio** Merlot Graf de la Tour★★ £E

LE VIGNE DI ZAMÒ   Friuli-Venezia Giulia   www.levignedizamo.com   *UK stockists:* **HSA**
Modern winery making well-made regular varietals. Oak used in premium Pinot Bianco, Tullio Zamò and
Ronco delle Acacie (Tocai, Chardonnay, Pinot Bianco) which can show impressive texture and complexity.
Tocai is a strength especially old-vine Cinquant'Anni. Reds include characterful Ronco dei Roseti (Merlot
and two Cabernets) and richly textured, concentrated Merlot Cinquant' Anni. Tiny amounts of Pignolo and
Schioppettino also made. (PW)

O **COF** Tocai Friulano Cinquant' Anni★★★ £C   Pinot Bianco Tullio Zamò★★ £C
O **COF Bianco** Ronco delle Acacie★★★ £C
● **COF** Merlot Vigne Cinquant' Anni★★★ £E   ● **COF** Ronco dei Roseti★★★ £D

ZENATO   Veneto   www.zenato.it   *UK stockists:* **Eur, Hrd**
High quality in special bottlings. As well as vibrant, chewy Valpolicella Ripassa there are 'signature' Riserva
wines – powerful Amarone and a concentrated Lugana (also good Vigneto Massoni version). Separate La
Sansonina estate for stylish blend of Merlot and Cab Sauv that shows a chocolaty, cedary complexity with 5
years' age or more. (PW)

Zenato:
O **Lugana** Vigneto Massoni★★ £C   Riserva Sergio Zenato★★ £C
● **Valpolicella** Sup. Ripassa★★ £C   ● **Amarone** Riserva Sergio Zenato★★★ £F

La Sansonina:
● **Sansonina**★★★ £D

ZUANI   Friuli-Venezia Giulia   *UK stockists:* **Bal,** JNi, UnC
Patrizia Felluga produces small amounts of two marvellous blended whites (from Tocai Friulano, Pinot Grigio,
Chardonnay, Sauvignon) that are site-specific. Unoaked Zuani Vigne is full, ripe and concentrated while oak-aged
Zuani Collio Bianco (from fruit harvested a little later) is more ambitious with greater breadth, complexity and
style. (PW)

O **Collio Bianco**★★★★   £D   Zuani Vigne★★★ £C

Other wineries of note
Borgo San Daniele (Friuli-Venezia Giulia), Dal Fari (Friuli-Venezia Giulia), Girolamo Dorigo (Friuli-
Venezia Giulia), Josko Gravner (Friuli-Venezia Giulia), Il Carpino (Friuli-Venezia Giulia), Nardello
(Veneto), Josef Niedermayr (Alto Adige), Ronco del Gelso (Friuli-Venezia Giulia), Matijaz Tercic (Friuli-
Venezia Giulia), Vignalta (Veneto)

An in-depth profile of every producer can be found in Wine behind the label 2006

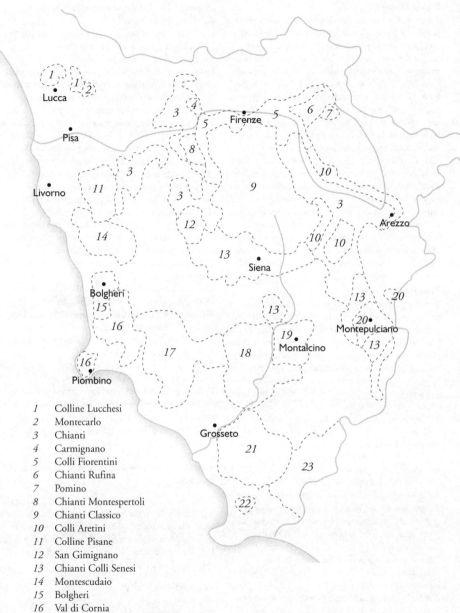

1   Colline Lucchesi
2   Montecarlo
3   Chianti
4   Carmignano
5   Colli Fiorentini
6   Chianti Rufina
7   Pomino
8   Chianti Montespertoli
9   Chianti Classico
10 Colli Aretini
11 Colline Pisane
12 San Gimignano
13 Chianti Colli Senesi
14 Montescudaio
15 Bolgheri
16 Val di Cornia
17 Monteregio di Massa Marittima
18 Montecucco
19 Brunello di Montalcino
20 Vino Nobile di Montepulciano
21 Morellino di Scansano
22 Parrina
23 Sovana

Tuscany

ITALY

Rinascimento

There's little excuse for ignorance of Tuscany's great wines as the region is awash with fine quality at all levels. But avoid the most strongly branded names and seek out smaller or newer producers. Tuscany's wine renaissance or *rinascimento* had its beginnings more than 30 years ago. Its artists include both individual producers and highly trained and experienced enologists that increasingly respond to what is required from both producer and site rather than imposing a uniform style. Outside investment and talent, including Swiss, English and American winemakers and entrepreneurs, also play a part. The current decade is seeing more emphasis placed on native grape varieties, new or revived wine growing areas and the importance of expressing something of the wine's origins or tipicità (typicality). As well as unprecedented quality from Sangiovese (topped up with Canaiolo, Colorino etc), and very good Cabernet Sauvignon, Merlot and Syrah, more can now be detected of the different permutations of place, soil and climate. There is also better balance and less oak, allied to greater finesse and elegance.

Tuscany Vintages

Tuscany produces plenty of red wine for short and medium-term cellaring but less that can provide real pleasure for a 15- or 20-year celebration. Many of the best reds, be it Chianti Classico Riserva, the best Vino Nobile, reds from the Tuscan coast or other blends including Cabernet or Merlot, are at or near their best with 5 to 10 years' age, the very best after 10 to 15 years, only exceptional wines should be kept for longer. Brunello from 1990, 93, 95, 97, 99 and 2001 should go the distance of 2 decades though most also have the balance to be ready to drink at half that age. The best Rosso di Montalcino (often with more fruit) might need 5 to 6 years' age. These guidelines need to be considered in conjunction with comments on style and quality within the producer profiles.

2004: Avoiding the demanding weather conditions of the previous 4 years, instead a long ripening season without extreme temperatures, and with measured and timely spells of rain. Good prospects for balanced, complex, long-lived wines.

2003: It's all about coping with the blistering conditions. Quality is somewhat variable but with highs as well as lows.

2002: Difficult vintage though good quality in the Maremma and southern zones. Most top reds not made (sometimes to the benefit of more humble labels).

2001: Heat affected but very good if somewhat variable quality. Plenty of fully ripe, very concentrated reds. Promising Brunello.

2000: The best reds show excellent richness and ripeness but many also show over-ripe fruit, a slight

hollowness and slightly coarse tannins. Decent if slightly lacklustre Brunello.

1999: Very fine vintage if not quite of the standard of 97. Excellent ageing potential in the best wines including full yet elegant Brunello.

1998: Successful but variable vintage. Real style and complexity where there was full ripeness. Most uneven in Chianti Classico, generally very good Brunello, much richer and more consistent than 96.

1997: Outstanding throughout Tuscany, unequalled in amount of high quality reds produced. That cellared will keep especially very rich, powerful and tannic Brunello - Riservas of great potential.

1996: Good yet overrated with some weak, relatively forward wines in most zones. Best wines from Bolgheri. Disappointing fast-evolving Brunello (if a few exceptions), many need to be drunk soon.

1995: Elegant, stylish Chianti Classico and fine quality in the premium blends or Super-Tuscans, filling out with age. Structured but keeping Brunello.

1994: Rain-affected with lighter wines. Some isolated successes but others tiring - not one to pay over the odds for. Reasonable if slightly hard-edged Brunello.

1993: Rich, gutsy if slightly rough-hewn reds, some will still keep. Solid powerful Brunello, the very best can be left to soften a little more.

1992: The worst vintage in recent times but some of 02 similar. Drink up, if at all.

1991: An uneven vintage although some wines showed good intensity should have been drunk up.

1990: A great year with excellent ripeness and balance. Some top wines now past their best but others will keep.

1989: Light and forward in Tuscany, little lasted. One to avoid, rare exceptions likely to be Brunello.

1988: Always a firm, relatively austere vintage now mature, only a few Super-Tuscans and Brunello might last a little longer.

Earlier years: Most earlier vintages now well past their best. This includes the initially under-rated 1986. Generally outstanding 85 with very ripe, flamboyant wines but only classics will drink well or possibly keep. 1983 and 1982 were also very good vintages but anything still alive is very rare.

Wizard's Wishlist

Classic Tuscans reds
ANTINORI ● Solaia
AVIGNONESI
● **Vino Nobile di Montepulciano** Riserva Grandi Annate
CASTELLO DI RAMPOLLA ● Vigna d'Alceo
ISOLE E OLENA ● Cepparello
LE PUPILLE ● Saffredi

New entries have producer's name underlined

MONTEVERTINE ● Le Pergole Torte

POGGIOPIANO ● Rosso di Sera

POLIZIANO ● Vino Nobile di Montepulciano Asinone

RUFFINO ● Romitorio di Santedame

QUERCIABELLA ● Camartina

SAN GIUSTO A RENTENNANO ● Percarlo

SETTE PONTI ● Crognolo

TENUTA DI TRINORO ● Tenuta di Trinoro

Outstanding Chianti

CASTELLO DI AMA

● Chianti Classico Vigneto Bellavista

CASTELLO DI FONTERUTOLI

● Chianti Classico Castello di Fonterutoli

FRESCOBALDI ● Chianti Rufina Montesodi

IL PALAZZINO ● Chianti Classico Grosso Sanese

LA MASSA ● Chianti Classico Giorgio Primo

POGGIO AL SOLE ● Chianti Classico Casasilia

FATTORIA SELVAPIANA

● Chianti Rufina Riserva Bucerchiale

ROCCA DI MONTEGROSSI

● Chianti Classico Riserva San Marcellino

Diverse top quality Brunello

CASANOVA DI NERI

● Brunello di Montalcino Tenuta Nuova

FULIGNI

● Brunello di Montalcino Vigneti dei Cottimelli

MASTROJANNI

● Brunello di Montalcino Schiena d'Asino

SILVIO NARDI

● Brunello di Montalcino Vigneto Manachiara

SIRO PACENTI ● Brunello di Montalcino

PERTIMALI/LIVIO SASSETTI

● Brunello di Montalcino Riserva

PIEVE SANTA RESTITUTA

● Brunello di Montalcino Sugarille

SALVIONI/LA CERBAIOLA ● Brunello di Montalcino

Coastal marvels

ANTINORI/GUADO AL TASSO ● Bolgheri Rosso

CASTELLO DEL TERRICCIO ● Lupicaia

LE MACCHIOLE ● Scrio

MONTEPELOSO ● Nardo

TENUTA DELL'ORNELLAIA

● Bolgheri Rosso Superiore Ornellaia

ENRICO SANTINI ● Bolgheri Rosso Montepergoli

SASSICAIA/TENUTA SAN GUIDO ● Bolgheri Sassicaia

TUA RITA ● Redigaffi

TENUTA DI VALGIANO ● Tenuta di Valgiano

Tuscan best buys

FATTORIA DI BASCIANO ● Vigna Il Corto

CASTELLO DI POPPIANO ● Toscoforte

LA PIEVE ● Chianti La Pieve

LAVACCHIO ● Chianti Rufino Cedro

LE MICCINE ● Chianti Classico

CANTINE LEONARDO DA VINCI ● Chianti Riserva

FATTORIA DI MAGLIANO ● Morellino di Scansano Heba

MALENCHINI ● Chianti Colli Fiorentini

FATTORIA DI PETROIO ● Chianti Classico Riserva

POGGIO ARGENTIERA

● Morellino di Scansano Bellamarsilia

SAN VINCENTI ● Chianti Classico

Tuscany / A-Z of producers

ALTESINO Brunello di Montalcino www.altesino.it *UK stockists:* **PFx**, N&P
Well-established source of Brunello under same ownership as Caparzo. Palazzo d'Altesi is best of barrique-aged varietals which also include Borgo d'Altesi (Cab Sauv) and Quarto d'Altesi (Merlot). Alte di Altesi is Sangiovese and Cabernet (70/30). Brunello is full, ripe and meaty, and best with 7-10 years' ageing. Also powerful Riserva, deep concentrated Montosoli, and Vin Santo. (PW)
● Brunello di Montalcino★★★ £E Riserva★★★★ £F Montosoli★★★★ £F
● Palazzo d'Altesi★★★ £D ● Alte d'Altesi★★ £D ● Borgo d'Altesi★★ £E

ANTINORI www.antinori.it *UK stockists:* **BWC**, AAA
Still expanding Tuscan empire of Piero Antinori and family. Famous Tignanello (Sangiovese, Cab Sauv - 80/20) and Solaia (Cab Sauv, Sangiovese) with added breadth and class. Also impressive Bramasole (since 2000) from Syrah, dependable Vino Nobile (better Santa Pia version from 2001). Brunello increasingly good, esp. late 90s vintages. Bolgheri red (Cab Sauv/Merlot) consistently excellent. Quality at the lower levels is less good. (PW)
Antinori:
● Solaia✪✪✪✪✪ £H ● Tignanello★★★★ £G
● Chianti Classico Riserva Badia a Passignano★★ £C Ris. Marchese Antinori★★ £D

163

ITALY

O **Vin Santo del Chianti Classico** Marchese Antinori★★ £E
La Braccesca:
● **Vino Nobile di Montepulciano**★★ £C   ● **Merlot**★★ £E
● **Cortona Syrah** Bramasole★★★★ £E
Pian delle Vigne:
● **Brunello di Montalcino**★★★ £E
Guado al Tasso:
● **Bolgheri Rosso**★★★★ £G   O **Bolgheri** Vermentino★★ £B

ARGIANO   Brunello di Montalcino   www.argiano.net   *UK stockists:* **Lib,** P&S, F&M, Sel, Las
Quality transformed during 1990s - structured, powerful Brunello very good in late 90s vintages. Solengo is consistently rich, stylish blend of Cab Sauv, Syrah and Merlot. Also Suolo (from 2000) special barrique-aged blend of oldest Sangiovese - refined, intense and classy. (PW)
● **Brunello di Montalcino**★★★★ £F   ● **Solengo**★★★★ £F
● **Rosso di Montalcino**★★ £C

AVIGNONESI   www.avignonesi.it   *UK stockists:* **Lib,** P&S, N&P, F&M, V&C
Most important producer in Montepulciano. Regular Vino Nobile of increasing consistency, purity and real class. Riserva Grandi Annate adds considerable depth and dimension. '50 & 50' (Merlot, Sangiovese) produced jointly with Capanelle. Desiderio is Merlot with up to 15% Cab Sauv while Il Marzocco is bold, powerful, toasty Chardonnay. Incomparable Vin Santo with great richness, texture and complexity (from Malvasia, Trebbiano and Grechetto) and Occhio di Pernice from Prugnolo (Sangiovese). (PW)
● **Vino Nobile di Montepulciano**★★★ £C   Riserva Grandi Annate★★★★★ £E
● **Cortona** Merlot Desiderio★★★ £F   O **Cortona** Chardonnay Il Marzocco★★★ £C

BANFI   Brunello di Montalcino   www.castellobanfi.com   *UK stockists:* **Vim,** Hrd, Maj
Banfi reshaped entire south-western corner of the Brunello zone. Increasing consistency with Sangiovese for Brunello that is rich, ripe and well-balanced. Fine single-vineyard Poggio alle Mura and excellent complex, structured Riserva Poggio all'Oro. Summus (Sangiovese, Cab Sauv, Syrah) and Excelsus (Cabernet/Merlot) best of premium blends. Also good rich Tavernelle and promising Colvecchio. Chardonnay Fontanelle can show real richness and depth. More affordable are Centine (Sangiovese, Cab Sauv and Merlot) and Col di Sasso; also newish Cum Laude (Sangiovese, Cab Sauv, Merlot and Syrah). (PW)
● **Brunello di Montalcino** Poggio alle Mura★★★★ £F   Poggio all'Oro★★★★ £G
● **Summus**★★★★ £E   ● **Excelsus**★★★★ £F   O **Sant'Antimo** Fontanelle★★ £C
● **Sant'Antimo** Cabernet Sauvignon Tavernelle★★ £D   Syrah Colvecchio★★ £D

BARICCI   Brunello di Montalcino
This is a fine example of authentic Sangiovese from Montalcino made in a traditional style – complex, savoury Brunello with real breadth and class. Particularly strong are 1995 and 97, while 98 is excellent in the vintage and a slightly lighter 2000 has atypical elegance for Brunello. Rosso is good from 01. (PW)
● **Brunello di Montalcino**★★★★ £F   ● **Rosso di Montalcino**★★ £C

FATTORIA DI BASCIANO   Chianti Rufina   *UK stockists:* **Bib**
High quality fruit and careful handling make for consistently excellent and affordable range. Chianti Rufina Riserva improves on good regular example with added richness and style in Sangiovese/Cabernet blends Vigna Il Corto and I Pini (90/10 and 50/50). Good source for Vin Santo too. Also Renzo Masi wines from purchased grapes including Erta & China (Sangiovese/Cabernet). (PW)
● **Chianti Rufina**★★ £B   Riserva★★★ £C   ● **Vigna Il Corto**★★★ £C
● **I Pini**★★★ £C   ● **Erta e China**★★ £B   O **Vin Santo**★★ £C

BIONDI-SANTI   Brunello di Montalcino   www.biondisanti.it   *UK stockists:* **Alv**
Famous estate with a traditional, non-interventionist approach. Wines are deep, powerful and forbidding when young, sometimes excessively structured but patience is key. Franco Biondi-Santi's son Jacopo handles distribution along with that from Villa Poggio Salvi where more forward, approachable Brunello is made. Also very good barrique-aged reds from Jacopo's Maremma estate, Castello di Montepò. Both Schidione (Sangiovese with Cab Sauv, Merlot) and Sassoalloro (pure Sangiovese) are rich and oak-influenced. (PW)

New entries have producer's name underlined

Tenuta Greppo:
● **Brunello di Montalcino**★★★ £H   Riserva★★★★ £H
Villa Poggio Salvi:
● **Brunello di Montalcino**★★★ £F
Castello di Montepò:
● **Schidione**★★★ £E   ● **Sassoalloro**★★★ £D

BOSCARELLI   Vino Nobile di Montepulciano   *UK stockists:* **Bal**, BBR
Small high quality estate with wines of richness and depth but also better proportions and greater refinement than nearly all others in zone. 'Boscarelli', like the Vino Nobile and single-vineyard Vigna del Nocio, is Sangiovese-based but barrique-aged. Rosso de Ferrari is better than most Rosso di Montepulciano. (PW)
● **Vino Nobile di Montepulciano**★★★ £C   Vigna del Nocio★★★★ £D
● **Boscarelli**★★★★ £E   ● **Rosso de Ferrari**★ £B

CA' MARCANDA   Bolgheri   *UK stockists:* **JAr**, F&M, Maj, IVV, FWC
Gaja's lavish new Bolgheri estate. Potential illustrated even in Promis (Merlot, Syrah and Sangiovese) with surprising complexity and class. Magari is estate's second wine (Merlot, Cab Sauv, Cab Franc) with top wine Ca' Marcanda, impressive from 01. (PW)
● **Ca' Marcanda**★★★★ £E   ● **Magari**★★★ £E   ● **Promis**★★★ £D

CAMIGLIANO   Brunello di Montalcino   www.camigliano.it   *UK stockists:* L&W, WSc
Rapid strides have been made at this large estate and investment is ongoing. Wines are expressive and well balanced: Gualto is lush, modern, *barrique*-influenced Brunello and doesn't lack for concentration or extract in both 1999 and 00 but the regular example is more of good Rosso level. Poderuccio is an attractive blend of Sangiovese and Cabernet Sauvignon. (PW)
● **Brunello di Montalcino**★★ £E   Gualto★★★ £F   ● **Poderuccio**★★ £C

CAMPOSILIO   www.camposilio.it   *UK stockists:* **C&B**
Camposilio's estate red has evolved into a deep, concentrated and complex *barrique*-aged blend of Sangiovese, Cab Sauv and Merlot (40/30/30 in 2001) needing 6–8 years' age. I Venti di Camposilio (100% Sangiovese) is only partly *barrique*-aged; there is more vibrancy and potential in 03 than an already richly textured 01. (PW)
● **Camposilio**★★★★ £E   ● **I Venti di Camposilio**★★★ £D
● **Rosso di Montepulciano**★★ £C   O **Vendemmia Tardiva**★★★ £D

TENUTA CAPARZO   Brunello di Montalcino   *UK stockists:* **Ast**, P&S, UnC, N&P
Large Brunello producer with high quality especially in Vigna La Casa version. Good late-90s vintages. with remarkable concentration, depth and power. Ca' del Pazzo (Sangiovese/Cab Sauv) and Le Grance (Chardonnay, also Sauvignon, Gewürz) show good fruit and intelligent use of oak. Also improved wines of Chianti Classico estate of Borgo Scopeto with newish single-vineyard Riserva Misciano, and Borgonero (Sangiovese, Syrah and Cab Sauv). (PW)
Tenuta Caparzo:
● **Brunello di Montalcino**★★★ £E Riserva★★★★★ £F Vigna La Casa✪✪✪✪✪ £F
● **Rosso di Montalcino** La Caduta★★★ £C   ● **Sant'Antimo** Ca' del Pazzo★★★ £D
Borgo Scopeto:
● **Chianti Classico** Riserva Misciano★★ £D

CAPEZZANA   Carmignano   www.capezzana.it   *UK stockists:* **Lib**, ACh, P&S, V&C
Foremost estate of small Carmignano zone. Riserva no longer made but Carmignano (Sangiovese with 20% Cab Sauv, 10% Canaiolo) has refined structure, lovely depth and touch of class. Ghiaie della Furba now adds a little Syrah to Cab Sauv and Merlot. Also lighter style Sangiovese Barco Reale and elegant, classic Vin Santo. Vin Ruspo (rosé) and Chardonnay too. (PW)
● **Carmignano** Villa di Capezzana★★★ £D   ● **Ghiaie della Furba**★★★ £E
● **Barco Reale di Carmignano**★ £B   O **Carmignano Vin Santo**★★★ £E

CARPINETO   Chianti Classico   www.carpineto.com   *UK stockists:* **Hal**, Nid, TPg
Well-known for IGT reds. Supple, scented Dogajolo (Sangiovese, Cab Sauv) made in largest quantities. Deep, chewy, intense, cedary Farnito (Cab Sauv) needs 10 years' age. Also Vino Nobile Riserva and oaky Chianti

165

ITALY

Classico Riserva. New series of 'Appodiati' single-vineyard wines first made in 99: Poggio Sant'Enrico (Sangiovese), Sillano (Sangiovese, Cab Sauv - 60/40) and Molin Vecchio (with 20% Syrah, 10% Cab Sauv). All are backward, extracted and need at least 8-10 years' age. (PW)

● **Chianti Classico★** £C Riserva★★★ £D ● **Farnito★★★** £E
● **Vino Nobile di Montepulciano** Riserva★★ £D ● **Dogajolo★** £B

CASANOVA DELLA SPINETTA Colline Pisane *UK stockists:* **Eno**, NYg
Giorgio Rivetti's (La Spinetta) small 8.5 ha estate in Pisa hills is focused on Sangiovese. Beautifully crafted Sezzana (includes a little Colorino) has real depth and intensity, with splendid purity to crushed cherry fruit. One to follow. (PW)

● **Sezzana★★★★** £E

CASANOVA DI NERI www.casanovadineri.com *UK stockists:* **Eur**, Far, JAr, Tur, Las
Increasingly rich, stylish meaty Brunello even in more difficult vintages like 1994 and 96. Both Tenuta Nuova and Riserva Cerretalto made as well as a regular Brunello. Superb 97s and very fine 99s too. Rosso is full and stylish while Pietradomice is deep, brash Brunello-like Cab Sauv that could use more refinement. (PW)

● **Brunello di Montalcino** Tenuta Nuova★★★★ £F Riserva Cerretalto★★★★★ £F
● **Rosso di Montalcino★★** £C ● **Pietradomice★★★** £E

CASTEL RUGGERO Chianti Classico www.castelruggero.it
High-profile enologist Nicolò d'Afflitto's family property. The 2 reds are unequivocally modern but from very low yields. Chianti Classico is plummy and berryish and very appealing (try from 2001, 02 or 03). The estate wine (60/30/10 Merlot/Cab Franc/Syrah in 03) is pure and stylish with lots of extract despite a lush, supple texture. Try from 01 or 03 but only with 6–8 years' age. (PW)

● **Chianti Classico★★** £B ● **Castel Ruggero★★★★** £D

CASTELLO DI AMA Chianti Classico *UK stockists:* **WTs**, JAr, F&M, P&S
Estate that always maintained emphasis on Chianti Classico. Two single-vineyard versions still made in the best years. Both Bellavista (includes Malvasia Nera) and richer La Casuccia (with some Merlot) combine intensity with nuance. Focus now on regular Chianti Classico that can improve for at least 5 years. Also Tuscany's first great Merlot, L'Apparita, attractive Chardonnay, Al Poggio, and Pinot Nero, Il Chiuso. (PW)

● **Chianti Classico★★** £C Bellavista★★★★ £E La Casuccia★★★★ £E
● **L'Apparita ★★★★** £F O **Al Poggio★★** £B

CASTELLO DI BOSSI www.castellodibossi.it *UK stockists:* **Wtr**, Gen, UnC, OxW
Well-established and very substantial estate, recently with better balance and finer structures. Wines include full and meaty Chianti Classico and deeper Riserva. Premium Girolamo (Merlot) and Corbaia (70/30 Sangiovese/Cab Sauv) have impressive depth and flavour and both need 6–8 years. Also promising Morellino and ripe Vermentino (Vento) from Maremma and from Montalcino a good Rosso and 2 other promising, bold 03 reds – Regina (Syrah) and powerful Re (Cab Sauv/Merlot/Petit Verdot) – both needing another 3 or 4 years' ageing. (PW)

Castello di Bossi:
● **Chianti Classico★★** £B Riserva Berardo★★★ £D ● **Girolamo★★★★** £E
● **Corbaia★★★★** £E

Terre di Talamo:
● **Morellino di Scansano** Tempo★★ £C O **Vento★** £B
Renieri:
Regina di Renieri★★★ £D ● **Re di Renieri★★★** £D

CASTELLO DI FONTERUTOLI www.fonterutoli.it *UK stockists:* **Eno**, JNi, F&M, Hrd, P&S, Vne
Historic estate and leader in restoring reputation of Chianti Classico. Best plots of Sangiovese go into rich, ripe modern example with excellent intensity and depth. Second selection (labelled simply Fonterutoli) of similar quality to good Chianti Classico. Siepi is rich, enticing blend (Sangiovese, Merlot). Belguardo estate in southern Maremma provides ever better Morellino di Scansano, and (from 2000) promsing, major new Cab Sauv-based estate wine (Tenuta di Belguardo) and well-priced, scented and characterful Serrata di Belguardo (Merlot/Sangiovese/Cab Sauv). (PW)

166 *Castello di Fonterutoli:*

● **Chianti Classico** Fonterutoli★★ £C Castello di Fonterutoli★★★★ £E
● **Siepi**★★★★ £F ● **Poggio alla Badiola**★★ £B
Tenuta Belguardo:
● **Morellino di Scansano** Poggio Bronzone★★★ £C
● **Tenuta di Belguardo**★★★★ £F ● **Serrata di Belguardo**★★ £C

CASTELLO LA LECCIA Chianti Classico
Small Chianti Classico estate producing stylish and expressive examples (03, 02 and 01 could be drunk now). The selection, Bruciagna, is really something: 100% Sangiovese and *barrique*-aged, it has great class and excellent texture and is deep, powerful and long. The superb 2001 deserves 5–6 years' age. (PW)
● **Chianti Classico**★★ £C Bruciagna★★★★ £D

CASTELLO DI MONSANTO Chianti Classico *UK stockists:* **Cib**
Illustrious reputation in 70s and 80s for Chianti Classico Riserva Il Poggio. More traditionally styled, slow evolving wine (with some Canaiolo and Colorino) of good breadth and excellent flavour depth. Also other premium wines - Fabrizio Bianchi (both pure Sangiovese and a Chardonnay), Tinscvil (Sangiovese, Cab Sauv), and Nemo, a very distinctive muscular cedary Tuscan Cab Sauv. (PW)
● **Chianti Classico** Riserva★ £D Riserva Il Poggio★★★ £E
● **Fabrizio Bianchi**★★ £E ● **Tinscvil**★ £D ● **Nemo**★★★ £E

CASTELLO DI POPPIANO Colli Fiorentini *UK stockists:* **GWW**
Historic estate making some of best wines of Colli Fiorentini. Chianti add Canaiolo and Colorino to Sangiovese. Newer style Tricorno, concentrated and powerful (Sangiovese, Cab Sauv, Merlot). Impressive Syrah includes 10% Sangiovese with reversed proportions in Tosco Forte. Also good old-style Vin Santo from Malvasia. Also Maremma property with Riserva Morellino di Scansano from 2001. (PW)
Castello di Poppiano:
● **Chianti Colli Fiorentini** Il Cortile★★ £B Riserva★★ £C
● **Tricorno**★★★★ £D ● **Syrah**★★★ £C ● **Tosco Forte**★★ £C
Massi di Mandorlaia:
● **Morellino di Scansano**★★ £B

CASTELLO DEI RAMPOLLA Chianti Classico *UK stockists:* **Bal**, UnC, Las
Sammarco (Cab Sauv with 20% Sangiovese) made this biodynamically-run estate famous - a firm, powerful, aristocratic red with great dimension. Now surpassed by sensational La Vigna d'Alceo (85% Cabernet, 15% Petit Verdot) from high density planting and of contrasting texture and profile. It shows terrific purity, depth and intensity in a superb 99. Ageworthy Chianti Classico usually shows how well Sangiovese does in these soils. (PW)
● **Vigna d'Alceo**✪✪✪✪✪ £G ● **Sammarco**★★★★★ £F
● **Chianti Classico**★★★ £C

CASTELLO DEL TERRICCIO www.terriccio.it *UK stockists:* **L&S**, F&M
Terriccio's fame has been spearheaded by flagship Lupicaia (Cab Sauv with 10% Merlot) - powerful, intense, oaky red with deep lush fruit. Cheaper Tassinaia (Cab Sauv, Merlot and Sangiovese) is similarly flattering. Whites Con Vento (Sauvignon) and Rondinaia (Chardonnay) are improving under Hans Terzer (San Michele Appiano). New estate blend of Syrah, Mourvèdre and Petit Verdot from 2000. Also unwooded Sangiovese, Capannino. (PW)
● **Lupicaia**★★★★ £G ● **Tassinaia**★★★ £D
O **Rondinaia**★★ £D O **Con Vento**★★ £C

CASTELLO VICCHIOMAGGIO Chianti Classico *UK stockists:* **Hal**, Vts
Producer of 3 very good Sangiovese-based reds. Best is Chianti Classico Riserva La Prima (includes Canaiolo and Colorino) from oldest vines. Riserva Petri (with a little Cab Sauv) hasn't quite the same intensity or structure. Ripa delle More (almost pure Sangiovese) aged entirely in barriques. Cheaper Ripa delle Mandorle and Chianti Classico San Jacopo for everyday drinking. New premium Semifonte di Semifonte (Cab Sauv, Sangiovese, Merlot) from 2001. (PW)
● **Chianti Classico** Riserva Petri★★ £D Riserva La Prima★★★ £E
● **Ripa delle Mandorle**★ £C ● **Ripa delle More**★★★ £E

ITALY

CASTELLO DI VOLPAIA   Chianti Classico   *UK stockists:* **Tri, Adm**, L&W, Odd, V&C
Elevated Radda estate with elegant, stylish wines, especially refined, graceful Coltassala (Sangiovese and little Mammolo) and Balifico (Sangiovese, Cab Sauv). Wines can struggle for ripeness and adequate richness in poorer vintages so stick with vintages such as 97 or 99. New consultant input should give greater consistency. Some Vin Santo and a little white also made. (PW)
● **Chianti Classico★** £B   Riserva★★ £C   Riserva Coltassala★★★ £E
● **Balifico★★★** £E

CERBAIONA   Brunello di Montalcino   *UK stockists:* **Bal**
Variable but potentially outstanding Brunello. Certifiable great vintages 97 or 90 (also very good 98) have concentration, depth and power combined with a thrilling aromatic and flavour complexity to make superb cellaring investment, even at the price. Second wine, Cerbaiona, adds Cab Sauv, Merlot, Syrah and Malvasia Nera to Sangiovese. (PW)
● **Brunello di Montalcino★★★★★** £F   ● **Cerbaiona★★★** £E

CIACCI PICCOLOMINI D'ARAGONA   www.ciaccipiccolomini.com   *UK stockists:* **Bal**, Vts, Las
Source of fine, ripe and full-textured, modern-styled Brunello best with 10 years' age. 1994, 95, 97, 98 and 99 are best recent vintages. Riservas from 95 and 97 add more extract and weight. Ripe, smoky, meaty Rosso better than most. Ateo (Sangiovese, Merlot, Cab Sauv) wants for a little more depth while intense, very ripe Syrah-based Fabius has wild Tuscan quality. (PW)
● **Brunello di Montalcino** Vigna di Pianrosso★★★ £E   Riserva★★★★ £F
● **Rosso di Montalcino** Vigna della Fonte★★ £C   ● **Sant'Antimo** Fabius★★★ £E

COL D'ORCIA   Brunello di Montalcino   www.coldorcia.it   *UK stockists:* **Alv**
Large, respected producer with sometimes too structured Brunello yet with richness and grip in 95, 97 and 99 examples. Riserva Poggio al Vento can develop a marvellous complexity with a decade's ageing. Also consistent gutsy, characterful Rosso di Montalcino, and bright, fruity forward Rosso degli Spezieri. Olmaia is very powerful, oaky, slightly rough-hewn Cab Sauv. Also very honeyed Moscadello di Montalcino, some Chardonnay (Ghiaie) and Pinot Grigio. (PW)
● **Brunello di Montalcino★★★** £E   Riserva Poggio al Vento★★★★ £F
● **Rosso di Montalcino★★** £C   ● **Rosso degli Spezieri★** £B   ● **Olmaia★★★** £F

COLOMBAIO DI CENCIO   Chianti Classico   www.wilhelm-chianti.com   *UK stockists:* **L&S**
Newish estate focused on two reds: Chianti Classico (with a little Merlot) and Il Futuro (Cab Sauv, Sangiovese, Merlot). Latter is oaky but also powerful, ripe, deep, lush berry richness and a sleek texture. Time is needed in order to see how much expression and finesse will be apparent with age. (PW)
● **Chianti Classico** I Massi★★★ £D   ● **Il Futuro★★★★** £E

CORZANO & PATERNO   Chianti   www.corzanoepaterno.it   *UK stockists:* **THt**, Han, UnC
Sleek, pure Tuscan reds from outer rim of the Classico zone. Il Corzano is individual despite blend (Sangiovese, Cab Sauv, Merlot) and finest expression with splendid texture and complexity. Stylish oak-influenced Chianti and Chianti Riserva with pure fruit and good depth. Also very fine and intense sweet white, Passito di Corzano. Dry whites are barrique-aged Chardonnays, Aglaia and Il Corzanello. (PW)
● **Il Corzano★★★★** £E   ● **Chianti** Terre di Corzano★★ £B   Ris. Tre Borri★★★ £D
O **Aglaia★★** £E   O **Passito di Corzano★★★** £E

LUIGI D'ALESSANDRO   Cortona   *UK stockists:* **L&S**
High quality producer in eastern Tuscany focused on Chardonnay, Viognier and Syrah. Fontarca from white varieties is ripe, aromatic with marvellous exotic, peachy fruit. Il Bosco red offers similarly impressive fruit but in black plum, herb, spice and floral spectrum but also has the structure to improve with age. Il Vescovo II is from younger Syrah vines. Also a little Vin Santo. (PW)
● **Cortona Syrah** Il Bosco★★★★ £D   Il Vescovo II★★ £B
O **Fontarca★★★** £C

DEI   Vino Nobile di Montepulciano   www.cantinedei.com   *UK stockists:* **L&S**, JNi
Supremely consistent Vino Nobile since the mid-90s. Riserva Bossona adds more weight and structure and some barrique influence but new oak mostly for Sancta Catharina - premium lush, ripe blend of Sangiovese, Syrah, Cab Sauv and Petit Verdot. Also round, fresh Rosso di Montepulciano if drunk young. (PW)

168

New entries have producer's name underlined

● **Vino Nobile di Montepulciano**★★★ £C Riserva Bossona★★★ £D
● **Sancta Catharina**★★★ £D

FATTORIA DI FELSINA Chianti Classico *UK stockists:* Lib, ACh, N&P, Vne, P&S
Classico heavyweight showing off best of southern commune with earthy, gutsy and fleshy examples. Riserva Rancia, premium oak-aged Sangiovese, Fontalloro, and rich Cabernet Sauvignon, Maestro Raro, show greater complexity and add a touch of refinement. Chardonnay, I Sistri, has never lacked for flavour either. Reds occasionally want for more finesse in structures. Very ripe 2000 Fontalloro and Rancia. (PW)
● **Chianti Classico**★★ £C Riserva★★ £D Riserva Rancia★★★ £E
● **Fontalloro**★★★★ £F ● **Maestro Raro**★★★ £F O **Chardonnay** I Sistri★★ £C

AMBROGIO E GIOVANNI FOLONARI www.tenutefolonari.com *UK stockists:* AWW
New project of Folonari family members previously part of Ruffino. Includes Cabreo and Nozzole estates and new additions: Vino Nobile estate TorCalvano (Gracciano Svetoni), Brunello La Fuga and in Bolgheri - Campo del Mare. Most outstanding ex-Ruffino wine is Il Pareto (Cab Sauv) but also depth and intensity in Cabreo Il Borgo (Sangiovese, Cab Sauv). Cabreo La Pietra is rich, creamy oak-fermented and aged Chardonnay. (PW)
Tenuta di Nozzole:
● **Chianti Classico** Riserva La Forra★★ £C ● **Il Pareto**★★★★ £F
Tenute del Cabreo:
● **Cabreo Il Borgo**★★★ £E O **Cabreo La Pietra**★★★ £D
Tenuta La Fuga:
● **Brunello di Montalcino**★★★ £E

FONTODI Chianti Classico *UK stockists:* Lib, ACh, BBR, P&S, Hrd, V&C, Vne
Fontodi Chianti Classico is a benchmark example rarely matched at price and shows marvellous vigour, intensity and style. Riserva Vigna del Sorbo (with 10% Cab Sauv) shows great refinement and style. Pure Sangiovese Flaccianello della Pieve still shows lovely dimension and evident class. Also increasingly good Syrah. (PW)
● **Chianti Classico**★★★ £C Riserva Vigna del Sorbo★★★★ £E

PODERE FORTE Orcia www.podereforte.it
Exciting new estate in the Orcia Valley south-east of Montalcino. The focus is on 2 wines. Both Petrucci (Sangiovese) and Guardiavigna (Sangiovese/Cab Sauv/Merlot/Petit Verdot) are vibrant, ripe and well oaked but have excellent balance and dense, compact fruit that will continue to unfurl with age. The 2002s are fine follow-ups to the very good 01s. (PW)
● **Orcia** Guardiavigna★★★★ £F Petrucci★★★★ £F

FOSSACOLLE Brunello di Montalcino *UK stockists:* Lib
Sergio Marchetti is most definitely one of the leaders of the latest wave of Brunello stars. He produces unashamedly modern, lush, approachable Brunello that is also solid and classy, deserving of 10 years' age. It's consistently good, as 1998 or a very good 00 show. Also perfumed, fruit-rich Rosso. (PW)
● **Brunello di Montalcino**★★★★ £F ● **Rosso di Montalcino**★★★ £D
● **Flaccianello**★★★★ £F ● **Syrah Case Via**★★★ £E ● **Pinot Nero**★ £E

FRESCOBALDI www.frescobaldi.it *UK stockists:* Hal, AAA
Recently richer and riper wines from one of Tuscany's biggest vineyard owners. Top wine is very fine, classy Montesodi from Chianti Rufina estate (Nipozzano) with great length and structure. Mormoreto (mostly Cab Sauv) from same. Very recently improved Brunello from Castelgiocondo while Lamaione (Merlot) of good fruit and consistency. Luce della Vite, also from Montalcino zone - estate wine (Sangiovese, Merlot) is dense and extracted. Second wine, Lucente is poor value. New Giramonte (since 99) is seductive and appealing. Basic brands are uninspiring. (PW)
Marchesi de' Frescobaldi:
● **Chianti Rufina** Riserva Nipozzano★★ £C Montesodi★★★★★ £E
● **Mormoreto**★★★ £E ● **Pomino**★ £C O **Pomino**★ £B Il Benefizio★★ £C
Tenuta di Castelgiocondo:
● **Brunello di Montalcino**★★★ £E Riserva★★★★ £F

ITALY

● Lamaione★★★ £E

Luce della Vite:
● Luce della Vite★★★ £G   ● Lucente la Vite★★ £D

FULIGNI   Brunello di Montalcino   *UK stockists:* **L&S**, N&P
Small Brunello estate with wines of classic muscle and size but also more elegance than is typical. After very good regular Brunello in 98, 97 and 95, outstanding 99 and Riserva 97. SJ or San Jacopo (includes Merlot) is lush with a seductive immediacy, while Rosso shows terrific intensity and vibrancy of fruit. (PW)
● **Brunello di Montalcino** Vigneti dei Cottimelli★★★★★ £E   Riserva★★★★★ £F
● **Rosso di Montalcino** Ginestreto★★★ £C   ● **San Jacopo**★★ £C

TENUTA DI GHIZZANO   Colline Pisane   www.tenutadighizzano.com   *UK stockists:* **L&S**, Eno
Leading property in Colline Pisane with two oak-aged lush modern-styled reds: Veneroso - mostly Sangiovese and Cab Sauv, Nambrot - Merlot with some Cabernet. Nambrot is a little fuller and more succulent but Veneroso has greater class. Also fruity Chianti Colline Pisane and tiny quantity of Vin Santo, San Germano. (PW)
● **Nambrot**★★★★ £E   ● **Veneroso**★★★★ £E   ● **Chianti Colline Pisane**★ £B

GUICCIARDINI STROZZI   San Gimignano   www.guicciardinistrozzi.it   *UK stockists:* **Bal**, Has
One of the exceptions in disappointing appellation. Vernaccia has good flavour, and more weight in the lightly oaked Perlato and Riserva versions. Reds have some style. Selvascura (Merlot), Sòdole (Sangiovese) and Millanni (Sangiovese/Cab Sauv/Merlot) are typically ripe and oaky with intense fruit, usually best with 5–6 years' age. (PW)
○ **Vernaccia di San Gimignano** San Biagio★ £B   Perlato★ £B   Riserva★★ £C
● **Sòdole**★★★ £D   ● **Selvascura**★★★ £D   ● **Millanni**★★★ £E

I GIUSTI & ZANZA   www.igiustiezanza.it   *UK stockists:* **Alv**
From densely planted vineyards nestled in Pisa's hills come 3 impressive reds. Both Dulcamara (Cab Sauv/Merlot) and Belcore (mostly Sangiovese) can be aggressive when young but are powerful and concentrated with sweet, intense fruit. Patience is the key: give Belcore 6 years, Dulcamara 8–10 years from the vintage. Perbruno (Syrah) is new (2003) and promising. (PW)
● **Dulcamara**★★★★ £E   ● **Belcore**★★★ £C   ● **Perbruno**★★★ £E

IL MOLINO DI GRACE   Chianti Classico   www.ilmolinodigrace.it   *UK stockists:* **MGF**, Goe
Amercian-owned estate committed to Chianti Classico based almost entirely on Sangiovese including perfumed, stylish *normale* and a denser, more structured Riserva. Better still are concentrated, powerful Riserva Il Margone and classy *barrique*-aged flagship Gratius (100% Sangiovese) from 55-year-old vines. Both deserve 8–10 years' age. (PW)
● **Chianti Classico**★★ £C   Riserva★★★ £D   Riserva Il Margone★★★ £E
● **Gratius**★★★★ £E   ● **Il Volano**★ £B

IL PALAZZINO   Chianti Classico   www.podereilpalazzino.it   *UK stockists:* **J&B**
Very committed estate that avoids style imposition from outside. Finest plot of vines is Grosso Sanese (30 year old Sangiovese) - now among top flight Chianti Classico. Small part as long-lived Riserva in best years. Also barrique-aged La Pieve with impressive depth but shares some youthful austerity with other wines. Argenina is more fruit-driven and simpler La Cascina Girasole from cooler origins. (PW)
● **Chianti Classico** Grosso Sanese★★★★ £C   Riserva Grosso Sanese★★★★ £D
● **Chianti Classico** Argenina★★ £C   La Pieve★★★ £C   ● **La Cascina Girasole**★ £B

IL POGGIONE   Brunello di Montalcino   www.tenutailpoggione.it   *UK stockists:* Eno, N&P
Excellent Brunello for 40-odd years. Full and structured, always with fair amount of tannin but balanced and long-lived - exhibits deep, savoury complexity and richness soon after release. Best recently in 95, 97, 98 and 99. Even more power, structure and breadth in Riserva (exceptional 97). Deep Rosso, too. San Leopoldo (Sangiovese, Cab Sauv, Cab Franc) is more overtly fruity. (PW)
● **Brunello di Montalcino**★★★★ £D   Riserva★★★★★ £E
● **Rosso di Montalcino**★★ £B   ● **San Leopoldo**★★★ £C

ISOLE E OLENA   Chianti Classico   *UK stockists:* Lib, Vne, ACh, F&M, Hrd, Sel, P&S, V&C
Very good wines for a long time but still being improved - from great Cepparello (Sangiovese) through powerful, long-lived Cab Sauv and stylish Syrah to vibrant Chianti Classico. All are intense, complete and expressive with both depth and elegance. Chardonnay is usually one of Tuscany's best, and consistently brilliant

170

Vin Santo. (PW)
● **Cepparello**★★★★★ £F ● **Chianti Classico**★★ £C O **Chardonnay**★★★ £D
● **Cabernet Sauvignon** Collezione De Marchi★★★★ £F ● **Syrah**★★★★ £E

LA BRANCAIA Chianti Classico *UK stockists:* **Eno,** JNi, NYg, Hrd,V&C,Vne
Fine Chianti Classico (pure Sangiovese) and Brancaia Il Blu (blue label) that includes 40% Merlot and 5% Cabernet. Both see some new wood - evident in wines that also show ripe stylish fruit and good depth. Third wine, Tre is supple and forward. 'Brancaia in Maremma' provided exceptionally good (new) Ilatraia in 2002 (Cab Sauv-based, also 30% Sangiovese, 10 % Petit Verdot). (PW)
● **Chianti Classico**★★★ £D ● **Brancaia Il Blu**★★★★ £E ● **Tre**★★ £C

LA FIORITA Brunello di Montalcino www.fattorialafiorita.it *UK stockists:* **Wtr**
Estate of renowned enologist Roberto Cipresso. His modern-style Brunello is open, deeply perfumed and appealing yet with good fruit depth and intensity too – for drinking quite young or with 10 years' age. The promise of 1997 was followed by a very good 98 Brunello and an even better 99. Laurus has upfront appeal and equates to Rosso di Montalcino but includes Merlot. (PW)
● **Brunello di Montalcino**★★★★ £F ● **Laurus**★★ £C

LA MASSA Chianti Classico *UK stockists:* **JAr,** Dec
Prime vineyards in much vaunted Panzano sub-zone. Wines are barrique-aged and always full of ripe, intense fruit from mostly Sangiovese but also some Cab Sauv and/or Merlot - less individual than some, but consistently high quality. Giorgio Primo deserves five years' or more. In 2001 the regular Chianti Classico replaced by 'La Massa' with reduction in Sangiovese but a step up in quality. (PW)
● **La Massa**★★★ £D ● **Chianti Classico** Giorgio Primo★★★★ £F

LA PIEVE Chianti *UK stockists:* **Wtr**
Simone Tognetti's dedicated approach to viticulture and vinification ensures high quality even in difficult vintages like 2002. Regular Chianti (up to 15% Canaiolo) has excellent fruit and structure. Fortebraccio (100% Sangiovese) has lovely style and purity while Rosso del Pievano (50/50 Cab Sauv/Sangiovese) is lush, deep and very long – almost as impressive in 2002 as 01. (PW)
● **Chianti** La Pieve★★ £B Fortebraccio★★★ £C ● **Rosso del Pievano**★★★★ £C

LA PODERINA Brunello di Montalcino www.saiagricola.it *UK stockists:* **Tri**
One of the Saiagricola blue-chip properties – others are Del Cerro (Vino Nobile) and Colpetrone (Montefalco Sagrantino). Brunello can be striking with a singular spiced herb and black fruit complexity and a dense, well-defined texture. Both this and small-production Poggio Banale are *barrique*-aged. Also fine, unusually elegant Moscadello di Montalcino. (PW)
● **Brunello di Montalcino**★★★★ £F Poggio Banale★★★★ £F
● **Rosso di Montalcino**★ £C
O **Moscadello di Montalcino** Vendemmia Tardiva★★★ £F

MAURIZIO LAMBARDI Brunello di Montalcino
Small quantities of often very good Brunello with a depth and fullness that show off the quality of fruit. Generally good quality across recent vintages with lushness and richness that make a vintage like 1995 or 98 both accessible now or capable of another 10 years' ageing. Also intense vibrant Rosso that can need 3-5 years to show its best. (PW)
● **Brunello di Montalcino**★★★ £E ● **Rosso di Montalcino**★★ £C
● **Brunello di Montalcino**★★★ £E ● **Rosso di Montalcino**★★ £C

LANCIOLA Chianti Classico www.lanciola.net *UK stockists:* **HSA,** Wat, The, UnC
Plenty of substance and vibrancy from top part of Classico zone. At the level of Riserva and premium Terricci (Sangiovese with Cab Sauv, Cab Franc), translates as broad, muscular wines slightly overdone in terms of oak and extract, needing at least 5 years' age. Regular Chiantis, both Classico and Fiorentini have a vigour and intensity well matched by a stylish fruit expression. (PW)
● **Terricci**★★★ £D ● **Chianti Classico** Le Masse di Greve★★ £B Riserva★★ £C
● **Chianti Colli Fiorentini**★★ £B

ITALY

LE CORTI/PRINCIPE CORSINI   Chianti Classico   *UK stockists:* **Ast**
High-quality wine made with view to restoring historic Villa di Corsini. Three fine Chianti Classicos, good
normale (Le Corti), more structured Riserva (Cortevecchia) and premium Don Tommaso. The wines are ripe,
intense with particularly good structure and depth in Don Tommaso. Also made is deep, characterful red at
Tenuta Marsiliana in Maremma (mostly Cab Sauv/Merlot but also Syrah and others). (PW)
Le Corti:
● **Chianti Classico** Le Corti★★ £B Ris. Cortevecchia★★ £C Don Tommaso★★★ £D
Tenuta Marsiliana:
● **Marsiliana**★★★ £E

LE MACCHIOLE   Bolgheri   www.lemacchiole.it   *UK stockists:* **L&S**, F&R
Outstanding Bolgheri producer. Main red is Macchiole (mostly Sangiovese) - sleek and compact, it opens out
with age. Tiny amounts of other reds: Paléo Rosso has evolved from Cab Sauv-based to Cabernet Franc only
(2001). Spellbinding quality in tremendously rich, classically varietal Merlot, Messorio, and deep, structured,
minerally Syrah, Scrio. Paléo Bianco, (Chardonnay, Sauvignon) is ripe and stylish. (PW)
● **Bolgheri** Rosso Superiore Paléo★★★★ £E ● **Macchiole Rosso**★★★ £D
● **Messorio**★★★★★ £H ● **Scrio**★★★★★ £H O **Paléo Bianco**★★ £D

LE MICCINE   Chianti Classico   www.lemiccine.com   *UK stockists:* Trf
An upcoming name in Chianti Classico. Fine, supple Chianti Classico *normale* includes a little Canaiolo and
Malvasia Nera (a real star in the tricky 2002 vintage). New French oak is evident in the lush spiced cherry fruit of
the Riserva (100% Sangiovese). (PW)
● **Chianti Classico**★★ £B Riserva Don Alberto★★★ £C

LE PUPILLE   www.elisabettageppetti.com   *UK stockists:* **Lib**, Vne, P&S, NYg
For long the one outstanding producer from the heart of the southern Maremma. Regular Morellino di
Scansano has wild herb and delightful berry fruit character. Marvellous style and complexity in excellent single-
vineyard Poggio Valente. Even better is rich, concentrated Saffredi (Cab Sauv, Merlot - 70/30). Solalto is
delicious sweet wine from Sauvignon, Traminer and Semillon. (PW)
● **Morellino di Scansano**★★ £C Poggio Valente★★★ £D
● **Saffredi**★★★★ £F O **Solalto**★★★ £E

CANTINE LEONARDO DA VINCI   Chianti   www.cantineleonardo.it   *UK stockists:* **Lib**
Modern co-op making wines in the Montalbano hills west of Carmignano. All the wines are very soundly made
with good fruit intensity and represent reasonable value at their respective quality levels. Single-vineyard San Zio
(mostly Sangiovese) and dense, black-fruited Sant'Ippolito (Merlot/Syrah) both deserve 5–6 years' age or more. (PW)
● **Chianti**★ £B Riserva★★ £C ● **Chianti Classico** Poggio de' Sassiduri★★ £B
● **San Zio**★★★ £D ● **Sant' Ippolito**★★★ £D
● **Morellino di Scansano**★★ £B O **Ser Piero**★ £B

LIVERNANO   Radda in Chianti   www.livernano.it   *UK stockists:* **L&S**
Restored medieval hamlet with 12.5 ha recently replanted at higher densities. Livernano blend (Cab Sauv,
Merlot, Sangiovese) shows good intensity and structure as well as increasing depth and concentration. Even
better is Puro Sangue, a very pure, powerful expression of Sangiovese. (PW)
● **Purosangue**★★★★ £E ● **Livernano**★★★ £E

FATTORIA DI MAGLIANO   Morellino di Scansano   www.fattoriadimagliano.it   *UK stockists:* **L&S**
A relatively new source of fine, fruit-intense Morellino di Scansano. Heba (Sangiovese with 15% Syrah) has classic
Maremma herbs and cherry, berry fruit. Better still is Poggio Bestiale (Merlot/Cab Sauv/Cab Franc). The rich and
concentrated 2003 deserves 6–7 years' age. Also exciting new varietal Syrah from 03 and delicious fruit-driven
Vermentino (Pagliatura) for drinking very young. (PW)
● **Morellino di Scansano**★★ £B ● **Poggio Bestiale**★★★★ £D
O **Pagliatura**★★ £C

MALENCHINI   Colli Fiorentini   www.malenchini.it   *UK stockists:* **Vxs**
A leading advocate for 'real Chianti'. From 90% Sangiovese, 10% Canaiolo the Malenchini's wine has classic
vibrancy, purity and intensity and archetypal Tuscan flavours. Cab Sauv is reserved for Bruzzico (with 20%
Sangiovese) which is ripe, characterful and deserving of 6–7 years' age. Vin Santo is in the more traditional mould

172

New entries have producer's name underlined

ITALY

that goes so well with *biscotti.* (PW)

● **Chianti Colli Fiorentini**★★ £B ● **Bruzzico**★★★ £D
○ **Vin Santo**★★★ £D

MASTROJANNI Brunello di Montalcino *UK stockists:* **Col**, F&R
Great Brunello producer in south-east of zone. Expansive Brunello is structured, dense but with ripe tannins, and real depth, class and complexity in vintages like 90, 93, 95 97 or 99. Also very small quantities of rich, complex Riserva and occasional special selection, Schiena d'Asino. San Pio (Sangiovese/Cab Sauv) is more accessible as is Brunello-like Rosso . (PW)

● **Brunello di Montalcino**★★★★ £F Riserva★★★★ £F Schiena d'Asino★★★★ £F
● **Rosso di Montalcino**★★ £D ● **San Pio**★★★ £D

MONTE BERNARDI Chianti Classico www.montebernardi.com *UK stockists:* **RsW**, Rae
Run by Schmelzer family (since 2004). High-quality French oak, used in ageing of all wines, has been evident in structure and flavour but expect a style evolution here. To date Sa'etta (Sangiovese) has been ripe, oaky and intense. Chianti Classico now includes a little Canaiolo. Tzingana is Bordeaux blend. (PW)

● **Chianti Classico**★★ £C ● **Sa'etta**★★★ £D ● **Tzingana**★★★ £F

MONTEPELOSO Val di Cornia *UK stockists:* **Bal**, UnC
One of Suvereto's stars, making wines of extraordinary concentration. Small quantities of Gabbro (Cab Sauv, Cab Franc) and Nardo (mostly Sangiovese with little Cab Sauv and Montepulciano). Eneo (Sangiovese with little Canaiolo and Ciliegiolo) made in greater quantities and better value. Also new very promising new varietal Syrah and Sangiovese made in 02. (PW)

● **Gabbro**★★★★★ £G ● **Nardo**★★★★★ £G ● **Eneo**★★★★ £D

MONTEVERTINE www.montevertine.it *UK stockists:* **Eur**, N&P
Source of seminal single-vineyard Sangiovese Le Pergole Torte from high altitude vineyards. Also Il Sodaccio and Montevertine (both include a little Canaiolo). All three can show marvellous quality, very stylish and harmonious, with excellent dimension on length, gaining in richness with age. Usually best from warmer years. (PW)

● **Le Pergole Torte**★★★★★ £F ● **Il Sodaccio**★★★★ £E
● **Montevertine**★★★ £E ● **Pian del Ciampolo**★ £B

MORIS FARMS Monteregio di Massa Marittima *UK stockists:* **Bal**, JNi, C&B,Vts, But
Generally sound if robust examples of both Monteregio di Massa Marittima and Morellino di Scansano, particularly an intense, extracted Riserva of latter. Real star is Avvoltore, powerhouse Sangiovese-based wine of great vigour and depth. Cab Sauv and Syrah also contribute to consistently rich, floral and crushed berry fruit complexity. (PW)

● **Avvoltore**★★★★ £E ● **Monteregio di Massa Marittima**★★ £C
● **Morellino di Scansano**★ £C Riserva★★ £D

SILVIO NARDI Brunello di Montalcino www.tenutenardi.com *UK stockists:* **C&C**, F&R, Blx
Rising star striving to be among the élite of Brunello producers. The rise in quality is best seen in single-vineyard Brunello Manachiara: outstanding in 1999, showing tremendous depth, complexity and class, but scarcely less complete in the less stellar vintages of 98 and 00. Regular Brunello is good too, pursued by a concentrated powerful Rosso; try the latter from 2001, 02 or 03. (PW)

● **Brunello di Montalcino**★★★★ £F Vigneto Manachiara★★★★★ £F
● **Rosso di Montalcino**★★★ £C

TENUTA DELL' ORNELLAIA Bolgheri www.ornellaia.it *UK stockists:* **JAr**, F&M, UnC, BBR, Las
Now solely owned by Frescobaldi but established by Lodovico Antinori. Focus is very fine estate blend, Ornellaia (Cab Sauv, Merlot and Cab Franc). Good second wine is Le Serre Nuove, also large volume basic Le Volte. Most sought-after wine is pure Merlot, Masseto with sheer fruit opulence that has no equal for some impassioned fans. (PW)

● **Bolgheri** Rosso Superiore Ornellaia★★★★★ £G ● **Masseto**★★★★★ £H
● **Bolgheri** Rosso Le Serre Nuove★★★ £E ● **Le Volte**★ £B

SIRO PACENTI Brunello di Montalcino *UK stockists:* **JAr**, Lay, BBR, Far
Now exemplary Brunello, excellent in 96 and outstanding 97, 98 and 99. Superb richness, breadth and power

but also great length, really fine tannins and impeccable balance. Also rich, concentrated Brunello-like Rosso di Montalcino and a little Riserva. (PW)

● Brunello di Montalcino❂❂❂❂❂ £F ● Rosso di Montalcino★★★ £D

PANIZZI San Gimignano *UK stockists:* **Eno**
Really decent Vernaccia di San Gimignano in a well-structured regular version and better oak-aged and fermented Riserva with minerally, leesy, spiced preserved citrus character as well as breadth and intensity. Also new (2003) single-vineyard version, Vigna Santa Margherita. Red Folgóre (Sangiovese/Merlot/Cab Sauv) is fully ripe, plummy and stylish, also one of the zone's best. (PW)

O Vernaccia di San Gimignano★★ £C Riserva★★★ £D
● Folgóre★★★ £E

PERTIMALI/LIVIO SASSETTI Brunello di Montalcino *UK stockists:* **J&B**, F&R, Fal
Slightly old-fashioned Brunello of great richness and depth within a sturdy frame. Also meaty, ripe Rosso di Montalcino. Vigna dei Fili di Seta (Sangiovese, Cab Sauv) is more modern, with rich, dense fruit to the fore. Brunello however, can be a little uneven with poor 96, a slightly bruising, monolithic 98, and slightly high-toned if otherwise promising 99. Riserva can be superb as in 97. (PW)

● Brunello di Montalcino★★★★ £F Riserva★★★★★★£F
● Rosso di Montalcino★★ £C ● Vigna dei Fili di Seta★★★ £D

PETROLO Colli Aretini www.petrolo.it *UK stockists:* **Lib**,Vne, But, P&S
One of Tuscany's finest pure Merlots: Galatrona has remarkable richness and concentration but also depth, spice and individuality. Bigger volume Torrione (Sangiovese) very impressive since 1997, if not of the same concentration or proportions as Galatrona. Terre di Galatrona (Sangiovese/Merlot) is at ripest and fullest in the best vintages. (PW)

● Galatrona★★★★ £F ● Torrione★★★ £D ● Terre di Galatrona★ £B

PIAGGIA Carmignano *UK stockists:* **J&B**, F&R
Cult Carmignano Riserva from late-picked fruit off very low-yielding vines. Very rich with concentrated black fruits, lots of extract but fine tannins. Excellent in 1997 and 99 and outstanding in every vintage since, including an uncommon 02; all require at least 6–8 years' ageing. Also small quantities of Il Sasso (vineyard-specific), a similar blend of Sangiovese/Cab Sauv/Merlot (70/20/10) but more international in style. (PW)

● Carmignano Riserva★★★★ £E ● Il Sasso★★★ £D

PIEVE SANTA RESTITUTA Brunello di Montalcino *UK stockists:* JAr, L&W, F&R
Angelo Gaja's first venture into Tuscany. Two Brunellos are made – Rennina, a superior selection and Sugarille, from single-vineyard site. Both wines show an elegance and structure since 95 that has set them apart from most other Brunello but need at least 10-12 years' age and will keep for longer. (PW)

● Brunello di Montalcino Rennina★★★★★ £G Sugarille★★★★★ £G

POGGERINO Chianti Classico www.poggerino.com *UK stockists:* **L&S**
High altitude estate producing consistently fine wines. Merlot supplements Sangiovese in Chianti Classico (with small amount single vneyard Riserva Bugialla, recently in 2000, 99 and 97) and matches it in Primamatera - characterised by new oak and concentrated sweet berry fruit but also an elegance and stylishness. Il Labirinto is from young vine Sangiovese. (PW)

● Chianti Classico★★ £B Riserva Bugialla★★★ £E
● Primamateria★★★★ £E ● Il Labirinto★ £B

POGGIO ANTICO Brunello di Montalcino www.poggioantico.com *UK stockists:* **BWC,** F&R
Established Brunello producer with elevated vineyards (450m). Recently wines show extra drive and intensity added to the elegance of site. Best is vineyard-specific Riserva with great depth, class and preserved-fruits intensity, deserving 10–15 years' or more. Regular Brunello is more classic, Altero slightly more international. New from 2001 is oaky and robust Madre (Cab Sauv/Sangiovese). (PW)

● Brunello di Montalcino★★★★ £E Altero★★★★ £E Riserva★★★★★ £F
● Madre★★★ £D

POGGIO ARGENTIERA Morellino di Scansano www.poggioargentiera.com *UK stockists:* **CdP**
Exciting new Maremma producer. Unwooded Bellamarsilia is ripe, spicy and characterful. Oak-aged Capatosta from

New entries have producer's name underlined

older vines has intense, concentrated fruit. Also small amounts of stylish, complex Finisterre (Syrah/Alicante) with a lightly mineral intensity. All impress from 2003, 02 and 01. New Lalicante (03) from late-harvested and dried Alicante grapes, has moderate sweetness and an intense, distinctive spicy fruit character. (PW)

● **Morellino di Scansano** Bellamarsilia★★ £B Capatosta★★★★ £D
● **Finisterre★★★★** £E

POGGIO SAN POLO   Brunello di Montalcino www.poggiosanpolo.com   *UK stockists:* **Lib**, P&S, NYg
One of Montalcino's rising stars. Real progress has already been made with Brunello in an intense, spicy, richly black-fruited 1999 and a very ripe but balanced 00. A little more refinement will put it amongst the best. Mezzo Pane, a powerful and complex blend of Sangiovese and Cabernet Sauvignon (80/20), has the less class but is impressive in 99, 00 and 01. Good Rosso too. (PW)

● **Brunello di Montalcino★★★★** £F ● **Rosso di Montalcino★★** £D
● **Mezzo Pane★★★** £E

POGGIO SCALETTE   *UK stockists:* **Mgi**, L&W
Consultant Vittorio Fiore's son Jurij makes one wine only from best grapes. Il Carbonaione (100% Sangiovese) is very fine with pure fruit, ample breadth and depth, and lovely harmony. Also consistently good since first (1992). 99 arguably has most promise of the recent fine trio of 01, 00 and 99. (PW)

● **Il Carbonaione★★★★★** £F

POGGIO AL SOLE   Chianti Classico   *UK stockists:* **THt**, UnC, P&S
Refined Chianti Classico, both splendid, sleek, intense *normale* and poised, elegant but graceful and beautifully defined Casasilia. Selvasera (Merlot/Cab Sauv) shows similar refinement while Syrah, although lacking concentration of top Côte-Rôtie, has fine fruit, and length of flavour that characterises all the wines. Elegance rather than power. (PW)

● **Chianti Classico★★★** £C Casasilia★★★★ £E
● **Seraselva★★★** £E ● **Syrah★★★** £E

POGGIOPIANO   Chianti Classico   *UK stockists:* **Mer**, Con, Fal
Most remarkable is limited production Rosso di Sera, which combines a high 15 per cent Colorino with Sangiovese. Delicious spicy, black-fruited depth and a lush texture and more individual than less interesting efforts which add Merlot to Sangiovese. Needs a little time, 2001 particularly good. Also Chianti Classico with excellent breadth, intensity and depth. (PW)

● **Chianti Classico★★** £C ● **Rosso di Sera★★★★** £E

POLIZIANO   www.carlettipoliziano.com   *UK stockists:* **Eno**, JNi, N&P, F&M, Vne, V&C
Top flight Tuscan producer taking quality consistently higher. Excellent regular Vino Nobile but better Asinone with more breadth, complexity and sheer style, and Le Stanze - outstanding Cab Sauv with wonderful depth but also increasing elegance. Also wines of Lohsa estate in Maremma for spicy, vibrant, pure fruit Morellino di Scansano (Sangiovese with 10% Ciliegiolo) and new Mandrone di Lohsa (Cab Sauv-based with Alicante, Petit Verdot) - from 2001. (PW)

Poliziano:
● **Vino Nobile di Montepulciano★★★** £C Asinone★★★★ £E
● **Le Stanze★★★★** £E ● **Rosso di Montepulciano★** £B
Azienda Agricola Lohsa:
● **Morellino di Scansano★★★** £C

QUERCIABELLA   Chianti Classico   www.querciabella.com   *UK stockists:* **Pol**, Cam, Han
Grand Chianti Classico estate with wines of strength as well as individuality. Chianti Classico and Riserva (last made 99) include Cab Sauv and Merlot yet retain distinctive Tuscan character. New (2000) rich, refined Palafreno (Merlot, Sangiovese) made to similar standard as Camartina (Sangiovese, Cab Sauv and some Merlot, Syrah), a wine of great class and intensity. Rich, powerful Batàr (Chardonnay, Pinot Bianco - 65/35 in 2001) has almost exotic fruit character. Reds deserve ageing. (PW)

● **Camartina★★★★★** £F ● **Palafreno★★★★** £E O **Batàr★★★** £E
● **Chianti Classico★★** £C Riserva★★★ £D

ITALY

RICASOLI/CASTELLO DI BROLIO   www.ricasoli.it   *UK stockists:* Eno, Cam, NYg, FWC, ThP, F&R
Large noble property with on-going vineyard improvements. Flagship Chianti Classico (100% Sangiovese) quite oaky but increasingly expansive and stylish. 'Brolio' is 'second' wine, also nutty, biscuity Vin Santo. Barone Ricasoli label includes concentrated consistently impressive Casalferro (Sangiovese, Merlot), increasingly refined barrique-aged Chardonnay Torricella, and new lightly oaked Sangiovese Campo Ceni. (PW)

Castello di Brolio:
● **Chianti Classico** Brolio★★ £C Castello di Brolio★★★★ £E   O **Vin Santo**★★★ £D

Barone Ricasoli:
● **Chianti Classico** Riserva Rocca Guicciarda★ £C
● **Casalferro**★★★ £E   O **Torricella**★★ £C

RIECINE   Chianti Classico   www.riecine.com   *UK stockists:* THt, Dec, Han, UnC, F&M
Wines that have always shown great concentration, intensity as well as purity and elegance. Recently with richer texture and greater suppleness than previously but all should have some age. No Riserva or La Gioia from difficult 2002 vintage but regular Chianti Classico even better as a result. Prices reflect quality. (PW)
● **Chianti Classico**★★★ £D Riserva★★★★ £E   ● **La Gioia**★★★★ £F

ROCCA DI CASTAGNOLI   Chianti Classico   www.roccadicastagnoli.it   *UK stockists:* Eur
Producer with established track record for Chianti Classico Riserva, recently further improved. Riserva Capraia is *barrique*-aged and has more flair than Poggio a' Frati (large oak). Stielle (Sangiovese/Cab Sauv) is best of 3 non-Classico premium reds. Neither Buriano (Cab Sauv) nor Le Pratola (Merlot) lack for ripe, intense fruit or character. Molino delle Balze is ripe but balanced Chardonnay. Also promise from a second estate, San Sano. (PW)

Rocca di Castagnoli:
● **Chianti Classico**★★ £B Riserva Poggio a' Frati★★★ £C Riserva Capraia★★★ £C
● **Buriano**★★★ £E   ● **Stielle**★★★★ £E   ● **Le Pratola**★★★ £E
O **Vin Santo del Chianti Classico**★★★ £E   O **Molino delle Balze**★★ £C

Castello San Sano:
● **Chianti Classico**★ £B Riserva Guarnellotto★★ £C
● **Borroalfumo**★★ £E

ROCCA DI MONTEGROSSI   Chianti Classico   *UK stockists:* HSA, UnC, P&S
Now a first-division estate and one to follow for ever finer Chianti Classico (Sangiovese with 10% Canaiolo) and Riserva (entirely Sangiovese from 99) which are becoming classic pure Tuscan wines. Previously Sangiovese Geremia is Cab Sauv/Merlot from 01. All have depth and structure to ensure they age well. Also marvellously rich Vin Santo. (PW)
● **Chianti Classico**★★★ £C Riserva San Marcellino★★★★ £D
● **Geremia**★★★★ £E   O **Vin Santo**★★★★ £E

RUFFINO   www.ruffino.com   *UK stockists:* Alv
Divided in 2000 (see Folonari) yet still includes great swathes of vineyard. Adequate Vino Nobile and Brunello but also Chianti Classico Riserva Ducale Oro of great class and breadth from top vintages. Better still is Romitorio di Santedame (Colorino/Sangiovese), a highly original wine of great character and superb fruit. New Chardonnay, Il Solatio, and newish Modus (Sangiovese, Cab Sauv, Merlot). Also Libaio (mostly Chardonnay) and large-volume Chianti Classico Aziano. (PW)

Tenimenti Ruffino:
● **Chianti Classico** Santedame★★ £C Riserva Ducale Oro★★★★ £E
● **Romitorio di Santedame**★★★★★ £G   ● **Modus**★★★ £F

Il Greppone Mazzi:
● **Brunello di Montalcino**★★ £E

Lodola Nuova:
● **Vino Nobile di Montepulciano**★★ £E

SALVIONI/LA CERBAIOLA   Brunello di Montalcino   *UK stockists:* JAr, Lay, F&R
Classic handmade Brunello of great elegance and complexity. Fine quality even in lesser vintages like 96. Traditionally produced, wine is rich, deep and powerful with superb texture, definition and great expression both

176

in aroma and flavour. Rosso is made to help maintain very high standards. (PW)
● **Brunello di Montalcino**⊕⊕⊕⊕⊕ £G ● **Rosso di Montalcino**★★★ £E

SAN FABIANO CALCINAIA   Chianti Classico   *UK stockists:* **GID**
Comprised of two estates and led by flagship Cerviolo Rosso (Sangiovese, Cab Sauv, Merlot - 50/25/25 in 2000) - a very distinguished concentrated red with old-vine fruit, earth and mineral complexity. Supple, stylish Chianti Classico though overly oaky Riserva 99 and 2000. (PW)
● **Cerviolo Rosso**★★★★ £E ● **Chianti Classico**★★ £B Riserva★★ £D

SAN FILIPPO - FANTI   Brunello di Montalcino
Owner Filippo Fanti in his third term as president of Brunello *consorzio* ensures own wines up with zone's best. Depth, drive and structure in 97, 98 and 99 most impressive with good harmony between fruit and oak and promise of delightful complexity and texture with 10 years' or more. In more internationally-styled Sant'Antimo Rosso, Sangiovese character snuffed out. Vin Santo also made. (PW)
● **Brunello di Montalcino**★★★★ £E ● **Rosso di Montalcino**★★ £C
● **Sant'Antimo Rosso**★ £B

SAN GIUSTO A RENTENNANO   www.fattoriasangiusto.it   *UK stockists:* **Bal**, UnC, NYg, JAr
Much venerated estate with wines of strength allied to an intense preserved fruits quality which makes for complex, classy wines with age. Fine Chianti Classico, more muscular Riserva (with 5% Canaiolo) with exquisite fruit and great length (replaced by new Le Baroncole in 2000). Percarlo (Sangiovese) more closely resembles top Brunello than most Classico wines. Also an outstanding, wonderfully complex Vin Santo and recently, blockbuster Merlot, La Ricolma. (PW)
● **Chianti Classico**★★ £C Riserva★★★ £D
● **Percarlo**★★★★ £E ● **La Ricolma**★★★★ £F ○ **Vin Santo**★★★★ £F

ENRICO SANTINI   Bolgheri   *UK stockists:* **C&B**, F&R
Most interesting new Bolgheri star. Already Montepergoli (Cab Sauv, Merlot, Syrah, Sangiovese) is worth contrasting with the zone's heavyweights - a profound red of real vigour, intensity and lovely berry fruit aroma and flavour. More Sangiovese in attractive, spicy, perfumed second wine, Poggio al Moro. White from Sauvignon and Vermentino. (PW)
● **Bolgheri Rosso** Poggio al Moro★★ £C Montepergoli★★★★ £E
○ **Bolgheri Bianco** Campo alla Casa★ £C

SASSICAIA/TENUTA SAN GUIDO   www.sassicaia.com   *UK stockists:* **Lib**, JAr, HHC, BBR, P&S, Las
Sassicaia is arguably Italy's single most famous wine, its production much expanded from first commercial, much celebrated vintage, 1968. Blend of 85% Cab Sauv, 15% Cab Franc now in excess of 12,000 cases a year. If efforts in 90s don't match exceptional vintages like 85, most still reveal a beautifully composed wine with delicious sweet black fruits intensity and elegant complexity sustained on a very long finish. Needs 5-20 years'. New sophisticated Guidalberto (Merlot, Cab Sauv, Sangiovese - 50/30/20) since 2000. (PW)
● **Bolgheri Sassicaia**★★★★★ £G ● **Guidalberto**★★★ £E

MICHELE SATTA   Bolgheri   www.michelesatta.it   *UK stockists:* **SCh**, F&R
Good if not great wines from 30 ha. Complex, characterful Piastraia (Sangiovese, Cab Sauv, Merlot and Syrah) can want for more refined tannins. Cavaliere (pure Sangiovese) can be more angular. Attractive, aromatic Costa di Guilia (Vermentino, Sauvignon) and very ripe, oak-influenced Viognier Giovin Re. Also basic Bolgheri Rosato and Bianco. (PW)
● **Bolgheri Rosso** Piastraia★★★ £E ● **Cavaliere**★★ £D
○ **Giovin Re**★★ £C ○ **Costa di Giulia**★ £B

FATTORIA SELVAPIANA   Chianti Rufina   www.selvapiana.it   *UK stockists:* **Lib**, Vne, ACh, Sel
Noble estate and champion of Chianti Rufina. Wines start out austere but have energy, purity and refinement. Best is single-vineyard Riserva Bucerchiale of great intensity and depth but requires 6-7 years' age or more. Another single-vineyard wine, Fornace is more obvious and fleshy from Cab Sauv component. Also very good Vin Santo with rich ripe fruit and refined nutty complexity. (PW)
● **Chianti Rufina**★★ £B Riserva Bucerchiale★★★★ £E
● **Fornace**★★★ £E ○ **Vin Santo**★★★ £E

177

ITALY

SESTI Brunello di Montalcino   *UK stockists:* **JAr, Tan**
With a traditional long ageing in wood, these wines have sometimes verged on the rustic but show real intensity and depth. Expansive and complex Riserva always has impressive flavour and definite class. 2000 Brunello is very good in the vintage and both 99 and 99 Riserva will not disappoint devotees of this style. Terra di Siena is a characterful Cab Sauv/Merlot blend, while light, supple Monteleccio is from Sangiovese. (PW)
- **Brunello di Montalcino★★★★** £F   Riserva Phenomena★★★★ £F
- **Sant'Antimo** Terra di Siena★★★ £E ● **Rosso di Montalcino★★** £C ● **Monteleccio★★** £C

SETTE PONTI www.tenutasetteponti.com   *UK stockists:* **C&C, Vts, Hfx**
Slick, professional operation with fabulous wines from eastern side of the Valdarno. Oreno (50/50 Sangiovese, Cab Sauv in 2003) and Crognolo (90% Sangiovese) are rich yet gently textured wines with a beautifully detailed fruit intensity. Oreno is more international but concentrated and very harmonious; Crognolo expresses more of its origins. Also reds from Poggio al Lupo in Maremma and Feudo Maccari in Sicily. (PW)

Sette Ponti:
- **Oreno★★★★** £F ● **Crognolo★★★** £D ● **Vigna di Pallino★** £B

Poggio al Lupo:
- **Morellino di Scansano★★** £C ● **Poggio al Lupo★★★** £D

SOLDERA Brunello di Montalcino   www.soldera.it   *UK stockists:* **Bal**, Fal, Sec, F&R, Rae
Small superbly sited (organic) Brunello estate. Natural winemaking with long stay in large oak. Wines often of extraordinary breadth and complexity if occasionally marred by high levels of volatility in past. Intistieti and Case Basse Riservas released after 6-7 years. Other years only a single Brunello (designated Riserva if considered worthy). Best recent vintages are 1997, 95 and 90 (all five stars). Prices are always £H. (PW)

TALENTI Brunello di Montalcino   *UK stockists:* **Bib**, Hfx
Riccardo Talenti continues work of his father Pierluigi (who established reputation of Il Poggione). Talenti Brunello is ageworthy with classic character, breadth and style. Decent 96, good 98 and promising 99. Both regular and Riserva 95 and 97 approachable but will keep another 10 years. Talenti Rosso is fruit-centred blend of Sangiovese, Syrah, Canaiolo and Colorino. (PW)
- **Brunello di Montalcino★★★★** £E   Riserva★★★★ £F
- **Rosso di Montalcino★★** £C ● **Talenti★★** £C

TERRABIANCA Chianti Classico   www.terrabianca.com   *UK stockists:* **GWW**
The emphasis here is on stylish, accessible reds with supple textures. Ceppate (Cab Sauv/Merlot) is refined with plummy fruits and cured meats complexity. Campaccio (Sangiovese/Cab Sauv) is deeper and more oaky in a Riserva version. Both Piano del Cipresso (100% Sangiovese) and Chianti Classico Riserva Croce are more distinctly Tuscan. Other wines include Il Tesoro (Merlot) and a sweet white from dried grapes, Il Fior di Fino. (PW)
- **Ceppate★★★** £E ● **Campaccio★★** £D   Riserva★★★ £E
- **Chianti Classico** Riserva Croce★★ £C ● **Piano del Cipresso★★★** £D

TENUTA DI TRINORO www.trinoro.com   *UK stockists:* Sec, C&B, F&R
High quality, original wines from very high vineyards in virgin wine territory near Umbrian and Lazio borders. Trinoro (mostly Cab Franc with Merlot, Cab Sauv, Petit Verdot) has pure, concentrated black fruit and a hint of wild herbs in refined structure. Also new second wine, Le Cupole di Trinoro and tiny amount of Cincinnato (from Cesanese d'Affile). Palazzi (Merlot, Cab Franc) made until 99. Also Passopisciaro - old-vine Nerello Mascalese from slopes of Mount Etna. (PW)
- **Tenuta di Trinoro★★★★★** £G ● **Le Cupole★★★** £D

TUA RITA Val di Cornia   www.tuarita.it   *UK stockists:* **L&S, JAr**, CdP, Fal, F&R, Las
Rita Tua set standard for Suvereto. Redigaffi, among top Tuscany Merlots. More is produced of Giusto di Notri (Cabernet/Merlot) an equally powerful, textured, expansive style. Both require patience. Bigger volumes of red Perlato del Bosco (Sangiovese)with seductive, forward fruit and good depth. White Lodano (prev. Sileno) is aromatic, creamy blend of Chardonnay, Gewürz and Riesling. (PW)
- **Redigaffi★★★★★** £H ● **Giusto di Notri★★★★★** £F
- **Perlato del Bosco★★★** £D ○ **Lodano★★** £C

178

VALDICAVA   Brunello di Montalcino   *UK stockists:* **VDu**, Tur, F&R
Brunello of real weight, power and richness without recourse to new oak with excellent complexity and
dimension. Will improve for at least a decade, longer in Riserva Madonna del Piano (from1998, 97, 95 or
90). Regular Brunello was very good in 95 and 97, and super in 99. More advanced in 96 and, to a lesser
extent, 98. (PW)
● **Brunello di Montalcino★★★★** £F   Riserva Madonna del Piano★★★★★ £G
● **Rosso di Montalcino★★★** £C

TENUTA DI VALGIANO   Colline Lucchesi   www.valgiano.it   *UK stockists:* Sec
Leading estate in Lucchese hills. Biodynamic methods employed to help achieve a sense of place in wines. Estate
red (Sangiovese with Syrah, Merlot) is rich and succulent with good depth. Palistorti is similar blend from
younger vines. Most stylish is racy Scasso dei Cesari (pure Sangiovese) from 40-year-old vines. Also characterful
white, Giallo dei Muri (Vermentino, Trebbiano, Malvasia, Chardonnay). (PW)
● **Colline Lucchesi** Tenuta di Valgiano★★★★ £E   Scasso dei Cesari★★★ £E
● **Colline Lucchesi** Rosso dei Palistorti★★ £C   O **Giallo dei Muri★** £B

VECCHIE TERRE DI MONTEFILI   Chianti Classico   *UK stockists:* **RsW**, Rae, N&P
Reputation built around two very fine Super-Tuscans. Bruno di Rocca (Cab Sauv/Sangiovese) is stylish but
concentrated fusion of berryish fruit and elegant oak with age. More distinctive and increasingly rich with age is
Anfiteatro (pure Sangiovese). Adequate regular Chianti Classico, and oak-aged white, Villa Regis (Chardonnay
with Sauvignon, Traminer) should both be drunk young. (PW)
● **Bruno di Rocca★★★★** £F   ● **Anfiteatro★★★★** £F
● **Chianti Classico★** £C   O **Vigna Regis★** £D

VILLA CAFAGGIO   Chianti Classico   www.villacafaggio.it   *UK stockists:* HWC, BBR, Amp, N&P, Vne
Professionally directed estate with ripe, vibrant, almost chewy wines. Interventionist winemaking ensures high
level of consistency. New oak also important in San Martino (pure Sangiovese) and Cortaccio (100% Cab
Sauv). Also very good Chianti Classico Riserva (single-vineyard Solatio Basilica even better but not made
recently). All wines benefit from some extra bottle age. (PW)
● **Chianti Classico★★** £C   Riserva★★★ £D   Riserva Solatio Basilica★★★ £D
● **Cortaccio★★★** £E   ● **San Martino★★★** £E

Other wineries of note
Erik Banti (Morellino di Scansano), Tenuta di Bibbiano (Chianti Classico), Fattoria del Buonamico
(Montecarlo), Canneto (Vino Nobile di Montepulciano), Capannelle (Chianti Classico), Casa di Terra
(Bolgheri), Casaloste (Chianti Classico), Casanova delle Cerbaie (Brunello di Montalcino), Castellare di
Castellina (Chianti Classico), Castello della Paneretta (Chianti Classico), Castello di Querceto (Chianti
Classico), Castello Romitorio (Brunello di Montalcino), Cennatoio (Chianti Classico), Giovanni
Chiappini (Bolgheri), Donatella Cinelli Colombini (Brunello di Montalcino), Colle Santa Mustiola,
Collelceto (Brunello di Montalcino), Costanti (Brunello di Montalcino), Gagliole, Bibi Graetz,
Grattamacco/Colle Massari (Bolgheri), Gualdo del Re (Val di Cornia), Tenuta Il Borro, Il Palazzone
(Brunello di Montalcino), La Togata (Brunello di Montalcino), Lavacchio (Chianti Rufina), Le Filigare
(Chianti Classico), Fattoria Le Fonti (Chianti Classico), Le Sorgenti (Colli Fiorentini), Lisini (Brunello di
Montalcino), Livernano (Chianti Classico), Marchesi Pancrazi, Nittardi (Chianti Classico), Fattoria di
Petroio (Chianti Classico), Poggio Gagliardo (Montescudaio), Russo (Val di Cornia), Salicutti (Brunello
di Montalcino), San Felice (Chianti Classico), San Vincenti (Chianti Classico), Sangervasio (Terre di
Pisa), Solaria (Brunello di Montalcino), Fattoria Valtellina (Chianti Classico), Villa Mangicane (Chianti
Classico), Villa Pillo

An in-depth profile of every producer can be found in Wine behind the label 2006

Appellations:
1   Colli Bolognesi
2   Albana di Romagna
3   Sangiovese di Romagna
4   Colli Pesaresi
5   Falerio dei Colli Ascolani
6   Verdicchio dei Castelli di Jesi
7   Verdicchio di Matelica
8   Rosso Conero
9   Rosso Piceno
10   Rosso Piceno Superiore
11   Colli del Trasimeno
12   Torgiano Rosso Riserva
13   Montefalco Sagrantino

14   Colli Martani
15   Orvieto
16   Est! Est!! Est!!!
17   Colli Amerini
18   Frascati
19   Montepulciano d'Abruzzo
20   Biferno

New entries have producer's name underlined

Background

Just as culturally there is so much to be discovered just beyond the bounds of Tuscany so it is when it comes to viticulturally derived masterpieces. This is not a section of also-rans but includes exciting top-quality producers – some working in a Tuscan vein but with much more to offer besides. Away from those famous appellations can be found an increasing number of fine reds from not only from the likes of Sangiovese, Sagrantino and Montepulciano, native in these diverse regions, but also Cabernet Sauvignon and Merlot, as well as stylish whites from Verdicchio.

Wizard's Wishlist

Excellent Sangiovese di Romagna
STEFANO BERTI
● Sangiovese di Romagna Superiore Calisto
CASTELLUCCIO ● Ronco delle Ginestre
DREI DONÀ - LA PALAZZA
● Sangiovese di Romagna Superiore Riserva Pruno
SAN PATRIGNANO
● Sangiovese di Romagna Riserva Avi
SAN VALENTINO
● Sangiovese di Romagna Riserva Terra di Covignano
ZERBINA
● Sangiovese di Romagna Riserva Pietramora

Top Montepulciano based reds
PODERE CASTORANI ● Montepulciano d'Abruzzo
GAROFOLI ● Rosso Conero Riserva Grosso Agontano
LE TERRAZZE ● Rosso Conero Sassi Neri
LEOPARDI DITTAJUTI ● Rosso Conero Pigmento
MASCIARELLI ● Montepulciano d'Abruzzo Villa Gemma
ANTONIO & ELIO MONTI
● Montepulciano d'Abruzzo Pignotto

NICODEMI
● Montepulciano d'Abruzzo Colline Teramane Neromoro
OASI DEGLI ANGELI ● Kurni
SAN SAVINO - PODERE CAPECCI ● Quinta Regio
VALENTINI ● Montepulciano d'Abruzzo

Individual stars
BOCCADIGABBIA ● Akronte Cabernet Sauvignon
CAPRAI ● Montefalco Sagrantino 25 Anni
FALESCO ● Montiano
LA FIORITA LAMBORGHINI ● Campoleone
FATTORIA MANCINI ● Blu
PIEVE DEL VESCOVO ● Lucciaio
POGGIO BERTAIO ● Crovèllo
SPORTOLETTI ● Villa Fidelia Rosso
TABARRINI ● Montefalco Sagrantino Colle Grimaldesco
ZERBINA ● Marzieno

Alternatives to Chardonnay
CASTEL DE PAOLIS O Vigna Adriana
CORONCINO
O Verdicchio dei Castelli di Jesi Classico Superiore Gaiospino
GAROFOLI
O Verdicchio dei Castelli di Jesi Classico Superiore Podium
LA MONACESCA
O Verdicchio di Matelica La Monacesca
FATTORIA MANCINI O Pinot Nero Impero Bianco
SARTARELLI
O Verdicchio dei Castelli di Jesi Classico Superiore Contrada Balciana
VALENTINI O Trebbiano d'Abruzzo

Central Italy/A-Z of producers

BOCCADIGABBIA Marche www.boccadigabbia.com *UK stockists:* **L&S**
Boccadigabbia make some of the best Rosso Piceno going. The single vineyard Saltapicchio shows herbs, smoke and cherry fruit together with good acidity and well-balanced tannin. French varieties planted since early 19th century also of high standard, too – best wine is a stylish, powerful but elegant, pure blackcurrant-fruited Cabernet Sauvignon, Akronte. Also promising Merlot, Pix. (PW)
● Akronte★★★★ £E ● Rosso Piceno★★ £C ● Sangiovese Saltapicchio★★ £C
● Pix★★★ £E O Chardonnay Montalperti★★ £C

BUCCI Marche www.villabucci.com *UK stockists:* **Alv**
Well-known Verdicchio producer owing to Villa Bucci Riserva from 40-year-old vines. Refined, complex and concentrated, it can also age impressively; 01 is perhaps the best to date. New (01) Villa Bucci version of Rosso Piceno is 70/30 Montepulciano/Sangiovese and richer and rounder than the 50/50 Pongelli. (PW)
O Verdicchio dei Castelli di Jesi Classico Superiore★★ £B Riserva Villa Bucci★★★ £D
● Rosso Piceno Tenuta Pongelli★ £B Villa Bucci★★ £C

ITALY

ARNALDO CAPRAI Umbria www.arnaldocaprai.it UK stockists: **L&S, Bal**, JAr, P&S, Hrd
Modern powerhouse operation bringing wide recognition to Montefalco and Sagrantino grape. Leading
Sagrantino wines are extremely concentrated, powerful and structured needing at least 7-10 years' age; Sagrantino
25 Anni is an Italian classic. Montefalco Rosso Riserva is 70% Sangiovese with Sagrantino and Merlot. New is
Outsider (from 2000), a plush, concentrated red from Merlot and Cab Sauv. Most accessible is Poggio Belvedere
(unoaked Sangiovese and Ciliegiolo - 80/20). (PW)
- Montefalco Sagrantino CollePiano★★★★ £E 25 Anni✪✪✪✪✪ £F Passito★★★£F
- Montefalco Rosso★★ £C Riserva★★★ £D O Grechetto dei Colli Martani★★ £B

CASTELLO DELLA SALA Umbria www.antinori.it UK stockists: **BWC**, UnC, Sel
Antinori outpost with 160 ha in the vicinity of the 14th-century castle. Cervaro della Sala is one of Italy's best
and most ageworthy Chardonnays (that includes a little Grechetto), with a refinement and gentle minerality.
Also good value second Chardonnay. Conte della Vipera mostly Sauvignon while Muffato della Sala is an oak-
aged botrytised sweet wine from blend of Sauvignon, Grechetto, Gewürz and Riesling. Also decent Superiore
Orvieto. (PW)
- O Cervaro della Sala★★★★ £E O Chardonnay★★ £C Conte della Vipera★★ £C
- Pinot Nero★★ £E O Muffato della Sala★★ £E O Orvieto Classico Sup.★ £B

CASTELLUCCIO Romagna www.ronchidicastelluccio.it UK stockists: **Nov, Mgi**, Bal
Leading Romagna producer of Sangiovese owned by renown Tuscan consultant Vittorio Fiore (Poggio Scalette).
Ciliegi shows more class and elegance than an increasingly rich-fruited and good-value Sangiovese di Romagna,
Le More. Ginestre, the top wine, comes from a 2-ha site and adds more weight, power and complexity. Also
good Sauvignon, Lunaria - better than richer 'barriqued' Ronco del Re. Reds need time. Massicone, Cab Sauv
and Sangiovese is new. (PW)
- Ronco dei Ciliegi★★★ £C ● Ronco delle Ginestre★★★★ £D
- Sangiovese di Romagna Le More★★ £B ● Massicone★★★ £E O Lunaria★★ £B

PODERE CASTORANI Abruzzo www.poderecastorani.it UK stockists: **Eno**
First-rate Montepulciano d'Abruzzo from owners that include Formula One racing driver Jarno Trulli's father
and his manager. A very good 2000, beautifully made with concentrated black cherry and spice, has been
followed by an even more convincing 01. One to follow. (PW)
- Montepulciano d'Abruzzo★★★ £E

COLPETRONE Umbria www.saiagricola.it UK stockists: **Tri**, Por
Like Caprai, an established benchmark for Sagrantino. Impressive black plum, smoke and herb-fuelled Sagrantino
has formidable power, extract and intensity, often needing a decade or longer. Montefalco Rosso too is typically
concentrated with plenty of extract. Also an intense, complex and well-balanced *passito*. (PW)
- Montefalco Sagrantino★★★★ £E Passito★★★ £F
- Montefalco Rosso★★ £C

CONTRADA CASTELLETTA Marche UK stockists: **Lib**, ACh
Domenico D'Angelo is the viticulturalist for Saladini Pilastri. His own wine, Vespro (70/30 Montepulciano/Syrah)
is produced from low yields and the 02 shows splendid black plum, spice, licorice and carob fruit in a modern style.
It currently represents great value. New is Rosso Piceno, Fausto. (PW)
- Vespro★★★★ £C

CORONCINO Marche UK stockists: **Mgi**, L&W
Better Verdicchio than Coroncino's Gaiospino is hard to find. The wine has a gentle pear and quince fruit
intensity, with definition and style that belie its body. A Fumé version was also made in 1998. A second
Verdicchio, Il Coroncino is less refined but has good fruit richness. New from 2000 is a pricey new premium
Verdicchio, Stracacio. (PW)
- O Verdicchio dei Castelli di Jesi Classico Superiore Il Coroncino★★ £B
- O Verdicchio dei Castelli di Jesi Classico Bacco★ £B Gaiospino★★★ £C

DI MAJO NORANTE Molise www.dimajonorante.com UK stockists: **L&S**
Molise's top producer is essentially organic and recently more consistent. Wines led by rich, oaky premium red
Don Luigi (90% Montepulciano) Long-established Ramitello Rosso is ripe, characterful Sangiovese and
Aglianico blend. Whites are ripe and clean with plenty of fruit - Biblos from Falanghina and Greco (70/30).

New entries have producer's name underlined

Generally well-priced for the fruit and character they deliver. (PW)
● **Molise** Don Luigi★★★ £E Aglianico Contado★★ £B ● **Biferno** Ramitello★★ £B
● **Sangiovese★** £B O **Biblos**★★ £B O **Molise** Greco★★ £B Falanghina★★ £B

FALESCO Lazio www.falesco.it *UK stockists:* **BWC**, N&P, Blx
Property of Italy's most famous winemaker brothers – Renzo Cotarella, Antinori's winemaker, and top enologist
Riccardo Cotarella. Atypically good Est! Est!! Est!!! - also made in late-harvest version. Reds are the stars:
Montiano - high-quality, lush, showy Merlot; at least as impressive Marciliano (since 1999) from Cab Sauv and
Cab Franc. Both need 8-10 years' age. More affordable are 'second' fruity Merlot (dell'Umbria) and large
volume Vitiano (Cab Sauv, Merlot and Sangiovese). (PW)
● **Montiano**★★★★★ £E ● **Marciliano**★★★★★ £E ● **Merlot**★★ £C
O **Est! Est!! Est!!!** Poggio dei Gelsi★★ £B Vendemmia Tardiva★★ £D

GAROFOLI Marche www.garofolivini.it *UK stockists:* **Hal**
Top-quality Verdicchio from low yields. Oak-aged Riserva Serra Fiorese shows
considerable richness and depth with 3-4 years' age, but best is unoaked Podium, with lovely breadth, weight
and a refinement. Also made are a *passito* version, Brumato, and a sparkling version. Both Rosso Conero are
100% Montepulciano - premium oak-aged Grosso Agontano has ample breadth and complexity. Good price
quality ratio. (PW)
O **Verdicchio dei Castelli di Jesi Classico** Podium★★★ £B Serra Fiorese★★★ £C
● **Rosso Conero** Vigna Piancarda★★ £B Riserva Grosso Agontano★★★ £D

LA FIORITA LAMBORGHINI Umbria www.lamborghinionline.it *UK stockists:* SCh, JAr, Las
Beautiful estate with two top reds. Campoleone, Sangiovese/Merlot shows terrific intensity, powerful new oak
and crushed small berry fruit within a vibrant structure. Needs 6-10 years' ageing. Second wine, Trescone is
ready sooner - a sleek and intense blend of Sangiovese, Ciliegiolo and Merlot (50/30/20) with distinctive plum
and cherry fruit. (PW)
● **Campoleone**★★★★★ £F ● **Trescone**★★ £C

LA MONACESCA Marche www.monacesca.it *UK stockists:* **Wtr**, Gen, Add, UnC, Las
Located in Matelica, the smaller, lesser of two Verdicchio zones. Ripe and concentrated unoaked Verdicchio
with good depth and character especially in superior La Monacesca bottling. Top white is richer Mirum, from
late-harvested grapes, giving added richness and complexity. All three keep well. Also Chardonnay, Ecclesia, and
increasingly good red, Camerte (Sangiovese/Merlot). (PW)
O **Verdicchio di Matelica★** £B La Monacesca★★ £B Riserva Mirum ★★★ £C
● **Camerte★★★** £D

LA VALENTINA Abruzzo www.fattorialavalentina.it *UK stockists:* UnC
In the past these wines were compromised by too much extract and tannin. Two special *cuvées* of Montepulciano
d'Abruzzo, Spelt and Bellovedere, are impressively complex and structured (cellar from 01). Binomio is produced
with Stefano INAMA (see North-East Italy). Aged in new French *barriques* it offers more cherry/berry and spice and
less coffee and herb; the 2002 has more charm than 01 or 00. (PW)
La Valentina
◉ **Montepulciano d'Abruzzo Cerasuolo★** £B
● **Montepulciano d'Abruzzo** Spelt★★★ £C Bellovedere★★★★ £E
Binomio
● **Montepulciano d'Abruzzo** Binomio★★★ £E

LE TERRAZZE Marche www.fattorialeterrazze.it
Bob Dylan-mad Antonio Terni's Rosso Conero (100% Montepulciano) shows better ripeness and richness than
most. Barrique-aged Sassi Neri shows real depth, succulence and elegance while Chaos is (new oak aged) lush,
black-fruited blend of Montepulciano, Syrah and Merlot. Visions of J is made in exceptional years. Also a little
unoaked Chardonnay, Le Cave. (PW)
● **Rosso Conero★** £B Sassi Neri★★★ £D ● **Chaos**★★★ £E O **Le Cave★** £B

FATTORIA MANCINI Marche www.fattoriamancini.com *UK stockists:* **BWC**, P&S, Vts
Pinot Nero is Luigi Mancini's grape of choice on slopes high above the rim of the Adriatic from which a white,

Impero Bianco, of exotic, almost decadent fruit character is made - as unoaked Roncaglia (which includes Albanella). Best Pinot, however, goes into 3 bold reds that require patience. Meaty Impero Rosso has old-fashioned Burgundian character and complexity. Powerful black-fruited Blu now adds Montepulciano to Pinot Nero and Ancellotto. (PW)

● **Blu★★★** £D   ● **Colli Pesaresi Focara** Pinot Nero Impero★★★ £D
O **Colli Pesaresi** Roncaglia★★ £B   O **Impero Bianco★★** £B

MASCIARELLI Abruzzo   www.masciarelli.it   *UK stockists:* CdP, P&S, N&P
Flag-bearer for Montepulciano d'Abruzzo. Villa Gemma is the top wine and impresses for its texture, depth and richness of fruit but increasingly good Marina Cvetic San Martino version too. Also improving Cab Sauv and white barrel-fermented Trebbiano d'Abruzzo with good depth and breadth and fine herbal, mineral complexity. Cerasuolo is also made. (PW)

● **Montepulciano d'Abruzzo** Villa Gemma★★★★ £F   San Martino Rosso★★★ £D
O **Trebbiano d'Abruzzo** Marina Cvetic★★★ £E

ANTONIO & ELIO MONTI Abruzzo   www.vinimonti.it
Small family producer making powerful, structured reds, although recently showing more oak influence, vigour and fruit purity. Top wine is wonderfully complex but powerful and extracted single-vineyard Pignotto that demands 10 years' ageing. Also characterful white Raggio di Luna (mostly Chardonnay and Trebbiano) and pretty Cerasuolo. (PW)

● **Montepulciano d'Abruzzo Colline Teramane** Pignotto★★★★ £E
● **Montepulciano d'Abruzzo** Senior★★★ £C
● **Controguerra** Riserva Rio Moro★★★ £C   O **Controguerra** Raggio di Luna★ £B

NICODEMI Abruzzo   *UK stockists:* Bli
Significant producer of Montepulciano d'Abruzzo Colline Teramane. Single-vineyard Neromoro is powerful and extracted. Rich and meaty with plenty of oak, it shows great promise from 2001 and 02 but give it 8–10 years. Notàri (from 03) has a sweet fruit core but less well-integrated oak and firmer tannins. A partly *barrique*-fermented white equivalent is stylish and creamy. (PW)

● **Montepulciano d'Abruzzo★** £B   O **Trebbiano d'Abruzzo★** £B   Notàri★★ £C
● **Montepulciano d'Abruzzo Colline Teramane** Notàri★★ £C   Neromoro★★★★ £E

OASI DEGLI ANGELI Marche   www.kurni.it   *UK stockists:* Wtr, PaV, BBR, F&R
Just one very sought-after wine. Kurni is a powerful, very ripe, complex example of Montepulciano. Fruit verges on the over-ripe but it usually achieves balance if teetering on the brink with a richness and extract balanced by fine tannins. Quantities are increasing but very small. (PW)

● **Kurni★★★★** £F

PALAZZONE Umbria   www.palazzone.com   *UK stockists:* J&B, Win
About as good as it gets – for Orvieto that is. Terre Vineate has ripe, pure fruit while Campo del Guardiano is richer with very ripe citrus fruit, even a touch of honey. Also perfumed Grechetto and good-value, zesty, minerally, citrusy Dubini Bianco. Rubbio (mostly Sangiovese) has good purity. Less consistent are Cab Sauv/Cab Franc blend Armaleo (try 2000) and sweet Muffa Nobile (Sauvignon). (PW)

O **Dubini Bianco★** £B   O **Grechetto★★** £B
O **Orvieto Classico** Terre Vineate★★ £B   Campo del Guardiano★★ £C
O **Muffa Nobile★★** £E   ● **Rubbio★★** £C   ● **Armaleo★★** £D

POGGIO BERTAIO Umbria   *UK stockists:* L&S
From close to Lago Trasimeno. Cab Sauv and Merlot really excel in *barrique*-aged Crovèllo – rich with blackberry, mineral, oak spice and a touch of carob and licorice. Cimbolo (Sangiovese) is more compact in profile and less of a blockbuster. Both are ageworthy. (PW)

● **Cimbolo★★★** £D   ● **Crovèllo★★★★** £E

SALADINI PILASTRI Marche   www.saladinipilastri.it   *UK stockists:* Lib, ACh
Increasingly organic estate. Best is concentrated Vigna Monteprandone (70% Montepulciano) with truffle, plum, blackberry and spice, but intense fruit in all Rosso Piceno. In Pregio del Conte, Aglianico instead of Sangiovese complements Montepulciano. Vigna Palazzi white includes Sauvignon and Chardonnay. Wine

director Domenico D'Angelo also makes own wine at Contrada Castelletta estate. (PW)
● **Rosso Piceno Superiore**★★ £B Montetinello★★ £B Monteprandone★★★ £C
● **Rosso Piceno** Piediprato★★ £B O **Falerio** Vigna Palazzi★★ £B

SAN PATRIGNANO   Romagna   www.sanpatrignano.org
Remarkable community for drug and social rehabilitation near Rimini. Wines made by Riccardo Cotarella (see
Falesco) are very good indeed. Very small amounts of top wine, Sangiovese di Romagna Riserva Avi which is
very concentrated, dense and structured but with a sleek and elegant texture. Also impressive Riserva
Zarricante. Regular Aulente exhibits lovely pure cherry fruit and good depth. All three need time as does
Montepirolo, a classy Bordeaux blend. (PW)
● **Sangiovese di Romagna** Aulente★★ £C Riserva Zarricante★★★ £D
● **Sangiovese di Romagna** Riserva Avi★★★★£E ● **Montepirolo**★★★ £E

SAN SAVINO – PODERE CAPECCI   Marche   www.sansavino.com
One of the most exciting estates in the southern Marche. White from Pecorino is arguably the most distinctive
made. Reds include lush, complex Picus (65/35 Montepulciano/Sangiovese) and stylish if oaky Fedus (100%
Sangiovese). Also pure, concentrated Ver Sacrum (unoaked Montepulciano) and rich, powerful and complete
Quinta Regio (oak-aged Montepulciano) – both deserve 5 years' ageing. (PW)
O **Offida Pecorino** Ciprea★★ £C
● **Rosso Piceno** Superiore Picus★★★ £D ● **Ver Sacrum**★★★ £E
● **Fedus**★★★ £E ● **Quinta Regio**★★★★ £E

SAN VALENTINO   Romagna   www.vinisanvalentino.com   _UK stockists:_ **Eno**
14-ha estate progressively improved over last 15 years. Two fine Sangiovese di Romagna: pure ripe-fruited Scabi
and classy intense Riserva Terra di Covignano, that also benefits from some old-vine fruit. Powerful Cab Sauv,
Luna Nuova has the blackberry, mineral and earth of good Romagna Cabernet. (PW)
● **Sangiovese di Romagna Superiore** Scabi★★ £B Ris.Terra di Covignano★★★★ £D
● **Luna Nuova**★★★ £E

SARTARELLI   Marche   www.sartarelli.it   _UK stockists:_ **Ast**, P&S, UnC, F&M
Source of ripe, flavoursome Verdicchio. Regular version is typically bright, fresh and fruit-driven with ripe
apple, floral and yellow plum flavours. Tralivio has richer texture from part barrique-ageing but less refinement
and fruit purity. Barrique-aged Contrada Balciana has good intensity and lots of depth and character if also
missing a little refinement. (PW)
O **Verdicchio dei Castelli di Jesi Classico**★★ £B Tralivio★★ £C
O **Verdicchio dei Castelli di Jesi Classico** Contrada Balciana★★ £D

SPORTOLETTI   Umbria   www.sportoletti.com   _UK stockists:_ **L&S**
One of the best of a new wave of producers in Umbria and Lazio. Top red, Villa Fidelia, is deep, concentrated
oak-aged blend (Merlot with Cab Sauv, Cab Franc) with splendid smoke, sweet spice and mineral individuality
- potentially a classic. Assisi Rosso (Merlot/Sangiovese) is ripe and plummy while Villa Fidelia Bianco is oak-
aged Chardonnay/Grechetto blend. (PW)
● **Villa Fidelia Rosso**★★★★★ £E ● **Assisi** Rosso★★ £B
O **Villa Fidelia Bianco**★★ £C O **Assisi** Grechetto★ £B

TABARRINI   Umbria   www.tabarrini.com
Newish Montefalco enterprise already producing fine Sagrantino. Fruit is picked very late to achieve fully ripe
tannins. 2001 shows oak spice, floral and truffle aromas and concentrated bitter chocolate, black cherry and black
plum fruit on the palate with lots of depth, breadth and extract. Best with 8–10 years' ageing. Also striking 03
Rosso, needing 3–5 years' age, and promising mineral-imbued white. (PW)
O **Bianco**★★ £B ● **Montefalco Rosso** Colle Grimaldesco★★ £C
● **Montefalco Sagrantino** Colle Grimaldesco★★★★ £E

UMANI RONCHI   Marche   www.umanironchi.it   _UK stockists:_ **Eno**, JNi,Vne,Vts, Sel
Reliable big volume producer if missing excitement of newer or smaller producers. Verdicchio in unwooded
Villa Bianchi and Casal di Serra versions (new Vecchie Vigne version shows more intensity, vigour), also
partially oak-aged/fermented Riserva Plenio. Le Busche is Verdicchio and Chardonnay. Characterful reds from

ITALY

Montepulciano include Rosso Conero San Lorenzo and Cúmaro. Pelago (Cab Sauv, Merlot) is richer, oakier flagship red. Also varietal Sangiovese, Medoro, and a sweet white botrytised Sauvignon, Maximo. (PW)

O **Verdicchio dei Castelli di Jesi** Casal di Serra★ £B Riserva Plenio★★ £C
● **Pelago**★★★ £E ● **Rosso Conero** San Lorenzo★ £B Cúmaro★★ £C

VALENTINI Abruzzo *UK stockists:* **Wtr**, CdP, BBR
One of the great alternatives to modern winemaking with only small volumes released (when ready to drink) under Valentini's distinctive label. At its best, red has great power, dimension and complexity of dried flowers, cedar, coffee, spice, pepper and berry fruit. Best are 1995, 92, 90, 88 and 85. White, more notable for texture than richness, shows a subtle range of floral, herbal and fruit-derived scents. Also pink Cerasuolo. (PW)
● **Montepulciano d'Abruzzo**★★★★ £F O **Trebbiano d'Abruzzo**★★★ £F

ZERBINA Romagna www.zerbina.com *UK stockists:* **CdP**
Brilliantly run with classy top red, Pietramora from single vineyard of old vines. Torre di Ceparano from denser but youner plantings. Unoaked Ceregio is supple, fruity - better as special selection, Vigna Querce (01,97). Marzieno (Sangiovese, Cab Sauv, Merlot) is lush and powerful. Scacco Matto is an excellent rich, botrytised white; second version, Arrocco, is lighter. (PW)
● **Sangiovese di Romagna Sup.** Torre di Ceparano★★ £C Ris. Pietramora★★★★ £E
● **Marzieno**★★★ £E O **Albana di Romagna** Arrocco★ £D Scacco Matto★★★ £F

Other wineries of note
Aurora (Marche), Giuseppe Beghelli (Emilia-Romagna), Stefano Berti (Emilia-Romagna), Cataldi Madonna (Abruzzo), Floriano Cinti (Emilia-Romagna), Dezi (Marche), Drei Donà - La Palazza (Emilia-Romagna), Goretti (Umbria), Leopardi Dittajuti (Marche), Madonna Alta (Umbria), Perticaia (Umbria), Pieve del Vescovo (Umbria), Scacciadiavoli (Umbria), Terre Rosse (Emilia-Romagna)

An in-depth profile of every producer can be found in Wine behind the label 2006

New entries have producer's name underlined

Foggia

VOLTURNO *A*
Benevento
Caserta • *2* • *4*
Napoli • *3* • Avellino
Vesuvio • Salerno

Bari

6

5

7

C

Brindisi

Potenza

B

Taranto *8* *10*
9

Arzachena
20
• Sassari
21
Alghero

Nuoro

SARDEGNA
22
Oristano *24*

Regions:
A Campania
B Basilicata
C Puglia
D Calabria

D

Cosenza
12

11

23 Cagliari

Messina
13 • Reggio di Calabria

Palermo

Trapani *17*
18
17 *19*

Etna *14*

16

SICILIA

Catania

15

Siracusa

Appellations:

1	Falerno del Massico	13	Faro
2	Greco di Tufo	14	Etna
3	Fiano di Avellino	15	Cerasuolo di Vittoria
4	Taurasi	16	Contea di Sclafani
5	Aglianico del Vulture	17	Marsala
6	Castel del Monte	18	Alcamo
7	Gioia del Colle	19	Contessa Entellina
8	Primitivo di Manduria	20	Vermentino di Gallura
9	Brindisi	21	Alghero
10	Salice Salentino	22	Vernaccia di Oristano
11	Cirò	23	Carignano del Sulcis
12	Savuto	24	Vermentino di Sardegna,
			Cannonau di Sardegna

ITALY

Background

For years fans of Italian wine have glimpsed the quality and originality of the south but have been frustrated by a lack of consistently fine examples. Since the mid- to late nineties, the once-isolated pockets of quality have been growing and spreading and there are now many excellent producers in the Mezzogiorno. As in much of Italy the general standard of winemaking is at an unprecedented level. Add this to some high-quality vineyard sources, both new and old, and a rich hoard of native grape varieties and you begin to see what is possible. Campania vies with Puglia and Sicily as the south's most important quality wine producing area but there are now both good-value bottles and world-class wines, often with prices to match, to be had in all regions.

Wizard's Wishlist

Southern red stars
ABBAZIA SANTA ANASTASIA ● Litra
ARGIOLAS ● Turriga
FEUDO MONTONI ● Vrucara Selezione Speciale
LIBRANDI ● Gravello
MONTEVETRANO ● Montevetrano
ODOARDI ● Scavigna Vigna Garrone
PALARI ● Faro
SANTADI ● Carignano del Sulcis Superiore Terre Brune
TASCA D'ALMERITA
● Contea di Sclafani Rosso del Conte
COSIMO TAURINO ● Patriglione
VALLONE ● Graticciaia
CONTI ZECCA ● Nero

Superior expressions of Aglianico
ANTONIO CAGGIANO
● Taurasi Vigna Macchia dei Goti
CANTINE DEL NOTAIO
● Aglianico del Vulture La Firma
D'ANGELO ● Canneto

MASSERIA FELICIA
● Falerno del Massico Etichetta Bronzo
FEUDI DI SAN GREGORIO ● Taurasi Selve di Luoti
GALARDI ● Terra di Lavoro
TENUTA LE QUERCE
● Aglianico del Vulture Vigna Corona
PATERNOSTER ● Aglianico del Vulture Rotondo

Brilliant inexpensive reds
ACCADEMIA DEI RACEMI/SINFAROSA
● Primitivo di Mandura Zinfandel
ALESSANDRO DI CAMPOREALE ● Kaid
LEONE DE CASTRIS ● Salice Salentino Riserva
MORGANTE ● Nero d'Avola
TELARO/LAVORO & SALUTE
● Galluccio Montecaruso
CANTINA DEL TABURNO
● Aglianico del Taburno Fidelis
TORREVENTO ● Castel del Monte Riserva Vigna Pedale
VALLONE ● Salice Salentino Vereto
VETRERE ● Tempio di Giano

Captivating whites
CAPICHERA O Capichera
GIOVANNI CHERCHI
O Vermentino di Sardegna Tuvaoes
GULFI O Carjcanti
CUSUMANO O Cubia
FEUDI DI SAN GREGORIO
O Sannio Falanghina
PLANETA O Cometa
TORMARESCA O Castel del Monte Pietrabianca

Delicious sweet whites
ARGIOLAS O Angialis
BOTROMAGNO O Gravisano Passito di Malvasia
DE BARTOLI O Passito di Pantelleria Bukkuram
FEUDI DI SAN GREGORIO O Privilegio
SALVATORE MURANA
O Passito di Pantelleria Martingana
SANTADI O Latinia

Southern Italy & Islands/A-Z of producers

ABBAZIA SANTA ANASTASIA Sicilia www.abbaziasantanastasia.it   *UK stockists:* **L&S**
Superbly sited estate high above the sea on the north coast of Sicily. Impressive top wine, Litra is 100 % Cab Sauv. Still-improving Passomaggio is Nero d'Avola with 20% Merlot. Whites include Baccante, a late-harvested, new oak-fermented and aged Chardonnay, and Gemelli, Chardonnnay with a little Sauvignon. Unwooded Bianco di Passamaggio is mostly Inzolia. Least expensive are a basic trio of red, white and rosé. (PW)
● Litra★★★★ £E   ● Montenero★★ £C   ● Passomaggio★★ £B
O Baccante★★ £C   O Gemelli★★ £C   O Bianco di Passamaggio★ £B

ALESSANDRO DI CAMPOREALE Sicilia www.alessandrodicamporeale.it   *UK stockists:* **Bia**
Brothers Rosolino, Antonino and Natale Alessandro currently produce 2 good-value reds. Donna Ta' is a good, supple everyday version of Nero d'Avola, while Kaid is an expressive, characterful Syrah with some propensity for ageing. (PW)
● Donna Ta'★★ £B   ● Kaid★★★ £C

188

ACCADEMIA DEI RACEMI Puglia www.accademiadeiracemi.it *UK stockists:* **Mer,** Wtr, UnC
Umbrella organisation for a network of growers in Salento peninsula promoting good-value reds especially from
old Primitivo vines. Led by Pervini and the younger generation of the Perrucci family (own estate is Felline),
typically all the wines have good fruit, balance and real character. Primo Amore is a sweet version of Primitivo.
Wines from Masseria Pepe, Casale Bevagna (Salice Salentino), Tenuta Pozzopalo and Torre Guaceto should not
be overlooked either, epecially the Primitivos. (PW)

Pervini
- **Primitivo di Manduria** Archidamo★★ £B Primo Amore★★ £C
- **Bizantino Rosso★★** £B ● **Squinzano** L'Evangelista★★ £B

Felline
- **Primitivo di Manduria★★★** £B ● **Vigna del Feudo★★** £B ● **Alberello★** £B

Sinfarosa
- **Primitivo di Manduria** Zinfandel★★★ £C ● **Primitivo★★** £B

ARGIOLAS Sardegna www.cantine-argiolas.it *UK stockists:* **Eur,** F&R
230-ha estate with the emphasis on local Sardinian varieties providing good examples of island's more widely seen
DOCs. Best wines are IGT Isola dei Nuraghi. Argiolas is mostly Vermentino, while Angialis, a fine light sweet
wine, is Nasco and Malvasia. Newish Cerdeña is a (pricey) *barrique*-fermented and aged Vermentino. Top red
is the deep but structured Turriga, based on Cannonau. Similarly structured is Korem, from Bovale,
Carignano and a little Cannonau. (PW)
- **Turriga★★★★** £F ● **Korem★★** £D ● **Cannonau di Sardegna** Costera★★ £C
○ **Angialis★★★** £D ○ **Vermentino di Sardegna** Costamolino★★ £B

BASILISCO Basilicata *UK stockists:* **GID**
Michele Cutolo's Aglianico del Vulture comes from volcanic soils on slopes at 400m. Quality is further improved in
a 2001 with distinctive personality – an amalgam of black fruits, mineral and earth. Only shows full potential with
6–8 years' age. (PW)
- **Aglianico del Vulture★★★** £D

BENANTI Sicilia www.vinicolabenanti.it *UK stockists:* **Nov**
Wines of character and individuality from old-vines on Mount Etna. Varietal reds less convincing but excellent
Lamorèmio red (Nerello Mascalese, Nero d'Avola, Cab Sauv). Rosso di Verzella, Rovittello and Serra della
Contessa all combine Nerello Mascalese and Nerello Cappuccio. Sound whites include scented and intense
Pietramarina (Carricante), flavoursome Edèlmio (Carricante, Chardonnay) and unique varietal Minnella. Also
very good sweet Passito di Pantelleria. (PW)
- **Lamorèmio★★★★** £E ● **Etna** Serra della Contessa★★ £D Rovittello★★ £C
○ **Passito di Pantelleria** Coste di Mueggen★★★ £E

BOTROMAGNO Puglia www.botromagno.it *UK stockists:* **Eno**
Co-op with 3 excellent wines. Dry white is perfumed and well-structured Gravina. Red, Pier delle Vigne, combines
Aglianico and Montepulciano and is very 'southern' in style with preserved black fruits and raisins. Gravisano is fine
southern Italy sweet white with preserved fruits, honey and spice intensity (try the 2000). (PW)
○ **Gravina★★** £B ○ **Gravisano** Passito di Malvasia★★★ £E
- **Pier delle Vigne★★★** £C ● **Primitivo★** £B

ANTONIO CAGGIANO Campania www.cantinecaggiano.it *UK stockists:* **J&B**
Single-vineyard Taurasi Vigna Macchia dei Goti has classic tar, earth, smoke and black plum fruit characters,
with no lack of depth or character and fine tannins. Also fine single vineyard Salae Domini. Taurì is inexpensive
Aglianico. White FiaGre is a barrique-aged blend of Fiano and Greco (70/30). Potent Greco di Tufo, Devon,
made in 2002. Also elegant sweet white, Mel, from dried Fiano and Greco grapes. (PW)
- **Taurasi** Vigna Macchia dei Goti★★★ £E ● **Salae Dominii★★★** £D
- **Taurì★★** £C ○ **Fiano di Avellino** Béchar★★ £C ○ **Mel★★★** £E

CANDIDO Puglia www.candidowines.it *UK stockists:* **Eno**
Synonymous with good-value, characterful Puglian reds; whites too are recently improved with more life and
intensity, notably the stylish VignaVinera. Reds include a very 'southern' savoury Salice; intense, meaty, black-fruited

ITALY

Cappello di Prete (Negroamaro); intense, black-fruited Immensum (70/30 Negroamaro/Cab Sauv); and full-bodied Duca di Aragona (80/20 Negroamaro, Montepulciano) – a composed and complex red with 5–10 years' age. Also Aleatico, an aromatic medium-sweet red. (PW)

● Salice Salentino Riserva★★ £B ● Cappello di Prete★★★ £B
● Immensum★★★ £C ● Duca di Aragona★★★ £C
O VignaVinera★★ £B ◉ Salice Salentino Le Pozzelle★ £B

CANTINE DEL NOTAIO Basilcata www.cantinedelnotaio.com *UK stockists:* BBR
New operation making exciting Aglianico del Vulture. Best La Firma (needing 5-6 years') is very promising in 2000 and 01. A second example, Il Repetorio, has less depth but is more immediate and fruit-accented. Sweet apricotty L'Autentica is from Moscato and Malvasia grapes. (PW)

● Aglianico del Vulture Il Repetorio★★ £C La Firma★★★★ £D
O L'Autentica★★ £E

CAPICHERA Sardegna www.capichera.it *UK stockists:* Bal, JNi
60 ha in far north of Sardinia for very good if pricey Vermentino whites and and Carignano reds. 'Capichera' is intense, perfumed estate white; Vigna'ngena - a more affordable version. Barrique-aged Vendemmia Tardiva is splendid, refined, late-harvested but dry. Both Carignanos are ripe and classy - powerful barrique-aged Mantènghja has added depth and concentration but needs 8 years' or more. (PW)

● Mantènghja★★★★ £F ● Assajé★★★ £D O Vendemmia Tardiva★★★ £F
O Capichera★★ £D O Vermentino di Gallura Vigna 'Ngena★★ £C

CEUSO Sicilia www.ceuso.it *UK stockists:* CdP
High-quality reds that combine the traditional and modern. Custera, a wonderfully characterful, concentrated and powerful red with deep smoky, earthy aromas combines Nero d'Avola with Cab Sauv and Merlot (50/30/20). Fastaia, added in 2000, is fine second wine. New from 2002 is Scurati, a reasonably priced varietal Nero d'Avola. (PW)

● Custera★★★ £D ● Fastaia★★ £C

COTTANERA Sicilia www.cottanera.it *UK stockists:* Ast, L&W
New Mount Etna winery with vineyards at 700 m. Top reds Grammonte (Merlot), Nume (Cab Sauv), Sole di Sesta (Syrah) and L'Ardenza (Mondeuse) show remarkable fruit intensity, concentration and definition. Intense, complex Fatagione is Nerello Mascalese/Nero d'Avola (90/10). Barbazzale red is similar blend but more open and immediate, the unoaked white is old vine Inzolia. (PW)

● Grammonte★★★ £E ● L'Ardenza★★★ £E ● Sole di Sesta★★★ £E
● Nume★★★ £E ● Fatagione★★★ £D ● Barbazzale Rosso★★ £B

D'ANGELO Basilicata *UK stockists:* Alv, Sel
D'Angelo reds are most impressive with age adding greater richness, harmony and a deep, savoury complexity. Impressive Riserva Caselle from single vineyard, Canneto from old vines and barrique-aged. Serra delle Querce adds Merlot to Aglianico. New Donato d'Angelo is expansive and very long (in 2000) but also needs time. (PW)

● Aglianico del Vulture★★ £B Riserva Vigna Caselle★★★ £C
● Canneto★★★★ £C ● Serra delle Querce★★★★ £D

MARCO DE BARTOLI Sicilia *UK stockists:* Cib
Crusader for the original unfortified Marsala. Vecchio Samperi Ventennale - unsweetened and unfortified blend including some very old wine shows rich, toffeed dry fruits, candied peel, dates and nuts. Vigna La Miccia is youngest, freshest style while Marsala Superiore (fortified) from *solera* type system. Also very good Passito di Pantelleria Bukkuram, and Pietranera (dry version of Zibibbo). New are dry white from Grillo, Grappoli del Grillo, and Merlot, Rosso di Marco. (PW)

O Vigna La Miccia★★ £C O Marsala Superiore★★★ £D O Pietranera★★ £B
O Vecchio Samperi Ventennale★★★★ £D O Passito Pantelleria Bukkuram★★★ £D

DE CONCILIIS Campania www.viticoltorideconciliis.it *UK stockists:* Rae
Fine wines predominantly from Fiano (whites) and Aglianico (reds). New (2003) is Antece, a rich, structured and complex white. The top red Naima is *barrique*-aged Aglianico. Brilliant in 2001 and 03 (★★★★★), it is lush, concentrated and splendidly complex. Ra! from partially dried, foot-trodden grapes is moderately sweet with an

190

intense ripe fruit, spice and earth character. (PW)
- **Donnaluna Aglianico★★** £C ● **Naima★★★★** £E ● **Ra!★★★** £D
- ○ **Donnaluna Fiano★** £B ○ **Antece★★★** £C ○ **Selim Brut★** £B

DONNAFUGATA Sicilia www.donnafugata.it   *UK stockists:* **Vim**, Hrd, F&M
Reds and whites grown at altitude in western Sicily. Reds recently much richer, softer with finer tannins including complex and classy Mille e Una Notte (Nero d'Avola), more refined Tancredi (esp. 2000, 01 - Nero d'Avola, Cab Sauv) and Angheli (Nero d'Avola/Merlot). Whites include scented stylish Vigna di Gabri (Inzolia) and Chardonnay Chiarandà del Merlo with a southern richness. Also aromatic Anthìlia (Ansonica/Cataratto) and intense, dried fruits Ben Ryé. (PW)
- **Contessa Entellina** Tancredi★★★ £D   Mille e Una Notte★★★★ £F
- ○ **Contessa Entellina** Vigna di Gabri★★ £C ○ **Passito Pantelleria** Ben Ryé★★★ £E

MASSERIA FELICIA Campania www.masseriafelicia.it_
What awesome vineyard sites there must exist in Campania! Here we have relatively young vines but already super wines. Reds of tremendous extract and richness are 80/20 Aglianico/Piedirosso. Etichetta Bronzo 2003 promises to be stunning but the 02 also promises much if you are patient. Quantities of all wines are very small. (PW)
- **Falerno del Massico** Ariapetrina★★★★ £C Etichetta Bronzo★★★★★ £E
- ○ **Anthologia** Falanghina★★ £C

FEUDI DI SAN GREGORIO Campania www.feudi.it   *UK stockists:* **Alv**, Odd, P&S, F&R, Wai
Region's leading producer. Modern, oak-enriched reds with fabulous fruit, concentration and depth. Very fine Taurasi and Serpico, a wine of majestic depth and length of flavour. Pàtrimo (since 1999) is prodigious Merlot, with marvellous fruit and depth. Good Fiano, Greco and Falanghina dry whites. Partly barrique-aged and late-harvested Campanaro is rich and exotic. Moderately sweet Privilegio (botrytised grapes) has intense ripe fruit. Blended Idem also sweet. Quality and value in Rubrato (Aglianico) and excellent newish Aglianico del Vulture and Primitivo di Manduria. (PW)
- **Taurasi★★★** £C   Piano di Montevergine★★★★ £E   Selve di Luoti★★★★ £E
- **Serpico★★★★★** £F ● **Pàtrimo★★★★** £F ● **Rubrato★★** £B
- ○ **Campanaro★★★** £D ○ **Idem★★★** £E ○ **Privilegio★★★** £E

FEUDO MACCARI Sicilia www.feudomaccari.it   *UK stockists:* SCh, Ssx
Sicilian outpost of Antonio Moretti (owner of Sette Ponti in Tuscany). Reds from low-altitude bush vines. Estate wine is *barrique*-aged Saia, from Nero d'Avola – ripe and powerful, best with 5 years' age or more. ReNoto (previously Rosso di Noto) is also Nero d'Avola but unwooded; a cooler, better-defined 2004 is a significantly improvement on the 03. (PW)
- **Saia★★★** £D ● **ReNoto★★** £B

FEUDO MONTONI Sicilia www.feudomontoni.it
A rather special source of Nero d'Avola. Vrucara is a selection of the best grapes aged in oak and bottled without fining or filtration. Elegant, classy and expansive, it has wonderful complexity including coffee, carob, mineral and plum aromas; best with 8–10 years' age. Also a stylish regular version; the 2001 could be drunk now. (PW)
- **Vrucara Selezione Speciale★★★★** £E ● **Nero d'Avola★★** £C

FIRRIATO Sicilia www.firriato.it
This is what is possible in Sicily given good winemaking direction. Top reds from local varieties include consistently impressive Harmonium (Nero d'Avola) and classy, individual Ribeca (with 40% Perricone) while Camelot (Cab Sauv/Merlot) shows a cool, somewhat Bordeaux-like complexity in 2002. Dual-variety Santagostino red (Nero d'Avola/Cabernet) and white (Cattaratto/Chardonnay) are made in larger quantities and show good character and depth. Well-priced Chiaramonte white (Inzolia) edges a flavoursome Grillo for depth and structure. (PW)
- **Harmonium★★★** £D ● **Camelot★★★** £D ● **Ribeca★★★** £D
- **Santagostino Baglio Soria★★** £C ○ **Santagostino Baglio Soria★★** £C
- ○ **Chiaramonte** Ansonica★★ £B ○ **Altavilla della Corte** Grillo★★ £B

GALARDI Campania   *UK stockists:* F&R
Small quantities of just one wine, Terra di Lavoro (Aglianico /Piedirosso - 80/20) - a superb, fabulously complex red of great depth and stunning length, with a wealth of black fruits, mineral and earth, spice and herbs. First

made in 1994 but continues to improve. Cult status means high prices. (PW)
● **Terra di Lavoro**★★★★★ £F

GULFI Sicilia www.gulfi.it *UK stockists:* **Nov, Odd**
Gulfi produce 2 good fruit-driven and mineral-imbued whites: Valcanzjria (50/50 Carricante/Chardonnay) and Carjcanti (pure Carricante) but reds are the real stars. All are from Nero d'Avola. Vineyard-designated versions range from the perfume and fruit of Nerosanlorenzj, elegance and persistence of Nerobufalefej, to the substance and density of Nerobaronj, and extract and power of Neromàccarj. All deserve at least 5 years' age. (PW)
● **Nerosanlorenzj**★★★ £D ● **Nerobufalefej**★★★ £D ● **Nerobaronj**★★★ £D
● **Neromàccarj**★★★ £D ● **Nerojbleo**★★ £C ● **Rossojbleo**★ £B
O **Valcanzjria**★★ £C O **Carjcanti**★★ £C

LA CORTE Puglia www.renideo.com *UK stockists:* Ast, JNi, F&M
Focused on great wines from Primitivo and Negroamaro. Superior 'La Corte' from old-vine fruit show very ripe fruit, considerable intensity and extract, and are much better than Zinfandel Anfora and Negroamaro Solyss. Top wine, Ré (first made 2001) combines best Negroamaro and Primitivo, and shows greatest complexity and style. (PW)
● **Ré**★★★ £D ● **Zinfandel La Corte**★★★ £C ● **Negroamaro La Corte**★★★ £C
● **Zinfandel Anfora**★★ £B ● **Negroamaro Solyss**★★ £B

TENUTA LE QUERCE Basilicata www.tenutalequerce.com *UK stockists:* **Tri,** But,VKg
Major new star and part of the wider wine revolution in Basilicata. Crowning glory is Vigna della Corona from a single plot of vines - marvellously expansive wine with much of the complexity, expression and nobility of Aglianico but needs 6-8 years' ageing. Rosso di Costanza, barrique-aged, also needs time. More affordable wines of Cantine Sasso made here too. (PW)
Tenuta Le Querce
● **Aglianico del Vulture** Vigna Corona★★★★★ £F
● **Aglianico del Vulture** Il Viola★★ £B Rosso di Costanza★★★ £D
Cantine Sasso
● **Aglianico del Vulture**★★ £B

LEONE DE CASTRIS Puglia www.leonedecastris.com *UK stockists:* Alv
More traditional face of Puglia. Large volume production of extensive range. Salice Riserva shows classic dark raisiny character and black fruits. Better again is the Donna Lisa Riserva, best 8-10 years'. Improving Ilemos from Primitivo, Montepulciano, Merlot and Negroamaro. White Donna Lisa is barrique-fermented/aged Chardonnay; more interesting is characterful, unoaked Messapia (from Verdeca). Five Roses is the widely seen rosé. New is Messere Andrea (Negroamaro/Cab Sauv). PW)
● **Salice Salentino** Riserva★★ £B Riserva Donna Lisa★★★ £C
● **Primitivo di Manduria** Santera★★ £B ● **Illemos**★★ £C O **Messapia**★★ £B

MASSERIA LI VELI Puglia www.liveli.it *UK stockists:* Lib
Exciting new undertaking with Avignonesi involvement. Atypical quality (and prices) for (Negroamaro-based) Salice Salentino: deep, powerful Pezzo Morgana (more structured than Passamante) best with 5-6 years' age. Riserva, Morgana Alta (2000) is given longest ageing and shows marvellous complexity with great depth and length of flavour. (PW)
● **Salice Salentino** Pezzo Morgana★★★ £C ● **Passamante**★★★ £B

LIBRANDI Calabria www.librandi.it *UK stockists:* **Eno,** F&M
Calabria's quality leader with 230 ha. Top red, Gravello (Gaglioppo/Cab Sauv) but also many local varieties being revived - first is increasingly persuasive barrique-aged Magno Megonio from Magliocco. Best value is characterful, gamey, earthy Duca San Felice. Le Passule is light yet intense honeyed sweet wine from Mantonico while Efeso is new rich, oaky dry version of same. (PW)
● **Gravello**★★★ £D ● **Magno Megonio**★★★ £E
● **Cirò Rosso** Riserva Duca San Felice★★ £B
O **Efeso**★★★ £E O **Le Passule**★★★ £D

<u>**ALBERTO LOI**</u> Sardegna www.cantina.it/albertoloi_
Good Sardinian reds from Cannonau. Riserva Cardedo has lots of soft red fruits and good concentration but top
New entries have producer's name underlined

Riserva has more class, intensity and power. Premium reds are based on Cannonau (around 70%): stylish, concentrated Astrangia is surpassed by Tuvara with more class, complexity and breadth. Loi Corona, aged only in *barrique*, includes Cab Sauv and is more international. Unusual is Leila, Canonau vinified as a white. Also fresh, attractive Vermentino. (PW)

● **Tuvara**★★★ £E ● **Loi Corona**★★★ £E ● **Astrangia**★★ £D
● **Cannonau di Sardegna Jerzu Riserva** Cardedo★★ £C Alberto Loi★★★ £C
O **Leila Vendemmia Tardiva**★★ £D

LUIGI MAFFINI Campania www.maffini-vini.com *UK stockists:* Bib
Very creditable red and white as well as 6,000 bottles of premium red. Intense, fruit-driven Kràtos (Fiano) scented of spice, herb, dried peach and apricot. Red Klèos also provides lots of attractive fruit (from Aglianico, Piedirosso and Sangiovese). Deep, oaky Cenito (Aglianico/Piedirosso) shows greatest promise but likely to be best with 8-10 years' age. (PW)

● **Cenito**★★★ £D ● **Klèos**★★ £B O **Kràtos**★★ £C

MASTROBERARDINO Campania *UK stockists:* BWC, Cib, Sel
For long Campania's leader with complex and refined Taurasi Radici that needs a decade's age. Now also richer and more modern-styled Naturalis Historia (Piedirosso, Aglianico). Best Greco di Tufo (Nova Serra) and Fiano di Avellino (Radici) are intense, ripe and varietal (More Maiorum oak-fermented and aged). Historic Pompeii vineyard - intriguing new (2001) Villa dei Misteri (Piedirosso, Sciascinoso - 90/10). Also relatively large volumes of Lacryma Christi del Vesuvio. (PW)

● **Taurasi** Radici★★★★ £E ● **Naturalis Historia**★★★ £F
O **Fiano di Avellino** Radici★★ £C O **Greco di Tufo** Nova Serra★★ £C

MONTEVETRANO Campania *UK stockists:* Wtr, Ast, CdP, UnC, F&M, NYg, Las, F&R
Small volume super-Campanian from from Cab Sauv, Merlot and Aglianico. It has great structure and depth with considerable complexity and elegance - not just another internationally styled red. (PW)

● **Montevetrano**★★★★★ £F

MORGANTE Sicilia www.morgante-vini.it *UK stockists:* Lib, NYg, But, N&P
Morgante family have made own wine since 98 from part of more than 200 ha of vines. Nero d'Avola is made in two versions: Don Antonio, aged in new French oak, has depth and intensity in a sleek structure and needs 3-5 years' age. Characterful regular example can be drunk sooner. (PW)

● **Nero d'Avola**★★ £B ● **Don Antonio**★★★ £D

SALVATORE MURANA Sicilia *UK stockists:* Eno
Top producer of Passito di Pantelleria with greater refinement than others. Martingana is the most concentrated and raisiny, very powerful but stylish. Khamma is also excellent with classic dried apricot and date aromas and flavours. Moscato di Pantelleria is lighter style. New is dry version of Zibibbo called Gadì. (PW)

O **Passito di Pantelleria** Khamma★★★ £F Martingana★★★★ £F
O **Moscato di Pantelleria** Mueggen★★ £E

ODOARDI Calabria
Remarkable Calabrian reds, mostly from Gaglioppo grapes, with seductive texture and considerable elegance. Most outstanding are the *barrique*-aged Vigna Mortillo and Vigna Garrone – the latter with a little Cab Sauv and Merlot, is richer but both consistently show well with 6–8 years' age. Promising new Polpicello (2001) is more overtly 'southern' in character with a powerful black fruits intensity. (PW)

● **Savuto**★★ £B ● **Savuto Superiore** Vigna Mortillo★★★★ £D
● **Scavigna** Vigna Garrone★★★★ £D ● **Scavigna** Polpicello★★★★ £E

PALARI Sicilia *UK stockists:* Wtr, CdP
Faro is DOC revived by Palari. Ageworthy red, from mostly Nerello Mascalese and Nerello Cappuccio aged in French barriques, impresses with nuanced complexity but also as wine of refined, discreet structure. Rosso del Soprano is a stylish second wine that can be drunk young or kept. (PW)

● **Rosso del Soprano**★★ £C ● **Faro**★★★★ £E

PATERNOSTER Basilicata www.paternostervini1925.com *UK stockists:* Eno, Hfx
Venerable producer and family enterprise with relatively traditional vinification and ageing. Top example, Don

193

ITALY

Anselmo is deep, powerful, classically tight and closed in youth, but rich and mesmerising with age. More modern in style is barrique-aged Rotondo which is richer and more immediate but stylish and sophisticated too. Bigger-volume Synthesi also good and ready sooner. (PW)

● **Aglianico del Vulture** Synthesi★★ £C   Rotondo★★★★ £E   Don Anselmo★★★★ £E

PLANETA   Sicilia   www.planeta.it   *UK stockists:* Eno, JNi, Vne, P&S, Vts, Hrd, F&M
Dynamic family powered enterprise with four estates/wineries and 350 ha of vineyards. Top wines are relatively pricey. Santa Cecilia (Nero d'Avola) and pure Syrah are often the best with excellent fruit and length. Also very good Cab Sauv and rich, intense Merlot. Cerasuolo di Vittoria has distinctive spice and red fruits perfume (Nero d'Avola/Frappato - 60/40). Also rich, ripe complex, powerful Chardonnay. Alastro, combines Grecanico and Chardonnay while concentrated Cometa (Fiano) is rich in exotic and dried stone fruits. Best value in La Segreta Rosso and Bianco. (PW)

● **Santa Cecilia**★★★ £D   ● **Syrah**★★★ £D   ● **Cerasuolo di Vittoria**★★★ £C
● **Cabernet Sauvignon**★★★ £D   O **Chardonnay**★★★ £D   O **Cometa**★★★ £C

RIVERA   Puglia   www.rivera.it   *UK stockists:* Mdl
Leading advocate of Castel del Monte DOC with characterful well-priced red in Il Falcone (Uva di Troia/Montepulciano - 70/30). Since 2000 new flagship red, Pier Apuliae (100% Uva di Troia) is deeper, more concentrated but with much of the personality and class of this grape. Cappellaccio, (100% Aglianico) is increasingly fine, Triusco is from Primitivo. Also new small-volume Chardonnay, Lama di Corvo. (PW)

● **Castel del Monte** Puer Apuliae★★★ £E   Riserva Il Falcone★★ £B
● **Castel del Monte** Aglianico Riserva Cappellaccio★★ £B   ● **Triusco**★★ £B

SANTADI   Sardegna   www.cantinadisantadi.it   *UK stockists:* Eno, Vne, Hrd, P&S
Co-op with deserved following for its combination of quantity and quality from Carignano. Top wine Terre Brune is rich, powerful and structured, best with 8 years' or more. Bigger volume Rocca Rubia with less weight and structure is ready sooner. Araja is unoaked (Carignano/Sangiovese). Several good whites are also made. Sweet Latinia (Nasco) is intense and stylish. Santadi are also partners in Agricola Punica, a new project involving Tenuta San Guido, Giacomo Tachis and Sebastiano Rosa - 2002, the first vintage of the 'super Carignano' Barrua reflects the sophisticated winemaking. know-how. (PW)

● **Carignano del Sulcis** Riserva Rocca Rubia★★★ £C   Sup. Terre Brune★★★★ £E
O **Vermentino di Sardegna** Villa Solais★ £B   Cala Silente★★ £B   O **Latinia**★★★ £E

SOLIDEA   Sicilia   www.solideavini.it   *UK stockists:* **Ast**
Good source for the sweet Muscats of Pantelleria. Passito is particularly lush, sweet and richly flavoured with powerful raisiny, grapy and dried apricot flavours as well as toffee, honey and other dried fruits. Also lighter but spicy, intense Moscato di Pantelleria – try both from 2002 or 03. (PW)

O **Passito di Pantelleria**★★★ £E   O **Moscato di Pantelleria**★★ £C

CANTINA DEL TABURNO   Campania   *UK stockists:* Eno, Han, NYg, Vts
Whites are a speciality at this co-op with excellent examples of Falanghina, Fiano and hitherto obscure Coda di Volpe. Oak is used for Coda di Volpe, subtly cradling its ripe, intense preserved fruit character. Bue Apis is limited bottling of Aglianico of great breadth and structure but grape's spice, earth, smoke and plum character also seen in Delius and decent Fidelis. (PW)

● **Bue Apis**★★★★ £F   ● **Delius**★★★ £D   ● **Aglianico del Taburno** Fidelis★★ £B
O **Serra Docile** Coda di Volpe★★ £C   O **Taburno Falanghina**★★ £C

TASCA D'ALMERITA   Sicilia   www.tascadalmerita.it   *UK stockists:* **BWC**, Vts
Large high altitude estate long ensuring fine quality from Sicily - led by composed yet characterful Rosso del Conte (mostly Nero d'Avola) and powerful, refined Cab Sauv. Also reds Cygnus (Nero d'Avola, Cabernet) and Camastra (Nero d'Avola, Merlot). Also rich, powerful Chardonnay and unoaked, flavoursome Nozze d'Oro (Inzolia based). Leone d'Almerita is Cataratto with Chardonnay and Sauvignon. Volume Regaleali basic red, white and rosé are excellent quaffing wines. (PW)

● **Contea di Sclafani** Rosso del Conte★★★★ £D   Cabernet Sauvignon★★★★ £E
O **Contea di Sclafani** Chardonnay★★★ £D   Nozze d'Oro★★ £C

194

COSIMO TAURINO Puglia www.taurinovini.it *UK stockists:* **Hal,** Maj
Source of rich, robust yet harmonious reds. Top wine Patriglione (Negroamaro/Malvasia Nera - 90/10) is wonderfully rich, complex, beautifully structured expression of southern Italy. Inexpensive Notarpanaro, also produced from old vines, is dense and flavoursome. Also popular Salice Salentino Riserva, white I Sierri (Chardonnay/Malvasia) and rosé Scaloti. (PW)
● **Patriglione**★★★★ £E ● **Notarpanaro**★★ £B ● **Salice Salentino** Riserva★ £B

TENUTA DELLE TERRE NERE Sicilia www.marcdegrazia.com *UK stockists:* **J&B**
Estate of Marc De Grazia, leading distributor of fine Italian wines, with 2 vineyards on northern slopes of Mount Etna: Guardiola and Calderara. Guardiola spends 18 months in *barriques* and displays the complexity, expansive qualities and class possible from old bush-vine Nerello Mascalese. 2002 has fine mineral-edged fruit and Burgundian texture; 03 promises even more. (PW)
● **Etna Rosso** Vigneto Guardiola★★★★ £D

TORMARESCA Puglia www.tormaresca.it *UK stockists:* **BWC,**Vts, Cam
Antinori venture into Puglia with 350 ha of vineyards. Top reds Masseria Maime (Negroamaro), and Bocca di Lupo (Aglianico with 10% Cab Sauv) show great fruit definition, excellent texture and balance. At least as good is a deep, blackberry, earth and spice-rich Torcicorda (old vine Primitivo). Also sound regular red and Chardonnay (also in impressively rich Pietrabianca version). (PW)
● **Masseria Maime**★★★ £D ● **Castel del Monte** Bocca di Lupo★★★ £C
● **Torcicoda**★★★ £C O **Castel del Monte** Pietrabianca★★★ £C

VALLONE Puglia www.agricolevallone.com *UK stockists:* **Mer,** L&W
170 ha Puglian estate producing wines of consistently high standard. Graticciaia, is from (mostly) Negroamaro grapes dried on mats (*graticci*) and resulting wine has rich, concentrated sweet fruit. Also Brindisi Rosso Vigna Flaminio red with very ripe fruit and intensely flavoured Salice Salentino. (PW)
● **Graticciaia**★★★ £E ● **Brindisi** Vigna Flaminio★★ £B
● **Salice Salentino** Vereto★ £B

VETRERE Puglia www.vetrere.it *UK stockists:* **Tri**
An accessible, affordable taste of Puglia. Whites are Chardonnay-based with the balance from Malvasia, Verdeca or Fiano, which add personality. Laureato is the oaked version. Reds are pure Negroamaro or Primitivo. Tempio di Giano (unoaked Negroamaro) has lovely fruit and can be as impressive as the oaked Lago della Pergola. Primitivo is supple, ripe and varietal; the oaked Barone Pazzo shows more depth and extract. (PW)
O **Finis Terrae**★★ £B O **Laureato**★★ £B
● **Tempio di Giano**★★ £B ● **Lago della Pergola**★★ £B
● **Livruni**★★ £B ● **Barone Pazzo**★★★ £B

Other wineries of note
Caputo (Campania), Roberto Ceraudo (Calabria), Giovanni Cherchi (Sardinia), Cusumano (Sicily), Tenuta Dell'Abate (Sicily), Dettori (Sardinia), Fatascià (Sicily), Masseria Del Feudo Grottarossa (Sicily), Pala (Sardinia), Feudo Principi di Butera (Sicily), Hauner (Isola di Salina), Maurigi (Sicily), Malaterra (Basilicata), Michele Moio (Campania), Pupillo (Sicily), San Paolo (Campania), Sella & Mosca (Sardinia), Telaro/Lavoro & Salute (Campania), Terre del Principe (Campania), Torrevento (Puglia), Conti Zecca (Puglia)

An in-depth profile of every producer can be found in Wine behind the label 2006

Spain

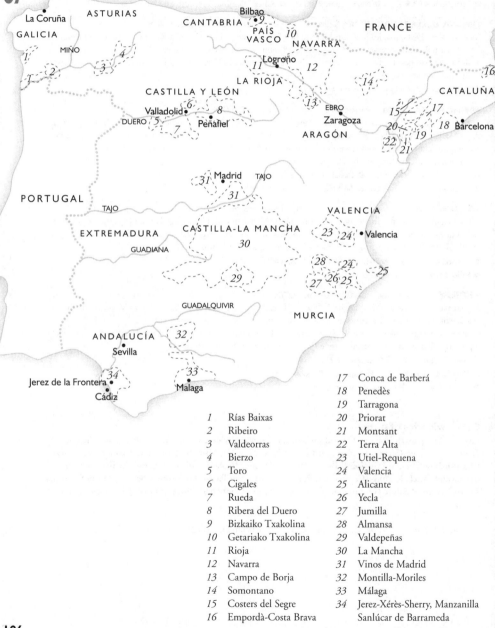

1	Rías Baixas
2	Ribeiro
3	Valdeorras
4	Bierzo
5	Toro
6	Cigales
7	Rueda
8	Ribera del Duero
9	Bizkaiko Txakolina
10	Getariako Txakolina
11	Rioja
12	Navarra
13	Campo de Borja
14	Somontano
15	Costers del Segre
16	Empordà-Costa Brava
17	Conca de Barberá
18	Penedès
19	Tarragona
20	Priorat
21	Montsant
22	Terra Alta
23	Utiel-Requena
24	Valencia
25	Alicante
26	Yecla
27	Jumilla
28	Almansa
29	Valdepeñas
30	La Mancha
31	Vinos de Madrid
32	Montilla-Moriles
33	Málaga
34	Jerez-Xérès-Sherry, Manzanilla Sanlúcar de Barrameda

The North-East

The Rioja wine zone spreads out of the administrative region of Rioja, its borders stretching into Navarra to its north-east and Castilla y León to the west. Of three sub-regions: Alavesa, Alta and Baja. Tempranillo performs well in the limestone soils of the Alavesa, Alta with heavier clay soils is more suitable for Garnacha, which also dominates plantings in the hotter Baja. **Navarra** shares the native Tempranillo, Garnacha and Viura with Rioja but also has plantings of international varieties. In Aragón are two DOs worth considering: **Campo de Borja** and **Somontano**.
Cataluña is home to a number of diverse wine regions. A few fine, traditional reds are made in the **Empordà-Costa Brava** DO. Good red and white is produced at **Costers del Segre**. To the east **Conca de Barberá** is cooled by altitude and source of good Chardonnay and Pinot Noir. At **Penedès** some fine reds and whites are produced from a mix of local and international varieties. This is also the centre of the vast **Cava** DO. Immediately to the west of Penedès is **Tarragona**, which has a superior new sub-region, **Monsant** DO, and the small, very high-quality region of **Priorat**. Reds excel, none more so than old-vine Garnacha.

The North-West

Ribera del Duero produces some of the finest reds in the country based on Tinto Fino (Tempranillo). Improving reds are emerging from **Cigales** and **Rueda** remains a source of interesting barrel-fermented wines from Sauvignon and Verdejo To the west **Toro** now produces some world class reds. The small DO of **Bierzo** is now producing wines of real substance. Next to Bierzo, in Galicia is **Valdeorras**. Reds are produced, like those in Bierzo, from Mencía but of particular note are the whites produced from the unusual, indigenous Godello. Some attractive, fruity whites are also produced in **Ribeiro** but the greatest interest lies in the coastal vineyards of **Rías Baixas**.

Central Spain

Increasing numbers of exciting reds are now emerging, particularly to the east of the area nearer the coast in **Valencia**, in the DOs of **Utiel-Requena** and **Jumilla**. The indigenous Bobal and Monastrell are both proving very successful. Some good fortified wine is produced from Monastrell at **Alicante**, as are some fine, sweet Moscatels.

The South

This is fortified-wine country, most specifically the sherries of **Jerez y Manzanilla**. Andalucía is also home to the fortified wines of **Montilla-Moriles** and **Málaga**. Sherries are raised in a *solera* system which is maintained by fresh young wines.

Spain Vintages

Although there is a reasonably uniform climate in most of Spain's more southerly regions, see also Vintage

Charts to get a good guide of what to expect with the premium red-wine areas. The maturity guide applies to top wines. Dry whites generally should be drunk on or shortly after release.

Wizard's Wishlist

The Spanish new wave

AALTO ● Ribera del Duero Aalto PS
ABADÍA RETUERTA ● Pago Valdellón Vino de Mesa
AGRO DE BAZÁN O Rías Baixas Granbazán Ambar
CELLER DE CAPÇANES ● Monsant Flor de Primavera
CASA CASTILLO ● Jumilla Pie Franco
CLOS I TERASSES ● Priorat Clos Erasmus
CLOS MOGADOR ● Priorat Clos Mogador
LEDA VINAS VIEJAS ● Vina Leda
DOMINIO DE VALDEPUSA ● Émeritus Montes de Toledo
MAURO ● Mauro Vendimia Seleccionada
MAURODOS ● Toro Viña San Román
CELLER VALL LLACH ● Priorat
TORRES ● Grans Muralles Conca de Barberá
RODA ● Rioja Cirsion
BODEGAS TILENUS ● Bierzo Tilenus Pagos de Posada

Established and emerging classics

FINCA ALLENDE ● Rioja Aurus
ISMAEL ARROYO
● Ribera de Duero Val Sotillo Gran Reserva
ARTADI ● Rioja Viña El Pisón Reserva
DOMINIO DE PINGUS ● Ribera del Duero Pingus
ALEJANDRO FERNÁNDEZ - PESQUERA
● Ribera del Duero Gran Reserva
MARQUÉS DE MURRIETA ● Rioja Dalmau
MARQUÉS DE RISCAL ● Rioja Reserva Baron de Chirel
ALVARO PALACIOS ● Priorat L'Ermita
PÉREZ PASCUAS
● Ribera del Duero Pérez Pascuas Gran Reserva
LA RIOJA ALTA ● Rioja 890 Gran Reserva
ALEMANY I CORRIO ● Penedès Sot Lefriec
ARTAZU ● Navarra Santa Cruz de Artazu
CELLER RIPOLL SANS ● Priorat Closa Battlet
MARQUÉS DE VARGAS ● Rioja Private Reserva
TORRES ● Mas la Plana Penedès

A selection of great Spanish values

AGRO DE BAZAN O Rías Baixas Granbazán Ambar
EL SEQUE ● Alicante El Seque
BODEGAS AS LAXAS O Rías Baixas Laxas
CELLER DE CAPÇANES ● Monsant Mas Turtò
BODEGAS SIERRA SALINAS ● Alicante Mira Salinas
BODEGAS CASTAÑO ● Yecla Coleccion
BODEGA RODERO ● Ribera de Duero Crianza
BODEGAS BALCONA ● Bullas Partal Crianza
GRAMONA ● Cava III Lustros

197

SPAIN

DEHESA LA GRANJA ● **Dehesa La Granja** Vino de Mesa

BODEGA NIÑO JESÚS ● **Calatayud** Estecillo Viña Viejas

MAS PERINET ○ **Montsant** Clos Maria

BODEGAS OSTATU ● **Rioja** Reserva

BODEGAS OLIVARES ● **Jumilla** Altos de la Hoya

JOSE PARIENTE ○ **Rueda** Verdejo

Spain/A-Z of producers

AALTO Ribera del Duero www.aalto.es *UK stockists:* F&R,N&P
Impressive new estate producing a richly concentrated, dense, modern Ribera del Duero. The wine is powerful, supple and very complex, full of dark fruits and oriental spices. The PS bottling adds an extra dimension and will only be released in the best vintages. (DM)
● **Ribera del Duero** Aalto★★★★ £E   Aalto PS★★★★★ £F

ABADÍA RETUERTA Castilla y León www.abadia-retuerta.com *UK stockists:* C&D,JAr
Based just outside the boundaries of Ribera del Duero. Arnaldo, Primicia and Rivola offer attractive early drinking. Retuerta Especial red is fuller. El Campanario Reserva and El Palomar are a step up. Top reds Pago Valdebellón from Cab Sauv, Pago Negrallada from Tempranillo and PV from Petit Verdot are all impressively ageworthy. (DM)
● **El Palomar**★★★★ £F   ● **Pago Negrallada**★★★★★ £G
● **Selección Especial**★★★ £D   ● **Cuvée El Campanario**★★★ £E

AGRO DE BAZÁN Rías Baixas
First-class producer in this potentially high-quality appellation in Galicia. Granbazán Verde is for early drinking; Ambar is richer and more concentrated than most, resembling a good Condrieu. It has a pure mineral structure and the depth to develop well over two or three years. (DM)
○ **Rías Baixas** Granbazán Verde★★ £B   Granbazán Ambar★★★ £C

ALEMANY I CORRIO Penedès *UK stockists:* Vne
Tiny warehouse winery. Output is less than 500 cases a year of the brilliant red Sot Lefriec, from very old Cariñena, Merlot and Cab Sauv. Now a very passable second wine, Pas Curtei, has been added to help ensure the integrity and quality of the top wine. (DM)
● **Penedès** Pas Curtei★★ £C   Sot Lefriec★★★★ £F

FINCA ALLENDE Rioja fallende@fer.es *UK stockists:* FMV
Top-flight Rioja producer. Fruit is mostly from owned vineyards in the Rioja Alta. Complex Calvario is mainly Tempranillo. From 60-year-old vines, pricey top wine Aurus will age gracefully. (DM)
● **Rioja**★★ £B   Calvario★★★★ £F   Aurus★★★★★ £G   ○ **Rioja** Blanco★★ £B

ISMAEL ARROYO Ribera del Duero www.valsotillo.com *UK stockists:* N&P, NYg
Dense, powerful and tannic Ribera del Duero, among the best in the DO. Top wines go under the Val Sotillo label and include Crianza, Reserva and Gran Reserva which has formidable extract with concentrated, dark fruit, subtle, spicy oak and real refinement. Wines that demand to be cellared. (DM)
● **Ribera de Duero** Val Sotillo★★ £B   Val Sotillo Crianza★★★ £C
● **Ribera de Duero** Val Sotillo Reserva★★★ £E   Val Sotillo Gran Reserva★★★★ £F

ARTADI Rioja *UK stockists:* BBR, GWW, NYg, Bal,F&M
Very impressive range of new-wave Rioja is produced here. Viñas de Gain Crianza and the more expensive Pagos Viejos Reserva are both fine, modern, fleshy styles. There are also two other very impressive Reservas: Viña El Pisón and Grandes Añadas, a very limited special bottling. (DM)
● **Rioja** Viñas de Gain Crianza★★ £C   Pagos Viejos Reserva★★★ £E
● **Rioja** Viña El Pisón Reserva★★★★ £F   ○ **Rioja** Viñas de Gain★ £B

ARZUAGA NAVARRO Ribera del Duero www.arzuaganavarro.com *UK stockists:* OWL
Substantial Ribera property making traditional sturdy examples. Special Reserve comes from 80–90-year-old Tinto Fino vines, while the Gran Arzuaga has a vibrancy not present in some older vintages. Second label La Colegada comes from Burgos. Promising new La Mancha property Pago Florentino produces ripe, fleshy, full-flavoured Tempranillo. (DM)

198

New entries have producer's name underlined

Bodegas Arzuaga
● **Ribera de Duero** Crianza★★ £D Reserva★★★ £E Gran Reserva★★★ £G
● **Ribera de Duero** Special Reserve★★★★ £F Gran Arzuaga★★★★★ £H

Bodega La Colegiada
● **Tinto Lerma** Vino de Calidad del Arlanza★★ £C

BODEGAS AS LAXAS Rías Baixas www.bodegaslaxas.com *UK stockists:* **Bur**, SVS
Very old estate with 19ha of vineyards with an ideal south-facing aspect. Two wines are produced, both based on the Albariño. The Laxas is relatively cool-fermented in stainless steel and has marked grassy, floral aromas with just a hint of citrus and a subtle minerality. The Bágos de Miño comes from the single-vineyard O Pucha estate and is more intense and piercing in character than its stablemate. Both wines should be enjoyed young.
O **Rías Baixas** Laxas★★ £B Bágos de Miño★★★ £C

DOMINIO DE ATAUTA Ribera del Duero & Bierzo *UK stockists:* **Gen**
Thoroughly modern Ribera reds and very different in style from some of the Reservas and Gran Reservas produced elsewhere. Bierzo is dark and characterful with an earthy old-vine character. (DM)

Dominio de Atauta
● **Ribera del Duero**★★★★ £E

Valtuille
● **Bierzo** El Castro de Valtuille★★★ £D

BODEGA BALCONA Bullas www.paralelo40.org/partal/
Fine example of one of many newly emerging producers from central Spain. Seleccion is mainly Monastrell and can be a bit four-square and rustic. The Crianza by contrast is vibrant and intense with piercing dark, spicy, berry fruit and supple, well-rounded tannins. (DM)
● **Bullas** Partal Seleccion★ £B Partal Crianza★★★ £C

BARBADILLO Jerez y Manzanilla www.barbadillo.com *UK stockists:* **JEF**
Based in Sanlúcar de Barrameda, a great producer of often exceptional Manzanilla with fine examples at all levels. Also releases a number of remarkable old wines from venerable soleras labelled as Relics, including Amontillado, Oloroso, Palo Cortado and Pedro Ximénez. (DM)
O **Solear** Manzanilla★★ £B O **Principe** Amontillado★★★ £C
O **Cuco** Oloroso Seco★★★ £C O **Amontillado de Sanlúcar**★★★ £C
O **Manzanilla Pasada**★★★ £C O **Obispo Gascón** Palo Cortado★★ £C

BODEGAS BORSAO Campo de Borja www.bodegasborsao.com *UK stockists:***Bur**,Wai
Standard-bearer for this DO with a range of well-priced reds. Crianza and Reserva Seleccion labels are both rich, spicy styles aged in a mix of French and American oak. Tres Picos, from old-vine Garnacha, has classical structure and depth. Top reds will develop well in the short term. (DM)
● **Campo de Borja** Reserva Selección★★★ £B Tres Picos★★★ £C
● **Campo de Borja** Vina Borgia★ £B Borsao★★ £B Crianza Selección★★ £B

CELLERS CAPAFONS-OSSÓ Montsant www.capafons-osso.com
Montsant-based operation with estates in Montsant and Priorat. Reds are supple and fruit-driven. Impressively rich, concentrated and darkly spicy Mas de Masos has a subtle mineral undercurrent which is less ferocious than some. (DM)
● **Priorat** Sirsell★★★ £C Masos d'En Cubells★★★ £D Mas de Masos★★★★ £E
● **Montsant** Vessants★★ £C Masia Esplanes★★★ £D ◉ **Montsant** Roigenc★★ £C

CELLER DE CAPÇANES Tarragona capsanes@retemail.es *UK stockists:* **Vni**,Wai
Arguably Spain's finest co-operative. The high quality achieved through the range has developed after producing a remarkable Kosher wine, Flor de Primavera, and the 120-strong membership provides some splendid old vineyards. Top reds are rich, complex and ageworthy. (DM)
● **Monsant** Mas Collet★★ £B Costers del Gravet★★★ £B Vall de Calàs★★ £B
● **Monsant** Mas Turtò★★★ £C Flor de Primavera★★★ £D Cabrida★★★★ £E

SPAIN

CASA CASTILLO Jumilla *UK stockists:* **FMV**
Among a number of rising stars from Spain's lesser-known southern regions. with some splendid old bush-vine Monastrell (Mourvèdre) of exceptional quality. The top two wines are rich, dense and spicy, and all offer very good value. (DM)
● **Jumilla** Monastrell★★ £B Las Gravas★★★★ £C Pie Franco★★★★ £D

BODEGAS CASTAÑO Yecla www.bodegascastano.com *UK stockists:* **Lib**
An extensive range based mainly on old-vine Monastrell as well as varietal Syrah, Merlot and Cabernet. Pozuelo-labelled reds are more traditional in style. Monastrell Dulce is a late-harvest fortified red. At Bodegas Sierra Salinas they are making a splendid Monastrell/Cabernet/Garnacha blend called Mira Salinas from old ungrafted vines. (DM)

Bodegas Castaño
● **Yecla** Pozuelo Crianza★ £B Pozuelo Reserva★★ £C Coleccion★★★ £C Dulce Monastrell★★★★ £C
● **Yecla** Syrah★★ £B Merlot★★ £B Monastrell★★ £B Hecula Monastrell★★ £B
● **Yecla** Cabernet Sauvignon★ £B O **Yecla** Macabeo/Chardonnay★★★ £B

Bodegas Sierra Salinas
● **Alicante** Mira Salinas★★★★ £D

CELLER DEL PONT Priorat www.cellerdelpont.com *UK stockists:* **Vni**
Recently established small Priorat property producing less than 400 cases a year of a sturdy, powerful and richly mineral-laden red, Lo Givot. Blended from Garnacha, Cariñena, Cab Sauv and Syrah. it deserves five or six years' ageing to show at its best. (DM)
● **Priorat** Lo Givot★★★★ £F

CIMS DE PORRERA Priorat cims@arrakis.es *UK stockists:* **JAr**
The Priorat Classic is Cariñena blended with Garnacha and Cab Sauv and is dark, spicy and beguiling in its fiery complexity. Two small-scale single-vineyard bottlings, Finca Pigat and Finca La Tena are both 100 per cent Cariñena. Also a good, much more forward second wine, Solanes. (DM)
● **Priorat** Classic★★★★ £F Solanes★★★ £D

CLOS DEL LLOPS Priorat closmogador@sendanet.es *UK stockists:* **GBa**
This is one of several properties with valuable input from winemaker René Barbier Ferrer. Output is relatively small, barely 1,000 cases a year, so the wine, Clos Manyetes, is inevitably scarce. It deserves cellaring for at least five years to better integrate its fierce, fiery nature. (DM)
● **Priorat** Clos Manyetes★★★★★ £E

CLOS FIGUERAS Priorat europvin@infonegocio.com
Excellent old-vine Garnacha/Cariñena blend. Second label, Font de la Figuera, is softer, rounder and much more approachable. Some Viognier vines contribute to theClos Nelin white. (DM)
● **Priorat** Font de la Figuera★★★ £D Clos Figueras★★★★ £F

CLOS I TERASSES Priorat closeramus@terra.es *UK stockists:* **JAr**, F&R
A Priorat pioneer established in 1989. Two wines are made here: the top wine, Clos Eramus, is a super-rich blend of Garnacha, Cab Sauv and Cariñena; the well-priced second wine, Laurel, is produced from Cab Sauv. Clos Erasmus demands six to seven years' ageing. (DM)
● **Priorat** Clos Erasmus★★★★★ £F

CLOS MOGADOR Priorat closmogador@sendanet.es *UK stockists:* **GBa,Bal**
Home property of talented owner and winemaker René Barbier Ferrer. A big, structured wine, it will develop very well with age. Barbier is also involved at Clos del Llops and works with Christopher Cannan in producing the stylish white Priorat Clos Nelin. (DM)
● **Priorat** Clos Mogador★★★★★ £F

CLOS NELIN Priorat closmogador@sendanet.es *UK stockists:* **GBa**
As well as producing his brilliant Clos Mogador red, René Barbier Ferrer has long been interested in making a benchmark white Priorat. Part vinified in oak and part in stainless steel Nelin has great style and intensity. (DM)
O **Priorat** Clos Nelin★★★★ £E

200

SPAIN

BODEGAS Y VIÑAS DOS VICTORIAS Toro www.dosvictorias.com *UK stockists:*GBa
The 2 Victorias make very good top-end Toro as well as 2 Ruedas that achieve a level of intensity and depth rarely found in this DO. Both the Crianza and the splendid Gran Elias Mora are serious and structured. (DM)

Elias Mora
● **Toro** Semi-Crianza★★ £D Semi-Crianza★★★ £D Semi-Crianza★★★★ £D

Jose Pariente
O **Rueda** Verdejo★★★ £B

BODEGAS ESTEFANIA Bierzo *UK stockists:*Ala
Like Cigales, Bierzo is beginning to emerge with good to very good reds alongside the more established appellations of Ribera del Duero and Toro. Two reds here of striking depth, character and quality appear under the Tilenus label. A good-value budget wine is called simply Tilenus. (DM)
● **Bierzo** Tilenus Crianza★★★ £C Tilenus Pagos de Posada★★★★ £E

EUROPVIN FALSET Montsant *UK stockists:*GBa
One of the three great red producers in Tarragona. There are two wines, both rich and concentrated. Malolactic is in barrel and the wines are kept on their lees during maturation. Expect both wines to develop well in the medium term; the Seleccio will add further complexity for up to a decade. (DM)
● **Montsant** Laurona★★★ £C Selecció de 6 Vinyes★★★★ £E

CELLERS J.M. FUENTES Priorat granclos@airtel.net *UK stockists:*Bal
Small Priorat producer established in 1995, making an impressively structured and concentrated Gran Clos *cuvée* as well as a decent second wine, El Puig, and a straightforward nutty white Vinya Llisarda. (DM)
● **Priorat** Gran Clos Joset Maria Fuentes★★★★ £E

ALEJANDRO FERNÁNDEZ Ribera del Duero *UK stockists:*JAr,May,Sel
Splendid wines are produced both at Pesquera and Condado de Haza, some of the very finest in Ribera del Duero at all quality levels from Crianza to the great Gran Reservas. Cuvée Janus is made only in great years and is not one massive in extract but remarkably fine. Two interesting new regional projects are Dehesa La Granja and El Viniculo. (DM)

Pesquera
● **Ribera del Duero** Crianza★★★ £C Reserva★★★★ £E
● **Ribera del Duero** Gran Reserva❁❁❁❁❁ £G

Condado de Haza
● **Ribera del Duero** Crianza★★ £C Alenza★★★★ £G

FERNÁNDEZ DE PIÉROLA Rioja www.pierola.com *UK stockists:* Msp,Ben
Three fine reds and a relatively light barrel-fermented wild-yeast white are made at this newly established Rioja estate located in the north of the region in the Rioja Alavesa. New-wave Litium Reserva is richer and fuller than the more piercingly fruit-driven Crianza and Reserva. (DM)
● **Rioja** Crianza★★ £C Reserva★★★ £D Litium Reserva★★★ £E
O **Rioja** Oak Fermented★★ £B

GONZÁLEZ BYASS Jerez y Manzanilla www.gonzalezbyass.com *UK stockists:* AAA
One of the most famous names in sherry production. Tio Pepe is an impressive Fino but of a different order are a number of super-rich Amontillados and Olorosos. These include the refined Oloroso Añada, as well as the full, rich Alfonso, Apóstoles, and most notably Matusalem. (DM)
O **Añada** Oloroso★★★ £E O **Apóstoles** Oloroso★★★★ £E
O **Matusalem** Oloroso★★★★★ £F O **Del Duque** Amontillado❁❁❁❁❁ £F
O **Tio Pepe** Fino★★ £B O **Noé Pedro** Pedro Ximénez★★★★ £E

GRAMONA Penedès
A fine range of dry whites and some of the finest Cavas are made by this well-established Penedès producer founded in 1921. Particularly unusual is the Collecion, an icewine produced from artificially frozen grapes.(DM)
O **Penedès** Gessami★★ £B Sauvignon Blanc★★★ £C Collecion★★★ £C
O **Cava** Imperial Gran Reserva★★ £C Illustros★★★ £D

SPAIN

HIDALGO Jerez y Manzanilla www.lagitana.es   *UK stockists:*AAA
Best-known is consistent La Gitana Manzanilla. Very striking though is an impressive collection of rare Viejo wines. The Amontillado and Oloroso stand out; the latter is almost bone dry but full of evolved *rancio* notes. Impressively complex. (DM)
O **La Gitana** Manzanilla★ £B   O **Manzanilla Pastrana**★★★ £B
O **Amontillado Viejo**★★★★ £E   O **Oloroso Viejo**★★★★ £E

BODEGA NIÑO JESÚS Calatayud   *UK stockists:* **Msp**,Ben
Fine co-op producing ripe, spicy, fruit-driven reds under the Estecillo label. The wines are basket-pressed and souced from old bush-vine Garnacha and Tempranillo grown at high altitude. Joven and Viña Viejas are particularly striking. (DM)
● **Calatayud** Joven★★ £B Viña Viejas★★★ £B Crianza★★ £B

LEDA VIÑAS VIEJAS Castilla y Leon   *UK stockists:* F&M ,N&P
Exciting new project producing first-class red just outside boundaries of the Ribera del Duero DO. Fruit is sourced from both Ribera and Cigales DO; the average age of the vines is 50 years. The wine is deep, dark and formidably extracted but with a fine balance and supple structure. (DM)
● **Viña Leda**★★★★ £E

BODEGA LÓPEZ HERMANOS Málaga www.lopezhermanos.com   *UK stockists:* **Mps**,Vts
Large producer of traditional Málaga based on Pedro Ximénez and Moscatel. The PX range is very good. The splendid Transañejo bottlings are aged in old soleras. Dark and extraordinarily rich, the Moscatel in particular has remarkable depth and a piercing intensity. (DM)
O **Málaga** PX Reserva de Familia★★ £C Transañejo PX Don Juan★★★★★ £F
O **Málaga** Transañejo Moscatel Don Salvador★★★★★ £F

EMILIO LUSTAU Jerez y Manzanilla   *UK stockists:* **FMV**,F&M,BBR,Wai
Splendid range of high-quality sherries. Good Reservas and better Almacenista labels. Old East India Solera is full of nutty, burnt toffee aromas. Very unusual and very rich is the Moscatel Superior Emilin. Some very fine old wines are offered from the company's oldest soleras under the Very Old, Very Old Rare and Single Cask labels. (DM)
O **Puerto Fino** Solera Reserva★★ £B   O **Almacenista** Manzanilla Pasada★★★ £D
O **Empertriz Eugenia** Oloroso★★★ £D   O **Moscatel Superior** Emilin★★★ £D
O **Old East India Solera** Oloroso★★★★ £D

MARQUÉS DE LA CONCORDIA Rioja   *UK stockists:* Maj
New-wave Rioja estate owned by the giant Berberana group. Concordia is 1 of 4 properties that the company has established under a project labelled Haciendas de Espana. Pride of place goes to the splendid single-vineyard Hacienda de Susar. Durius Magister MMII is sourced from the firm's best Duero vineyards. Also decent Penedès although more interesting varietal Petit Verdot and an Andalus red from Principe de Hohenlohe. (DM)
● **Rioja** Tempranillo★ £B Crianza★★ £C Hacienda de Susar★★★★ £E

MARQUÉS DE GRIÑÓN Castilla la Mancha   *UK stockists:* Maj,CeB,Sel,Wai
Part-owned by the giant Arco Bodegas Unidas group (whose brands include Berberana and Marqués de Monistrol). The main focus is on the Dominio de Valdepusa wines produced on the Marqués's private 30-ha estate to the south of Madrid. Marqués de Griñón Rioja is also well established. (DM)
Dominio de Valdepusa
● **Cabernet Sauvignon**★★ £C   ● **Petit Verdot**★★★ £C
● **Syrah**★★★ £C   ● **Émeritus**★★★★ £E
Marqués de Griñón Rioja
● **Rioja** Reserva Colección Personal★★ £D

MARQUÉS DE MURRIETA Rioja   *UK stockists:* **MMD**,Sel,F&M
Very conservative Rioja bodega producing traditional reds and whites exposed to considerable periods in oak. Gran Reservas are now all released under the Castillo d'Ygay label and Reservas are now simply Murrieta. Also produced is a lightly exotic Rías Baixas, Pazo de Barrantes. (DM)
● **Rioja** Gran Reserva Especial Castillo d'Ygay★★★ £E Dalmau Reserva★★★★ £F
● **Rioja** Reserva★★ £C O **Rioja** Reserva El Dorado★★ £B
New entries have producer's name underlined

SPAIN

MARQUÉS DE VARGAS Rioja www.marquesderiscal.com *UK stockists:* **Bur**, BBR
This 65-ha family-owned property is unusual for the region in producing wines solely from its own vineyards. Recently quality has been increasingly high, with major investment in a new winery facility and consultancy from Michel Rolland. The style is traditional but the winemaking and the purity and depth in the wines are second to none. (DM)
● **Rioja** Reserva★★★ £D Private Reserva★★★★ £F

MAS MARTINET Priorat martinet@arrakis.es *UK stockists:* N&P, Rae
Clos Martinet has more elegance and less raw power than other Priorats. It is a blend of Garnacha, Syrah, Cab Sauv and Cariñena. Second wine, Martinet Bru, is relatively soft and accessible, if lacking the depth and quality of some of the other secondary labels now emerging. (DM)
● **Priorat** Martinet Bru★★ £C Clos Martinet★★★★ £F

MAURO Castilla y León www.bodegasmauro.com *UK stockists:* **JAr**,Sel,F&M
Three reds are produced: the supple, opulent, forward Mauro; a Vendimia Seleccionada, which is richer and firmer; and a single-vineyard *cuvée*, Terreus, which is produced in limited volumes and only when the vintage conditions are particularly fine. (DM)
● **Mauro**★★★ £D Vendimia Seleccionada★★★★ £F Terreus★★★★★ £F

MAURODOS Toro
As well as the excellent wines he has been involved in developing at Mauro, enologist Mariano Garcia established this benchmark Toro property in the mid 1990s. Just one very fine and structured wine is made, Viña San Roman, a varietal Tinta de Toro. (DM)
● **Toro** Viña San Román★★★★ £F

BODEGA ABEL MENDOZA Rioja
Small new-wave bodega producing three reds and a barrel-fermented white Rioja. Reds are solely Tempranillo and aged in French rather than American oak. Top wine, the Selección Personal, is aged in new oak. Powerful, dense and impeccably balanced, it is edging towards five stars. (DM)
● **Rioja** Jarrarte Maceracion Carbonica★★ £B Jarrarte★★★ £C
● **Rioja** Seleccion Personal★★★★ £E

MUGA Rioja www.bodegasmuga.com *UK stockists:* **C&D**,N&P,Wai
Traditional range and at best the wines can be very good. Reserva and Gran Reserva can display classically mellow, rounded Tempranillo character with vanilla and coconut notes infused from extended time in cask. Modern-style Torre Muga, is loaded with vibrant blackberry fruit and velvety tannin. (DM)
● **Rioja** Gran Reserva Prado Enea★★★ £D Torre Muga★★★★ £F
● **Rioja** Reserva★★ £C O **Rioja** Bianco★ £B

MUSTIGUILLO V d T El Terrerazo *UK stockists:* **Lib**,NYg
Much of the vineyard is planted to very old, unirrigated Bobal, which provides potentially exceptional raw material. Two wines are produced. Finca Terrerazo is the more forward of the two, Quincha Corral is more structured and firm. Likely to improve in bottle for five years or more. (DM)
● **Finca Terrerazo**★★★ £D ● **Quincha Corral**★★★★ £F

BODEGAS OLIVARES Jumilla *UK stockists:* **Gen**
Olivares is emerging as one of the more exciting of Spain's new wave of producers from lesser regions. The key is old ungrafted Monastrell planted in sandy soils. Particularly rare is the rich, concentrated, purely varietal, late-harvested and occasionally botrytis-affected Dulce Monastrell. (DM)
● **Jumilla** Panarroz★ £A Altos de la Hoya★★★ £B Dulce Monastrell★★★★ £E

BODEGAS OSTATU Rioja www.ostatu.com *UK stockists:* Gen
Family-run bodega producing Rioja of exemplary quality, white as well as red. They have just 26ha in the higher-altitude vineyards of the Rioja Alavesa planted on chalky-clay soils. The top wine, Gloria de Ostatu, is amongst the best modern reds in Rioja. (DM)
● **Rioja** Crianza★★★ £C Reserva★★★★ £D Gloria de Ostatu★★★★ £F

SPAIN

PAGO DE CARRAOVEJAS Ribera del Duero
There are 60ha of vineyards planted to a mix of 75% Tempranillo and 25% Cabernet Sauvignon. Crianza is rich and concentrated with impressive dark berry fruit and full, supple tannins. The Riserva, which gets longer ageing, is fuller and offers greater depth and dimension. (DM)
● **Ribera del Duero** Crianza★★★ £E Reserva★★★★ £F

PALACIOS REMONDO Rioja www.ddnet.esvinhos/herenciaremondo *UK stockists:* FMV
Some impressive modern reds are made at the family property of Alvaro Palacios in the Rioja Baja. The 150 ha of vineyards are covered with large pebbles and provide a great resource for intensely flavoured fruit. Dos Viñedos is cellarworthy. (DM)
● **Rioja** Propriedad H Remondo★★★ £C Dos Viñedos★★★★ £F
● **Rioja** La Vendimia★ £B La Montesa Crianza★★ £B O **Rioja** Plácet★ £B

ALVARO PALACIOS Priorat alvaropalacios@ctv.es *UK stockists:* C&B, BBR,Sel
Alvaro Palacios established this excellent property in the late 1980s and he produces very good to quite exceptional examples of the Priorat DO from his 10 ha of vineyards. Finca Dofi and the cult L'Ermita are both refined and very ageworthy, improving effortlessly for a decade or more. (DM)
● **Priorat** Les Terasses★★★ £C Finca Dofi★★★★★ £F L'Ermita✪✪✪✪ £H

PARÉS BALTÁ Penedès www.paresbalta.com
Sizeable and ancient Penedès producer, established in 1790 as commemorated by its top micro-production red, Dominio Cusiné 1790. There is an extensive range, with a number of good small-production limited-release *cuvées*, both red and white. (DM)
● **Penedès** Mas Elena★ £B Mas Irene★★ £C Absis★★★★ £H
O **Penedès** Mas de Carol★★ £C Electio★★★ £E

PAZO SAN MAURO Rías Baixas *UK stockists:* **Bur**
This single estate was purchased by the Marqués de Vargas in 2003. The vineyards overlook the Miño River right on the border between Spain and Portugal and are in the most southerly and mountainous of the Rías Baixas sub-zones, Condado de Tea. The wines should be drunk young and fresh. (DM)
O **Rias Baixas** Albariño★★ £B San Amaro★★★ £C

PÉREZ PASCUAS Ribera del Duero *UK stockists:* Rs**W**, BBR
Fine Ribera del Duero under the Viña Pedrosa label including structured Crianza and Reserva as well as a denser, richer Gran Reserva. Pérez Pascuas, from a single vineyard, is powerful,refined and complex. A very small amount of a Pérez Pascuas Gran Seleccion is also made. (DM)
● **Ribera del Duero** Pérez Pascuas Gran Reserva★★★★ £G
● **Ribera del Duero** Pedrosa Reserva★★★ £E Pedrosa Gran Reserva★★★★ £G
● **Ribera del Duero** Pedrosa★★ £C Pedrosa Crianza★★★ £D

DOMINIO DE PINGUS Ribera del Duero *UK stockists:* C&B,BBR,Sel,F&M
Now a cult wine, Pingus was in fact only established as recently as 1995. Very modern in style and approach, the wine is massively extracted but has remarkably intense, pure, dark and spicy fruit. Second label, Fleur de Pingus, is also impressive. (DM)
● **Ribera del Duero** Pingus✪✪✪✪ £H

CELLER VINOS PIÑOL Terra Alta www.vinospinol.com
One of the very best producers in this small DO in the far north-east of the country. Whites are good enough at the top level although they lack the quality and depth of the reds. The top wine is the Mather Teresina, a selection of the oldest vines and a non-vintage blend. (DM)
● **Terra Alta** Sacra Natural★★★ £C L'Avi Arrufi★★★ £C Mather Teresina★★★★ £E
● **Terra Alta** Raig de Raïm★★ £C Señora del Portal★★★ £E
O **Terra Alta** Señora del Portal★ £B L'Avi Arrufi★★ £C

REJADORADA Toro www.rejadorada.com *UK stockists:*Msp,Ben
Founded only in 1999, although the vineyards are some of the oldest in the region. Sango Reserva is rich, dense and powerful, full of dark spicy fruit and underpinned by toasty vanilla oak. Surprisingly approachable, this

204

should develop well over five or six years. (DM)
- **Toro** Tinto Roble★★ £C Crianza★★★ £C Sango Reserva★★★★ £E

REMELLURI Rioja remelluri@sea.es *UK stockists:***Adm**
90 ha planted in the Rioja Alavesa and the vineyards are tended organically. Reserva and Gran Reserva, particularly, are structured and will stand some ageing – the latter will be all the better for five or six years in your cellar. The Crianza is supple and approachable. (DM)
- **Rioja** Crianza★★ £C Reserva★★★ £D Gran Reserva★★★ £E

REMÍREZ DE GANUZA Rioja www.remirezdeganuza.com *UK stockists:***Vni**
Top-quality Rioja bodega based in the Rioja Alavesa with 57 ha under vine. Three good to exceptional reds of real distinction are produced and the Trasnocho is one of the region's great wines. It will add complexity with age. (DM)
- **Rioja** Fincas de Ganuza Reserva★★★ £D Remirez de Ganuza Reserva★★★ £E Trasnocho★★★★★ £F

CELLERS RIPOLL SANS Priorat www.closabatllet.com *UK stockists:* **Vni**
Very good recently established small Priorat estate. Both red and white examples are made in artisan style and quantity. Marc Ripoll has some excellent terraced vineyards and vines up to 90 years of age which contribute significantly to the dense, black-fruited, mineral-laden red. (DM)
- **Priorat** Closa Batllet★★★★ £E

RODA Rioja *UK stockists:* Odd,N&P,F&R,Tur
Impressive 50-ha Rioja property producing two Reservas and a new-wave Rioja *super-cuvée*, the very pricey Cirsion. Roda I is the flagship of the two Reservas, powerful and concentrated but with the characteristic underlying spicy, berry fruit character of Tempranillo. (DM)
- **Rioja** Roda I★★★ £E Roda II★★★★ £E Cirsion★★★★★ £G

BODEGA RODERO Ribera del Duero www.bodegasrodero.com *UK stockists:* **Msp,Ben**
Traditional range of good Ribera del Duero with some fine, increasingly old vineyards at high altitude. The top wines are impressively ageworthy and the Gran Reserva offers real depth and power. Backward and restrained in its youth, it demands six or seven years' patience. (DM)
- **Ribera del Duero** Reserva★★★★ £E Gran Reserva★★★★★ £G
- **Ribera del Duero** Joven★★ £C Roble★★ £C Crianza★★★ £C

TELMO RODRÍGUEZ Rioja *UK stockists:* **Adm**
Telmo Rodriguez is one of Spain's great winemaking stars. From his base in Logroño he produces an extensive range of wines from throughout the country in highly diverse styles. Some very fine reds are joined by the splendid Moscatel-based Málaga, Molino Real. (DM)
- **Ribera del Duero** M2★★★ £E Matellana★★★★★ £G
- **Rioja**Altos de Lanzaga★★★★ £F ● **Toro**Pago La Jara★★★★ £E
- **Cigales** Vina 105★★ £C O **Málaga** Molino Real★★★★ £E

ROTLLÁN I TORRA Priorat www.closabattlet.com *UK stockists:* **Mor,F&R,Tur**
Jordi Rotlan's family estate of 24 ha was founded in 1984 and now offers some excitingly dark, spicy and fiery examples of this appellation, arguably Spain's greatest now for reds. Better with at least five years' ageing. (DM)
- **Priorat** Balandra★★★ £D Amadís★★★ £E Tirant★★★★ £E

CELLER JOAN SANGENIS Priorat *UK stockists:* **Bur**
The 80ha here are planted on south-facing slopes and the winery is modern and well equipped. Cal Pla labels are light and fruit-driven, Mas d'En Compte Crianza comes from mostly old Cariñena and Garnacha and the white is barrel-fermented Garnacha Blanca/Picapoll/Pansal. (DM)
- **Priorat** Cal Pla★★ £C Mas d'en Compte Crianza★★★★ £E
- O **Priorat** Cal Pla★★ £D Mas d'en Compte Barrel-Fermented★★★ £E

DOMINIO DE TARES Bierzo www.dominiodetares.com
Newly established bodega producing good to excellent reds plus 2 Godello-based whites. Baltos is soft and forward, Cepas Viejas is from 60-year-old vines and the opulent Bembibre is aged only in American oak. The top red, the

SPAIN

Tares P3, is altogether subtler and finer. (DM)

● **Bierzo** Baltos★★ £C Cepas Viejas★★★ £D Bembibre★★★★ £E Tares P3★★★★ £F

TORRES Penedès www.torres.es   *UK stockists:* **JFe**,Sel,Wai

Very important producer, now making wines at all quality levels from grapes sourced throughout Cataluña. The Penedès firm of Jean León has been added to the operation and its wines are now of a uniformly much higher quality than they were before the acquisition by Torres. Top reds are undoubtedly ageworthy; Reserva Real requires considerable patience. (DM)

● **Mas la Plana** Penedès★★★ £E   ● **Reserva Real** Penedès★★★★ £H
● **Grans Muralles** Conca de Barberá★★★ £E   O **Waltraud** Penedès★★★ £C
O **Fransola** Penedès★★★ £D   O **Milmanda** Conca de Barberá★★★ £E

VALDESPINO Jerez y Manzanilla   *UK stockists:* **HWC**,Wai

Marvellous, old-fashioned sherry producer with an impressive holding of old soleras to provide some of the best examples to be found in Jerez. The extraordinary intense, nutty and fragrant Coliseo is one of the greatest sherries. (DM)

O **Inocente** Fino★★ £B   O **Su Majestad** Oloroso★★★★ £D
O **Don Tomás** Amontillado★★★ £C   O **Coliseo** Amontillado❂❂❂❂❂£E

CELLER VALL LLACH Priorat www.fm2.com/vallllach   *UK stockists:* F&R

Singer Luis Llach founded this first-class Priorat property in the early 1990s. He also has an interest in Cims de Porrera. Vall Llach is dominated by old-vine Cariñena, with Garnacha and Cab Sauv blended in. It is a dark, spicy, brooding beast, full of fiery *sauvage* character. (DM)

● **Priorat★★★★★ £F** Embruix★★★ £C

BODEGAS VALSACRO Rioja www.valsacro.com

The Escudero family produce wines under the Escudero label as well as from their premium label, Valsacro. The Escudero wines are well made but lack the depth and intensity of the top reds. The splendidly complex and intense Dioro is modern and fleshy with malolactic in French oak barrels. (DM)

● **Rioja**★★★ £D Dioro★★★★ £E O **Rioja** Oloroso★★★ £D

VEGA SICILIA Ribera del Duero www.vega-sicilia.com   *UK stockists:* **FMV**,BBR,F&M

Spain's most famous red wine producer. Top wine, Unico, is still given extended cask-maturation, although this has been reduced to help preserve the wine's fruit character. Second wine, Valbuena, has more obvious fruit character. Alión offers a more modern, richly complex, contemporary style. (DM)

Bodegas Vega Sicilia
● **Ribera del Duero** Valbuena★★★★ £F Reserva Especial★★★★★ £H Unico❂❂❂❂❂ £H

Bodegas y Viñedos Alión
● **Ribera del Duero** Alión★★★★★ £E

Other wineries of note

Bodegas Agnusdei (Rias Baixas), Ameztoi (Getariako Txakolina), Artazu (Navarra), Bodegas Crianza Castilla La Vieja (Rueda), Castell del Remei (Costers del Segre), Contino (Rioja), Cortijo La Monjas (Vino de Mesa), Costers del Siurana (Priorat), Hermanos Cuadrado (Ribera del Duero), Dehesa La Granja (Vino de Mesa), Pedro Domecq (Jerez y Manzanilla), El Seque (Alicante), El Vinculo (La Mancha), Bodegas Emeterio Fernández (Cigales), Bodegas Escudero (Rioja), Hacienda Unamuna (Castille y León), Heretat Vall-Ventós (Penedès), Ijalba (Rioja), La Rioja Alta (Rioja), Marqués de Riscal (Rioja), Mas Perinet (Priorat), Masia l'Hereu (Penedès), Pazo de Señoráns (Rias Baixas), Quinta de la Quietud (Toro), Senorio de Otazu (Navarra), Terras Gauda (Rias Baixas), Hermanos del Villar (Rueda)

An in-depth profile of every producer can be found in Wine behind the label 2006

New entries have producer's name underlined

1 Vinho Verde
2 Douro, Port
3 Bairrada
4 Dão
5 Alenquer
6 Palmela, Setúbal

RIOS DO MINHO

TRÁS-OS-MONTES

TUA

DOURO

1

Pinhão

2

Porto

DOURO

Peso da Régua

Viseu

3   *4*

Coimbra

BEIRAS

ESTREMADURA

RIBATEJO

TEJO

5

Portalegre

ALENTEJO

Estremoz

Lisboa

6

Évora

Setúbal

TERRAS DO SADO

Reguengos de Monsaraz

Vidigueira

Moura

GUADIANA

ALGARVE

Faro

Background

The fantastic revolution taking place in the quality of Portuguese wines continues. At the cutting edge are some brilliant winemakers making both everyday wines of great value and character and also exciting new wines of unprecedented quality for this ancient wine-producing country. The Douro, followed by Alentejo, provides the greatest riches but there are exciting wines from nearly all the major regions. Wines from leading producers can be tried with confidence.

Styles of Port

There are two basic styles of port: bottle matured and wood aged. In the first category, **Vintage Port** applies equally to shipper's ports from a 'declared' vintage, single-quinta ports and 'off-vintage' ports (or 'second label' – a shipper's port from a non-declared year). All require decanting. Late Bottled Vintage Port (or **LBV**) spends 4-6 years in large vats and most are fined and filtered. 'Traditional' examples, closer to Vintage Ports in character and depth might age further 5 or 6 years after release. **Crusted Port** (a blend of 2 or 3 vintages), like Traditional LBVs and Vintage Port, will throw a sediment.

The best wood-matured are tawnies with an indication of age. The best fresh, balanced **10-year-old Tawny Port** show a date, nut, fig and toasty complexity but this is seen more often in examples of the more pricey **20-year-old Tawny Port**. **30-and 40-year-old** can have an intense, nutty *rancio* character and complexity not dissimilar to an aged sherry. **Colheita Port** is effectively a tawny port of a single vintage - labelled with both *colheita* (vintage) and bottling year. The best **Vintage Character** or **Premium Ruby** are relatively inexpensive and offer good fruit intensity in an easy-drinking style. Good regular **Ruby Port** is young and fruity port. **White Port** is made from white grapes but turning amber with age, better examples are dry and nutty.

...and Madeira

The best **Madeira** come from one of four traditional varieties - either Malvasia (Malmsey), Bual (Boal), Verdelho or Sercial - and are of a particular style and degree of sweetness. The richest and sweetest, Malmsey – often pungent, full and toffeed – is usually the most easily appreciated but most examples miss the elegance and definition associated with the smoky, spicy, dried-fruits Bual (Boal), which is less sweet but still a dessert-style wine. The best Verdelho (of moderate sweetness) is often tangy yet lightly honeyed with dried citrus fruits and a certain delicacy of flavour and aroma. The dry Sercial, often with daunting acidity, can show a fine citrusy (orangey), nutty and dried-fruit complexity with age. The best commercial examples are the 10-year-old and 15-year-old wines. Vintage Madeira spends at least 20 years in cask but many of the very best have spent 50 years or even 100 years in wood. Once bottled it continues to age but at a very slow rate.

Port Vintages

The best vintages are 'declared' by port shippers while in other years of sufficient quality the same wine is bottled under the name of a leading estate or quinta. In addition estate-based ports from true single quintas will produce a Vintage Port in almost every year. For a true guide to longevity both the vintage assessment and that of the individual producer's style and reputation must be taken together. **Those years underlined denote a wide declaration.**

2003: In the year of Europe's extreme heat Portugal's Douro fared better than most. Cask samples of the top names reveal deeply perfumed, richly berried wines of great potential.

2002: Rains fell to spoil a potentially fine vintage. Some good, forward, fruit-emphasised single-quinta ports were made by those who care about quality.

2001: Preceded by an incredibly wet winter which has dampened quality to some extent, though volumes are up.

2000: Yields were very low and best wines have an incredible intensity of fruit - will be long-lived with great expression and classic character in the top names.

1999: Top quality was hard to achieve and while most small estates made Vintage Port, the shippers opted for their single-quinta ports.

1998: The best single-quinta ports are reasonably concentrated and intense but more modestly structured and lack real stuffing - attractive in the medium term.

1997: Ports with quite firm but ripe structures and the best are well-concentrated too. Less successful than 1994 or 2000 yet still a very promising vintage.

1995: Good concentration and often very ripe and with more raisiny characters and a lack of flavour finesse in some. Mostly single-quinta port.

<u>**1994:**</u> The most outstanding port vintage in recent times. Remarkably seductive fruit and a deep, tannic backbone suggests classic wines with 20, 30 or more years' age.

1992: A very high-quality vintage declared by a few who preferred this to 1991. Taylor's, Vesúvio and Niepoort made ports of real class and concentration.

<u>**1991:**</u> Full and firm, with plenty of power in the best examples. The best such as Dow, Graham and Warre deserve considerably longer.

1987: Few declarations but whether Vintage or single-quinta, one for drinking up.

<u>**1985:**</u> Much-touted vintage but highly variable - Symington group coped the best (Graham is superb); also Fonseca.

<u>**1983:**</u> Muscle and structure typified many of the wines

but the best have added flesh and richness with age. Another Symington year, also Taylor and Niepoort very good.

1982: Some declared 82 instead of the superior 83 and got it badly wrong. Sandeman and Niepoort did rather better but one for drinking up.

1980: Dow, Graham and Warre made remarkably good and well-priced port in this under-rated vintage.

1977: A classic year but in many instances now near its best. Some variation but brilliant Fonseca and fine efforts from Graham, Niepoort, Smith Woodhouse and Warre.

1975: A relatively light and fast-maturing vintage.

1970: Generally a very good vintage with most wines showing excellent balance and fine tannins. Dow, Graham, Fonseca, Noval's Nacional, Niepoort and Taylor will continue to improve.

1966: Very powerful long-lasting ports though most miss the extra finesse and harmony of 63. Look for Cálem, Delaforce, Dow, Fonseca, Graham, Noval's Nacional and Taylor.

1963: The finest proven vintage of the second half of the 20th century. Cockburn, Croft, Delaforce, Dow, Fonseca, Graham, Noval's Nacional, Taylor and Warre provide the evidence.

Earlier Years: Great port years extend back the length of the entire 20th century if increasingly scarce and expensive). 1960 is a fully mature vintage - Cockburn's seems the most likely to keep much longer. 1955 has more vigour and richness and well-sourced bottles of Dow, Graham, Fonseca and regular Noval will live on. Older vintages (48, 45, 35, 34, 31, 27 and others) should only be be bought where the wines have been impeccably stored and from a reliable bottler.

Portuguese red wine vintages
The best Portuguese table wines have considerable ageing potential. In general, the best reds, whatever their origins, will keep for 5-10 years but the majority of such wines have been made in the last decade and do not come from earlier vintages. Therefore while the vintage chart needs to be considered in conjunction with comments in the specific producer entry, in most instances buy from a recent good vintage whether for drinking young or to cellar for a substantial period.

Wizard's Wishlist

Classic Vintage Ports
CHURCHILL ● Vintage Port
DOW'S ● Vintage Port
FONSECA ● Vintage Port
GRAHAM'S ● Vintage Port
NIEPOORT ● Vintage Port
QUINTA DE RORIZ ● Vintage Port
QUINTA DO NOVAL ● Vintage Port Nacional
QUINTA DO VESUVIO ● Vintage Port
SMITH WOODHOUSE ● Vintage Port
TAYLOR'S ● Vintage Port
WARRE'S ● Vintage Port

Alternative 'single Quinta' type ports
COCKBURN ● Vintage Port Quinta dos Canais
DELAFORCE ● Vintage Port Quinta da Corte
DOW ● Vintage Port Quinta do Bomfim
FONSECA ● Vintage Port Guimaraens
GRAHAM ● Vintage Port Malvedos
QUINTA DE LA ROSA ● Vintage Port
QUINTA DO VALE DOÑA MARIA ● Vintage Port
TAYLOR'S ● Vintage Port Quinta de Vargellas
WARRE ● Vintage Port Quinta da Cavadinha

Leading new order Portuguese reds
ALVES DE SOUSA ● Douro Quinta da Gaivosa
CAVES ALIANÇA ● Alentejo Quinta da Terrugem
CORTES DE CIMA ● Reserva
FERREIRA ● Douro Quinta da Leda
NIEPOORT ● Douro Redoma
LUIS PATO ● Vinha Barrosa
PINTAS ● Douro
QUINTA DO CRASTO ● Douro Vinha da Ponte
QUINTA DO VALE DOÑA MARIA ● Douro
QUINTA DO VALE MEÃO ● Douro
QUINTA DO PASSADOURO ● Douro Reserva
QUINTA DOS ROQUES ● Dão Reserva
JOÃO PORTUGAL RAMOS ● Alentejo Marqués de Borba Reserva
QUINTA DO ZAMBUJEIRO ● Zambujeiro

Good Value Portuguese reds
CASAL BRANCO ● Ribatejo Falcoaria
CAVES ALIANÇA ● Palmela Particular
CORTES DE CIMA ● Chaminé
DFJ VINHOS ● Manta Preta
ESPORÃO ● Alentejo Reserva
QUINTA DE LA ROSA ● Douro
QUINTA DO VALLADO ● Douro
JOÃO PORTUGAL RAMOS ● Vila Santa
SOGRAPE ● Douro Reserva
VINHA D'ERVIDEIRA ● Vinha d'Ervideira

Portugal A-Z of producers

DOMINGOS ALVES DE SOUSA   Douro
Several estates for Douro reds. Stylish and refined Quinta da Gaivosa is Touriga Nacional, Tinta Cão and Tinta Roriz – as is deep, powerful, ageworthy Grande Escolha from Quinta do Vale da Raposa. Inexpensive but well made Estação, Caldas and Aveleira wines. New powerful, earthy Alves de Sousa Pessoal from Gaivosa and supple and berryish inexpensive Cume red. Whites are variable. (PW)

Quinta da Gaivosa:
● **Douro★★★** £C

Quinta do Vale da Raposa:
● **Douro★** £B Tinta Roriz★★ £B Touriga Nacional★★ £B Grande Escolha★★★ £C

BACALHÔA   Terras do Sado   www.bacalhoa.com   *UK stockists:* **Ehr**
Significant and sizeable producer previously known as JP Vinhos. Wines of good flavour and intensity, including gutsy Tinto da Ânfora (mostly Aragonês) and superior Grande Escolha version. Quinta do Bacalhôa (Cab Sauv, Merlot) is ripe, meaty and characterful. Má Partilha Merlot can be slightly raisiny if savoury. In whites, Cova da Ursa is flavoursome barrel-fermented Chardonnay. Also light Catarina white, J P basics and sparkling wine. New Só Syrah and Touriga show increasing richness and style. (PW)
● **Tinto da Ânfora★** £B Grande Escolha★★★ £C
● **Quinta do Bacalhôa★★★** £C ● **Só Syrah★★★** £C ● **Só Touriga Nacional★★★** £C
O **Cova da Ursa★** £B O **Moscatel de Setúbal★★** £C

BARBEITO   Madeira   *UK stockists:* **RyR**, BBR, F&M, P&S, Hfx, RGr, F&R
Interesting commercial Madeiras and old vintage examples. Wines are subject only to natural heating and are drier, with higher acidities than some. Flavoursome Single Harvest shows what is possible from Tinta Negra Mole. Basic Boal (Bual) Veramar has excellent fruit and intensity, the 10-year-old is fine, while the 20 adds still more power, intensity and length. Elegant, pure vintage single-cask Malvasia (currently 1994 Cask 18a) and stylish vintage Verdelho (1981). (PW)
O **Single Harvest★★★** £D O **Madeira** Boal Veramar★★★ £C
O **Madeira** 10-year-old Boal Reserve★★★ £E 10-year-old Sercial Reserve★★★ £E
O **Madeira** 20-year-old Special Reserve Malvasia★★★★ £F

C.A.R.M   Douro   www.carm.pt   *UK stockists:* **RyR**
C.A.R.M stands for Casa Agrícola Roboredo Madeira. Trained winemaker Rui Madeira makes 3 excellent wines under the C.A.R.M label and several others named for individual quintas. Best is oak-aged and ageworthy Praemium. Aromatic Quinta da Urze varietals can be drunk fairly young. Quinta do Côa includes an organic Reserva. (PW)

C.A.R.M:
● **Douro** Classico★★ £B Reserva★★★ £C Praemium★★★★ £D

Quinta da Urze:
● **Douro** Touriga Nacional★★ £B Tinta Roriz★★ £B Touriga Franca★★ £B

CASAL BRANCO   Ribatejo   www.casalbranco.com   *UK stockists:* **Oak**, Wai
Large estate more famous for breeding horses. Cool-fruited Merlot and Cab Sauv under the Capucho label but much more concentrated Petit Verdot (from 2003). More original is Falcoaria (Castelão/Trincadeira); the Reserva (try from 2001) has more depth and cedary, herbal black fruits. Also sound inexpensive dual-variety Cork Grove wines (sold in the UK). (PW)
● **Ribatejo** Falcoaria★★ £B Falcoaria Reserva★★★ £B
● **Merlot** Capucho★★ £B ● **Cabernet Sauvignon** Capucho★★ £B
● **Petit Verdot** Capucho★★★ £D O **Ribatejo** Falcoaria★ £B

CAVES ALIANÇA   Beiras   www.caves-alianca.com   *UK stockists:* **Mer**,ACh
Much-improved big company. The better wines from large estates show regional character and savoury intensity with age. Francisco Antunes works with Michel Rolland on the flagship reds. Very fine Quinta da Terrugem in Alentejo is Aragonês/Trincadeira with smoke, earth and black plum. Classy T da Terrugem combines power and

New entries have producer's name underlined

finesse. The Quatro Ventos (Douro), primarily Touriga Franca/ Tinta Barocca, shows real potential (also exciting new Reserva). Baceladas is characterful Bairrada from Merlot/Cab Sauv/Baga. New Garrida is classic Dão with floral and mineral notes. (PW)

Aliança:
- **Douro** Foral Grande Escolha★★ £B   ● **Bairrada** Garrafeira★★ £B
- **Dão** Particular★★ £B   ● **Palmela** Particular★★ £B

Quinta da Terrugem:
- **Alentejo** Quinta da Terrugem★★★ £C T da Terrugem★★★★★ £F

CHURCHILL Port   *UK stockists:* **EdV**, HHB, CPp, L&S, Tan, P&S, FWC
Port house established 20 years ago by Johnny Graham, with important Quinta da Gricha and Quinta do Rio sites since 1999 (complementing fine Agua Alta made in 1998, 96, 95 and 92). The ports show rich, ripe fruit and good balance. Vintage continues to improve (best recent years 2003, 2000, 97, 94 and 91). Other ports are good value. Good dry white port. Also Douro reds. (PW)
- **Vintage Port**★★★★ £F Quinta da Gricha★★★ £E   ● **Crusted Port**★★★ £C
- **Late Bottled Vintage Port** Traditional★★ £C   ● **10-year-old Tawny Port**★★ £C
- **Finest Vintage Character Port**★★ £B   O **White Port** Dry Aperitif★ £B

COCKBURN Port   www.cockburns-usa.com   *UK stockists:* **ADo**, AAA
One of the best-known port names with popular basic Special Reserve Vintage Character. Substantial vineyards include excellent Quinta do Tua and Quinta dos Canais. Vintage is back on form since 1991 (excellent 94 and 00), while 1963 and earlier can be superb. Single-quinta Canais shows a lovely fruit purity and intensity. Modest LBV; good tawnies. (PW)
- **Vintage Port**★★★★ £F Quinta dos Canais★★★ £E
- **10-year-old Tawny Port**★ £C   ● **20-year-old Tawny Port**★★ £E

CORTES DE CIMA Alentejo   www.cortesdecima.pt   *UK stockists:* Adm, JNi, Maj
Ripe, modern reds made by Hans Kristian Jørgensen; fruit-driven with excellent varietal expression, particularly from Portuguese grapes. Ripe, fleshy Cortes de Cima is a varying blend featuring Syrah, Aragonês and Trincadeira; the dark, dense Reserva marries new oak to complex fruit. Powerful, very ripe Syrah Incógnito. Enticingly aromatic Touriga Nacional and a second Syrah in 2002. Good-value forward, fruity Chaminé; also basic Courela. New varietal Antão Vaz is the first white. (PW)
- **Cortes de Cima**★★ £C **Reserva**★★★★ £E
- **Incógnito**★★★ £E   ● **Aragonez**★★★ £E   ● **Chaminé**★ £B

CROFT Port   www.croftport.com   *UK stockists:* **Men**, AAA
Long-established house of variable quality set to improve under Taylor-Fonseca ownership. Quinta da Roêda is the backbone of all its best Vintage Ports, giving muscularity. Decent 10-year-old Tawny and filtered LBV with upfront fruit. Big-volume basics include 'Distinction' Vintage Character. (PW)
- **Vintage Port**★★★ £F Quinta da Roêda★★ £E   ● **10-year-old Tawny Port**★★ £E

D F J VINHOS www.dfjvinhos.com   *UK stockists:* **D&F**, Wai
A large modern range focused on native varieties offering good flavour and supple textures even at very modest price points. Grand' Arte varietals combine quality and value. Also 3 new premium wines: Escada is a Douro blend with classic character and real depth; Francos is from Alenquer and is classy and individual; best of all is Consensus (2003) from Ribatejo which should age well. (PW)
- O **Grand' Arte Chardonnay**★★ £B   ● **Manta Preta**★★ £B
- **Senda do Vale Reserva**★★ £B   ● **Douro Patamar Reserva**★★ £B   ,
- **Grand' Arte Touriga Nacional**★★ £B   ● **Douro Escada**★★★ £C
- **Alenquer Francos**★★★ £C   ● **Ribatejo Consensus**★★★★ £C

DELAFORCE Port   *UK stockists:* **Men**, AAA
Delaforce, like Croft, should improve under Taylor-Fonseca. The wines are noted for being fruit-rich, stylish and refined at best (1977 and earlier, although good 92, 94, 2000 and 2003). The Quinta da Corte is key to fruit quality and the source of a delicious, relatively forward single-quinta port. LBV can have good fruit, while the tawnies show more finesse than most yet have good intensity too. (PW)
- **Vintage Port**★★★ £E Quinta da Corte★★ £E

● **20-year-old Tawny Port** Curious and Ancient★★★ £E
● **10-year-old Tawny Port** His Eminence's Choice★★ £C   ● **LBV Port**★ £C

DOW Port www.dows-port.com *UK stockists:* **JEF,**AAA
Part of the Symington empire but with a very distinct profile. Weight and dimension combined with an elegance
and poise put the top examples among the best (recently 1994, 97, 2000 and 2003). It is quite a structured port
but its fine tannins are covered in layers of ripe fruit. Fine single-quinta ports come from the important Quinta
do Bomfim in non-declared years; also Quinta Senhora da Ribeira since 1998. Tawnies tend to be quite vigorous
with good complexity at the 20-and 30-year level. Trademark is acceptable Vintage Character port. (PW)
● **Vintage Port**✪✪✪✪✪ £F Bomfim★★★★ £E Senhora da Ribeira★★★★ £F
● **30-year-old Tawny Port**★★★ £F   ● **20-year-old Tawny Port**★★★ £D
● **10-year-old Tawny Port**★★ £C   ● **Crusted Port**★★★ £C   ● **LBV Port**★★ £C

ESPORÃO Alentejo www.esporao.com *UK stockists:* **JEF,** Hrd,Wai
Winemaker David Baverstock has set a high standard at the 600-ha Alentejo venture of the Roquette family
(behind Quinta do Crasto). Esporão and varietal wines are bold, powerful, ripe, intense, fruit-driven and oak-
influenced. Esporão Reserva is Trincadeira/Aragonês/Cab Sauv; the white is Antão Vaz/Arinto/Roupeiro. Private
Selection white resembles concentrated Barossa Sémillon. At an everyday level the best vintages of Monte Velho
red can provide decent value. (PW)
● **Alentejo** Esporão Reserva★★ £B Esporão Private Selection★★★★ £E
● **Alicante Bouschet**★★★ £C   ● **Aragonês**★★★ £C   ● **Syrah**★★★ £C
O **Alentejo** Esporão Reserva★★ £B Esporão Private Selection★★ £C

FERREIRA Port *UK stockists:* **BWC,** Sel, F&R
The most gutsy and earthy of the leading Vintage Ports. It is declared more frequently than most and it can age
impressively. LBV has character and depth, while tawnies maintain fruit intensity. The famous Barca Velha dry
red is based Tinta Roriz, now aged in new French oak and released at 5 to 10 years. Lesser years are released as
Casa Ferreirinha Reserva. New Quinta da Leda and Callabriga are Touriga Nacional/Tinta Roriz/Touriga Franca
with power and depth but need 7 to 10 years. (PW)
Ferreira:
● **Vintage Port**★★★ £E   ● **Late Bottled Vintage Port**★★ £C
● **Tawny Port** 10-year-old Quinta do Porto★★ £D
● **20-year-old Tawny Port** Duque de Bragança★★★ £E
Casa Ferreirinha:
● **Douro** Casa Ferreirinha Reserva★★ £E Barca Velha★★★★ £F
● **Douro** Quinta da Leda★★★ £C Quinta da Leda Touriga Nacional★★★ £C
● **Douro** Callabriga★★ £C Vinha Grande★★ £B

FONSECA Port www.fonseca.pt *UK stockists:* **Men,** AAA
One of the truly great Vintage Ports – a rich and expansive style with often
explosive fruit intensity and marvellous depth of flavour. Great vintages include 2003, 2000, 97, 94, 92, 85, 77,
70, 66, 63 and 55. Fonseca Guimaraens is the consistently very fine 'off-vintage' port. Occasional single-quinta
Quinta do Panascal. Tawnies show good vigour and intensity; good fruit in a filtered LBV. Bin 27 is one of the
best of the big-brand Vintage Character ports. Also dry White Port, Siroco. (PW)
● **Vintage Port**✪✪✪✪✪ £G Fonseca Guimaraens★★★★ £E Panascal★★★ £E
● **10-year-old Tawny Port**★★ £C   ● **20-year-old Tawny Port**★★★ £E

JOSÉ MARIA DA FONSECA Terras do Sado www.jmf.pt *UK stockists:* **HMW**
Long-established family producer with 850 ha in Terras do Sado and Alentejo. Some attractive volume brands.
Periquita Clássico, released with some age, shows classic spicy, berry, savoury and chocolaty Castelão character.
Garrafeira wines show excellent complexity, depth and intensity (best with 6 to 10 years). Promising new
Colecção Privada varietals and new powerful, oaky Hexagon (from 2000). Domini wines are a joint venture with
Cristiano van Zeller (Quinta do Vale Doña Maria). Domini Plus shows classic Douro character and intensity in
a modern style. The other great strength is fortified sweet Setúbal. (PW)
José Maria da Fonseca:
● **Hexagon**★★★ £F   ● **Periquita** Clássico★★ £C

212

● **Garrafeira** CO★★ £C RA★★ £C FSF★★★ £C
O **Setúbal** Superior★★ £E Moscatel Roxo 20-year-old★★ £E
O **Moscatel de Setúbal** Alambre★ £B
Domingos Soares Franco & Cristiano Van Zeller:
● **Douro** Domini★ £B Domini Plus★★★ £C

GRAHAM   Port   www.grahams-port.com   *UK stockists:* **JEF**, AAA
Brilliant Vintage Port is perhaps the most consistent of all – big, rich and sweet-fruited with a lush opulence that conceals ripe, compact tannins. Excellent in 2000, 97, 94, 91, 85, 83, 80, 77, 70, 66, 63, 55 and 45; often excellent Malvedos Vintage Port in non-declared years. Adequate aged tawnies; filtered LBV is fruity, round and agreeable. Intense, grapey Six Grapes Premium Ruby and now a Crusted. (PW)
● **Vintage Port**✪✪✪✪✪ £F Malvedos★★★★ £E
● **10-year-old Tawny Port**★ £D ● **20-year-old Tawny Port**★★ £E

HENRIQUES & HENRIQUES   Madeira   *UK stockists:* **HWC**, F&M, Evg
Consistent commercial Madeira from a historic producer with a modern winery, excellent in 10-year-old and 15-year-old versions. Vibrant citrusy Sercial, elegant honeyed Verdelho, rich nutty Bual and still richer, sweeter but less refined Malmsey. Extra intensity and richness in 15-year-old versions better balance the assertive acidities. Very small amounts of venerable Vintage Madeira. (PW)
O **Madeira** 15-year-old Sercial★★★ £E Verdelho★★★ £E Bual★★★ £E
O **Madeira** 15-year-old Malmsey★★★ £E 10-year-old Malmsey★★ £D
O **Madeira** 10-year-old Sercial★★ £D Verdelho★★★ £D Bual★★★ £D

LAVRADORES DE FEITORIA   Douro   www.lavradoresdefeitoria.pt   *UK stockists:* **RyR**
New project using grapes from 15 estates that were previously sold to port companies. Três Bagos red offers plenty of character and fruit. White is fresh and perfumed. Basic Douro bottlings are forward, fruity quaffers. Top Grande Escolha red has classy black-fruited depth – 2003 is even better than 01. Also promising special single-quinta Quinta da Costa das Aguaneiras No. 6 (2003). (PW)
● **Douro** Três Bagos★★ £B Três Bagos Grande Escolha★★★★ £E
● **Douro** Quinta da Costa das Aguaneiras No. 6★★★ £C
O **Douro**★ £B Três Bagos★★ £B

MADEIRA WINE COMPANY   www.madeirawinecompany.com   *UK stockists:* **JEF**, AAA
The leading producer of Madeira, encompassing Blandy's, Cossart Gordon and Leacocks. Noble varieties are made using the *canteiro* system and aged in used American oak. Blandy's wines are generally richer and sweeter than those of Cossart Gordon. Cossart 10-year-old Verdelho and Bual are particularly fine for this level. Blandy's concentrated and elegant 15-year-old Malmsey is a significant step up from the 10-year-old version. Also many fine Vintage Madeiras. (PW)
Blandy's:
O **Madeira** 15-year-old Malmsey★★★ £E 10-year-old Malmsey★★ £D
O **Madeira** 5-year-old Malmsey★★ £C Dry Duke of Sussex★ £C
Cossart Gordon:
O **Madeira** 15-year-old Bual★★★ £E 10-year-old Bual★★★ £D
O **Madeira** 10-year-old Verdelho★★★ £D 5-year-old Bual★★ £C
Leacocks:
O **Madeira** 10-year-old Bual★★ £D

NIEPOORT   Port   *UK stockists:* **RyR**, Bib, Rae, Han, P&S, OxW, BBR, F&M, FWC
Dirk Niepoort produces both outstanding Douro table wines and an extraordinary array of fine ports. The Vintage Port is marked by its raw power and vigour in youth but with almost unequalled intensity and length of flavour. Secundum is a lighter second selection. 10-year-old Tawny Port shows great subtlety and complexity and there are very fine *colheitas*. Also the best White Port going. The red wines from old, low-yielding vines have excellent structure and weight. (PW)
● **Vintage Port**✪✪✪✪✪ £F Secundum★★★★ £E
● **Colheita Port**★★★★ £E ● **10-year-old Tawny**★★★ £E ● **30-year-old**★★★★ £F
● **Senior Tawny Port**★★★ £C ● **Junior Tinto Port**★★ £B

Portugal

- **Douro** Vertente★★★ £C   Redoma★★★★ £E   Batuta★★★★★ £F
- **Douro** Redoma★★ £B   O **Douro** Redoma★★★ £C

LUIS PATO   Bairrada   *UK stockists:* **LyS**,Vne, Hrd, Sel
Bairrada' great moderniser, creating excellent, ageworthy wines that show off the earthy, truffly flavours at Baga at their best. Top wine is old-vine Vinha Barossa. Baga Pé Franco is from ungrafted vines. A regular Baga has more forward, spicy, black-plum fruit and is lightly structured. Premium white Vinha Formal from Bical is subtle yet intense. The wines are labelled as Vinho Regional Beiras. (PW)
- **Quinta do Ribeirinho Baga Pé Franco★★★★ £F** ● **Baga★ £B**
- **Vinha Barrosa★★★★ £D** ● **Vinha Pan★★★ £D** ● **Vinha Moinho★★★ £D**
- **Vinha Barrio★★★ £D** O **Vinha Formal★★★ £C** O **Maria Gomes★★ £B**

PINTAS   Douro/Port   *UK stockists:* **C&B**
Profound Douro red from just 1.8 ha belonging to Jorge Serôdio Borges (ex-Niepoort) and his wife Sandra Tavares (Quinta do Vale Doña Maria). More than 30 different grape varieties from 80-year-old vines are fermented and foot-trodden in *lagares* and aged in *barriques*. Fabulous fruit and depth in 2001 and promising classy 2003 - also vintage port from the latter vintage. (PW)
- **Douro★★★★ £E**

POEIRA/QUINTA DE TERRA FEITA DE CIMA   Douro   *UK stockists:* **FMV**, Han, Hfx
Jorge Moreira consults for Quinta de la Rosa but also makes a few thousand bottles of his own from Quinta de Terra Feita de Cima. This is an elegant, classy Douro red with both red and black fruits. While not in a blockbuster mould, it shows intensity, depth and evident ageing potential (give it 6–10 years from 2003 or 01). (PW)
- **Douro** Poeira★★★★ £D

QUINTA DE CHOCAPALHA   Estremadura   *UK stockists:* **C&B**
Family estate of talented Sandra Tavares da Silva (also see Quinta do Vale Doña Maria), using robotic *lagares* and plenty of French oak. Top wine Chocapalha is mostly Touriga Nacional/Tinta Roriz with a depth and texture not encountered in other Estremadura reds. Also a distinctive blackcurrant, mint and mineral Cabernet Sauvignon. White Chardonnay/Arinto from 2003. (PW)
- **Chocapalha★★★ £C** ● **Quinta de Chocapalha★★ £B**
- **Cabernet Sauvignon** Quinta de Chocapalha★★ £B

QUINTA DO CRASTO   Douro/Port   *UK stockists:* **Adm, Eno**, NYg, Hrd,ARe,Vts
Crasto has built an enviable reputation for both splendid table wines and fruit-rich ports. The regular red offers good Douro character within a modern structure and a somewhat oaky Reserva adds extra intensity. Varietal Tinta Roriz shows marvellous fruit, oak, smoke and spice and small-volume premium Vinha da Ponte and Maria Teresa are among the Douro's very best. Excellent medium-weight Vintage Port with stylish, ripe fruit intensity and attractive traditional LBV. (PW)
- **Douro★ £B** Reserva★★ £C Tinta Roriz★★★ £D Touriga Nacional★★★ £D
- **Douro** Vinha da Ponte★★★★ £E Vinha Maria Teresa★★★★ £E
- **Vintage Port★★★ £E** ● **Late Bottled Vintage Port★★ £C**

QUINTA DAS HEREDIAS   Port   *UK stockists:* **Gau**
Emerging port house under Mauricette Mordant with 82 ha in the Cima Corgo. Well-defined, balanced ports with expressive fruit include a marvellously complex 40-year-old Tawny. Vintage Port from 2001 shows both elegance and depth. Stylish traditional LBV and a dry White Port has good balance between spiced fruit and nutty tertiary flavours. Excellent Ruby. Also some Douro red. (PW)
- **Late Bottled Vintage Port★★ £D** ● **40-year-old Tawny Port★★★★★ £G**
- **10-year-old Tawny Port★★★ £D** ● **20-year-old Tawny Port★★★★ £E**
- **Ruby Port★★ £B** O **White Port** Meio Seco★★ £C

QUINTA DO INFANTADO   Port   *UK stockists:* **Lib**,ACh
João Roseira works with the talented Luís Soares Duarte and all the wines, even a Ruby, are made in *lagares*. Powerful Vintage Port and traditional LBV are both and intense and extracted. 10-year-old Tawny is vigorous and refined. (PW)
- **Vintage Port★★★★ £E** Late Bottled Vintage Port★★★ £D
- **10-year-old Tawny Port★★★ £E** ● **Douro★★ £B**

214

New entries have producer's name underlined

QUINTA DO NOVAL Douro/Port www.quintadonoval.com *UK stockists:* **Par**, AAA
Just 2.5 ha of ungrafted vines produce Nacional, the most sought-after of all ports, with great breadth, power
and dimension and a distinctive earthy, spicy dark plum character; riveting after 20, 30 or more years. 2000, 97,
94, 70, 66, 63 and 62 are great vintages. The regular Quinta do Noval Vintage has been very exciting since
1991. Second selection Silval is a high-quality, medium-full style. Concentrated tradional LBV and fine aged
tawnies and *colheitas*. Raven is a Premium Ruby. (PW)
● **Vintage Port**★★★★★ £F   Nacional❂❂❂❂❂ £H   Silval★★★★ £E
● **40-year-old Tawny Port**★★★ £G   ● **20-year-old Tawny Port**★★★ £F
● **10-year-old Tawny Port**★★ £D   ● **Colheita Port**★★★ £E

QUINTA DO PASSADOURO Douro www.quintadopassadouro.com *UK stockists:* **RsW**, BBR
Superb quinta in the Pinhão Valley. Stylish, expressive and complex Douro red, with black fruits, spice, clove and
floral characters that become more savoury with 5 years' age or more. Also very concentrated old-vines Reserva
(2003) and fine single-quinta Port (as in 2000). (PW)
● **Douro** Passadouro★★★★ £E   Reserva★★★★★ £F
● **Port** Quinta do Passadouro★★★★ £F

QUINTA DOS ROQUES Dão *UK stockists:* **RyR**, Han, C&R, P&S, F&M, Evg
Arguably the Dão's leading estate, producing modern, accessible wines under renowned Professor Virgílio
Loureiro. Characterful, medium-weight red and separate varietal bottlings show excellent fruit expression and
good concentration and structure. Reserva comes from an old vineyard of mixed plantings. Wines from the
nearby Quinta das Maias emphasise the local Jaen grape with smoky, spicy, wild berry flavours; exciting new
premium Rótulo Preto. Subtly oaked Encruzado white. (PW)
Quinta dos Roques:
● **Dão** Tinto★★ £B   Reserva★★★★ £D   **O Dão** Encruzado★★ £C
● **Dão** Tinto Cão★★ £C   Alfrocheiro Preto★★ £C   Touriga Nacional★★★ £D
Quinta das Maias:
● **Dão** Tinto★ £B   Jaen★★ £C   **O Dão** Malvasia Fina★ £B

QUINTA DE RORIZ Douro/Port www.quintaderoriz.com *UK stockists:* **JEF**, Hrd, BBR, F&R
Famous old individual-quinta port re-established by the van Zeller family with help from the Symington family.
The Vintage Port (especially 2003 and 2000) has sheer class with a dimension, definition and complexity seen only
among the top names. Douro Reserva (Touriga Nacional/Touriga Franca/Tinta Roriz) aged in new French
barriques has lots of depth and extract. (PW)
● **Vintage Port**❂❂❂❂❂ £E
● **Douro** Prazo de Roriz★★ £B   Quinta de Roriz Reserva★★★ £C

QUINTA DE LA ROSA Douro/Port *UK stockists:* **FMV**, JNi, Hrd, Sel, OxW
The Bergqvists make Vintage Port every year in the manner of a Bordeaux château. It is medium-weight with
balance and excellent fruit intensity and quality has steadily improved. Finest Reserve is a superior Vintage
Character port with elegance and
intensity; LBV is unfiltered. Excellent, well-priced reds. (PW)
● **Vintage Port**★★★★ £E   ● **10-year-old Tawny Port** Tonel No. 12★★ £C
● **LBV Port**★★★ £C   ● **Finest Reserve**★★ £B   ● **Ruby Port** Lote 601★ £B
● **Douro**★★ £B   Reserva★★★ £D   ● **Douro** Vale di Clara★ £B   **O Douro**★ £B

QUINTA DO VALE DOÑA MARIA Douro/Port *UK stockists:* Bib, L&S, C&B
Cristiano van Zeller is involved in several Douro estates, here with a mixed planting of old vines. Grapes are
foot-trodden in *lagares*, for a rich, fleshy, characterful and seductive red and an increasingly fine Vintage Port.
Winemaker Sandra Tavares' home estate is Quinta de Chocapalha. (PW)
Quinta do Vale Doña Maria:
● **Douro**★★★★ £C   ● **Vintage Port**★★★★ £E

QUINTA DO VALE MEÃO Douro/Port *UK stockists:* **RyR**, N&P, C&R
Francisco Javier de Olazabal was president of Ferreira until 1998 and his 62 ha of vineyards used to provide the
basis of Barca Velha. An outstanding estate red, mostly Touriga Nacional/Touriga Franca/Tinta Roriz, is foot-
trodden and spends two years in new Allier oak. An excellent second wine, Meandro, aged in used oak, is

215

medium-bodied with intense, juicy, plummy fruit. Complex, aromatic Vintage Port since 2000. (PW)
● **Douro** Quinta do Vale Meão★★★★★ £E Meandro★★★ £C

QUINTA DO VESUVIO Port www.quinta-do-vesuvio.com *UK stockists:* **JEF**,AAA
Grand old property, now one of the new breed of true (château-like) quintas. The wine is outstanding in top
years, with extraordinary ripeness in the tannins – and tempting when quite young. High percentages of Tinta
Roriz and Tinta Barroca contribute to its unique character. (PW)
● **Vintage Port**✪✪✪✪✪ £F

QUINTA DO ZAMBUJEIRO Alentejo www.zambujeiro.com *UK stockists:* **RyR**
Swiss-owned estate making impressive wines from the outset. 2001 releases are of a different order to all but the very
best Alentejo wines. Outstanding estate wine is neither fined nor filtered but very expansive, lush and complex with
excellent depth and expression. Also fine second wine, Terra do Zambujeiro, with similar composure and style. (PW)
● **Zambujeiro**★★★★★ £G ● **Terra do Zambujeiro**★★★ £E

JOÃO PORTUGAL RAMOS Alentejo www.jportugalramos.com *UK stockists:* **Oak**,ARe
For more than 20 years, João Ramos has been the leading consultant enologist in the south of Portugal. Top
own-label wine Marqués de Borba Reserva is a powerful but composed Aragonês/Trincadeira/Alicante
Bouschet/Cab Sauv blend needing 5-10 years. Good-value Vila Santa is a similar blend. Varietals have good
fruit. Very ripe and powerful Quinta de Viçosa Syrah/Trincadeira stands out elsewhere. (PW)

João Portugal Ramos:
● **Alentejo** Marqués de Borba★ £B Marqués de Borba Reserva★★★★ £E
●**Vila Santa**★★★ £B ● **Trincadeira**★★ £B ● **Aragonês**★★ £B
● **Syrah**★★ £B ● **Tinta Caiada**★★ £B O **Antão Vaz**★ £B

Quinta da Viçosa:
● **Syrah/Trincadeira**★★★ £C

Quinta de Foz de Arouce:
● **Quinta de Foz de Arouce**★★ £B

RAMOS PINTO Douro/Port *UK stockists:* **MMD**, JNi, BBR, L&W, Hfx, FWC
One of the leading proponents of Douro table wines – variable but culminating in deep, vigorous and classy
Reserva Especial from a field blend of old vines. A little white is also made. Most consistent and refined of the
ports is a 20-year-old Tawny from Bom-Retiro. Vintage Port wants for more depth and richness. LBV can be
remarkably full and powerful. Modest Vintage Character Urtiga. (PW)

Ramos Pinto:
● **Vintage Port**★★★ £E ● **Late Bottled Vintage Port**★★ £C
● **20-year-old Tawny Port** Quinta do Bom-Retiro★★★ £E

Duas Quintas:
● **Douro**★ £B Reserva★★ £E Reserva Especial★★★★ £F

RIBEIRA D'ERVIDEIRA www.ervideira.com *UK stockists:* **RyR,** Cam, But, Hfx, Han, F&M
Around 60,000 cases of consistent and characterful wine from re-established family vineyards. Herbal, citrusy
white and bright, red-fruited red Terras d'Ervideira are typical Alentejo blends. Ambitious oaked Conde
d'Ervideira Reserva needs a minimum of 5-6 years. A mealy, spicy white equivalent is slightly overdone but
with good fruit and structure. (PW)
● **Conde d'Ervideira Reserva**★★★ £C
● **Terras d'Ervideira**★★ £B ● **Vinha d'Ervideira**★★ £B
O **Terras d'Ervideira**★★ £B O **Conde d'Ervideira Reserva**★★ £B

SMITH WOODHOUSE Port www.smithwoodhouse.com *UK stockists:* **JEF**,AAA
The Vintage Port has spicy individuality and is typically succulent, intense and
well-balanced. Top vintages: 2003, 2000, 97, 94, 92, 91, 85, 83, 80 and 77. Distinguished Madalena single-
quinta port in 1995 and 99. Traditional LBV maintains house style. Decent Vintage Character Lodge Reserve.
(PW)
● **Vintage Port**★★★★★ £E Madalena★★★ £D
● **Late Bottled Vintage Port**★★★ £C ● **Lodge Reserve**★ £B

New entries have producer's name underlined

PORTUGAL

SOGRAPE www.sogrape.pt *UK stockists:* **SsG**, Hrd, Con, Maj
Portugal's largest producer includes the port companies of Ferreira, Offley and Sandeman but the focus is in Dão with flagship Quinta dos Carvalhais. Varietals from relatively young vines so far lack a little richness. Powerful, profound and complex Carvalhais Reserva (Touriga Nacional/Tinta Roriz/Alfrocheiro Preto) needs 8 to 10 years. Good-value 'regional' Reservas and Herdade do Peso Aragonês are softly textured with good flavour intensity and a regional stamp. Agreeable, inexpensive brands such as Terra Franca, Vila Régia and Duque de Viseu. Adequate Vinho Verde. (PW)

Sogrape:
● **Douro** Reserva★★ £B ● **Dão** Reserva★★ £B ● **Alentejo** Reserva★★ £B
● **Herdade do Peso Aragonês★★★** £C O **Bairrada** Reserva★★ £B

Quinta dos Carvalhais:
● **Dão** Tinta Roriz★★★ £C Touriga Nacional★★★ £C Reserva★★★★ £E
O **Dão** Encruzado★★★ £C

SYMINGTON www.symington.com *UK stockists:* **JEF**, NYg, Hrd, BBR, F&R
The Symington family runs the Douro's leading port shippers, owning Dow, Graham, Quinta do Vesúvio, Smith Woodhouse and Warre, and, through the Madeira Wine Company, is also the leading producer of Madeira. Gould Campbell and Quarles Harris are minor brands. Basic Douro Altano is uninspiring but 2003 of premium Chryseia will be best yet. Post Scriptum is the quite striking, well-balanced second wine, not unlike a good Haut-Médoc. (PW)

Gould Campbell:
● **Vintage Port★★** £E ● **Late Bottled Vintage Port★** £C

Quarles Harris:
● **Vintage Port★★★** £E

Prats & Symington:
● **Douro** Chryseia★★★★ £E Post Scriptum★★★ £C

TAYLOR'S Port www.taylor.pt *UK stockists:* **Men**, AAA
Exemplary port producer, and with Fonseca, part of an expanding group that now includes Croft and Delaforce. Taylor's structure, depth and class set it apart and occasionally it is unrivalled for its completeness. Best in 2003, 2000, 97, 94, 92, 85, 83, 80, 77, 70, 66 and 63. In good non-declared years, Quinta de Vargellas can be stunning; single-quinta Terra Feita has also been produced. Disappointing 10-year-old Tawny, spicy, fruity filtered LBV and good First Estate Vintage Character. (PW)
● **Vintage Port✪✪✪✪✪** £F Quinta de Vargellas★★★★ £E Terra Feita★★★ £D
● **20-year-old Tawny Port★★** £E ● **Late Bottled Vintage Port★★** £B

WARRE Port www.warre.com *UK stockists:* **JEF**, AAA
Symington-owned Warre makes consistently fine, very ageworthy Vintage Port, perfumed, with a rich, spice, fig and black fruit intensity and lushness. Best in 2003, 2000, 97, 94, 91, 85, 83, 80, 77, 70, 66, 63, 60 and 55. Quinta da Cavadinha can be excellent in non-declared years. Top traditional LBV (can be kept) and Warrior Vintage Character. Fine tawnies include mould-breaking Otima. (PW)
● **Vintage Port★★★★★** £F Quinta da Cavadinha★★★ £E
● **Late Bottled Vintage Port★★★** £C ● **20-year-old Tawny Port★★★** £E
● **10-year-old Tawny Port** Otima★ £C Sir William★ £C

Other wineries of note
Fojo (Douro), Herdade Grande (Alentejo), Monte da Ravasqueira (Alentejo), Quinta de Cabriz/Dão Sul (Dão), Quinta do Côtto (Douro), Quinta de Macedos (Douro), Quinta do Mouro (Alentejo), Quinta do Portal (Douro/Port), Quinta da Portela da Vilariça (Douro), Quinta do Vallado (Douro/Port), Real Campanhia Velha (Douro/Port), Sandeman (Port), Sidónio de Sousa (Bairrada)

An in-depth profile of every producer can be found in Wine behind the label 2006

RHEIN

Bonn

AHR

1 2

Koblenz

2

MOSEL   Bacharach   Wiesbaden   Frankfurt

3

Mainz

Bernkastel-Kues   Nackenheim

6   MAIN   11

Trier   Bad Kreuznach   11

4   NAHE   8   11

Saarburg   RUWER   10   13   Würzburg

5   13

SAAR   Bad Dürkheim

Deidesheim   Heidelberg

RHEIN

9   13

Karlsruhe

FRANCE   12   NECKAR

Stuttgart

13

Freiburg

13   13

13   Bodensee   12   13

SCHWEIZ

1	Ahr
2	Mittelrhein
3	Mosel
4	Ruwer
5	Saar
6	Nahe
7	Rheingau
8	Rheinhessen
9	Pfalz
10	Hessische Bergstrasse
11	Franken
12	Württemberg
13	Baden

Background

Germany's often exquisite white wines deserve wider recognition and support. Wines are now riper and cleaner and are increasingly marketed in a direct modern way with a growing number of inexpensive and consistently well made dry or off-dry Rieslings. There are also excellent examples of Weissburgunder (Pinot Blanc), Silvaner and other grapes. More clarity is still needed in terms of what degree of sweetness to expect but there are ever more outstanding producers with wines across a range of styles.

The quality German label

There are two basic quality levels, QbA and QmP (*Qualitätswein mit Prädikat*).Quality really begins with the latter which includes Six Prädikat (or classifications) of ripeness. **Kabinett** is the lowest level, a dry or off-dry wine but quality is producer dependent. **Spätlese** wines are riper - dry examples are labelled Trocken (off-dry, Halb-Trocken), otherwise expect some sweetness. **Auslese** wines are made from riper grapes again (sometimes botrytis affected) and usually sweeter but Trocken versions are also made. Still riper and sweeter categories of **Beerenauslese** and **Trockenbeerenauslese (TBA)** are made from handpicked, botrytis enriched grapes. **Eiswein**, high in both sugar and acidity, is made from frozen grapes. Critical to quality at all levels is the balance between residual sugar and acidity.

Most Prädikat wines come from a single site - an *Einzellagen* name, usually suffixed with a village name (often dropped in the Pfalz). The best parcels within a single top site (often more botrytis-affected) may be differentiated as Gold Capsule (*Goldkapsel*) or even Long Gold Capsule (*Lange Goldkapsel*). Alternatively small stars may be used to distinguish between bottlings of increasing quality ('1 Stern', '2 Sterne' or '3 Sterne'). Many top German estates belong to the VDP consortium (labels bear its emblem of an eagle) and their best and rarest sweet wines are sold at the annual VDP auction (as *Versteigerungswein*). Specialist wine merchants may stock such wines following a successful bid.

The VDP also promotes the establishment of a vineyard classification system. An increasing number of producers now labelled some or all of their wines from the best vineyards under the top level of the classification. All must be a minimum of Spätlese ripeness. In Rheingau sites are designated *Erstes Gewächs* (EG), in the Mosel it is *Erste Lage* (EL) while in the Pfalz and other regions it is *Grosses Gewächs* (GG). When looking for good-quality wines from Germany, avoid wines bearing a village name in conjunction with a *Grosslage* name (referring to a broader sweep of inferior vineyards). Piesporter Michelsberg or Niersteiner Gutes Domtal are infamous examples.

German Vintages

What is produced each year from German vineyards is dependent on the climatic conditions – especially during the months of October and November. Top years provide greater ripeness and plentiful Spätlese and Auslese and, if the conditions are right, botrytis enrichment for Beerenauslese and Trockenbeerenauslese styles. In a poor year only Kabinett and a little Spätlese might be made.

The vintage chart is based on Spätlese and Auslese levels of ripeness but when to drink and potential longevity are very producer dependent. While well-made Kabinett can be drunk within a year or two of the vintage, most Spätlese or Auslese needs three or four years' age to start to show well. Whether they will keep for another couple of years or a further five or 10 or 15 (or more) depends on the specific wine and vintage quality. Eiswein from a great vintage like 1998 can age very impressively but even when well-balanced from the outset it usually retains its penetrating acidity. Recent vintages are very exciting, the outstanding 2001 followed by some exceptional ageworthy wines in 2002 (if very little of the very sweet styles) and the super-rich, ripe 2003s which are exceptional when the balance is right. 2004 is another fine vintage, characterised in particular by excellent late-harvested Spätlese with fine acidities and cool but fully ripe fruit. Also some superb Eiswein.

Wizard's Wishlist

Classic dry or off-dry Mosel Riesling

WGT. FRITZ HAAG
O **Brauneberger Juffer-Sonnenuhr** Riesling Spätlese
WGT. REINHOLD HAART
O **Piesporter Goldtröpfchen** Riesling Spätlese
HEYMANN-LÖWENSTEIN
O **Winninger Uhlen** Riesling 'Roth Lay' Erste Lage
KARLSMÜHLE O **Kaseler Nies'chen** Riesling Spätlese
WGT. KARTHÄUSERHOF
O **Eitelsbacher Karthäuserhofberg** Riesling Spätlese Trocken
DR LOOSEN O **Wehlener Sonnenuhr** Riesling Spätlese
ST. URBANS-HOF
O **Ockfener Bockstein** Riesling Spätlese
WILLI SCHAEFER
O **Graacher Domprobst** Riesling Spätlese
SCHLOSS LIESER
O **Lieser Niederberg Helden** Riesling Spätlese

Germany

GERMANY

More superior dry or off-dry Riesling

BASSERMANN-JORDAN
O **Deidesheimer Hohenmorgen** Riesling Grosses Gewächs
REICHSRAT VON BUHL
O **Forster Pechstein** Riesling Grosses Gewächs
BÜRKLIN-WOLF
O **Forster Kirchenstück** Riesling Grosses Gewächs
CHRISTMANN
O **Gimmeldingen Mandelgarten** Riesling Trocken GG
DÖNNHOFF
O **Niederhäusen Hersmannshöhle** Riesling Spätlese
EMRICH-SCHÖNLEBER
O **Monzinger Frühlingsplätzchen** Riesling Spätlese
PETER JAKOB KÜHN
O **Oestricher Lenchen** Riesling Kabinett
WGT. KELLER
O **Dalsheimer Hubacker** Riesling Spätlese Trocken
FRANZ KÜNSTLER
O **Hochheimer Hölle** Riesling Auslese Trocken
ANDREAS LAIBLE
O **Durbacher Plauelrain** Riesling Auslese Trocken
WEINGUT JOSEPH LEITZ
O **Rudesheimer Berg Schlossberg** Riesling Spätlese
REBHOLZ
O **Birkweiler Kastanienbusch** Riesling Grosses Gewächs
SCHÄFER-FRÖHLICH
O **Bockenauer Felseneck** Riesling Spätlese Trocken
SCHLOSSGUT DIEL
O **Dorsheimer Pittermännchen** Riesling Spätlese
WGT. WITTMANN
O **Westhofener Kirschspiel** Riesling Grosses Gewächs

Stupendous German sweet wines

GEORG BREUER
O **Rauenthal Nonnenberg** Riesling Auslese Gold Capsule
DÖNNHOFF O **Oberhäuser Brücke** Riesling Eiswein
GUNDERLOCH
O **Nackenheimer Rothenberg** Riesling Beerenauslese
DR LOOSEN O **Bernkasteler Lay** Riesling Eiswein
MARKUS MOLITOR
O **Zeltinger Sonnenuhr** Riesling Beerenauslese
MÜLLER-CATOIR
O **Mussbacher Eselshaut** Rieslaner TBA
JOH JOS PRÜM
O **Wehlener Sonnenuhr** Riesling Auslese Gold Capsule
MAX FERD. RICHTER
O **Mülheimer Helenenkloster** Riesling Eiswein
HORST SAUER O **Escherndorfer Lump** Riesling TBA
ROBERT WEIL
O **Kiedricher Gräfenberg** Riesling Auslese Gold Capsule

Fine German whites not from Riesling

WGT. BERCHER
O **Burkheimer Feuerberg** Weissburgunder Spätlese Tr. GG
DR HEGER
O **Ihringer Winklerberg** Muskateller Spätlese 3 sterne
ANDREAS LAIBLE
O **Durbacher Plauelrain** Gewürztraminer Auslese
MÜLLER-CATOIR
O **Haardter Mandelring** Scheurebe Auslese
HORST SAUER O **Escherndorfer Lump** Silvaner Auslese
JULIUSSPITAL
O **Würzburger Stein** Silvaner Spätlese Trocken
REBHOLZ
O **Siebeldingen im Sonnenschein** Weisser Burgunder GG

Germany/A-Z of producers

BASSERMANN-JORDAN Pfalz www.bassermann-jordan.com *UK stockists:* **WBn,** Wai
Famous Pfalz estate, revitalised since the mid-1990s. 42 ha include some of the best sites of Forst and Deidesheim. Ulrich Mell makes intense, ripe, balanced Rieslings - especially *Grosses Gewächs* versions in 2001 and 02. Almost anything of Spätlese level or above made since 1997 is worth trying. (PW)
O **Forster Kirchenstück** Riesling Auslese★★★ £D
O **Deidesheimer Hohenmorgen** Riesling Spätlese Trocken GG★★★ £E
O **Deidesheimer Kalkofen** Riesling Spätlese Trocken GG★★★ £E

WGT. BERCHER Baden www.weingutbercher.de *UK stockists:* **WBn**
Southern Baden estate dominated by the three Pinots. *Grosses Gewächs* (GG) wines have real richness and depth. Weissburgunder is stylish, intense and long, while the Spätburgunder shows splendid flavour complexity. Intense and tangy Eiswein when conditions allow. Drink dry whites fairly young. (PW)
O **Burkheimer Feuerberg** Weissburgunder Spätlese Trocken GG★★★ £C
O **Chardonnay** Spätlese Trocken★★ £C
● **Burkheimer Feuerberg** Spätburgunder Spätlese Trocken GG★★★ £E

New entries have producer's name underlined

GEORG BREUER Rheingau www.georg-breuer.com *UK stockists:* **NYg**, N&P
Bernhard Breuer was a passionate advocate for Rheingau Riesling until his death in 2004. *Erstes Gewächs* vineyards at this 26-ha estate include the entire 5 ha of Rauenthaler Nonnenberg, with good botrytis richness in stylish and distinctive sweet Gold Capsule Auslese. Also some Grauburgunder and Spätburgunder. Recent vintages are particulary good but prices are high. Joint ventures in South Africa (Mont du Toit) and Portugal's Douro (Quinta da Carvalhosa). (PW)
O **Rüdesheim Berg Rottland** Riesling Auslese Gold Capsule★★★★ £F
O **Rüdesheim Berg Schlossberg** Riesling Auslese Gold Capsule★★★ £G
O **Rauenthal Nonnenberg** Riesling Auslese Gold Capsule★★★★ £F

REICHSRAT VON BUHL Pfalz www.reichsrat-von-buhl.de *UK stockists:* **FEM**, **JNi**, SVS
Japanese investment has put this once-famous estate with top Pfalz vineyards back on form since 1994. Very classy, mineral-imbued Forster Pechstein and initially more austere Ruppertsberger Reiterpfad with underlying concentration, white peach and spice. Fine sweet wines as well as *Grosses Gewächs*, including Forster Ungeheuer Riesling and Ruppertsberger Reiterpfad Scheurebe. (PW)
O **Forster Pechstein** Riesling GG★★★★ £C
O **Forster Kirchenstück** Riesling GG★★★ £C
O **Ruppertsberger Reiterpfad** Riesling GG★★★ £C

BÜRKLIN-WOLF Pfalz www.buerklin-wolf.de *UK stockists:* **AWs**, **CPp**, Lay, Tan, N&P
Since the mid-1990s Christian von Guradze has restored the reputation of this large and historic estate with several of the Pfalz's top *Grosses Gewächs* sites (only a selection are given below). These dry wines resemble top Alsace, each with a distinctive character. Budget Bürklin Estate Riesling offers good fruit character. Good very sweet wines teeter on the brink of imbalance. Also some Chardonnay and Spätburgunder. (PW)
O **Forster Kirchenstück** Riesling GG★★★★★ £E
O **Forster Ungeheuer** Riesling GG★★★★ £E
O **Deidesheimer Hohenmorgen** Riesling GG★★★ £D

A CHRISTMANN Pfalz www.weingut-christmann.de *UK stockists:* F&R
Steffen Christmann has vines in four leading Pfalz sites. The wines show intense, ripe fruit and a full, lush, almost creamy character yet with good intensity and acidity. Sweet wines are very sweet, intense and succulent but generally well-balanced. Small amounts of Trockenbeerenauslese and Eiswein are also made as is a Spätburgunder (Pinot Noir) from Königsbacher Idig. (PW)
O **Königsbacher Idig** Riesling Trocken GG★★★ £C Riesling Auslese★★★ £E
O **Gimmeldinger Mandelgarten** Riesling Trocken GG★★★ £C
O **Ruppertsberger Reiterpfad** Riesling Trocken GG★★★ £C

J J CHRISTOFFEL Mittel Mosel www.moenchhof.de *UK stockists:* **RsW**, HRp
Christoffel's neighbour Robert Eymael (Mönchhof/Robert Eymael) has taken on responsibility for the wines from this minute holding of Riesling. The Ürziger Würzgarten wines are excellent with lovely spice, citrus (and riper peach and nectarine in the riper styles), and penetrating intensity and depth, particularly in reasonably priced special selections. also fine Erdener Treppchen. (PW)
O **Ürziger Würzgarten** Riesling Kabinett★★ £B Riesling Spätlese★★ £C
O **Ürziger Würzgarten** Riesling Auslese 3 Sterne★★★★ £D
O **Ürziger Würzgarten** Riesling Eiswein★★★★★ £G

DÖNNHOFF Nahe *UK stockists:* **WSS**, HRp, Gen, Tan, L&W, L&S, JNi, SVS, P&S
Helmut Dönnhoff, one of Germany's most celebrated winemakers, makes prodigious Rieslings from 14.5 ha mostly in Schlossböckelheim, Niederhausen and Oberhäusen (with solely owned Brücke vineyard). Spätlese and Auslese show concentration, minerally intensity and elegance with vivid flavours, from cool blackcurrant, apple and citrus to ripe peach. Also some Weissburgunder and Grauburgunder. Even modest wines shine. Brilliant in 2001, 02 and 03. (PW)
O **Schlossböckelheimer Kupfergrube** Riesling Spätlese★★★ £D
O **Niederhäusen Hermannshöhle** Riesling Spätlese★★★ £D Auslese★★★★★ £F
O **Oberhäuser Brücke** Riesling Auslese★★★★★ £F Riesling Eiswein✪✪✪✪✪ £H

EMRICH-SCHÖNLEBER   Nahe   www.emrich-schoenleber.com   *UK stockists:* **CTy**, HRp
Arguably the second great Nahe estate (after Dönnhoff) under Werner Schönleber with tight, sleek, intense Rieslings from previously unsung Monzingen. Elegant Frühlingsplätzchen Riesling Kabinett contrasts with vigorous Halbtrocken that needs a little age. Minerally, refined Halenberg wines include beautifully delineated citrusy Eiswein. Ripe, fruity Grauburgunder. (PW)
O **Monzinger Frühlingsplätzchen** Riesling Kabinett★★ £B   Riesling Spätlese★★★ £C
O **Monzinger Halenberg** Riesling Spätlese★★★ £C   Riesling Auslese★★★★ £D
O **Monzinger Halenberg** Riesling Auslese 3 Sterne★★★★★ £F   Eiswein★★★★★ £H

WGT. GÖTTELMANN   Nahe   *UK stockists:* **WBn**
Enologists Götz Blessing and Ruth Göttelmann-Blessing have 12.5 ha of classic steep slate-covered slopes. Wines of often piercing minerally citrus and blackcurrant fruit can be a little too sharp in some of the drier styles. Dautenpflänzer Riesling Spätlese shows a Mosel-like elegance. All Rieslings need age; also the pure lemony, minerally Weissburgunder. (PW)
O **Münsterer Dautenpflänzer** Riesling Spätlese★★ £B
O **Münsterer Kapellenberg** Riesling Spätlese Trocken★★★ £B
O **Münsterer Rheinberg** Riesling Spätlese★★ £B   Riesling Beerenauslese★★★ £F

GUNDERLOCH   Rheinhessen   *UK stockists:* **WSS**, JNi, BBR, ACh, C&R, Hrd, Has
Fritz and Agnes Hasselbach produce some of the richest, most intense German Rieslings from the famed Rothenberg site. Spätlese has explosive fruit richness; higher ripeness levels even more. Wines can be drunk fairly young, though most deserve at least 5 years. '3 Sterne' Auslese is a Trocken style. Newish Red Stone is a light, racy, commercial Riesling. Also some Nierstein wines. (PW)
O **Red Stone** Riesling QbA★ £B   O **Jean Baptiste** Riesling Kabinett★★ £C
O **Nackenheimer Rothenberg** Riesling Spätlese★★★ £D   Auslese 3 Sterne★★★ £E
O **Nackenheimer Rothenberg** Riesling Auslese★★★★ £E   Beerenauslese✪✪✪✪ £H

WGT. FRITZ HAAG   www.weingut-fritz-haag.de   *UK stockists:* **J&B**, Rae, JAr, HRp, L&W
Wilhelm Haag produces some of the finest, most elegant Mosel Riesling from the great Brauneberger Juffer-Sonnenuhr and promotes quality throughout the region. The wines start out very taut and concentrated with a remarkably fine, minerally intensity and sulphur can be intrusive when they are young, but they gradually open out. Some individual cask bottlings. (PW)
O **Brauneberger Juffer-Sonnenuhr** Riesling Spätlese★★★ £C   Auslese★★★★ £D
O **Brauneberger Juffer-Sonnenuhr** Riesling Auslese Gold Capsule★★★★★ £E

WGT. REINHOLD HAART   Mittel Mosel   www.haart.de   *UK stockists:* **RsW**
6 ha centred on the great Piesporter Goldtröpfchen site. Theo Haart's style responds to the vintage, but intensely blackcurrant fruit is characteristic, as is a profusion of peach, apricot and citrus in Spätlese and Auslese wines and exotic fruits in the sweetest styles. Other sites such as Dronhofberger give cooler green apple and citrus flavours but share intensity. The wines need age. Haart to Heart is a light attractive quaffing Riesling. (PW)
O **Piesporter Domherr** Riesling Spätlese★★★ £C   Auslese★★★★ £D
O **Piesporter Goldtröpfchen** Riesling Spätlese★★★ £C   Auslese★★★★ £D
O **Wintrich Ohligsberg** Riesling Auslese★★★ £C

HEYL ZU HERRNSHEIM   Rheinhessen   www.heyl-zu-herrnsheim.de   *UK stockists:* **WBn**
Markus Ahr and Michael Burgdorf are giving a real lead to the Nierstein area with much improved sweet, intense and concentrated riper styles. A full hand of top sites between Nierstein and Nackenheim includes sole ownership of Brudersberg. The *Grosses Gewächs* is minerally, dry and rather austere. Rotschiefer bottlings come only from red slate soils. (PW)
O **Niersteiner Pettenthal** Riesling Trocken GG★★ £D   Riesling Auslese★★★ £E
O **Niersteiner Oelberg** Riesling Auslese Gold Capsule★★★★ £F
O **Riesling** Trocken Rotschiefer★★ £C   O **Weisser Burgunder** Rotschiefer★★ £C

HEYMANN-LÖWENSTEIN   *UK stockists:* **FMV**, HRp, Sel, ACh
Reinhard Löwenstein's steep terraces in the Terrassenmosel yield excellent fruit and wines with a very different expression of the Mosel – either fully dry or in Auslese and above sweet styles with exquisite fruit and

222

New entries have producer's name underlined

definition. Long and complex Winninger Uhlen wines recommended in 2001 and 02. Schieferterrassen indicates a vineyard blend while a vom Blauem Schiefer Riesling comes from a different 'blue' type of slate within Uhlen. (PW)

O **Winninger Uhlen** Riesling 'Blaufüsser Lay' EL★★★ £C Riesling 'Laubach' EL★★★ £D
O **Winninger Uhlen** Riesling 'Roth Lay' EL★★★ £D
O **Schieferterrassen** Riesling Eiswein★★★★★ £H

VON HÖVEL Saar *UK stockists:* Tan, OWL
Long-established Saar estate of monastic origins. Most wines come from the excellent Scharzhofberg or Oberemmeler Hütte sites. Top Rieslings include pure, racy Scharzhofberger Auslese and *Goldkapsel* Oberemeler Hütte with terrific intensity and definition in a long, honeyed finish. Very good 2004s including light, basic, off-dry QbA. (PW)

O **Oberemmeler Hütte** Riesling Kabinett★★ £B Riesling Spätlese★★ £B
O **Oberemmeler Hütte** Riesling Auslese I Stern★★★ £D Goldkapsel★★★★ £F
O **Scharzhofberger** Riesling Spätlese★★ £B Riesling Auslese★★★ £C

KARLSMÜHLE Ruwer www.karlsmuehle.com *UK stockists:* **HRp**, F&R
Peter Geiben has 12 ha in excellent Ruwer sites. Quality since the late 1990s puts him among the best growers in the Mosel-Saar-Ruwer. Ripe (in a cool, mineral, citrus/apple vein) and intense wines range from light, stylish Mäuerchen Kabinett to concentrated, sweet Nies'chen Auslese. Ultra-sweet and tangy Eiswein deserves plenty of age. Excellent value. (PW)

O **Lorenzhöfer** Riesling Spätlese★★ £B Riesling Auslese Gold Capsule★★★ £D
O **Kaseler Nies'chen** Riesling Spätlese★★★ £B Auslese Long Gold Capsule★★★★ £E
O **Kaseler Kehrnagel** Eiswein★★★★★ £G

WGT. KARTHÄUSERHOF *UK stockists:* **OWL, CTy**, F&R, SVS, Has, Sel
Christoph Tyrell's great and historic Ruwer estate. Vivid, intense, elegant Riesling, very well made by Ludwig Breiling – with flavours of apple, white peach, blackcurrant, citrus and mineral in Kabinett and Spätlese (sweet and dry), nectarine, peach and exotic fruits in rich but vibrant Auslese and Eiswein. Superb Auslese from numbered casks. Also dry Weissburgunder. (PW)

O **Eitelsbacher Karthäuserhofberg** Riesling Kabinett★★ £B Riesling Spätlese★★★ £C
O **Eitelsbacher Karthäuserhofberg** Riesling Spätlese Trocken★★★ £C
O **Eitelsbacher Karthäuserhofberg** Riesling Auslese★★★★ £D Eiswein❍❍❍❍ £H

WGT. KELLER Rheinhessen www.weingut-keller.de *UK stockists:* **HRp**, F&R
Klaus Keller and his son Klaus-Peter are showing that outstanding wines are possible in the unsung hilly countryside around Flörsheim-Dalsheim with Riesling, Weissburgunder and Grauburgunder. Fine dry wines but even better exuberant sweeter styles with scintillating fruit richness and excellent balance and length of flavour. Also outstanding Trockenbeerenauslese and some Spätburgunder. All the better wines deserve some age and will keep for a decade. (PW)

O **Dalsheimer Hubacker** Riesling Spätlese★★ £C Riesling Spätlese Trocken★★ £C
O **Dalsheimer Hubacker** Riesling Auslese★★★ £F Riesling Auslese 3 Sterne★★★★ £G

VON KESSELSTATT Mosel *UK stockists:* **Lay, ABy**, BBR, Cam, Odd, JNi
The Günter Reh family possess 38 ha of Riesling, much of it in leading sites. Their natural, unmanipulated wines emphasise fruit and at best reflect something of their origins although sulphur can be a problem. 'RK' Riesling and new dry Palais Kesselstatt Riesling are not recommended. (PW)

O **Graacher Domprobst** Riesling Spätlese★★ £C
O **Kaseler Nies'chen** Riesling Spätlese★★ £C Riesling Eiswein★★★★ £G
O **Piesporter Goldtröpfchen** Riesling Spätlese★★★ £C Riesling Auslese★★★ £D

KOEHLER-RUPRECHT Pfalz *UK stockists:* **Win**
Dry wines with good structure from the Pinots, Chardonnay and Riesling. Ripe barrel-fermented 'Philippi' whites with integrated lees and oak. Pinot Noir best in warm vintages. Vigorous, ripe and minerally Riesling; ageworthy 'R' bottlings add concentration and spicy botrytis. Bernd Philippi is a partner in the Douro estate Quinta da Carvalhosa. Also Gewürztraminer and Scheurebe. (PW)

O **Kallstadter Saumagen** Riesling Spätlese Trocken★★ £C Auslese Trocken★★★ £D

Germany

GERMANY (vertical sidebar)

O **Kallstadter Saumagen** Riesling Auslese 'R'★★★★ £D Riesling Eiswein★★★★★ £G
O **Chardonnay** Philippi★★ £C ● **Pinot Noir** Philippi★★ £D Philippi 'R'★★★ £E

PETER JAKOB KÜHN Rheingau www.weingutpjkuehn.de *UK stockists:* **C**Ty, Tan
Long-established and greatly improved organic estate; Peter Jakob Kühn now makes exemplary Rheingau
Rieslings. Oestrich Lenchen wines combine the richness of the Rheingau with the elegance of the Mosel.
Doosberg provides complex, expressive dry wines. All deserve some age; sweeter styles at least five years. Also
some Spätburgunder. (PW)
O **Oestricher Doosberg** Riesling Zwei Trauben QbA★★ £C Riesling EG★★★ £D
O **Oestricher Lenchen** Riesling Kabinett★★★ £C Riesling Spätlese★★★ £C
O **Oestricher Lenchen** Riesling Auslese★★★★ £F Riesling Beerenauslese★★★★★ £H

FRANZ KÜNSTLER Rheingau *UK stockists:* **RsW**, HRp, DWS, NYg, Has, Wai
Gunter Künstler draws on extensive vineyards spread over the Hochheim slopes. Traditionally made wines such
as a fine Kirchenstück Spätlese and Domdechanay Auslese show wonderful richness with good acidity. Dry
Auslese wines are a feature including powerful honeyed Kirchenstück and a splendidly complex Hölle. Elegant if
oaky (and pricey) Pinot Noir, also attractive Pinot-dominated fizz. (PW)
O **Hochheimer Hölle** Riesling Spätlese Trocken★★ £D Auslese Trocken★★★ £E
O **Hochheimer Kirchenstück** Riesling Spätlese★★★ £D Auslese Trocken★★★ £E
O **Hochheimer Domdechaney** Riesling Auslese★★★ £E ● **Pinot Noir** Auslese★★ £F

SYBILLE KUNTZ Mittel Mosel www.sybillekuntz.de *UK stockists:* **OWL**, Hrd, Sel
A rising star in the Mosel with the focus on dry wines. Optimal ripeness is sought from old vines, resulting in
atypical breadth and depth and making them good food wines. A regular bottling is surpassed by Gold-
Quadrat and Dreistern. Also small quantities of fine Beerenauslese and very sweet, very intensely flavoured
TBA. (PW)
O **Riesling Trocken**★★ £B O **Riesling Gold-Quadrat**★★ £C
O **Lieser Niederberg Helden** Riesling Spätlese Trocken **Dreistern**★★★ £D
O **Lieser Niederberg Helden** Riesling Auslese Halbtrocken★★★ £E

ANDREAS LAIBLE Baden www.weingut-laible.de
Wines of unprecedented quality from the Ortenau area of Baden, not just Riesling (aka Klingelberger) but also
lush, ripe Gewürztraminer and rich, fruity Scheurebe. Top Rieslings have lovely concentrated fruit, with depth,
body and good acidity. Rich, honeyed yet dry Auslese Trocken; Achat is the richer of two Spätlese. Also good
Chardonnay, Grauburgunder and Spätburgunder. (PW)
O **Durbacher Plauelrain** Riesling Auslese Trocken★★★★ £D
O **Durbacher Plauelrain** Riesling Spätlese Trocken Achat★★★ £C
O **Durbacher Plauelrain** Gewürztraminer Auslese★★★ £C

LANGWERTH VON SIMMERN Rheingau www.langwerth-von-simmern.de *UK stockists:* **Win**
Recently revived famous Rheingau estate. Even Kabinett-level wines from 2003 and 04 show off the class of
vineyards such as Rauenthaler Baiken, Hattenheimer Nussbrunnen and Erbacher Marcobrunn. The intensity,
definition, vibrancy and splendid expression make for excellent drinking whether the wines are young or
aged. (PW)
O **Rauenthaler Baiken** Riesling Kabinett★★ £B Riesling Spätlese★★★ £C
O **Hattenheimer Nussbrunnen** Riesling Kabinett★★★ £B Auslese★★★★ £E
O **Hattenheimer Mannberg** Riesling Spätlese Blaukapsel★★★★ £D
O **Hattenheimer Wisselbrunnen** Riesling Spätlese★★★ £C Beerenauslese★★★★ £E

WGT JOSEF LEITZ Rheingau www.leitz-wein.de *UK stockists:* **WSS**, L&W, Gen, JNi, HRp
Johannes Leitz is one of the Rheingau's rising stars; top Rudesheim sites lend themselves to his elegant, intense
style of Riesling. Quality is consistently high from ripe, attractive QbA to richer, ripe mineral, peach and
apricot in the riper styles (only a selection is given below). Eiswein is tight, intense and long. (PW)
O **Rudesheimer Berg Roseneck** Riesling Kabinett★★ £B Riesling Spätlese★★★ £D
O **Rudesheimer Berg Schlossberg** Riesling Spätlese★★★ £D
O **Rudesheimer Kirchenpfad** Riesling Auslese★★★★ £F

224

New entries have producer's name underlined

CARL LOEWEN Mittel Mosel www.weingut-loewen.de *UK stockists:* **HRp, JAr**
Karl-Josef Loewen champions the Laurentiuslay vineyard where he produces minerally, spicy Riesling with a suggestion of elderflower. Exceptional individual cask bottlings. Varidor is a dry generic Riesling; dry Alte Reben (old vine) is full and New World-like. Wines from under-rated Thörnicher Ritsch show bright intense fruit. Classy citrus and tropical Klostergarten Eiswein. Good value. (PW)
O **Leiwener Klostergarten** Riesling Kabinett★★ £B Riesling Eiswein★★★★★ £F
O **Thörnicher Ritsch** Riesling Spätlese★★★ £B Riesling Auslese★★★★ £C
O **Leiwener Laurentiuslay** Spätlese★★★ £B Riesling Auslese★★★ £C

DR LOOSEN www.drloosen.com *UK stockists:* **WSS, GWW, JNi,** HRp, Tan, NYg, L&S
High-profile, high-quality organic producer with old vines in some choice Mittel Mosel plots. Ernst Loosen's wines have lovely depth and intensity but also real elegance and a distinctive expression of their origins – succulent Wehlener Sonnenuhr, spice-lined Ürziger Würzgarten and exotic Erdener Prälat. Sulphur can show in young wines. Keep all except attractive Dr L for at least 3-4 years. Ernst Loosen also produces excellent dry Rieslings at the J L Wolf estate, and another in Washington State in conjunction with Ch. Ste Michelle. (PW)
O **Ürziger Würzgarten** Riesling Spätlese★★★ £D Riesling Auslese★★★★ £E
O **Wehlener Sonnenuhr** Riesling Spätlese★★★ £D Auslese Gold Capsule★★★★★ £F
O **Erdener Prälat** Riesling Auslese★★★★ £F Riesling Auslese Gold Capsule★★★★★ £F
O **Bernkasteler Lay** Riesling Kabinett★★ £C Riesling Eiswein★★★★★ £H

FÜRST LÖWENSTEIN Franken & Rheingau www.lowenstein.de *UK stockists:* **WKe**
Two estates – 30ha in Franken and 22ha in Rheingau – give consistently good quality. Top Franken Silvaner, Asphodill, is ripe and exotic; Coronilla, the Riesling equivalent, is stylish, concentrated and more seductive. Rheingau Rieslings have good intensity and flavour even at Kabinett level. Top Rheingau Pinot Noir from French clones is classy and Burgundian. Sweet wines are also made. (PW)
Franken
O **Homburger Kallmuth** Riesling Spätlese Trocken GG Coronilla★★★ £D
O **Homburger Kallmuth** Silvaner Spätlese Trocken GG Asphodill★★★ £D
O **Homburger Kallmuth** Tradition★★★ £C
Rheingau
O **Hallgarten Schönhell** Riesling Erstes Gewächs★★★ £D
O **Hallgarten Jungfer** Riesling Kabinett Trocken★★ £B Riesling Spätlese Trocken★★ £C
● **Hallgarten Schönhell** Pinot Noir Spätlese Trocken★★★ £E

MARKUS MOLITOR Mittel Mosel www.wein-markus-molitor.de *UK stockists:* **BBR, F&R**
Sweet Rieslings from the excellent Zeltinger Sonnenuhr are extraordinarily rich, concentrated, intense and ripe for the Mosel but retain sufficient acidity and balance. Kabinett can disappoint but there is a honeyed peach richness in Spätlese; luscious Auslese and a Beerenauslese show a deep marmalady botrytis character. Vibrant citrusy Eiswein. Very high prices. (PW)
O **Zeltinger Sonnenuhr** Riesling Spätlese★★★ £C Riesling Auslese 3 Sterne★★★★ £H
O **Zeltinger Sonnenuhr** Riesling Beerenauslese★★★★ £H
O **Bernkasteler Badstube** Riesling Eiswein★★★ £H

MEYER-NÄKEL Ahr www.meyer-naekel.de *UK stockists:* **WBn**
The most highly rated red wine producer in Germany. Top wines are oaky single-vineyard examples with high alcohol levels. Raspberryish and Volnay-like Frühburgunder ripens earlier and can show the better balance while Spätburgunder has perhaps the greater potential complexity, but both are intense, deep and long. (PW)
● **Spätburgunder Trocken** Blauschiefer★ £C Selection 'S'★★★ £E
● **Dernauer Pfarrwingert** Spätburgunder Auslese Trocken★★★ £E
● **Dernauer Pfarrwingert** Frühburgunder Auslese Trocken★★★ £E

MÖNCHHOF/ROBERT EYMAEL Mittel Mosel *UK stockists:* **RsW,** Rae
Robert Eymael's vineyards are concentrated on some of the finest Mittel Mosel sites. Wines show classic delicacy, intensity and refined fruit flavours, especially Spätlese and Auslese. Würzgarten gives characteristic spiciness and mineral, ripe peach and nectarine hints. See also J J Christoffel. (PW)

O **Ürziger Würzgarten** Riesling Spätlese £C Riesling Auslese★★★★ £D
O **Erdener Prälat** Riesling Auslese★★★ £D
O **Erdener Treppchen** Riesling Spätlese Trocken★★ £C Riesling Auslese★★★ £D

GEORG MOSBACHER Pfalz www.georg-mosbacher.de UK stockists: **HRp**
The Mosbacher family make excellent expressions of leading Pfalz vineyards. *Grosses Gewächs* wines have fresh, ripe intense fruit and good flavour depth with real differentiation: striking mineral intensity and depth in the powerful Forster Ungeheuer; open, expressive, exotic Deidesheimer Kieselberg. Also good Rieslings from lesser sites and Forster Freundstück Eiswein plus some Weissburgunder and Gewürz. (PW)
O **Forster Ungeheuer** Riesling Spätlese Trocken GG★★★ £D
O **Forster Freundstück** Riesling Spätlese Trocken GG★★★ £D
O **Deidesheimer Kieselberg** Riesling Spätlese Trocken GG★★★ £D

MÜLLER-CATOIR Pfalz www.mueller-catoir.de UK stockists: **HRp, N&P, F&R**
Winemaker Hans-Günther Schwarz has made this estate great with very intense, fine wines from lesser-known Pflaz vineyards. Power and thrilling intensity have earned the wines an almost fanatical following. Characterful Rieslaner, with remarkable sweetness and power at Auslese level and higher. Intense Riesling but not Pfalz's best. Sweet, exotic Scheurebe and good dry Grauburgunder, Weissburgunder and Muskateller are also made. (PW)
O **Gimmeldinger Mandelgarten** Riesling Auslese★★★ £F
O **Mussbacher Eselshaut** Rieslaner Auslese★★★ £E Rieslaner TBA✪✪✪✪✪ £H
O **Haardter Mandelring** Scheurebe Spätlese★★ £C Scheurebe Auslese★★★ £F

EGON MÜLLER/SCHARZHOF Saar UK stockists: **J&B, DAy, OWL, HRp**
One of the most prestigious domaines in the world, run by Egon Müller IV. The top sweet wines (with superior numbered versions) start out firm, intense and taut but have tremendous underlying concentration with the potential to last for decades. All need at least 10 years' age. Almost all the wines are sold at auction (so prices vary). Also produces wines from the 4-ha Le Gallais estate. (PW)
O **Scharzhofberger** Riesling Auslese★★★★ £G Riesling Beerenauslese✪✪✪✪✪ £H
O **Scharzhofberger** Riesling Kabinett★★ £C Riesling Spätlese★★★ £E
Le Gallais
O **Wiltinger Braune Kupp** Riesling Spätlese★★ £D Auslese Gold Capsule★★★★ £H

JOH JOS PRÜM Mittel Mosel UK stockists: **J&B, OWL, JAr, HRp**
Famed estate centred on the great Wehlener Sonnenuhr but also including Zeltinger Sonnenuhr, Graacher Himmelreich and Bernkasteler Lay. The wines are renowned for their longevity and a wonderful, racy intensity and minerally elegance with age (although the most recent vintages can be drunk quite young). Five-star Beerenauslese and TBA are sold at auction. (PW)
O **Wehlener Sonnenuhr** Riesling Kabinett★★ £C Riesling Spätlese★★★ £C
O **Wehlener Sonnenuhr** Riesling Auslese Gold Capsule✪✪✪✪✪ £H
O **Graacher Himmelreich** Riesling Kabinett★★ £C Riesling Spätlese★★★ £C

RATZENBERGER Mittelrhein www.weingut-ratzenberger.de
One of the very best Mittelrhein estates in recent vintages. There is lovely purity in the Steeger St Jost wines while the best Wolfshöhle wines are stylish and classy with the distinctive Mittelrhein mineral, floral and preserved nectarine quality. Even basic QbAs are decent, especially a tangy Trocken version. Also very sweet, powerful, intense Eiswein. (PW)
O **Steeger St Jost** Riesling Kabinett Halbtrocken★★ £B Riesling Spätlese Trocken★★ £B
O **Bacharacher Wolfshöhle** Riesling Spätlese I Sterne★★★ £C
O **Bacharacher Wolfshöhle** Riesling GG★★★★ £D
O **Bacharacher Kloster Fürstental** Riesling Eiswein★★★★★ £F

ÖKONOMIERAT REBHOLZ Pfalz www.oekonomierat-rebholz.de UK stockists: **vLw**
Hansjörg Rebholz makes some of the Pfalz region's best wines in the less-celebrated southern part. Very fine, intense, *terroir*-derived expressions of Riesling – cool, pure mineral intensity in the Kastanienbusch, Im Sonnenschein with minerally warmth. Various Pinots and Chardonnay make up half the plantings and include very composed and complex Siebeldingen Im Sonnenschein Weisser Burgunder. (PW)
O **Birkweiler Kastanienbusch** Riesling Spätlese Trocken GG★★★★ £E

226

New entries have producer's name underlined

O **Siebeldingen im Sonnenschein** Riesling Spätlese Trocken GG★★★ £D
O **Siebeldingen im Sonnenschein** Weisser Burgunder Spätlese Trocken GG★★★ £D

MAX FERD. RICHTER Mosel   *UK stockists:* **CTy**, Tan, BBR, SVS, F&M
Dr Dirk Richter brings out the fine acidity and class of some top Mittel Mosel sites in ripe and intense wines including complex, apricotty Juffer-Sonnenuhr Spätlese and the citrus elegance of Graacher Himmelreich Spätlese. Outstanding Eiswein from solely owned Mülheimer Helenenkloster. Also fine Riesling from Veldenzer Elisenberg. Prices are fair, a good QbA included. (PW)
O **Graacher Himmelreich** Riesling Kabinett★★ £B   Riesling Spätlese★★★ £B
O **Brauneberger Juffer-Sonnenuhr** Riesling Spätlese★★★ £C   Riesling Auslese★★★★ £D
O **Mülheimer Helenenkloster** Riesling Eiswein★★★★★ £H

ST. URBANS-HOF Mittel Mosel   www.urbans-hof.de   *UK stockists:* **FEM**, SVS
Winemaker Rudolf Hoffmann harnesses the potential of fruit that is riper and more concentrated than most. Piesporter Goldtröpfchen wines show rich, intense blackcurrant, citrus and peach fruit, yet elegance too. Individual Ockfener Bockstein wines include smoky and minerally, very ripe citrus Auslese. Sulphur can detract in young Kabinett wines but all will age. Eiswein from Leiwener Klostergarten. (PW)
O **Piesporter Goldtröpfchen** Riesling Spätlese★★★ £C   Riesling Auslese★★★★ £E
O **Ockfener Bockstein** Riesling Spätlese★★★ £C   Riesling Auslese★★★★ £E
O **Wiltinger Schlangengraben** Riesling Auslese Gold Capsule★★★★ £E

HORST SAUER Franken   www.weingut-horst-sauer.de   *UK stockists:* **NYg**, J&B
The best producer in Franken and a new star of Germany. Elegance and well-detailed fruit are evident even in Riesling Kabinett. Escherndorfer Lump Silvaner is as good as Riesling; both superb in Trockenbeerenauslese with intense, long spice, mineral and dried fruit flavours. Notable Scheurebe and even Müller-Thurgau. Part-barriqued Sennsucht Silvaner succeeds. Also Pinot Noir rosé. (PW)
O **Escherndorfer Lump** Riesling Spätlese Trocken★★★ £C   Riesling Eiswein★★★★★ £G
O **Escherndorfer Lump** Riesling TBA✪✪✪✪ £G   Silvaner TBA✪✪✪✪ £G
O **Escherndorfer Lump** Silvaner Spätlese Trocken★★★ £C   Silvaner Auslese★★★★ £E

SCHÄFER-FRÖHLICH Nahe
Tim Fröhlich is a new star in the Nahe with some quite superb wines from 2002, 03 and 04. Kabinett and Spätlese from two excellent sites are very refined with excellent balance and definition. Also pure Weissburgunder, especially the richer, more textured, lightly oaked 'S' version. Super regular Auslese and sweeter styles include exquisite TBA and Eiswein as well as Goldkapsel versions. (PW)
O **Monzingen Halenberg** Riesling Kabinett Trocken★★ £B   Spätlese★★★ £C
O **Bockenauer Felseneck** Riesling Spätlese★★★ £C   Riesling Auslese★★★★ £E
O **Bockenauer** Weisser Burgunder Trocken★★ £B   Weissburgunder 'S'★★★ £C

SCHLOSS LIESER Mittel Mosel   *UK stockists:* **J&B**, HRp, Tan, F&R
Thomas Haag, son of Wilhelm Haag of the Fritz Haag estate, has revitalised this once-famous 7.5-ha estate centred on the Lieser Niederberg Helden site with taut, intense and ripe Rieslings that age well. Auslese wines capture the essence of Mittel Mosel finesse and richness. Recently some sulphur noticeable in young wines. Also a little 3 Sterne Auslese and some Beerenauslese. Reasonable prices. (PW)
O **Lieser Niederberg Helden** Riesling Auslese 2 Sterne★★★★ £E
O **Lieser Niederberg Helden** Riesling Spätlese★★ £B

SCHLOSS SAARSTEIN Saar   www.saarstein.de   *UK stockists:* **CTy**, Has, SVS, C&R
Christian Ebert's wholly owned Serriger Schloss Saarsteiner vineyard is the top site in this marginal location. Wines are low in alcohol with a very cool green fruits character, especially in cooler vintages. Auslese offer the best acid/sugar balance and becomes increasingly enticing with age. A little Beerenauslese and Eiswein, also some Weissburgunder. (PW)
O **Serriger Schloss Saarsteiner** Riesling Kabinett★ £B   Riesling Spätlese★★ £C
O **Serriger Schloss Saarsteiner** Riesling Auslese Gold Capsule★★★★ £E

SCHLOSS VOLLRADS Rheingau   www.schlossvollrads.com   *UK stockists:* **Lib**, FSt, Sel
Celebrated ancient Rheingau estate with a massive 58 ha of vineyards, now owned by a bank and returning to

GERMANY

form. 2002 seems a significant leap forward with good minerality and depth even at Kabinett level but there is the potential for more. Promising Spätlese with intense ripe peach and citrus fruit. Beerenauslese and TBA were also made in 2002. (PW)

O **Schloss Vollrads** Riesling QbA★ £B Riesling Kabinett★★ £C
O **Schloss Vollrads** Riesling Spätlese★★★ £D Riesling Auslese★★★ £E

SCHLOSSGUT DIEL Nahe *UK stockists:* **Win, OWL,** HRp, F&R
Armin Diel, a leading expert on German wines and a German television celebrity, makes very good wines from Dorsheim's top sites. His Rieslings are rich and intense but usually well-balanced and all share a floral, herbal, mineral, blackcurrant and nectarine profile. Barrique-fermented Pinots include plump, ripe Cuvée Caroline Pinot Noir in 2002. Characterful basic Diel de Diel white blend. (PW)

O **Dorsheimer Pittermännchen** Riesling Spätlese★★★ £D Riesling Auslese★★★★ £E
O **Dorsheimer Burgberg** Riesling Auslese★★★★ £E Riesling Eiswein★★★★ £H
O **Grauburgunder**★★ £C O **Weissburgunder**★★ £C O **Cuvée Victor**★★ £E

VON SCHUBERT/MAXIMIN GRÜNHAUS *UK stockists:* Rae, OWL,HRp
The most famous estate of the Ruwer Valley, in the capable hands of Dr Carl-Ferdinand von Schubert. Sublime Rieslings from solely owned Abtsberg site. Class and finesse are paramount; delicious lime, mineral, floral, apple and white peach flavours prevail, but with the structure and intensity to age for years. Numbered Ausleses of varying richness (£E to £F) are almost always of at least 4-star quality. All the wines need at least three to four years. (PW)

O **Maximim Grünhauser Abtsberg** Riesling Spätlese★★★ £C
O **Maximim Grünhauser Abtsberg** Riesling Auslese★★★ £D Eiswein★★★★ £H
O **Maximim Grünhauser Herrenberg** Riesling Spätlese★★ £C

SELBACH-OSTER Mittel Mosel *UK stockists:* **FMV**, BBR, JNi, Rae, JAr, HRp, L&W
Fine Mosel wines with depth, elegance and fine, cool, apple, citrus and white peach flavours. Particularly stylish Zeltinger Sonnenuhr Riesling Auslese. Sulphur can be a problem. A little Beerenauslese and Trockenbeerenauslese are also made from Zeltinger Sonnenuhr. Wines labelled J&H Selbach are produced from bought-in grapes as part of a *négociant* business. (PW)

O **Wehlener Sonnenuhr** Riesling Kabinett★★ £B
O **Zeltinger Sonnenuhr** Riesling Spätlese★★★ £C Riesling Auslese★★★ £C
O **Graacher Domprobst** Riesling Spätlese★★ £C Riesling Auslese★★ £D

TESCH Nahe www.weingut-tesch.de *UK stockists:* **HRp**
Biochemist Dr Martin Tesch focuses on dry Rieslings. Labels indicate only the vineyard: vigorous, fruit-driven Karthäuser, mineral and herbal Krone and St Remigiusberg (potentially the top wine) are from Laubenheim; big, ripe spiced citrus Königsschild and Löhrer Berg from Langenlonsheim. Good basic Riesling Unplugged. (PW)

O **Karthäuser** Riesling Spätlese Trocken★★★ £B
O **Krone** Riesling Spätlese Trocken★★★ £B
O **Königsschild** Riesling Spätlese Trocken★★★ £B

GEHEIMRAT J WEGELER Rheingau, Mosel & Pfalz www.wegeler.com
The Wegeler family's outstanding vineyard sites total some 80 ha, mostly in the Rheingau. Oliver Haag, son of Wilhelm Haag (of Fritz Haag), directs winemaking. Very good Rheingau wines include refined and well-defined Winkeler Jesuitengarten and Berg Schlossberg with more weight and power. Also Berg Rottland, Oestricher Lenchen and Geisenheimer Rothenberg. Mosel wines from Wehlener Sonnenuhr and Bernkasteler Doctor that show depth, richness and ripeness. (PW)

Gutshaus Oestrich:
O **Winkeler Jesuitengarten** Riesling GG★★★ £C
O **Rüdesheimer Berg Schlossberg** Riesling GG★★★ £C
Gutshaus Bernkastel:
O **Bernkasteler Doctor** Riesling Spätlese★★★ £D Riesling Auslese★★★★ £E
O **Wehlener Sonnenuhr** Riesling Auslese★★★ £E

228

ROBERT WEIL   Rheingau   www.weingut-robert-weil.com   *UK stockists:* **HBJ,DWS,**F&M
Since the 1990s Wilhelm Weil's wines from the very fine Kiedricher Gräfenberg site have shown intensity and richness, especially sweeter styles, where the rich, sweet, apricot and dried-peach fruit, braced by tangy acidity, becomes more honeyed and magnificent with age. Less elegant wines from other vineyards. Also Spätburgunder and tiny amounts of TBA. (PW)
O **Kiedricher Gräfenberg** Riesling Spätlese★★★ £D   Riesling EG★★★★ £E
O **Kiedricher Gräfenberg** Riesling Auslese Gold Capsule★★★★★ £H
O **Kiedricher Gräfenberg** Riesling Eiswein❍❍❍❍❍ £H

WGT. WITTMANN   Rheinhessen   www.wittmannweingut.com   *UK stockists:* **WBn,** Bal
Steadily improving 25-ha organic family estate. The best Rieslings, both dry and sweet, have vibrant acidityare and are now really first class. 'S' selection wines have an extra intensity and rich fruit. Powerful but austere *Grosses Gewächs* bottling need time. Good Silvaner and Weisser Burgunder plus some Chardonnay and more esoteric sweet Huxelrebe and Albalonga (a Rieslaner-Silvaner crossing). (PW)
O **Westhofener Kirschspiel** Riesling GG★★★ £D
O **Westhofener Morstein** Riesling GG★★★ £D   Riesling Auslese 'S'★★★★ £E
O **Westhofener Aulerde** Riesling GG★★★ £D   Riesling TBA★★★★ £H

J L WOLF   Pfalz   www.jlwolf.com   *UK stockists:* **WSS,GWW,** Has,CPp, P&S
Here Ernst Loosen (Dr Loosen, Mosel) makes broad, powerful 'grand cru' wines, including Pechstein, Ungeheuer and Jesuitengarten from Forst, and Deidesheimer Leinhöhle. 'Premiers crus' from Wachenheim are also fine: Belz is dry, intense and gently refined. Good character too in 'village' wines, especially Wachenheimer Riesling. Least expensive are the Villa Wolf varietals; most widely seen is the Grauburgunder, exported as Pinot Gris. 'J L' labelled versions more pricey. (PW)
O **Forster Pechstein** Riesling Spätlese Trocken★★★★ £D
O **Deidesheimer Leinhöhle** Riesling Spätlese Trocken★★★ £D
O **Wachenheimer Belz** Riesling Spätlese Trocken★★★ £C

ZILLIKEN   Saar   www.zilliken-vdp.de   *UK stockists:* **J&B,** HRp
Based in large part on the fine Saarburger Rausch vineyard. Rieslings with a fine mineral undercurrent are ripe and intense with no harshness. Flavours range from cool lemon and lime fruit in Kabinett to nectarine and peach at higher levels. Sweeter Auslese and above are the real stars with much greater concentration, superb definition and a stylish elegance that showcases the vineyard. (PW)
O **Saarburger Rausch** Riesling Kabinett★ £B   Riesling Spätlese★★ £C
O **Saarburger Rausch** Riesling Auslese★★★★ £E   Riesling Auslese Goldkapsel★★★★★ £F
O **Saarburger Rausch** Riesling Eiswein❍❍❍❍❍ £G

Other wineries of note
Aldinger (Württemberg), Bergdolt (Pfalz), Josef Biffar (Pfalz), Castell (Franken), Dautel (Württemberg), Domdechant Werner'sches (Rheingau), Duijn (Baden), Rudolf Fürst (Franken), Grans-Fassian (Mosel-Saar-Ruwer), Dr Heger (Baden), Prinz von Hessen (Rheingau), Bernhard Huber (Baden), Wgt. Toni Jost (Mittelrhein), Juliusspital (Franken), August Kesseler (Rheingau), Knipser (Pfalz), Kruger-Rumpf (Nahe), Hans Lang (Rheingau), von Othegraven (Mosel-Saar-Ruwer), Paulinshof (Mosel-Saar-Ruwer), Dr Pauly-Bergweiler (Mosel-Saar-Ruwer), Balthasar Ress (Rheingau), Josef Rosch (Mosel-Saar-Ruwer), Salwey (Baden), Willi Schaefer (Mosel-Saar-Ruwer), Schloss Schönborn (Rheingau), Schloss Wallhausen (Nahe), Schmitt's Kinder (Franken), Spreitzer (Rheingau), Jean Stodden (Ahr), Dr Wehrheim (Pfalz), Hans Wirsching (Franken)

An in-depth profile of every producer can be found in Wine behind the label 2006

Austria

AUSTRIA

ČESKÁ REPUBLIKÁ (CZECH REPUBLIC)

SLOVENSKÁ
REPUBLIKÁ
(SLOVAKIA)

KAMP

3

2 • Langenlois

1 Krems

• Spitz

5

6

4

DONAU

7 Wien

DONAU

NIEDER-ÖSTERREICH

9

8

11

10 Neusiedler See

Rust • • Illmitz

1   Wachau
2   Kremstal
3   Kamptal
4   Traisental
5   Donauland
6   Weinviertel
7   Wien
8   Thermenregion
9   Carnuntum
10 Neusiedlersee-Hügelland
11 Neusiedlersee
12 Mittelburgenland
13 Südburgenland
14 Süd-Oststeiermark
15 Südsteiermark
16 Weststeiermark

BURGENLAND

12

MAGYARORSZAG
(HUNGARY)

STEIERMARK

13

• Graz

14

16

15

SLOVENIJA (SLOVENIA)

AUSTRIA

Background
From a growing band of small producers, Austria provides the world with outstanding dry whites, superb sweet wines and ever more interesting, good quality reds. Great Rieslings and Grüner Veltliner come from steep hillside vineyards above the Danube (Donau) in the Wachau but also from neighbouring Kremstal and Kamptal. In Burgenland, especially around the broad shallow lake of Neusiedlersee, are produced outstanding sweet wines and ever better reds.

Emerald lizards
Wachau's full powerful Riesling and Grüner Veltliner are labelled Steinfeder, Federspiel or Smaragd. The relatively low-alcohol style of Steinfeder is for early drinking but the best Federspiel are more structured and concentrated and will keep for at least 3 or 4 years. The best quality however always comes from usually long-lived Smaragd examples, named after a little emerald green lizard. German classifications of ripeness are used for sweeter styles - Auslese, Beerenauslese, Trockenbeerenauslese (TBA) - both here and elsewhere in Austria. Specific to Neusiedlersee-Hügelland, around the town of **Rust**, the traditional **Ausbruch** style is made- now generally a full, sweet white with higher alcohol than wines made in the Germanic style (with a must weight between Beerenauslese and TBA). Wines from the leading vineyards are sometimes labelled with only the vineyard (*Ried*) name (eg. *Ried* Klaus) and not the associated village.

Austria Vintages
In Austria vintages are of considerable importance, particularly in the Wachau for its leading Rieslings and Grüner Veltliners. Ratings for Wachau wines apply to Smaragd examples and Kremstal or Kamptal equivalents. Most are better with 3-4 years' age but might keep for 10 or more. The rarer sweet Wachau styles, Auslese and Beerenauslese, will also prove ageworthy. The dramatic flooding in 2002 ruined grapes from vines on the flat ground but quality appears very promising from terraced vineyards. 2003 was the hottest vintage ever and the wines have more alcohol and less acidity and quality is very good indeed from a good producer. Both 2002 and 2003 are very good for reds from Burgenland and Styria. In contrast to 2003, 2004 lacked heat and was a protracted vintage requiring diligence to get fully ripe healthy fruit, particularly in Wachau-Kremstal-Kamptal. There is, however, very pure, classic intense Riesling and Grüner Veltliner from the best producers.
The sweet wines of Neusiedlersee and Neusiedlersee-Hügelland, while producer-dependent, will nearly always benefit from at least five years' age and will keep for a decade or more. See Vintage Charts.

Wizard's Wishlist

Superior Austrian Riesling
LEO ALZINGER O Loibner Steinertal Riesling Smaragd
BRÜNDLMAYER
O Zöbinger Heiligenstein Riesling Alte Reben
FRANZ HIRTZBERGER O Singerriedel Riesling Smaragd
EMMERICH KNOLL
O Dürnsteiner Ried Schütt Riesling Smaragd
LOIMER O Langenloiser Steinmassl Riesling
NIGL O Riesling Privat
F-X PICHLER
O Dürnsteiner Kellerberg Riesling Smaragd
RUDI PICHLER
O Weissenkirchener Achleiten Riesling Smaragd
PRAGER O Weissenkirchen Achleiten Riesling Smaragd

Superb Grüner Veltliner
BRÜNDLMAYER O Kammerner Lamm Grüner Veltliner
BIRGIT EICHINGER
O Strasser Gaisberg Grüner Veltliner
FRANZ HIRTZBERGER
O Honivogl Grüner Veltliner Smaragd
JOSEF JAMEK
O Ried Achleiten Grüner Veltliner Smaragd
NIGL O Grüner Veltliner Alte Reben
NIKOLAIHOF
O Im Weingebirge Grüner Veltliner Smaragd
F-X PICHLER O Loibner Berg Grüner Veltliner Smaragd
SCHLOSS GOBELSBURG
O Kammerner Lamm Grüner Veltliner

Sweet whites
BRÜNDLMAYER O Zöbinger Heiligenstein Riesling TBA
FEILER-ARTINGER O Ruster Ausbruch Pinot Cuvée
KRACHER O Grande Cuvée Trockenbeerenauslese
HEIDI SCHROCK O Ruster Ausbruch
VELICH O Welschriesling Trockenbeerenauslese

Leading reds
ARACHON T FX T ● Arachon Evolution
FEILER-ARTINGER ● Solitaire
JURIS ● St. Laurent Reserve
KOLLWENTZ-RÖMERHOF ● Steinzeiler
KRUTZLER ● Perwolff
ANITA & HANS NITTNAUS ● Pannobile
ERNST TRIEBAUMER ● Ried Marienthal
Blaufränkisch

Best value Austrians
KURT ANGERER O Grüner Veltliner Spies
BIRGIT EICHINGER O Strasser Gaisberg Riesling
FELSNER O Grüner Veltliner Moosburgerin Kabinett
GRAF HARDEGG O Weinviertel DAC Grüner Veltliner

Austria

LOIMER O Riesling Langenlois
NEUMAYER O Rafasetzen Grüner Veltliner
ANITA & HANS NITTNAUS ● Heideboden
BERNHARD OTT O Der Ott Grüner Veltliner
SALOMON O Undhof Wieden Grüner Veltliner

Austria /A-Z of producers

LEO ALZINGER Wachau www.alzinger.at *UK stockists:* **NDb**
Some of the best wines of the Wachau. Slightly more Grüner Veltliner than Riesling that is intense, taut and steely when young but with an underlying richness and concentration. True class, minerality and considerable complexity with age. Liebenberg pair are more accessible than Steinertal wines. Also several other good examples and Chardonnay. (PW)
O **Loibner Loibenberg** Riesling Smaragd★★★★ £D
O **Loibner Steinertal** Riesling Smaragd★★★★ £D Grüner V. Smaragd★★★ £D
O **Dürnsteiner Liebenberg** Riesling Smaragd★★★ £D Grüner V. Smaragd★★★ £D

KURT ANGERER Kamptal www.kurt-angerer.at *UK stockists:* **NYg**
3 unoaked Grüner Veltliners (Kies, Loam and Spies) from differing soils are arguably the most consistent and balanced of this fine and diverse range of whites and reds. Unfiltriet is an impressive barrel-fermented and aged version. Riesling is very ripe, concentrated and powerful. Reds are increasingly good. (PW)
O **Grüner Veltliner** Kies★★ £C Loam★★★ £C Spies★★★ £C
O **Grüner Veltliner** Unfiltriert★★★ £D O **Riesling** Donatus★★★ £C
● **Zweigelt Barrique★** £C ● **Zweigelt Granit★★** £D ● **St Laurent★★** £C
● **Cabernet Sauvignon/Zweigelt★★** £C ● **Merlot★★★** £C

BRÜNDLMAYER Kamptal www.bruendlmayer.com *UK stockists:* **RsW**, Gen, NYg, N&P
Top (organic) estate for superb Rieslings. Most outstanding are Zöbinger Heiligenstein with depth, power and vibrant ripe fruit, especially complex Alte Reben (old vines) example. Also full flavoursome Grüner Veltliner, similarly ageworthy. Regular Kamptaler Terrassen examples drink sooner. Also good Chardonnay, traditional-method sparkling wine, Pinot Noir (Cécile) and occasional superb sweet Beerenauslese (1998) or Trockenbeerenauslese (2000). (PW)
O **Riesling** Alte Reben★★★★★ £D O **Zöbinger Heiligenstein** Riesling★★★★ £C
O **Langenloiser Steinmassel** Riesling★★★ £C Berg Vogelsang Grüner V.★★ £B
O **Grüner Veltliner** Alte Reben★★★★ £C O **Ried Lamm** Grüner V.★★★ £D

BIRGIT EICHINGER Kamptal www.weingut-eichinger.at *UK stockists:* **JAr**
Emerging star with vines in two top sites, Heiligenstein and Gaisberg. Fine Grüner Veltliner and Riesling from Gaisberg with more structured Riesling from Heiligenstein. Goliath is partially oaked blend of ripest Grüner grapes from Gaisberg and Heiligenstein but struggles for balance. Good unoaked Chardonnay but a second from Strasser Stangl is oaked and more international. (PW)
O **Zöbinger Heiligenstein** Riesling★★★★ £D O **Grüner Veltliner** Goliath★★★ £D
O **Strasser Gaisberg** Riesling★★★ £C Grüner V.★★★ £C Chardonnay★★ £C

FEILER-ARTINGER Neusiedlersee-Hügelland *UK stockists:* **FWW**, SVS
Very fine, elegant sweet Ruster Ausbruch (from Pinot Blanc, Welschriesling) - honeyed, refined with lots of ripe botrytised fruit intensity. Pinot Cuvée version (Pinot Gris, Pinot Blanc) shows lovely balance between sweetness and acidity. Also balanced reds: peppery, brambly Solitaire (Blaufränkisch, Zweigelt, Merlot, Cab Sauv) and very convincing Cab Sauv/Merlot blend. Dry white Cuvée Gustav is barrel-fermented Pinot Gris, Chardonnay and Neuburger. (PW)
O **Ruster Ausbruch★★★★** £E Pinot Cuvée★★★★★ £F ● **Solitaire★★★** £E
O **Cuvée Gustav★★** £C ● **Cabernet Sauvignon/Merlot★★** £E

FELSNER Kremstal www.weingut-felsner.at *UK stockists:* **FWW**, Wai
Good, reasonably priced family estate in Kremstal. Grüner Veltliner from loess soils shows yellow plum, lentil, spice and pepper in several different bottlings. Also expressive, stylish Riesling from Gebling vineyard. Reds include soft,

232

AUSTRIA

New entries have producer's name underlined

supple St-Laurent and a spicy, flavoursome Zweigelt. (PW)

O **Grüner Veltliner** Alte Reben★★ £C O **Grüner Veltliner Lössterrassen**★★ £B
O **Vordenberg** Grüner Veltliner★★ £B O **Moosburgerin** G Veltliner Kabinett★★ £B
O **Gebling** Grüner Veltliner★★ £B Riesling★★★ £C
● **Sankt Laurent**★ £B ● **Zweigelt Weitgasse** ★★ £B

FREIE WEINGÄRTNER WACHAU Wachau www.fww.at *UK stockists:* **FWW,** Wvr
Co-op with 600 growers with some of most readily available and affordable Grüner Veltliner and Riesling from Wachau. Generally wines of good definition and intensity if lacking a little zip, however 02 and 03 promise to be the best yet. Domäne Wachau label is for wines from individual vineyards. Dry wines generally best with 2-5 years'. (PW)

O **BA** Beerenauslese★★ £D
Domäne Wachau
O **Dürnsteiner Kellerberg** Grüner V. Smaragd★★ £C Riesling Smaragd★★★ £C
O **Loibener Loibenberg** Riesling Smaragd★★★ £C O **Riesling Exceptional**★★★ £C
O **Achleiten** Grüner V. Smaragd★★★ £C Riesling Smaragd★★★ £C

GRAF HARDEGG Weinviertel www.grafhardegg.at *UK stockists:* **NYg,**
Peter Veyder-Malberg achieves high standard in this quality wilderness with good Grüner Veltliner, especially richer old-vine Alte Reben version, but also Viognier (Austria's first), Syrah, Merlot and Pinot Noir. Tethys is oak-fermented and aged Chardonnay/Pinot Blanc/Grüner/Viognier; Forticus, a fortified red from Blauburger and Merlot. (PW)

O **Grüner Veltliner Veltlinsky**★★ £B O **Weinviertel DAC**★★ £B
O **Grüner Veltliner** Alte Reben★★★ £C O **Riesling Steinbügel**★★★ £C
O **Viognier V**★★ £E O **Tethys**★★ £C ● **Pinot Noir Steinbügel**★★ £C

HIEDLER Kamptal www.hiedler.at *UK stockists:* **FMV,** BBR, FWC
Wide range of wines but focus on Grüner Veltliner and Riesling. Wines are fruit emphasized but missing extra class or expression of some. Grüner Veltliner Thal Novemberlese has extra depth while Rieslings Steinhaus and Heiligenstein show atypically rich fruit. Riesling Maximum is big, rich and powerful but develops well. Also Riesling from Gaisberg and Loiserberg, and cool minerally Sauvignon. (PW)

O **Riesling Maximum**★★★★ £E O **Heiligenstein** Riesling★★★ £D
O **Steinhaus** Riesling★★★ £C O **Thal** Grüner V. Novemberlese★★★ £C

FRANZ HIRTZBERGER Wachau *UK stockists:* **FWW,** NYg, P&S, SVS, N&P, F&M
There is a pure pristine fruit intensity to Hirtzberger's Smaragd examples of Grüner Veltliner and Riesling - wines that are structured, taut and concentrated, but beautifully balanced. Hochrain is classic Wachau Riesling with great length while splendid minerally Singerriedel has superb structure. Honivogl Grüner Veltliner has underlying strength and intensity. All deserve at least 5 years' ageing. (PW)

O **Hochrain** Riesling Smaragd★★★★ £F O **Singerriedel** Riesling Smaragd★★★★★ £F
O **Axpoint** Grüner V. Smaragd★★★★ £D O **Honivogl** Grüner V. Smaragd★★★★ £E

JOSEF JAMEK Wachau www.jamekweingut.at *UK stockists:* **NDb**
Pioneer of dry Riesling and Grüner Veltliner. Low yields contribute to an intense varietal expression as well as something of the individual *terroir*. Wines are pure, intense and very classy but need time to soften and become easier to drink. (PW)

O **Ried Klaus** Riesling Smaragd★★★★ £E
O **Ried Achleiten** Grüner V. Federspiel★★ £C Grüner V. Smaragd★★★ £D

JURIS Neusiedlersee www.juris.at *UK stockists:* **Sav**
Axel and Herta Stiegelmar produce a huge range. Dry whites include distinctive elderberry-scented Sauvignon and clean, pure Chardonnay (Altenberg). Selection reds are supple and flavoursome, especially Blaufränkisch and St-Laurent. Also elegant, stylish Reserves of Pinot Noir, St-Laurent, Blaufränkisch, Cab Sauv, and blended Ina'mera. Sweet whites are even better. (PW)

● **Blaufränkisch** Reserve★★★ £D ● **Pinot Noir** Reserve★★★ £D
● **St. Laurent** Reserve★★★ £D ● **Cabernet Sauvignon** Reserve★★★ £D
● **Ina'mera**★★★ £D O **Strohwein**★★★ £F O **Chardonnay** TBA★★★★ £F

AUSTRIA

JURTSCHITSCH SONNHOF Kamptal www.jurtschitsch.com *UK stockists:* **VDu**, Odd
Traditional family estate, run along ecological principles. Reduced yields are reflected in intensity and length of flavour in Grüner Veltliner, and fine fruit and gentle minerality in best Rieslings. Most wines drink well with just 2-3 years' age. Small quantities of sweet wines when conditions favour it. (PW)
O **Zöbinger Heiligenstein** Riesling Auslese★★★ £D Riesling Reserve★★★★ £E
O **Riesling Alte Reben**★★★ £D O **Grüner Veltliner TBA**★★★★ £F
O **Grüner Veltliner Alte Reben**★★★ £C O **Grüner Veltliner Reserve**★★★ £D

EMMERICH KNOLL Wachau *UK stockists:* RsW, NYg, Sec, Rae, N&P, F&M, P&S
Historic family vineyard making wines with almost overwhelming intensity and concentration that need ageing. Great vigour and superb length of flavour in Smaragd Loibenberg Loibner Riesling, more elegant, refined Dürnsteiner Schütt. Slightly less good Grüner Veltliner but most concentration and style in Loibenberg Loibner or Loibner Schütt. Ripest fruit goes into 'Vinothekfüllung' Grüner Veltliner and Riesling. (PW)
O **Loibenberg Loibner** Riesling Federspiel★★ £C Riesling Smaragd★★★★★ £E
O **Dürnsteiner Ried Schütt** Riesling Smaragd★★★★★ £E
O **Loibenberg Loibner** Grüner V. Smaragd★★★ £D Grüner V. Vinothefüllung★★★★ £E

KRACHER Neusiedlersee www.kracher.at *UK stockists:* **NYg**, P&S, Fal, Bal, N&P, SVS, Tan
Outstanding sweet wine producer. A series of very sweet, very intense Trockenbeerenauslese (TBA) are produced every year - wines labelled Zwischen den Seen ('between the lakes') are unoaked, usually from naturally spicy, aromatic indigenous varieties, while Nouvelle Vague wines are oaked. Barrique-aged reds, Blend I and Blend II, from Zweigelt and Blaufränkisch, are also made. (PW)
O **Grande Cuvée** TBA✪✪✪✪ £G O **Scheurebe Zwischen den Seen** TBA★★★★ £E
O **Chardonnay Nouvelle Vague** TBA✪✪✪✪ £G
O **Welschriesling Zwischen den Seen** TBA★★★★★ £E

KRUTZLER Südburgenland www.krutzler.at *UK stockists:* **Sav**
Blaufränkisch is the main focus here with great care going into maximising fruit quality. A supple, round basic is surpassed by deeper Reserve from older vines that needs 3–4 years'. Perwolff needs 8–10 years to fully reveal its refined cedar, plum, bramble and black cherry character; 2002 and 03 should be the best yet. (PW)
● **Blaufränkisch**★★ £B Reserve★★★ £D ● **Perwolff**★★★★ £E

LOIMER Kamptal www.loimer.at *UK stockists:* **Lib**, ACh
Fred Loimer excels with both Grüner Veltliner and Riesling. Top cuvées are precise but pure and expressive with real depth and length. LOIS is a light but expressive introductory Grüner Veltliner. Regular Langenlois varietals with more depth and intensity are excellent value for money. (PW)
O **LOIS**★ £B O **Spiegel** Grüner V.★★★ £C O **Käferberg** Grüner V.★★★ £C
O **Seeberg** Riesling★★★★ £C O **Steinmassl** Riesling★★★★ £D

NEUMAYER Traisental *UK stockists:* **WKe**
Good wines from scattered parcels of vineyard on the Traisen. Wines can sometimes struggle for full ripeness and flavours are cool and citrusy, but there is good intensity and length. Wein vom Stein wines (a special selection) show fine fruit expression, purity and length of flavour. If youthfully austere they should be given some time. (PW)
O **Rafasetzen** Grüner V.★ £B O **Berg** Riesling★★ £C
O **Der Wein vom Stein** Grüner V.★★ £C Riesling★★★ £C

NIGL Kremstal www.weingutnigl.at *UK stockists:* **Gau**
Contrasting Rieslings from racy, minerally, elegant Piri to taut, intense and concentrated Hochäcker or deep, pure and stylish Privat. Grüner Veltliner Privat is full-bodied and powerful with very ripe fruit, yet balanced; Alte Reben version is atypically rich and profound for this variety. All have good ageing potential. (PW)
O **Senftenberger Piri** Grüner V.★★★ £D Riesling★★★ £D O **Riesling Privat**★★★★ £E
O **Grüner Veltliner Privat**★★★★ £D O **Grüner Veltliner Alte Reben**★★★★ £D

NIKOLAIHOF Wachau www.nikolaihof.at *UK stockists:* **RsW**, Rae, SVS, P&S
Biodynamically produced Riesling and Grüner Veltliner from vines with high average age. Long-lived Riesling, whether restrained, minerally vom Stein, intense, refined Im Weingebirge or

234

New entries have producer's name underlined

steely, elegant Steiner Hund. Characterful Im Weingebirge Grüner Veltliner in both full, fat Smaragd version or ripe Federspiel. Also Weissburgunder of good depth and structure. (PW)

O **vom Stein** Riesling Smaragd★★★ £E   O **Steiner Hund** Riesling Reserve★★★★ £E

O **Im Weingebirge** Grüner V. Smaragd★★★ £D   Riesling Smaragd★★★ £E

ANITA & HANS NITTNAUS Neusiedlersee www.nittnaus.at   *UK stockists:* **L&S**

Reds from Zweigelt and Blaufränkisch are most important here. Elegant Heideboden is the principal estate wine, topped up with other varieties. Top reds Comondor (Merlot/Cab Sauv/Zweigelt) and Pannobile (80/20 Zweigelt/Blaufränkisch) are deep and stylish – richer and riper in 02 than 01. Also good dry white blends and sweet wines – dense, concentrated TBA and refined sweet red Kurzberg TBA (Pinot Noir/Zweigelt/Blaufränkisch). (PW)

● **Zweigelt★** £B   ● **Heideboden★★** £B

● **Pinot Noir Kurzberg★★** £D   ● **Comondor★★★** £E   ● **Pannobile★★★** £D

O **Heideboden★★** £B   O **TBA★★★★** £F   ● **Kurzberg** TBA★★★ £E

BERNHARD OTT Donauland/Wagram www.ott.at   *UK stockists:* **Sav**

Estate close to Kamptal on loess soils highly suited to Grüner Veltliner, making only unoaked whites. All Grüners are expressive, fruity and characterful, from cool, spicy Am Berg and more floral Rosenberg to Fass 4, a selection of the best vineyards, through late-harvested old-vine Der Ott, to powerful Rosenberg Reserve. (PW)

O **Am Berg** Grüner Veltliner★ £B   O **Rosenberg** Grüner Veltliner★★ £B

O **Fass 4** Grüner Veltliner★★ £B   O **Der Ott** Grüner Veltliner★★★ £C

O **Rosenberg** Reserve Grüner Veltliner★★★ £D   O **von Rotem Schotter** Riesling★★ £C

F-X PICHLER Wachau   *UK stockists:* **RsW**, NYg, Gen, Rae, F&R, N&P, Sec, P&S

Extremely high quality Riesling and Grüner Veltliner of great extraction and concentration. Loibner Berg most classy Riesling but also very fine examples from Dürnsteiner Kellerberg, von den Terrassen and slow evolving Steinertal. Grüner Veltliners are marvellous too led by deep, structured Loibner Berg. Also special supercharged, very concentrated selections of Riesling (Unendlich) and Grüner Veltliner ('M'). (PW)

O **Loibner Berg** Riesling Smaragd✪✪✪✪✪ £E   Grüner V. Smaragd★★★★ £E

O **Dürnsteiner Kellerberg** Riesling Smaragd★★★★★ £E   Grüner V. Smaragd★★★★ £E

O **Von den Terrassen** Riesling Smaragd★★★★ £E   Grüner V. Smaragd★★★ £E

RUDI PICHLER Wachau   *UK stockists:* **Gau**, NYg

Concentrated wines with almost exotic quality in riper styles but good definition and minerality too. Less austere than some but still needing at least 5 years' ageing. Well-illustrated by 'Smaragd' Kollmütz and Hochrain Grüner Veltliner, or Steinriegl and Achleiten Riesling. Also very good blended Terrassen examples and vigorous cool Wachauer Federspiel wines. A name to track down. (PW)

O **Weissenkirchner Achleiten** Riesling Smaragd★★★★★ £E

O **Weissenkirchner Steinriegl** Riesling Smaragd★★★★ £E

O **Wösendorfer Hochrain** Grüner V. Smaragd★★★★ £D

PRAGER Wachau www.weingutprager.at   *UK stockists:* **FMV**, NYg, Fal, P&S, F&M

Dry wines of harmony and longevity as well as fine sweet wines when conditions permit. Several fine Smaragd Rieslings from Weissenkirchen including Steinriegl, Wachstum Bodenstein and Klaus. Achleiten provides fine Grüner Veltliner as well as Riesling - also made in Auslese and (occasionally) Trockenbeerenauslese versions. Also an intense, fruit-rich Chardonnay Smaragd. (PW)

O **Weissenkirchen Steinriegl** Riesling Smaragd★★★★ £E

O **Weissenkirchen Achleiten** Riesling Smaragd★★★★ £E   Grüner V. Smaragd★★★ £D

O **Dürnsteiner Kaiserberg** Riesling Smaragd★★★ £D

SALOMON-UNDHOF Kremstal www.undhof.at   *UK stockists:* **L&S**

Historic family estate with increasingly good wines. Initially austere Von Stein Grüner Veltliner of lovely minerality and intensity; fine Grüner from old vines in Lindberg too. Fine Kögl Riesling including very pure, elegant Reserve. Also an attractive Gelber Traminer. (PW)

O **Undhof Wieden** Grüner V.★★ £C   O **Von Stein** Grüner V. Reserve★★★ £D

O **Pfaffenberg** Riesling★★ £C   O **Kremser Kögl** Riesling★★★ £C   Reserve★★★★ £D

AUSTRIA

SCHLOSS GOBELSBURG Kamptal www.gobelsburg.at *UK stockists:* **FWW**, NYg, P&S, SVS
Ancient estate still belonging to a Cistercian monastery. Radically improved wines - now fully ripe Grüner Veltliner and Riesling of superb definition and concentration. Great style and refinement in Alte Reben Riesling (from Gaisberg) and composed, classy Heiligenstein. Regular Gobelsburger Riesling and Renner Grüner Veltliner are good value. (PW)

○ **Zöbinger Heiligenstein** Riesling★★★★★ £C   ○ **Gaisberg** Riesling★★★★ £C
○ **Riesling Alte Reben**★★★★★ £D   ○ **Riesling Gobelsburger**★★ £B
○ **Kammerner Lamm** Grüner V.★★★★ £D   ○ **Kammerner Grub** Grüner V.★★★ £C

TEMENT Südsteiermark www.tement.at
Standard-bearer for southern Styria with superbly balanced and expressive whites. Beyond sound, varietally pure *Steirische Klassik* basics, he makes very good Chardonnay (Morillon) and at times brilliant Sauvignon from Grassnitzberg and Sernau vineyards. Zieregg is richly textured, powerful but balanced. Also blended 'Pino. T', mineral-and-elderflower Roter Traminer, and floral, elegant sweet wines. (PW)

○ **Grassnitzberg** Sauvignon Blanc★★ £C   Roter Traminer★★ £C
○ **Sernau** Sauvignon Blanc★★★ £D   ○ **Zieregg** Sauvignon Blanc★★★★ £E   Morillon★★★ £E
○ **Pino. T**★★ £C   ○ **Sulz** Morillon★★★ £D   Welschriesling TBA★★★★ £F

ERNST TRIEBAUMER Neusiedlersee-Hügelland *UK stockists:* **GWW**
One of the best known names of Burgenland with wide range of styles. Dry whites include Neuburger, Welschriesling, Weissburgunder, Chardonnay and Sauvignon. Also under son Herbert's label are aromatic Gelber Muskateller and Grüner Veltliner. Best grape is Blaufränkisch with up to 4 versions: Aus den Rieden, Gmärk, Oberer Wald and Ried Marienthal, the last only in best years. All soften and more complex with age. Also fine sweet Ruster Ausbruch. (PW)

Ernst Triebaumer
● **Blaufränkisch** Aus den Rieden★★ £B   Ried Marienthal★★★ £E
○ **Chardonnay Ried Pandkräftn**★★ £C   ○ **Ruster Ausbruch**★★★★ £F

Herbert Triebaumer
● **Cabernet Sauvignon/Blaufränkisch**★ £C
○ **Grüner Veltliner**★★ £B   ○ **Gelber Muskateller**★ £B

VELICH Neusiedlersee www.velich.at *UK stockists:* **FMV**, BBR, SVS
Austria's finest Chardonnay, Tiglat combines depth and richness with real poise and elegance. Also good second version, Darscho and attractive Chardonnay-based Cuvée OT. Fine sweet wines: rich Seewinkel Beerenauslese (Chardonnay, Neuburger, Bouvier) and sweet, intense very refined Welschriesling Trockenbeerenauslese (TBA) - 99, 98 and 95. Also powerful TBA from Tiglat vineyard. (PW)

○ **Apetlon Chardonnay Darscho**★★ £C   Chardonnay Tiglat★★★ £E
○ **Seewinkel** Beerenauslese★★★ £D   ○ **Welschriesling** TBA★★★★ £F

WOHLMUTH Südsteiermark www.wohlmuth.at *UK stockists:* **Ham**
Large, quality southern Styria estate producing 70% white, including 2 contrasting Sauvignons – ripe, mineral-infused Steinriegel, and barrel-fermented and aged Elite from Altenberg vineyard. Ripe-fruited GG (Sauvignon/Sémillon) has impressive depth and intensity. Riesling is also fine while reds include plummy Aristos (Blaufränkisch/Cab Sauv) and more ambitious single-vineyard Rabenkropf. (PW)

○ **Steinriegel** Sauvignon Blanc★★★ £C   Gewürztraminer★★ £C
○ **Sauvignon Blanc Elite**★★★ £D   ○ **GG**★★★ £C
○ **Altenberg** Riesling★★★ £C   ● **Aristos**★★ £C   ● **Rabenkropf**★★ £D

Other wineries of note
Arachon T FX T (Mittelburgenland), Ehn (Kamptal), Gross (Südsteiermark), Hirsch (Kamptal), Holzapfel (Wachau), Kollwentz-Römerhof (Neusiedlersee-Hügelland), Lagler (Wachau), Helmut Lang (Neusiedlersee), Prieler (Neusiedlersee-Hügelland), Schmelz (Wachau), Heidi Schröck (Neusiedlersee-Hügelland), Dr Unger (Kremstal)

236   *An in-depth profile of every producer can be found in* Wine behind the label 2006

New entries have producer's name underlined

Background

England offers the occasional wine of depth and character, from Seyval Blanc. The best bets, though are some first-class sparkling wines, including those from Chardonnay and Pinot Noir. In Eastern Europe the **Czech** and **Slovak Republics** both produce some decent dry whites. In **Romania** the best potential would appear to rest with the sweet botrytised wines of **Cotnari** and **Murfatlar**. Outside investment would be a real advantage. In **Hungary**, apart from Tokaji, few wines of real quality have been produced. **Tokaji**, though, is a different matter. Investment aplenty has flooded into the region and some of the results are stunning. In South-Eastern Europe **Slovenia** produces some crisp dry whites and a few reasonable sweet wines close to the Austrian border. **Croatia** has a few gutsy reds, while **Bulgaria** ought to produce much more in the way of quality than it does.

Greece has real potential and an increasing number of stylish modern whites and rich plummy reds are now being made as well as a few established classics like the sweet **Muscats** from the island of **Samos**. The industry in **Israel** is still largely focused on the production of kosher wines, many from the **Golan Heights**, but an increasing number of stylish reds and whites are being produced there as well. In **Lebanon**, after decades of war and strife, new producers are now making dense, powerful wines of heady character. Dense and concentrated reds are also emerging from **Morocco** and **Algeria**.

A-Z of producers

ALPHA ESTATE   Greece   www.alpha-estate.gr   *UK stockists:* **Vbr**
The Alpha White is 100% Sauvignon, with a piercing varietal character and intensity to match some of the best examples elsewhere. The characterful Xinomavro red is aged in American oak, as is the top Alpha Red, 60/20/20 Syrah/Merlot/Xinomavro. (DM)
● **Alpha Estate Red** Macedonia★★★ £C   ● **Amyndeon** Alpha Red Xinomavro★★ £C
O **Alpha Estate White** Florina★★ £B   O **Alpha Estate Dessert White** Florina★★ £B

BIBLIA CHORA ESTATE   Greece   *UK stockists:* **Ecl**
The vineyards are planted in the sparse flinty soils of Mount Pangeon in the cooler north of the country. Estate White blends Sauvignon and Assyrtiko, the Estate Red is a Bordeaux blend. 12 months in new oak result in a rich, characterful wine with marked dark berry fruit. (DM)
● **Estate Biblia Chora**★★★ £C   O **Estate Biblia Chora**★★★ £C
O **Estate Biblia Chora**★ £B

DOMAINE LOUIS BOVARD   Lavaux, Switzerland   www.domainebovard.com   *UK stockists:* Tan
From terraced slopes above Lac Léman, Chasselas-based wines that are remarkably stylish and finely balanced with mineral, citrus, apple and a delicately nutty character. Added depth, structure in ageworthy Dézaley Grand Cru Médinette. From Saint-Saphorin, both a varietal Chasselas, and blend with Chenin. (PW)
O **Dézaley** Grand Cru Médinette★★★ £C   O **Calamin** Cuvée Speciale★★ £C
O **Saint-Saphorin** L'Archevesque★★ £C   Chasselas/Chenin★★ £C

DISZNÓKŐ   Tokaji, Hungary   *UK stockists:* **PFx**
Created in 1992 with investment in major new cellars. A full range of Tokaji styles is produced and top sweet wines have marvellous botrytis complexity. With as much care lavished on the base wine as the *aszu*, the wines are very opulent and exotic with comfortably enough acidity for balance. (DM)
O **Tokaji** Aszú 5 Puttonyos★★★★ £E   Aszú 6 Puttonyos★★★★ £F

DENBIES   Surrey, England   www.denbiesvineyard.co.uk
Very substantial operation with more than 100 ha planted on limestone soils near Dorking. An extensive range is offered and, as elsewhere in England, sparkling wines have good potential and there have been some impressive sweet whites over the past few vintages. (DM)
O **Classic Brut** Vintage★ £B

EVHARIS ESTATE   Greece   www.evharis.gr   *UK stockists:* **Ecl,Han,NYg**
Small 30-ha Greek estate located between Athens and Corinth with vineyards planted in the foothills of the Gerania Mountains. Good red and white blends from indigenous grapes are joined by impressive unfiltered Merlot and one of Greece's better Syrahs. (DM)

EUROPE, N AFRICA & MIDDLE EAST

● Estate Red★★★ £C   ● Syrah★★★ £C   ● Merlot★★ £C
O Estate White★★ £B   O Asyrtiko★★ £B

GAIA ESTATE Greece www.gaia-wines.gr *UK stockists:* Odd
One of the finest producers in Greece with two wine estates. The island of Santorini is source of striking
Thalassitis whites, while fine reds based on Agiorgitiko come from coastal Nemea. Good rosé and a benchmark
retsina, Ritinis Nobilis, too. The Gaia Estate is firmly structured with real depth. (DM)
● Notios Nemea★ £B   ● Agiorgitiko Nemea★★ £B   ● Gaia Nemea★★★★ £D
O Thalassitis Santorini★★★ £C   O Thalassitis Oak Santorini★★★ £C

JEAN-RENÉ GERMANIER Switzerland www.jrgermanier.ch *UK stockists:* **Las**
One of the finest producers in Switzerland, making top-class red and white from native as well as international
varieties. The wines are all impressively ripe and full as well as firmly structured. Humagne du Valais is from the local
variety of the same name. Amigne de Vétroz is a characterful late-harvest white.(DM)
● Vétroz Dôle Grand Cru★★ £C Pinot Noir Grand Cru★★★ £C   ● Valais Humagne du Valais★★★ £D
O Vétroz Fendant Grand Cru★★★ £C   O Valais Mitis Amigne de Vétroz★★★★ £F

GEROVASSILIOU Greece www.gerovassiliou.gr *UK stockists:* Odd
Relatively small estate of 33ha in northern Greece with an interesting mix of international and local varieties. The
characterful Malagousia is a rare local variety marked by hints of citrus and and underlying spicy herbs. The best red
is Avaton, produced from indigenous varieties. (DM)
● Epanomi Syrah/Merlot★★ £B Avaton★★★ £D
O Epanomi Viognier★★ £C Malagousia★★★ £C Chardonnay★★★ £C

HATZIDAKIS Greece www.hatzidakiswines.gr *UK stockists:* **Ecl**,
Some impressive whites and a stunning Vin Santo are made here on the barren landscape of the island of
Santorini. These are wines marked by a piercing minerality. Nykteri Santorini comes from the oldest vines on the
property. and is richer and more opulent than the other whites. Mavrotragano red lacks the intensity of the
whites. (DM)
● Mavrotragano★ £C   O Santorini★★ £B   O Aidani-Assyrtiko★★ £B
O Santorini Barrel★★★ £C   O Nykteri★★★ £C   O Vin Santo★★★★ £E

KTIMA PAVLIDIS Greece www.ktima-pavlidis.gr
Ktima Pavlidis white is a cool-fermented Sauvignon/Assyrtiko blend, the red is an impressively structured Cab
Sauv/Limnio/Merlot aged in French (80%) and American oak with malolactic in barrel. Syrah and Tempranillo are
soft, supple and fruit-driven. (DM)
● Drama Ktima Pavlidis★★ £C Tempranillo★★ £B Syrah★★ £B
O Drama Ktima Pavlidis★★ £B

LUMIÈRE Morocco
Gérard Depardieu's 6-ha estate at Meknes in the Guerrouane appellation produces a remarkable old-vine
Grenache/Carignan/Syrah blend. Attractive young, the wine benefits from four or five years' age. (DM)
O Guerrouane Cuvée Lumière★★★★ £E

MASSAYA Lebanon www.massaya.com *UK stockists:* **THt**
Arguably now the finest producer in Lebanon. Red, white and rosé are produced and it is the reds that stand out.
Classic is forward and fruit-driven; Selection is bigger and sturdier. The Reserve red is dense, powerful and
concentrated, a blend dominated by Cab Sauv with some Mourvèdre and Syrah. (DM)
● Classic★★ £B   ● Selection★★★ £C   ● Selection★★★★ £D

NYETIMBER West Sussex, England *UK stockists:* **RyR, Wai**
Very good sparkling wines are made here from the Champagne varieties. Classic Cuvée blends mainly
Chardonnay with lesser amounts of the Pinots. The Blanc de Blancs is leaner, more intense and piercing and
will add more with a little age after release. (DM)
O Classic Cuvée★★★ £D Première Cuvée★★★ £D

OREMUS Tokaji, Hungary *UK stockists:* **FMV**,F&M,BBR
Venture between Tokaji Kereskedöhóz (the former state-run commercial house) and Spain's Bodegas Vega

238

Sicilia. It is named after the vineyard where the original Tokaji was produced in 1650. A full range of styles is made, from basic dry Furmint to exceptional and heady Essencia. (DM)

O **Tokaji** Aszú 5 Puttonyos★★★ £E   Essencia✪✪✪✪✪ £H

DOM. DE SAINT AUGUSTIN   Algeria

Gérard Depardieu-owned property. Regular bottling La Confession blends Grenache, Carignan and Syrah, whereas the Cuvée Monica more unusually comprises Grenache, Carignan and Alicante. Dense, very rich and loaded with dark berry fruit,the concentration is impressive. Exciting and characterful wines. (DM)

O **Coteaux de Tlemcen** Cuvée Monica★★★ £E

ISTVAN SZEPSY   Tokaji, Hungary   *UK stockists:* **RsW**,F&M

Istvan Szepsy has emerged as one of the most exciting winemakes in the region. Quality is reflected in wines which are unusually fresh. The Aszú 6 Puttonyos is remarkably intense. Szepsy is also involved in a new venture, Kiralyudvar, where similarly impressive fresh Tokaji styles are being produced. (DM)

O **Tokaji** Noble Late Harvest★★★ £D   Aszú 6 Puttonyos✪✪✪✪✪ £G

ROYAL TOKAJI WINE COMPANY   Tokaji, Hungary   *UK stockists:* RTo, BBR,Wai

First of the foreign investments in the Tokay region. The wines are rich and intense, without a hint of oxidation, and have a more overtly orange peel and nutty character than other examples. (DM)

O **Tokaji** Blue Label 5 Puttonyos★★ £E   Aszú Nyulaszo 6 Puttonyos★★★★ £G

O **Tokaji** Essencia✪✪✪✪✪ £H

SAMOS CO-OPERATIVE   Greece   www.greekwinemakers.com   *UK stockists:* **Ecl**

Fine, long-established producer of sweet Muscat. Vin Doux, Grand Cru and Anthemis are fortified in a similar manner to other Muscats in France and elsewhere. Nectar differs; it is vinified from dried grapes and is not fortified, having less oxidative character and impressive, piercing intensity. (DM)

O **Samos** Vin Doux★ £B   Grand Cru★★ £B   Anthemis★★ £B   Nectar★★★ £C

THREE CHOIRS   Gloucestershire, England   www.three-choirs-vineyards.co.uk

Top-quality English property with 28 ha of vineyards. Decent quality dry and sweet whites are made as well as sparkling non-vintage and vintage bottlings. (DM)

O **Bacchus** Reserve★★ £B

TOKAJ CLASSIC   Tokaji   www.tokaj-classic.com   *UK stockists:* **May**

New cellar in Tokaj, established by 3 musicians. Noble Late Harvest is both rich and elegant with a subtle, sweet peachy character. The 5 Puttonyos is fuller and impressively intense with piercing botrytis character. The magnificently opulent 6 Puttonyos is one of the best examples from the region. (DM)

O **Tokaji** Noble Late Harvest★★★ £C   Aszú 5 Puttonyos★★★★ £F   Aszú 6 Puttonyos★★★★★ £F

An in-depth profile of every producer can be found in Wine behind the label 2006

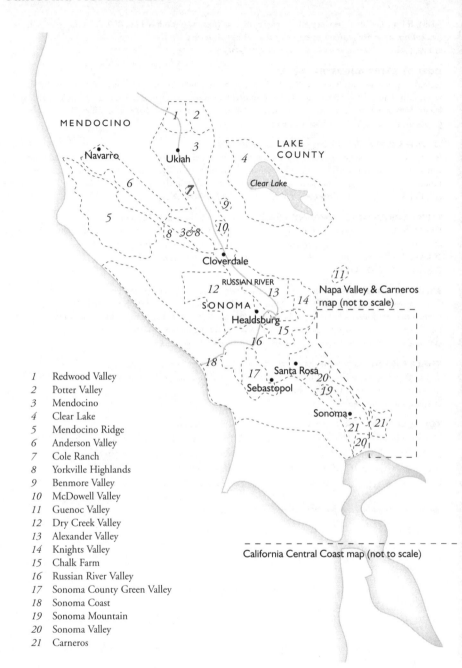

1   Redwood Valley
2   Potter Valley
3   Mendocino
4   Clear Lake
5   Mendocino Ridge
6   Anderson Valley
7   Cole Ranch
8   Yorkville Highlands
9   Benmore Valley
10   McDowell Valley
11   Guenoc Valley
12   Dry Creek Valley
13   Alexander Valley
14   Knights Valley
15   Chalk Farm
16   Russian River Valley
17   Sonoma County Green Valley
18   Sonoma Coast
19   Sonoma Mountain
20   Sonoma Valley
21   Carneros

The Region

Vast area, taking in Mendocino and Lake Counties, as well as Sonoma County. The whole viticultural area is encompassed under the **North Coast** AVA. What enables such diverse vinegrowing are cool coastal breezes and sea fogs that drift in through coastal gaps, creating a cooling fan for the whole vineyard area. Mendocino is mostly cool and particularly suitable for Pinot Noir and Chardonnay. The **Anderson Valley**, produces a number of restrained, stylish examples as well sparkling wine. To the north-east of the sector are the warmer AVAs of **Redwood Valley** and **Potter Valley**. **Clear Lake** AVA and **Guenoc** sub-AVA are best-suited to growing reds – Cab Sauv and Zin. **Benmore Valley** AVA is cooled by elevation and provides restrained Chardonnays.

In Northern Sonoma **Dry Creek** and **Alexander Valleys** provide fine Zin and Syrah. **Knights Valley** is a source of first-class Chardonnay and Cab Sauv. The **Russian River Valley** produces exemplary Pinot Noir and Chardonnay and, in the warmer eastern sites, very good Syrah and Zin. Fine cool climate Chardonnay and Pinot Noir are also now being produced in the **Sonoma Coast** and **Sonoma Green Valley** AVAs. The **Sonoma Valley** AVA is home to some of the largest producers on the North Coast. The western range has its own AVA, **Sonoma Mountain**, and provides impressive examples of restrained Chardonnay, Pinot Noir and Cab Sauv. The southern sector that borders Carneros produces stylish whites and good Pinot Noir. Fine Cab Sauv blends and Zins come from the Mayacamas Mountains.

California North Coast Vintages

Cab Sauv, Zin and other late ripening varieties working best in the warmer sites and early-ripening Chardonnay and Pinot Noir performing better in the cooler sectors. With regard to earlier years, the occasional 1987, 1985, 1984 and 1980 Cabernet and perhaps really top-flight Zinfandel might be worth a punt. 1978 and 1970 were also classic Cabernet years. (See also Vintage Charts)

Wizard's Wishlist

A selection of Sonoma blockbuster reds

BEHRENS AND HITCHCOCK
● Cabernet Sauvignon Kenefick Ranch
DEHLINGER ● Syrah Estate
FOPPIANO ● Petite Sirah Russian River Reserve
GALLO OF SONOMA ● Cabernet Sauvignon Estate
HARTFORD ● Zinfandel Russian River Valley
KENDALL JACKSON ● Cabernet Sauvignon Stature

MARTINELLI ● Zinfandel Jackass Hill
PETER MICHAEL ● Les Pavots Knights Valley
SEGHESIO ● Omaggio Alexander Valley
VÉRITÉ ● La Joie Sonoma County
LAUREL GLEN ● Cabernet Sauvignon Sonoma Mountain
DUTTON-GOLDFIELD ● Syrah Cherry Ridge Vineyard
PAX WINE CELLARS ● Syrah Alder Springs Vineyard
FISHER VINEYARDS
● Cabernet Sauvignon Wedding Vineyard
VÉRITÉ ● La Muse Sonoma County

Benchmark Pinot Noirs

GARY FARRELL ● Pinot Noir Rochioli Vineyard
HANZELL ● Pinot Noir Estate
HARTFORD COURT
● Pinot Noir Dutton Sanchietti Vineyard
PAUL HOBBS ● Pinot Noir Cuvée Agustina
KISTLER ● Pinot Noir Kistler Vineyard Vineyard
LYNMAR WINERY ● Pinot Noir Five Sisters Vineyard
PAPAPIETRO PERRY ● Pinot Noir Peters Vineyard
J ROCHIOLI ● Pinot Noir Estate
SIDURI ● Pinot Noir Van der Kamp Vineyard
WILLIAMS SELYEM ● Pinot Noir Hirsch Vineyard
MARIMAR TORRES ● Pinot Noir Sonoma Green Valley
DUTTON-GOLDFIELD
● Pinot Noir Devil's Gulch Ranch Marin County
SKEWIS ● Pinot Noir Floodgate Vineyard
TANDEM
● Pinot Noir Sonoma Mountain Van der Kamp Vineyard

A selection of cool climate Sonoma whites

ARROWOOD O Viognier Saralee's Vineyard
KISTLER O Chardonnay Hudson Vineyard
LA CREMA O Chardonnay Russian River Valley
LANDMARK O Chardonnay Damaris Reserve
LYNMAR WINERY O Chardonnay Five Sisters Vineyard
MARCASSIN O Chardonnay Marcassin Vineyard
MARTINELLI O Chardonnay Charles Ranch
PETER MICHAEL O Chardonnay Cuvée Indigene
ROEDERER ESTATE O Brut L'Ermitage
STEELE O Chardonnay Durrell Vineyard
BENZIGER O Chardonnay Los Carneros
DUTTON-GOLDFIELD
O Chardonnay Dutton Ranch Rued Vineyard

A selection of affordable Sonoma values

DRY CREEK ● Zinfandel Old Vine Sonoma County
EDMEADES ● Zinfandel Mendocino Ridge
LA CREMA O Chardonnay Russian River Valley
FLOWERS ● Ponot Noir Sonoma Coast
FOPPIANO ● Petite Sirah Reserve
DRY CREEK ● Syrah Owl Hill

241

California North Coast

GALLO OF SONOMA ● **Zinfandel** Frei Ranch
IRON HORSE VINEYARDS O **Chardonnay** Estate
LYNMAR ● **Pinot Noir** Quail Hill Vineyard

MARTINELLI O **Gewürztraminer** Martinelli Vineyard
ROEDERER ESTATE O **Brut** L'Ermitage
PAPAPIETRO PERRY ● **Pinot Noir** Russian River

California North Coast/A-Z of producers

ARROWOOD Sonoma Valley www.arrowoodvineyards.com *UK stockists:* **RMi**
Now owned by Mondavi this continues to make impressive Cab Sauv and Chardonnay as well as Sonoma fruit sourced Rhône styles. Saralee's Vineyard has long been a very good source for Viognier and others. Grand Archer is a decent second label. (DM)
● **Cabernet Sauvignon** Réserve Spéciale★★★★ £G Sonoma County★★★ £F
● **Syrah** Sonoma Valley★★★ £F O **Viognier** Saralee's Vineyard★★★ £D

BENZIGER Sonoma Mountain www.benziger.com *UK stockists:* **N&P**
Large, family-run operation producing an extensive range of wines. The best are very good and of relatively good value. The family also owns the Imagery Estate winery, which sells a good-quality range from lesser varieties at the cellar door only. (DM)
● **Cabernet Sauvignon** Reserve Sonoma County★★ £E
● **Merlot** Reserve Sonoma County★★ £E O **Chardonnay** Reserve Carneros★★★ £D

DEHLINGER Russian River Valley
Dehlinger remains among the very top echelon in the Russian River, continually crafting outstanding unfiltered Pinot Noir, Syrah and Chardonnay. Cab Sauv does not quite hit the same heady heights, although it is rich, structured and impressive in top years. (DM)
● **Cabernet Sauvignon** Estate★★★ £E ● **Syrah** Estate★★★★ £E
● **Pinot Noir** Estate★★★★ £E O **Chardonnay** Estate★★★★ £D

DRY CREEK VINEYARDS Dry Creek www.drycreekvineyard.com *UK stockists:* **Bal**
Medium-sized winery notable for good, well-priced Fumé Blanc in a very much more herbaceous style than many. Also a number of rich and impressive Zins. (DM)
● **Merlot** Reserve★★ £D ● **Cabernet Sauvignon** Reserve★★ £D
● **Zinfandel** Heritage Clone★★ £C Old Vines★★★ £C Reserve★★★ £D

DUTTON-GOLDFIELD Russian River Valley www.duttongoldfield.com
Very impressive Chardonnay, Pinot Noir and Syrah from a range of sites, mostly in the cool Green Valley. Cherry Ridge Syrah comes from one of the area's warmer sites, whereas Chardonnay and Pinot Noir are both sourced from the cooler Dutton Ranch, which is family owned. (DM)
● **Pinot Noir** Devil's Gulch Ranch Marin County★★★★ £E McDougall Vineyard★★★★ £E
● **Pinot Noir** Dutton Ranch★★★ £E ● **Syrah** Cherry Ridge Vineyard★★★★ £E
O **Chardonnay** Dutton Ranch★★★★ £D Dutton Ranch Rued Vineyard★★★★ £E

EDMEADES Anderson Valley www.kjsales.com/brands/edmeades *UK stockists:* **KJn, WTs**
Kendall-Jackson Mendocino-based winery, producing an extensive range of full, brambly Zinfandels and well-structured Petite Sirah and Syrah. Cool Anderson Valley vineyards provide the source for Pinot Noir and Chardonnay. (DM)
O **Chardonnay** Anderson Valley★★ £C ● **Petite Sirah** Eaglepoint Vineyard★★★ £D
● **Zinfandel** Eaglepoint Vineyard★★★ £D Mendocino Ridge★★★ £D

GARY FARRELL Russian River Valley www.garyfarrell.com *UK stockists:* **Vin**
Now owned by Allied Domecq, Farrell produces stylish, elegant Chardonnay and Pinot Noir and decent Merlot and Encounter, a meritage blend. (DM)
● **Pinot Noir**★★★ £E Starr Ridge Vineyard★★★ £E Rochioli Vineyard★★★★ £F
O **Chardonnay**★★★ £E Bien Nacido★★★ £E Rochioli Vineyard★★★★ £F

242

FISHER VINEYARDS Russian River Valley www.fishervineyards.com
Long-established property producing top class reds and whites from some superbly sited high-density vineyards in both Sonoma and Napa. Of the 2 great single-vineyard Cabs, the Napa Valley-sourced Lamb Vineyard is marginally richer, the Sonoma County Wedding Vineyard offers a touch more elegance. Chardonnay is both very impressive and well priced. (DM)
● **Cabernet Sauvignon** Lamb★★★★★ £H Wedding★★★★ £H Coach Insignia★★★★ £F
● **Cameron Red** Napa Valley★★★★ £E ● **Merlot** RCF★★★ £E
O **Chardonnay** Mountain Estate★★★★ £E Whitneys★★★★ £E

FLOWERS Sonoma Coast www.flowerswinery.com *UK stockists:* **Vin**
Very good Sonoma coastal property with vineyards planted in volcanic soils and moderated by cooling maritime breezes making an ideal environment for cultivating top quality Chardonnay and Pinot Noir. Vinification follows age-old Burgundian techniques for both varieties. (DM)
● **Pinot Noir** Camp Meeting Ridge★★★★ £E Andreen-Gale★★★★ £F
O **Chardonnay** Camp Meeting Ridge★★★★ £E Andreen-Gale★★★★ £E

FOPPIANO Russian River Valley www.foppiano.com *UK stockists:* **WTs**
There are good solid, earthy reds here: the Sangiovese is one of the better California examples but the real stars are the two Petite Sirah *cuvées*. Both are dense, powerful and supple examples of this sometimes raw and tannic variety. (DM)
● **Sangiovese** Alexander Valley★★ £C ● **Zinfandel** Reserve★★ £C
● **Petite Sirah** Russian River★★★ £C Reserve★★★ £E

FRICK Dry Creek Valley www.frickwinery.com
Small Rhône specialist with some Merlot as well. Not huge blockbusters the wines show rich and concentrated fruit with balance and finesse. New is C Squared, a Rhône-style blend of Cinsault and old-vine Carignan from Mendocino. All offer good value. (DM)
● **Syrah** Owl Hill★★★ £C ● **Cinsault** Dry Creek★★ £C
● **Merlot** Dry Creek★★ £C O **Viognier** Gannon Vineyard★★ £C

FRITZ WINERY Dry Creek Valley www.fritzwinery.com
Grapes come from both the Dry Creek Valley and the cooler Russian River, which provides an excellent source for Chardonnay. Zins are vibrant and full of rich fruit. Range is completed by well-priced Carignane and two restrained cedary Cabernet Sauvignons. (DM)
● **Zinfandel** Old Vine★★ £C O **Sauvignon Blanc** Sonoma County★★ £B
O **Chardonnay** Dutton Ranch★★★ £C Dutton Ranch Shop Block★★★ £E

GALLO OF SONOMA Dry Creek Valley www.gallosonoma.com *UK stockists:* **EJG**
One of the world's largest wine companies, E & J Gallo, is known the world over for its Gallo and Turning Leaf volume labels. Much more exciting are the wines made from its seven vineyards owned throughout Sonoma. Estate Vineyard Chardonnay and Cab Sauv are very classy. (DM)
● **Cabernet Sauvignon** Estate★★★★ £F ● **Zinfandel** Barelli Creek★★★ £D
O **Chardonnay** Estate★★★ £E Laguna Vineyard★★ £D Two Rock★★ £D

HANZELL Sonoma Valley www.hanzell.com *UK stockists:* **Vin**
Small producer located high up in the Mayacamas Mountains. Hanzell was established way back in 1953 and has long been a pioneer of first-class Chardonnay and Pinot Noir from its hillside estate vineyard. Both will age well. (DM)
● **Pinot Noir** Estate★★★ £F O **Chardonnay** Estate★★★★ £F

HARTFORD FAMILY WINERY Sonoma Green Valley *UK stockists:* **May**
Founded in 1993 by Don Hartford and his wife Jennifer Jackson-Hartford, of the Kendall-Jackson clan. Burgundian Chardonnay and Pinot Noir and rich spicy Zinfandel of great class and depth. Hartford Court labels coming from a range of single vineyard sources. (DM)
Hartford
● **Pinot Noir** Sonoma Coast★★★ £C ● **Zinfandel** Russian River Valley★★★★ £D

NORTH AMERICA

O **Chardonnay** Sonoma Coast★★★ £C

Hartford Court
O **Chardonnay** Three Jacks Vineyard★★★★ £E   ● **Pinot Noir** Marin County★★★ £E
● **Pinot Noir** Velvet Sisters Vineyard★★★ £E   Dutton Sanchietti★★★★£E

PAUL HOBBS Sonoma County www.paulhobbs.com
Paul Hobbs makes a stunning range of single vineyard wines, his top Chardonnay and Pinot Noirs labelled Cuvée Agustina. He also now produces, in partnership, own premium Argentine Malbec, Cobos, from high altitude vineyards in the Upper Mendoza. (DM)
● **Cabernet Sauvignon** Napa Valley★★★ £F   ● **Pinot Noir** Hyde Vineyard★★★★ £F
O **Chardonnay** Russian River★★★ £E

IRON HORSE VINEYARDS Sonoma-Green Valley www.ironhorsevineyards.com
Some of the best sparkling wines in California. Impressively structured and elegant Blanc de Blancs is only a touch below the quality of the much pricier Brut LD. An extensive range of still wines is also produced from Green Valley as well as the T-bar-T estate in Alexander Valley. (DM)
● **Pinot Noir** Sonoma-Green Valley★★ £D   ● **T-bar T-Benchmark** Alexander Valley★★★ £F
O **Chardonnay** Estate★★★ £C   Corral★★★ £D   O **Classic Vintage Brut** Sonoma-Green Valley★★ £D
O **Blanc de Blancs** Sonoma-Green Valley★★★ £E   O **Brut LD** Sonoma-Green Valley★★★★ £F

KAMEN ESTATE WINES Sonoma Valley www.kamenwines.com
The meagre, volcanic, rocky soils at this south-western Mayacamas estate never produce yields beyond 1.5 tons/acre, resulting in a pure varietal Estate Cab Sauv with great intensity and depth. (DM)
● **Cabernet Sauvignon** Sonoma Valley★★★★ £F

KENDALL-JACKSON Sonoma County www.kj.com   *UK stockists:* **KJn**
Vast, private wine company, founded by Jess Jackson, producing an extensive range under its own label and also owning or part-owning a considerable number of wine operations in the premium-wine sector throughout California. Some leading brands include Stonestreet, Verite, Lokoya, Atalon and Cardinale. (DM)
● **Cabernet Sauvignon** Great Estates Alexander Valley★★★ £F   Stature★★★★ £G
O **Chardonnay** Great Estates Arroyo Seco ★★★ £E   Stature★★★★ £F

KISTLER Russian River Valley   *UK stockists:* **WTs**
One of the greatest producers of both Chardonnay and Pinot Noir in California. Great bottles are produced from Les Noisetiers, Durrell, McCrea, Vine Hill, Hirsch and Camp Meeting Ridge vineyards as well as those below. Cuvée Cathleen is the top Chardonnay, while the ultimate expressions of Pinot Noir here are Cuvée Elizabeth from the Occidental Vineyard and the Cuvée Catherine. (DM)
● **Pinot Noir** Sonoma County★★★ £E   Kistler Vineyard❂❂❂❂❂ £G
O **Chardonnay** Sonoma County★★★ £E   Kistler Vineyard❂❂❂❂❂ £G

LANDMARK Sonoma Valley www.landmarkwine.com   *UK stockists:* **Lay**
Very fine and stylish Chardonnays, the main focus, are produced in a rich, lightly tropical vein. Structured Grand Detour Pinot Noir comes from altitude at the Van der Kamp vineyard on Sonoma Mountain. (DM)
● **Pinot Noir** Sonoma County★★★ £E   Grand Detour★★★★ £E
O **Chardonnay** Damaris Reserve★★★★ £E   Lorenzo Vineyard★★★★ £E

LAUREL GLEN Sonoma Mountain www.laurelglen.com   *UK stockists:* **AWM**
As well as a brilliant Cab Sauv Patrick Campbell makes a fine second wine Counterpoint as well as two youthful gluggers. Reds is sourced from old bush vines at Lodi, Terra Rosa is a Cab Sauv from Chile's Central Valley. More serious are Za Zin and Quintana, a dark vibrant Cab Sauv. (DM)
● **Cabernet Sauvignon** Sonoma Mountain★★★★ £E   ● **Za Zin** Lodi★★ £B
● **Counterpoint** Sonoma Mountain★★ £D   ● **Reds** Lodi★ £B

LYNMAR WINERY Russian River Valley www.lynmarwinery.com   *UK stockists:* **Vin**
Very good newly established Russian River winery with vineyards at their own Quail Hill Ranch. The top wines are the Five Sisters bottlings which are a significant step up in both quality and price. The Chardonnay, particularly, is marked by super-ripe opulent fruit and layer upon layer of flavour. (DM)

244

● **Pinot Noir** Quail★★★ £D   Reserve★★★★ £E   Five Sisters★★★★★ £F
○ **Chardonnay** Estate★★★★ £D   Quail Cuvée★★★★ £E   Five Sisters★★★★★ £F

MARCASSIN   Sonoma Coast
Helen Turley has achieved a cult reputation among California winemakers. The Marcassin winery was established in 1990 and an extraordinary number of brilliant Chardonnays and Pinots have been made from both the home Marcassin as well as other vineyards. (DM)

MARIMAR TORRES   Sonoma Green Valley   *UK stockists:* **JEF**
Based in the cool Sonoma Green Valley sub-appellation, Miguel Torres' sister Marimar produces consistently fine Chardonnay and Pinot Noir, in a restrained and European in style. (DM)
● **Pinot Noir** Don Miguel★★★★ £E   ○ **Chardonnay** Don Miguel★★★ £E

MARTINELLI   Russian River Valley   www.martinelliwinery.com   *UK stockists:* AWM,Vin
Steve Martinelli and winemaker Helen Turley produce brilliant Zin, some of the very best in the state; the Jackass Hill is a benchmark for all. You can also find very classy Chardonnay and Pinot Noir here sourced from a number of sites. (DM)
● **Zinfandel** Giuseppe & Luisa★★★★ £E   Jackass Hill✪✪✪✪✪ £E
● **Pinot Noir** Blue Slide Ridge★★★★ £F   ○ **Chardonnay** Martinelli Road★★★★ £E

MATANZAS CREEK   Sonoma County   www.matanzascreek.com   *UK stockists:* **May**
Much improved property under new Jackson family ownership. Small amounts of a powerful Reserve Merlot, very pricey Journey meritage blend, a Sonoma Valley Syrah and a promising Mendocino Viognier are also now being made. Hopefully quality is likely to support price from now on. (DM)
● **Merlot** Sonoma Valley★★★ £E   ○ **Sauvignon Blanc** Sonoma Valley★★★ £C
○ **Chardonnay** Sonoma Valley★★★★ £E

PETER MICHAEL   Knights Valley   www.petermichaelwinery.com   *UK stockists:* **Vin**
A range of dazzling Chardonnays and meritage red and white as well as Pinot Noir are made at this increasingly brilliant property. Both Les Pavots, a blend of Cab Sauv, Merlot and Cab Franc, as well as Chardonnay Indigene are among the State's great wines. (DM)
● **Pinot Noir** Le Moulin Rouge★★★ £F   ● **Les Pavots** Knights Valley✪✪✪✪✪ £G
○ **Sauvignon** Les Après-Midi★★★★ £F   ○ **Chardonnay** Indigene✪✪✪✪✪ £G

ROBERT MUELLER   Russian River Valley   *UK stockists:* **Vin**
Chardonnay is in a ripe, classically forward California style. The Pinots show impressive deep berry fruit, with some gamey character and supple, well-balanced tannins. As well as Emily's Cuvée, tiny quantities of pricey Pinot have also been produced from the Sonoma Coast Summa Vineyard. (DM)
● **Pinot Noir** Emily's Cuvée★★★★ £E   ○ **Chardonnay** LB★★★ £E

PAPAPIETRO PERRY   Russian River Valley   *UK stockists:* **WTs**
Tiny warehouse winery producing ripe, full-blown Burgundian style Pinot Noir. Dark and richly concentrated, the wines are aged in 60 per cent new oak and are bottled unfined and unfiltered. The Peters Vineyard, from the Sonoma Coast offers just a little more depth and intensity. (DM)
● **Pinot Noir** Russian River★★★★ £E   Peters Vineyard★★★★ £E

PAX WINE CELLARS   Russian River Valley   www.paxwines.com
Very impressive warehouse winery producing some of the best small-lot Syrah in California. The wines are characterised by ripe, opulent, full-blown dark fruit, loads of depth and concentration, and marvellous varietal purity throughout. 2 whites are also released – a Roussanne labelled Venus and a Viognier dubbed Aphrodite. (DM)
● **Syrah** Alder Springs★★★★★ £E Kobler Family★★★★★ £F Walker Vine Hill★★★★★ £F
● **Syrah** Castelli-Knight★★★★★ £F Obsidian★★★★ £E Griffins Lair★★★★ £E

A RAFANELLI   Dry Creek Valley
Dave Rafanelli has some excellent hillside vineyard sites producing superlative old-vine, highly complex and characterful Zin, as well as some impressive Cab Sauv. The estate vineyards are dry-farmed (i.e. without recourse to irrigation) and yields are always kept to a minimum. (DM)
● **Zinfandel** ★★★★ £C   ● **Cabernet Sauvignon** ★★★ £D

RAVENSWOOD Sonoma Valley www.ravenswood-wine.com *UK stockists:* **JAr,** Wai
Well established Sonoma winery making good to very good Zin and decent Cab Sauv, Merlot and Chardonnay
Ranch Salina is a meritage Bordeaux blend. Top reds are fine cellar prospects. (DM)
- ● **Rancho Salina** Moon Mountain★★★ £E ● **Merlot** Sonoma County★★ £C
- ● **Zinfandel** Monte Bello ★★★★ £E Old Hill Ranch★★★★ £E

J ROCHIOLI Russian River Valley *UK stockists:* **RsW**
The Rochioli family produce some of the best Pinot Noir and Chardonnay from various sources throughout the
Russian River, along with impressive Sauvignon Blanc and big, full, very rich Zinfandel, of which there is a
striking Sodini Vineyard bottling. (DM)
- ● **Pinot Noir** Estate★★★★ £E ● **Zinfandel** Estate★★★ £D
- O **Chardonnay** Estate★★★★ £E O **Sauvignon Blanc** Estate★★★ £C

ROEDERER ESTATE Anderson Valley www.roederer-estate.com *UK stockists:* **MMD,**F&M
Louis Roederer has set up its California outpost in the cool Anderson Valley. Regular Brut NV is made from all
three Champagne grapes, and Rosé, from Pinot Noir. Brut L'Ermitage is more serious, a well structured blend of
Pinot Noir and Chardonnay that is both long and complex. (DM)
- O **Brut** L'Ermitage★★★★ £E O **Brut** NV★★ £D ● **Brut** Rosé BV★★ £E

SAUSAL Alexander Valley www.sausalwinery.com
As the top Zinfandel label suggests, some of the vines here are over 100 years showing in the quality of the
reds. Private Reserve and Century Vines are barrel-aged in French oak to add complexity and depth. The
resulting wines are supple but finely structured. (DM)
- ● **Cabernet Sauvignon** Estate★★★ £D
- ● **Zinfandel** Family★★ £C Private Reserve★★★ £D Century Vines★★★★ £D

SEGHESIO Dry Creek Valley www.seghesio.com *UK stockists:* **Lib,**Sel
The Seghesio family make a range of striking Italian varietals including Barbera, Pinot Grigio and Arneis as well
as Sangiovese. Omaggio blends Sangiovese with Cab Sauv. Particularly impressive are the Zins which all have
marvellous depth and purity. (DM)
- ● **Pinot Noir** Keyhole Ranch★★★ £E ● **Omaggio** Alexander Valley★★★★ £E
- ● **Sangiovese** Old Vine "Chianti Station"★★★ £E 'Venom'★★★★ £E
- ● **Zinfandel** Home Ranch★★★★ £E Cortina★★★★ £E Old Vine★★★★ £E

SIDURI Russian River Valley www.siduri.com *UK stockists:* **Vin**
An extensive range of fine and stylish Pinot Noirs, as well as impressive Syrah from the Novy Vineyard among
others, have been made by this small warehouse operation on the outskirts of Santa Rosa. All are bottled
unfiltered. (DM)
- ● **Pinot Noir** Santa Lucia★★★★ £F Van der Kamp Vineyard★★★★ £F
- ● **Syrah** Novy Vineyard★★★ £D

SKEWIS WINES Russian River Valley www.skewiswines.com
Specialist producer of superb small-lot Pinot Noir. From the Russian River Salzgeber is the lightest, Montgomery is
more gamy and Bush Vineyard is darker and plummier. Finely structured Floodgate and Demuth from the
Anderson Valley offer a touch more depth and intensity. (DM)
- ● **Pinot Noir** Salzgeber★★★ £E Montgomery★★★★ £E Bush Vineyard★★★★ £E
- ● **Pinot Noir** Floodgate Vineyard★★★★ £E Demuth Vineyard★★★★ £E

WH SMITH Sonoma County *UK stockists:* **Vin**
Bill Smith established his reputation at La Jota on Howell Mountain. He now vinifies stylish and elegant Pinot
Noir on the Sonoma Coast. As well as the intense and complex Hellenthal Vineyard, a Sonoma Coast bottling
is also offered. (DM)
- ● **Pinot Noir** Hellenthal Vineyard★★★ £E

SONOMA-CUTRER Russian River Valley www.sonomacutrer.com *UK stockists:* **BFW,**L&S
Sonoma-Cutrer produces consistent Chardonnay, particularly the two leading *cuvées*. Tiny-production top wine
is the Founders Reserve, selected from the five best barrels of the vintage and bottled without filtration. (DM)

246

New entries have producer's name underlined

O **Chardonnay** Russian River Ranches★★ £C The Cutrer★★★ £E Les Pierres★★★£E

ST FRANCIS VINEYARDS Sonoma Valley www.stfranciswine.com *UK stockists:* **HMA**
An extensive range is produced, solely from Sonoma County fruit and at the top end the quality is striking. Zinfandels, both Old Vines and Pagani Ranch, are huge, brooding, super-ripe examples of the variety. Cab Sauv Kings Ridge Reserve, the top label, is powerful, refined and very well crafted. (DM)
● **Zinfandel** Old Vines★★★£D Reserve Pagani Vineyard★★★★ £E
● **Cabernet Sauvignon** Kings Ridge Vineyard Reserve★★★★£G

STEELE Lake County www.steelewines.com *UK stockists:* **Vin**
Jed Steele produces a huge range of mostly single vineyard bottlings from a range of red and white varieties. Chardonnay and Pinot Noir are both significant. Shooting Star is the winery's second label, providing good fruit-driven wines at very fair prices. (DM)
● **Pinot Noir** Bien Nacido★★★ £E ● **Zinfandel** Catfish Vineyard★★★ £D
● **Syrah** Parmalee-Hill★★★ £D O **Chardonnay** Durrell Vineyard★★★★ £E

STONESTREET Alexander Valley www.stonestreetwines.com *UK stockists:* KJn, WTs
High-quality, medium-sized winery in the Jackson family empire. Merlot, Chardonnay and the meritage red Legacy, a blend dominated by Cabernet Sauvignon, are all impressive. Chardonnay is in a rich, tropical style, reds are big, powerful and brooding, marked by high alcohol. (DM)
● **Merlot** Alexander Valley★★★ £C ● **Legacy** Alexander Valley★★★★ £F
O **Chardonnay** Block Sixty-Six★★★ £D Upper Barn★★★★ £E

TANDEM Sonoma Coast www.tandemwinery.com
Warehouse operation sourcing fruit from some of the best vineyards in the area. Pinot Noir is the key variety, but Chardonnay, Sangiovese, Zin and red blends are all made. Vineyard sources include Kent Ritchie, Sangiacomo, Pisoni, Halleck, Van der Camp, Auction Bridge, and Porter Bass. (NB)
● **Pinot Noir** Sonoma Mountain Van der Kamp Vineyard★★★★★ £F

VÉRITÉ Sonoma Valley www.veritewines.com *UK stockists:* **May**
Brilliant Jackson family premium operation specialising in richly textured meritage reds. La Joie is a blend of roughly two-thirds Cab Sauv with the balance Merlot. La Muse is 90% Merlot and 10% Cab Sauv. Le Désir, a Saint-Emilion style dominated by Cab Franc and Merlot. (DM)
● **La Joie** Sonoma County★★★★★ £G **La Muse** Sonoma County★★★★★ £G
● **Le Désir** Sonoma County★★★★★ £G

WILLIAMS SELYEM Russian River Valley *UK stockists:* **Vin**
One of Sonoma's great Pinot Noir producers. Rich and concentrated wines, marked by their powerful, earthy tannins. Chardonnay can be lusciously rich. A plethora of single-vineyard labels are produced every vintage. Zin and two intense sweet wines from Gewürztraminer and Muscat are also made. (DM)
● **Pinot Noir** Russian River★★★★★ £F Hirsch Vineyard★★★★★ £F
O **Chardonnay** Allen Vineyard★★★★ £F Hirsch Vineyard★★★★ £F

Other wineries of note
Chalk Hill Winery (Chalk Hill), Château St Jean (Sonoma Valley), Clos du Bois (Alexander Valley), Fetzer Vineyards (Redwood Valley), Geyser Peak (Alexander Valley), Goldeneye (Anderson Valley), La Crema (Russian River Valley), Moon Mountain Vineyard (Sonoma Valley), Sonoma Cutrer (Russian River Valley)

An in-depth profile of every producer can be found in Wine behind the label 2006

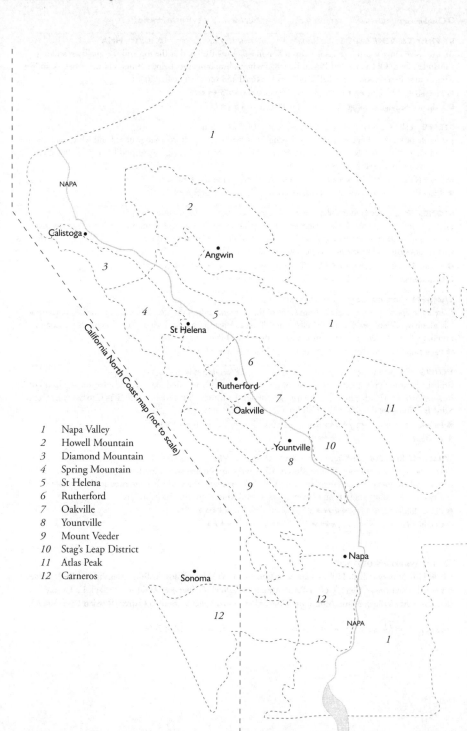

NAPA

Calistoga •

Angwin •

St Helena •

Rutherford •

Oakville •

Yountville •

Napa •

Sonoma •

NAPA

1   Napa Valley
2   Howell Mountain
3   Diamond Mountain
4   Spring Mountain
5   St Helena
6   Rutherford
7   Oakville
8   Yountville
9   Mount Veeder
10 Stag's Leap District
11 Atlas Peak
12 Carneros

California North Coast map (not to scale)

The Region

The **Napa Valley** AVA runs from Calistoga to south of the town of Napa edging towards San Pablo Bay. South-west of Napa, the Carneros AVA is located south of the Mayacamas Mountains and effectively divides the Sonoma and Napa Counties viticultural regions.

Calistoga's benchland vineyards are the warmest in the Napa Valley with the topography becoming semi-mountainous to the west with the **Spring Mountain District** AVA and to the east the **Howell Mountain** AVA.. A number of exceptional Cab Sauvs, Merlots and meritage blends emerge from these mountain AVAs. The central sector of the Napa Valley is the heart of the best benchland vineyards for Cab Sauv and Bordeaux-style red blends. The area runs from **St Helena** to cooler **Yountville** encompassing **Rutherford** and **Oakville**. As well as the Bordeaux styles, good Zin and Syrah are grown throughout this stretch of vineyards.

Some very fine wines and some that should be better are produced at **Stags Leap District**. To the west **Mount Veeder** provides sturdy reds with Zin and Syrah increasingly successful; some fine, tightly structured Chardonnay and peachy Viognier are also produced. Part-Sonoma County and part-Napa County, **Carneros** AVA is just inland to the north of San Pablo Bay and affected by cool, marine breezes. This is key for the production of sparkling base wine. Pinot Noir and Chardonnay are also successful and, in warmer mesoclimates Syrah.

Napa Valley Vintages

As elsewhere in California, it is difficult to provide a locally specific guide but there is a reasonable consistency through the region and the charts in the Vintage charts section give a fair indication of what you should expect. If you have cellared or are considering purchasing some older top Cab Sauv then earlier vintages that are looking particularly good are 1987, 1986 and more speculatively 1978, 1974 and 1970.

Wizard's Wishlist

15 premium Napa reds

ATALON ● **Cabernet Sauvignon** Napa Valley
ARAUJO ● **Cabernet Sauvignon** Eisele Vineyard
ARIETTA ● **H Block One Red** Napa Valley
BACIO DIVINO ● **Bacio Divino Red** Napa Valley
COLGIN CELLARS
● **Cabernet Sauvignon** Herb Lamb Vineyard

DALLA VALLE ● **Cabernet Sauvignon** Estate Oakville
DIAMOND CREEK ● **Cabernet Sauvignon** Volcanic Hill
LOKOYA ● **Cabernet Sauvignon** Diamond Mountain
DUNN VINEYARDS
● **Cabernet Sauvignon** Estate Howell Mountain
HARLAN ESTATE ● **Estate Red** Napa Valley
ROBERT MONDAVI
● **Cabernet Sauvignon** Reserve Napa Valley
STAGS LEAP WINE CELLARS
● **Cabernet Sauvignon** Cask 23
SHAFER ● **Cabernet Sauvignon** Hillside Select
PAHLMEYER ● **Proprietary Red** Napa Valley
VIADER ● **Cabernet Sauvignon** Napa Valley

A selection of diverse Napa whites

FAR NIENTE O **Chardonnay** Napa Valley
FROG'S LEAP O **Sauvignon Blanc** Rutherford
HESS COLLECTION O **Chardonnay** Napa Valley Collection
JADE MOUNTAIN O **Viognier** Para's Vineyard
KONGSGAARD O **Roussanne/Viognier** Napa Valley
LUNA O **Pinot Grigio** Napa Valley
MINER FAMILY O **Chardonnay** Wild Yeast
NIEBAUM-COPPOLA O **Blancaneaux** Rutherford
PAHLMEYER O **Chardonnay** Napa Valley
STAGLIN FAMILY O **Chardonnay** Rutherford

The best of Carneros

ACACIA ● **Pinot Noir** Beckstoffer Vineyard
CLINE CELLARS ● **Mourvedre** Small Berry Vineyard
CUVAISON O **Chardonnay** Estate Selection
DOMAINE CARNEROS ● **Pinot Noir** Famous Gate
GLORIA FERRER O **Carneros Cuvée** Carneros
HAVENS ● **Syrah** Napa Valley
JADE MOUNTAIN ● **Syrah** Hudson Vineyard
KONGSGAARD ● **Syrah** Napa Valley
SAINTSBURY ● **Pinot Noir** Reserve
RAMEY O **Chardonnay** Hudson Vineyard

The best Napa values

STORYBOOK MOUNTAIN ● **Zinfandel** Mayacamas Range
GREEN & RED ● **Zinfandel** Chiles Mill Vineyard
BROWN FAMILY ● **Zinfandel** Estate Chiles Valley
PETER FRANUS ● **Zinfandel** Brandlin Vineyard
GRGICH HILLS ● **Zinfandel** Napa Valley
HAVENS ● **Bourriquot** Napa Valley
BENESSERE ● **Zinfandel** BK Collins Old Vines
CLINE CELLARS ● **Mourvedre** Small Berry Vineyard
GARGIULO VINEYARDS
● **Aprile Super Oakville Blend** Napa Valley
LUNA ●**Sangiovese** Napa Valley

NORTH AMERICA

Napa Valley & Carneros/A-Z of producers

ABREU Napa Valley *UK stockists:* **THt**
As well as being one of the most sought after viticultural consultants, David Abreu fashions a massive, super-ripe Cab Sauv with a hint of Merlot and Cab Franc from this first-class vineyard. The wine is one of the most 'collectable' in California(DM)
● **Cabernet Sauvignon** Madrona Ranch❶❶❶❶❶ £H

ARAUJO Napa Valley www.araujoestatewines.com *UK stockists:* **THt**
As well as the Cab Sauv there is a first class Syrah and most recently Altagracia, a Bordeaux red blend of Cab Sauv, Petit Verdot and Merlot. Both are sadly produced in tiny quantities. Even scarcer is the occasional bottling of Viognier. The lightly-oaked Sauvignon Blanc has a hint of Viognier. (DM)
● **Cabernet Sauvignon** Eisele Vineyard❶❶❶❶❶ £H
○ **Sauvignon Blanc** Eisele Vineyard★★★ £C

ARIETTA Napa Valley www.arietta.com *UK stockists:* **Vin**
Three magnificent reds made by John Kongsgaard. Merlot is 100%. The Hudson H Block blends Cab Franc with Merlot. The exotic Variation One is dominated by Syrah. All will cellar well. (DM)
● **Merlot** Napa Valley★★★★★ £G ● **H Block One Red** Napa Valley★★★★★ £G
● **Variation One Red** Napa Valley★★★★★ £G

ATALON Napa Valley www.atalon.com *UK stockists:* **May**
Recently established super-premium winery owned by Jess Jackson, producing wines which complement his Lokoya and Cardinale brands. A wide range of Napa vineyard sources are being called on. The Cabernets stand out from the Merlots. (DM)
● **Merlot** Napa Valley★★★ £F Napa Mountain Estates★★★★ £F
● **Cabernet Sauvignon** Napa Valley★★★★ £F Napa Mountain Estates★★★★★ £G

BACIO DIVINO Rutherford www.baciodivino.com *UK stockists:* **WTs**
Small even by California cult-winery standards. The Bacio Divino red is a very stylish, impressive and unusual blend of Cab Sauv, Sangiovese and Petite Sirah. Second label Pazzo is a reverse blend of Sangiovese, Cab Sauv and Petite Sirah it should be enjoyed sooner rather than later. (DM)
● **Bacio Divino** Napa Valley★★★★★ £G

BARLOW VINEYARDS Napa Valley www.barlowvineyards.com
Small property south of Calistoga, producing fat and showy unfiltered Merlot and Barrouge (Cab Sauv/Merlot). Quality is impressively high and the wines at present offer very good value for Napa. (DM)
● **Merlot** Napa Valley★★★ £D ● **Barrouge** Napa Valley★★★★ £E

BARNETT VINEYARDS Spring Mountain www.barnettvineyards.com
Spectacularly sited property with steeply terraced vineyards at 600m (2,000ft). The highest point, Rattlesnake Hill, provides a superbly intense and balanced super-premium Cab. Pinot Noir from the Santa Lucia Highlands is ripe and full; fat, citrusy Chardonnay is sourced from Sangiacomo in Carneros. (DM)
● **Cabernet Sauvignon** Spring Mountain★★★★ £F Rattlesnake Hill★★★★★ £G
● **Merlot** Spring Mountain★★★★ £D ● **Pinot Noir** Sleepy Hollow Vineyard Block A★★★★ £E
○ **Chardeonnay** Sangiacomo Vineyard★★★ £C ○ **Sauvignon Blanc** Napa Valley★★ £C

BEHRENS AND HITCHCOCK Spring Mountain *UK stockists:* THt,F&M
Very impressive small producer specialising in tiny lots of startling, massive, super-rich reds from a number of varieties sourced throughout the North Coast. Ode to Picasso is a fat, forward combination of Syrah, Cab Sauv, Merlot and Cab Franc. (DM)
● **Cabernet Sauvignon** Kenefick Ranch★★★★★ £F
● **Merlot** Fortuna Vineyard★★★★ £E

BENESSERE VINEYARDS St Helena www.benesserevineyards.com
Good, well-priced wines with a focus on Italian varieties and old-vine Zins. Top label Phenomenon is an opulent, vibrant Sangiovese-dominated blend with some Cab Sauv, Syrah and Merlot. (DM)

250

New entries have producer's name underlined

● **Phenomenon** Napa Valley★★★★ £F ● **Sangiovese** Napa Valley★★ £D
● **Zinfandel** Napa Valley★★★ £D BK Collins Old Vines★★★ £D ● **Merlot** Napa Valley★★★ £D
○ **Pinot Grigio** Napa Valley★★ £C ○ **Sauvignon Blanc** Napa Valley★★ £C

BERINGER St Helena www.beringer.com *UK stockists:* **BWC,AAA**
Now a part of the global Beringer Blass group, a huge range is offerred here. Two lower level ranges are Stone
Cellars and the superior Founders Estate. Top wines though are the great Reserve Private Reserve and Limited
Release wines. Private Reserve Cab Sauv is one of California's great reds. (DM)
● **Cabernet Sauvignon** Private Reserve★★★★★ £G
○ **Chardonnay** Private Reserve★★★★ £E Sbragia Limited Release★★★★ £E

ROBERT BIALE Napa Valley www.robertbialevineyards.com *UK stockists:* **OWL**
The Biale family have owned vineyards in the Napa Valley for decades. They are now a very impressive small
producer of mainly old-vine Zinfandel from a range of sources including their home vineyard, along with Petite
Sirah and a little Syrah, Barbera and Sangiovese. (DM)
● **Zinfandel** Estate★★★★ £E Monte Rosso Vineyard★★★★ £E
● **Petite Sirah** Estate★★★ £E

BLOCKHEADIA RINGNOSII Napa Valley *UK stockists:***WTs**
The wines are very much in the fruit-driven mould with minimal oak influence. The Zins are marked by spicy,
dark fruits and they are medium weight rather than blockbusters. The Sauvignon Blancs are vinified without
oak and offer a mix of lightly tropical fruit with a soft mineral undercurrent. (DM)
● **Zinfandel★★** California £C Mendocino County★★ £D Napa Valley★★★ £E
○ **Sauvignon Blanc** California★★ £C Napa Valley★★ £C

BROWN ESTATE Napa Valley
Fine Zin and subtly-oaked 100% varietal Cab Sauv from the Chiles Valley District in the eastern Napa. A second
Napa Valley-labelled Zin is also made from estate grapes. (DM)
● **Cabernet Sauvignon** Estate Napa Valley★★★★ £F ● **Zinfandel** Estate Chiles Valley★★★★ £E

BRYANT FAMILY Napa Valley
The Bryant Cabernet has become one of a handful of blue-chip California examples of the variety alongside
such illustrious names as Araujo, Colgin, Grace Family, Harlan and Screaming Eagle. Expect the wine to age
gracefully and be prepared to pay a very high price for it.(DM)
● **Cabernet Sauvignon**〇〇〇〇〇 £H

CAFARO Napa Valley www.cafaro.com *UK stockists:* **Lib**
Joe Cafaro produces stylish, supple and complex Cab Sauv, Merlot and most recently a small amount of Syrah
from the Cafaro Family Vineyard. His property is on slopes just to the south of Stags Leap. and the wines are all
marked by their purity of fruit and fine, elegant structure. (DM)
● **Merlot** Napa Valley★★★★ £F ● **Cabernet Sauvignon** Napa Valley★★★★ £F
● **Syrah** Cararo Family Vineyard★★★★ £E

OLIVER CALDWELL Napa Valley
Cab Sauv, Petite Sirah and Zin from the small Aida Vineyard. Pure varietal Esedra Cab Sauv is impressively rich and
concentrated; densely structured, powerful Petite Sirah is one of the region's better examples. (DM)
● **Cabernet Sauvignon Esedra** Napa Valley★★★★ £F ● **Petite Sirah** Aida Vineyard★★★ £E

CARDINALE Napa County www.cardinale.com *UK stockists:*WTs,KJn
Jewel in the crown of the Kendall-Jackson empire, a blend of Cab Sauv and Merlot sourced from prime
vineyards in Napa and Sonoma, which explains the generic California appellation. A concentrated red with
copious quantities of super-ripe cassis and hints of cedar. (DM)
● **Cardinale Proprietary Red** California★★★★★ £H

CAYMUS Rutherford www.caymus.com *UK stockists:* **Vin**
Two very good Cab Sauvs are vinified here. Conundrum is blended from an unusual mix of Sauvignon ,
Semillon, Chardonnay, Viognier and Muscat Canelli. It is ripe and aromatic with a hint of new oak. Special
Selection, one of California's great reds, needs cellaring and will improve in bottle for 5 to 10 years. (DM)

● **Cabernet Sauvignon** Napa Valley★★★ £F Special Selection★★★★★ £H
O **Conundrum** California★★★ £C

CHÂTEAU MONTELENA Napa Valley www.montelena.com *UK stockists:* **Vin**
Produces one of the greatest Cabernet-based reds in California along with sound Zin and Chardonnay. Even in lesser years the Montelena Estate red has a reputation for real quality. It is a backward and powerfully structured wine that needs time. (DM)
● **Zinfandel**★★★ £D   O **Chardonnay**★★★ £E
● **Cabernet Sauvignon**★★★ £E Montelena Estate★★★★★ £H

CLINE CELLARS Carneros www.clinecellars.com *UK stockists:* **WTs**
Fred Cline was one of the original Rhône Rangers. He produces a vast range of very well made reds from Rhône varieties as well as some great Zin as well. Some solid whites are also produced but they lack the same excitement as the reds, with their vibrant, spicy, berry fruit character. (DM)
● **Syrah** Carneros★★★ £C   ● **Mourvèdre** Small Berry Vineyard★★★★ £D
● **Syrah** Sonoma County★★★ £D   ● **Zinfandel** Fulton Road★★★ £E

CLOUD VIEW Napa Valley www.cloudviewvineyards.com
Just 1 wine is made – a big, full, dense and quite extracted proprietary red with a good firm tannic backbone, blended fom roughly equal proportions of Cab Sauv and Merlot. (DM)
● **Proprietary Estate Red** Napa Valley★★★★ £F

COLGIN CELLARS Napa Valley www.colgincellars.com *UK stockists:* **Vin**
Colgin now offers three super-premium bottlings Cariad, Tychson Hill and Herb Lamb. All are extremely expensive (the $175-plus winery release prices can rapidly be dwarfed by trading prices at auction) and all are based on Cab Sauv. (DM)

CORISON Napa Valley www.corison.com *UK stockists:*DDr
Cathy Corison produces a small amount of Napa Cabernet Sauvignon sourced from a variety of top quality benchland vineyard sites. A very limited amount of a special *cuvée* from the Kronos Vineyard is also produced, which requires more patience and a deeper pocket. (DM)
● **Cabernet Sauvignon**★★★★ £F

ROBERT CRAIG Napa Valley www.robertcraigwine.com *UK stockists:***THt,MyC**
Small, high-quality Napa operation established in 1992 and sourcing fruit from a number of locations, producing forward approachable wines. Affinity is a typical Bordeaux-style blend of Cab Sauv, Merlot and Cab Franc. Drink the reds over the short to medium term. (DM)
● **Cabernet Sauvignon** Mount Veeder★★★★ £E Howell Mountain★★★★ £E
● **Affinity** Napa Valley★★★★ £E   ● **Syrah** Central Coast★★★ £D
O **Chardonnay** Carneros★★ £C Sonoma County★ £C

DALLA VALLE Oakville www.dallavallevineyards.com *UK stockists:* **THt**
Super-premium winery with a first-class hillside site to the east of Oakville. Three wines are produced under the guidance of Mia Klein of Selene. The main focus of production is Cab Sauv plus a small amount of the even more impressive Maya. A stylish, dark cherry-laden Sangiovese, Pietre Rosse, is also made. (DM)
● **Cabernet Sauvignon** Estate★★★★★ £H

DIAMOND CREEK Diamond Mountain *UK stockists:* **L&W**
Supreme Cabernet Sauvignon has been made here for a great deal longer than most of the new generation of *super-cuvées*. These are wines sourced from prime mountain sites and each individually stating its own *terroir*, they are wines of grace, power and above all immense refinement. (DM)
● **Cabernet Sauvignon** Gravelly Meadow❂❂❂❂❂ £H Volcanic Hill❂❂❂❂❂ £H
● **Cabernet Sauvignon** Red Rock Terrace❂❂❂❂❂ £H

DIAMOND TERRACE Diamond Mountain www.diamondterrace.com
Barely more than 250 cases are made, but very reasonably priced for Napa. It is an elegant and structured mountain red but with a sufficiently supple feel to its tannin. 2002 was right on the cusp of ★★★★. (DM)
● **Cabernet Sauvignon** Diamond Mountain★★★ £E

DOMINUS ESTATE   Yountville   www.dominusestate.com   *UK stockists:* **C&B**,FMV
Magnificent, structured red dominated by Cab Sauv. The ripe fruit character of the Napanook Vineyard shows through and the wine also possesses a classically powerful tannic structure. It requires up to a decade or more. Napanook is an impressive second label. (DM)
● **Dominus**✪✪✪✪✪ £H   **Napanook**★★★ £E

DUCKHORN   St Helena   www.duckhorn.com   *UK stockists:* **L&W**
The main focus here is Merlot with two premium labels from Howell Mountain and the Three Palms vineyard. Cab Sauv is also good. Paraduxx is an unusual blend of Zin with a touch of Merlot and Cab Sauv, while the Decoy maintains the integrity of the top wines. (DM)
● **Cabernet Sauvignon** Napa Valley★★★ £F ● **Merlot** Napa Valley★★★ £E
● **Merlot** Howell Mountain★★★★ £F   Three Palms★★★★ £F

DUNN VINEYARDS   Howell Mountain   *UK stockists:* **AWM**
One of the pioneers of great mountain-grown Cabernet. Output remains small at around 4,000 cases a year. Of the two wines the Howell Mountain from estate fruit is denser, fuller and more tannic than the Napa Valley label. Both are very cellarworthy, the Howell Mountain needs eight to 10 years. (DM)
● **Cabernet Sauvignon** Napa Valley★★★★ £F   Howell Mountain✪✪✪✪✪ £F

FANTESCA   Spring Mountain   www.fantesca.com
Tiny property on the south-eastern reaches of the small Spring Mountain AVA. The wine is a big, sturdy mountain Cabernet with firm tannins and dark, spicy black fruits. (DM)
● **Cabernet Sauvignon** Spring Mountain★★★★ £F

FAR NIENTE   Oakville   www.farniente.com   *UK stockists:* Hal,T&W
There are just two main wines here. Cabernet is a typically powerful Napa expression requiring several years' cellaring to be enjoyed at its best. The Chardonnay has been fine-tuned over recent vintages and is both elegant and refined and will develop well with age. (DM)
● **Cabernet Sauvignon**★★★★ £G   O **Chardonnay**★★★★ £F

FIFE VINEYARDS   Oakville   www.fifevineyards.com
Dennis Fife and wine writer wife Karen MacNeil produce an extensive range of mainly red wines from Zin and the Bordeaux and Rhône varieties. Reserve Cabernet will eventually come from their own Spring Mountain vineyard. Max Cuvée is Petite Syrah/Syrah/Carignane. (DM)
● **Cabernet Sauvignon Reserve** Napa Valley★★★ £F ● **Max Cuvée** Napa Valley★★★ £E
● **Zinfandel Old Vines** Napa Valley★★ £D

FLORA SPRINGS   St Helena   www.florasprings.com   *UK stockists:* **Vin**,Win
Family-owned operation with a broad selection of wines. The two flagships are the Cab Sauv Hillside Reserve and the proprietary red Trilogy, a blend of Cab Sauv, Merlot, Cab Franc and Malbec. Poggio del Papa is a new Tuscan style blend. (DM)
● **Cabernet Sauvignon** Wild Boar Vineyard★★★ £F   Hillside Reserve★★★★ £G
● **Merlot** Windfall Vineyard★★★ £E   ● **Trilogy** Napa Valley★★★★ £F

FORMAN   St Helena   *UK stockists:* **AWM**
Ric Forman makes impressive examples of both Chardonnay and Cabernet Sauvignon as well as a little Merlot. Chardonnay is bottled without malolactic fermentation for structure. Rich, cedary Cabernet from volcanic soils will develop very well with age.(DM)
● **Cabernet Sauvignon** Napa Valley★★★★ £E
O **Chardonnay** Napa Valley★★★★ £D
● **Magnificat**★★★ £F O **Chardonnay** Napa Valley★★ £C   Cuvée Sauvage★★★ £E

PETER FRANUS   Rutherford   www.franuswine.com   *UK stockists:* THt
Franus Cabernet is elegant and stylish, Zinfandel is always ripe, brambly and vibrant. Best of the three is the Brandlin Vineyard. Sauvignon comes in two guises: Farella-Park is barrel-fermented; the Stewart Vineyard bottling from Carneros sees no wood. (DM)
● **Zinfandel** Planchon Vineyard★★★ £C   Brandlin Vineyard★★★ £D
● **Cabernet Sauvignon** Napa Valley★★★ £E

NORTH AMERICA

FROG'S LEAP Rutherford www.frogsleap.com *UK stockists:* L&W, FMV,F&M
The emphasis here is on fun, reflected in the labelling. Pull a cork and you'll see what I mean. However, the wine is serious and can be very impressive. The style is for forward, ripe, fleshy reds with sufficient structure to age nicely in the medium term and for rich, fruity whites. (DM)
● **Cabernet Sauvignon** Napa Valley★★★ £E ● **Rutherford** Napa Valley★★★ £F
● **Merlot** Napa Valley★★★ £D ● **Zinfandel** Napa Valley★★★ £C

GEMSTONE Napa Valley www.gemstonewine.com
Small property producing an impressive meritage red from Cab Sauv with a little Merlot, Cabernet Franc and Petit Verdot. Second label Facets has much more Merlot and a tiny amount of Chardonnay is available only on the mailing list. (DM)
● **Proprietary Red** Napa Valley★★★★ £G

GRACE FAMILY VINEYARDS St Helena www.gracefamilyvineyards.com
This tiny operation was the first of the now numerous California cult wineries and the Grace Family is one of the most exalted premium Cabernets in California. Big, richly textured and immensely powerful, it is a wine respected for its balance and finesse as much as its sheer concentration. (DM)

GREEN AND RED VINEYARD Napa Valley *UK stockists:*AWM,Win
Small estate in the Chiles Valley on the eastern side of the Napa Valley whose main focus is Zinfandel. The California label is the lightest of the three. Chardonnay is barrel-fermented using native yeasts and spends nine months in oak. (DM)
● **Zinfandel** California★★ £C Chiles Valley Vineyards★★★ £C
● **Zinfandel** Chiles Mill Vineyard★★★ £C O **Chardonnay** Napa Valley★ £C

HL VINEYARDS Napa Valley www.herblambvineyard.com *UK stockists:* **Vin**
The Lambs' tiny but famous vineyard was the source for some benchmark wines from Colgin Cellars. They make just 80 cases a year under their own label, producing a rich, powerful and brooding red. (DM)
● **Cabernet Sauvignon** Napa Valley★★★★★ £H

HARLAN ESTATE Oakville www.harlanestate.com *UK stockists:* **THt**
Small, very high-quality producer dedicated solely to super-premium Bordeaux-style reds. The Harlan Estate Red meritage is a blend of Cab Sauv, Merlot, Cab Franc and Petit Verdot. Maiden is a very impressive second label. (DM)
● **Estate Red** Napa Valley✪✪✪✪ £H

HARRISON VINEYARDS Napa Valley www.harrisonvineyards.com
Small, family operation producing opulent richly textured reds that now also includes Merlot, Syrah and a meritage red with unusually some Syrah blended in. Chardonnay is barrel-fermented and like the reds bottled unfiltered.(DM)
● **Cabernet Sauvignon** Estate★★★ £F Reserve★★★★ £G
● **Zebra Zinfandel**★★ £C O **Chardonnay** Napa Valley★★★ £E Reserve★★★ £F

HAVENS Carneros www.havenswine.com *UK stockists:* **All**
Good Merlot and better Syrah are made here. The Hudson Syrah is strikingly elegant. Bourriquot is a Bordeaux-style blend, but Right Bank rather than Left, a mix of Cab Franc and Merlot. The Bourriquot and Hudson Syrah are real cellaring propositions. (DM)
● **Bourriquot** Napa Valley★★★★ £E ● **Merlot** Reserve Carneros★★★ £E
● **Syrah** Napa Valley★★★ £E Hudson Vineyard★★★★ £E

HEITZ CELLARS St Helena www.heitzcellar.com *UK stockists:* J&B
One of the original benchmark producers of premium Napa reds. Quality has been up and down during the 1980s and 1990s but the wines are now sounder. Chardonnay is in a tighter style than some of its neighbours and is only lightly oaked. (DM)
● **Cabernet Sauvignon** Bella Oaks Vineyard★★★ £F Trailside Vineyard★★★ £F
● **Cabernet Sauvignon** Martha's Vineyard★★★★ £H

HESS COLLECTION Mount Veeder www.hesscollection.com *UK stockists:* **BWC**
Particularly striking are the Cab Sauv and Chardonnay, produced under the Hess Collection label. In addition

254

New entries have producer's name underlined

NORTH AMERICA

to the Hess Collection is the Hess Estate Cabernet Sauvignon blended from a range of Napa sources, while Hess Select Cab Sauv, Merlot, Syrah and Chardonnay come from Monterey. (DM)
- ● **Cabernet Sauvignon** Collection★★★ £E   Collection Reserve★★★★ £F
- ● **Cabernet Sauvignon** Hess Estate★★ £C   O **Chardonnay** Collection★★★ £C

JADE MOUNTAIN   Napa Valley   www.chalonewinegroup.com   *UK stockists:* **FMV**
Now owned by the Chalone Wine Group, Jade Mountain has been a source of elegant, finely structured Merlot and Rhône style blends for a decade and a half. The sheer quality here is often misunderstood: these are wines that need time to fully unfurl and show at their best. (DM)
- ● **La Provençale**★★★ £C   ● **Merlot** Paras★★★★ £E   O **Viognier** Paras★★★★ £D
- ● **Mourvèdre** Contra Costa★★★★ £C   ● **Syrah** Hudson★★★★★ £F

JUSLYN   Spring Mountain   www.juslynvineyards.com
Three fine reds are produced, an Estate Cab Sauv, a Vineyard Select from the Beckstoffer Vineyard and a regular Napa Valley Cab Sauv, which has a larger proportion of Merlot. (DM)
- ● **Cabernet Sauvignon Vineyard Select** Napa Valley★★★★ £F

KONGSGAARD   Napa Valley   *UK stockists:* **Vin**
John Kongsgaard produces wines of formidable weight and concentration. Wild yeasts are used for fermentation and the wines are neither fined nor filtered. Very fine Chardonnay and a Roussanne/Viognier blend, are barrel-fermented. The richly, exotic Syrah is produced from Carneros fruit. (DM)
- ● **Syrah** Napa Valley✪✪✪✪✪ £H   O **Chardonnay** Napa Valley★★★★★ £G
- O **Roussanne/Viognier** Napa Valley★★★★★ £G

KULETO   St Helena   www.kuletoestate.com
Pat Kuleto has plantings of Cab Sauv, Syrah, Sangiovese, Zin, Pinot Noir and Chardonnay, all now released varietally, as well as some Muscat. Both Syrah and Cab Sauv are marked by elegance, purity of fruit and finely honed structure. (DM)
- ● **Cabernet Sauvignon Estate** Napa Valley★★★★ £F   ● **Syrah Estate** Napa Valley★★★★ £E

LAGIER MEREDITH   Mount Veeder   www.lagiermeredith.com   *UK stockists:* **AMW**
One wine is made here, a richly textured, very pure and intense Syrah. with the tiniest proportion of Viognier. Bottled without filtration, expect the wine to develop very well over five to seven years. The only problem is there's very little available. (DM)
- ● **Syrah** Mount Veeder★★★★ £F

LAIL VINEYARDS   Rutherford   www.lailvineyards.com   *UK stockists:* **Vin**
The J Daniel Cuvée is a Bordeaux blend of two-thirds Cab Sauv and one-third Merlot. Sourced from a mere 2.3 ha (5.6 acres) it is a stylish, elegant and very finely structured meritage red. (DM)
- ● **J Daniel Cuvée** Napa Valley★★★★ £F

LARKIN WINES   Yountville   www.larkinwines.com   *UK stockists:* **Vin**
Small Yountville operation producing a very fine Cab Franc-based red, one of the best of this style in the region. Merlot, Cab Sauv and Petit Verdot are blended in to add weight and depth. (DM)
- ● **Cabernet Franc** Napa Valley★★★★ £F

LARKMEAD   Napa Valley   www.larkmead.com
The Bordeaux red varieties are the main focus here although new blocks of Syrah, Zin and Sauvignon Blanc have been established. Top label Cab Sauv Solari Reserve is a pure varietal sadly only available in tiny quantities. Loaded with mouth-coating dark, spicy fruits it comes from the oldest Cab vines. (DM)
- ● **Cabernet Sauvignon Solari Reserve** Napa Valley★★★★★ £F   ● **Merlot** Napa Valley★★★★ £F

LITTORAI   St Helena   www.littorai.com   *UK stockists:* **Vin**
A range of Chardonnays and Pinot Noirs which are distinctly Burgundian in style and come from a number of North Coast sources. Chardonnay is subtle, structured and only lightly tropical. Pinot Noir shows intense, subtle berry fruits and is always well meshed by firm but supple tannin. (DM)
- ● **Pinot Noir** Hirsch Vineyard★★★★ £E   Savoy Vineyard★★★★★ £F
- O **Chardonnay** Charles Heintz Vineyard★★★★ £F   Theriot Vineyard★★★★ £F

California Napa & Carneros

NORTH AMERICA

LIVINGSTON MOFFETT Rutherford www.livingstonwines.com *UK stockists:* **Vin**
Two very good Cab Sauvs are produced: the Moffett is from the family estate vineyard, as well as a dark, spicy Syrah. Gemstone is the flagship red; a blend of Cab Sauv, Cab Franc, Merlot and Petit Verdot. The range is completed by a Genny's Vineyard Chardonnay, vinified with wild yeasts. (DM)
● **Cabernet Sauvignon** Moffett Vineyard★★★★ £F Stanley's Selection★★★★ £E
● **Gemstone**★★★★ £F ● **Syrah** Mitchell Vineyard★★★ £E

LOKOYA Oakville www.lokoya.com *UK stockists:* **WTs**
Jess Jackson's super-premium label, producing distinctive Cab Sauvs from prime mountain and benchland-grown fruit. They are all very big, dense and powerfully structured wines, needing time to shed their early youthful austerity. (DM)
● **Cabernet Sauvignon** Diamond Mountain★★★★ £G Howell Mountain★★★★ £G
● **Cabernet Sauvignon** Mount Veeder★★★★ £G Rutherford★★★★ £G

LUNA Napa Valley www.lunavineyards.com *UK stockists:* **MyC**
Regular Merlot, Pinot Grigio and Sangiovese are good value for money, while the pricier Canto is a proprietary Super-Tuscan-style blend of Sangiovese and Merlot with a touch of Cab Sauv for grip. Sangiovese Riserva is also now produced along with a little Petite Sirah/Zinfandel. (DM)
● **Merlot**★★★ £E ● **Canto**★★★★ £F ○ **Pinot Grigio**★★★ £C
● **Sangiovese**★★★ £C Riserva★★★★ £F

MINER FAMILY VINEYARDS Oakville www.minerwines.com *UK stockists:* **Vin**
The top wines here are the gamey, vibrant Pinot Noirs and Chardonnays, which are barrel-fermented with full malolactic. Zinfandel is straightforward, fruit-driven and blended with a little Petite Sirah for structure. Bordeaux varietals and the Oracle a meritage blend are also offerred. (DM)
● **Zinfandel** Napa Valley★★ £D ● **Pinot Noir** Gary's Vineyard★★★★ £F
● **Cabernet Sauvignon** Oakville★★★ £F ○ **Chardonnay** Wild Yeast★★★★ £F

ROBERT MONDAVI Oakville www.robertmondavi.com *UK stockists:* **RMi,BBR,F&M**
The most famous wine name in California, now owned by Constellation Brands. A vast range is produced including the ordinary budget Mondavi-Woodbridge and Coastal ranges and the company has widespread interests throughout California. The Cab Sauv Reserve is one of Napa's great reds. (DM)
● **Cabernet Sauvignon** Oakville★★★★ £F Reserve Napa Valley✪✪✪✪ £H
● **Pinot Noir** Reserve★★★ £F ○ **Chardonnay** Reserve★★★ £E

NEWTON Spring Mountain www.clicquot.com *UK stockists:* **Par,N&P,Bal,C&R**
Now a part of Moët Hennessey. Decent Red Label and Special Cuvées although better are the Unfiltered wines. The Epic is a firm, powerfully structured Merlot and there is a top-quality rich and cedary premium Cab Sauv, Le Puzzle. Both of these are very ageworthy. (DM)
● **Cabernet Sauvignon** Unfiltered★★★★ £E Le Puzzle★★★★★ £F
● **Epic** Napa Valley★★★★ £F ○ **Chardonnay** Unfiltered★★★★ £E

NIEBAUM-COPPOLA ESTATE Rutherford *UK stockists:* **MyC**
A fairly extensive range now including The Diamond Series sourced throughout the North Coast. Better are the Directors Reserve and Estate Wines labels. At the pinnacle there are Blancaneaux a blend of Chardonnay, Viognier, Marsanne and Roussanne. Rubicon is a very structured meritage red. It requires at least six to seven years' patience. (DM)
● **Cask Cabernet** Estate★★★ £F ● **Rubicon** Rutherford★★★★★ £G
● **Zinfandel** Edizione Pennino★★★★ £E ○ **Blancaneaux** Rutherford★★★£E

PAHLMEYER Napa Valley www.pahlmeyer.com *UK stockists:* **RWs**
Top-quality, low-volume winery producing three super-premium wines and occasional declassified lots under the Jayson label. These are all wines of depth, concentration and great finesse. They are bottled with neither fining nor filtration. (DM)
● **Merlot** Napa Valley★★★★★ £F ● **Proprietary Red** Napa Valley★★★★★ £F
○ **Chardonnay** Napa Valley★★★★ £F

256

New entries have producer's name underlined

PARADIGM   Oakville   www.paradigmwinery.com   *UK stockists:* **DDr**
At the Harris's excellent small estate the Cab Sauv (blended with Cab Franc and Merlot), is a round supple style with richly textured blackberry fruit and a hint of oak. A tiny amount of Zinfandel, Merlot and, most recently, Cabernet Franc is also produced. (DM)
● **Cabernet Sauvignon** Estate★★★★ £E

PATZ AND HALL   Napa Valley   www.patzhall.com   *UK stockists:* **T&W**
Small operation producing top-quality Pinot Noir and Chardonnay. The regular bottlings of both are impressive but even more so are the small volume runs produced from a number of single vineyards. Always bottled unfiltered, these are big, forward, explosive examples of both varieties. (DM)
● **Pinot Noir** Sonoma County★★★ £E   Russian River★★★ £E
○ **Chardonnay**★★★ £D   Dutton Ranch★★★★ £E   Woolsey Road Vineyard★★★★ £E

JOSEPH PHELPS   Napa Valley   www.jpvwines.com   *UK stockists:* **WTs**
Sizeable operation with a range of well made Rhône styles including Syrah/Grenache blend Le Mistral, as well as Bordeaux varieties and good Chardonnay. Top two wines are the structured and ageworthy Cab Sauv from the Backus Vineyard and the magnificent Insignia blended from all five Bordeaux varieties. (DM)
● **Insignia**★★★★★ £G   ● **Merlot**★★★ £E   ● **Syrah**★★★ £E
● **Cabernet Sauvignon** Backus Vineyard★★★★★ £G

PLUMPJACK   Oakville   www.plumpjack.com   *UK stockists:* **Vin**
The vineyards are still young and the best must surely yet emerge. Chardonnay is ripe, forward and toasty, the Cabernet powerful and structured. The very expensive Reserve offers an extra dimension at a not inconsiderable premium. New from 2001 is a Russian River Valley Syrah. (DM)
● **Cabernet Sauvignon** Estate★★★ £F   Reserve★★★★★ £H
● **Merlot** Napa Valley★★ £E   ○ **Chardonnay** Reserve★★★ £E

PRIDE MOUNTAIN VINEYARDS   Spring Mountain   www.pridewines.com
One of the finest sources of great Napa red. The vineyards have a southerly exposure as well as mountain, volcanic and sandstone soils providing an exceptional *terroir*. The key Bordeaux red varieties as well as Syrah, Sangiovese, Chardonnay and Viognier are all now planted. (DM)
● **Cabernet Sauvignon** Napa Valley★★★★★ £F

RAMEY   Oakville   *UK stockists:* **FMV**
David Ramey produces remarkably fine Chardonnay, impressive for its finesse, intensity and sheer quality as much as for its weight and texture. Two potentially great meritage reds have been added: Jericho Canyon and the younger vine Diamond Mountain Red. (DM)
○ **Chardonnay** Carneros★★★★ £E   Russian River★★★★ £E
○ **Chardonnay** Hudson Vineyard★★★★★ £F   Hyde Vineyard★★★★★ £F

REVERIE   Diamond Mountain   www.reveriewine.com
The Daydream wines from bought-in Napa fruit are cool-fermented to emphasise varietal character. The Reverie range are more serious with the Bordeaux varieties dominating plantings. Top label Special Reserve is emerging as one of Napa's better premium reds. Barbera is bright and forward. (DM)
● **Special Reserve** Diamond Mountain★★★★ £F   ● **Cabernet Franc** Diamond Mountain★★★★ £E
● **Barbera** Napa Valley★★★ £E   ● **AS Kiken** Napa Valley★★★ £D

RUDD ESTATE   Oakville   www.ruddwines.com   *UK stockists:* **Vin**
Seriously powerful, rich and structured reds come from vineyards that neighbour Screaming Eagle. Both the whites are barrel-fermented with natural yeasts. They are marked by their sophisticated and restrained style.(DM)
● **Estate Red** Oakville★★★★★ £G   ● **Cabernet Sauvignon** Oakville★★★★★ £F
○ **Chardonnay** Bacigalupi★★★★ £F   ○ **Sauvignon Blanc** Napa Valley★★★ £E

SAINTSBURY   Carneros   www.saintsbury.com   *UK stockists:* **Adm, J&B**
One of the top producers of the Burgundian varietals in Carneros, two-thirds of which are Pinot Noir. Carneros and Reserve labels of both Chardonnay and Pinot Noir are serious and refined examples. The only other variety produced is a tiny amount of Pinot Gris. (DM)

California Napa & Carneros

- ● **Pinot Noir**★★★ £D Reserve★★★★ £F Brown Ranch★★★★ £F
- ○ **Chardonnay**★★★ £C Reserve★★★★ £E

SCHRAMSBERG Napa Valley www.schramsberg.com *UK stockists:* **Vin**
First California winery to produce quality sparkling wines from the classic Champagne varieties. The off-dry Crémant Demi-Sec is produced from Flora, a crossing of Gewürztraminer and Semillon. The J Schram *cuvée* is part barrel-fermented and blended from the best lots in a single vintage. (DM)
- ○ **Blanc de Blancs**★★★ £D ○ **Blanc de Noirs**★★ £D
- ○ **Reserve**★★★★ £F ○ **J Schram**★★★★ £F ○ **Crémant Demi-Sec**★★ £D

SCREAMING EAGLE Oakville www.screamingeagle.com *UK stockists:* Sel,F&M,Vin
Perhaps first among all the recent Cabernet and meritage superstars of the Napa, certainly if rated by price achieved at auction. It is a classic blend dominated by Cab Sauv, with Merlot and Cab Franc from some exceptionally sited Oakville vineyards. (DM)

SHAFER Stags Leap www.shafervineyards.com *UK stockists:* **THt**
As well as great reds from Stags Leap, Red Shoulder Ranch Chardonnay comes from Carneros. Firebreak is a stylish blend of Sangiovese and Cab Sauv and Relentless is a rich and powerful Syrah blended with a little Petite Sirah. Hillside Select is one of California's very great reds. (DM)
- ● **Cabernet Sauvignon** Napa Valley★★★★ £F Hillside Select✪✪✪✪✪ £H
- ● **Firebreak** Napa Valley★★★★ £E ● **Relentless** Napa Valley★★★★ £F
- ○ **Chardonnay** Red Shoulder Ranch★★★★ £E

SHERWIN FAMILY Spring Mountain www.sherwinfamilyvineyards.com
Small Spring Mountain property producing top-class Cab Sauv. The wine is aged in 100% new oak, seamlessly integrated with the rich and concentrated dark berry-laden fruit. A second wine is planned. (DM)
- ● **Cabernet Sauvignon** Spring Mountain★★★★ £F

SPOTTSWOODE St Helena www.spottswoode.com *UK stockists:* **DDr**
The Cab Sauv is sourced fully from estate fruit, with a small component of Cab Franc. It is a deep, finely structured wine, with refined tannins and great ageing potential. The Sauvignon, part barrel-fermented with lees-enrichment, is ripe and stylish. (DM)
- ● **Cabernet Sauvignon** Napa Valley★★★★★ £G
- ○ **Sauvignon Blanc** Napa Valley★★★ £E

SPRING MOUNTAIN VINEYARD Spring Mountain www.springmtn.com
Grand Spring Mountain District property that has been up and down over the years but is now producing wines of real style that are representative of the area. Top red Elivette (Cab Sauv with just a little Merlot and Petit Verdot) is rich and opulent with dark and spicy berry fruit. (DM)
- ● **Elivette** Estate Napa Valley★★★★ £G ● **Cabernet Sauvignon** Estate Napa Valley★★★ £F
- ○ **Sauvignon Blanc** Estate Napa Valley★★ £D

SWITCHBACK RIDGE Napa Valley
As well as the Cabernet Sauvignon, varietal Merlot and Petite Sirah are also produced here. The richly textured Cabernet is opulent and loaded with exotic dark fruits and smoky oak. Expect it to drink well at a surprisingly young age. (DM)
- ● **Cabernet Sauvignon** Napa Valley★★★★ £F

STAG'S LEAP WINE CELLARS Stags Leap www.cask23.com *UK stockists:* **WTs**,Sel
Warren Winiarski's Stag's Leap Wine Cellars will forever be famous in wine circles as a result of the 1976 Paris tasting, when the Cask 23 outgunned the best from Bordeaux. Both SLV and Cask 23 are still among the best. The lesser bottles do pale in comparison. (DM)
- ● **Cabernet Sauvignon** Fay Estate★★★ £F SLV★★★★ £G Cask 23★★★★ £H
- ○ **Chardonnay** Arcadia★★★ £E Beckstoffer Ranch★★★ £E

STAGLIN FAMILY Rutherford www.staglinfamily.com *UK stockists:* Las
Estate Chardonnay and Cab Sauv are both very impressive. A second label Salus is now released to ensure the integrity of the estate wines. All the wines are marked by their weight, rich texture and extract. Sragliano, a

NORTH AMERICA

New entries have producer's name underlined

decent Sangiovese is also produced. (DM)

● **Cabernet Sauvignon** Salus★★★ £F   Rutherford★★★★★ £G
○ **Chardonnay** Salus★★★ £E   Rutherford★★★★ £F

DR STEPHENS ESTATE   Napa Valley   www.drstephenswines.com   *UK stockists:* **WTs**
Just Chardonnay and richly textured, cedary, minty Cab Sauv are produced at this small St Helena property.
The lightly tropical Chardonnay drinks young the Cab Sauv will develop for five or six years. (DM)

● **Cabernet Sauvignon** Moose Valley Vineyard★★★★ £F
○ **Chardonnay** Carneros★★★ £E

STORYBOOK MOUNTAIN   Napa Valley   www.storybookwines.com   *UK stockists:* **AWM**
This is a Zinfandel-only winery and a very good one, located on the red clay and loam slopes of the
Mayacamas. The wines are full-bodied and structured, tight and firm in their youth but with the kind of
cellaring potential the variety very often lacks. (DM)

● **Zinfandel** Atlas Peak★★★★ £C   Mayacamas Range★★★★ £C

PHILIP TOGNI   Spring Mountain   *UK stockists:* **Vin**, JAr,Rew
Philip Togni produces one of the more impressive Cab Sauvs to be found in the Napa. It is a dense, powerful
wine, with considerable tannin reinforcing its mountain origins, its texture rounded by malolactic fermentation
in barrel. It requires 8-10 years. (DM)

● **Cabernet Sauvignon** Spring Mountain★★★★★ £G

TOR KENWARD   St Helena   www.torwines.com   *UK stockists:* **Vin**
Small amounts of top-class Cab Sauv, a little Syrah from Carneros and Chardonnay from Two Rivers Vineyard in
the Napa and Durrell Vineyard in Carneros. Cab is concentrated and elegant, Chardonnay full of piercing citrus and
toasty oak. (DM)

● **Cabernet Sauvignon** Rutherford Clone 4 Oak Knoll★★★★ £F
○ **Chardonnay** Two Rivers Ranch★★★★ £E

TURLEY CELLARS   St Helena   www.turleywinecellars.com   *UK stockists:* **THt**
Larry Turley produces perhaps the modern benchmark for Zinfandel – massive, dark, brooding examples of the
variety. The wines are increasingly made from a wide range of sources and generally bottled as single-vineyard
cuvées. A number of very good Petite Sirahs are also made. (DM)

● **Zinfandel** Juvenile★★★ £C   Duarte★★★★ £D   Old Vines★★★★★ £E

VIADER   Napa Valley   www.viader.com   *UK stockists:* Bib,DDr
Very stylish and refined red wines are crafted here. Viader red is a powerful blend of Cab Sauv and Cab Franc.
Rare and impressively structured Petit Verdot V blended with Cab Sauv and Cab Franc. Estate Syrah is full of
exotic dark licorice and black pepper fruit. New is dare a fine, juicy Tempranillo with a little Cab Franc. All the
wines are very ageworthy. (DM)

● **Viader** Estate★★★★★ £F   ● **Viader** V Estate★★★★★ £F
● **Viader** Syrah Estate★★★★★ £F   ● **Dare** Estate★★★★★ £E

Other wineries of note

Acacia (Carneros), Amici Cellars (Napa Valley), Cakebread (Napa Valley), Clos Pegase (Napa Valley), Beaulieu
Vineyard (Rutherford), Cain Cellars (Spring Mountain), Chappellet (Napa Valley), Château Potelle (Mount
Veeder), Cuvaison (Napa Valley), Darioush (Napa Valley), Domaine Carneros (Carneros), Domaine Chandon
(Yountville), Franciscan (Oakville), Gargiulo Vineyards (Napa Valley), Gloria Ferrer (Carneros), Grgich Hills
(Napa Valley), La Jota (Howell Mountain), Lewis Cellars (Napa Valley), Mumm Napa (Rutherford), Opus
One (Oakville), Pine Ridge (Stags Leap), Quintessa (Rutherford), Silver Oak Cellars (Napa Valley), Stony Hill
(Spring Mountain), Swanson (Rutherford), Wolf Family Vineyards (St Helena)

An in-depth profile of every producer can be found in Wine behind the label 2006

California Central Coast

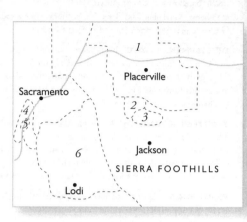

California North Coast map (not to scale)

San Francisco

7

SANTA CRUZ 9

San Jose 8

SANTA CLARA

10

Santa Cruz

11

12

Sacramento

1

Placerville

2

3

Jackson

4

5

6

Lodi

SIERRA FOOTHILLS

15

14

17

16

18

Monterey

13

SALINAS

21

19

20

MONTEREY

22

23

24

25

Paso Robles

26

SAN LUIS OBISPO

San Luis Obispo

27

28

SANTA MARIA

Santa Maria

29

SANTA BARBARA

30

31

SANTA YNEZ

Santa Barbara

NORTH AMERICA

1   El Dorado
2   Shenandoah Valley
3   Fiddletown
4   Clarksburg
5   Merritt Island
6   Lodi
7   Livermore Valley
8   Santa Clara Valley
9   Santa Cruz Mountains
10   Ben Lomond Mountain
11   San Ysidro
12   Pacheco Pass
13   Monterey
14   Cienega
15   San Benito
16   Paicines
17   Mount Harlan
18   Limekiln Valley
19   Carmel Valley
20   Santa Lucia Highlands
21   Chalone

22   Arroyo Seco
23   San Lucas
24   Hames Valley
25   Paso Robles
26   York Mountain
27   Edna Valley
28   Arroyo Grande
29   Santa Maria Valley
30   Santa Ynez Valley
31   Santa Rita Hills

NORTH AMERICA

The Regions

Santa Barbara County embraces the AVAs of **Santa Maria, Santa Ynez** and **Santa Rita Hills**. It is an excellent source of top Pinot Noir and Chardonnay. Pinot Blanc and Syrah are also successful. The northern tip of the Santa Maria lies within San Luis Obispo County. Four AVAs are contained within its boundaries. **Arroyo Grande** and **Edna Valley** are sources of Chardonnay and Pinot Noir, the Edna Valley also providing some excellent Rhône styles. **Paso Robles** is warmer and the wines are fuller and riper in style. **York Mountain** is cooled by altitude. Monterey AVA stretches down from the coast Paso Robles. On the coast are the **Carmel Valley, good for Cab Sauv and Merlot** and, further inland, the **Santa Lucia Highlands,** a source of impressive Pinot Noir. The area also includes the tiny monopole appellation of **Chalone**. Further south are the AVAs of **Arroyo Seco** and **San Lucas**. The **Santa Cruz** area includes a whole range of mesoclimates both Chardonnay and Pinot Noir are successful in Santa Cruz as well as warmer-grown Cab Sauv.

The huge geographical area of the Sierra Foothills encompasses Amador County and stretches into the Sierra Mountains. The AVAs here are **El Dorado, Fiddletown** and the **Shenandoah Valley**. The area is mainly a source of top old bush vine Zin but a number of Italian varieties, particularly Barbera, also enjoy some success. To the south is the giant irrigated Central Valley, heart of California's vast bulk wine industry.

California Central Coast Vintages

The Vintage Chart section gives an overall view of what to expect. The AVAs in the main are large by European standards and there can be significant variation from one mesoclimate to another within a single AVA. With the exception of the top Santa Cruz Cabernets most styles will be fading by 12 years or so.

Wizard's Wishlist

A diverse selection of Central Coast reds

ALBAN ● **Syrah** Seymour Vineyard
AU BON CLIMAT ● **Pinot Noir** Cuvée Isabelle
TABLAS CREEK ● **Esprot de Beaucastel** Paso Robles
TESTAROSSA ● **Pinot Noir** Palazzio
CALERA ● **Pinot Noir** Jensen Vineyard
BONNY DOON ● **Le Cigare Volant** California
LORING WINE CO ● **Pinot Noir** Cargasacchi Vineyard
JUSTIN ● **Isosceles** Paso Robles
OJAI ● **Syrah** Thompson Vineyard
RIDGE VINEYARDS ● **Monte Bello** Santa Cruz Mountains

SANFORD WINERY
● **Pinot Noir** Sanford and Benedict Vineyard
SEAN THACKREY ● **Orion** Rossi Vineyard
RIDGE VINEYARDS ● **Monte Bello** Santa Cruz Mountains
L'AVENTURE ● **Estate Cuvée** Paso Robles
LINNE CALODO ● **Sticks and Stones** Paso Robles

A selection of exciting whites

ANDREW MURRAY ○ **Enchante** Santa Ynez
BREWER CLIFTON ○ **Chardonnay** Mount Carmel
LINNE CALODO ○ **Contrarian** Paso Robles
CHALONE ○ **Pinot Blanc** Reserve
COLD HEAVEN ○ **Viognier** Alban Vineyard
MOUNT EDEN VINEYARDS ○ **Chardonnay** Estate
QUPÉ ○ **Viognier** Ibarra Young Vineyard
ROSENBLUM CELLARS ○ **Marsanne** Dry Creek
TALBOTT ○ **Chardonnay** Diamond T Estate
TESTAROSSA ○ **Chardonnay** Sleepy Hollow Vineyard
TALLEY ○ **Chardonnay** Arroyo Grande
TANTARA ○ **Chardonnay** Dierberg Vineyard

A selection of good values from the Central Coast

BECKMEN VINEYARDS ● **Cuvée Le Bec** Santa Barbara
BRANDER VINEYARDS
○ **Sauvignon Blanc** Santa Ynez Valley
BONNY DOON ○ **Critique of Pure Riesling**
CA DEL SOLO ● **Sangiovese Il Fiasco** Monterey
DOVER CANYON
● **Zinfandel** Old Vine Benito Dusi Vineyard
ETHAN ● **Grenache** Rancho Arroyo Grande Vineyard
GARRETSON WINE CO ◉ **The Celeidh** Paso Robles
ROBERT HALL ○ **Sauvignon Blanc** Paso Robles
HITCHING POST ● **Generation Red** Santa Barbara County
JAFFURS WINE CELLARS ● **Syrah** Santa Barbara County
RANCHO SISQUOC ○ **Silvaner** Santa Barbara
RENWOOD ● **Zinfandel** Old Vine
ROSENBLUM CELLARS ○ **Rousanne** Sanata Barbara
LANE TANNER ● **Lano Rouge** Central Coast
TOBIN JAMES CELLARS ● **Zinfandel Ballistic** Paso Robles

California Central Coast/A-Z of producers

ALBAN   Edna Valley   *UK stockists:* **WTs**
One of the finest Rhône specialists on the Central Coast. Estate vineyards are located in a cool sector of the Edna Valley, and this is reflected in the style, intensity and refinement of the wines. Limited-release Pandora is a cellar blend of Alban's best lots of Syrah and Grenache. (DM)
● **Syrah** Reva★★★★ £F   Lorraine★★★★★ £G   Seymour Vineyard★★★★★ £G
● **Grenache** Paso Robles★★★★ £F   O **Roussanne** Estate★★★★ £E

ARCADIAN   Santa Ynez Valley   www.arcadianwinery.com
Richly textured unfiltered Pinot Noir and subtle, lightly tropical Chardonnay come from a number of sources. Newly added Pinot Noir Fiddlestix is tight and restrained, an elegant cool climate example from the Santa Rita Hills. The Pisoni is richer, more opulent with remarkable depth. (DM)
● **Pinot Noir** Fiddlestix Vineyard★★★★ £F   Pisoni Vineyard★★★★★ £F
● **Pinot Noir** Bien Nacido★★★★ £F   O **Chardonnay** Sleepy Hollow★★★★ £E

AU BON CLIMAT   Santa Maria Valley   *UK stockists:* **FMV**,Sel,F&M
One of the very finest exponents of Pinot Noir and Chardonnay in California. The wines are marked by their restrained elegance, Burgundian in style and come from a wide range of sources. Jim Clendennen also makes a range of Italian-style reds and whites under the Il Podere dell' Olivos label. (DM)
● **Pinot Noir** La Bauge au-dessus★★★★ £E   Cuvée Isabelle✪✪✪✪ £F
O **Chardonnay** Nuits Blanches au Bouge★★★★★ £F

BABCOCK VINEYARDS   Santa Rita Hills   www.babcockwinery.com   *UK stockists:* **Vin**
Bryan Babcock produces a range of well priced reds and whites. Results are generally impressive, particularly with Pinot Noir. Limited bottlings come from Mount Carmel and the Cargasacchi Vineyard in Santa Barbara County. A simple, fruit-driven range labelled Troc provides affordable easy drinking. (DM)
● **Pinot Noir** Grand Cuvee★★★★ £E   ● **Syrah** Black Label Santa Barbara★★★ £E
O **Sauvignon Blanc** Eleven Oaks★★ £C   O **Chardonnay** Grand Cuvée★★★ £E

BECKMEN VINEYARDS   Santa Ynez Valley   *UK stockists:* **AWM**
Established in 1994 Tom Beckmen produces a small range of red and white Rhône styles of impressive quality. Cuvée Le Bec is a soft, forward blend of Grenache, Syrah, Mourvèdre and Counoise. A little Cab Sauv and meritage blend Atelier (Cab Franc and Merlot) are also produced. (DM)
● **Cuvée Le Bec** Santa Barbara★★ £C   ● **Grenache** Purisma Mountain★★★ £D

BERNARDUS   Carmel Valley   www.bernardus.com   *UK stockists:* **Goe**
Marinus, is crafted from high-density plantings of Cab Sauv, Merlot, Cab Franc and Petit Verdot, is traditionally vinified and matured. Sauvignon and Chardonnay, both sourced from a number of Monterey County vineyards are subtly oaked with barrel-fermentation and lees-stirring. (DM)
● **Marinus** Carmel Valley★★★★ £E   O **Sauvignon** Monterey County★★★ £C
O **Chardonnay** Monterey County★★★ £D

BONACCORSI   Santa Barbara County   www.bonawine.net
Small range of excellent Pinot Noir – supple, ripe and full of dark exotic spices. Sanford & Benedict is more opulent than the tighter, more structured Fiddlestix Vineyard. (DM)
● **Pinot Noir** Santa Rita Hills★★★ £E   Fiddlestix Vineyard★★★★ £E   Sanford & Benedict★★★★ £F

BONNY DOON   Santa Cruz Mountains   *UK stockists:* **FMV**,Sel,NYg
Splendidly eccentric operation dominated by Rhône styles. There are also some good Rieslings and a French Syrah and Madiran and three Italian offerings. Long established is a fine late-harvest Muscat. Top two reds Le Cigare Volant (Grenache and Syrah) and Old Telegram (Mourvèdre) are both modelled on Châteauneuf-du-Pape.(DM)
● **Le Cigare Volant** California★★★★ £E   ● **Old Telegram** California★★★★ £E
● **Syrah** California★★★★ £E   ● **Cardinal Zin**★★ £C   ● **Carignane**★★ £C
O **Critique of Pure Riesling**★★ £B   O **The Heart has its Rieslings**★★★ £C

New entries have producer's name underlined

BREWER CLIFTON   Santa Rita Hills   *UK stockists:* **THt**
Very small, recently established operation producing tiny amounts of very rich and extracted, full- blown Chardonnay and Pinot Noir from a number of vineyards in the Santa Rita Hills. Greg Brewer is also the winemaker at the recently established Melville Winery outside Lompoc in the Santa Rita Hills. (DM)
● **Pinot Noir** Rozak Ranch★★★★ £E   Melville★★★★ £F
O **Chardonnay** Sweeney Canyon★★★★ £E   Mount Carmel★★★★★ £F

CALERA   San Benito County   *UK stockists:* **Bib**
Best-known for its quartet of single-vineyard Pinot Noirs that have at times apporached cult status. On occasion the results are less than perfect but generally these are benchmarks for the state. Regular Central Coast wines are good if unspectacular and the Viognier is very good when not overly alcoholic. (DM)
● **Pinot Noir** Reed★★★ £F   Selleck★★★★ £F   Jensen★★★★ £F   Mills★★★★ £F
O **Chardonnay** Mount Harlan★★★ £E   O **Viognier** Mount Harlan★★★ £E

CARINA CELLARS   Santa Barbara County   www.carinacellars.com
Joey Tensley makes a small and impressive range of Rhône-style reds and whites as well as a Napa Valley-sourced Cab Sauv and an unusual (for California) richly textured Syrah/Cab Sauv, the Iconoclast. He also produces a small range under his own Tensley label. (DM)
● **Syrah** Westerly Vineyard★★★ £D   7 Percent★★★ £E Thompson Vineyard★★★ £E   Watch Hill★★★★ £E
● **Iconoclast**★★★★ £E   O **Viognier** Stolpman Vineyard★★★ £D

CHALONE   Chalone   www.chalonewinegroup.com   *UK stockists:* **Bib**
Part of the wider Chalone Wine Group, this is one of the most exciting sources on the Central Coast for tight and restrained ageworthy Chardonnay and Pinot Blanc. Chenin is also impressive, Pinot Noir has struggled in recent vintages. The estate possesses its own AVA. Syrah has now been added. (DM)
● **Pinot Noir** Estate★★ £E   O **Chardonnay** Estate★★★★ £E   Reserve★★★★★ £F
O **Pinot Blanc** Estate★★★ £D   Reserve★★★★ £E   O **Chenin Blanc** Estate★★★ £D

CLOS MIMI   Santa Maria Valley   www.closmimi.com   *UK stockists:* **AWM**
Solely artisan styled Syrah is made from a small range of vineyards within the Paso Robles region. Petite Rousse is the entry-level wine, Bunny Slope is a richly dense, dark-fruited more structured wine loaded with dark pepper and spice. It will be replaced with another top source from the 2001 vintage. (DM)
● **Syrah** Petite Rousse★★★ £C   Bunny Slopes★★★★★ £F

COLD HEAVEN   Santa Maria Valley   *UK stockists:* **FMV**
Small, operation focusing on Viognier, the brainchild of Morgan, wife of Jim Clendenen of Au Bon Climat. The wines are sourced from cool climate vineyards, providing depth and more structure than is normally found with the variety. She also releases a little Pinot Noir from husband Jim's Le Bon Climat Vineyard. (DM)
O **Viognier** Vogelzang Vineyard★★★ £C   Sanford and Benedict★★★ £D

DOVER CANYON   Paso Robles   www.dovercanyon.com
This small artisan winery is a source of great smoky, vibrant and spicy old vine Zinfandel, sadly only produced in very small quantities.. Viognier is richly-textured and barrel-fermented and some Westside Syrah is also produced. (DM)
● **Zinfandel** Old Vine Benito Dusi Vineyard★★★ £D   Bella Vineyard★★★ £D
O **Viognier** Hansen Vineyard★★★ £C

EDMUNDS ST JOHN   www.edmundsstjohn.com   *UK stockists:* **WTs,AWM**
Benchmark among California Rhône Rangers. Rocks and Gravel and the the more structured Los Viejos are both blends of Grenache, Mourvèdre, Syrah. Los Viejos white blends Viognier, Marsanne and Roussanne. Pallini Rosso, is a spicy blend of mainly Zinfandel with some Grenache. A Pinot Grigio is also produced. (DM)
● **Syrah** Parmalee Hill Vineyard★★★★ £E   Durell Vineyard★★★★ £E
● **Rocks and Gravel** California★★★ £C   ● **Los Robles Viejos** Rozet Vineyard★★★ £D
● **Pallini Rosso** Mendocino★★★ £C   O **Los Robles Viejos** Rozet Vineyard★★★ £D

ETHAN   Santa Rita Hills
Ethan Lindquist's father Bob is one of the original Rhône specialists on the Central Coast at QUPÉ. Ethan produces

his own small range. Purisima Syrah is particularly striking. (DM)

● **Syrah** Rancho Arroyo GrandeVineyard★★★ £D Purisima Mountain★★★★ £D
● **Grenache** Rancho Arroyo Grande Vineyard★★★ £D ● **Sangiovese** Paso Robles★★★ £D

GARRETSON WINE CO Paso Robles www.garretsonwines.com
Newly established and very fine Rhône style specialist. Syrah is the main focus, although good whites as well as rosé are also produced. Top label Reliquary red and white are respectively Syrah, Mourvedre, Grenache and a touch of Viognier and Marsanne and Roussanne. (DM)

● **Syrah** Mon Amie Bassetti Vineyard★★★★ £C The Craic Central Coast★★★ £D
◉ **The Celeidh** Paso Robles★★★ £D

HITCHING POST Santa Barbara County www.hitchingpostwines.com
Restaurateur Frank Ostini's Hitching Post II in Buellton was featured in the film *Sideways*. He and Gray Hartley also produce a number of fine small-lot reds from Pinot Noir, Syrah and the red Bordeaux varieties, drawing on a range of Santa Barbara County vineyard sources. (DM)

● **Pinot Noir** Highliner★★★★ £E ● **Generation Red** Santa Barbara County★★★ £C

JAFFURS WINE CELLARS Santa Barbara County www.jaffurswine.com
An impressive small range of Rhône styles. In addition to the wines below, Syrah is sourced from Stolpman, Melville and Bien Nacido, Roussanne and Grenache from the Stolpman Vineyard and a Syrah-based rosé Matiltja is also produced. (DM)

● **Syrah** Santa Barbara County★★★ £C Thompson Vineyard★★★★ £E
○ **Viognier** Santa Barbara County★★★ £D

TOBIN JAMES CELLARS Paso Robles www.tobinjames.com
There is a sense of fun here – the wines all have tongue-in-cheek names, many relating to less than lawful characters from the old American West. Blue Moon Zinfandel and Syrah have great depth and dimension. (DM)

● **Syrah Blue Moon** Paso Robles★★★★★ £F ● **Zinfandel Blue Moon** Paso Robles★★★★ £E
● **Syrah James Gang Reserve** Paso Robles★★★★ £E ● **Estate Private Stash** Paso Robles★★★ £E
○ **Chardonnay James Gang Reserve** Monterey County★★★ £E

JUSTIN Paso Robles www.justinwine.com *UK stockists:* Vin
Good operation producing decent Bordeaux-style reds along with a fine full-blown Syrah from the Halter Vineyard. These wines may share similar grapes to their French counterparts but are altogether fuller and riper without any hint of the rusticity or jamminess often found in warm-climate Cab Sauv. (DM)

● **Justification** Paso Robles★★★ £E ● **Isosceles** Paso Robles★★★ £E
● **Cabernet Sauvignon** Paso Robles★★★ £D ● **Syrah** Halter Vineyard★★★ £E

KATHRYN KENNEDY Santa Cruz Mountains
The Estate Cabernet is highly sought after, the most likely way of obtaining any at all is to join the mailing list. A secondary label is also produced, as well as a Merlot-based proprietary red, Lateral, from bought-in fruit. A small amount of Syrah comes from the Maridon Vineyard and a Sauvignon Blanc has been added. (DM)

● **Cabernet Sauvignon** Estate★★★★★ £G

KUNIN WINES Santa Barbara www.kuninwines.com
Well-priced Syrah, Viognier and Zin. Syrah is crafted in an opulent, rich, brambly vein and aged in a mix of French and American oak. (DM)

● **Syrah** Santa Barbara★★★ £D Alisos Vineyards★★★★ £E

L'AVENTURE Paso Robles www.aventurewine.com
Frenchman Stephan Asseo's property is located in the favourable climes of Paso Robles Westside and provides fruit of excellent quality. Two lower-level blends are also made: Stephan Ridge and Optimus. Top wines are impressively ageworthy. (DM)

● **Estate Cuvée** Paso Robles★★★★★ £F ● **Cuvée Côte à Côte Estate** Paso Robles★★★★ £F
● **Syrah Estate** Paso Robles★★★★ £F ● **Cabernet Sauvignon** Estate Paso Robles★★★★ £F

LINNE CALODO Paso Robles www.linnecalodo.com
Some of the finest and most vibrantly exciting Rhône-style reds and whites as well as the Zin-dominated Cherry

Red, are being produced at this small Paso Robles Westside property. The key is low-yielding fruit of the highest quality from some of the finest vineyards in the area. (DM)
- **Nemesis★★★★★** £F ● **Sticks and Stones★★★★★** £F ● **Problem Child★★★★** £E
- **Cherry Red★★★★** £E ● **Rising Tides★★★★** £E ● **The Slacker★★★★** £D
- ○ **Contrarian★★★★★** £E ○ **Disciple★★★★** £E

LORING WINE CO Santa Barbara County www.loringwinecompany.com
Pinot Noir is the sole wine here. Fruit comes from some of the best vineyard sites for the variety and the wines are marked by their rich texture and piercing varietal purity. (DM)
- **Pinot Noir** Cargasacchi Vineyard★★★★ £F Rancho Ontiveros Vineyard★★★★ £F
- **Pinot Noir** Clos Pepe Vineyard★★★★ £F

MOUNT EDEN VINEYARDS Santa Cruz Mountains *UK stockists:* **Vin**
Pinot is in a big, rich style, whereas the Cab Sauvs are tight and backward needing time. Chardonnay is particularly good: restrained in style with subtle citrus fruit and fine-grained oak. Newly added Edna Ranch West Slope Chardonnay is lusher, more tropical in style. (DM)
- **Cabernet Sauvignon** Estate★★★ £D Old Vine Reserve★★★★ £F
- **Pinot Noir** Estate★★★ £E ○ **Chardonnay** Estate★★★★ £E

ANDREW MURRAY Santa Ynez Valley *UK stockists:* **Bib**
Very good Rhône specialist. Syrah ranges from ripe forward Estate to rich, structured Hillside Reserve. Esperance blends of Grenache, Syrah and Mourvèdre, full of ripe berry fruit, spices and herbs. White Enchanté has slightly more Roussanne than Marsanne. Drink the whites young. (DM)
- **Esperance★★★** £E ● **Syrah** Estate★★★ £D Hillside Reserve★★★★ £F
- ○ **Enchante★★★** £D ○ **Roussanne** Estate★★★ £D

OJAI Ventura County ojaivineyard.com *UK stockists:* **THt,Vin,AWM**
Adam Tolmach produces some of the most striking and elegant Syrah on the Central Coast. A bewildering number of single vineyard bottlings are released, all very impressive. Chardonnay, Pinot Noir and Sauvignon are also very fine. Newly established are Vin du Soleil red and white Rhône blends. (DM)
- **Pinot Noir** Bien Nacido★★★ £E Pisoni Vineyard★★★★★ £G
- **Syrah** Roll Ranch★★★★ £E Bien Nacido★★★★ £E Thompson★★★★★ £F

QUPÉ Santa Maria Valley www.qupe.com *UK stockists:* **FMV,SVS,Sel,F&M**
One of the finest of the Rhône Rangers. The wines here are of a uniformly high standard; both reds and whites. Bien Nacido Cuvée blends Chardonnay and Viognier while the red Los Olivos Cuvée is a southern Rhône style comprising Syrah, Mourvèdre and Grenache. (DM)
- **Syrah** Bien Nacido Hillside Estate★★★★★ £E ● **Los Olivos Cuvée★★★** £E
- ○ **Bien Nacido Cuvée★★★** £C ○ **Viognier** Ibarra Young★★★★ £D

RANCHO SISQUOC Santa Maria www.ranchosisquoc.com
A relatively long-established name in Santa Barbara County with 130ha (320 acres) of vineyard. Sisquoc River red is a fruit-driven Cab Sauv/Merlot/Syrah/Sangiovese/Malbec blend. (DM)
- **Cabernet Sauvignon** Santa Barbara★★★ £C ● **Cellar Select Meritage** Santa Barbara★★★★ £D
- **Sisquoc River Red** Santa Barbara★★ £C ● **Merlot** Santa Barbara★★ £C
- ○ **Chardonnay** Santa Barbara★★★ £C ○ **Silvaner** Santa Barbara★★ £B
- **Zinfandel** Sierra Series★★ £B Old Vine★★★ £C D'Agostini★★★ £E

RIDGE VINEYARDS Santa Cruz Mountains www.ridgewine.com *UK stockists:* **FMV,Sel,F&M**
This is one of California's great wineries. Very fine Chardonnay, both Santa Cruz Mountains and Monte Bello, are joined by benchmark examples of Zinfandel and Petite Sirah. The regular Cab Sauv is impressive, the Monte Bello one of the great reds of California, elegant, powerful and very long-lived. (DM)
- **Cabernet Sauvignon★★★★** £E ● **Monte Bello✪✪✪✪✪** £G
- **Mataro★★★** £E ● **Petite Sirah** York Creek★★★★ £E
- **Zinfandel** Pagani★★★★ £E ● **Geyserville★★★★★**£E ○ **Chardonnay★★★★** £E

ROSENBLUM CELLARS Santa Lucia Highlands *UK stockists:* **Vin**
Warehouse winery in the San Francisco Bay area. The main focus here is very good Zin from a huge number of

sources. Red and white Rhône styles also stand out along with a late harvest Black Muscat from Gallagher Ranch. Château La Paws is a cheerful Rhône blend. (DM)
- **Zinfandel** Samsel Maggie's Reserve★★★★ £E   St Peters Church★★★★ £E
- **Syrah** Fess Parker★★★★ £E   **O Marsanne** Dry Creek★★★ £C

SANFORD WINERY   Santa Rita Hills   *UK stockists:* **WTs**
Located in the cool Santa Rita Hills AVA, Sanford produces good to very good lightly tropical Chardonnay, Sauvignon Blanc and berry-laden, gamey Pinot Noir. Particularly striking are the Sanford and Benedict and Riconada Pinot bottlings. (DM)
- **Pinot Noir** Santa Barbara★★ £C   La Riconada★★★★ £F
O **Chardonnay** Santa Barbara★★ £C   Sanford and Benedict★★★★ £E

SAXUM   Paso Robles   www.saxumvineyards.com
Excellent small-scale Rhône specialist. As well as Broken Stones, there is an additional Syrah, Bone Rock and the formidable Heartstone a blend of Grenache, Mourvedre and Syrah. All the wines come from Paso Robles Westside vineyards. (DM)
- **Syrah** Broken Stones Paso Robles★★★★ £E

SINE QUA NON   Ventura County
This really is the quintessential California garage winery. Some great Rhône styles have been made along Chardonnay and Pinot Noir from Oregon. In almost every vintage there are name changes so the range is very difficult to keep up with and produced in tiny quantities. Those wines below were from 2000. (DM)
- **A Capella** Pinot Noir Shea Vineyard Willamette Valley★★★★ £F
- **Incognito** Grenache/Syrah California★★★★★ £H
O **The Boot** Chardonnay/Roussane/Viognier California★★★★ £F

TABLAS CREEK   Paso Robles   www.tablascreek.com   *UK stockists:* **Mis**
Partnership between Château de Beaucastel and Robert Haas. Reserve Cuvée and Clos Blanc have been re-labelled Esprit de Beaucastel. A 100% Roussanne is part barrel-fermented and there are tiny amounts of Antithesis, a full-blown Chardonnay. The Panoplie red is based on Mourvèdre.The range is completed by the ripe, forward red and white Côtes de Tablas and a juicy rosé. (DM)
- **Esprit de Beaucastel** Paso Robles★★★★ £E   ● **Côtes de Tablas** Paso Robles★★★ £C
O **Esprit de Beaucastel** Paso Robles★★★★ £D   O **Côtes de Tablas** Paso Robles★★★ £C
O **Roussanne** Paso Robles★★★★ £D   ◉ **Tablas Rosé** Paso Robles★★★ £C

ROBERT TALBOTT   Monterey County   www.talbottvineyards.com   *UK stockists:* **Vin**
Small operation with vineyard resources in the Salinas Foothills and Santa Lucia Mountains. The three top Chardonnays, Kali-Hart, Sleepy Hollow and Cuvée Cynthia, are marvellously stylish cool-climate wines. A Kali-Hart Vineyard Pinot Noir bottling has also now been released. (DM)
O **Chardonnay** Logan★★ £D   Kali-Hart★★★ £E   Diamond T Estate★★★★ £E
O **Chardonnay** Sleepy Hollow★★★★ £E   Cuvée Cynthia★★★★ £E

TALLEY VINEYARDS   Arroyo Grande   www.talleyvineyards.com
First-class estate Chardonnay and Pinot Noir here. The Rosemary and Rincon vineyards have tremendous potential and as yet are still young. Both are capable of five-star quality. Sauvignon Blanc has not reached the same stellar heights. It is blended with Semillon and part barrel-fermented. (DM)
- **Pinot Noir** Estate★★★ £D   Rincon★★★★ £E   Rosemary's Vineyard★★★★ £E
O **Chardonnay** Estate★★★ £D   Rincon★★★★ £E   Rosemary's Vineyard★★★★ £E

LANE TANNER   Santa Maria Valley   lanetanner@sbwines.com
Lane Tanner operates a small warehouse winery in Santa Maria where she has been making first-rate Pinot Noir for a decade. Cool, peppery Syrah from the French Camp Vineyard has been added that shows equally impressive potential. (DM)
- **Pinot Noir** Santa Maria★★★ £D   Bien Nacido★★★ £D

TANTARA WINERY   Santa Maria   www.tantarawinery.com
266   Jeffrey Fink and Bill Cates make some very classy Chardonnay and some of the best Pinot to emerge from the

Central Coast. Pinot Blanc and Syrah are also produced and early vintages included Sangiovese. Also excellent generic wines from Santa Maria. (DM)

● **Pinot Noir** Rio Vista★★★★ £E Gary's★★★★ £F Pisoni★★★★★ £F Evelyn★★★★★ £F
● **Pinot Noir** Solomon Hills Ranch★★★★ £E Bien Nacido Adobe★★★★ £E Dierberg★★★★ £E
○ **Chardonnay** Bien Nacido★★★★ £E Dierberg★★★★ £E Chalone Brosseau★★★★ £E

DOM. DE LA TERRE ROUGE Shenandoah Valley UK stockists: **Vin**
Rhône styles come under the Terre Rouge label, while the Easton label supplies good fruit-driven, spicy Barbera and more serious Zinfandel. Shenandoah Valley vineyards are cooled by elevation and the top wines are both elegant and concentrated. They will benefit from four or five years' ageing. (DM)

Domaine de la Terre Rouge
● **Syrah** Sentinel Oak Pyramid Block★★★ £E Ascent★★★★ £F
○ **Viognier** Shenandoah Valley★★★ £E
Easton
● **Barbera** Shenandoah Valley★★ £C ● **Zinfandel** Shenandoah Valley★★★ £C

TESTAROSSA Arroyo Grande www.testarossa.com UK stockists: P&S,Por
The focus here is top-quality Pinot Noir and Chardonnay. from an almost bewildering number of single-vineyard *cuvées*. They are invariably good to very good indeed, Pinots are rich and gamey with no shortage of oak; the Chardonnays are ripe and full. Richly textured, forward wines for enjoying with a year or two in bottle. (DM)

● **Pinot Noir** Sleepy Hollow Vineyard★★★★ £E Pisoni Vineyard★★★★ £F
○ **Chardonnay** Chalone-Michaud★★★★ £E Bien Nacido★★★★ £E

SEAN THACKREY Marin County www.wine-maker.net
Just two wines. Orion is produced from Syrah sourced from the Rossi Vineyard in St Helena, a burly, massive wine with tremendous potential. Pleiades by contrast is a ripe, altogether more forward non-vintage blend from a varying mix of Syrah, Grenache, Mourvèdre and Petite Sirah. (DM)

● **Pleiades** California★★★ £C **Orion** Rossi Vineyard★★★★★ £F

VILLA CREEK CELLARS Paso Robles www.villacreek.com
Warehouse operation producing modern, fleshy, vibrant Paso Robles-sourced reds. Avenger and Willow Creek are both Rhône blends, Mas de Maha is Tempranillo/Grenache/Mourvèdre. Top label High Road is a dense and very powerful Syrah/Mourvèdre/Grenache. (DM)

● **High Road**★★★★ £E ● **Avenger**★★★ £D ● **Garnacha**★★★ £D
● **Willow Creek**★★★ £D ● **Mas de Maha**★★★ £D

WESTERLY VINEYARDS Santa Maria www.westerlyvineyards.com
Some impressive wines are produced here, particularly from the Bordeaux red varieties, all sourced from Santa Ynez Valley. W Blanc is Roussanne/Viognier, the red Cab Franc/Merlot. (DM)

● **Merlot**★★★ £C Estate Reserve★★★★ £E ● **W Red**★★★ £E
○ **Sauvignon Blanc**★★ £C ○ **W Blanc**★★★ £C ○ **Viognier**★★ £C

Other wineries of note
Brander (Santa Ynez Valley), **Ca del Solo** (Santa Cruz Mountains), **Cambria** (Santa Maria Valley), **Castoro Cellars** (Paso Robles), **Clos LaChance** (Santa Cruz Mountains), **Eberle** (Paso Robles), **Edna Valley** (Edna Valley), **Gainey** (Santa Ynez Valley), **Robert Hall** (Paso Robles), **Austin Hope** (Paso Robles), **Il Podere dell' Olivos** (Santa Maria Valley), **Laetitia** (Arroyo Grande), **Longoria** (Santa Ynez Valley), **Mer Soleil** (Monterey County), **Morgan Winery** (Monterey County), **Nadeau** (Paso Robles), **Peachy Canyon** (Paso Robles), **Pipestone** (Paso Robles), **Quady** (Madera County), **Renwood** (Amador County), **Silver Stone** (Paso Robles), **Summer Wood** (Paso Robles), **Treana** (Paso Robles), **Zaca Mesa** (Santa Barbara County)

An in-depth profile of every producer can be found in Wine behind the label 2006

Oregon & Washington

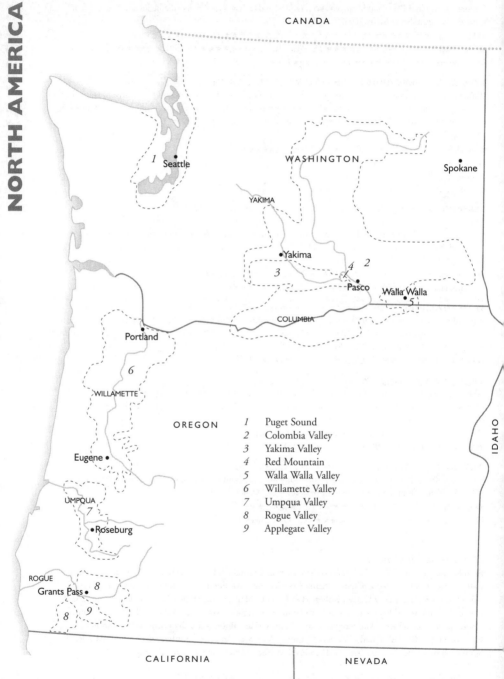

NORTH AMERICA

CANADA

WASHINGTON

Seattle

Spokane

YAKIMA

Yakima

Pasco

Walla Walla

COLUMBIA

Portland

WILLAMETTE

OREGON

Eugene

UMPQUA

Roseburg

ROGUE

Grants Pass

CALIFORNIA

NEVADA

IDAHO

1   Puget Sound
2   Colombia Valley
3   Yakima Valley
4   Red Mountain
5   Walla Walla Valley
6   Willamette Valley
7   Umpqua Valley
8   Rogue Valley
9   Applegate Valley

Oregon

As well as the **Willamette Valley** there are two other AVAs to the south, **Umpqua Valley** and **Rogue Valley.** The main viticultural activity, though, is in the Willamette, a vast stretch of vineyards with varied soils and an extensive array of mesoclimates. The majority of vineyards are found in the northern half of the region between Monmouth and Portland; the greatest concentration in Yamhill County, in the centre of that area. This is mainly Pinot Noir country although a number of white varieties are also successful, with Pinot Gris and Pinot Blanc having the best potential.

Washington State

The vineyard area is vast and dominated by the giant **Columbia Valley** AVA, within which there are two sub-AVAs, the **Yakima Valley** and the **Walla Walla Valley** in the east. A newly established AVA close to the coast is **Puget Sound,** too cool and damp to provide wines of any substance. Columbia Valley east of the Cascades, it is suitable for quality wine because of its northerly latitude and long, sunny days.

Oregon & Washington State Vintages

With such a sprawling viticultural expanse, providing meaningful detail on vintages is difficult. In Oregon Pinot Noir in 2003 should be good, 2001 was reasonable; 2002, 2000, 1999 and 1998 were good to very good. In Washington, for reds, 2003 and 2002 are very good, and only 1996 looks average over the last eight or nine years.

Wizard's Wishlist

The best of the Willamette Valley

ARCHERY SUMMIT ● **Pinot Noir** Arcus Estate
BEAUX FRÈRES ● **Pinot Noir** Beaux Frères Vineyard
CHEHALEM ● **Pinot Noir** Rion Reserve
CRISTOM ● **Pinot Noir** Louise Vineyard
DOMAINE DROUHIN O **Chardonnay**
PATRICIA GREEN CELLARS ● **Pinot Noir** Estate

PENNER ASH ● **Pinot Noir** Willamette Valley
PONZI O **Pinot Gris** Willamette Valley
DOMAINE SERENE O **Chardonnay** Clos du Soleil
KEN WRIGHT CELLARS ● **Pinot Noir** Shea Vineyard
OWEN ROE ● **Pinot Noir** Wollamette Valley
LEMELSON ● **Pinot Noir** Jerome Reserve

A selection of new classics from Washington State

ANDREW WILL ● **Merlot** Klipsun Vineyard
CHATEAU STE MICHELLE ● **Col Solare** Columbia Valley
NORTHSTAR ● **Merlot** Walla Walla Valley
DELILLE CELLARS ● **Chaleur Estate**
DUNHAM CELLARS
● **Cabernet Sauvignon** Columbia Valley
L'ECOLE NO 41 O **Semillon** Seven Hills
LEONETTI CELLAR ● **Reserve** Walla Walla Valley
PEPPER BRIDGE WINERY ● **Merlot** Walla Walla Valley
QUILCEDA CREEK VINEYARDS
● **Cabernet Sauvignon** Columbia Valley
WOODWARD CANYON O **Chardonnay** Celilo Vineyard
MCCREA CELLARS ● **Syrah** Cuvée Orleans
SPRING VALLEY ● **Nina Lee** Boushey Vineyards

A selection of good value reds and whites

AMITY VINEYARDS O **Gewurztraminer** Oregon
CRISTOM ● **Pinot Noir** Mt Jefferson Cuvée
LEMELSON O **Chardonnay** Wascher Vineyard
OWEN ROE O **Pinot Gris** Willamette Valley
O' REILLY'S ● **Pinot Noir** Oregon
BOOKWALTER WINERY
● **Cabernet Sauvignon** Columbia Valley
CHATEAU STE MICHELLE O **Riesling** Eroica
JANUIK WINERY O **Chardonnay** Cold Creek Vineyard
KIONA ● **Syrah** Reserve Estate
MCCREA CELLARS O **Viognier** Red Mountain
L'ECOLE NO 41 O **Semillon** Fries Vineyard
REININGER WINERY ● **Helix Pomatia** Columbia Valley

Oregon & Washington State/A-Z of producers

Oregon

ARCHERY SUMMIT Willamette Valley www.archerysummit.com UK *stockists:* **Dis**
Small, bespoke operation owned by the Andrus family, ofPine Ridge in Napa's Stags Leap District. Very classy Pinot Noir is produced across a number of *cuvées.* The Vireton Blanc des Collines Rouges is an elegant part barrel-fermented blend of Pinot Gris, Chardonnay and Pinot Blanc. (DM)
● **Pinot Noir** Premier Cuvée★★★£E Arcus Estate★★★★£F
O **Vireton** Blanc des Collines Rouges★★★£D

BEAUX FRÈRES Willamette Valley www.beauxfreres.com UK *stockists:* **Vin**
Producer of some of the best Pinot Noir in the Willamette Valley, this operation is as well known for the involvement of wine critic Robert M Parker as for anything else. Belles Soeurs is not a second label but an

NORTH AMERICA

addition to the estate wine, sourced from the excellent Shea Vineyard. (DM)

● **Pinot Noir** Beaux Frères Vineyard★★★★ £F Belles Souers Vineyard★★★★ £F

CHEHALEM Willamette Valley www.chehalemwines.com
Some exemplary Pinot Noir is sourced from three estate vineyards, Ridgecrest, Stoller and Corral Creek, Special *cuvée* Rion Reserve, is firmer and more structured and will evolve well over four or five years. Barrel-fermented Chardonnay, and dry and late-harvest Riesling, Pinot Gris are also made. (DM)

● **Pinot Noir** Ridgecrest Vineyards★★★ £E Rion Reserve★★★★ £E
○ **Chardonnay** Willamette Valley★★ £D

CRISTOM Willamette Valley www.cristomwines.com *UK stockists:* **WTs**,Sel
Excellent Pinot Noirs and some very good whites. As well as the lightly oaked, quite restrained Chardonnay and floral Viognier there is a stylish, mineral-scented Pinot Gris. Pinot Noir is rich and opulent, it will evolve well in the short term. (DM)

● **Pinot Noir** Reserve★★★★ £E Louise★★★★ £E
○ **Chardonnay** Celilo★★★ £C ● **Viognier** Willamette Valley★★ £D

DOMAINE DROUHIN Willamette Valley *UK stockists:* **FMV**,Sel,F&M
Established the firm Joseph Drouhin and run by Véronique Drouhin. Distinctly Burgundian examples show more structure and restraint than most Willamette Pinot Noir and Chardonnay. Low-volume special release Cuvée Louise, is a special barrel selection of the best of the material used in the Laurène. (DM)

● **Pinot Noir** Willamette Valley★★★★ £E Cuvée Laurene★★★★ £F
○ **Chardonnay** Cuvée Arthur★★★★ £E

PATRICIA GREEN CELLARS Willamette Valley
Impressive new property established by former Torii Mor winemakers Patty Green and Jim Anderson. As well as their Estate label they produce richly textured opulent Pinot Noir from a range of sources including Quail Hill, Four Winds and Shea Vineyards. Well-priced Chardonnay, Sauvignon and Oregon Pinot Noir are also produced. (DM)

● **Pinot Noir** Estate★★★★ £E Shea Vineyard★★★★ £E

KING ESTATE Willamette Valley www.kingestate.com *UK stockists:* **BBR**
Largest producer of Pinot Noir in Oregon. Quality ranges from good to very good. There is also a second label, Lorane. King Estate wines are a serious step up in quality and there a couple of classy limited-volume bottlings in the Tower series: Domaine Pinot Noir and a Pfeiffer Vineyard bottling. (DM)

● **Pinot Noir** Oregon★★ £C Reserve★★★ £E ○ **Pinot Gris** Reserve★★ £C

LEMELSON VINEYARDS Willamette Valley *UK stockists:* **JAr**
A small and impressive range of well priced Pinot Noirs is produced here along with a good melony Burgundian styled Chardonnay. The Stermer Vineyard and top Pinot Jerome Reserve are the firmest of the reds.and should develop well in bottle for five years or more. (DM)

● **Pinot Noir** Stermer Vineyard★★★ £E Jerome Reserve★★★★ £E
○ **Chardonnay** Wascher Vineyard★★★ £D

PANTHER CREEK Willamette Valley www.panthercreekcellars.com *UK stockists:* **AWM**
Excellent producer of first-class Pinot Noir as well as Chardonnay, Pinot Gris and a bit of Melon de Bourgogne. The winery purchases fruit from 10 different vineyard sources and there is a plethora of single-vineyard bottlings of Pinot Noir, of which Freedom Hill and Shea Vineyard are produced in greater volume. (DM)

● **Pinot Noir** Winemakers Cuvée★★★★ £E Freedom Hill★★★★ £E

PENNER-ASH Willamette Valley www.pennerash.com
Ron and Lynn Penner-Ash produce some rich and concentrated Willamette Valley Pinot Noir as well as small quantities of hand-crafted Syrah and Viognier. The Syrah comes from several different Oregon growers, while the Viognier has been added with the 2002 vintage and is sourced from the Del Rio Vineyard in the south of the state. (DM)

● **Pinot Noir** Willamette Valley★★★★ £E

PONZI Willamette Valley www.ponziwines.com
270 Pinot Noir is good here and there is a superior Reserve bottling, as well as the tiny production of Abetina

New entries have producer's name underlined

Vineyard Reserve. Particularly interesting is one of the better Pinot Gris and a good fruit-driven Arneis. These offer particularly good value. (DM)

● **Pinot Noir** Reserve★★★ £F O **Chardonnay** Reserve★★ £D
O **Pinot Gris** Willamette Valley★★ £B O **Arneis** Willamette Valley★ £C

REX HILL Willamette Valley www.rexhill.com *UK stockists:* **Mor**
This winery has consistently produced first-class Pinot Noir from a number of sites. There are a number of stylish low-volume, single-vineyard offerings as well as a good regular Willamette Valley bottling and a consistent Reserve. Pinot Gris Reserve is one of the more striking Oregon examples. (DM)

● **Pinot Noir** Kings Ridge★ £B Willamette Valley★★ £D Reserve★★★★ £E
O **Pinot Gris** Reserve★★★ £C

OWEN ROE Willamette Valley www.owenroe.com
This small Newberg-based winery produces wines under two labels. The Owen Roe label is for top-quality, small-lot wines, while the O'Reilly's generics are sourced from throughout the Pacific Northwest. Quality is extremely high and the Owen Roe wines consistently offer a level of subtlety, elegance and purity of fruit rarely encountered in either state.(DM)

Owen Roe
● **Cabernet Sauvignon** Dubrol Vineyard★★★★★ £F ● **Red Wine** Yakima Valley★★★★ £E
● **Cabernet Franc** Yakima Valley★★★★ £E ● **Pinot Noir** Willamette Valley★★★★ £E
O **Pinot Gris** Willamette Valley★★★ £C

O'Reilly's
● **Pinot Noir** Oregon★★ £B

DOMAINE SERENE Willamette Valley www.domaineserene.com *UK stockists:* **Vin**
Top-class producer of both Pinot Noir and Chardonnay. Considerable investment has gone into the estate and the results are impressive. Tiny lots of various single-vineyard bottlings are available through the winery and there is also a flagship Pinot Noir, Grace Vineyard. The most recent development is the Rockblock Syrah, produced from Dundee Hills fruit. (DM)

● **Pinot Noir** Evenstad Reserve★★★★ £E Mark Bradford Vineyard★★★★ £F
O **Chardonnay** Clos du Soleil★★★★ £E Cote Sud★★★★ £E

KEN WRIGHT Willamette Valley www.kenwrightcellars.com *UK stockists:* **Vin**
Willamette champion of single-vineyard Pinot Noir. Excellent examples emerge from throughout the AVA as the wines display the varied *terroirs* of the region. Two Chardonnays, from the Columbia River Celilo Vineyard site – Carabella and McCrone are also produced as well as a floral, subtly oaked Pinot Blanc. (DM)

● **Pinot Noir** Guadalupe Vineyard★★★★ £E Shea Vineyard★★★★ £E
● **Pinot Noir** Canary Hill Vineyard★★★★ £E McCrone Vineyard★★★★ £E

Washington State

ANDREW WILL Washington State *UK stockists:* **FMV**,NYg,Sel
A range of very good quality, finely made reds. Both Cab Sauv and Merlot offer a seamless mix of fruit and oak. Sorella is a fine, spicy meritage blend of Cab Sauv, Cab Franc and Merlot. The single vineyard Merlots particularly stand out. (DM)

● **Cabernet Sauvignon** Seven Hills★★★★ £E Pepper Bridge★★★★ £E
● **Merlot** Klipsun★★★★★ £E Ciel du Cheval★★★★★ £E ● **Sorella**★★★★ £F

BOOKWALTER WINERY Columbia Valley www.bookwalterwines.com
Fruit sources include top Columbia Valley vineyards Andrews Horse Heaven, Ciel du Cheval and Conner-Lee as well as the home Bookwalter Estate. Chapter One Meritage is a sumptuously rich red, very supple and forward, and like the other wines it will drink well relatively young. (DM)

● **Meritage Chapter One** Columbia Valley★★★★ £F
● **Cabernet Sauvignon** Columbia Valley★★★ £D
● **Merlot** Columbia Valley★★★ £E

CAYUSE VINEYARDS Walla Walla Valley www.cayusevineyards.com
Christophe Baron's family roots are in Champagne and there is a marked French influence in his Walla Walla sourced wines. They tend to be tighter and more structured than a number of his neighbours' offerings, with a subtler, defter hand and very well-integrated fruit and oak. Camaspelo is a Bordeaux blend. (DM)
● **Syrah** Cailloux Vineyard★★★★ £F   En Cerise Vineyard★★★★ £F
● **Camaspelo** Walla Walla Valley★★★ £E

CHÂTEAU STE MICHELLE Columbia Valley www.ste-michelle.com   *UK stockists:* **PRc**
The largest producer in Washington State and the jewel in the Stimson Lane crown. A considerable array of wines is produced , including two partnerships. These are Col Solare a premium blend of Cab Sauv, Merlot, Syrah and Malbec produced with Antinori and Eroica, an intense, opulent but crisp, mineral-scented Riesling made with Ernst Loosen. (DM)
● **Cabernet Sauvignon** Cold Creek★★★ £E   ● **Syrah** Reserve★★★ £C
● **Col Solare** Columbia Valley★★★★ £G   ○ **Riesling** Eroica★★★ £D

COLUMBIA WINERY Washington State www.columbiawinery.com   *UK stockists:* **For**
Pioneering Washington State operation under the winemaking guidance of David Lake MW. A considerable range is now offered. The bulk of the winery's top wines is sourced from five prime vineyards – Red Willow, Otis, Wyckoff, Alder Ridge and Sagemoor – in both the Yakima and Columbia Valleys. (DM)
● **Cabernet Sauvignon** Otis Vineyard★★★ £D   Red Willow★★★ £D
● **Syrah** Red Willow★★★ £D   ○ **Chardonnay** Otis Vineyard★★★ £D

DELILLE CELLARS Washington State www.delillecellars.com   *UK stockists:* **WTs,Sel**
Top-quality Bordeaux blends are made from a range of Yakima Valley fruit sources, the majority from the Red Mountain AVA. Both the Chaleur Estate and the D2 are made in an open-knit, ripe, supple style, Single vineyard Harrison Hill is more backward in style. White Chaleur Estate blends Sauvignon and Semillon. (DM)
● **Chaleur Estate**★★★★ £F   ● **Harrison Hill**★★★★ £F   ● **D2**★★★ £E
● **Doyenne Syrah**★★★★ £F   ○ **Chaleur Estate**★★★ £E

JANUIK WINERY Washington State www.januikwinery.com
Mike Januik works with a whole host of vineyards including Ciel du Cheval, Seven Hills, Klipsun, Connor Lee, Lewis, Red Mountain and draws on Cold Creek for his Chardonnay and Champoux for an elegant and poised single-vineyard Cabernet Sauvignon. (DM)
● **Cabernet Sauvignon** Columbia Valley★★★ £D   Champoux Vineyard Columbia Valley★★★★ £E
● **Merlot** Columbia Valley★★★ £D   ● **Syrah** Columbia Valley★★★ £E
○ **Chardonnay** Cold Creek Vineyard Columbia Valley★★★ £C

KIONA Yakima Valley www.kionawine.com
One of the longest-established Washington wineries, founded in 1972, and is located in the Yakima Valley's Red Mountain sub-appellation. The top wines are the Reserve Estate bottlings from the firm's own 26ha (65 acres) of Red Mountain vineyards. (DM)
● **Cabernet Sauvignon** Reserve Estate★★★ £E   ● **Merlot** Reserve Estate★★★ £D
● **Syrah** Reserve Estate★★★ £D

L'ECOLE NO 41 Walla Walla Valley www.lecole.com   *UK stockists:* **PDn**
Consistently good producer. The reds are well-crafted and stylish with refined supple tannins; not blockbusters, rather good, medium-term cellar prospects. The principal varieties here are Merlot and Semillon and the winery is one of the very best sources of the latter. (DM)
● **Cabernet Sauvignon** Walla Walla Valley★★★ £E   ● **Merlot** Seven Hills★★★ £E
○ **Chardonnay** Columbia Valley★★ £C   ○ **Semillon** Fries Vineyard★★★ £C

LEONETTI CELLAR Walla Walla Valley www.leonetticellar.com
One of the very best producers of Bordeaux-style reds in Washington State. These are wines of massive proportions – powerful and sturdy but refined and very long-lived. Stylish Sangiovese is also produced in a softer, lighter style, displaying very good intense, dark cherry fruit. (DM)
● **Reserve**❂❂❂❂ £G   ● **Cabernet Sauvignon**★★★★★ £F
● **Merlot** Columbia Valley★★★★★ £F   ● **Sangiovese**★★★★ £F

272

New entries have producer's name underlined

MCCREA CELLARS Washington State   www.mccreacellars.com
Small warehouse operation specialising in Rhône styles although Chardonnay has been made in the past from the
Elerding Vineyard. The other two vineyard sources are Boushey, purely for Syrah, and Ciel du Cheval for a range of
varieties. All the reds are bottled without fining or filtration. (DM)
● **Syrah** Ciel du Cheval★★★ £E Boushey Vineyard★★★★ £E Cuvée Orleans★★★★ £F
O **Viognier** Red Mountain★★★ £D

NORTHSTAR Walla Walla   www.northstarmerlot.com
Merlot is the focus here in a ripe and oaky style but with real depth and character. A dark and plummy regular
Columbia Valley Merlot has been joined by a more concentrated and marginally more opulent Walla Walla Valley
bottling sourced in part from the potentially great Spring Valley vineyard. (DM)
● **Merlot** Columbia Valley★★★ £E Walla Walla Valley★★★★ £F
● **Stella Maris** Columbia Valley★★★ £E

PEPPER BRIDGE WINERY Walla Walla Valley   www.pepperbridge.com
Cab Sauv and plummy Merlot are sourced from Pepper Bridge and Seven Hills vineyards. Second label Amavi
offers a lightly peppery Cab Sauv and more impressive Syrah, which is dark and spicy with impressive fruit. (DM)
● **Merlot** Walla Walla★★★ £E ● **Syrah** Amavi Walla Walla★★ £C

QUILCEDA CREEK VINTNERS Washington State   *UK stockists:* **AWM**
For many, this is Washington State's greatest source of Cab Sauv and Merlot. Certainly along with Leonetti they
vie for that accolade. The Cab Sauv is sourced from Ciel du Cheval, Taptiel and Klipsun vineyards from Red
Mountain and Champoux (which is now estate owned) from Yakima Valley. (DM)
● **Cabernet Sauvignon** Columbia Valley★★★★★ £F

REININGER WINERY Walla Walla Valley   www.reiningerwinery.com
Fine Bordeaux-style reds and Syrah from a range of sources. Helix Pomatia is a supple, soft, berry-laden
Merlot/Syrah/Cab Sauv/Cab Franc blend. The other wines are denser and more seriously structured. (DM)
● **Cabernet Sauvignon** Walla Walla Valley★★★ £E ● **Merlot** Walla Walla Valley★★★ £D
● **Syrah** Walla Walla Valley★★★ £E ● **Helix Pomatia** Columbia Valley★★ £C

SPRING VALLEY Walla Walla   www.springvalleyvineyard.com
This is rare in Washington State, a property that produces wines solely from its own estate vineyards, which were
planted in 1993. Uriah is a richly opulent Merlot blend, whereas Frederick is based on Cab Sauv. Nina Lee is a
100% Syrah with lots of dark pepper, oriental spices and exotic dark fruits. (DM)
● **Frederick** Champoux Vineyard★★★★ £E ● **Uriah** Columbia Valley★★★★★ £E
● **Nina Lee** Boushey Vineyards★★★★ £E

WOODWARD CANYON Walla Walla Valley   woodwardcanyon.com   *UK stockists:* **Vin**
An extensive range of wines is produced. Chardonnay is restrained and minerally, almost Burgundian in style but
with a rich, toasty character. Reds are good to very good particularly the Estate Red, a blend of Cab Sauv, Merlot
and Cab Franc. Small amounts of Barbera, Syrah and Pinot Noir are produced as well as Riesling and an Orange
Muscat. (DM)
● **Charbonneau Red**★★★ £F ● **Estate Red**★★★★ £E
O **Chardonnay** Columbia Valley★★★ £E Celilo Vineyard★★★★ £E

Other wineries of note
**Amity Vineyards (Willamette Valley), Argyle (Willamette Valley), Canoe Ridge Vineyard (Columbia Valley),
Columnbia Crest (Columbia Valley), Domaine Ste Michelle (Washington State)**

An in-depth profile of every producer can be found in Wine behind the label 2006

Rest of North America

Background

Besides California, Oregon and Washington State, quality wine production is limited to just a handful of states. Grapes other than vinifera varieties are grown throughout the country. In New York State, for example, hybrid varieties are popular in the production of kosher wines and grape juice. Wines from these tend to have what is quaintly referred to as a 'foxy' character. The best developments have been on New York's Long Island, in Maryland, in Virginia and to the far south in Arizona. The odd reasonable bottle has also emerged from Texas and the state may have real potential. Canadian quality wine has traditionally been Niagara icewine, but the developing region of the Okanagan Valley in British Columbia is also providing an increasing number of stylish dry whites and reds.

USA

New York State remains the best bet for quality wines outside the big sources on the western coast. In the north-west of the state the **Finger Lakes** region, just to the south of Lake Ontario, has a protected, very localised climate moderated by the lakes themselves. Both Chardonnay and Riesling are successful here along with a few sparkling wines. Among the best wineries, Fox Run, Dr Konstantin Frank, Lamoreaux Landing and Hermann J Wiemer stand out.

Directly north of New Jersey is the small **Hudson River** AVA where some decent Chardonnay is produced. Perhaps of most significance from a quality point of view are the wineries of **Long Island** and particularly The **North Fork of Long Island**. The climate is strongly maritime and both regions have proved to be impressive sources in recent years of Cabernet Sauvignon, Merlot and Cabernet Franc, along with the occasional striking Chardonnay. Bedell, Corey Creek, Gallucio, Jamesport, Palmer, Paumanok and Pellegrini are all worth a look.

Maryland with its warm maritime climate, has real potential despite the odd wet harvest and better mesoclimates are being established. One winery in particular, Basignano, stands out for the impressive quality of its Cabernet Sauvignon and meritage wines. There have been attempts to grow vines in Virginia since Thomas Jefferson's days, but only recently have these proved to be successful. Piedmont Vineyards is making some impressive Chardonnay and others have proved successful with a range of varieties, including those of Rhône and Bordeaux origin. Horton, Prince Michel and Barboursville are also worth looking at.

There is just one winery that stands out in **Arizona**: Callaghan Vineyards, based in the **Sonoita** AVA. The region is cooled by its elevation and the winery has some impressive, well-drained, gravel-dominated vineyards. From a volume rather than a quality point of view, **Idaho** is significant - the wines so far have been sound but uninspirational.

Canada

The country has one sizeable wine region at Niagara in Ontario and more recently one in the far west in British Columbia. As well as the **Niagara Peninsula** good whites and icewine are also produced in Ontario from **Pelee Island** and **Lake Eyrie North Shore**. Although the majority of the country's vineyard area is in Ontario, wines of some style are emerging from British Columbia and in particular in the **Okanagan Valley**. Pinot Gris, Chardonnay, Merlot and Syrah have all shown potential in this dry, sparse inland region to the immediate north of the international border with Washington State.

Mexico

Quality wine production remains very sparse. This is largely down to a scarcity of local consumers to support a small wine industry. However, the potential of the area is there and in particular in the Baja Peninsula.

SOUTH AMERICA

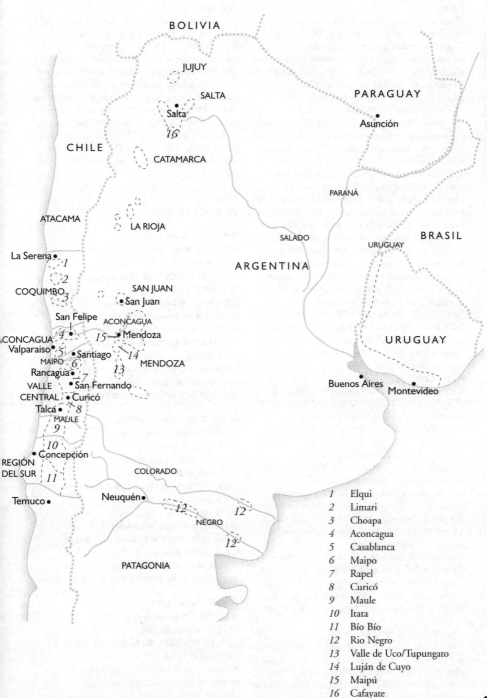

BOLIVIA

JUJUY

SALTA

Salta

16

PARAGUAY

Asunción

CHILE

CATAMARCA

PARANÁ

BRASIL

ATACAMA

LA RIOJA

SALADO

URUGUAY

La Serena
1

2

ARGENTINA

COQUIMBO
3

SAN JUAN
San Juan

San Felipe

ACONCAGUA

URUGUAY

CONCAGUA
4
15
Mendoza

Valparaiso
5
Santiago

MAIPO
6

14
MENDOZA

Rancagua
7

13

VALLE
CENTRAL
San Fernando

Buenos Aires

Montevideo

Talca
8

Curicó

MAULE
9

10

Concepción

REGIÓN
DEL SUR
11

COLORADO

Temuco

Neuquén

12

12

NEGRO

12

PATAGONIA

1	Elqui
2	Limari
3	Choapa
4	Aconcagua
5	Casablanca
6	Maipo
7	Rapel
8	Curicó
9	Maule
10	Itata
11	Bío Bío
12	Rio Negro
13	Valle de Uco/Tupungato
14	Luján de Cuyo
15	Maipú
16	Cafayate

SOUTH AMERICA

Chile

The country is split into five viticultural zones. Running from north to south, they are: **Atacama, Coquimbo, Aconcagua, Valle Central** and the **Región del Sur**. These zones contain a number of sub-regions and these may also be further subdivided. Atacama and Coquimbo are hot and dry, producing basic table grapes. You have to travel further south to find vineyards capable of providing good quality wines in any volume. Aconcagua includes the cool sub-region of **Casablanca** a source for some fine whites. **Valle del Aconcagua** is warmer and some of the best sites are on well-drained slopes.

The Valle Central includes the vineyards of **Maipo,, Rapel, Maule** and **Curicó**. The best reds from Maipo have traditionally been Cabernet-based but increased plantings of Rhône varieties is a continuing trend. Rapel is very promising with Cab Sauv, Merlot and particularly Carmenère successful in the warmer south of the region at **Colchagua**, while Chardonnay, Sauvignon and Pinot Noir are more successful in cooler **Cachapoal**. Promising reds and whites come from Curicó. **Maule** is largely dominated by whites but there is some good Merlot too.

To the south is the Región del Sur including the two sub-regions of Itata and **Bío Bío**. The climate is cool and sophisticated trellising and the planting of early-ripening Pinot Noir and Chardonnay as well as Alsace varieties have shown potential.

Argentina

Argentina appears to have real promise for good and indeed premium wine production and a number of impressive reds and whites are now being made. In the north of the country are the hot and dry vineyards of **Salta**. Within the region there are a number of better sites with vineyards planted at high altitude, in particular those in the Calchaquies Valley. Mendoza is the main focus for quality wine production and the two sub-regions **Luján de Cuyo** and **Tupungato**. Malbec is very successful as are Cab Sauv, Syrah and Sangiovese. Bonarda is important both varietally and as a component in blends. Chardonnay produces very striking wines in cooler sites.

The climate at **Río Negro**. is cool and early-ripening Sauvignon, Sémillon and Chardonnay have all been successful. However, stylish, elegant examples of the red Bordeaux varieties and Syrah are also appearing and there are ongoing efforts to realise the potential of Pinot Noir.

The Rest of South America

The only other country that would appear to have any real potential for quality wine production is Uruguay. Cab Sauv, Merlot, Chardonnay and Sauvignon are all cultivated successfully. Most important from a quality wine perpective is Tannat.

Vintages

Almost all whites with the exception of the top barrel-fermented Chardonnays should be drunk on release. Top reds, though, can develop well in bottle. Early indications suggest 2005 will be good in Chile and the harvest also looks good in Argentina which enjoyed cooler late summer temperatures than normal and good wines are expected.2004 looks good for reds and whites in Chile, and for reds in Argentina. 2003 produced good Malbec in Argentina. 2003 was good for both red and white in Chile. Top reds emerged from Chile in 2002, 2001, 2000, 1999, 1996 and 1995; in Argentina 2002, 2000, 1999, 1997, 1996 and 1995.

Wizard's Wishlist

A top Chilean selection

ALMAVIVA ● **Almaviva Red** Maipo Valley
CASA LAPOSTOLLE ● **Clos Apalta** Rapel
VIÑA VON SIEBENTHAL ● **Montelig** Valle de Colchagua
EL PRINCIPAL ● **El Principal** Maipo
ERRÁZURIZ ● **Don Maximiano** Aconcagua Valley
GRACIA ● **RR Reserva** Caminante
MONTES ● **Montes Folly** Santa Cruz
ODFJELL VINEYARDS ● **Aliara** Maipo
SEÑA ● **Seña** Aconcagua Valley
VIÑEDO CHADWICK ● **Red** Maipo Valley
VIÑA ALTAIR ● **Altaïr** Cachapoal
VIÑA QUEBRADA DE MACUL ● **Domus Aurea** Maipo

A top Argentine selection

ACHAVAL-FERRER ● **Quimira**
ALTA VISTA ● **Alto** Vistalba
SUSANA BALBO ● **Brioso** Mendoza
BEN MARCO ● **VMS** Mendoza
CATENA ZAPATA ● **Nicolás Catena Zapata** Luján de Cuyo
LUCA O **Chardonnay** Mendoza
TIKAL ● **Corazon** Mendoza
CLOS DE LOS SIETE ● **Lindaflor** Mendoza
NIETO SENETINER ● **Malbec** Cadus Tupungato
YACOCHUYA ● **Yacochuya** Cafayate
POESIA ● **Poesia** Mendoza
BODEGA NOEMIA PARTAGONIA ● **Malbec** Mendoza

A value selection

ALTA VISTA ● **Grande Reserve** Vistalba
ANUBIS ● **Syrah/Bonarda** Mendoza
CLOS DE LOS SIETE ● **Clos de los Siete** Mendoza
NIETO SENETINER
● **Cabernet-Shiraz** Nieto Reserva Mendoza
POESIA ● **Clos des Andes** Mendoza
MICHEL TORINO ● **Malbec** Don David Cafayate

New entries have producer's name underlined

CARMEN ● **Merlot** Reserve Rapel
VIÑA VON SIEBENTHAL
● **Carmenere** Panquehue Valle de Aconcagua
CASA SILVA ● **Syrah** Colchagua

EL PRINCIPAL ● **Memorias** Maipo
ERRÁZURIZ ● **Syrah** Aconcagua
VIÑA CASABLANCA
○ **Sauvignon Blanc** Santa Isabel Casablanca

South America/A-Z of producers

Argentina

ACHAVAL-FERRER Mendoza www.achaval-ferrer.com *UK stockists:* **C&B**
Newly established but top-quality Mendoza winery. The 100% Malbec comes from the estate-owned Finca Altamira vineyard planted to vines over 80 years old. The Quimera red is a blend of Malbec, Cab Sauv and Merlot and is the mainstay of the winery. Dense and powerful wines which will keep well for a decade or more. (DM)
● **Quimera**★★★★ £E ● **Malbec** Finca Altamira★★★★ £F

ALTA VISTA Mendoza www.altavistawines.com *UK stockists:* J&B, L&W
Based in Argentina's high-quality Luján de Cuyo. Two basic blends, Cosecha Blanco and Tinto, offer attractive, fruity easy drinking. More serious is the Malbec Grande Reserve. The unfiltered Alto is a serious step up, a very powerfully structured blend of Malbec and Cab Sauv. Full of dark, spicy fruit, supple firm tannins and well-judged oak. (DM)
● **Alto** Vistalba★★★★ £F ● **Grande Reserve** Vistalba★★ £B
● **Malbec** Luján de Cuyo★ £B ○ **Chardonnay** Luján de Cuyo★ £B

ANUBÍS Mendoza sbalbo@impsat1.com.ar *UK stockists:* **Lib**, Wai
A decent small range of juicy, characterful reds are made by a partnership between Susana Balbo, of Dominio del Plata, and Alberto Antonini, formerly of Antinori. Fruit is sourced from Luján de Cuyo and Tupungato and a range of vibrant, forward varietals is now being produced. (DM)
● **Syrah/Bonarda** Mendoza★★ £B ● **Tempranillo** Mendoza★ £B
● **Malbec** Mendoza★★ £B

CATENA ZAPATA Mendoza www.nicolascatena.com *UK stockists:* **Bib**, Wai
Good straightforward varietal styles under the Argento and more serious Alamos labels. Premium bottlings appear under the Catena Alta label.of which the top wine is the Cab Sauv Zapata. Daughter Laura Catena produces the Luca brand independently and son Ernesto three Tikal reds: Corazon (Bonarda/Malbec), Jubilo which is based on Cab Sauv; and Amoria, based on Malbec. Caro, a blend of Malbec and Cab Sauv, is a new joint venture with Baron de Rothschild of Lafite-Rothschild. (DM)
Catena
● **Nicolás Catena Zapata**★★★★ £F ● **Cabernet Sauvignon** Alta★★★ £E
● **Malbec** Alta★★★★ £E ○ **Chardonnay** Alta★★★ £E
Luca
● **Syrah**★★★ £E ● **Malbec**★★★ £E ○ **Chardonnay**★★★ £E
Tikal
● **Corazon**★★★ £D ● **Jubilo**★★★ £D

CLOS DE LOS SIETE Mendoza *UK stockists:* **Eno**
Major new French investment spearheaded by Michel Rolland. Wines are produced at the Bodega Monteviejo, owned by Catherine Péré-Vergé, the owner of Château Montviel in Pomerol. Upfront brambly Clos de Los Siete red, blends Merlot, Cab Sauv, Syrah and Malbec. Val de Flores comes from some of the best-sited Malbec, Lindaflor is a vineyard selection. (DM)
● **Clos de los Siete** Mendoza★★★ £C ● **Val de Flores** Mendoza★★★★ £E
● **Lindaflor** Mendoza★★★★ £E

DOMINIO DEL PLATA Mendoza www.dominiodelplata.com
Home winery of Pedro Marchevsky and Susana Balbo who are the manager and winemaker at Anubis. Good Crios Torrontes is joined by some serious reds. The Ben Marco VMS is a blend of Malbec Cab Sauv, Bonarda, Tannat and a little Merlot. Brioso is an impressively structured Bordeaux blend. (DM)

277

Chile

Crios
○ **Crios Torrontes** Cafayate★ £B

Ben Marco
● **Malbec**★★ £D   ● **VMS**★★★ £E

Susana Balbo
● **Malbec**★★★ £E   ● **Cabernet Sauvignon**★★★ £E   ● **Brioso**★★★★ £F

NIETO SENETINER Mendoza www.nietosenetiner.com   *UK stockists:* Cap
Some good wines are made here as Nieto Reservas. These include an extracted, oaky, dark Malbec, good stylish Cabernet-Shiraz and a good but quite austere Cab Sauv. New is a premium Bordeaux blend Con Nicanor. Best of all is the splendid premium Malbec, Cadus, made from 80-year-old vines. (DM)
● **Malbec** Cadus Tupungato★★★★ £D Nieto Reserva Mendoza★★ £B
● **Cabernet-Shiraz** Nieto Reserva Mendoza★★ £B

BODEGA NOEMIA PATAGONÍA Rio Negro www.bodeganoemia.com   *UK stockists:* **Lib**
Partnership between Contessa Noemi Marone Cinzano of Tenuta Argiano in Tuscany and Hans Vinding-Diers is responsible for Argentina's most expensive red wine to date. It is an impressively rich and opulent Malbec, loaded with dark spicy berry fruit but firmly structured too, with great potential. (DM)
● **Malbec** Mendoza★★★★★ £G

BODEGA POESIA Mendoza   *UK stockists:* **Gen**
Hélène Garcin, owner of Clos l'Eglise in Pomerol discovered this vineyard planted to some remarkably old Malbec dating back to 1935 as well as a little Cabernet Sauvignon. Soft and easy Clos des Andes is purely Malbec, Poesia is an altogether more seriousred, aged for 18–20 months in all-new oak. (DM)
● **Poesia** Mendoza★★★★ £F   ● **Clos des Andes** Mendoza★★★ £C

MICHEL TORINO Salta www.micheltorino.com.ar   *UK stockists:* **Hal**
Sizeable producer with some good reds produced under the Colección and Don David labels, the latter offering wines of character, density and some structure. A new flagship red, Altimus, combines Malbec, Cabernet Sauvignon and Syrah. (DM)
● **Cabernet Sauvignon** Don David Cafayate★★ £B
● **Malbec** Colección Cafayate★ £B Don David Cafayate★★ £B

YACOCHUYA Salta www.yacochuya.com   *UK stockists:* His
Small winery part owned by Michel Rolland producing a magnificent striking, ageworthy red, a blend of Malbec and Cab Sauv, is produced from vineyards with vines up to 80 years old. A second wine, San Pedro de Yacochuya, is also being made to ensure the integrity of the *Grand Vin*. (DM)
● **Yacochuya** Cafayate★★★★★ £F

Chile

ALMAVIVA Maipo www.conchaytoro.com   *UK stockists:* **CyT**,Sel
Recently established joint venture between Concha y Toro and Baroness Philippine de Rothschild (Mouton-Rothschild). The ambitious project is aimed at producing one of, possibly *the* finest red wine yet from Chile. Undoubtedly impressive but as yet Almaviva falls some way short of its lofty price tag and on a global scale faces formidable opposition. (DM)
● **Almaviva Red** Maipo Valley★★★★ £G

CARMEN Maipo www.carmen.com   *UK stockists:* **SsG**,Wai
Carmen's best wines, are produced under the Reserve and Winemakers Reserve labels along with impressive organic Nativa Chardonnay and the deep, concentrated and minty Nativa Cabernet Sauvignon. The flagship red Gold Reserve, comes from a small 45-year-old parcel of vines in Maipo. (DM)
● **Cabernet Sauvignon** Nativa★★★ £C Gold Reserve★★★ £E
● **Merlot** Reserve Rapel★★ £B   ● **Cabernet Syrah** Reserve★★ £C

CASA LAPOSTOLLE Rapel www.casalapostolle.com   *UK stockists:* **MMD**
With consultancy from Michel Rolland Casa Lapostolle produces some of the best reds in Chile, particularly

278

under the Tanao (Cab Sauv, Merlot and Carmenère), Cuvée Alexandre and premium Clos Apalta labels. Whites are sound enough, if not on a par with the reds, particularly Chardonnay Cuvée Alexandre from Casablanca. (DM)

● **Clos Apalta**★★★★ £E   ● **Tanao**★★ £C   ● **Merlot** Cuvée Alexandre★★★ £C
O **Chardonnay** Cuvée Alexandre Casablanca★★ £C

CASA SILVA   Rapel   www.casasilva.cl   *UK stockists:* JNV
Only established in 1997, the winery owns three different estates. Top wines are the Reservas and Quinta Generación Gran Reserva Tinto, a blend of both Cab Sauv and Carmenère. A number of impressive Single Vineyard Reserve wines have now been released. (DM)

● **Carmenère** Single Vineyard Reserve Los Linques★★★★ £D
● **Merlot** Single Vineyard Reserve Angostura★★★ £D
● **Quinta Generación** Colchagua★★★ £C

CONCHA Y TORO   Maipo   www.conchaytoro.com   *UK stockists:* CyT, Wai
This is a massive operation with a huge range of commercial wines throughout the vinous spectrum at all price points. It is also involved with Mouton-Rothschild in the super-premium Almaviva project. Amelia Chardonnay and Don Melchor Cab Sauv both stand out. (DM)

● **Cabernet Sauvignon** Don Melchor★★★ £E   ● **Carmenère** Terrunyo★ £C
O **Chardonnay** Trio★ £B Terrunyo ★★£B Amelia★★ £C

CONO SUR   Rapel   www.conosur.com   *UK stockists:* WWs, Wai
Good Reserve, and 20 Barrels wines come from vineyards at Casablanca, Maipo, Rapel and the Bío Bío Valley. Under the Isla Negra label some attractively fruity reds and whites are also produced. Pinot Noir also comes in a superior Limited Edition bottling. (DM)

● **Cabernet Sauvignon** Reserve★ £B 20 Barrels★★ £C
● **Merlot** 20 Barrels★★ £C   ● **Pinot Noir** Limited Edition★★ £C

EL PRINCIPAL   Maipo Valley   vinaep@ctcinterneyt.cl   *UK stockists:* WEx
This is a modern Bordeaux style with a second wine Memorias produced to shore up the quality of the Grand Vin. El Principal is aged in 100% new oak with malolactic in barrel. The wine is typically a blend of Cab Sauv and Carmenère. (DM)

● **Memorias**★★ £B   ● **El Principal**★★★★ £E

ERRÁZURIZ   Aconcagua   www.errazuriz.com   *UK stockists:* HMA, AAA
Top producers based in the Panquehue sub-region of Aconcagua. Fruit is sourced from home vineyards as well as cool Casablanca for whites with stylish wines at all levels. Top reds include Don Maximiano Founders Reserve. Also make the Super-premium Sena and wines from the La Arboleda Estate. 1999 was also the first vintage of super-premium Vinedo Chadwick. (DM)

● **Sangiovese** Single Vineyard★★ £C   ● **Carmenère** Single Vineyard★★ £D
● **Don Maximiano** Reserve★★★ £E   O **Chardonnay** Wild Ferment★★ £C

GRACIA   Rapel   www.graciawinery.cl   *UK stockists:* Pat, Wai
With estate-owned vineyards in the Aconcagua, Maipo, Rapel and Bío Bío valleys, there are some well-crafted Reserva wines and the style is full-on and opulent: Chardonnay, is ripe, and toasty; Merlot, plummy and smoky; and Carmenère brambly and supple. Top red is the premium Cab Sauv RR Reserva Caminante. (DM)

● **Carmenère** Reserva Especial Callajero Maipo★ £B   ● RR Reserva Caminante★★★ £D
● **Cabernet Sauvignon** Reserva Lo Mejor Porquenó★★ £C

MONTES   Curicó   www.monteswines.com   *UK stockists:* HWC, Wai
Large somewhat variable producer with some impressive wines and some less so. Best wines are produced under Montes Alpha label. Dark, smoky Syrah is one of Chile's best. This has now been joined by the Montes Folly, 100% Syrah aged in new French oak. (DM)

● **Montes Alpha M** Colchagua★★ £E   ● **Montes Folly** Santa Cruz★★★★ £D
● **Montes Alpha Syrah** Santa Cruz★★★ £D   ● **Alpha Merlot** Colchagua★ £C

ODFJELL VINEYARDS   Maipo   www.odfjellvineyards.com   *UK stockists:* WTs
By Chilean standards a small, almost boutique style of operation. Some good wine comes under the budget Armador label. The Orzada wines are a level up and some very characteristic Cabernet Franc, Carmenère and

SOUTH AMERICA

Carignan stand out. Top of the range is a 100% Cabernet Sauvignon Aliara which is full and rich with dark berry fruit and abundant oak needs. (DM)
- **Cabernet Franc** Orzada Maule★★ £B ● **Carignan** Orzada Maule★★ £B
- **Carmenère** Orzada Maule★★★ £B ● **Aliara** Maipo★★★ £D

SANTA RITA Maipo www.santarita.com   UK stockists: **BWC**,Wai
120 range offers some reasonable straightforward easy drinking; the reds are a better bet generally than the whites. Some good Reserva and Medalla reds as well as Medalla Chardonnay. Floresta reds recently added. The two stand out wines are the red Triple C (Cab Franc/Cab Sauv/Carmenère) and Casa Real Cab Sauv. (DM)
- **Cabernet Sauvignon Floresta Apalta**★★ £B ● **Triple C**★★ £C
- **Syrah/Cabernet/Carmenère Floresta**★★ £B

SEÑA Aconcagua www.senawines.com   UK stockists: **HMA**,Sel
Super-premium red now solely owned by Eduardo Chadwick. A blend of Cab Sauv, Merlot and Carmenère the wine is impressively dense, structured and concentrated. It is planned that the wine will eventually be sourced entirely from its own single estate. (DM)
- **Seña** Aconcagua Valley★★★★ £F

VALDIVIESO Curicó www.vinavaldivieso.cl   UK stockists: **Bib**
Extensive range of wines at all levels. Barrel Selections offer reasonable value. Some impressive red is produced under the Reserve label, Single Vineyard Cabernet Franc and Merlot stand out. The top wines are The Don, part aged in American and French oak, and the non-vintaged Caballo Loco, a blend that changes by the year. (DM)
- **Cabernet Franc** Single Vineyard Reserve★★ £B
- **Malbec** Single Vineyard Reserve★★ £B ● **Caballo Loco**★★★ £D

VIÑA ALTAIR Cachapoal www.vinaaldair.com
New Franco-Chilean joint venture with vineyards in the Upper Cachapoal, one of the cooler areas of the country, nestled into the foothills of the Andes. Estate sourced Altaïr is an impressively structured and concentrated blend of Cabernet Sauvignon, Carmenère, Cabernet Franc and Syrah. (DM)
- **Altaïr** Cachapoal★★★★ £E ● **Sideral** Cachapoal★★★ £C

VIÑA CASABLANCA Casablanca rbeckdor@santacarolina.cl   UK stockists: **Mor**
Consistently impressive producer of good, sometimes very good cool-grown whites. Reds are more variable. Neblus is a pricey blend of Cab Sauv, Merlot and Carmenère. Chardonnay is one of the best in the country, particularly the Barrel Fermented label, which is very intense with marked citrus, subtle lees and oak character. (DM)
- **Neblus**★★ £D ○ **Chardonnay**★★ £B Barrel Fermented★★★ £C
- ○ **Gewurztraminer**★ £B ○ **Sauvignon Blanc**★★ £B

VIÑA VON SIEBENTHAL Aconcagua www.vinavonsiebenthal.com   UK stockists:**May**
Based in warm Panquehue, new Swiss-owned property producing excellent reds. Carabantes is dominated by Syrah while the top wine, Montelig is blended from Cabernet Sauvignon, Petit Verdot and just a little Carmenère. (DM)
- **Montelig** Colchagua★★★★ £D ● **Carabantes** Panquehue Valle de Aconcagua★★★ £C
- **Carmenere** Panquehue Valle de Aconcagua★★ £B
- **Parcela 7** Panquehue Valle de Aconcagua★★ £B

VINEDO CHADWICK Maipo www.vinedoschadwick.com   UK stockists: **HMA**
Recently established premium label owned by Errázuriz, with a vineyard located on the northern bank of the Maipo river into the foothills of the Andes. The wine is aged in 100 per cent new French oak. Firmly structured with a cedary edge to its fruit, it needs at least five years to soften. (DM)
- **Vinedo Chadwick** Maipo★★★★ £F

An in-depth profile of every producer can be found in Wine behind the label 2006

New entries have producer's name underlined

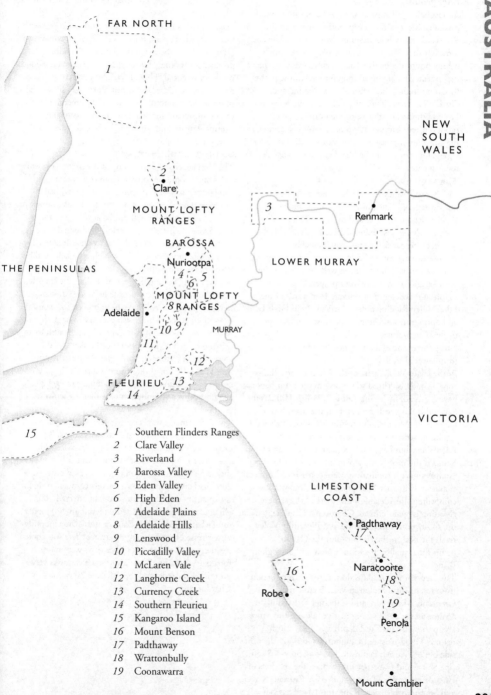

AUSTRALIA

FAR NORTH

1

NEW
SOUTH
WALES

2
Clare

MOUNT LOFTY
RANGES

3

Renmark

BAROSSA

Nuriootpa

THE PENINSULAS

LOWER MURRAY

7   *4* *5*
           6
     MOUNT LOFTY
Adelaide *8* RANGES

       9
    10
     11   MURRAY

          12

FLEURIEU   *13*
     14

VICTORIA

15

1   Southern Flinders Ranges
2   Clare Valley
3   Riverland
4   Barossa Valley
5   Eden Valley
6   High Eden
7   Adelaide Plains
8   Adelaide Hills
9   Lenswood
10   Piccadilly Valley
11   McLaren Vale
12   Langhorne Creek
13   Currency Creek
14   Southern Fleurieu
15   Kangaroo Island
16   Mount Benson
17   Padthaway
18   Wrattonbully
19   Coonawarra

LIMESTONE
COAST

Padthaway
17

Naracoorte
18

16

Robe

19

Penola

Mount Gambier

AUSTRALIA

Background

Almost half of all Australian wine comes from South Australia. Most of the cheap stuff comes from the Riverland area, while premium wines (red, white and fortified) are made from regions that range from baking hot to distinctly cool. Quality is very producer-dependent, as many have chosen to maximise profits by concentrating their efforts on marketing and distribution rather than producing ever better wines. From both the latest wave of high-quality small producers and some of the more established names, the wines are increasingly vineyard-specific but great wines also continue to be blended from a range of mesoclimates.

The regions

The **Barossa Valley** has a rich resource of often unirrigated, old-vine Shiraz, Grenache and Mourvèdre. Besides rich, lushly textured old-vine Shiraz and Rhône-style blends, there's distinctive dense, black-fruited Cabernet Sauvignon-based blockbusters. Barossa also a great tradition of very high quality fortified wines. Whites do less well, Semillon is the most successful in the Barossa proper. Over in the significantly cooler, more elevated vineyards of the **Eden Valley** Riesling excels, particularly in **High Eden** and **Springton** subregions which also produce high-quality Chardonnay, Viognier, Pinot Noir and Merlot. Great Shiraz and Cabernet, notably Henschke's, come from lower altitudes.

In the **Clare Valley**, part of the Mount Lofty Ranges zone altitude is critical to success. Several sub-regions have emerged, including **Auburn, Polish Hill River, Sevenhill, Watervale** and around the township of **Clare** itself. Most Rieslings from the Clare Valley offer less immediate fruit sweetness than those from the Eden Valley but have better structure and greater style. Shiraz is the most widely planted variety and the best examples have a captivating smoke, earth and mineral character. Cabernet Sauvignon is also important if less compelling. In **Adelaide Hills**, part of the same zone, elevation is again critical. Chardonnay, especially from the sub-regions of **Lenswood** and **Piccadilly Valley**, rivals the best in the country but there's also compelling quality from Pinot Noir and Sauvignon Blanc.

The Fleurieu Peninsula is dominated by production from the historic **McLaren Vale**. Here Shiraz, Grenache, Mourvèdre and Cabernet Sauvignon assume ascendancy. Care must be taken if the wines are to show balance and depth as well as a lush texture. Flood-irrigated **Langhorne Creek** on the other side of the Fleurieu Peninsula has long provided soft, ripe Shiraz and Cabernet fruit while other pockets of vineyard now officially sanctioned are **Currency Creek** and **Southern Fleurieu. Kangaroo Island** has but a few

vines yet shows good potential for Bordeaux-style reds. The Limestone Coast zone is essentially flat yet its magic emerges from low limestone ridges topped with the famous terra rossa (or terra rosa) soil. **Coonawarra** is famous for Cabernet Sauvignon but can also produce great Shiraz but quality is variable and a good producer essential. Though warmer **Padthaway** has a reputation for Chardonnay but Shiraz also shows real promise. **Wrattonbully** is now rapidly emerging as an important region for quality Cabernet Sauvignon. In **Mount Benson** and adjoining Robe Cabernet Sauvignon and Shiraz lead the plantings.

South Australia Vintages

The Vintage charts cover some of the most ageworthy styles and should be considered in conjunction with comments on style and ageing within individual producer entries. Many wines can be drunk young but an increasing number will not be at their best for at least 5 years, whether a powerful, full-bodied red or a more structured example of Clare Valley Riesling. Top-quality Chardonnay and Pinot Noir are likely to show at their best only with 3-6 years'. In terms of longer-term cellaring potential, great Australian Rieslings have been shown to age for a decade or more, while some famous Australian reds have been proven to age for 30 or even 40 years. While it is necessary to be prepared to buy only the best if you want to add breadth to an existing French or European-based cellar, this doesn't always mean purchasing only the most expensive. It should also be noted that those indicated (in producer entries) as needing a minimum amount of ageing should be given it; underestimate their structure at your peril.

The 2005 vintage was another record harvest for Australia, due to healthy yields as well as the still expanding area given over to growing grapes. South Australia received the most variable weather but quality should be high if not as consistently so as in other states. 2004 had also been a record harvest compensating for the quantity shortfall of the drought-affected 2003 vintage. In terms of quality the picture in 2004 looks somewhat varied. While Barossa and Clare vineyards were stressed by a February heatwave there was cooler weather closer to harvest. Other parts were more fortunate, including Coonawarra, which looks very promising for reds, and the Adelaide Hills, for Chardonnay.

AUSTRALIA

Wizard's Wishlist

Powerful Barossa/Eden Valley Shiraz-based reds

BAROSSA VALLEY ESTATE ● Shiraz E&E Black Pepper
GRANT BURGE ● Shiraz Meschach
BURGE FAMILY ● Shiraz Draycott
DUTSCHKE ● Shiraz Oscar Semmler
GLAETZER ● Shiraz Amon-Ra
GREENOCK CREEK ● Shiraz Seven Acre
HENSCHKE ● Shiraz Mount Edelstone
PETER LEHMANN ● Shiraz Stonewell
CHARLES MELTON ● Shiraz
MT BILLY ● Shiraz Antiquity
ROCKFORD ● Shiraz Basket Press
TORBRECK ● Shiraz The Factor

Other top Shiraz

TIM ADAMS ● Shiraz Clare Valley Aberfeldy
JIM BARRY ● Shiraz Clare Valley The Armagh
BOWEN ESTATE ● Shiraz Coonawarra
CORIOLE ● Shiraz McLaren Vale Lloyd Reserve
D'ARENBERG ● Shiraz McLaren Vale Dead Arm
FOX CREEK ● Shiraz McLaren Vale Reserve
HARDYS ● Shiraz Eileen Hardy
HENRY'S DRIVE ● Shiraz Padthaway Reserve
KILIKANOON ● Shiraz Clare Valley Covenant
REYNELLA ● Shiraz McLaren Vale Basket Pressed
ROSEMOUNT ● Syrah McLaren Vale Balmoral
ULITHORNE ● Shiraz Frux Frugis
WENDOUREE ● Shiraz Clare Valley

Leading Cabernet-based reds

GROSSET ● Gaia
HENSCHKE ● Cabernet Sauvignon Cyril Henschke
HOLLICK ● Cabernet Sauvignon Ravenswood
LECONFIELD ● Cabernet Coonawarra
PARKER COONAWARRA ● Terra Rossa First Growth
PENFOLDS ● Cabernet Sauvignon Bin 707
PENLEY ESTATE ● Cabernet Sauvignon Reserve
PRIMO ESTATE ● Cabernet Sauvignon/Merlot Joseph
WYNNS ● Cabernet Sauvignon John Riddoch

Ageworthy whites

TIM ADAMS O Semillon Clare Valley
BARRATT O Chardonnay Adelaide Hills
GROSSET O Riesling Polish Hill
HARDYS O Chardonnay Eileen Hardy
LENSWOOD VINEYARDS O Chardonnay Lenswood
MOUNT HORROCKS O Riesling Watervale
PETALUMA O Chardonnay Tiers
PEWSEY VALE (Yalumba) O Riesling The Contours

Best buys

ANNIE'S LANE O Riesling Clare Valley
CASCABEL O Riesling Eden Valley
D'ARENBERG O Roussanne Money Spider
KILIKANOON O Riesling Clare Valley Morts Block
PETER LEHMANN ● Shiraz Barossa Valley
TORBRECK ● Woodcutters Red
WAKEFIELD ● Shiraz Clare Valley
WYNNS ● Shiraz Coonawarra
YALUMBA O Viognier Y

South Australia/A-Z of producers

TIM ADAMS Clare Valley *UK stockists:* **AWA**, ACh, HoM, Por
Brilliant Clare Valley producer. Adams Brothers Shiraz (sold only in the UK) combines Barossa and Clare fruit. Aberfeldy, the top red, has a certain elegance as well as masses of fruit. The Fergus combines Grenache with a little Shiraz, Cab Sauv and Cab Franc. Prices are exemplary for the quality. (PW)
● Shiraz★★★ £C Adams Brothers★★★ £C Aberfeldy★★★★★ £E
● The Fergus★★ £B ● Cabernet★★★ £C
O Semillon★★★ £C O Riesling★★★ £B O Botrytis Riesling★★★ £C

ASHTON HILLS Adelaide Hills *UK stockists:* **Cac**, Rae
Small estate known first and foremost for two refined yet ripely fruity sparkling wines. Biscuity Salmon Brut is mainly Chardonnay, the balance Pinot Noir. An intense structured Riesling, piercingly fruity Pinot Noir and richly textured Chardonnay stand out. (PW)
O Blanc de Blancs★★ £C ◉ Salmon Brut★★★ £C
O Chardonnay★★★ £C O Riesling★★★★ £C ● Pinot Noir★★★ £D

BALNAVES Coonawarra www.balnaves.com.au *UK stockists:* **Lib**, Vne, ACh, But, P&S
The Blend (Merlot/Cab Franc/Cab Sauv) and Cab Sauv/Merlot both offer round and pleasurable drinking. Cab Sauv adds more breadth and intensity, while Shiraz is ripe and concentrated. Flagship is The Tally Reserve, a big, powerful, oaky Cab Sauv. A sweetish Sparkling Cabernet is worth a try. (PW)
● The Blend★★ £C ● Cabernet Sauvignon/Merlot★★ £D

● Cabernet Sauvignon★★★ £D
● Shiraz★★★ £D   O Chardonnay★★ £C   ● Sparkling Cabernet★★ £D

BAROSSA VALLEY ESTATE   Barossa   *UK stockists:* **Cst**, WSc, N&P, Nid, P&S
Co-op now in partnership with BRL Hardy. Ebenezer Shiraz is full of berry fruit and American oak. Pricey flagship E & E Black Pepper Shiraz is an explosively rich, powerful but balanced expression of old-vine Barossa fruit. Moculta second label includes good Grenache, Shiraz and Chardonnay. (PW)
● Shiraz Ebenezer★★★ £D   E & E Black Pepper★★★★ £F
● Cabernet Sauvignon/Merlot Ebenezer★★ £C

BARRATT WINES   Adelaide Hills   *UK stockists:* **Gun**
Unfiltered Pinot Noir, including a richly textured Reserve, and Chardonnay are both powerful and balanced. They will keep for at least five years, Reserve Pinot even longer. A new Merlot (from 2001) is aged in French oak (part of it new). 2002 was the first vintage of an unwooded Sauvignon. (PW)
● Pinot Noir Bonython★★ £C   Reserve★★★ £D
O Chardonnay Piccadilly Valley★★★ £D   O Sauvignon Blanc Piccadilly Valley★★ £C

JIM BARRY   Clare Valley   *UK stockists:* **Neg**, CPp, DWS, Tan, ACh, Sel
Reds are the mainstay: deep, concentrated if relatively unrefined Shiraz, Cab Sauv and Cab Sauv/Malbec under the McRae Wood label. However, it is for the uncompromisingly big, thick, extracted and oaky Armagh that Jim Barry is best known. (PW)
● Shiraz The Armagh★★★★ £F   McCrae Wood★★ £C
● Cabernet Sauvignon★ £C   McCrae Wood★★★ £C
● Cabernet/Malbec McCrae Wood★★ £C   O Riesling★★ £B

WOLF BLASS   Barossa Valley   www.wolfblass.com.au   *UK stockists:* **BBI**, AAA
Now part of the Beringer Blass wine portfolio. The lower level can be uninspiring although Presidents Selection wines offer a lot of upfront fruit and oak and adequate depth and structure. The top Gold label wines though are of a different order. Richly textured Black Label Cab Sauv/Shiraz (subjected to a delayed release) is consistently fine, if pricey. (PW)
● Cabernet Sauvignon/Shiraz Black Label★★★★ £F
● Shiraz/Viognier Gold Label★★★ £C   O Riesling Gold Label★★ £B
● Cabernet Sauvignon/Cabernet Franc Gold Label★★★ £C

BLEASDALE   Langhorne Creek   www.bleasdale.com.au   *UK stockists:* **JEF**, Odd, Nid, FWC
All the wines show an accentuated varietal character and lots of flavour intensity. Frank Potts, is a savoury, cedary Cab Sauv-based blend and the complex Generations Shiraz (from a parcel of old vines) is full of eucalypt, plum and berry character. Petrel Reserve is another premium Shiraz, first produced in 1999. (PW)
● Shiraz Bremerview★★★ £B   Generations★★★★ £D   ● Frank Potts★★★ £C
● Cabernet Sauvignon Mulberry Tree★★ £B   ● Shiraz/Cabernet★★ £B
● Malbec★★ £B   ● Sparkling Shiraz★★ £B   O Verdelho★★ £B

BOWEN ESTATE   Coonawarra   *UK stockists:* **AWA**, Tan, NYg, P&S
Reds are of consistently high quality: deep, fleshy and textured with very ripe flavours. The Blend is composed of Cab Sauv, Merlot and Cab Franc. Ripe and creamy Chardonnay is also made while Ampelon is a new single-vineyard Shiraz. (PW)
● Shiraz★★★★ £C   ● Cabernet Sauvignon★★★ £C   ● The Blend★★★ £C
O Chardonnay★ £B

BREMERTON   Langhorne Creek   www.bremerton.com.au   *UK stockists:* **Sec**, ACh
Sisters Rebecca and Lucy Willson run this large Langhorne Creek winery. Excellent top reds: Old Adam Limited Release Shiraz is an old-style blockbuster but with fine structure and lots of character; Tamblyn is Cab Sauv/Shiraz/Malbec/Merlot. Verdelho has spiced citrus fruit and good structure. (PW)
● Shiraz Selkirk★★★ £B   Old Adam★★★★ £D   ● Cabernet Sauvignon Walter's★★★ £C
● Tamblyn★★ £B   O Verdelho★★ £B

GRANT BURGE Barossa Valley   *UK stockists:* **HMA**, Vne, ACh, P&, LasS
Good Shiraz includes sweet-fruited Miamba, oaky and characterful Filsell, and, from the same vineyard, Meschach, a powerful, super-stylish American-oaked Barossa Shiraz from 80-year-old vines. Rich and intense Shadrach is aged in French oak. Holy Trinity, comprises Grenache, Shiraz and Mourvèdre. (PW)
- **Shiraz** Miamba Barossa★★ £B   Filsell Barossa★★★ £C   Meschach★★★★★ £F
- **Cabernet Sauvignon** Cameron Vale★★ £C   Shadrach★★★★ £F
- **Merlot** Hillcot Barossa★ £C   ● Holy Trinity★★★ £D   O **Semillon** Zerk★★ £B

BURGE FAMILY Barossa Valley   www.burgefamily.com.au   *UK stockists:* **NYg**, Fal, UnC
Classic oak-lined, rich, lush, sweet-fruited Barossa reds. Garnacha is mostly old-vine Grenache with a little Shiraz and Mourvèdre. Semillon has plenty of rich citrus and herb character but is not for long keeping. New from the 2002 vintage is G3, a premium blend of Grenache, Shiraz and Mourvèdre. (PW)
- **Shiraz** Draycott★★★★ £D   ● **Shiraz/Grenache/Mourvèdre** Olive Hill★★★ £D
- **Shiraz/Merlot/Cabernet Sauvignon** The Renoux★★ £C
- **Grenache** Garnacha★★ £D   O **Semillon** Olive Hill★★ £C

CLARENDON HILLS McLaren Vale   *UK stockists:* **J&B**, F&R, N&P, Las, Hrd
Impressive unfiltered and unfined, ripe, extracted reds. Shiraz and Grenache are powerful, broadly structured as well as very concentrated and marvellously complex in the best bottlings. Intense, muscular and ageworthy Chardonnay and Semillon have also been made. (PW)
- **Shiraz** Australis✪✪✪✪ £H   Piggot Range★★★★★ £G   Brookman★★★★ £F
- **Grenache** Romas★★★★★ £F   Blewitt Springs★★★★ £E   Clarendon★★★★ £E
- **Cabernet Sauvignon** Hickinbotham★★★★ £E   ● **Merlot** Hickinbotham★★ £E

COLONIAL ESTATE Barossa Valley   www.colonialwine.com.au   *UK stockists:* **J&B**, BBR, NYg
Jonathan Maltus of Château Teyssier in Saint-Emilion has brought his intelligence and dynamism to the Barossa. There are 3 premium wines: Éxile (old vines Shiraz and Mourvèdre) with enormous breadth, depth and intensity; concentrated Émigré (from a mix of parcels and varieties); and Exodus (Piccadilly Valley Chardonnay). Much less expensive are stylish reds Explorateur Shiraz, Étranger Cab Sauv and Envoy (Grenache, Shiraz, Mouvrèdre). Also good Semillon Expatrié. Plentiful new releases all seem certain to be worth a try. (PW)
- **Éxile**★★★★★ £H   ● **Émigré**★★★★ £F

Colonial Estate range:
- **Explorateur Shiraz** Barossa Valley★★★ £C   ● **Envoy** Barossa Valley★★★ £C
- **Étranger Cabernet Sauvignon** Barossa★★★ £C   O **Expatrié Semillon** Barossa★★ £C

CORIOLE McLaren Vale   www.coriole.com   *UK stockists:* **Sec**, Tan, ACh, P&S, Las
Coriole has been long known for its intense old-vine Shiraz and Sangiovese. Shiraz is richly textured with deep, ripe fruit. Lloyd Reserve is the premium bottling. Powerful, minty Mary Kathleen is a sometimes over-structured blend of Cab Sauv, Merlot and Cab Franc. Rich, concentrated, citrusy Semillon is easily the best of the whites. (PW)
- **Shiraz**★★★ £C   Lloyd Reserve★★★★ £E   ● **Sangiovese/Cabernet** Lloyd★★ £C
- **Mary Kathleen**★★★ £D   O **Semillon** Lalla Rookh★★ £B

D'ARENBERG McLaren Vale   *UK stockists:* **Bib**, Odd, WSc, NYg, Hrd, P&S, Wai
Sizeable producer of good, if at times, overhyped wines. The best reds have exuberant fruit, offering enjoyable youthful drinking. Flagship is the Dead Arm Shiraz, with super fruit and excellent concentration. Other premium reds are also very good. Whites are fruit-driven if sometimes a little coarse. (PW)
- **Shiraz** Dead Arm★★★★★ £E   ● **Cabernet Sauvignon** Coppermine Road★★★★ £E
- **Mourvèdre** Twenty-Eight Road★★★ £C   ● **Shiraz/Grenache** D'Arry's Original★★ £C
- O **Riesling** Noble★★★ £D   O **Roussanne** Money Spider★★ £B

DUTSCHKE Barossa Valley   www.dutschkewines.com   *UK stockists:* **C&R**, UnC
Shiraz is the thrust of this operation. St Jakobi, with an almost coconutty American-oak influence displays a deep fruit succulence. Oscar Semmler, the top *cuvée*, is aged in 100 per cent French oak. It is marvellously profound with terrific potential if

AUSTRALIA

cellared for at least five to eight years. (PW)
● **Shiraz** St Jakobi★★★ £D Oscar Semmler★★★★ £E

ELDERTON Barossa Valley www.eldertonwines.com.au *UK stockists:* **Fie, BBR**, F&R, The, P&S, Las
Unashamedly oaky, full-throttle style reds. Most successful and sought-after is the Command Shiraz epitomising
the richly extracted, lusciously fruity style. CSM is not a Rhône style but a blend of Cab Sauv, Shiraz and
Merlot. Riesling and Chardonnay are also made and offer plenty of upfront flavour. (PW)
● **Shiraz★** £C Command★★★ £E ● CSM★★ £D ● **Merlot★** £C
● **Cabernet Sauvignon★** £C Ashmead Single Vineyard★★ £E

FOX CREEK McLaren Vale *UK stockists:* **NYg**, UnC, F&R, N&P, P&S, Las
Rich, ripe and succulent reds. Reserve Shiraz is the leading wine displaying all the potency and character of
McLaren Vale. Also impressive is a more forward but ripe and stylish JSM Shiraz/Cabernet Franc. Pick of the
whites is a Verdelho with an intense, flavoursome varietal character. (PW)
● **Shiraz** Reserve★★★★ £E ● **Shiraz/Cabernet Franc** JSM★★★ £C
● **Sparkling Shiraz/Cabernet Franc** Vixen★★ £C
● **Cabernet Sauvignon** Reserve★★ £D O **Verdelho★★** £B

GLAETZER Barossa Valley www.glaetzer.com *UK stockists:* **GWW**, Nid, Fal, NYg, F&R
Colin Gaetzer and son Ben (also see Mitolo) now make superb reds from unirrigated vineyards. Top is the very
complete Amon-Ra, an unfiltered Shiraz from 100-year-old vines. Also very stylish Barossa Valley Shiraz with classic
black plum, licorice, tar, earth and berry richness. Bishop Shiraz and Wallace Shiraz/Grenache are supple and
characterful. (PW)
● **Amon-Ra Shiraz★★★★★** £F ● **Shiraz★★★★** £E Bishop★★★ £D
● **Shiraz/Grenache** Wallace★★ £C

GREENOCK CREEK Barossa Valley *UK stockists:* **THt**, C&B, Bal, NYg, F&M, Hrd, P&S
From very low yields these are wines which reveal unusual, almost exotic, ripe flavours. Very striking is the
Seven Acre Shiraz which reveals real power and intensity. Made in tiny quantities and sold for astronomical
prices are Roennfeldt Road Cab Sauv and Shiraz. New from 2000 is Alice's Block Shiraz. (PW)
● **Shiraz** Seven Acre★★★★ £F Creek Block★★★ £F Apricot Block★★★ £E
● **Grenache** Cornerstone★★★ £E ● **Cabernet Sauvignon★★★** £E

GROSSET Clare Valley www.grosset.com.au *UK stockists:* **MSd**, Bal, BBR, Mar, Tur, WSc, P&S, Las
Outstanding Rieslings, Chardonnay and the Gaia Bordeaux blend all show pristine fruit, wonderful symmetry
and excellent concentration with proven ageability. A delicious Semillon/Sauvignon blend is one of the best
Australian examples of its type. (PW)
● **Gaia★★★★** £E ● **Pinot Noir★★★** £E
O **Riesling** Polish Hill★★★★ £C watervale★★★★ £C
O **Chardonnay** Piccadilly★★★★ £D O **Semillon/Sauvignon Blanc★★★** £C

HAMILTON'S EWELL Barossa Valley *UK stockists:* **Str**, FWC, Nid, NYg
These are wines of impressive breadth, depth and character. All show excellent flavour intensity and good
ageing potential. As well the bold Limestone Quarry Chardonnay a Shiraz and Cab Sauv are also made from
Wrattonbully fruit. Other wines include Stonegarden Riesling from Eden Valley and a very small amount of
Barossa Fuller's Barn Shiraz. (PW)
● **Shiraz** Railway Barossa Valley★★★ £C O **Chardonnay** Limestone Quarry★★ £C
● **Cabernet Sauvignon** Ewell Barossa Valley★★★ £C
● **Grenache/Shiraz** Stonegarden Barossa Valley★★★ £B

HARDYS McLaren Vale www.hardys.com.au *UK stockists:* **Cst**, Vne, P&S, N&P, Wai
One of the great names of Australian wine. Eileen Hardy label is reserved for an outstanding Shiraz and a rich,
powerful oaky Chardonnay. Thomas Hardy Cab Sauv has terrific depth. Tintara Limited Release Shiraz and
Grenache are full, concentrated and more affordable. Also produces the brands Nottage Hill and Stamps of
Australia. (PW)
● **Shiraz** Eileen Hardy★★★★★ £F ● **Cabernet Sauvignon** Thomas Hardy★★★★ £F

New entries have producer's name underlined

● **Shiraz** Tintara Limited Release★★★ £C
● **Grenache** Tintara Limited Release★★★ £C   O **Chardonnay** Eileen Hardy★★★ £C

HEARTLAND   *UK stockists:* **GWW,** Jas, Nid, NYg
Joint venture involving Ben Glaetzer (Glaetzer) and drawing in grapes from leading regions in South Australia. Early efforts combine quality and volume with reasonable prices. Top wine is Director's Cut Shiraz but also good Limestone Coast Shiraz, Cab Sauv and Petit Verdot. Unusual white Viognier/Pinot Gris and red Dolcetto/Lagrein have lots of fruit and character. (PW)
● **Shiraz** Limestone Coast★★★ £B   Directors' Cut★★★★ £C
● **Cabernet Sauvignon** Limestone Coast★★★ £B   ● **Dolcetto/Lagrein** Langhorne Creek★★ £B
● **Petit Verdot** Limestone Coast★★ £B   O **Viognier/Pinot Gris** Langhorne Creek★★ £B

HENRY'S DRIVE   www.henrysdrive.com   *UK stockists:* **THt,** JNi, Bal, F&M, NYg, But, Tur
Shiraz and Cab Sauv are both distinctive and intense. Shiraz is aged in new American oak, Cab Sauv in mostly French oak. Reserve Shiraz was added in 1999 and a Reserve Cab Sauv has been made since 2000; both are more full-on with greater extract and structure. A Sparkling Shiraz is also made. (PW)
● **Cabernet Sauvignon**★★★ £D   Reserve★★★ £D
● **Shiraz**★★★ £D   Reserve★★★★ £E

HENSCHKE   Eden Valley   www.henschke.com.au   *UK stockists:* **L&W,** JNi, NYg, WSc, Wai, Las
The Hill of Grace vineyard includes a parcel of vines that date in part from the 1860s. Mount Edelstone is arguably more consistent, with more pepper and spice character. Cyril Henschke Cab Sauv now includes Merlot and Cab Franc. All are very ageworthy. Abbott's Prayer is based on Merlot and like the Grenache-dominated Johann's Garden, is immediately drinkable yet deep and concentrated. Whites now show quality across several different varieties. (PW)
● **Shiraz** Hill of Grace✪✪✪✪✪ £H   Mount Edelstone★★★★★ £E
● **Cabernet** Cyril Henschke★★★★ £F   ● **Abbott's Prayer**★★★★ £E
● **Henry's Seven**★★★ £C   ● **Grenache/Mourvèdre/Shiraz** Johann's Garden★★★ £C
O **Chardonnay** Croft★★★ £D   O **Semillon** Louis★★★ £C   O **Riesling** Julius★★ £C

HEWITSON   www.hewitson.com.au   *UK stockists:* **FMV,** BBR, ACh, The, Sel
Accomplished range of wines. Beyond an intense, powerfully flavoured if broad Riesling are four fine reds. Miss Harry Dry Grown & Ancient is from old-vine Grenache, Shiraz and Mourvèdre. The top wine is a superb Mourvèdre from probably the oldest vineyard (planted 1853) of this variety in the world. (PW)
● **Shiraz** Ned & Henry's Barossa Valley★★★ £C   L'Oizeau McLaren Vale★★★ £D
● **Mourvèdre** Old Garden Barossa Valley★★★★ £D
● **Miss Harry** Dry Grown & Ancient★★ £C   O **Riesling** Eden Valley★★ £C

HILLSTOWE   Adelaide Hills   www.hillstowe.com.au   *UK stockists:* **D&D,** Lwt
Buxton labels indicate a McLaren Vale origin while Udy's Mill is Adelaide Hills. Pinot is at the ripe end of the spectrum but is intense and stylish, while Chardonnay has a cool, citrusy vigour. Mary's Hundred Shiraz includes some 100-year-old McLaren Vale fruit. Rich and deeply characterful. (PW)
● **Shiraz** Mary's Hundred★★★★ £C   Buxton★★ £B   ● **Pinot Noir** Udy's Mill★★★ £C
O **Pinot Gris** Scrub Block★ £B   O **Chardonnay** Udy's Mill★★ £C

HOLLICK   Coonawarra   www.hollick.com   *UK stockists:* **Sec,** JNi, ACh, NYg
First-rate producer that shows what Coonawarra is all about across a range of varieties. Top reds add refinement and complexity with age. Tempranillo is being developed and an intensely berryish Sparkling Merlot, a Pinot Noir/Chardonnay sparkler are also produced. (PW)
● **Cabernet Sauvignon** Ravenswood★★★★ £D   ● **Shiraz** Wilgha★★★ £C
● **Merlot** Neilson's Block★★★ £D   ● **Cabernet Sauvignon/Merlot**★★★ £B
● **Pinot Noir**★★★ £B   O **Chardonnay** Reserve★★★ £B

JACOB'S CREEK/ORLANDO   Barossa Valley   *UK stockists:* **PRc,** AAA
The success of a single brand, namely Jacob's Creek, seems to have swallowed the image of the parent company here. Increasingly Orlando labels are giving way to the expanding Jacob's Creek range. Riesling has long been a strength here. Jacob's Creek Limited Release Chardonnay from Padthway and Limited Release Shiraz/Cabernet

287

AUSTRALIA

(from Barossa and Coonawarra fruit respectively) stand out. (PW)
- **Shiraz** Lawson's Padthaway★★★ £D ● **Cabernet** Jacaranda Ridge★★ £E
- **Shiraz/Cabernet** Jacob's Creek Limited Release★★★ £E
- O **Chardonnay** Jacob's Creek Limited Release★★★ £C O **Riesling** Steingarten★★ £C

JAMIESONS RUN Coonawarra www.jamiesonsrun.com.au *UK stockists:* **BBI**, AAA
Major commercial label offering rather light and simple wines as well as some significantly better individual vineyard bottlings. McShane's Block Shiraz and Alexander's Block Cabernet show concentrated fruit, and reasonable depth. O'Dea's Cabernet, was first made in 2000. A rich, powerful Jamieson's Run Winemaker's Reserve is the flagship wine based on Cab Sauv. (PW)
- **Winemakers Reserve**★★★ £E
- **Shiraz** McShane's Block★★★ £D ● **Cabernet** Alexander's Block★★★ £D

KATNOOK ESTATE Coonawarra *UK stockists:* **Frt, Bib**, Tan, WWs, NYg
Reds characterised by their intense, concentrated, ripe (often very ripe), sweet fruit and tight structures when young. Whites can show good intensity too but typically lack subtlety and flair. Some attractive, softly textured fruit-driven wines for early consumption have been made under a second label, Riddoch. (PW)
Katnook Estate:
- **Cabernet Sauvignon**★★ £C Odyssey★★★ £E ● **Merlot**★★ £C
- **Shiraz**★★ £C Prodigy★★★ £E O **Chardonnay**★★ £C
Riddoch:
- **Shiraz**★ £B O **Chardonnay**★ £B

KILIKANOON Clare Valley *UK stockists:* **THt**, JNi, Rae, NYg, UnC, P&S
Shiraz is a star, showing off the regional characteristics superbly in both Oracle and Covenant versions. Cab Sauv shows both its orgins and the style and balance typical of the wines here. Riesling has deep fruit intensity if not always the structure of Clare's finest. New is Medley, a very stylish blend of Grenache, Shiraz and Mourvèdre. (PW)
- **Shiraz** Oracle★★★★ £C Covenant★★★★ £C ● **Grenache** Prodigal★★★ £C
- **Cabernet Sauvignon** Blocks Road★★★★ £C ● **Medley**★★★ £C
- O **Riesling** Morts Block★★ £B

KNAPPSTEIN Clare Valley www.knappsteinwines.com.au *UK stockists:* **LNa**, Odd
Reliable varietals remain moderately priced and widely available but there is now a greater emphasis on Shiraz. Premium wines include very promsing new Single Vineyard wines. A sparkling Shiraz, rather unnervingly called Chainsaw, has also been introduced. (PW)
- **Cabernet Sauvignon** Enterprise★★ £C Single Vineyard★★★ £D
- **Shiraz** Enterprise★★ £C ● **Cabernet/Merlot**★ £B
- O **Semillon/Sauvignon Blanc**★★ £B O **Gewürztraminer** Dry Style★★ £B
- O **Riesling** Hand Picked★★ £B Single Vineyard★★★ £C

LAKE BREEZE www.lakebreeze.com.au *UK stockists:* **THt**, UnC, F&M, Nid, NYg, Rae, Sel
One of the emerging quality producers from Langhorne Creek. The reds are very competently made, Bernoota is from Shiraz and Cab Sauv with good complexity, Cab Sauv is of similar quality. Winemaker's Selection Cab Sauv and Shiraz, made in the best years, are more oaky and concentrated. (PW)
- **Cabernet Sauvignon**★★★ £C ● **Cabernet/Shiraz** Bernoota★★★ £C
- **Shiraz** Winemaker's Selection★★★ £D

LEASINGHAM Clare Valley www.leasingham-wines.com.au *UK stockists:* **Cst**, AAA
Simple and consistent range. The Classic Clare wines are the most exciting, high in alcohol but packed full of rich, ripe fruit and abundant new oak. Reds deserve four or five years ageing. Riesling is good with excellent limey, mineral intensity to the Bin 7. Classic Clare Riesling is made in a tighter, more ageworthy style. (PW)
- **Shiraz** Classic Clare★★★ £E Bin 61★★ £B ● **Cabernet** Classic Clare★★★ £E
- O **Riesling** Bin 7★★ £B ● **Sparkling Shiraz** Classic Clare★★ £C

LECONFIELD Coonawarra www.leconfield.com.au *UK stockists:* **Eno**, Nid, Hrd
288 The leading wine is the Cabernet, it includes a little Merlot, Cab Franc and Petit Verdot. Most other wines are

New entries have producer's name underlined

100% varietal. All show archetypal Coonawarra character and fruit intensity when on form. The 2002 reds and whites show what is possible. (PW)

● Cabernet★★★★ £D ● Merlot★★★ £D ● Shiraz★★★★ £D
○ Chardonnay★★★ £B ○ Riesling Old Vines★★ £B

PETER LEHMANN Barossa Valley   UK stockists: **PLh**, Odd, WSc, Wai, Las
Peter Lehmann is a Barossa institution and a consistently sound bet for accessible, fruit-rich and well-structured Barossa reds. Stonewell Shiraz is released with five years' age. Mentor, is Cabernet-based, GSM blends Grenache, Shiraz and Mourvèdre. A powerful, ageworthy Reserve Riesling from Eden Valley is the best of the whites. Clancy's red is an everday Barossa blend. (PW)

● Shiraz Barossa★★ £B Eight Songs★★★★ £E Stonewell★★★★★ £E
● Mentor★★★★ £D ● GSM★★ £B ● Grenache Barossa★★ £B
○ Riesling Reserve Eden Valley★★★ £C ○ Semillon Reserve Barossa★★★ £C

LENSWOOD VINEYARDS   UK stockists: **McK**, UnC, Hrd
Good whites include Sauvignon Blanc, one of Australia's best; taut, attractively herbal, subtly oaked Semillon as well as powerful, oaky, citrus and melon Chardonnay. A complex, richly textured Pinot Noir is ripe and intense. Palatine is a blend of Cab Sauv, with a cool fruit complexity but ripe tannins and good ageing potential. (PW)

● Pinot Noir★★★ £D ● Palatine★★★ £D ○ Chardonnay★★★ £C
○ Semillon★★★ £B ○ Sauvignon Blanc★★★ £B ○ Gewürztraminer★★ £C

LINDEMANS Coonawarra & Padthaway   www.southcorp.com.au   UK stockists: **ScE**, AAA
In Coonawarra, Lindemans makes a trio of decent reds which lack the depth of the best examples of the region. Pyrus is a Bordeaux blend, St George a Cab Sauv and Limestone Ridge a Shiraz/Cabernet. Good value is to be had in the Padthaway wines, particularly the Reserve Chardonnay with its pronounced barrel-fermentation character. (PW)

● Pyrus Coonawarra★★★ £D ● Cabernet Sauvignon St George★★ £D
● Shiraz/Cabernet Limestone Ridge★★ £D ● Shiraz Padthaway Reserve★★ £C
○ Chardonnay Limestone Coast★ £B Padthaway Reserve★★ £C

MAGLIERI McLaren Vale   www.maglieri.com.au   UK stockists: **BBI**
Now owned by Beringer Blass. Reds, show intense ripe fruit and well-integrated oak. Steve Maglieri Shiraz is structured, and oaky and needs the best part of a decade's ageing. Semillon and Chardonnay are both well crafted and better than is typical for McLaren Vale. (PW)

● Shiraz★★★ £C Steve Maglieri★★★ £E ● Cabernet Sauvignon★★ £B
● Merlot★ £B ○ Chardonnay★ £B ○ Semillon★ £B

MAJELLA Coonawarra   www.majellawines.com.au   UK stockists: **All**, Odd, Fsp, FFW
A label gaining in recognition and importance. Cab Sauv and Shiraz make up the blend of a very impressive, rich and concentrated flagship, Malleea. Varietal Shiraz and Cab Sauv are in a similar mould with potent berry fruit and evident oak. Sparkling Shiraz is also made but you may need to visit the winery to get your hands on it. (PW)

● Malleea★★★★ £F ● Cabernet Sauvignon★★★ £D ● Shiraz★★★★ £D

CHARLES MELTON   UK stockists: **Lib**, JNi, Vne, ACh, BBR, Hrd, P&S
One of the key figures in the revival of the Barossa. Shiraz is arguably the best wine made but a varietal Grenache (from old bush vines) is always very ripe and sweet-fruited. Nine Popes is a blend of Shiraz, Grenache and Mourvèdre. The exotic Sotto di Ferro is made from dried Pedro Ximenez and Muscadelle grapes. New is a Kirsche Vineyard Shiraz. (PW)

● Nine Popes★★★★ £E ● Grenache★★★ £C
● Shiraz★★★★ £E Laura★★ £D ● Cabernet Sauvignon★★★ £E
◉ Rose of Virginia★★ £C ● Sparkling Red★★★v£E ● Sotto di Ferro★★★ £F

GEOFF MERRILL McLaren Vale   UK stockists: **Eve**, GWW, HWC
One of the great characters of Australian wine Geoff Merrill makes wines which at their best achieve a certain elegance and subtlety. New Henley Shiraz is being sold at a stratospheric price but does have impressive depth and complexity.. Top labels are released with extended bottle-age. Mount Hurtle label ofers upfront, simple

AUSTRALIA

fruity wines. (PW)

● **Shiraz** Reserve★★ £D   ● **Cabernet Sauvignon** Reserve★★ £D
○ **Chardonnay**★ £B   Reserve★★ £C

MITOLO   McLaren Vale   www.mitolowines.com.au   *UK stockists:* **Lib**, L&W, Lay, NYg
Formed in 2000 remarkably high standards have been achieved from the outset. Three differing Shirazes are notable for their depth, extract and complexity. Serpico, a Cab Sauv made from dried grapes is very concentrated and powerful without any raisiny character. (PW)

● **Shiraz** Reiver Barossa Valley★★★ £D   Savitar McLaren Vale★★★★ £E
● **Shiraz** Jester McLaren Vale★★ £C   G.A.M McLaren Vale★★★★ £E
● **Cabernet Sauvignon** Serpico McLaren Vale★★★★ £E

MOUNT HORROCKS   Clare Valley   *UK stockists:* **Lib**, ACh, WSc, Hrd
Classy range of wines which all have good structure and ripeness, coming from unirrigated vines. All the whites show good weight and intensity and need a little ageing. Cabernet/Merlot is ripely berryish. Shiraz has a hint of the Clare mineral, earth character. A sweet version of Riesling, Cordon Cut, is made from grapes de-hydrated and dried on the vine. (PW)

○ **Riesling** Watervale★★★ £C   Cordon Cut★★★ £D   ○ **Semillon** Watervale★★★ £C
○ **Chardonnay**★★ £C   ● **Cabernet/Merlot**★★ £D   ● **Shiraz**★★★ £D

MOUNTADAM   Eden Valley   *UK stockists:* **VCq**, JNi, N&P, Amp, Cam, Hrd
High-profile, often overhyped winery, now owned by LMVH. Chardonnay has some style and structure, while Riesling has had better structure of late than previously. The leafy Red is a blend of Cab Sauv and Merlot. Red berry-fruited Pinot Noir can age well. DW, is rich, composed and seductive. (PW)

● **Shiraz** DW★★★★ £D   ● **Pinot Noir**★★★ £C   ● **The Red**★★★ £D
○ **Chardonnay**★★★ £C   ○ **Riesling**★★ £B

NEPENTHE   Adelaide Hills   *UK stockists:* **Str, GWW**, Odd, WSc, WTs, Wai
Wines from ripe yet cool Lenswood fruit. All the wines have excellent fruit, texture and balance. Zinfandel and Tempranillo are interesting and unusual for the area. Cabernet/Merlot blend the Fugue, has been joined by The Rogue, (Merlot, Cab Sauv and Shiraz). Whites are intense and expressive. Most affordable are unusual Tryst red and white. (PW)

● **Pinot Noir**★★★ £C   ● **Zinfandel**★★★ £D   ● **Tempranillo**★★ £C
● **The Fugue**★★★ £C   ● **The Rogue**★★ £B   ○ **Chardonnay**★★★ £B
○ **Riesling**★★★ £B   ○ **Semillon**★★★ £B   ○ **Sauvignon Blanc**★★ £B

PARKER COONAWARRA ESTATE   *UK stockists:* **C&B**, Sel, Las
The focus of production is a single premium wine, a Bordeaux-like approach that is also reflected in the provocative name, Terra Rossa First Growth. It is based on Cab Sauv and includes Merlot and Cab Franc and is aged in 100% new French oak. Second wine, Terra Rossa Cab Sauv has recently been only a shade behind. (PW)

● **Terra Rossa First Growth**★★★★ £F
● **Cabernet Sauvignon** Terra Rossa★★★ £E

PENFOLDS   Barossa Valley   www.penfolds.com.au   *UK stockists:* **ScE**, AAA
Part of Southcorp. Grange, Australia's most consistently great wine over five decades, is the pinnacle of production. RWT, 100 per cent Barossa Shiraz aged in French oak, has good drive and intensity. Top Cabernet is fleshy, blackberry, uncompromisely structured Bin 707 which like Grange is aged in American oak. Bin 138 Old Vine Shiraz/Grenache/Mourvèdre and long-established Bin 389 are best of other Bin-labelled reds. Yattarna, the top Chardonnay, is a classic rich, concentrated Australian expression of the grape. Koonunga Hill and Rawson's Retreat brands are cheaper brands. (PW)

● **Grange**✪✪✪✪✪ £H   ● **Cabernet Sauvignon** Bin 407★★★ £C   Bin 707★★★★ £F
● **Shiraz** RWT★★★★ £F   Magill Estate★★★ £E   St Henri★★★ £E
○ **Chardonnay** Adelaide Hills★★ £C   Bin 98A★★★ £E   Yattarna★★★★ £G

PENLEY ESTATE   Coonawarra   www.penley.com.au   *UK stockists:* **L&W**, NYg, N&P
Small but consistently high-quality range of wines. The style is for rich, ripe, smooth wines with lush fruit and unobtrusive tannins but with good ageing potential. Cab Sauv Reserve is consistently impressive while Ausvetia

New entries have producer's name underlined

is a pricey flagship Shiraz. Phoenix and Hyland are lighter, more forward examples. (PW)
- **Cabernet Sauvignon** Reserve★★★ £D   Phoenix★★ £C   ● **Merlot★★** £C
- **Shiraz** Ausvetia★★★ £E   Hyland★★ £B   ● **Shiraz/Cabernet★★** £C

PETALUMA   Adelaide Hills   *UK stockists:* **LNa**,Tan, Odd,Vne, F&M, Sel, FFW
Brian Croser conceived wines that are subtle, intense and ageworthy. All the wines are site-specific from classic, tightly structured, minerally Riesling to brilliant, individual Tiers Chardonnay. Complex berry-fruited Coonawarra (Cabernet, Merlot) always reveals greater concentration with age. Croser is an elegant traditional-method sparkling wine. New are a promising Shiraz (since 2001) and Viognier (since 2002). Also blended Bridgewater Mill 3 Districts wines. (PW)
- **Coonawarra★★★** £D   ● **Merlot★★★** £D   O **Riesling** Hanlin Hill★★★★ £B
- O **Chardonnay** Piccadilly Valley★★★★ £C   Tiers★★★★★ £F   O **Croser★★★** £C

PIKES   Clare Valley   www.pikeswines.com.au   *UK stockists:* **L&S**, NYg
One of the most reliable names in Clare with full, flavoursome wines across the range. Both Shiraz and Cabernet show good Clare character with a mineral, earth influence in the rich berry fruit. Decent value too though occasional very good Reserves are more pricey. Also made are Sauvignon/Semillon, Sangiovese (Premio) and Viognier (from 2001). (PW)
- O **Riesling★★** £B   O **Chardonnay★★★** £B   ● **Shiraz★★★** £B
- ● **Shiraz/Grenache/Mourvèdre★★** £B   ● **Cabernet Sauvignon★★★** £B

PRIMO ESTATE   Adelaide   *UK stockists:* **AWA**, NYg, ACh, N&P
An exceptional range from the hot Adelaide plains. Richly textured, exuberant Cabernet/Merlot (mostly Cabernet) uses partially dried grapes and is best with 5-10 years'. La Magia is late-harvested, mostly Riesling. Vibrant fleshy Sparkling Red is from Shiraz. Il Briccone, a Shiraz/Sangiovese blend and zesty Colombard white, La Biondina are more modestly priced. (PW)
- ● **Cabernet Sauvignon/Merlot** Joseph★★★ £D   ● **Sparkling Red★★★** £E
- ● **Shiraz/Sangiovese** Il Briccone★ £B   O **Riesling** La Magia Joseph★★★ £C

REYNELLA/REYNELL   McLaren Vale   *UK stockists:* **Cst,** TPg, C&B, N&P,Wai
Historic property now headquarters for Hardy Wine Company group. From a wealth of old-vine McLaren Vale material deep, intense, muscular wines are made. Open fermenters and old basket presses are utilised for reds of great depth, complexity and structure yet with ripe, smooth tannins. Chardonnay is bold and oaky. (PW)
- ● **Cabernet Sauvignon** Basket Pressed★★★ £D   ● **Shiraz** Basket Pressed★★★ £D
- ● **Cabernet Sauvignon/Merlot** Basket Pressed★★★ £D

ROCKFORD   Barossa Valley   www.rockfordwines.com.au   *UK stockists:* **AHW**, P&S, HoM
Rockford wines still taste like true classics. Basket Press Shiraz shows the depth and richness that the best old-vine Barossa fruit delivers with ease. Riesling is picked late and a very full-flavoured example. Moppa Springs is Grenache-based with some Shiraz and Mourvèdre. The Sparkling Shiraz is one of the best going. (PW)
- ● **Shiraz** Basket Press★★★★ £D   ● **Cabernet Sauvignon★★** £C
- ● **Sparkling Shiraz** Black Shiraz★★★★ £F   ● **Moppa Springs★★** £C
- O **Semillon** Local Growers★★ £C   O **Riesling** Eden Valley★★★ £B

ROSEMOUNT (MCLAREN VALE)   www.rosemountestates.com   *UK stockists:* **ScE**,AAA
Rosemount South Australian quality outpost. Includes rich, harmonious Balmoral Syrah with an extra dimension over most other Australian examples. Show Reserve Cabernet is from Coonawarra while Show Reserve Shiraz comes from McLaren Vale and Langhorne Creek. Traditional is a Bordeaux blend aged in American oak; characterful GSM is Grenache, Shiraz and Mourvèdre. All wines show lush fruit and oak, good depth and fine tannins, needing only 5 or 6 years'. Also see Rosemount (under New South Wales & Queensland). (PW)
- ● **Syrah** Balmoral★★★★★ £F   ● **Shiraz** Show Reserve★★★ £C   ● **GSM★★★** £C
- ● **Cabernet Sauvignon** Show Reserve★★★ £C   ● **Traditional★★★** £C

ST HALLETT   Barossa Valley   *UK stockists:* **LNa**,AWA, Por, HoM,WSc
Leading estate in Barossa revival now making sound but less exciting wines. Old Block Shiraz recently improved after dip in form while irregular Eden Valley Riesling can be intense, weighty, if slightly coarse. Big

volumes in blended Gamekeeper's Reserve (red) and Poacher's Blend (white). Also barrique-fermented Blackwell Semillon (since 2001) and GST - Touriga (Nacional), Grenache, Shiraz - from 2002. (PW)
- ● **Shiraz** Faith★ £B Blackwell★★★ £C Old Block★★★★ £E
- ○ **Riesling** Eden Valley★★ £B

SALTRAM Barossa Valley www.beringerblass.com.au *UK stockists:* **BBI**, NYg
Beringer Blass owned since 96 and fortunes somewhat restored under Nigel Dolan. Occasional great bottles from the late 50s, 60s and 70s can still be unearthed from Australian cellars. Recently wines have greater richness and depth. Ageworthy Metala Original Plantings from 100-year-old vines. Mamre Brook now offers good value, Pepperjack is a second label. (PW)
- ● **Shiraz** No. 1 Reserve★★★ £D Metala Original Plantings (Black Label)★★★ £D
- ● **Shiraz** Mamre Brook★★ £B ● **Shiraz/Cabernet** Metala (White Label)★ £B
- ● **Cabernet Sauvignon** Mamre Brook★★ £B ○ **Chardonnay** Mamre Brook★ £B

SEPPELT Barossa Valley www.seppelt.com.au *UK stockists:* **ScE**
Seppelt's historic Seppeltsfield winery is centre for some marvellous intense, powerful Australian fortified wines. Outstanding examples include 'sherries' Amontillado DP 116, Show Fino DP 117 and Show Oloroso DP 38; and Show 'port' Tawny DP 90. Para Liqueur Port is produced in two versions, non-vintage and a 100-year-old version. From Rutherglen come outstanding Muscat (Show Reserve DP 63) and Tokay (Show Reserve DP 57). Also see Seppelt Great Western (Victoria & Tasmania). (PW)

SHAW & SMITH Adelaide Hills *UK stockists:* **Lib**, Tan, Vne, ACh, FFW, Hrd, Wai
Now estate-based with stunning new winery. Success with distinctive Sauvignon followed by deep, complex and ageworthy Reserve Chardonnay replaced by single vineyard M3 (since 2000). Also stylish varietal Merlot since 2001 (made since 99, previously only under second label, Incognito). New are Riesling and a superb, classy Shiraz (especially 2002). (PW)
Shaw & Smith:
- ○ **Chardonnay** M3 Vineyard★★★★ £D Unoaked★★ £B
- ○ **Sauvignon Blanc**★★ £B ● **Merlot**★★★ £D
Incognito:
- ○ **Riesling**★ £B ○ **Chardonnay**★★ £B ● **Merlot**★ £B

STONEHAVEN Padthaway www.stonehavenvineyards.com.au *UK stockists:* **Cst**
State-of-the-art winery processes fruit from Constellation group's Limestone Coast vineyards. Top tier is Limited Vineyard Release for intense, powerful Chardonnay that needs age, and two concentrated, extracted reds that both need 8-10 years'. Second varietal (Limestone Coast) range includes excellent well-defined Chardonnay. Coonawarra Cab Sauv and Padthaway Chardonnay best of Stepping Stone range. (PW)
- ○ **Chardonnay** Limestone Coast★★★ £B Limited Vineyard Release★★★ £C
- ● **Cabernet Sauvignon** Limestone Coast★★ £C Limited Vineyard Release★★★ £D
- ● **Shiraz** Limestone Coast★★ £C Limited Vineyard Release★★★ £D

THE LANE WINE COMPANY Adelaide Hills www.thelane.com.au *UK stockists:* **Cap**, Amp
Estate-based wines (previously as Ravenswood Lane) include exciting lush, peppery, fleshy Shiraz and deep, lemony Chardonnay. Also Starvedog Lane wines in collaboration with Hardys. Vibrant, nettly Sauvignon contrast with barrel-fermented The Lane version with more breadth. Cool, complex, but ripe Starvedog Cabernet and good Shiraz; also Merlot, an unwooded 'No Oak' Chardonnay, and a traditional-method sparkler. (PW)
The Lane:
- ● **Shiraz** Reunion★★★ £E ● **Cabernet Sauvignon** 19th Meeting★★★ £E
- ○ **Sauvignon Blanc** Gathering★★ £C ○ **Chardonnay** Beginning★★★ £C
Stavedog Lane:
- ● **Cabernet Sauvignon**★★★ £C ● **Shiraz**★★ £C
- ○ **Chardonnay**★★ £C ○ **Sauvignon Blanc**★★ £B

TIN SHED Eden Valley *UK stockists:* **DMT**, FFW, Cam
New small Eden/Barossa operation. Wines are made without added yeasts, enzymes or acidity and are vibrant, fruit-intense and expressive. Wild Bunch Riesling has exaggerated limey, toasty aromas and bursts with flavour. Stylish Melting Pot Shiraz has exuberant very berryish fruit while foot-trodden Single Wire Shiraz has fabulous fruit and

New entries have producer's name underlined

impressive depth and length. Also made is Three Vines Mataro Shiraz & Grenache. (PW)
● **Shiraz** Melting Pot★★★ £C Single Wire★★★★ £D
○ **Riesling** Wild Bunch Eden Valley★★ £C

TORBRECK Barossa Valley UK stockists: **HBJ**, Bal, NYg, Rae, BBR, UnC, Hrd, P&S, Las
Genuinely outstanding wines (from very old unirrigated vineyards) with breadth and extract other Aussie
blockbusters lack. Sensational top wine Runrig (Shiraz with 3% Viognier) has great depth, class and dimension.
More open, perfumed Descendant (more Viognier) contrasts with tighter, more ageworthy The Factor (100%
Shiraz). Also stylish blend Struie (from 2001) while Juveniles and The Steading are blends of Grenache, Shiraz
and Mourvèdre. New white, VMR is Viognier, Marsanne, Roussanne. There's good fruit in cheaper
Woodcutters red (Shiraz) and white (Semillon). (PW)
● **Runrig**✪✪✪✪✪ £H ● **The Factor**★★★★★ £G ● **Descendant**★★★★ £G
● **The Struie**★★★ £D ● **The Steading**★★★ £D ● **Juveniles**★★★ £D
● **Woodcutter's Red**★★ £C ○ **Woodcutter's White**★ £C

TWO HANDS www.twohandswines.com UK stockists: **All**, P&S, Nid
Now changed from acclaimed first releases but standards still high. Most wines have both style, *typicité* and an
intense fruit expression. Lily's Garden McLaren Vale Shiraz is most consistently fine red. Also very intensely
flavoured Riesling. In addition to rated wines are Deer in the Headlights Shiraz (Barossa) and Samantha's
Garden Shiraz (Clare Valley) while new (2003) are Brilliant Disguise Moscato and Yesterday's Hero (Barossa
Grenache). Flagship Shiraz Ares, since 2001. (PW)
● **Shiraz** Lily's Garden McLaren Vale★★★★ £E Angel's Share McLaren Vale★★★ £C
● **Shiraz** Bad Impersonator Single Vineyard Barossa Valley★★★ £E
● **Shiraz/Grenache** Brave Faces Barossa Valley★★★ £D
● **Shiraz/Cabernet Sauvignon** The Bull and the Bear Barossa Valley★★★ £E

ULITHORNE McLaren Vale www. ullithorne.com.au UK stockists: **Gun**, Odd
Revived McLaren Vale vineyard (under conversion to organic practices) currently producing a single Shiraz, Frux
Frugis. Oak-aged for 18 months, it reveals deep pepper, rich blackberry and black plum fruit and oak together with
impressive flesh, intensity and length. Drink with 5–15 years' age. (PW)
● **Shiraz** Frux Frugis★★★★ £E

VERITAS/ROLF BINDER Barossa Valley www.veritaswinery.com UK stockists: **Sec**, L&W, NYg, Hrd
Much-lauded Barossa star. Reds have lost some of their oomph and richness of late but are still deep, powerful,
extracted. Best are Heysen and Hanisch Shirazes that need at least 8-10 years' age. Pressings (subtitled Binder's
Bull's Blood) has rich black plum and berry fruit, while Heinrich is more backward, extracted. One or two
recent reds marred by odd musty and/or menthol-like characters. Also inexpensive Retro 55 red and white. (PW)
● **Shiraz** Heysen Vineyard★★★★ £C ● **Shiraz/Mourvèdre** Pressings★★★ £C
● **Shiraz/Mourvèdre/Grenache** Heinrich★★★ £C ● **Cabernet Sauvignon/Merlot**★★★ £B
● **Shiraz/Grenache** Christa-Rolf★★ £B ○ **Semillon** Christa-Rolf★★ £B

WAKEFIELD Clare Valley www. wakefieldwines.com.au UK stockists: **Str**, Odd, OzW
Family-owned Taylor's (as it is known in Australia) is the Clare's biggest producer. Best are the premium St Andrew's
varietals including intense toasty, limey Riesling with splendid depth after 5 years', and ripe, full old-style
Chardonnay. Shiraz has a classic Clare berry/mineral stamp while Cab Sauv has terrific complexity and dimension.
Also ripe, fruit-intense Estate reds, best with at least 3–4 years' age. Budget label is Promised Land. (PW)
○ **Riesling** Estate★★ £B St Andrews★★★ £D
○ **Chardonnay** Estate★ £B St Andrews★★★ £D
● **Shiraz** Estate★★ £B St Andrews★★★ £E ● **Merlot** Estate★★ £B
● **Cabernet Sauvignon** Estate★★ £B St Andrews★★★★ £E

WENDOUREE Clare Valley UK stockists: NYg
Cult producer of tiny volumes of massive uncompromising, extracted and tannic reds - dense, earthy
impenetrable fruit when young but complex and compelling after 20 years or more. Shiraz/Mataro (Mourvèdre)
and Shiraz/Malbec (both mostly Shiraz) together with varietal Shiraz, are perhaps more consistent than the
Cabernet-based reds. Above all a cellaring investment. (PW)
● **Shiraz**★★★★ £F ● **Shiraz/Mataro**★★★★ £F ● **Shiraz/Malbec**★★★★ £F
● **Cabernet/Malbec**★★★ £F ● **Cabernet Sauvignon**★★★★ £F

South Australia

AUSTRALIA

WIRRA WIRRA McLaren Vale www.wirra.com.au   *UK stockists:* **HBJ**, WSc, P&S
Well regarded high quality wines but missing flair and natural expression. Flagship Cabernet Sauvignon, The Angelus, and Shiraz, RSW but also small volume premium Vineyard Series reds made in exceptional vintages: impressive Cabernet (Penley), Shiraz (Chook Block) and Grenache (Allawah). More affordable are Church Block and Original Blend. Whites are flavoursome but don't match reds for quality. Also sparkling wine, The Cousins and Scrubby Rise brand. (PW)
● **Cabernet Sauvignon** The Angelus★★★ £D ● **Grenache/Shiraz** Original Blend★★ £B
● **Shiraz** McLaren Vale★★ £C RSW★★★ £D ● **Grenache** McLaren Vale★★ £C

WYNNS Coonawarra www.wynns.com.au   *UK stockists:* **ScE**, Maj, Odd, Nid, BBR, Sel, WSc
Famous Coonawarra colossus with 900 ha. Magnificent rich, powerful John Riddoch Cabernet, based on unirrigated vines in the heart of region, needs 10 years' or more. Michael Shiraz at similar level but more oaky. Black Label Cabernet now big volume but retains blackcurrant/blackberry fruit intensity of old. Impressive well-priced Chardonnay and Riesling too. (PW)
● **Cabernet Sauvignon** Black Label★★★ £C John Riddoch★★★★★ £F
● **Shiraz**★★ £B Michael★★★★ £F ● **Cabernet/Shiraz/Merlot**★ £B
O **Chardonnay**★★ £B O **Riesling**★ £B

YALUMBA Barossa Valley   *UK stockists:* **Neg**, BBR, WSc, F&M, Hrd, P&S, Sel, Wai
Big but family-owned for richly oaky old-vine Barossa Shiraz, Octavius and suave, flattering vanilla-streaked Signature. New is MGS (Barossa Mourvèdre, Grenache, Shiraz). Viognier pioneers in state and better than most. Y is inexpensive varietals series; basics are simple Oxford Landing wines. Other wineries include Eden Valley estates Pewsey Vale (for revitalised Riesling, especially Contours) and Heggies (stylish whites); also Jansz for cool, well-defined Tasmanian sparkler. Excellent Mesh Riesling (with Jeffrey Grosset) almost Pfalz-like. Smith & Hooper (from Wrattonbully) includes ambitious Limited Edition Merlot. (PW)
Yalumba:
● **Shiraz** Octavius★★★ £F ● **Cabernet/Shiraz/Merlot** Mawson's★★ £B
● **Shiraz/Viognier** Handpicked★★★ £C ● **Cabernet Sauvignon** Menzies★★★ £D
● **Cabernet/Shiraz** Signature★★★ £D O **Chardonnay** Adelaide Hills★★★ £C
O **Viognier** Eden Valley★★ £C Virgilius★★★ £D O **Jansz** Vintage★★★ £C
Heggies:
O **Chardonnay**★★ £B O **Riesling**★★ £B O **Viognier**★★ £C ● **Merlot**★★ £C
Pewsey Vale:
O **Riesling**★★ £B The Contours★★★ £C
Grosset - Hill-Smith:
O **Riesling** Mesh★★★ £C

ZEMA ESTATE Coonawarra www.zema.com.au   *UK stockists:* **MSd**, Lwt
Wines that express much of the best of Coonawarra with dense, powerful fruit lent a little more structure from oak-ageing. Also lusher, oakier Family Selection Cabernet. If slightly less good in cooler years like 1997, very good in 2000, 99 and 98. Cluny, a lighter, softer Bordeaux blend is the most accessible. Also Family Selection Shiraz from 2000 vintage. (PW)
● **Cabernet Sauvignon**★★★ £C Family Selection★★★ £D
● **Shiraz**★★★ £C ● **Cluny**★★ £C

Other wineries of note
Annie's Lane (Clare Valley), Cascabel (McLaren Vale), Chain of Ponds (Adelaide Hills), Chapel Hill (McLaren Vale), M Chapoutier Australia (Mount Benson), Charles Cimicky (Barossa Valley), Crabtree (Clare Valley), Ralph Fowler (Mount Benson), Hamilton (McLaren Vale), Haselgrove (McLaren Vale), Heathvale (Eden Valley), Trevor Jones (Barossa), McWilliams of Coonawarra (Coonawarra), Maxwell (McLaren Vale), Mitchell (Clare Valley), Mt Billy (Barossa Valley), Tatachilla (McLaren Vale), Three Rivers/Chris Ringland (Barossa Valley), Turkey Flat (Barossa Valley), Geoff Weaver (Adelaide Hills), Woodstock (McLaren Vale)

An in-depth profile of every producer can be found in Wine behind the label 2006

294

New entries have producer's name underlined

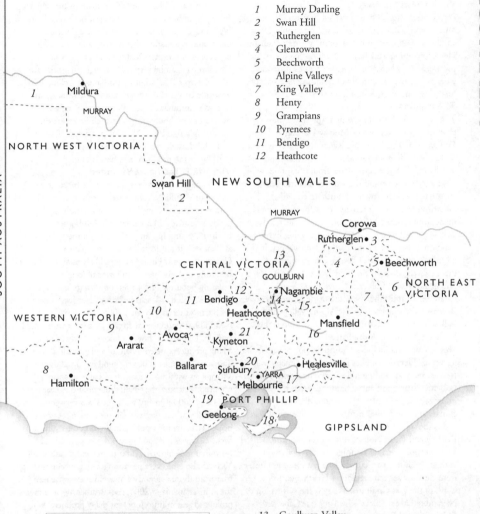

1   Murray Darling
2   Swan Hill
3   Rutherglen
4   Glenrowan
5   Beechworth
6   Alpine Valleys
7   King Valley
8   Henty
9   Grampians
10 Pyrenees
11 Bendigo
12 Heathcote

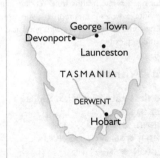

13 Goulburn Valley
14 Nagambie Lakes
15 Strathbogie Ranges
16 Upper Goulburn
17 Yarra Valley
18 Mornington Peninsula
19 Geelong
20 Sunbury
21 Macedon Ranges

AUSTRALIA

Background

Victoria offers a diversity of site and climate permutations arguably unequalled in Australia, while much more is being made of Tasmania's cool climatic conditions. As an example of an increasing regionality, Heathcote Shiraz and Tasmanian Pinot Noir – which previously only boasted isolated successes – are now emerging as two potentially outstanding regional styles following a mini-explosion in quality.

The regions

The North-West Victoria zone is the state's most productive - the regions of **Murray Darling** and **Swan Hill** are shared with the Big Rivers zone of New South Wales. Best wines are sound and inexpensive and usually much better equivalents from other bulk wine producing areas around the world. In North-East Victoria, aroud the towns of **Rutherglen** and **Glenrowan**, unique, intensely sweet fortified wines are made from raisined Muscat and Muscadelle (sold as Tokay) grapes - often subject to long ageing in hot conditions. Beyond a basic Rutherglen category, in ascending order, are the Classic, Grand and Rare quality levels. Robust, earthy reds are also made from Shiraz, Durif and Cabernet Sauvignon. Fine Chardonnay and Pinot Noir are made in much cooler **Beechworth**. Vineyards in the **Alpine Valleys** and **King Valley** (known for Italian varieties) extend into the lower reaches of the Australian Alps.

Western Victoria includes **Grampians** long famous for its Shiraz. Elevation makes for a cooler climate as is the case with the rolling hills of **Pyrenees** where Shiraz, Cabernet Sauvignon and Chardonnay can be impressive. The **Henty** region is not dissimilar in climate and soil to South Australia's Limestone Coast and is the source of the fine sparkling wines and Riesling and Pinot Noir of much promise. The Central Victoria zone is led by **Bendigo**, now synonymous with great Shiraz, particularly a new wave of examples from the now separate region of **Heathcote**. In the south of the vast **Goulburn Valley** is the sub-region of **Nagambie Lakes**. Shiraz is brilliant but Cabernet Sauvignon and Riesling as well as Marsanne and other white and red Rhône varieties are beginning to excel. Vineyards in the **Upper Goulburn** and **Strathbogie Ranges** are most suited to aromatic white varieties. The zone surrounding state capital, Melbourne is Port Phillip. **Yarra Valley** is the leading region and produces great examples of Pinot Noir and Chardonnay but also fine Bordeaux blends and Shiraz - the best are fruit-rich but softly textured and stylishly complex. There is also fine fizz. **Geelong** has a reputation for intense, powerful Shiraz, Pinot Noir and Chardonnay and the same theme is echoed in the cool **Mornington Peninsula** whose many small producers, though focusing on Pinot Noir and Chardonnay, can produce elegant, stylish Shiraz too. In **Sunbury,** and especially the higher-altitude **Macedon Ranges,** Shiraz and Cabernet-based blends are at the margins for achieving full ripeness but can be super in warmer years. Pinot Noir and Chardonnay have even more potential. Gippsland is a vast, cool zone with a few isolated pockets of vineyards. Quality from Pinot Noir or Chardonnay can be very high though quantities are scarce. Across Bass Strait in Tasmania the climate is generally cooler and wetter than in Victoria. Apart from the dominant Pipers Brook group there are dozens of tiny holdings from which tiny quantities of increasingly fine Pinot Noir are produced. Riesling and Chardonnay are also successful while premium sparkling wine production is flourishing.

Victoria & Tasmania Vintages

The Vintage Chart covers some of the most ageworthy styles but should be considered in conjunction with comments on style and ageing within individual producer entries. Many powerful, full-bodied red can be drunk young but an increasing number will not be at their best for at least 5 years. Top-quality Chardonnay and Pinot Noir are likely to show at their best only with 3-6 years'. In terms of longer-term cellaring potential, great premium Victorian Shiraz or Cabernet-based reds can improve for at least a decade. Of the most recent vintages, 2005 in Victoria was a plentiful harvest (a record crop in Australia) with a mild summer followed by hot conditions in early March. Many producers are confident of a high quality vintage. Tasmania promises to be very good too. In 2004 in Victoria, as with the other small eastern states, quantity bounced back after the small, drought-affected early harvest of 2003. Quality-wise, 2004 was very good in the Yarra Valley where heat early in the growing season helped facilitate full ripening in the Bordeaux varieties. Pinot Noir was less good here but very promising from Mornington Peninsula. Shiraz from Central and Western Victoria also looks very promising with concentrated ripe fruit from those vineyards that avoided excessive heat stress. In Tasmania in 2004, cool weather meant a much prolonged season (into June) for many producers with a struggle for ripeness and healthy fruit. Yet despite it being a difficult vintage, wines from producers who achieved full ripening could be very good – with good acidities and flavour complexity.

Wizard's Wishlist

Diverse first-rate Victorian Shiraz

CRAIGLEE ● Shiraz
DALWHINNIE ● Shiraz Moonambel
JASPER HILL ● Shiraz Georgia's Paddock
MITCHELTON ● Shiraz Print
MOUNT LANGHI GHIRAN ● Shiraz
PARINGA ESTATE ● Shiraz

SEPPELT GREAT WESTERN ● Show Sparkling Shiraz
SUMMERFIELD ● Shiraz Reserve
TAHBILK ● Shiraz 1860 Vines
YARRA YERING ● Shiraz Underhill

Victorian classics
CAMPBELLS O Rutherglen Tokay Rare Isabella
CHAMBERS ROSEWOOD O Rutherglen Grand Muscat
MOUNT LANGHI GHIRAN ● Cabernet/Merlot
MOUNT MARY ● Quintet
VIRGIN HILLS ● Virgin Hills
YARRA YERING Dry Red No. 1
YERINGBERG ● Dry Red

Top Victorian/Tasmanian Pinot Noir
BANNOCKBURN ● Pinot Noir Geelong
BASS PHILLIP ● Pinot Noir Reserve
BINDI ● Pinot Noir Original Vineyard
DIAMOND VALLEY ● Pinot Noir Estate
GIACONDA ● Pinot Noir
KOOYONG ● Pinot Noir Mornington Peninsula
STEFANO LUBIANA ● Pinot Noir Tasmania
PIPERS BROOK ● Pinot Noir Reserve Tasmania
STONIER ● Pinot Noir Reserve Mornington Peninsula

Whites with personality
COLDSTREAM HILLS
O Chardonnay Yarra Valley Reserve
DALWHINNIE O Chardonnay Moonambel
DELATITE O Gewürztrminer Deadman's Hill
GIACONDA O Nantua Les Deux
JASPER HILL O Riesling Georgia's Paddock
MÉTIER O Chardonnay Schoolhouse Vineyard
MITCHELTON
O Marsanne/Roussanne/Viognier Airstrip
PIPERS BROOK O Riesling Estate
TALTARNI O Clover Hill (sparkling)
YERINGBERG O Marsanne/Roussanne

Undervalued wines
BALGOWNIE ● Shiraz Bendigo
BEST'S ● Shiraz Great Western
R L BULLER & SON
O Rutherglen Tokay Premium Fine Old
DELATITE O Riesling
DROMANA ESTATE O Arneis i Garry Crittenden
MITCHELTON O Riesling Blackwood Park
MOUNT LANGHI GHIRAN ●
Shiraz/Grenache/Cabernet Billi Billi Creek
TAHBILK O Marsanne
TAMAR RIDGE O Riesling

Victoria & Tasmania/A-Z of producers

BAILEYS OF GLENROWAN Glenrowan www.beringerblass.com.au *UK stockists:* **BBI**, FFW
Beringer Blass-owned source of fortified Muscat and Tokay. Particularly rich, sweet examples with plenty of power and flavour if not the greatest elegance. Finest are Winemaker's Selection made in tiny quantities. Robust and gutsy Shirazes are more refined in recent vintages. (PW)
● Shiraz 1920 Block★★£C 1904 Block★★★£D ● Cabernet Sauvignon★ £B
O Liqueur Tokay Founder★★★£B O Liqueur Muscat Founder★★£B

BALGOWNIE Bendigo www.balgownie.com *UK stockists:* **Cap**, WRk, GGg
Recently returned to form and undergoing major vineyard expansion; the quality of recent releases of Shiraz and Cab Sauv in particular has been generally very good. Maiden Gully is the new second label, producing fresh, fruit-driven Cab/Shiraz and Chardonnay. (PW)
● Shiraz★★★£C ● Cabernet Sauvignon★★★£C
● Pinot Noir★£C O Chardonnay★★£D

BANNOCKBURN Geelong www.bannockbumvineyards.com *UK stockists:* **L&S**, ACh, NYg
High profile Geelong estate thanks to winemaker Gary Farr (By Farr) – inspired by Domaine Dujac in Burgundy. Produced deep, rich, extracted, structured and ageworthy Pinot Noir when almost unheard of in Australia. Serré version is from close-planted vines. Also Shiraz with superb texture and complexity and concentrated Chardonnay. Sometimes leafy Cab/Merlot less good. Sauvignon Blanc and Riesling are also made. (PW)
● Shiraz★★★★£D ● Cabernet/Merlot★★£C
● Pinot Noir★★★★£D O Chardonnay★★★£D

BASS PHILLIP Gippsland *UK stockists:* **Box**, NYg
Cult wine estate of Phillip Jones in the vast vinous wilderness of Gippsland for at times unrivalled (in Australia) **297**

AUSTRALIA

Pinot Noir from closely spaced vines. All are characterised by excellent structure, length and purity of fruit whether regular forward Pinot, more intense, complex Premium or deep, structured Reserve (needing 5 years' age or more). Newer are cheaper Crown Prince and the Village versions. (PW)

● **Pinot Noir**★★★ £F   Premium★★★★ £G   Reserve★★★★ £H

BEST'S Grampians www.bestswines.com   *UK stockists:* **Cac**, JNi, WIE, Fsp, FWC, CeB, Hrd
A family tradition of grape growing/winemaking since 19th century. Vineyards favour Shiraz, both deep, peppery Bin O and limited-release Thomson Family version. Unusual varietal Pinot Meunier is savoury and complex. Also good Riesling and Chardonnay while Merlot, Cab Franc, Pinot Noir and a Late Harvest Muscat are also made. Budget Victoria range include decent Shiraz. (PW)

● **Shiraz** Great western★★★ £C   ● **Cabernet Sauvignon** Great Western★★ £C
● **Pinot Meunier** Great Western★★ £C   O **Chardonnay** Great Western★★ £C

BINDI Macedon Ranges   *UK stockists:* **Sec**
One of Australia's best boutique growers with very small quantities of supremely rich and concentrated Chardonnay and Pinot Noir. All *cuvées* have excellent balance and an intense fruit-filled finish. Both Chardonnays and Original Vineyard Pinot Noir deserve 5–10 years' age. Also made are Bundaleer Shiraz (from Heathcote) and a little sparkling wine. (PW)

● **Pinot Noir** Original Vineyard★★★★ £E
O **Chardonnay**★★★★ £D   Quartz★★★★★ £E

R L BULLER & SON Rutherglen www.buller.com.au   *UK stockists:* **PWt**, OWL, Las
The Buller family's outstanding (very old) Rare Tokay and Muscat (from unirrigated vineyards) have splendid complexity and length. Exceptional value Premium Fine Old examples (also made in a solera system) have great intensity and unexpected elegance. Also made are Premium Fine Old Tawny, powerful, robust Calliope Shiraz, Limited Release Durif, and Rhône and Bordeaux-style blends. (PW)

O **Rutherglen Tokay** Premium Fine Old★★★★ £C   Calliope Rare★★★★★ £F
O **Rutherglen Muscat** Premium Fine Old★★★★ £C   Calliope Rare★★★★★ £F

CAMPBELLS Rutherglen & Glenrowan   *UK stockists:* **WSS**, ACh
Consistent top-quality producer of Rutherglen fortifieds. Marvellous complexity, intensity and refinement in the Rare-level Isabella Tokay and Merchant Prince Muscat and impressive flavour at lower levels. Barkly Durif with real intensity is best of robust high alcohol reds. Also some white wine. (PW)

O **Rutherglen Tokay** Classic★★★★ £C   Grand★★★★★ £E   Rare Isabella✪✪✪✪✪ £G
O **Rutherglen Muscat** Grand★★★★ £E   Rare Merchant Prince★★★★★ £G
● **Shiraz** Bobbie Burns★ £C   ● **Durif** The Barkly★★ £C

CHAMBERS ROSEWOOD Rutherglen & Glenrowan   *UK stockists:* **L&W**
Leading Rutherglen producer dating from 1858. Stocks of extremely old wines give incredible concentration as well as remarkable texture and extraordinary flavour complexity to Rare versions. The tea-leaf elegance of the Tokay contrasts with the more dried-fruits, raisiny character of the Muscat. Grand level also very fine. Table wines are also made. (PW)

O **Rutherglen Muscat**★★ £D   Grand★★★★ £F   Rare✪✪✪✪✪ £G
O **Rutherglen Tokay**★★★ £D   Grand★★★★★ £F   Rare✪✪✪✪✪ £G

COLDSTREAM HILLS Yarra Valley www.coldstreamhills.com.au   *UK stockists:* **ScE**, PFx
High-profile, much expanded Southcorp winery created by wine critic James Halliday in 1985. Reserves of ageworthy but fruit-emphasized Pinot Noir and Chardonnay come from the best fruit and see more new French oak. Cab Sauv and Merlot Reserves show good texture as does the Bordeaux blend, Briarston. Sauvignon Blanc and Pinot Gris are also made. (PW)

● **Cabernet Sauvignon** Reserve★★★ £E   ● **Merlot**★★ £C   Reserve★★★ £E
● **Pinot Noir**★★ £C   Reserve★★★ £E   O **Chardonnay**★★ £C   Reserve★★★ £D

CRAIGLEE Sunbury www.craiglee.com.au   *UK stockists:* **FMV**, The, NYg, P&S, FFW
Replanted 19th century vineyards of Pat Carmody give structured, elegant wines with a real capacity to age. Best are restrained melony Chardonnay and at times minty/spearmint-influenced Shiraz (at margins for achieving full ripeness) though shows classic pepper and black fruits character in warmer years. Also very small

298

amounts of Cabernet Sauvignon, Pinot Noir and Sauvignon Blanc. (PW)

● Shiraz★★★ £D   O Chardonnay★★★ £C

CRAWFORD RIVER   Henty   *UK stockists:* **J&B**
Long-established boutique operation in little-known Henty region. Riesling is consistently best with impressive depth, intensity and concentration but Semillon/Sauvignon Blanc has real style and length too, with vivid herb and ripe citrus fruit. Cabt Sauv from old vines succeeds in warm years like 2000. Also made is a Cabernet/Merlot and elegant, moderately sweet white, Nektar. (PW)

O Riesling★★★ £C   O Semillon/Sauvignon Blanc★★ £C
● Cabernet Sauvignon★★★ £D

CURLY FLAT   Macedon Ranges   www.curlyflat.com   *UK stockists:* **Lib**
One of a small but growing band of high-quality producers in Macedon Ranges. Both Pinot Noir and Chardonnay are rich and fleshy with impressive breadth and depth. Declassified fruit goes into a second label, Williams Crossing. Also sparkling wine, Pinot Gris and rosé. (PW)

● Pinot Noir★★★★ £E   O Chardonnay★★★★ £D

DALWHINNIE   Pyrenees   www.dalwhinnie.com.au   *UK stockists:* **J&B**, P&S, NYg, FFW
Outstanding winery in the Pyrenees region with 18 ha of organic vineyards in granite soils. Shiraz (including Eagle Series from 1.2-ha) and Chardonnay of excellent structure and finesse. Also increasingly impressive Pinot Noir. Both the Cabernet and Shiraz best with 5 to 10 years' age. (PW)

● Cabernet Sauvignon Moonambel★★★ £D   ● Shiraz Moonambel★★★★ £E
● Pinot Noir★★★ £D   O Chardonnay Moonambel★★★★ £D

DELATITE   Upper Goulburn   www.delatitewinery.com.au   *UK stockists:* **JEF**, ACh, Por
Cool, steep slopes here favour light aromatic, floral Riesling and spicy, fuller Gewürz that are intense and ageworthy. Reds are cool and minty, but Devil's River (Cab Sauv, Malbec and Shiraz) increasingly shows ripe tannins. Also made are Sauvignon, Pinot Gris, Pinot Noir, Merlot, Shiraz and sparkling Delmelza Pinot/Chardonnay. (PW)

O Riesling★★ £B   O Gewürztraminer Dead Mans Hill★★★ £B
O Chardonnay★★ £C   ● Devil's River★★ £C

DIAMOND VALLEY   Yarra Valley   www.diamondvalley.com.au   *UK stockists:* **Cac**, T&W
Small winery established in 1982 making excellent Estate wines, both superb Pinot Noir and rich, lightly tropical Chardonnay. Pinot is marked by concentrated, almost gamey, plum and black fruit underpinned by plenty of oak. With real structure too, it is best with five years' ageing. (DM)

● Cabernet Merlot★★ £C Estate★★★ £D   ● Pinot Noir★★ £C Estate★★★★ £D
O Chardonnay★★ £C Estate★★★ £D

DOMAINE A   Tasmania   www.domaine-a.com.au   *UK stockists:* **All**, BFs
11 ha of highish-density vineyards in the Coal River Valley are pruned and harvested by hand. Domaine A is the top selection: Cab Sauv epitomises cool-grown elegance, Pinot Noir has rich plum and cherry fruit, while barrel-fermented and aged Sauvignon Lady A is usually balanced. Stoney Vineyard varietals are cool, elegant but with sufficient ripeness in the Cabernet. (PW)

Domaine A:
O Fumé Blanc Lady A★★★ £E   ● Pinot Noir★★★ £E
● Cabernet Sauvignon★★★ £E

Stoney Vineyard:
O Sauvignon Blanc★★ £C   ● Cabernet Sauvignon★★ £C

DROMANA ESTATE   Mornington Peninsula   *UK stockists:* **Cac**, CeB, Hrd
Rollo Crittenden makes premium estate wines under the Dromana label, especially Pinot Noir and Chardonnay (more complex Reserves) but also increasingly ripe, spicy berry-fruited Cabernet/Merlot and stylish Shiraz. Interesting, recently improved 'i' Italian varietals from King Valley fruit, though Nebbiolo and Sangiovese still want for finesse. Schinus is a cheaper label for varietals from diverse sources. Also Yarra Valley Hills wines from Yarra fruit. (PW)

Dromana Estate:
● Pinot Noir★ £B Reserve★★★ £D   ● Cabernet/Merlot★ £B

AUSTRALIA

● Shiraz★★ £B   O Chardonnay★ £B   Reserve★★★ £D

i Garry Crittenden:
● Barbera★ £B   ● Dolcetto★ £B   O Arneis★★ £B

GIACONDA   Beechworth   www.giaconda.com.au   *UK stockists:* **FMV**, NYg, P&S, Sel
Rick Kinzbrunner's Pinot Noir and Chardonnay are Australian cool-climate classics, mirroring the the best of the Côte d'Or in their vinification. Rich, opulent Pinot Noir, structured and refined Chardonnay and Bordeaux blend 'Cabernet' have been complemented by new stars. Full-on Nantua Les Deux (Chardonnay and Roussanne), rich powerful and exotic varietal Roussanne, Aeolia, and richly textured, stylish Shiraz. All age very well. Prices reflect both quality and demand. (PW)
● Cabernet★★★ £F   ● Pinot Noir★★★★ £F   ● Shiraz Warner Vineyard★★★★ £F
O Chardonnay★★★★★ £F   O Aeolia★★★★ £F   O Nantua Les Deux★★★ £E

GREEN POINT   Yarra Valley   www.greenpointwines.com.au   *UK stockists:* **MHn**, Vne
Prestigious Yarra Valley operation owned by Moët-Hennessey. Still Pinot Noir and Chardonnay are characterised by clarity, intensity and good breadth, with richer, more structured Reserves. Vintage Brut is high-quality sparkling wine and a little Blanc de Blancs, Blanc de Noirs and Brut Rosé are also made. All show fine texture, rich, ripe fruit and improve with a little age. Premium Cuvée Prestige in a richer, late-disgorged (with six years on its lees) style was first produced in 1995. (PW)
O Vintage Brut★★★ £C   O Vintage Blanc de Blancs★★★ £C
O Chardonnay★★ £C   Reserve★★★ £D   ● Pinot Noir★ £C   Reserve★★★ £D

HANGING ROCK   Macedon Ranges   *UK stockists:* **TWS**, AWA
Cool estate vineyards on the Jim Jim (an extinct volcano), are mostly planted to Pinot Noir and Chardonnay for top Australian sparkler, Macedon Cuvée – a blend of vintages enriched by reserve wines. Also a cool, crisp Sauvignon while rich, powerful Shiraz is Heathcote-derived. 'Victoria' wines are from diverse sources and inexpensive 'Rock' a second label. (PW)
● Shiraz Cambrian Rise★★★ £C   Heathcote★★★ £C
● Cabernet Sauvignon Turners Crossing★★ £B
O Macedon Cuvée★★★ £C   O Sauvignon Blanc Jim Jim★ £B

JASPER HILL   Heathcote   *UK stockists:* **Yap**, P&S, NYg, N&P
Small production based on minimal intervention and tiny yields provides two remarkable Shiraz. Both are rich, concentrated, and very ageworthy, full of exotic dark berry fruit and spice with a marvellous supple texture. A powerful, structured Riesling is citrusy, minerally and toasty with three to four years' age. Also very small quantities of Nebbiolo and Semillon since 2001. (PW)
● Shiraz Georgia's Paddock★★★★★ £F   O Riesling Georgia's Paddock★★★ £D
● Shiraz/Cabernet Franc Emily's Paddock★★★★★ £F

KOOYONG   Mornington Peninsula   www.kooyong.com   *UK stockists:* **L&S**
Australian-trained Sandro Mosele makes compelling Chardonnay and Pinot Noir. Regular Pinot Noir is structured and dense with immaculate concentrated ripe cherry/berry fruit. Similarly powerful and ageworthy Chardonnay shows a touch of minerality. Also single-vineyard examples. (PW)
● Pinot Noir★★★ £D   O Chardonnay★★★ £C

STEFANO LUBIANA   Tasmania   www.stefanolubiana.com   *UK stockists:* NYg, UnC
5.6 ha above the Derwent River are the source for Pinot Noir and Chardonnay of a persuasive style and refinement. With very pure and intense fruit, the wines are elegant and vibrant, improving for at least three to four years. Chardonnay Sur Lie and Pinot Noir Primavera are second versions. Sauvignon and Pinot Grigio are also made. Sparkling non-vintage Brut is Pinot Noir-based. (PW)
● Pinot Noir★★★ £D   O Chardonnay★★★ £D   O Riesling★★ £C

MÉTIER WINES   Yarra Valley   www.metierwines.com.au   *UK stockists:* **HHB**
Small though expanding operation of top winemaker Martin Williams (also see Tallarook). Tarraford Chardonnay is extremely well crafted with subtle use of oak and lees. Finely textured Pinot Noir is more variable. Schoolhouse versions are also Yarra but tiny amount of Viognier and promising new Manytrees Shiraz/Viognier come from higher altitudes. Milkwood is a second range. (PW)

300

● **Pinot Noir** Schoolhouse Vineyard★★ £E   Tarraford Vineyard★★ £D
○ **Chardonnay** Schoolhouse Vineyard★★★★ £C   Tarraford Vineyard★★★★ £D

MITCHELTON   www.mitchelton.com.au   *UK stockists:* **LNa,** WSc, FWC, Hrd, F&M, Sel
Recognised quality from the banks of the Goulburn River. Vigorous whites combine citrusy and more exotic flavours. Intense floral and lime-scented Blackwood Park Riesling is also made in Late Harvested and Botrytis versions. Top red, Print Shiraz, exudes class and finesse. New Parish Shiraz includes 10% Viognier. Also fine red and white Rhône blends. Intense honeysuckle Marsanne is a speciality. Central Victoria or Preece wines can be good value for money. (PW)
● **Shiraz** Central Victoria★★ £C   Print★★★★ £E   ● **Shiraz/Viognier** Parish★★ £C
● **Shiraz/Mourvèdre/Grenache** Crescent★★ £C   ○ **Riesling** Blackwood Park★★★ £C
○ **Viognier** Central Victoria★ £C   ○ **Marsanne/Roussanne/Viognier** Airstrip★★ £C

MOUNT LANGI GHIRAN   Grampians   *UK stockists:* **Eno, Lib,** ACh, Vne, Hrd, P&S
Same ownership as Yering Station but owes reputation, centred on outstanding Shiraz, to Trevor Mast. Richly textured Cab/Merlot contrasts with cool, minty Joanna Cabernet (from Wrattonbully). Also improving Sangiovese and second Shiraz, Cliff Edge (since 1999). Attractive Billi Billi Creek is mostly Shiraz (with Grenache and Cabernet). Four Sisters wines are fruit-accented. (PW)
● **Shiraz**★★★★★ £E   Cliff Edge★★★ £C   ● **Cabernet/Merlot**★★★★ £D
● **Cabernet Sauvignon** Limestone Coast Joanna★★★ £C   ○ **Riesling**★★ £B
● **Sangiovese** Nut Block★★ £C   ● **Shiraz/Grenache/Cabernet** Billy Billy Creek★★ £B

MOUNT MARY   Yarra Valley   *UK stockists:* **Bal, VdV,** JAr, BBR, F&R, Las
Highly esteemed estate with small volumes from unirrigated vineyards. Quintet (Cab Sauv, Merlot, Cab Franc, Malbec and Petit Verdot) is graceful, refined and very ageworthy. Pure-fruited Pinot Noir can age for about half as long while two fine whites, Chardonnay and Triolet (Sauvignon, Semillon and Muscadelle) also age well.(PW)
● **Quintet**★★★★ £G   ● **Pinot Noir**★★★ £G
○ **Triolet**★★★ £F   ○ **Chardonnay**★★★ £F

PARINGA ESTATE   Mornington Peninsula   *UK stockists:* **Adm,** NYg
Top-notch small estate both for Chardonnay and Pinot Noir but also Shiraz, the latter especially when benefitting from a long ripening period. Peninsula label is from a combination of bought-in fruit and younger Paringa vines. An unoaked Pinot Gris is also made. (PW)
● **Pinot Noir**★★★ £E   Peninsula★★ £C   ● **Shiraz**★★★★ £D
○ **Chardonnay**★★★ £D   Peninsula★★ £C

PIPERS BROOK   Tasmania   www.pbv.com.au   *UK stockists:* **Cap,** ACh, FWC
The dominant force in Tasmanian wine production. Lovely varietal fruit character with extra nuance, richness (and oak) in Reserves. Also very fine sparkling wine in Pirie. Small amounts of single-site Pinot Noir (The Blackwood and The Lyre) and Chardonnay (The Summit) have been made recently. Ninth Island is a separate entity for both varietals and sparkling wines from wider sources. (PW)
Pipers Brook:
● **Pinot Noir** Estate★★ £C   Reserve★★★ £D
○ **Chardonnay** Estate★★ £C   Reserve★★★ £D   ○ **Riesling** Estate★★ £C
○ **Gewürztraminer** Estate★★ £C   ○ **Pirie Vintage**★★★★ £D
Ninth Island:
● **Pinot Noir**★ £B   ○ **Chardonnay**★ £B

PONDALOWIE   Bendigo   *UK stockists:* **AWA**
Much travelled Dominic Morris brings considerable experience to his small Bendigo winery. Shiraz is the star (esp. 2002); also unwooded MT Tempranillo with vibrant blueberry fruit and excellent substance, and supple, characterful fruit-driven Shiraz/Cab Sauv/Tempranillo. (PW)
● **Shiraz**★★★★ £C   ● **Shiraz/Cabernet/Tempranillo**★★★ £C
● **Tempranillo** MT★★ £C   ● **Shiraz/Cabernet**★★ £B

PORT PHILLIP ESTATE   Mornington Peninsula   www.portphillip.net   *UK stockists:* **P&S**
Same ownership as Kooyong. Wines are characterised by fine pure fruit, good texture and soft, ripe tannins in the

AUSTRALIA

AUSTRALIA

reds. Minerally, berryish Shiraz is best in warm vintages. Rich, mealy, oaky Chardonnay has a ripe stone-fruit core and should age well. Also Sauvignon Blanc. (PW)

● **Pinot Noir**★★★ £D   ● **Shiraz**★★★ £D   O **Chardonnay**★★★ £D

SCOTCHMANS HILL   Geelong   *UK stockists:* **Orb**, Odd, Bal, WSc
Medium-sized Bellarine Peninsula winery with a cool maritime climate. Pinot Noir is a strength, also good individual Shiraz, Cab/Merlot and well-made Chardonnay and Sauvignon. New and very pricey Norfolk Vineyard Pinot and Sutton Vineyard Chardonnay. Swan Bay is the second label. (PW)

● **Pinot Noir**★★★ £C   Swan Bay★ £B   ● **Cabernet/Merlot**★★★ £C
● **Shiraz**★★★ £C   O **Chardonnay**★★★ £C   O **Sauvignon Blanc**★★ £B

SEPPELT GREAT WESTERN   Grampians   www.seppelt.com.au   *UK stockists:* **ScE**
Seppelt's renowned sparkling-wine operation but also many fine cool-climate varietals. Riesling and Pinot Noir highlight the potential of the Henty region. Also cedary cool Cab Sauv which contrasts with Dorrien version from old-vine Barossa fruit. Fine Partalunga Chardonnay is from the Adelaide Hills. Sparkling wines are led by creamy, citrusy Salinger and Drumborg Show Sparkling Reserve. Most exceptional is the red Great Western Show Sparkling Shiraz – arguably the best of its type. (PW)

● **Cabernet Sauvignon** Dorrien★★★ £C   ● **Shiraz** Great Western★★★ £C
● **Pinot Noir** Drumborg★★ £D   ● **Sparkling Shiraz Vintage Show**★★★ £D
O **Chardonnay** Partalunga★★★ £C   O **Salinger Vintage**★★ £C

SEVILLE ESTATE   Yarra Valley   www.sevilleestate.com.au   *UK stockists:* **Lib**, Vne, NYg, ACh
Yarra Valley pioneer in the modern era, lately owned by Brokenwood. Fine varietals from cool side of valley are ageworthy, powerful and fruit-accented with good structure and definition in warmer vintages. Also small amounts of Reserve Cabernet and Shiraz from 30-year-old vines. (PW)

● **Shiraz**★★★ £C   ● **Cabernet Sauvignon**★★ £C
● **Pinot Noir**★★★ £C   O **Chardonnay**★★ £C

SHADOWFAX   Geelong   *UK stockists:* **FMV**, The, NYg, RGr, P&S
Newish operation buying in only the best grapes. Atypically good Sauvignon/Semillon, also full but tightly structured Chardonnay, characterful, textured Pinot Noir, and vibrant, spicy, fruit-driven Shiraz. Premium versions include Geelong Pinot Noir (since 2001) and concentrated, intense, meaty single-vineyard Heathcote Shirazes: Pink Cliffs and One Eye. Viognier, Pinot Gris and unusual K Road Sangiovese/Merlot/Shiraz are also made. (PW)

● **One Eye** Heathcote★★★★ £E   ● **Pink Cliffs** Heathcote★★★★ £E
● **Pinot Noir**★★ £C   ● **Shiraz** McLaren Vale★★★ £C
O **Sauvignon Blanc/Semillon**★★ £B   O **Chardonnay**★★★ £C

STONIER   Mornington Peninsula   www.stonier.com.au   *UK stockists:* **LNa**, Bib, Vne, NYg, Vts
Long-established premium Mornington Peninsula winery under same ownership as Petaluma since 98. Regular Chardonnay and Pinot Noir show fine fruit but excellent Reserves much better than price differential suggests. Also small quantities of single-vineyard wines from KBS Vineyard. (PW)

● **Pinot Noir**★★ £C   Reserve★★★ £D   O **Chardonnay**★★★ £C   Reserve★★★★ £D

SUMMERFIELD   Pyrenees   www.summerfieldwines.com   *UK stockists:* BBR, NYg
Input from Drew Noon down the years has resulted in increasingly rich, ripe and more consistent reds if always with a noticeable dash of oak. Shiraz is the real star, particularly the Reserve. Muscular, minty Reserve Cabernet now benefits from the use of some French oak. Both Reserves will keep for a decade or more (PW)

● **Shiraz**★★ £C   Reserve★★★ £E   ● **Cabernet/Merlot**★★ £C
● **Cabernet Sauvignon**★★ £C   Reserve★★★ £D

TAHBILK   Nagambie Lakes   www.tahbilk.com.au   *UK stockists:* **PLh**, Fsp, The
Historic winery with plantings of Shiraz dating back to 1860, contributing to the structured, tannic style of the wines when young. Patience is required for reds, up to 10 years for the Reserves and 1860 Vines. Marsanne is a regional benchmark. New and promising are Roussanne and Viognier. (PW)

● **Cabernet Sauvignon**★★ £B   Reserve★★★ £D

302   ● **Shiraz**★★ £B   Reserve★★★ £D   1860 Vines★★★★ £F
O **Marsanne**★★ £B   O **Chardonnay**★ £B   O **Riesling**★★ £B   O **Semillon**★★ £B

New entries have producer's name underlined

AUSTRALIA

TALLAROOK Upper Goulburn www.tallarook.com *UK stockists:* **HHB,** F&M
Wines made by Martin Williams MW of Métier from elevated, cool vineyards include a little Viognier, Marsanne, Roussanne as well as more substantial amounts of Chardonnay, Pinot Noir and Shiraz. Best are a toasty Chardonnay, gently creamy Marsanne and cool, peppery Shiraz. (PW)
O Chardonnay★★ £C   O Marsanne★ £C   ● Shiraz★★ £C

TAMAR RIDGE Tasmania www.tamarridgewines.com.au *UK stockists:* VsV, L&W
60-ha estate based winery producing clear-fruited if sometimes slightly austere whites. Led by an intense, well-structured Riesling but also complex, cool (barrel-fermented) Chardonnay and Pinot Noir. Also Cabernet Sauvignon and Josef Chromy Selection for late-harvest Riesling and sparkling Blanc de Noirs. Inexpensive Devil's Corner label includes Pinot Noir and Chardonnay. (PW)
O Riesling★★ £C   O Sauvignon Blanc★ £B   O Pinot Gris★★ £B
O Chardonnay★★ £C   O Gewürztraminer★★ £B   ● Pinot Noir★★ £C

TARRAWARRA Yarra Valley www.tarrawarra.com.au *UK stockists:* CRs, May, WSc, Vts
Producer of top-quality Chardonnay and Pinot Noir modelled on white and red Burgundy. Rich, structured, concentrated and complex examples of each result from both winemaking skill and increasingly high-quality fruit. Both are best with three to five years' age. Tin Cows label also includes Merlot and Shiraz while Kosher Chardonnay and Shiraz are made under the Kidron label. (PW)
Tarrawarra:
● Pinot Noir★★★ £D   O Chardonnay★★★ £D
Tin Cows:
O Chardonnay★★ £C

VIRGIN HILLS Macedon Ranges www.virginhills.com.au *UK stockists:* **Str,** Vne
Just one wine is made here, a blend of Cab Sauv, Shiraz and Merlot – one of the best Cabernet-based reds in Victoria. Organically produced it excels in top vintages (such as 98) when it is a magnificent, elegant, cedary red. In cooler years there can be a marked green undercurrent. (PW)
● Virgin Hills★★★★ £E

YARRA BURN Yarra Valley www.brlhardy.com.au *UK stockists:* **Cst,** Sav
Headquarters of BRL Hardy's substantial Yarra Valley operations, though quantities are small. Wines show characteristic BRL Hardy style with a rich fruit core, balance, complexity and well-integrated oak, if slightly overdone in bold premium Bastard Hill Pinot Noir. Yarra Burn sparkling wine, from all three Champagne grapes, is an elegant Yarra Valley example. (PW)
O Chardonnay★★ £B   Bastard Hill★★★ £D   O Yarra Burn★★ £C
● Pinot Noir★★ £C   ● Shiraz★★★ £C

YARRA YARRA Yarra Valley *UK stockists:* JAr, Rae
Very small but first-rate Yarra Valley estate. Plenty of style in ripe but cool-grown Syrah while Cabernets (Cab Sauv with both Cab Franc and Merlot) has a cool, leafy Yarra Valley trait but fine, ripe tannins. Classy, sophisticated, richly textured Yarra Yarra from similar blend is riper and more concentrated. All deserve at least five to six years' age. Semillon/Sauvignon is also made. (PW)
● The Yarra Yarra★★★★ £E   ● Cabernets★★★ £E   ● Syrah★★★ £D

YARRA YERING Yarra Valley *UK stockists:* **Adm,** JNi, ACh, BBR, NYg, P&S
Bailey Carrodus's often exceptional reds from well-established vines attract a cult following. Dry White No.1 is a fine Sauvignon/Semillon blend, Dry Red No.1 is a powerful Bordeaux blend. Dry Red No.2, with terrific fruit richness and depth, is Shiraz with a little Viognier, while Pinot Noir is in a rich, powerful, extracted style. Newer are Dry Red No.3 based on Sangiovese, and a Young Vines Cab Sauv. (PW)
● Dry Red No.1★★★★ £E   ● Dry Red No.2★★★★★ £E
● Shiraz Underhill★★★★ £E   ● Pinot Noir★★★★ £F   ● Merlot★★★★ £H
O Dry White No.1★★★ £E   O Chardonnay★★★ £E

YERING STATION/YARRABANK Yarra Valley *UK stockists:* **Eno,** ACh, P&S
Well-structured wines have real style and intensity with added class, depth and expression in the Reserves. New MVR (Marsanne, Viognier, Roussanne) has excellent fruit while Barak's Bridge is a decent second label.

303

AUSTRALIA

Intense, rich, vintage-dated Yarrabank Brut Cuvée (joint venture with Champagne Devaux) is among Australia's best. (PW)

Yarrabank:
O **Yarrabank Brut Cuvée**★★★★ £C

Yering Station:
O **Chardonnay**★★★ £C   Reserve★★★★ £E   O **Pinot Gris** Late Harvest★★ £C
● **Pinot Noir**★★ £C   Reserve★★★ £E   ● **Shiraz/Viognier** Reserve★★★★ £E
● **Cabernet Sauvignon**★★ £C   Reserve★★★★ £E   ● **Merlot**★★★ £C

Barak's Bridge:
O **Chardonnay**★ £B   ● **Pinot Noir**★ £B   ● **Shiraz**★★ £B

YERINGBERG   Yarra Valley   *UK stockists:* **JAr**
Gentle, pure artisanal wines with an underlying strength and intensity. Both whites are subtle and restrained but possess real elegance and flair. Dry Red (a Bordeaux blend) develops richness and a savoury complexity with age as well as elegance and finesse seen in few other Australian reds. (PW)

● **Pinot Noir**★★ £E   ● **Yeringberg Dry Red**★★★★ £E
O **Marsanne/Roussanne**★★★ £C   O **Chardonnay**★★★ £D

Other wineries of note
All Saints (Rutherglen & Glenrowan), Armstrong Vineyards (Grampians), Cobaw Ridge (Macedon), De Bortoli (Victoria), By Farr (Geelong), Heathcote Winery (Heathcote), Main Ridge (Mornington Peninsula), Moorilla Estate (Tasmania), Morris (Rutherglen & Glenrowan), Taltarni (Pyrenees), Wellington (Tasmania), Wild Duck Creek (Heathcote)

An in-depth profile of every producer can be found in Wine behind the label 2006

New entries have producer's name underlined

1 •Kingaroy

•Toowoomba •Brisbane

QUEENSLAND

2 •Stanthorpe

NORTHERN
RIVERS

•Tamworth

MACQUARIE

3•
Port Macquarie

HUNTER VALLEY
4 •Muswellbrook
•Dubbo *6*
HUNTER
•Mudgee
5•Cessnock
CENTRAL •Newcastle
LACHLAN *8* •Orange
7
•Cowra
•Sydney
BIG *9*
RIVERS •Young SOUTH
13 COAST
10 SOUTHERN NSW
MURRUMBIDGEE *12* *14*
•Wagga Wagga
•Canberra
11
•Tumbarumba AUSTRALIAN
MURRAY CAPITAL
TERRITORY

VICTORIA

1	South Burnett
2	Granite Belt
3	Hastings River
4	Hunter
5	Broke Fordwich
6	Mudgee
7	Orange
8	Cowra
9	Hilltops
10	Gundagai
11	Tumbarumba
12	Canberra District
13	Southern Highlands
14	Shoalhaven Coast

AUSTRALIA

Background
New South Wales not only makes a sizeable contribution to Australia's production of bulk wine but 160 km north-west of its largest city, Sydney, has a wine region of magnetic tourist attraction in the Hunter Valley. Thanks to the Great Dividing Range much potential remains and new regions will continue to make an impact if developed with quality as the foremost consideration.

The regions
The **Hunter Valley**, New South Wales' most traditional region, is not the most suited region to viticulture. The Lower Hunter Valley is peppered with estates but, despite regular cloud cover, conditions are very hot and much of the rain fall as the growing season reaches its climax. Great vintages are the exception rather than the norm yet some marvellous ageworthy Shiraz and Semillon are produced, the best of the latter in a long-lived, minerally, toasty-but-unoaked style. Regions in the Central Ranges zone (encompassing the western side of the Great Dividing Range) are better protected from cyclonic deluges, making them both cooler and drier. **Mudgee** produces intensely flavoured Cabernet Sauvignon, Shiraz, Chardonnay and Semillon while **Cowra** Chardonnay has a well-established distinctive, lush, full style of its own. Gaining increasing significance are **Orange**, **Hilltops** and, from close to the border with Victoria, the chilly, elevated **Tumbarumba** region. Similarly cool and elevated is the **Canberra District** where the best reds are Cabernet/Merlot blends and expressive, cool-climate Shiraz; also whites from Riesling, Chardonnay and Viognier. The Big Rivers zone incorporates the commercially important bulk-producing regions of **Riverina** and, shared with Victoria on the Murray River, **Murray Darling** and **Swan Hill**. In sub-tropical Queensland wine is produced from **South Burnett**, around Kingaroy, and in the **Granite Belt** around Stanthorpe, in the Great Dividing Range, where it is cooler and elevated. Despite sometimes difficult vintage conditions Shiraz can be good.

New South Wales Vintages
The generalised Vintage charts cover some of the most ageworthy styles and will prove most useful when taken together with comments on style and ageing within individual producer entries. Many wines can be drunk young but an increasing number will not be at their best for at least five years. Hunter Valley Semillon can take two decades in its stride while top Hunter or Mudgee Shiraz and Cabernet have similar ageing

potential. Both the vintage ratings and when to drink assessments generally only apply to the top rated examples (three star wines or higher). Following on from the record early, drought-affected and outstanding quality harvest of 2003, 2004 was a difficult vintage in the Hunter Valley. Two summer heatwaves were followed by two torrential downpours, which for many came before the grapes were picked. The chances of classic long-lived Hunter Shiraz and Semillon from 2004 look slight. 2005 brought better conditions as with very promising Semillon and Verdelho for the whites and potentially long-lived Shiraz from Hunter, if less rich than 2003.

Wizard's Wishlist

Classic Hunter/Mudgee reds
BROKENWOOD ● **Shiraz** Graveyard Vineyard
HUNTINGTON ESTATE ● **Shiraz**
LAKE'S FOLLY ● **Lake's Folly red**
MCWILLIAM'S MOUNT PLEASANT
● **Shiraz** Old Hill & Old Paddock
ROSEMOUNT ● **Shiraz/Cabernet** Mountain Blue
KEITH TULLOCH ● **Shiraz** Hunter Valley Kester
TYRRELL'S ● **Shiraz Vat 9**

Definitive Hunter/Mudgee whites
ALLANDALE ○ **Chardonnay**
BROKENWOOD ○ **Chardonnay** Graveyard Vineyard
LAKE'S FOLLY ○ **Chardonnay**
MCWILLIAM'S MOUNT PLEASANT
○ **Semillon** Lovedale
ROSEMOUNT ○ **Chardonnay** Roxburgh
KEITH TULLOCH ○ **Semillon** Hunter Valley
TYRRELL'S ○ **Chardonnay** Vat 47
TYRRELL'S ○ **Semillon** Vat 1

Other Wines not to be missed
BLOODWOOD ● **Shiraz**
BLOODWOOD ○ **Chardonnay**
CLONAKILLA ● **Shiraz Viognier** Canberra District
CLONAKILLA ○ **Viognier**
CHALKERS CROSSING ● **Cabernet Sauvignon** Hilltops
DE BORTOLI ○ **Botrytis Semillon** Noble One
GLENGUIN
○ **Botrytis Semillon** Griffith Individual Vineyard
MEEREA PARK ○ **Semillon** Hunter Valley Epoch
ROSEMOUNT ○ **Chardonnay** Orange Vineyard
KEITH TULLOCH ● **Shiraz** Hunter Valley Kester

New entries have producer's name underlined

A-Z of producers

ALLANDALE   Hunter Valley   www.allandalewinery.com.au   *UK stockists:* **AWA**, HoM
Relatively small Hunter Valley operation with a reputation for intensely flavoured, individual wines including
full-flavoured, complex Chardonnay, very ripe, oak-influenced Shiraz and classic Hunter-grown Verdelho and
Semillon. New Allandale Reserve red is based on Mudgee Shiraz. (PW)
● **Shiraz** Matthew★★★ £C   ● **Cabernet Sauvignon** Hilltops★★ £C
○ **Chardonnnay**★★★ £B   ○ **Semillon**★★ £B   ○ **Verdelho**★★ £B

BLOODWOOD ESTATE   Orange   www.bloodwood.com.au   *UK stockists:* **Sav**
Orange's first vineyard. Expressive, elegant wines with typical regional fruit character are not in the least bit 'made' or
over-manipulated. Bright, limey, gently mineral Riesling; refined, well-balanced Chardonnay rich in stone fruits and
melon; intense, flavoursome, peppery Shiraz; and a black-fruited, spicy, cedary/minty Cab Sauv. Also aromatic
strawberryish rosé, Big Men in Tights. (PW)
○ **Chardonnnay**★★★ £C   ○ **Riesling**★★ £B   ◉ **Big Men in Tights**★★ £B
● **Shiraz**★★★ £C   ● **Cabernet Sauvignon**★★ £C

BROKENWOOD   Hunter Valley   *UK stockists:* **Lib**, ACh, Ben, P&S, Vne, Odd
Benchmark Lower Hunter winery with impressively rich Rayner (McLaren Vale) and Graveyard (Hunter)
Shiraz. The Semillons, especially ILR, are classic expressions: very honeyed and intense with 8 to 10 years.
Premium Graveyard Chardonnay has real depth and intensity with three or four years. New is a very
promising Forest Edge Vineyard Chardonnay from Orange. Relatively inexpensive Harlequin and Cricket Pitch
reds and whites have immediate appeal and drinkability. (PW)
● **Shiraz** Mistress Block★★★ £C   Rayner★★★★ £D   Graveyard Vineyard★★★★★ £F
● **Cabernet Sauvignon**★★★ £C   ○ **Semillon**★★★ £B   ILR Reserve★★★★ £C
○ **Chardonnay**★★ £C   Forest Edge★★★ £C   Graveyard Vineyard★★★★ £D

CAPERCAILLIE   Hunter Valley   *UK stockists:* **WIE**, Fin, Luv
Scot Alasdair Sutherland makes Hunter Chardonnay and Semillon that are arguably more impressive than reds,
with classic Hunter flavours, structure and depth. Best red is intense, very berryish Ceilidh Shiraz; also
characterful The Clan (Cab Sauv/Merlot/Petit Verdot). The Ghillie Shiraz is special Hunter selection. Gewürz,
red Chambourcin and a sparkling red are also made. (PW)
○ **Chardonnay**★★★ £C   ○ **Semillon**★★★ £C   ● **The Clan**★★ £C
● **Shiraz** Ceilidh★★★ £C   ● **Merlot** Orange Highlands★ £C

CHALKERS CROSSING   Hilltops   www.chalkerscrossing.com..au   *UK stockists:* **ABy**
First wines only made in 2000 but already very good thanks to French-born winemaker Celine Rousseau. Better in
warmer 2002 and 04. Semillon and Sauvignon both made in stainless steel in 04. Chardonnay is restrained and
pure; Shiraz and Cab Sauv are full, soft and concentrated. Cabernet deserves 10 years; Shiraz can be drunk sooner.
Some promise in Pinot Noir too. (PW)
○ **Riesling** Hilltops★ £B   ○ **Sauvignon Blanc** Tumbarumba★★ £B
○ **Chardonnay** Tumbarumba★★★ £B   ○ **Semillon** Hilltops★★ £B
● **Shiraz** Hilltops★★★ £C   ● **Cabernet Sauvignon** Hilltops★★★ £C

CLONAKILLA   Canberra District   www.clonakilla.com.au   *UK stockists:* **Lib**, ACh, P&S, FFW
Tim Kirk makes outstanding Canberra District Shiraz Viognier, an elegant red with distinctive pepper, spice,
floral and berry amalgam – one of the best in the country. Very good Viognier with delightful mayblossom and
ripe peach aromas is unusually well-structured in an Australian context. Chardonnay, Riesling,
Semillon/Sauvignon and Cabernet/Merlot are also produced. (PW)
● **Shiraz**★★★★ £E   Hilltops★★ £C   ○ **Viognier**★★★ £D

CUMULUS   Central Ranges/Orange   www.cumuluswines.com.au   *UK stockists:* **D&D**
Large new operation under the winemaking direction of Philip Shaw (ex-ROSEMOUNT). There are 3 ranges:
Climbing, Rolling and Chasing. Rolling wines lack a little depth but have attractive fruit and adequate structure at
the price. Lightly oaked Climbing Chardonnay and soft-textured Merlot highlight these grapes potential here. Also
look out for the new wines of Philip Shaw from his own vineyards. (PW)

○ **Sauvignon Blanc/Semillon** Rolling★★ £B
○ **Chardonnay** Rolling★ £B Climbing★★ £B ● **Shiraz** Rolling★★ £B
● **Cabernet/Merlot** Rolling★★ £B ● **Merlot** Climbing★★ £B

DE BORTOLI Riverina *UK stockists:* **DeB**, BBR, FWC, ARe, Cam, SFW, F&M
De Bortoli's vast Riverina operation includes budget labels Deen De Bortoli, Willowglen and Sacred Hill ranges. Exceptions are botrytis-influenced Semillons. Noble One is classic Australian sweet wine – rich, concentrated and remarkably complex and honeyed with age. Rich, raisiny fortified Black Noble is produced in a similar fashion to the liqueur Tokays of Rutherglen. (PW)
○ **Noble One**★★★★ £F ○ **Black Noble**★★★★ £E

GLENGUIN Hunter Valley *UK stockists:* **Bib**
Estate-based bottlings from Lower Hunter show real intensity and ripeness with good Hunter Shiraz character, led by complex Aristea. Also lots of flavour and character in Semillon and Chardonnay. Orange-sourced Maestro reds are less interesting; better to try Botrytis Semillon with spiced honey, preserved citrus and marmalade character. (PW)
Glenguin
● **Shiraz** Stonybroke★★ £C Schoolhouse Block★★ £C Aristea★★★ £E
○ **Semillon** Old Broke Block★★ £B ○ **Botrytis Semillon** Griffith Individual Vineyard★★★ £D
○ **Chardonnay** River Terrace★★ £B
Maestro
○ **Pinot Grigio** Adelaide Hills★★ £C
● **Sangiovese Cabernet** Orange★ £C ● **Merlot** Orange★★ £C

HUNTINGTON ESTATE Mudgee www.huntingtonestate.com.au
Relatively small producer and Mudgee's best. Cab Sauv, Shiraz and Cabernet/Shiraz are now identified with FB or MB Bin numbers. Rich ensemble of fruit and oak in Special Reserves of Cab Sauv and Shiraz. Semillon (unwooded) is top white, also a rich, barrel-fermented Chardonnay and a fruit-filled, early-drinking Semillon/Chardonnay. Good value for money, if difficult to track down. (PW)
● **Cabernet Sauvignon**★★★ £B Special Reserve★★★ £C
● **Shiraz**★★★ £B Special Reserve★★★★ £C
○ **Chardonnay** Barrel Fermented★★ £B ○ **Semillon**★★★ £B

LAKE'S FOLLY Hunter Valley www.lakesfolly.com.au *UK stockists:* **Lay**, NYg, P&S, FFW
Top-quality Lower Hunter producer, back on form since the late 90s. Cabernet blend, mostly Cab Sauv with some Shiraz, Merlot and Petit Verdot is restrained, well-structured, avoiding overripeness seen in some Hunter reds. The Chardonnay is rich, opulent and buttery. Both are ageworthy. (PW)
● **Cabernet blend**★★★ £E ○ **Chardonnay**★★★★ £E

MCWILLIAM'S MOUNT PLEASANT Hunter Valley www.mcwilliams.com.au
The gems of McWilliams' sizeable output. Unwooded Semillons, subject to delayed release, have marvellous toasty, citrus and herb intensity with extended bottle-ageing. Shiraz too is deep and individual with a flavour complexity that you just won't get anywhere else – especially long-lived Old Paddock & Old Hill. Wines are very reasonably priced if difficult to find. (PW)
● **Shiraz** Maurice O'Shea★★★ £C Old Paddock & Old Hill★★★★ £D
○ **Semillon** Elizabeth★★★ £B Lovedale★★★★ £D
○ **Chardonnay** Maurice O'Shea★★★ £C

MEEREA PARK Hunter Valley **Lib**, ACh, Ben, V&C, FFW, Hrd
Pokolbin-based, with 10,000 cases per year from bought-in fruit. Ripe, complex Chardonnay, intensely honeysuckle Viognier and fresh Verdelho are good Hunter examples. Characterful Aunts Shiraz but greater depth in powerful spice and smoky black-fruited Alexander Munro. Also aromatic Shiraz Viognier (since 2001) and good Orchard Road Pinot Gris and Barbera (from Orange fruit). (PW)
● **Shiraz** The Aunts★★ £C Alexander Munro★★★ £D
● **Shiraz Viognier**★★ £C ○ **Viognier** Lindsay Hill★★ £C
○ **Chardonnay** Alexander Munro★★ £D ○ **Semillon** Epoch★★ £B

New entries have producer's name underlined

ROSEMOUNT ESTATE   Hunter Valley   *UK stockists:* **ScE, AAA**
Merged with huge Southcorp in 2001 but maintaining generally high standards throughout an extensive portfolio. Dense concentrated Mountain Blue Shiraz/Cab Sauv is from Mudgee. Intense, complex Roxburgh Chardonnay contrasts with spicy, ripe-fruited Orange Vineyard version. Show Reserve Chardonnay is less good than previously – Semillon equivalent much better but needs at least 3-4 years'. Varietal reds, including classy Shiraz, from very high altitude Orange Vineyard show cooler climate origins. Chardonnay and Shiraz best of Hill of Gold (Mudgee) varietals. Diamond label reds and whites for everyday drinking. (PW)
- **Shiraz/Cabernet Sauvignon** Blue Mountain★★★★ £F
- **Shiraz** Orange Vineyard★★★ £D   ● **Cabernet** Orange Vineyard★★★ £D
- ○ **Chardonnay** Orange Vineyard★★★ £D Roxburgh★★★★ £F

KEITH TULLOCH   Hunter Valley   www.keithtullochwine.com.au   *UK stockists:* **Gun, Bal, WSc**
Only a few hundred cases of classy, complex wines with super Hunter fruit and excellent intensity, texture and length. All will age impressively: Forres Blend (mostly Cab Sauv but also Merlot, Petit Verdot), excellent Shiraz, splendid Chardonnay and Semillon (both great value for money). (PW)
- ○ **Semillon**★★★★ £C ○ **Chardonnay**★★★★ £C
- **Shiraz** Kester★★★★ £D   ● **Forres Blend**★★★★ £D

TYRRELL'S   Hunter Valley   www.tyrrells.com.au   *UK stockists:* **Par,** CPp WSc, Hrd, Sel
Family-owned and run winery making around half a million cases even after the recent sale of the Long Flat brand. Top Winemakers Selection (Vat numbered) series includes the classic bold, powerful and complex Vat 47 Chardonnay, Vat 1 Semillon of great breadth and nuance, and good Vat 9 Shiraz. Hunter-sourced Brokenback Shiraz, Moon Mountain Chardonnay and Shee-Oak Chardonnay are full-flavoured if sometimes lacking balance; unwooded Lost Block Semillon is better. Old Winery label includes decent Shiraz and Semillon. Moore's Creek is new budget label . (PW)
- **Shiraz** Old Winery★ £B Brokenback★★ £C Vat 9★★★ £E
- ○ **Chardonnay** Shee-Oak★ £C Moon Mountain★★ £C Vat 47★★★★ £E
- ○ **Semillon** Old Winery★ £B Lost Block★★ £C Vat 1★★★★ £E

Other wineries of note
Tower Estate (Hunter Valley), Sirromet (Queensland)

An in-depth profile of every producer can be found in Wine behind the label 2006

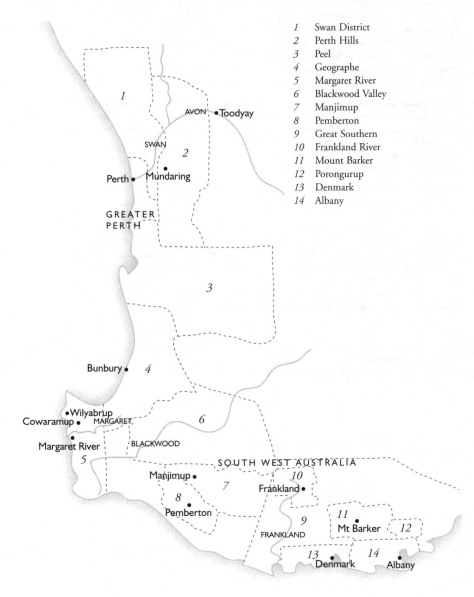

1   Swan District
2   Perth Hills
3   Peel
4   Geographe
5   Margaret River
6   Blackwood Valley
7   Manjimup
8   Pemberton
9   Great Southern
10 Frankland River
11 Mount Barker
12 Porongurup
13 Denmark
14 Albany

1

AVON   •Toodyay

SWAN

2

Perth• •Mundaring

GREATER
PERTH

3

Bunbury•   *4*

•Wilyabrup
Cowaramup•   MARGARET

Margaret River•
5   BLACKWOOD

6

SOUTH WEST AUSTRALIA

Manjimup•   *7*   Frankland•   *10*

8

Pemberton•   *9*   *11*
Mt Barker•   *12*

FRANKLAND

13   *14*
Denmark   Albany

Background

Australia's biggest state is virtually all desert but it does have a cool coastal skirt that runs south from the state capital, Perth, and around the south-western corner to parts kept cool and damp under the influence of the Southern Ocean. WA contributes only a tiny amount to Australia's total wine production (3 per cent) but by our reckoning accounts for an unequal share of its premium wine. That said some have dropped the quality baton in the race for bigger volumes and healthier profits so care is needed when choosing from amongst some of the better known names.

The regions

The **Swan District** (Swan Valley) is historic heart of Western Australian viticulture. It is extremely hot and dry but from Verdelho, Chenin Blanc, Chardonnay and Semillon surprisingly good whites are produced. Reds, including Shiraz and Cabernet Sauvignon, can be characterful and well-made though the best wines are likely to include a Great Southern component. The celebrated **Margaret River** continues to grow apace with Cabernet Sauvignon and Chardonnay of remarkably rich, pure, deeply textured fruit. Sauvignon Blanc and Semillon (both individually and combined), and Shiraz are made to a high standard too. Quality in **Geographe** which incorporates a large swathe of countryside is led by Capel Vale. **Great Southern**, as its name suggests, is an especially large region. **Frankland River** is currently the most planted of five sub-regions, and often excels with Riesling, Chardonnay, Shiraz, Cabernet Sauvignon and Cabernet Franc. From **Mount Barker** comes particularly fine Shiraz as well as excellent Riesling and Chardonnay. **Porongurup** lies east of Mount Barker while scattered vineyards in **Albany** and **Denmark** can provide marvellous fruit. Between Great Southern and Margaret River even more far-flung vineyards are appearing in the gaps between extensive tracts of forest in three emerging areas, **Blackwood Valley**, **Manjimup** and **Pemberton**. Pinot Noir, Chardonnay, Shiraz and the Bordeaux varieties are all successful.

Western Australia Vintages

The vintage chart covers the most ageworthy styles and should be used in conjunction with comments on style and ageing within individual producer entries. While many wines can be drunk young, top full-bodied Margaret River Cabernet demands at least 5 years' cellaring. Great Southern Shiraz is usually a little more approachable but can also be long-lived. Top-quality Chardonnay and Pinot Noir only show their full potential with 3-5 years' ageing, while exceptions like Leeuwin Estate Art Series Chardonnay can age for more than 10 years. The best Great Southern Riesling is up there with the best from the eastern states and will keep for at least 5-6 years.

In 2003 Western Australia largely escaped the draught conditions that ravaged the eastern states but intermittent rain, and a mix of humid and drier conditions in the late summer took the edge off the vintage in both Great Southern and Margaret River. In 2004 in the Margaret River the season finished with a heatwave but this followed predominantly cool dry growing conditions (for good whites). The healthiest, more established vineyards of Cabernet Sauvignon are thought to have withstood the stress well. But while vintage prospects are generally excellent some reds may lack full physiological ripeness. 2005 could be outstanding with even ripening and good harvest conditions.

Wizard's Wishlist

Top Margaret River reds

CAPE MENTELLE ● Cabernet Sauvignon
CULLEN ● Cabernet Sauvignon/Merlot Diana Madeline
HOWARD PARK ● Cabernet Sauvignon Leston
LEEUWIN ESTATE ● Cabernet Sauvignon Art Series
MOSS WOOD ● Cabernet Sauvignon
PIERRO ● Cabernet Sauvignon/Merlot
VASSE FELIX ● Heytesbury

Distinguished WA whites

CAPE MENTELLE
O Semillon/Sauvignon Blanc Margaret River
CAPEL VALE O Riesling Whispering Hill
CULLEN O Sauvignon Blanc/Semillon Margaret River
HOWARD PARK O Riesling
LEEUWIN ESTATE O Chardonnay Arts Series
MOSS WOOD O Chardonnay Margaret River
PIERRO O Chardonnay Margaret River

Great Southern red stars

ALKOOMI ● Shiraz Frankland River Jarrah
CHATSFIELD ● Shiraz Mount Barker
FERNGROVE VINEYARDS ● Malbec King
FRANKLAND ESTATE ● Olmo's Reward
HOUGHTON ● Jack Mann
HOWARD PARK ● Cabernet Sauvignon/Merlot
PICARDY ● Shiraz Pemberton
PLANTAGENET ● Shiraz Mount Barker

Excellent value for money wines

ALKOOMI O Riesling Frankland River
CAPE MENTELLE ● Cabernet/Merlot Trinders
CAPEL VALE O Verdelho
CULLEN ● Ellen Bussell Red Margaret River
FONTY'S POOL ● Shiraz Pemberton
HOUGHTON'S O HWB
PLANTAGENET OMRAH O Riesling
STELLA BELLA O Sauvignon Blanc Margaret River

A-Z of producers

AUSTRALIA

ALKOOMI Frankland River www.alkoomiwines.com.au *UK stockists:* **Lay**
82 ha of estate vineyards provide refined Cab Sauv and Shiraz full of spicy berry fruit (especially in concentrated Jarrah, from the oldest vines). Also structured Blackbutt, from Cab Sauv, Cab Franc, Malbec and Merlot. Top white, Wandoo, is part oak-fermented Semillon. Others include zesty Sauvignon, well-structured Chardonnay and toasty Riesling. Fruit-driven basics under the Southlands label. (PW)
● **Cabernet Sauvignon**★★ £C ● **Blackbutt**★★★ £D
● **Shiraz**★★★£C Jarrah★★★ £D ○ **Sauvignon Blanc**★ £B
○ **Wandoo**★★★ £E ○ **Chardonnay**★★ £C ○ **Riesling**★★★ £B

CAPE MENTELLE *UK stockists:* **VCq,** JNi, ACh, Maj, P&S, F&M, Sel, Wai
A top Margaret River winery (also see Cloudy Bay). Ripe, spicy Semillon/Sauvignon also in single-vineyard selection, Wallcliffe (with more Sauvignon). Chardonnay is rich, powerful and complex. Ripe, dark berry-fruited Cabernet/Merlot is surpassed by bold, concentrated Cab Sauv that requires cellaring. Also dark fruits and black pepper Shiraz and rare gutsy Australian Zinfandel. (PW)
● **Cabernet Sauvignon**★★★★ £D ● **Cabernet/Merlot** Trinders★★★ £C
● **Shiraz**★★★ £C ● **Zinfandel**★★★ £C ○ **Wallcliffe**★★★ £D
○ **Chardonnay**★★★ £C ○ **Semillon/Sauvignon Blanc**★★★ £C

CAPEL VALE Geographe www.capelvale.com *UK stockists:* **D&D,** Por
150,000 cases a year. Best are top black label wines, especially ageworthy whites: intense, deep toast, smoke and lime Whispering Hill Riesling (Mount Barker) and rich, opulent Frederick Chardonnay (Geographe). Also good regular Verdelho, Riesling, pungent Sauvignon/Semillon and intense subtly oaked Chardonnay. Top reds are concentrated with plenty of oak. Kinnaird Shiraz (from Whispering Hill) surpasses more variable Howecroft Merlot (Geographe). Good everyday CV range. (PW)
● **Merlot**★★£C Howecroft★★★ £D ● **Shiraz**★★ £C Kinnaird★★★★ £E
○ **Chardonnay**★★ £C Frederick Reserve★★★★£D
○ **Riesling**★★ £B Whispering Hill★★★ £C ○ **Verdelho**★★ £B

CHATSFIELD Mount Barker www.chatsfield.com.au *UK stockists:* **Cac, DWS**
An impressive 16-ha family operation. Well-crafted and very well-priced wines include Gewürz and Riesling in a dry, structured and ageworthy style. Reds include Loire Valley-like elegant Cab Franc and great-value, refined Shiraz – chock full of dark fruit, liquorice and black pepper. (PW)
● **Cabernet Franc**★★ £B ● **Shiraz**★★★ £C
○ **Riesling**★★ £B ○ **Chardonnay**★★ £C ○ **Gewürztraminer**★★ £B

CULLEN Margaret River *UK stockists:* **Lib,** ACh, Vne, P&S, F&M, Hrd, Wai
Vanya Cullen's winery is arguably WA's best. Finesse, superior structure and complexity put the organic wines in a different class. Cab Sauv/Merlot matches top Bordeaux with superb fruit, outstanding breadth, depth and structure. Magnificent Chardonnay of great length and part barrel-fermented Sauvignon/Semillon with lovely texture and balance. Powerful new red blend, Mangan is Malbec/Petit Verdot/Merlot. Also new and promising Ellen Bussell red (Cab/Merlot) and white (Semillon/Sauvignon/Verdelho). (PW)
● **Cabernet Sauvignon/Merlot** Diana Madeline★★★★★ £E
● **Mangan**★★★ £D ● **Pinot Noir**★★ £D
○ **Chardonnay**★★★★ £E ○ **Sauvignon Blanc/Semillon**★★★ £C

EVANS & TATE Margaret River *UK stockists:* **AWs, IRW,** P&S
Now a very substantial operation. Of an extensive Margaret River collection, very ripe berryish Cabernet/Merlot (previously Barrique 61) and intense spicy Shiraz are better than the whites. Better still are the Redbrook Vineyard wines. Burgundian-styled Chardonnay is surprisingly restrained, while spicy, intense Shiraz (one of the region's best) and impressive Cab Sauv are ageworthy. (PW)
● **Shiraz** Margaret River★★ £B Redbrook★★★ £D
● **Cabernet Sauvignon** Redbrook★★★ £E
○ **Chardonnay** Margaret River★ £B Redbrook★★★ £D

312

FERNGROVE VINEYARDS Frankland River   *UK stockists:* **O&L,** Odd, NYg

A thriving, expanding operation offering good value in the regular varietals and dual-variety blends. Superior Orchid bottlings of reds show greater concentration and style (especially in 2001) including striking blackberry and black plum Special Late Harvested King Malbec, and The Stirlings, a Merlot/Cab Sauv/Malbec blend. White equivalents (not tasted) are Cossack Riesling and Butterfly Chardonnay. Also made is Margaret River label, Leaping Lizard. (PW)

Ferngrove Vineyards:
- **Shiraz★★** £B Dragon★★★ £C ● **Cabernet/Shiraz★** £B
- **Malbec** King★★★ £C ● **Cabernet Sauvignon** Majestic★★★ £C
○ **Semillon/Sauvignon Blanc★★** £B ○ **Riesling★★** £B ○ **Chardonnay★★** £B

Leaping Lizard:
○ **Semillon/Sauvignon Blanc★★** £B ● **Cabernet/Merlot★★** £B

FONTY'S POOL Pemberton www.fontyspoolwines.com.au   *UK stockists:* **Cap,** Vnf

Made by Cape Mentelle, Fonty's Pool reds offer good value against some of WA's more established labels. Stylish Shiraz has real depth and character while a smoky, plummy Pinot Noir has good breadth and a refined structure. Chardonnay has potential and Sauvignon Blanc/Semillon is a fruit-driven quaffer. Viognier and Cabernet/Merlot are also made. (PW)
- **Shiraz★★★** £B ● **Pinot Noir★★** £C
○ **Chardonnay★★** £C ○ **Semillon/Sauvignon Blanc★** £B

FRANKLAND ESTATE Frankland River   *UK stockists:* **FMV,** P&S

Flagship red is sleek and stylish Olmo's Reward, mostly Merlot and Cab Franc. Also impressive estate-sourced Isolation Ridge wines: ageworthy Riesling stands out with its tight, apple and mineral fruit (now in two single-vineyard versions: Cooladerah and Poison Hill) but also good black pepper, brambly Shiraz and intensely berryish Cab Sauv. Rocky Gully wines are made from contract-grown fruit. (PW)
- **Olmo's Reward★★★** £D
- **Cabernet Sauvignon** Isolation Ridge★★ £C ● **Shiraz** Isolation Ridge★★★ £C
○ **Chardonnay** Isolation Ridge★★ £C ○ **Riesling** Isolation Ridge★★★ £B

GILBERTS Mount Barker   *UK stockists:* **Gun, RHW**

Small range from well-established vines includes floral Riesling, and Chardonnay with good richness and nicely integrated oak. 3 Devils Shiraz, from younger vines, has good spiciness and soft tannins; Reserve Shiraz, from 20-year-old vines is a different proposition – rich but with finesse and complexity. (NB)
○ **Riesling★★** £B ○ **Chardonnay★★★** £B
- **Shiraz/Cabernet★★** £B ● **Shiraz** 3 Devils★★ £B Reserve★★★★ £C

HOUGHTON Swan District   *UK stockists:* **Cst,** WSc, P&S, Maj

Now part of Constellation Wines and the biggest operation in WA, sourcing grapes throughout the state. Flagship is Jack Mann red, a dense, powerful and sometimes oaky blend of Cab Sauv, Shiraz and Malbec that demands ageing. Regional wines from Frankland River, Pemberton and Margaret River are also impressive. Basic Line range includes highly successful HWB (Chenin, Muscadelle, Verdelho and others), almost unique among big-volume whites in its ability to age. (PW)
- **Jack Mann★★★★** £F ● **Shiraz** Frankland River★★★ £C ○ **HWB★★** £B
- **Merlot** Pemberton★★★ £C ● **Cabernet Sauvignon** Margaret River★★ £C
○ **Riesling** Frankland River★★★ £B ○ **Sauvignon Blanc** Pemberton★★ £B

HOWARD PARK Denmark   *UK stockists:* **Bib,** L&W, JNi, P&S, NYg

Fast rising and rapidly expanding quality WA producer with over 200 ha of estate vineyards. Three top wines are labelled simply Howard Park: a superb complex Riesling, dense, powerful and profound Cab Sauv/Merlot, and restrained, structured and ageworthy Chardonnay. Also good are region-specific Scotsdale (Great Southern) and Leston (Margaret River) Shiraz and Cab Sauv. The Madfish label offers immediate fruit character and appeal. (PW)

Howard Park:
- **Cabernet Sauvignon/Merlot★★★★** £E ○ **Riesling★★★★** £C
- **Cabernet Sauvignon** Scotsdale★★★ £C Leston★★★ £C

AUSTRALIA

● **Shiraz** Scotsdale★★★ £C Leston★★★ £C ○ **Chardonnay**★★★★ £C
Madfish:
● **Premium Red**★ £B   ● **Shiraz**★★ £B   ● **Pinot Noir**★★ £B
○ **Chardonnay**★★ £B   ○ **Premium White**★ £B

LEEUWIN ESTATE Margaret River   *UK stockists:* **DDr**, BBR, P&S, F&M, Hrd, Sel, Wai, Las
One of the very best in the Margaret River with excellent Art Series wines: extraordinarily rich and and powerful, yet balanced Chardonnay and very intense Riesling with mineral, lime and a marvellous toasty persistence with age. Also very stylish Sauvignon, while reds include a fine Cab Sauv which shows a complex fusion of cooler and riper fruit with excellent structure and length. Prelude is a second tier of wines with generally good richness and structure but faster evolving. (PW)
● **Cabernet Sauvignon** Art Series★★★★ £E   ● **Cabernet/Merlot** Prelude★★★ £C
● **Pinot Noir** Art Series★★ £D   ○ **Riesling** Art Series★★★ £C
○ **Chardonnay** Art Series★★★★★ £E   ○ **Sauvignon Blanc** Art Series★★★ £C

MOSS WOOD Margaret River www.mosswood.com.au   *UK stockists:* Lay, NYg, P&S
Very fine, small but long-establed Margaret River estate of 12 ha. Excellent unwooded Semillon and full, opulent Chardonnay. Complex, powerful and structured Cab Sauv is one of the region's finest. The range now includes three Ribbon Vale vineyard wines following purchase of this 6-ha vineyard and winery. Also produced from growers' vineyards are Cabernet Sauvignon from Amy's Vineyard (previously Glenmore), a tiny amount of Green Valley Chardonnay, and Chardonnay and Pinot Noir from the Lefroy Brook Vineyard in Pemberton.(PW)
● **Cabernet Sauvignon**★★★★ £F Amy's Vineyard★★★ £C
● **Cabernet Sauvignon/Merlot** Ribbon Vale Vineyard★★★ £D
○ **Chardonnay**★★★★ £E Lefroy Brook Vineyard★★★ £D   ○ **Semillon**★★★★ £C

PICARDY Pemberton www.picardy.com.au   *UK stockists:* **Lay**, CPp
Arguably Pemberton's top producer, owned by Bill Pannell (who established Moss Wood). Chardonnay has excellent structure and texture, judiciously oaked Pinot Noir is full of dark, berry-fruit and Shiraz shows a real intensity of spice, pepper and berry fruits. Cab Sauv, Merlot and Cab Franc are also planted – Merlot/Cabernet is a roughly equal blend of all three. (PW)
● **Merlot/Cabernet**★★ £C   ● **Shiraz**★★★ £C
● **Pinot Noir**★★★ £C   ○ **Chardonnay**★★★ £C

PIERRO Margaret River   *UK stockists:* **MSd**, BBR, P&S, Las
Home to one of the most complete WA Chardonnays, possessing excellent fruit and an array of secondary flavours with great breadth and intensity in the mouth. LTC is a fine, grassy, melony Semillon/Sauvignon with good intensity and structure. Berryish, slightly earthy Cab Sauv/Merlot misses the concentration of the very best Margaret River examples. Pinot Noir is flavoursome if very ripe. Fire Gully reds lack richness and depth; whites are better. (PW)
Pierro:
○ **Chardonnay**★★★★ £E   ○ **Semillon/Sauvignon Blanc** LTC★★★ £C
● **Cabernet Sauvignon/Merlot**★★★ £E   ● **Pinot Noir**★★ £D
Fire Gully:
● **Cabernet/Merlot**★ £C   ○ **Semillon/Sauvignon Blanc**★★ £B

PLANTAGENET www.plantagenetwines.com   *UK stockists:* **Lib**, ACh, Ben, Luv, V&C, Vne, P&S
Mount Barker's top winery with over 100,000 cases a year of a consistently high standard. Highlights include ripe, smoky Pinot Noir, expressive and undervalued Chardonnay, great value, limey Riesling and distinctive, elegant Cab Sauv. Shiraz is mightily impressive – as much Northern Rhône as Western Australia. Estate Rocky Horror Vineyard now a source of Merlot and excellent Cab Franc. 'Off the Rack' Chenin is from partially dried grapes. Second label Omrah of good quality. (PW)
Plantagenet:
● **Shiraz** Mount Barker★★★★ £D   ● **Cabernet Sauvignon** Mount Barker★★★ £C
● **Pinot Noir** Great Southern★★★ £C
○ **Chardonnay** Mount Barker★★★ £C   ○ **Riesling** Mount Barker★★★ £B

314

Omrah:
● **Shiraz★★** £B ● **Cabernet/Merlot★** £B
○ **Chardonnay** Unoaked★★ £B ○ **Sauvignon Blanc★** £B

SUCKFIZZLE/STELLA BELLA Margaret River *UK stockists:* **All**, Odd, P&S, Sel, Wai
Encompassing three labels: the single-vineyard Suckfizzle wines, Stella Bella and a third, Skuttlebutt. Stella Bella whites have intense, ripe fruit flavours (herbal, fruit-accented Sauvignon/Semillon contrasts with barrel-fermented and lees-stirred Suckfizzle version) but the reds are more interesting. Cool, cedary and ageworthy Suckfizzle Cab Sauv is a notch or two higher. (PW)

Suckfizzle Augusta:
○ **Sauvignon Blanc/Semillon★★★** £D ● **Cabernet Sauvignon★★★** £D
Stella Bella:
○ **Sauvignon Blanc★★** £B ○ **Semillon/Sauvignon Blanc★★** £B
● **Cabernet Sauvignon/Merlot★★★** £C ● **Sangiovese/Cabernet★★★** £C

VASSE FELIX Margaret River *UK stockists:* **Neg**, L&W, Tan, CPp, P&S, Han, Hrd, Sel
Sizeable Margaret River operation producing some 125,000 cases a year. Reputation built on top reds. Cab Sauv is denser and better structured than berryish Cabernet/Merlot while Shiraz is intense and refined. Rich, concentrated Heytesbury red is from Cab Sauv, Shiraz, Merlot and Malbec. Chardonnay impresses, including powerful Heytesbury version when balance is maintained. The same goes for Semillon. Rich and concentrated Noble Riesling is made when conditions allow. (PW)

● **Heytesbury★★★★** £E ● **Cabernet Sauvignon★★★** £D
● **Shiraz★★★** £D ○ **Semillon★★** £B ○ **Semillon/Sauvignon Blanc★★** £B
○ **Chardonnay★★** £B Heytesbury★★★ £C ○ **Noble Riesling★★★** £E

VOYAGER ESTATE Margaret River www.voyagerestate.com.au *UK stockists:* **J&B**, Odd
A Margaret River tourist magnet with rich and powerful wines, if occasionally disjointed and overly made. Secondary flavours can be slightly exaggerated at the cost of purity or sense of origin but will appeal more to some palates than others. Also made are premium Tom Price red and white from single vineyard sources. (PW)

○ **Sauvignon Blanc/Semillon★★** £B ○ **Semillon★★★** £B ○ **Chardonnay★★★** £C
● **Cabernet Sauvignon/Merlot★★★** £C ● **Shiraz★★★** £C

WILLOW BRIDGE ESTATE Geographe www.willowbridgeestate.com *UK stockists:* **SsG**
Large Ferguson Valley estate with strengths in Semillon, Sauvignon and Shiraz. The top Shiraz, Black Dog, reveals intense black plum and licorice fruit on an expansive palate. Basic Dragonfly range includes good everyday Sauvignon Blanc/Semillon and Shiraz. (PW)

○ **Sauvignon Blanc/Semillon** Dragonfly★ £B
○ **Sauvignon Blanc** Reserve★★ £B ○ **Semillon/Sauvignon Blanc** Reserve★★★ £C
● **Shiraz** Dragonfly★ £B Reserve★★ £C Black Dog★★★ £E

WOODSIDE VALLEY ESTATE Margaret River *UK stockists:* **May**
An exceptional new project where vines have been planted on south-facing slopes rather than the usual north-facing slopes. Production of four varietals is small: Le Bas Chardonnay, Bissy Merlot, Bonnefoy Shiraz and Baudin Cabernet Sauvignon. All are distinguished by their elegance, purity and a beautifully delineated fruit expression, though Merlot and Chardonnay want for more depth. All are potentially four star but prices are high (£E/F). (PW)

○ **Chardonnay** Le Bas★★★ £E ● **Merlot** The Bissy★★★ £E
● **Cabernet Sauvignon** The Baudin★★★★ £E
● **Shiraz** The Bonnefoy★★★★ £E

Other wineries of note
Goundrey (Mount Barker), Gralyn Estate (Margaret River), Hackersley (Geographe), Higher Plane (Margaret River), Rickety Gate (Denmark), Talijancich (Swan Valley)

An in-depth profile of every producer can be found in Wine behind the label 2006

1 Northland
2 Matakana
3 Kumeu/Huapai
4 Waiheke Island
5 Waikato
6 Bay of Plenty
7 Gisborne
8 Hawke's Bay
9 Martinborough/Wairarapa
10 Nelson
11 Marlborough
12 Waipara
13 Canterbury
14 Waitaki
15 Central Otago

NORTHLAND
Whangarei
AUCKLAND
Auckland
Hamilton
WAIKATO
WAIKATO
Rotorua
BAY OF PLENTY
GISBORNE
Gisborne
Taupo
HAWKE'S BAY
New Plymouth
TARANAKI
Napier
Hastings
MANAWATU-WANGANUI

TASMAN
Nelson
Martinborough
Westport
WAIRAU
Blenheim
Wellington
WELLINGTON
MARLBOROUGH
WEST COAST
Greymouth
CANTERBURY
Waipara
WAIMAKARIRI
Christchurch
Tekapo
RANGITATA
Timaru
Wanaka
WAITAKI
Wakatipu
Te Anau
Queenstown
Alexandra
OTAGO
CLUTHA
SOUTHLAND
Dunedin
Invercargill

Background

New Zealand's wine profile, with an image first centred on intense, vibrant, fruit-driven whites for immediate consumption is now in a state of perpetual evolution. It's true many winemakers have fashioned wines based on a dogma of technological expertise but the influence of the European quality revival (underpinned by better health in the vineyard) is also apparent. Slowly too, the best sites are being unearthed and planted to the most suited varieties.

Changing colours

Despite rapid expansion in the 1990s, first the record harvest of 2002 and now unprecedented production of 2004 (166,000 tonnes), New Zealand's output (three-quarters white) is still small in the global context. Gradually the industry has moved southwards from **Auckland** (with the greatest success in **Kumeu, Huapai, Waiheke Island** and **Matakana**) through **Gisborne** and **Hawkes Bay** (includes **Gimblett Gravels**) before confirming **Marlborough** as its leading region (with Sauvignon its most important grape). The regions of **Nelson, Martinborough, Waipara** and **Central Otago** contribute little quantity wise but significantly broaden the quality spectrum. Fine Chardonnay has been produced in all leading regions and Cabernet Sauvignon, Merlot and other Bordeaux grapes have found their place (best in Hawkes Bay, Waiheke Island and Matakana). Central Otago seems set to prove the best region for Pinot Noir but Martinborough, Marlborough, Waipara provide serious competition while the newest region, **Waitaki Valley** is also generating excitement. Other varieties taking hold include Pinot Gris, Gewürztraminer, Riesling and Syrah - with some excellent examples from diverse sources. There is increasing regional or even site-specific identification for many quality wines with less cross-regional blending than previously.

New Zealand Vintages

With a few exceptions, New Zealand whites haven't enjoyed a good reputation for ageing and many Chardonnays that were attractive with one or two years' age were falling apart with three or more. However this is changing even if only rare examples of Marlborough Sauvignon can improve in the way a top Sancerre or Pouilly-Fumé can. In fact the majority still need to be consumed within the first year after the vintage. The few exceptions have been noted in the producer entries. Riesling and sweet wines will generally keep a little longer. Reds have a growing reputation for keeping thanks to improved viticultural and winemaking practices. The best Cabernet Sauvignon and Merlot-based reds show an increasing propensity to age. Top examples, coming in the main from Waiheke or Hawkes Bay, now usually need 5 years' ageing but can keep for 10 from an excellent vintage. In addition to those styles

rated in the chart below, the best Waiheke vintages (no recent top vintages) include 2000, 99, 98, 94, 93, 91 and 90, while 97 and 96 aren't bad. Shiraz and Pinot Noir are also ageworthy. For most good examples, 3-6 years' age is likely to be the window of optimum drinking but it is very producer dependent - some of the bigger, more extracted styles might need 5 years or more.

The 2005 vintage in New Zealand was the second largest ever but from more normal yields than the record harvest of 2004 - the latter more than twice that of the frost-decimated 2003 (worst felt in Hawkes Bay). 2005 was characterised by a very cool early summer and wet March in both Marlborough and Hawkes Bay but fine, dry conditions in April will ensure good quality from the healthiest vineyards. Most producers are also happy with quality in 2004 despite significant late summer rain. The exception was Central Otago which suffered frost and a drop in both quality and quantity. This was the reverse of 2003 when Central Otago was the exception to a difficult vintage.

Wizard's Wishlist

Most arresting Sauvignon Blanc

CLOUDY BAY O **Sauvignon Blanc** Marlborough
CRAGGY RANGE
O **Sauvignon Blanc** Marlborough Old Renwick
DOG POINT O **Sauvignon Blanc** Marlborough Section 94
GRAVITAS O **Sauvignon Blanc** Marlborough
HUNTER'S O **Sauvignon Blanc** Marlborough
ISABEL ESTATE O **Sauvignon Blanc** Marlborough
STAETE LANDT O **Sauvignon Blanc** Marlborough
VAVASOUR
O **Sauvignon Blanc** Marlborough Single Vineyard
VILLA MARIA
O **Sauvignon Blanc** Marlborough Taylor's Pass

Most convincing Chardonnay

ATA RANGI O **Chardonnay** Martinborough Craighall
CRAGGY RANGE
O **Les Beaux Cailloux Chardonnay** Gimblett Gravels
ESK VALLEY O **Chardonnay** Hawkes Bay Reserve
FELTON ROAD
O **Chardonnay** Central Otago Barrel-Fermented
GRAVITAS O **Chardonnay** Marlborough
KUMEU RIVER O **Chardonnay** Kumeu
MATUA VALLEY O **Chardonnay** Gisborne Judd Estate
MILLTON O **Chardonnay** Gisborne Opou Vineyard
PEGASUS BAY O **Chardonnay** Waipara
TE MATA O **Chardonnay** Hawkes Bay Elston
VAVASOUR O **Chardonnay** Marlborough Awatere Valley
VILLA MARIA
O **Chardonnay** Marlborough Fletcher Vineyard

New Zealand

Diverse high quality whites
ATA RANGI O **Pinot Gris** Martinborough Lismore
DRY RIVER O **Pinot Gris** Martinborough
FELTON ROAD O **Riesling** Central Otago Dry
MILLTON O **Chenin Blanc** Gisborne Te Arai Vineyard
STONECROFT O **Gewürztraminer** Hawkes Bay

Top Cabernet or Merlot based reds
ALPHA DOMUS ● **AD The Aviator** Hawkes Bay
CRAGGY RANGE ● **The Quarry** Gimblett Gravels
ESK VALLEY ● **The Terraces** Hawkes Bay
MATAKANA ESTATE ● **Moko** Matakana
OBSIDIAN ● **Obsidian** Waiheke Island
RED METAL ● **The Merlot** Hawkes Bay
STONYRIDGE ● **Larose Cabernets** Waiheke Island
TE MATA ● **Coleraine** Hawkes Bay
UNISON ● **Selection** Gimblett Gravels

Leading Pinot Noir
ATA RANGI ● **Pinot Noir** Martinborough
FELTON ROAD ● **Pinot Noir** Central Otago Block 3
FROMM
● **La Strada Pinot Noir** Marlborough Fromm Vineyard

MOUNTFORD ● **Pinot Noir** Waipara
MURDOCH JAMES ESTATE
● **Pinot Noir** Martinborough Fraser
NEUDORF ● **Pinot Noir** Moutere
OLSSENS ● **Pinot Noir** Central Otago Jackson Barry
PISA RANGE ● **Pinot Noir** Central Otago Black Poplar Block
SCHUBERT ● **Pinot Noir** Wairarapa
TERRAVIN ● **Pinot Noir** Marlborough Hillside Selection
TWO PADDOCKS
● **Pinot Noir** Central Otago Last Chance
VILLA MARIA
● **Pinot Noir** Marlborough Seddon Vineyard

Most promising Syrah
CRAGGY RANGE ● **Syrah** Gimblett Gravels Block 14
DRY RIVER ● **Syrah** Martinborough
MURDOCH JAMES ESTATE ● **Syrah** Martinborough
SCHUBERT ● **Syrah**
STONECROFT ● **Syrah** Hawkes Bay
TE MATA ● **Syrah** Hawkes Bay Bullnose

New Zealand A-Z of producers

ALPHA DOMUS Hawkes Bay www.alphadomus.co.nz *UK stockists:* **McK**, NYg, Has, Hrd
Leading Hawkes Bay producer; wines from own 20 ha since 1995. AD is premium label. Ripe, composed reds: Merlot-dominated The Navigator and impressive, concentrated Bordeaux blend Aviator. Richly textured AD Chardonnay contrasts with tangy, peachy unoaked version. Very ripe Semillon also made in a rich botrytised version, AD Noble Selection. (PW)
● **AD The Aviator**★★★★ £E   ● **The Navigator**★★★ £D
O **Chardonnay** Unoaked★★ £B AD★★★ £C   O **Semillon**★★ £B

ATA RANGI Martinborough www.atarangi.co.nz *UK stockists:* **Lib**, MHv, WSc, Hrd
Winery with an enviable reputation thanks to consistently fine Pinot Noir that is rich and complex with three to five years. The 34.5 ha of low-yielding vineyards (now including 2.2-ha Walnut Ridge) are mostly on Martinborough Terrace. Vine age is over 20 years. Also good but vintage-dependent is cedary, berryish Célèbre (Cabernet/Syrah/Merlot). Very good premium Chardonnay, Craighall. Top quince-like Pinot Gris, also Sauvignon, a botrytised Riesling (Kahu), and new Syrah. (PW)
● **Pinot Noir**★★★★ £E   ● **Célèbre**★★★ £C
O **Chardonnay** Craighall★★★ £C Petrie★★ £B   O **Pinot Gris** Lismore★★ £C

BLACK RIDGE Central Otago www.blackridge.co.nz *UK stockists:* **BFs**
Central Otago pioneer, commenced 1981. Riesling and Gewürz both show good depth, varietal intensity and structure to age at least two to three years. Ripe and concentrated mineral-tinged Chardonnay will also keep. Improving smoky-fruited Pinot Noir has density and grip, needing time. (PW)
● **Pinot Noir**★★ £D   O **Chardonnay**★★ £C
O **Gewürztraminer**★★ £C   O **Riesling**★★ £C

CABLE BAY Waiheke Island www.cablebayvineyards.co.nz *UK stockists:* **Str**, NZH
Newish 20-ha Waiheke estate with several sites. Chardonnay already shows breadth, intensity and class and red Five Hills (Merlot/Malbec/ Cab Sauv) shows good promise if from young vines. Viognier and Pinot Gris are also planted. Good Sauvignon and velvety Pinot Noir from Marlborough grapes. Culley label indicates bought-in grapes. (PW)
O **Sauvignon Blanc** Marlborough★★★ £B

318

New entries have producer's name underlined

○ **Chardonnay** Waiheke★★★ £C   Culley Marlborough★★ £B   ○ **Riesling** Culley Marlborough★ £B
● **Pinot Noir** Marlborough★★★ £D   ● **Five Hills** Waiheke★★ £D

CARRICK   Central Otago   www.carrick.co.nz   *UK stockists:* **GWW**, P&S, NYg, NZH
Winemaker Steve Davies seems to be getting into his stride with Pinot Noir of real depth, concentration and spicy, plummy fruit complexity in 2002. Chardonnay is also one of the region's best and will improve for at least 2–3 years. Also cool, zesty 04 Sauvignon, Riesling, Pinot Gris, a more richly oaked Chardonnay, and everyday Pinot Noir (Unravelled). (PW)

● **Pinot Noir**★★★ £D   ○ **Chardonnay**★★★ £C
○ **Sauvignon Blanc**★★ £C   ○ **Pinot Gris**★★ £C

CHURCH ROAD   Hawkes Bay   www.churchroad.co.nz   *UK stockists:* **ADo**, Odd
Montana's relatively small Hawkes Bay operation with input from Bordeaux *négociant* Cordier. Good Reserve Cab Sauv, especially with five years' age. Also Montana's flagship red, Tom – a small-volume, complex, cedary Bordeaux-like red from Merlot, Cab Sauv and Cab Franc (1995, 96 and 98) that requires patience. (PW)

○ **Chardonnay**★ £B   Reserve★★ £C
● **Cabernet/Merlot** Reserve★★ £C   ● **Tom**★★★ £F

CLOUDY BAY   Marlborough   *UK stockists:* **MHn**, Maj, Ni, NYg, Rae, UnC
NZ's best-known winery internationally, producing its most famous Sauvignon – still among Marlborough's best despite bigger volumes, also unusual in ability to age. Barrel-fermented Te Koko has style and finesse. Pinot Noir and Chardonnay good but could be more. Fruit-rich sparkling Pelorus best in more structured vintage-dated version. (PW)

○ **Sauvignon Blanc**★★★ £C   Te Koko★★★ £D   ○ **Chardonnay**★★ £C
○ **Pelorus** Non-Vintage★★ £C   Vintage★★★ £D   ● **Pinot Noir**★★ £D

CRAGGY RANGE   Hawkes Bay   www.craggyrange.com   *UK stockists:* **Cap**, ACh, NYg, Wai
NZ's most dynamic winery in recent vintages, processing grapes from outstanding vineyard sites in Hawkes Bay, Martinborough and Marlborough. Concentrated, well-structured wines with an extra intensity and definition not seen in most NZ wines. 'Prestige' wines from Gimblett Gravels include: Les Beaux Cailloux Chardonnay; The Quarry, mostly Cab Sauv; Sophia, Merlot-based but with Cab Franc and Malbec; and Syrah, Le Sol. All show great promise as does classy, black-fruited Block 14 Syrah. (PW)

○ **Sauvignon Blanc** Te Muna★★★ £B   Avery★★★ £B   Old Renwick★★★★ £C
○ **Chardonnay** Seven Poplars★★★ £C   ○ **Riesling** Rapaura Road Vineyard★★★ £C
○ **Les Beaux Cailloux**★★★ £D   ● **Syrah** Block 14★★★ £D   ● **Le Sol**★★★★ £E
● **Sophia**★★★ £E   ● **The Quarry**★★★ £E

THE CROSSINGS ESTATE   Marlborough   www.thecrossings.co.nz   *UK stockists:* **HBJ**, NZH
Large Awatere Valley development with 140ha and a focus on Sauvignon. The regular version has excellent structure with classic Awatere style, showing subtle mineral, citrus and passionfruit aroma and flavour. Catherine's Run Reserve, partly fermented and aged in barrel, has more breadth and texture. Chardonnay, Pinot Noir and Cab Sauv are also made. (PW)

○ **Sauvignon Blanc**★★★ £C   Catherine's Run Reserve★★★ £C

DOG POINT VINEYARD   Marlborough   www.dogpoint.co.nz   *UK stockists:* **FMV**, NYg, P&S, Sel, Hrd
Arguably the hottest of Marlborough' s new names. Both the owners have had a long relationship with Cloudy Bay before starting their own small, hands-on operation. Section 94 Sauvignon Blanc from a specific plot is oak-fermented and aged and has atypical density and extract. Also stainless steel version in 2004 and concentrated yet restrained Chardonnay with intense grapefruit and mealy complexity. (PW)

○ **Sauvignon Blanc**★★★ £C   Section 94★★★ £D   ○ **Chardonnay**★★★ £D

DRY RIVER   Martinborough   *UK stockists:* **J&B**, NYg, Rae
Small estate with 10 ha of prime Martinborough vineyards and an enviable cult following due to the unstinting efforts of Dr Neil McCallum. All wines are ageworthy with complexity, depth and richness of texture, including the best Gewürz and Riesling in the country. Under new (American) ownership from 2003 but with the same direction. Mostly sells through a mailing list but a little is exported. (PW)

● **Pinot Noir**★★★★ £E   ● **Syrah**★★★ £E   ○ **Pinot Gris**★★★ £D
○ **Riesling** Craighall★★★★ £D   ○ **Gewürztraminer**★★★★ £D

319

ESK VALLEY Hawkes Bay www.eskvalley.co.nz *UK stockists:* **HMA**, Odd, WSc
Villa Maria-owned winery run by Gordon Russell. Rich, intense and powerful The Terraces red (Malbec, Merlot and Cab Franc) is made in top vintages only – 2000, 98 and 95; next will be 2002. Very good if more variable Reserve Merlot/Cab Sauv/Malbec. Good whites include Meursault-like Reserve Chardonnay. Other reasonably priced varietals are attractive, ripe and fruit-accented. (PW)
● The Terraces★★★★ £G ○ Chardonnay★★ £B Reserve★★★ £C
● Merlot/Cabernet Sauvignon /Malbec★★ £B Gimblett Gravels Reserve★★★ £D

FELTON ROAD www.feltonroad.com *UK stockists:* **CPW**, BBR, ACh, Rae, P&S
Leading Central Otago winery owned by Englishman Nigel Greening. Inspired winemaking from Walter Blair gives Pinot Noir with great richness and complexity. Chardonnay and Riesling too are very good as are Pinot Gris and new Pinot Noir fom Cornish Point Vineyard. Single-vineyard Block 1 Riesling (made in a rich medium-dry Spätlese style) from 2001 and Block 2 Chardonnay from 2002. (PW)
Felton Road:
● Pinot Noir★★★ £D Block 3★★★★ £E Block 5★★★★ £E
○ Chardonnay★★ £C Barrel Fermented★★★ £C Block 2★★★ £D
○ Riesling★★★ £C Dry★★★ £C
Cornish Point Vineyard:
● Pinot Noir★★★ £D

FROMM Marlborough www.frommwineries.com *UK stockists:* **L&W**, NYg, Hrd
Leading Marlborough winery for Pinot Noir (including Clayvin Vineyard) based on low yields, fully ripe grapes and minimal intervention. Also Chardonnay and Riesling. All show good character, flavour intensity and structure but the range varies from year to year. Impressive Reserve Syrah. Reserve Merlot includes a little Cab Franc and Malbec. Small quantities of Gewürz and Sauvignon Blanc and, since 1999, a Malbec/Merlot blend. (PW)
La Strada:
● Pinot Noir★ £C Fromm Vineyard★★★ £E Clayvin Vineyard★★★ £D
○ Chardonnay★★ £C ○ Riesling★★ £C

GOLDWATER ESTATE Waiheke Island www.goldwaterwine.com *UK stockists:* **Hal**, ACh, Hrd
Waiheke pioneer Kim Goldwater has long produced a structured and powerful yet elegant Cab Sauv/Merlot that needs a minimum of five years' age. Also from Waiheke are impressive Esslin Merlot and premium Zell Chardonnay. Marlborough vineyards provide aromatic New Dog Sauvignon (previously Dog Point). New vineyard too in Hawkes Bay's Gimblett Gravels. (PW)
● Cabernet Sauvigon/Merlot★★★ £E ● Merlot Esslin★★★ £F
○ Chardonnay Roseland★★ £B Zell★★★ £D ○ Sauvignon Blanc New Dog★★ £B

GRAVITAS Marlborough www.new-zealand-wines.com *UK stockists:* **OWL**, JNi, UnC, Sel
New and exciting young Marlborough operation with 30 ha in Wairau Valley (Saint Arnaud's Vineyard) including some steep slopes from which a Pinot Noir was first produced in 2004. Early reputation for Sauvignon Blanc and Chardonnay with vibrancy, purity and concentration from atypically low yields. Also Vin de Paille, a new sparkling wine and, from 2005, Pinot Gris. (PW)
○ Sauvignon Blanc★★★ £B ○ Chardonnay★★★ £B Unoaked★★ £B
● Pinot Noir★★★ £D
○ Chardonnay★★ £B ○ Pinot Gris★★ £B ● Pinot Noir★ £C

HERZOG Marlborough www.herzog.co.nz *UK stockists:* NYg
Tiny quantities of handmade wines from Swiss immigrants Hans and Therese Herzog. Unfined, unfiltered wines from low-yielding, hand-picked grapes include Spirit of Marlborough – a stylish, nuanced Bordeaux-style red. Also, unusually, Montepulciano that is ripe and characterful with plenty of the grape's flesh and depth. Pinot Noir is from young vines. Also small amounts of Chardonnay, Pinot Gris and Viognier (with cult following). Winery restaurant very highly regarded. (PW)
● Montepulciano★★★ £D ● Spirit of Marlborough★★★ £D
● Pinot Noir★★ £D

320

HUNTER'S   Marlborough   www.hunters.co.nz   *UK stockists:* **Lay, WIE**, WSc, NYg, Kwi, P&S
Jane Hunter's wines show a harmony, charm and gentler character in contrast to brasher Marlborough efforts.
Two fine Sauvignons – a stylish unoaked version and a seamless, gently creamy Winemakers Selection
(previously 'Oak-aged'). Also perfumed raspberry and cherry Pinot Noir of moderate intensity and
concentration and ripe, well-structured sparkling wine. A little Merlot is also made. (PW)

O **Sauvignon Blanc★★★** £B   Winemakers Selection★★★ £C
O **Riesling★★** £B   O **Gewürztraminer★** £C   O **Chardonnay★★** £C
O **Miru Miru** Brut Vintage★★ £C   ● **Pinot Noir★★** £C

ISABEL ESTATE   www.isabelestate.com   *UK stockists:* **FMV**, NYg, Kwi, UnC, P&S, Sel
50-ha Marlborough estate with well-established, densely planted vineyards. First-rate Sauvignon. Pinot Noir
impresses with vivid fruit and improving texture and breadth while bright, crunchy Riesling shows typical Isabel
fruit intensity and Pinot Gris has attractive pear and quince fruit. Also Noble Sauvage, a botrytised Sauvignon,
in 2000 and 02. (PW)

O **Sauvignon Blanc★★★★** £C   O **Pinot Gris★★** £C
O **Chardonnay★★** £C   O **Riesling** Dry★★★ £C   ● **Pinot Noir★★★** £D

KUMEU RIVER   Kumeu, Auckland   *UK stockists:* **Box, Far**, Ben, WSc, Hrd
Family estate of top winemaker Michael Brajkovich with the country's leading Chardonnays – richly
textured, complex wines with well-integrated oak and atypically ageworthy. Ripe, characterful Merlot/Malbec/
Cab Franc blend Melba. Recently also promising Pinot Noir and a rich yet floral Pinot Gris. Second label is
now called Kumeu River Village. All wines bottled under Stelvin caps. (PW)

O **Chardonnay★★★★** £D   Maté's Vineyard★★★★ £D
O **Pinot Gris★★** £C   ● Melba★★ £C

MARTINBOROUGH VINEYARD   www.martinborough-vineyard.co.nz   *UK stockists:* **B-S**, NYg
Important estate that helped to establish Martinborough's reputation for Pinot Noir. Recent releases made by
Claire Mulholland show more restraint and refinement – also seen in rich, ripe Chardonnay and full, intense
Riesling (Manu is late-picked, off-dry style). Pinot Gris and Sauvignon (Pirinoa Block) are also made as is
newish second Pinot Noir, Te Tera. (PW)

● **Pinot Noir★★★★** £D   Te Téra★★ £C
O **Chardonnay** Martinborough Terrace★★★ £C
O **Riesling** Jackson Block★★ £C

MATAKANA ESTATE   Matakana, Auckland   *UK stockists:* **BWC**, Vts
34-ha estate with a classy, individual premium red, Moko, from Bordeaux varieties. Composition varies
significantly but usually includes around 20 per cent Malbec. Excellent in recent vintages but not produced in
2003 or 01. Also very good ripe pear and quince Pinot Gris. Goldridge Estate wines are sourced both from
estate vineyards in Marlborough and contract growers in Hawkes Bay. (PW)

Matakana Estate:
O **Pinot Gris★★★** £C   ● **Moko★★★** £D

MILLTON   Gisborne   www.millton.co.nz   *UK stockists:* **Vcs**, ARe
The Milltons are best known for their biodynamic stance, making 'natural' wines of good fruit richness,
intensity and purity. Most successful from 20 ha are Chenin (country's best), Riesling and Chardonnay. Under a
Growers Series label, there's Viognier from the Tietjen Vineyard and Gewürz. Also late-harvested 'Special Bunch
Selection' Riesling and Gewürz, and red Merlot/Cab. (PW)

O **Riesling** Opou Vineyard★★★ £B   O **Chardonnay** Opou Vineyard★★★ £B
O **Chenin Blanc** Te Arai Vineyard★★★ £B

MONTANA   Gisborne, Marlborough & Auckland   *UK stockists:* **ADo**, AAA
New Zealand's largest producer with extensive vineyard holding across the three major regions. Consistent
regular Chardonnay and Sauvignon, better Reserves and Estate-labelled wines which can add more
sophistication, structure and concentration. Newest is 'T' Terraces Estate Pinot Noir (from 2002) from
Marlborough. Also fine sparkling wines in collaboration with Deutz (Champagne house) and sweet wine, Virtu
from botrytised Semillon. See Church Road for Hawkes Bay reds. (PW)

321

Gisborne:
O **Chardonnay** Gisborne Reserve★ £B Ormond Estate★★ 'O' £C
O **Gewürztraminer** Gisborne Reserve★ £B Patuthai Estate 'P'★ £C
Montana Brancott Winery:
O **Sauvignon Blanc** Reserve★ £B Brancott Estate 'B'★★ £C
● **Pinot Noir** Reserve★ £B ● **Cabernet Sauvignon** Fairhall Estate 'F'★★ £C
O **Deutz Marborough** Cuvée Non-Vintage★★★ £C Blanc de Blancs Vintage★★★ £C

Corbans (Marlborough):
O **Sauvignon Blanc** Cottage Block★★ £C O **Chardonnay** Cottage Block★★ £C

MT DIFFICULTY Central Otago *UK stockists:* **BFs**,Vne, JNi, NYg, P&S
One of the best new Central Otago wineries with small amounts of single-vineyard Pinot Noirs. 2002 and 01 estate versions shows more weight and density than previously. Attractive Chardonnay and Sauvignon plus lively, fruit-driven Pinot Gris (Mansons Farm version is late-harvested). Riesling too comes in in different versions, varying both in origin and the degree of sweetness. (PW)
● **Pinot Noir**★★★ £D O **Pinot Gris**★★ £C

MOUNT EDWARD Central Otago www.mountedward.co.nz *UK stockists:* **BFs, BBR**,Vne, JNi, WSc, P&S
Very small, virtual one-man operation run by Gibbston Valley founder Alan Brady. Ripe yet sappy Pinot Noir adds good richness with age, improving with successive vintages – one of the classier Central Otago offerings. A small amount of Riesling is also planted. (PW)
● **Pinot Noir**★★★ £E

MOUNTFORD Waipara, Canterbury www.mountfordvineyard.co.nz *UK stockists:* **FMV**, Han, The, NYg
From Waipara's limestone-rich soils and outperforming others thanks to specialist vineyard and winemaking expertise. Blind winemaker C P Lin increasingly realises an extra class and complexity in Pinot Noir. Chardonnay is also made in a full-bodied, concentrated, oak-influenced style. (PW)
● **Pinot Noir**★★★ £E O **Chardonnay**★★ £D

MURDOCH JAMES ESTATE www.murdochjames.co.nz *UK stockists:* **CdP**, Odd, P&S
Expanding organic Martinborough estate focusing on Pinot Noir and Syrah. Pinot, especially in Fraser and Blue Rock bottlings (subject to 100 per cent French oak), is very ripe, rich and fleshy with Pommard-like strength. Bold, promising Syrah is in the same mould with lots of extract, while minty blackcurrant and textured Cab Franc is also good. Riesling, Chardonnay and Pinot Gris are also made. (PW)
● **Pinot Noir** Waiata★ £C Blue Rock★★★ £D Fraser★★★ £D
● **Syrah**★★★ £C ● **Cabernet Franc**★★★ £C O **Sauvignon Blanc**★★ £C

NEUDORF Nelson www.neudorf.co.nz *UK stockists:* **RsW**, Cam, UnC, P&S, WSc, Sel
Nelson's quality leader producing concentrated but not overworked wines. Fine aromatic Sauvignon and Riesling contrast with rich, complex Moutere Chardonnay. Pure, silky Pinot Noir has become a speciality, the fine Moutere example surpassed by a Moutere Home Vineyard version. Wine also comes from younger vineyards at Brightwater. Pinot Gris is made too. (PW)
O **Chardonnay** Moutere★★★ £E O **Chardonnay** Nelson★★ £C
O **Sauvignon Blanc** Marlborough★★ £C O **Sauvignon Blanc** Nelson★★ £C
O **Riesling** Moutere★★ £B ● **Pinot Noir** Moutere★★★ £E

OLSSENS Central Otago www.olssens.co.nz *UK stockists:* **BFs**,Vne, Han, Swg
A husband-and-wife partnership with vineyards in the superior Bannockburn sub-region of Central Otago. Expansive Jackson Barry Pinot Noir; also Reserve Slapjack Creek in best years. Whites include lime, citrus and floral Riesling, Sauvignon, Gewürz and Chardonnay, the latter in unoaked, barrel-fermented and Reserve versions. Late-harvest Riesling, Desert Gold, is also made. (PW)
● **Pinot Noir**★★ £D Jackson Barry★★★ £E O **Riesling**★★ £B

PEGASUS BAY Waipara, Canterbury *UK stockists:* **MHv**, WSc, BBR
Leading Canterbury winery under winemakers Matthew Donaldson and his wife Lynette. Good plummy, fleshy Pinot Noir (superior selection is Prima Donna) and more variable Cab/Merlot (Maestro is the special selection). Whites are more consistent: richly textured Chardonnay and Sauvignon/Semillon and fruit-rich Riesling

New entries have producer's name underlined

(especially late-harvested, botrytis-affected, Aria). Also botrytised Chardonnay, Finale. (PW)

O **Riesling**★★ £B Aria★★★ £B O **Sauvignon Blanc/Semillon**★★ £C
O **Chardonnay**★★★ £B ● **Pinot Noir**★★ £C

PISA RANGE Central Otago www.pisarangeestate.co.nz *UK stockists:* **L&W**
Just one wine here at present – and no prizes for guessing what that might be! This is a deep, complex Pinot Noir with good breadth and length as well as a touch of class. The 2003 is arguably the best of the fine trio of 01, 02, 03, deserving 5–6 years' age. (PW)
● **Pinot Noir** Black Poplar Block★★★ £D

SCHUBERT Martinborough www.schubert.co.nz *UK stockists:* **GVS**
Martinborough/Wairarapa's most exciting new producer. German owners craft very impressive artisanal reds from high-quality fruit. Two very good Pinot Noirs, especially the estate version with more density, class. Also berryish, succulent Cab Sauv/Merlot and tiny amounts of a deep, concentrated Syrah. Tribianco white is ripe and perfumed. Also good Hawkes Bay wines from grapes bought from friends. (PW)
● **Pinot Noir** Wairarapa★★★★ £E Marion's Vineyard★★★ £D
● **Cabernet/Merlot** Wairarapa★★ £D ● **Cabernet Sauvignon** Hawkes Bay★★★ £E
● **Syrah**★★★★ £E O **Sauvignon Blanc** Hawkes Bay★★ £C O **Tribianco**★★ £C

STAETE LANDT Marlborough www.staetelandt.co.nz *UK stockists:* **L&W**
Young winery producing wines with atypical intensity, concentration and breadth for Marlborough. Sauvignon enhanced by small percentage barrel-fermented and aged. Also complex, delicately mineral Chardonnay. Pinot Gris is ripe and powerful, while distinctive berry and floral Pinot Noir will develop a fine silky texture with a little age. (PW)
O **Chardonnay** Marlborough★★ £C O **Sauvignon Blanc** Marlborough★★ £C
O **Pinot Gris** Marlborough★★ £C ● **Pinot Noir** Marlborough★★★ £D

STONECROFT Hawkes Bay www.stonecroft.co.nz *UK stockists:* **L&S**, NYg, Rae
Dr Alan Limmer's rich-textured and concentrated Syrah and Gewürz from 10 ha have advanced these varieties in New Zealand. Mineral, blackcurrant and plum Syrah is the real star; also bold Chardonnay with uncommon depth and substance. Stylish, ageworthy Ruhanui is blend of Cab Sauv, Merlot and Syrah (cheaper Crofters is similar blend). Zin was added in 1999 (no 2001) while unusual spicy, tropical-fruited Sauvignon was resurrected in 2003. (PW)
● **Syrah**★★★★ £D ● **Ruhanui**★★ £B
O **Chardonnay**★★★ £C O **Gewürztraminer**★★★ £C O **Sauvignon Blanc**★★ £C

STONYRIDGE Waiheke Island www.stonyridge.co.nz *UK stockists:* **MHv**, Kwi, NYg, Hfx
Stephen White's small north-facing vineyard produces Waiheke's most famous Bordeaux-style red, Larose. Low yields underpin a rich, harmonious blend with impressive ripeness, depth and balance. Best with three to six years' age, though keeps longer. Second wine, Airfields. Also varietal Merlot and Chardonnay (Row 10). (PW)
● **Larose Cabernets**★★★★ £F

TE MATA Hawkes Bay www.temata.co.nz *UK stockists:* **JEF**, NYg, Kwi, Hrd
John Buck's inspirational winery is still a leading light. Wines of style and elegance yet good fruit and intensity. Coleraine (from both Cabs and Merlot) ages gracefully, at best giving soft, caressing fruit on a long richly textured finish. Stylish Syrah and *barriqued* Elston Chardonnay. Also fine Bordeaux-like Cape Crest Sauvignon. Less exciting Woodthorpe range, but promising new Syrah/Viognier. (PW)
Te Mata:
● **Cabernet/Merlot** Awatea★★ £C Coleraine★★★★ £D ● **Syrah** Bullnose★★★ £C
O **Chardonnay** Elston★★★ £C O **Sauvignon Blanc** Cape Crest★★ £C
Woodthorpe:
● **Cabernet/Merlot**★ £B O **Chardonnay**★★ £B O **Sauvignon Blanc**★ £B

TRINITY HILL Hawkes Bay www.trinityhill.com *UK stockists:* **L-P**, NZH
John Hancock has always produced ripe, concentrated, fruit-driven wines that ooze fruit. Gimblett Road Chardonnay is a classic deep, powerful example while Pinot Gris is super-concentrated with an almost preserved-pear character. Reds include cedary Gimblett Road Cab Sauv/Merlot with cassis and berry fruit. Also varietal Merlot,

occasional varietal Cab Sauv and super-premium Homage Chardonnay and red. Part-owned by owners of London restaurants Bleeding Heart and The Sign of the Don. (PW)

O **Chardonnay** Hawkes Bay★★ £B Gimblett Road★★★ £C
O **Pinot Gris** Gimblett Road★★ £C ● **Trinity Merlot/Cabernet Franc/Syrah**★ £D
● **Syrah** Gimblett Road★★★ £C ● **Cabernet Sauvignon/Merlot** Gimblett Road★★★ £D

UNISON Hawkes Bay www.unisonvineyard.co.nz UK stockists: **SFW**, N&P
Dedicated to producing top-quality blended red from 6 ha of high-density, low-yielding vineyard (with Merlot, Syrah and Cab Sauv) in Gimblett Gravels since 1993. Unison red spends one year in oak (one-third in *barriques*). Selection is based on the very best fruit and undergoes a longer maceration (three weeks) and has one year exclusively in *barriques*. Both need at least five years' age. (PW)

● **Unison** Gimblett Gravels★★★ £C ● **Unison Selection** Gimblett Gravels★★★★ £D

VAVASOUR Marlborough www.vavasour.com UK stockists: **C&B**, SVS, Kwi
Leading Marlborough winery in now increasingly planted Awatere Valley. Two excellent Sauvignons both show their Awatere origins and a minerally, ripe fruit intensity and structure and depth matched by few others. Single Vineyard Sauvignon shows restrained oak influence with two to three years' age. Tight but creamy Chardonnay and aromatic Riesling are also impressive. Much improved Pinot Noir since 2002. Dashwood is excellent second label. (PW)

Vavasour:
O **Sauvignon Blanc**★★★ £B Single Vineyard★★★ £C
O **Chardonnay**★★★ £B O **Riesling**★★★ £B ● **Pinot Noir**★★ £C
Dashwood
O **Sauvignon Blanc**★★ £B O **Chardonnay**★★ £B

VILLA MARIA Auckland & Marlborough www.villamaria.co.nz UK stockists: **HMA**, Odd, WSc
Formidable group (includes Esk Valley and Vidal) with enviable record of quality and consistency. Best are the Reserve-level and impressive series of new single-vineyard wines, particularly Sauvignon and Chardonnay but also including intense Pinot Gris and Riesling. Pinot Noir is ambitious and concentrated, most individual and expansive in single vineyard versions. Reserve Hawkes Bay reds (Merlot, Cab Sauv) show impressive fruit intensity. The premium Vidal red is Joseph Soler Cab Sauv. Villa Maria's third tier is fruit-driven early drinking Cellar Selection joined by simple Private Bin basics. All wines under Stelvin caps since 2004. (PW)

Villa Maria:
● **Merlot/Cabernet Sauvignon** Gimblett Gravels Reserve★★★ £D
● **Pinot Noir** Seddon Vyd★★★ £E Taylor's Pass Vyd★★★ £E
O **Sauvignon Blanc** Reserve Wairau River★★★ £C Reserve Clifford Bay★★★ £C
O **Sauvignon Blanc** Taylor's Pass Vyd★★★ £C Peter Jackson Vyd★★★ £C
O **Chardonnay** Cellar Selection★★ £B Reserve★★★ £B
O **Chardonnay** Fletcher Vyd★★★ £C Keltern Vyd★★★★ £C

Other wineries of note

Borthwick (Wairarapa), Churton (Marlborough), Escarpment (Martinborough), Forrest Estate (Marlborough), Grove Mill (Marlborough), Huia (Marlborough), Margrain Vineyard (Martinborough), Matua Valley (Kumeu, Auckland), Mud House/Le Grys (Marlborough), Obsidian (Waiheke Island), Palliser Estate (Martinborough), Redmetal Vineyards (Hawkes Bay), Seresin (Marlborough), Spy Valley (Marlborough), TerraVin (Marlborough), Two Paddocks (Central Otago)

An in-depth profile of every producer can be found in Wine behind the label 2006

New entries have producer's name underlined

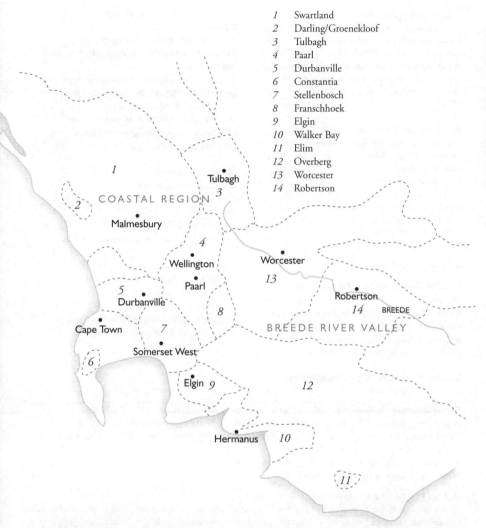

1 Swartland
2 Darling/Groenekloof
3 Tulbagh
4 Paarl
5 Durbanville
6 Constantia
7 Stellenbosch
8 Franschhoek
9 Elgin
10 Walker Bay
11 Elim
12 Overberg
13 Worcester
14 Robertson

The Regions

Quality wine production is centred around **Stellenbosch** WO. There is a wide variation of mesoclimates with maritime breezes and the Simonsberg and Helderberg mountains playing a role in tempering conditions. In the coolest areas Sauvignon and Chardonnay are both successful, as is the occasional Riesling. Chenin tends to be much in the local style with some residual sugar. Stellenbosch reds are among the best in the country. Pinotage coming from warm vineyards to the north-east of the WO. Decent Bordeaux-style reds abound and a number of wineries are achieving excellent results with Shiraz. Merlot can be good but also a touch vegetal. A marked minty note found in a number of reds can tend to be overpowering.

Paarl is warm and reds include successful Shiraz and Merlot. Cooler mesoclimates provide some decent Sauvignon, Semillon, Chardonnay and Pinot Noir. White Rhône varieties are also increasing. The **Franschhoek** Valley here gets cooler as you move east to higher altitude. Again, very good Shiraz and Cab Sauv are produced as well as earlier-ripening whites and Pinot Noir. **Durbanville** is cool and then south of Cape Town **Constantia** is home to a small number of good producers. The climate is cool and moderated by both Indian and Atlantic Some way east of Stellenbosch are **Worcester** and **Robertson**, which

produces some good whites.
The vast, semi-desert and arid expanse of the **Klein Karoo**, several hundred kilometres inland, provides reasonable fortifieds. **Swartland** just to the north-west of Paarl appears to have real potential. Hillside vineyards planted on well-drained granite soils are a source of excellent Pinotage, Shiraz, Carignan and Merlot.

South Africa Vintages

The top Cape reds will develop and keep well, the best for up to a decade. Whites generally need drinking as soon after release as possible although the odd barrel-fermented Chardonnay will develop in the short term. 2004 is potentially good for reds but there has been uneven ripening. Earlier years to consider for premium reds are 2003, 2002, 2001, 2000, 1998, 1997, 1995 and 1994.

Wizard's Wishlist

A selection of emerging Cape new classics

BEYERSKLOOF ● **Cabernet Sauvignon** Stellenbosch
BOEKENHOUTSKLOOF
● **Cabernet Sauvignon** Estate Franschhoek
GLEN CARLOU ● **Chardonnay** Reserve Paarl

HAMILTON RUSSELL VINEYARDS
● **Pinot Noir** Walker Bay
DE TRAFFORD ● **Shiraz** Stellenbosch
NICO VAN DER MERWE ● **Mas Nicolas** Stellenbosch
RUSTENBERG
● **Cabernet Sauvignon** Peter Barlow Stellenbosch
SADIE FAMILY WINES ● **Columella** Swartland
SAXENBURG ● **Shiraz** Select Stellenbosch
SPICE ROUTE COMPANY ● **Syrah** Swartland
RUDERA ● **Cabernet Sauvignon** Stellenbosch
VERGELEGEN ● **Vergelegen** Stellenbosch

10 finer values

BOUCHARD FINLAYSON
O **Chardonnay** Missionvale Walker Bay
BWC ● **Syrah** Paarl
SAXENBURG ● **Pinotage** Private Collection Stellenbosch
MORESON O **Premium Chardonnay** Franschoek
KANU
O **Chenin Blanc** Limited Release Wooded Stellenbosch
QUOIN ROCK O **Sauvignon Blanc** Stellenbosch
BON CAP O **Viognier** Robertson
KANONKOP ● **Pinotage** Stellenbosch
VERGELEGEN O **Sauvignon Blanc** Stellenbosch
WILDEKRANS ● **Pinotage** Barrel Selection Walker Bay

South Africa/A-Z of Producers

BEYERSKLOOF · Stellenbosch heidi@beyerskloof.co.za *UK stockists:* **RSo**
Beyers Truter makes a stylish and vibrant Pinotage in a juicy forward style and a dense, burly Cab Sauv with abundant new oak. New are a fruity rosé and a well-priced ripe and plummy red blend, Synergy, a blend of Merlot, Pinotage and Cab Sauv. (DM)
● **Pinotage** Stellenbosch★ £B ● **Synergy** Stellenbosch★★ £B
● **Cabernet Sauvignon** Stellenbosch★★★★ £D

BLACK PEARL Paarl www.blackpearlwines.com
As well as fine traditionally vinified and impressively opulent Cabernet Sauvignon and Shiraz varietals a softer more fruit driven blend of the two varieties, Oro is also produced. Richly textured dark berry fruited Shiraz gains additional depth and structure from 13 months in 60% new French oak, the more elegant and lightly minty Cabernet Sauvignon gets just a touch less new wood. (DM)
● **Cabernet Sauvignon** Paarl★★★ £D ● **Shiraz** Paarl★★★ £C

BON CAP Robertson www.boncaporganic.co.za *UK stockists:***RsW**,SVS,Wai
Michelle and Rolf du Preeze make a well-crafted range of organic reds at their small Robertson farm and have recently added Viognier. Fruit-driven Ruins Pinotage is aged in tank, Bon Cap wines are all aged in oak, part American part new. (DM)
● **Pinotage** The Ruins★ £B Eilandia★★ £B ● **Syrah** Eilandia★★ £C
● **Cabernet Sauvignon** Eilandia★★ £C

BOEKENHOUTSKLOOF Franschhoek boeken@mweb.co.za *UK stockists:* **Orb**,F&M,Wai
Located on the higher and cooler slopes of Franschhoek and producing some of the best wines in the Cape under the Boekenhoutskloof label. There is also a range of attractively fruity and characterful varietal wines under the Porcupine Ridge label, which are sourced from Coastal Region fruit. (DM)

● Cabernet Sauvignon Estate★★★★★ £E   ● Shiraz★★★★ £E
○ Semillon Estate★★★ £C

___

BOUCHARD FINLAYSON   Walker Bay   bf.overstrand.co.za   *UK stockists:* **Bib**,Wai
The style of Pinot here differs from neighbouring Hamilton Russell: the wine is denser and more extracted and there is a barrel selection Tête de Cuvée. Of two Chardonnays, the more opulent Missionvale comes from homegrown fruit. A recent addition is Hannibal, a blend of Sangiovese, Nebbiolo and Pinot Noir. (DM)
● **Pinot Noir** Galpin Peak★★★ £D   ○ **Sauvignon Blanc**★ £B
○ **Chardonnay** Kaaimansgat Overberg★★ £C   Missionvale★★ £C

___

CEDERBERG   Clanwilliam   www.cederbergwine.com   *UK stockists:* **SVS**
Located on the west coast of South Africa, some way to the north of Cape Town and the larger wine regions, Cederbergs vineyards are the highest in the country. Full blown reds as well as grassy, herb-spiced whites from Sauvignon Blanc and Chenin Blanc are made. Flagship Cabernet Sauvignon, V Generations is only released in top years. (DM)
● **V Generations** Cederberg★★★ £D   ○ **Chenin Blanc** Cederberg★★ £B
○ **Sauvignon Blanc** Cederberg★★ £B

___

CLOS MALVERNE   Stellenbosch   www.closmalverne.com   *UK stockists:* **Cap**
Medium sized producer with wines released under both the Clos Malverne and Shepherds Creek labels. Top label Auret is an unusual blend of Cabernet Sauvignon and Pinotage. Ripe and opulent with loads of dark, mulberry and chocolatey fruit the wine is aged for 12 months in a mix of French and American oak. (DM)
● **Auret** Stellenbosch★★★ £C   ● **Pinotage Reserve** Stellenbosch★★★ £C
● **Cabernet Sauvignon** Stellenbosch★★ £C
● **Pinotage** Stellenbosch★★ £B   ● **Cabernet Shiraz** Stellenbosch★ £B

___

PAUL CLUVER   Elgin   www.cluver.com   *UK stockists:* FWC, OxW, ARe
Pioneering wine farm in the cooler vineyards of Elgin. Reds are sound enough but whites are very striking. Sauvignon is fresh and grassy, Riesling citrusy and toasty, while Chardonnay is particularly stylish with impressive depth and concentration, a subtle barrel-fermentation character and a rich leesy texture. (DM)
● **Pinot Noir** Elgin★★ £C   ● **Cabernet Sauvignon** Elgin★★ £C
○ **Chardonnay** Elgin★★★ £C   ○ **Sauvignon Blanc** Elgin★★ £B
○ **Weisser Riesling** Elgin★★ £B

___

ANTHONY DE JAGER   Paarl   *UK stockists:* **SVS**
Fairview winemaker Anthony de Jager makes one wine under his own label, a richly expressive Shiraz, blended with a small touch of Viognier. The wine is produced from 20 to 25 year old Paarl vines and is aged for just under a year in all used oak to emphasise its fruit. (DM)
● **Shiraz Homtini** Paarl★★★★ £C

___

DE TOREN   Stellenbosch   www.de-toren.com   *UK stockists:* **WSS**,BBr, Rae,ACh
De Toren makes just 3,000 cases of one of the more striking Bordeaux red blends in the region. Named for the varieties which make up the blend: Cab Sauv, Malbec, Merlot, Cab Franc and Petit Verdot. Second label, Diversity, is a blend of whichever grapes are not felt to be suitable for the Grand Vin. (DM)
● **Fusion V** Coastal Region★★★ £D   ● **Diversity** Coastal Region★★ £C

___

DE TRAFFORD   Stellenbosch   www.de-toren.com   *UK stockists:* P&S
One of the Cape's finest producers, producing a small range of brilliant reds and Chenin Blanc of a depth and intensity rarely found in the variety in the Cape. Some very low-yielding old vine fruit is used. A straw wine is also made, again from Chenin Blanc. (DM)
● **Shiraz** Stellenbosch★★★★ £D   ● **Cabernet Sauvignon** Stellenbosch★★★ £C
● **Merlot** Stellenbosch★★★ £C   ○ **Chenin Blanc** Stellenbosch★★ £C

___

ENGELBRECHT-ELS   Stellenbosch   www.ernieelswines.com   *UK stockists:* **Sec**
Joint venture between Jean Engelbrecht of Rust en Vrede and his friend golfer Ernie Els produces two very striking and in the case of the limited release Ernie Els label red one of the most expensive wines yet to have emerged from the Cape. (DM)
● **Engelbrecht Els** Western Cape★★★★ £E

SOUTH AFRICA

FAIRVIEW ESTATE   Paarl   www.fairview.co.za   *UK stockists:* **CHk**,WSc,Wai
An extensive range is made, centred on Rhône styles. Goats do Roam are well-crafted if simple Rhône blends.
These have been supplemented by Goat Roti, which blends Shiraz with Grenache, Carignan and Viognier.
Some fine premium Red Seal labelled Shiraz and Pinotage are rich and concentrated as is the Rhône blend
SMV. (DM)
● **Shiraz** Cyril Back★★ £C   Beacon★★★ £C   Solitude★★★ £C
● **Zinfandel/Cinsault**★ £B   ● **SMV**★★ £B   O **Viognier**★★ £B

THE FOUNDRY   Stellenbosch   thefoundry@mweb.co.za   *UK stockists:* **RsW**
Brilliant boutique style Syrah sourced from vineyards across the Cape. Malolactic is in barrel after a relatively short
vatting to avoid over-extraction and limited new oak is used during maturation. Dark, blackberry-scented, spicy and
penetratingly pure. (DM)
● **Syrah** Coastal Region★★★★ £E

GLEN CARLOU   Paarl   glencarl@mweb.co.za   *UK stockists:* AWs, NYg
Particularly impressive Chardonnay, stylish and restrained. Regular bottling is tight and minerally, the Reserve is
concentrated, with citrus, cheesy lees notes and toasty oak. Pinot Noir and Grand Classique Bordeaux blend are
good and ripe but lack the flair of the Chardonnays. Shiraz and Zinfandel are also now produced. (DM)
● **Grand Classique**★★ £C   ● **Pinot Noir**★ £C
O **Chardonnay**★★ £B   Reserve★★★ £C

GRANGEHURST   Stellenbosch   www.grangehurst.co.za   *UK stockists:* **Bib**
Pinotage is impressively ripe and full-bodied with plenty of spicy, dark berry fruit. Nikela is an unusual blend of
Cab Sauv,Merlot and Pinotage. It shows a vibrant dark berry fruit character with a hint of menthol. Top wine is
the structured Cab Sauv/Merlot. Future plans include a move towards Rhône varieties. (DM)
● **Cabernet Sauvignon/Merlot**★★★ £C   ● **Nikela**★★ £B   ● **Pinotage**★★ £B

HAMILTON RUSSELL VINEYARDS   Walker Bay   *UK stockists:* **Hal**,WSc,F&M
The original and most impressive producer of rich, gamey Pinot Noir and intense, minerally Chardonnay in the
cool and visually stunning Walker Bay. A second label, Southern Right, has Sauvignon and Pinotage from the
Western Cape. (DM)
● **Pinot Noir**★★★★ £D   O **Chardonnay**★★★ £D

JORDAN   Stellenbosch   www.jordanwines.com   *UK stockists:* **AWs**
The Jordans make good regular Chardonnay, largely barrel-fermented and as well as the Nine Yards which is
richly textured very concentrated and sourced from higher altitude vineyards. The Cobblers Hill red, a
Bordeaux blend of Cabernet Sauvignon and Merlot is the top red here. (DM)
● **Cobblers Hill** Stellenbosch★★★ £D   ● **Cabernet Sauvignon** Stellenbosch★★ £C
O **Chardonnay** Stellenbosch★★ £C   Nine Yards Stellenbosch★★★ £D

KAAPZICHT   Stellenbosch   www.kaapzicht-wines.com   *UK stockists:* **Sec**
Magnificently sited vineyards look west towards Table Mountain. A comprehensive range is offerred including
fruity forward reds, Chenin, Sauvignon and the Combination which blends the two. The most important wines
are the richly textured Steytler Bordeaux blend Vision and Cab Sauv. Also some excellent Pinotage. (DM)
● **Vision** Steytler★★★ £D   ● **Cabernet Sauvignon**★★ £B
● **Pinotage**★★★ £C   Steytler★★★ £D

KANONKOP   Stellenbosch   www.kanonkop.co.za   *UK stockists:* **RSo**
One of the best Pinotage producers, an extensive holding of old bush vines a major contributing factor. Very
good Cab Sauv is also produced; the Paul Sauer label is blended with Cab Franc and Merlot and has an extra
dimension. Kadette is a cheerful soft and plummy blend of Pinotage, Cab Sauv and Merlot. (DM)
● **Cabernet Sauvignon**★★★ £D   ● **Paul Sauer**★★★★ £D   ● **Pinotage**★★★ £C

LANDAU DU VAL   Franschoek   *UK stockists:* **SVS**
A rarity in the Cape is the characterful Semillon made from 90 to 100 year old bush vines. Microscopic yields of 2
to 3 tons to the ha results in a wine that rivals the great examples from South Australia and the Hunter Valley in
New South Wales. (DM)
O **Semillon** Franschoek★★★ £C

328

New entries have producer's name underlined

MEERLUST Stellenbosch www.meerlust.co.za *UK stockists:* **MMD**, Tan, F&M
Reds, produced from the Bordeaux varieties, and rich and toasty Chardonnay are among the very best of their kind in the Cape. Merlot is very good and the Cabernet/Merlot/Cabernet Franc Rubicon blend is rich, concentrated and marked by cedar and exotic dark fruits. (DM)
● **Merlot**★★ £C   ● **Pinot Noir** Reserve★★ £C   ● **Rubicon**★★★ £D
O **Chardonnay**★★★ £C

MEINERT Stellenbosch meinert@netactive.co.za *UK stockists:* **TWS**
Good plummy varietal Merlot and a better Bordeaux blend, Devon Crest Cab Sauv/Merlot are both well established. Also produces a premium red blend, Synchronicity a rich and stylish combination of mainly Cab Sauv (60%), with the balance comprising Merlot, Pinotage and Cab Franc. (DM)
● **Devon Crest** Devon Valley★★★ £C   ● **Merlot** Devon Valley★★ £C
● **Synchronicity** Devon Valley★★★ £D

NICO VAN DER MERWE Stellenbosch wilhelmshof@xsinet.co.za
Nico van der Merwe is the winemaker at Saxenberg. Under his own label he has a very fine dense and minty blend of Shiraz and Cab Sauv. It will drink well young but evolve over a decade or more. (DM)
● **Mas Nicolas**★★★★ £D

MORESON Franschoek www.moreson.co.za *UK stockists:* **Pol**, YnG, V&C
A small range of well crafted and very good value reds and whites. The whites are sourced from Franschoek vineyards the reds from Stellenbosch and Paarl. Premium Chardonnay is one of the best value examples of the variety anywhere on the planet. Magia red is a Bordeaux based blend with dense, very ripe fruit and spends 18 months in oak. (DM)
● **Magia** Coastal Region★★ £C   ● **Pinotage** Coastal Region★★ £B
O **Premium Chardonnay** Franschoek★★★ £B   O **Chenin Blanc** Franschoek★★ £B

MORGENHOF Stellenbosch www.morgenhof.com *UK stockists:* **McK**
An extensive range includes sparkling and fortified wines. Chardonnay is in an oaky style, Sauvignon is zesty and fresh. There is a barrel-fermented Chenin. Best reds are the Cab Sauv and Première Selection, a blend of Cab Sauv, Merlot and Cab Franc. Merlot and Cab Sauv Reserve labels have been introduced and look promising. (DM)
● **Cabernet Sauvignon**★★ £C   ● **Première Selection**★ £C
● **Pinotage**★ £C   O **Chardonnay**★★ £B

MULDERBOSCH Stellenbosch www.mulderbosch.co.za *UK stockists:* **JAr**
Producer of one of the best piercing varietal Sauvignons. Subtly oaked Chardonnay, now in Barrel Fermented and regular bottlings, and a Barrel Fermented Sauvignon Blanc are also good. The red blend, Faithful Hound, comprises Merlot, Cabs Sauv and Franc and a touch of Malbec. Sister company Kanu is a source of well-priced reds and whites, particularly characterful Chenin Blanc. (DM)

Mulderbosch
● **Faithful Hound** Stellenbosch★★ £C
O **Chardonnay** Barrel-fermented Stellenbosch★★★ £C
O **Sauvignon Blanc** Stellenbosch★★ £C Barrel-fermented Stellenbosch★★ £C

Kanu
● **Kanu Red** Stellenbosch★★ £B
O **Chenin Blanc** Stellenbosch★ £B Limited Release Wooded Stellenbosch★★ £B
O **Sauvignon Blanc** Limited Release Stellenbosch★★ £B

THE OBSERVATORY Cape Town *UK stockists:* **BBR**, Odd
Two strikingly original Rhône-style reds are produced from organically tended vineyards at this Cape Town warehouse winery from old Swartland bush vines. These are very atypical wines possessing a mineral, almost fiery *sauvage* edge to their fruit. The Syrah needs two or three years to settle down in bottle. (DM)
● **Syrah** Swartland★★★★ £E   ● **Carignan/Syrah** Swartland★★★ £D

QUOIN ROCK Stellenbosch www.quoinrock.com *UK stockists:* **RsW**
Some very good cool climate whites are made at this recently established Stellenbosch property. Vineyards are also planted at Agulhas the southernmost tip of Africa. Oculus is a subtle barrel-fermented Sauvignon.Merlot while showing a lot of new oak is displaying increasing complexity. (DM)
● **Merlot**★★ £C   O **Chardonnay**★★ £C   O **Oculus**★★ £C
O **Sauvignon Blanc**★★ £B

RIDGEBACK Paarl www.ridgebackwines.co.za *UK stockists:***SVS**
Very impressive reds, particularly a smoky dense and opulent Shiraz. As well as the reds, Viognier, Sauvignon Blanc and a Dry White and Dry Red are also made. Rich toasty oak is a characteristic of all the wines and winemaker Cathy Marshall always lets the fruit have its head. (DM)
● **Cabernet Sauvignon** Paarl★★★ £E   ● **Cabernet Franc/Merlot** Paarl★★★ £E
● **Shiraz** Paarl★★★ £E   ● **Merlot** Paarl★★★ £E

ROZENDAL Stellenbosch www.rozendal.co.za *UK stockists:* **RsW**
Just one top-quality Bordeaux-style blend is produced biodynamically from the Jonkershoek Valley sub-region in the foothills of the Jonkershoek Mountains. It is a Right Bank-style mix of Merlot, Cab Sauv and Cab Franc, finely structured, elegant and almost European in style. (DM)
● **Rozendal Red** Jonkershoek Valley★★★ £D

RUDERA Stellenbosch www.rudera.co.za *UK stockists:***DDr**
Small artisan winery with Chenin Blanc a particular focus. Syrah and very classy Cab Sauv, one of the best examples from the Cape, are also made. Chenin Blanc is produced in a rich, tropical style. Robusto is not dissimilar in style to a good Vouvray or Montlouis demi-sec. The late harvest bottling offers a rich concentrated peachy character. (DM)
● **Syrah** Stellenbosch★★ £C   ● **Cabernet Sauvignon** Stellenbosch★★★★ £E
O **Chenin Blanc** Stellenbosch★★ £B   Stellenbosch Robusto★★★ £C
O **Chenin Blanc** Stellenbosch Noble Late Harvest★★★ £E

RUPERT & ROTHSCHILD Franschhoek *UK stockists:***HoK**
South African/French partnership producing three fine and elegant, almost European styled, wine. Red Classique is a blend of Cab Sauv, Merlot and unusually a little Pinotage. The more structured Baron Edmond is purely Cab Sauv and Merlot. The Baroness Nadine is a lightly citrus infused, elegant Chardonnay. (DM)
● **Classique** Coastal Region★★ £C   ● **Baron Edmond** Coastal Region★★★ £D
O **Chardonnay** Coastal Region★★★ £C

RUST EN VREDE Stellenbosch www.rustenvrede.com *UK stockists:* **L&S, P&S, Swg**
Old established winery producing very characterful warm grown reds. The wines are richer and more opulent and earthy in character than many others from the Cape. Some of the overtly minty character found elsewhere is absent here. (DM)
● **Cabernet Sauvignon** Stellenbosch★★★ £C   ● **Estate Red** Stellenbosch★★★★ £D
● **Shiraz** Stellenbosch★★★ £C   ● **Merlot** Stellenbosch★★ £C

RUSTENBERG Stellenbosch www.rustenberg.co.za *UK stockists:* **Men, L&S,F&M,Wai**
Some decent fruit driven wines red and white are made under the Brampton label. Of greater substance are the Rustenberg wines. Two Chardonnays are produced with intense citrus notes and well-judged oak, as well as the Bordeaux-style blend Rustenberg John X Merriman and the structured Peter Barlow reds. (DM)
● **Cabernet Sauvignon Peter Barlow**★★★ £D   ● **John X Merriman**★★ £C
O **Chardonnay**★★ £B   Five Soldiers★★★ £C

SADIE FAMILY WINES Swartland sadiefamily@mail.com *UK stockists:* **RsW,NYg,F&M**
Eben Sadie's very fine red, Columella, is an almost varietal Syrah with just a tiny proportion of Mourvèdre. It is a wine of remarkable dark, spicy complexity; rich, almost exotic, with a supple texture and great intensity. A tiny amount of Palladius, a white blend of Viognier, Chardonnay, Chenin and Grenache Blanc was first made with the 2002 vintage. (DM)
● **Columella** Swartland★★★★★ £E

330

New entries have producer's name underlined

SANCTUM Stellenbosch
Mulderbosch winemaker Mike Dobrovic now has his own label producing a Shiraz that is emerging among the best from the Cape. At present the wine is produced from leased Overberg vineyards however the Dobrovics are in the process of establishing their own small Elgin farm. (DM)
● **Shiraz Sanctum** Western Cape★★★★ £E

SAXENBURG Stellenbosch www.saxenburg.co.za *UK stockists:* **Fie**
A first class range of wines made under the Private Collection label. A Sauvignon shows good varietal fruit and there is stylishly handled oak in the Chardonnay. The Private Collection reds comprise a warm, plummy Merlot; a tightly structured Cab Sauv; and impressive Shiraz full of dark black fruit and Rhône-like licorice and black pepper. Shiraz Select is richer and fuller. (DM)
● **Pinotage** Private Collection★★ £C ● **Merlot** Private Collection★★ £C
● **Shiraz** Private Collection★★★ £C Select★★★★ £D

SPICE ROUTE COMPANY Swartland *UK stockists:* **Eno,Wai**
Good reds and whites are released under the Spice Route label as well as straightforward Andrew's Hope Sauvignon and Cab Sauv/Merlot. The Flagship range of three red varietals, though, is a real step up. All will develop well in the medium term. (DM)
● **Merlot**★★★ £C ● **Pinotage**★★★ £C ● **Syrah**★★★ £C

SPRINGFIELD Robertson www.springfieldestate.com *UK stockists:* **Bib,SVS,Wai**
Springfield is producing decent fresh, grassy Sauvignon Blanc Life from Stone and some good to very good Chardonnay with close-to-organic practices. Cab Sauv has been less impressive, although an unfiltered Méthode Ancienne has been added. (DM)
O **Chardonnay** Wild Yeast★★ £B Méthode Ancienne★★★ £C
O **Sauvignon Blanc** Life from Stone★ £B

STARK-CONDÉ Stellenbosch www.stark-conde.co.za *UK stockists:* **Str**
Small family-run producing some striking Cab Sauvs along with a Pinotage and most recently a Pinot Noir. The top red is the impressive Condé Cab Sauv, which comes from the best blocks on the property. It is very much in a minty, berry and light cassis style with just the merest hint of cedar. (DM)
● **Condé Cabernet Sauvignon**★★★ £C ● **Stark Cabernet Sauvignon**★★ £C

STELLENZICHT Stellenbosch www.stellenzicht.co.za *UK stockists:* **Hal**
An extensive range is produced at this Stellenbosch farm, with Semillon Reserve and particularly striking and well structured Syrah is one of the Cape's very best examples. A premium Bordeaux blend Stellenzicht has also now been added. (DM)
● **Cabernet Sauvignon**★ £B ● **Stellenzicht**★★ £C ● **Syrah**★★★ £C
● **Pinotage**★★ £B O **Chardonnay**★★ £B O **Semillon** Reserve★★★ £C

STONEWALL Stellenbosch *UK stockists:* **Las**
Firm and fleshy berry laden Cabernet Sauvignon comes from old bush vine plantings. Pinotage is dark and spicy with the typically raw, acetone character of the variety but good grip and depth. The Sauvignon Blanc has some subtle, lightly tropical hints and is vinified in small oak. (DM)
● **Cabernet Sauvignon**★★★ £C ● **Pinotage** Stellenbosch★★ £B
O **Sauvignon Blanc** Stellenbosch★★ £B

THELEMA Stellenbosch www.thelema.co.za *UK stockists:* **Eno**, NYg,F&M
Now a benchmark among Cape wineries. There's good Chardonnay and Cab Sauv as well as steely, minerally Riesling. Merlot is reasonably concentrated and ripely plummy. Sauvignon is piercing and full of lightly tropical, green fruits. Reserves of Merlot and Cab Sauv are a step up from the regular examples. (DM)
● **Cabernet Sauvignon**★★★ £C Reserve★★★★ £D ● **Merlot**★★ £C
O **Chardonnay**★★ £C O **Sauvignon Blanc**★★ £B O **Riesling**★★ £B

VEENWOUDEN Paarl *UK stockists:* **Sec**,NYg
The reputation of this property is based on three wines, all of which have their roots in Bordeaux. Merlot in particular has been among Cape examples: supple and rich. The Classic, a typical Bordeaux blend,

is also impressive. Similar in style, the Vivat Bacchus has a touch of Malbec and is more open and approachable. (DM)

● **Merlot**★★★ £C   ● **Vivat Bacchus**★★ £C   ● **Classic**★★★ £C

VERGELEGEN Stellenbosch   www.vergelegen.co.za   *UK stockists:* NYg, WSc

Now one of the best wineries in the Cape. Striking varietal Sauvignon and Chardonnay both impress, particularly the Reserves, which have real structure and grip. Bordeaux style reds are all rich and concentrated, Vergelegen Red is one of the Capes best. Dark and brooding Shiraz and a white Bordeaux style promise much. (DM)

● **Cabernet Sauvignon**★★★ £C   ● **Shiraz**★★★ £C   ● **Vergelegen**★★★★ £D
O **Chardonnay** Reserve★★★ £C   O **Sauvignon Blanc** Reserve★★ £C

WARWICK ESTATE Stellenbosch   *UK stockists:* **LLt**, WSc, F&M, Wai

Good examples of all the Bordeaux varieties here, as well as decent, leesy Chardonnay. There is also a vibrant, brambly, powerful Pinotage from old bush vines as well as a structured Bordeaux blend, Trilogy produced from Cab Sauv, Merlot and Cab Franc. A lighter red blend of Cab Sauv, Merlot and some Pinotage, Three Cape Ladies, can be enjoyed young. (DM)

● **Cabernet Franc**★★ £C   ● **Cabernet Sauvignon**★★★ £C   ● **Trilogy**★★ £C
● **Pinotage** Old Bush Vines★★ £C   ● **Three Cape Ladies**★★ £C

WELGEMEEND Paarl   *UK stockists:* **RsW**

The main focus here is a finely crafted and elegant Estate Reserve red made from a Right Bank blend of Merlot, Cab Sauv and Cab Franc. Two further Bordeaux reds are also produced. Soopieshooghte from the same varieties and Douelle comprising Cab Sauv, Malbec, Cab Franc and Merlot. Amadé by contrast is a Rhône-dominated blend of Shiraz, Grenache and Pinotage. (DM)

● **Estate Reserve**★★★ £C   ● **Amadé**★★ £B

WILDEKRANS Walker Bay   www.wildekranswines.co.za   *UK stockists:* **WhW**

Located further inland than most of the Walker Bay estates and particularly suited to producing elegant finely structured Pinotage as well as medium weight, restrained examples of the red Bordeaux varieties. Some refreshing straightforward, fruit-driven whites also offer excellent value. (DM)

● **Pinotage**★★ £B Barrel Selection★★★ £C   ● **Cabernet Franc/Merlot**★★ £C
O **Caresse Marine**★ £B   O **Chenin Blanc**★ £B

Other wineries of note

BWC (Stellenbosch), Guardian Peak (Stellenbosch), Morgenhof (Stellenbosch), Iona (Elgin), Mischa (Wellington), Paradyskloof (Stellenbosch)

An in-depth profile of every producer can be found in Wine behind the label 2006

New entries have producer's name underlined

Introduction

Whilst this book calls upon you to consider our ratings of the best wines in the world from the best producers in the world, the pricing therein is geared to home consumption. Supposing, however, you are out at a restaurant and are confronted with the wine list. What should you be looking for? Well, unless you are on a strict budget, the first thing you should be looking for is quality. Does this restaurant have a good selection of quality wines? And if so, are there any such wines that demand attention as being value for money. It has often been said that any fool can produce a list of top Clarets and Burgundies - money no object, but does this constitute a great wine list? There are many places in the world today where great wine is produced and we look to the enterprising restaurateur to produce a list which is quality driven all round, innovative and exciting. Does the restaurant have an interesting selection of half bottles? If so, I, for one, would be delighted to forego a bottle of wine with the meal for three halves! Does the restaurant have an interesting selection of wines by the glass to allow me to experiment? (And I don't mean the cheapest "House" red and white the proprietor can lay his hands on, which probably taste like you have licked the backs of a thousand envelopes), nor a selection of pudding wines by the glass, although they are useful, but there is little point in having six sweet wines by the glass and only two dry ones - as we have seen). Is the list an easy read, with helpful tasting notes (geared to the cuisine and not to some wine merchant's blather), or is there a helpful and knowledgeable sommelier to guide you through it?

In our quest to find some wine list paradigms, we have selected 100 of the top U.K. wine lists submitted to us and put them under the microscope to see if they meet up to our expectations. The criteria we have used is a somewhat complicated combination based on (a) the percentage of 4 and 5 star wines on the list, (b) the percentage of 3 star wines on the list (with a coefficient factor), (c) the percentage of 3, 4 and 5 star wines listed at under £50, £30, and £20 (again with a coefficient factor), (d) the proportion of the total number of half bottles

and wines by the glass on the list (with an adjustment for dessert wines), (e) the percentage of 3, 4 and 5 star half bottles and wines by the glass on the list and (f) an overall impression of the list generally. The score is then tallied and the lists are set out in the following pages in their order of merit with a brief comment on the top 20. It is interesting to note that although the emphasis is on overall quality in the list, those establishments who can list quality at very low prices score heavily, even though they may not have as many quality wines as some of the more expensive ones. Thus there are eight London establishments in the top 20 and four from rural Wales.

Caveats. 1. This list has been compiled from wine lists submitted to us between March and June 2005. Some establishments did not submit their list, so if you do not find your favourite wine list there, it could be that we did not see it and you should not therefore assume that it wasn't good enough to make the top 100. Obviously, we cannot make a judgement on what we haven't seen, so if you think that there is a glaring omission, please persuade the restaurant to submit their wine list for next year's edition. After all, it doesn't cost them anything - there is absolutely no charge for admission. **2.** This review is solely on the wine list. It does not take into account the quality or price of the food (although many of the restaurants listed are highly rated for it - you will have to look at other guides for that), nor the quality of the wine service, since we have not visited most of these establishments although, again, you will find comments on this in other guides.

If you would like to read a more detailed appraisal of these lists with the actual scores and a wander through each list pointing out the best drinking recommendations, there is a dedicated book *The Top 100 UK Restaurant Wine Lists* available from October 2005. As well as a brief comment on the top 20, included below is the full list of the Overall Top 100 as well as the top 25 by Quality alone and the top 25 for Value.

WINE LISTS

Overall Top 100

1	BURLINGTON RESTAURANT -	
	DEVONSHIRE ARMS	190.35
2	TATE GALLERY	177.36
3	RSJ	171.35
4	SHARROW BAY	163.38
5	GORDON RAMSAY	161.97
6	RANSOME'S DOCK	156.42
7	DYLANWAD DA	155.25
8	YE OLDE BULL'S HEAD	154.95
9	PENHELIG ARMS	153.14
10	CROOKED BILLET	152.69
11	CHERWELL BOATHOUSE	151.67
12	SYCAMORE HOUSE	
	LITLE SHELFORD	149.96
13	DARROCH LEARG	145.87
14	LA TROMPETTE	144.52
15	OLD BRIDGE, HUNTINGDON	141.64
16	THE GLASSHOUSE	140.61
17	TYDDYN LLAN	139.46
18	LOCANDA LOCATELLI	135.83
19	BENTLEY KEMPINSKI 1880	135.52
20	SIR CHARLES NAPIER	131.58
21	OPERA HOUSE LEICESTER	131.14
22	FIFTH FLOOR HARVEY NICHOLS	130.70
23	THE BELL AT SKENFRITH	130.58
24	KILLIECRANKIE HOUSE	130.49
25	PEAT INN	129.78
26	OLD FIRE ENGINE HOUSE	128.21
27	GREAT EASTERN HOTEL - AURORA	126.01
28	ENOTECA TURI	125.78
29	THE GRANGE BRAMPTON	124.53
30	LUMIERE	124.39
31	THE WILDEBEEST ARMS	123.39
32	THE DON	120.91
33	JSW	120.78
34	SANGSTER'S	118.49
35	WITCHERY BY THE CASTLE	117.70
36	36 ON THE QUAY	117.41
37	OXO TOWER	117.30
38	PLAS BODEGROES	114.06
39	SUMMER ISLES HOTEL	113.95
40	MORSTON HALL	112.06
41	PENMAENUCHAF HALL	111.87
42	CHAMPANY INN	111.45
43	UBIQUITOUS CHIP	111.40
44	THE ALBANNACH	111.23
45	THE CHESTER GROSVENOR -	
	ARKLE	111.13
46	FISHERS IN THE CITY	111.00
47	HAMBLETON HALL	110.78
48	BRIAN MAULE - GLASGOW	110.55
49	SHANKS	110.34
50	HOTEL DU VIN BIRMINGHAM	109.58
51	FAIRY HILL	109.40
52	LITTLE BARWICK HOUSE	108.23
53	THE OLD VICARAGE RIDGEWAY	107.56
54	ETAIN GLASGOW	105.98
55	CORSE LAWN	104.89
56	NOVELLI AT AUBERGE DU LAC	103.41
57	CHAMPIGNON SAUVAGE	103.26
58	THE STAR INN HAROME	101.11
59	LES MIRABELLES	101.03
60	THE LIME TREE	100.82
61	HOTEL DU VIN HARROGATE	97.92
62	LE CAFÉ DU JARDIN	96.84
63	GRAVETYE MANOR	96.37
64	NORTHCOTE MANOR	95.97
65	THE CROSS AT KINGUSSIE	95.89
66	WHITE MOSS HOUSE	95.03
67	KENSINGTON PLACE	94.64
68	THE THREE CHIMNEYS	93.96
69	HOLBECK GHYLL	92.79
70	CROWN AT WHITEBROOK	92.51
71	COTSWOLD HOUSE	91.95
72	60 HOPE STREET	91.05
73	LEWTRENCHARD MANOR	89.92
74	HOTEL DU VIN - BRIGHTON	88.28
75	LINTHWAITE HOUSE HOTEL	85.59
76	MC CLEMENTS	83.79
77	HOTEL DU VIN -	
	TUNBRIDGE WELLS	83.05
78	FIRENZE	82.11
79	LONGUEVILLE MANOR	81.82

80	THE WEAVER'S SHED	81.25
81	LE DEUXIEME	80.38
82	BLEEDING HEART	78.55
83	COMBE HOUSE	78.13
84	EYRE BROTHERS RESTAURANT	77.68
85	THE WINDMILL	76.79
86	THE JOLLY SPORTSMAN	76.38
87	CHARLTON HOUSE THE MULBERRY RESTAURANT	75.19
88	THE GREYHOUND INN STOCKBRIDGE	75.11
89	THE GRIFFIN INN FLETCHING	74.97
90	SWINTON PARK	73.55
91	AL DUCA	73.07
92	YORKE ARMS RAMSGILL	71.92
93	MAES-Y-NEUADD	68.03
94	PORTMEIRION HOTEL	67.20
95	BRADLEYS	65.39
96	LOWRY HOTEL	63.91
97	THE MANSION HOUSE POOLE	60.80
98	CAYENNE	59.11
99	THYME	56.72
100	ROSCOFF	55.36

Top 25 by QUALITY

1	GORDON RAMSAY	140.30
2	BURLINGTON RESTAURANT - DEVONSHIRE ARMS	135.84
3	TATE GALLERY	121.05
4	LOCANDA LOCATELLI	117.72
5	BENTLEY KEMPINSKI 1880	109.12
6	RANSOME'S DOCK	109.05
7	SHARROW BAY	107.74
8	GREAT EASTERN HOTEL - AURORA	103.36
9	LA TROMPETTE	102.03
10	THE GLASSHOUSE	98.89
11	THE DON	96.01
12	CHERWELL BOATHOUSE	95.33
13	36 ON THE QUAY	93.90
14	JSW	90.31
15	ENOTECA TURI	90.24

16	THE CHESTER GROSVENOR - ARKLE	87.98
17	HOTEL DU VIN BIRMINGHAM	86.58
18	NOVELLI AT AUBERGE DU LAC	85.79
19	PEAT INN	85.70
20	OXO TOWER	85.34
21	HAMBLETON HALL	84.45
22	SIR CHARLES NAPIER	83.94
23	CHAMPANY INN	83.52
24	FIFTH FLOOR HARVEY NICHOLS	82.63
25	OLD BRIDGE, HUNTINGDON	78.60

Top 25 for value

1	SYCAMORE HOUSE LITLE SHELFORD	105.83
2	DYLANWAD DA	104.17
3	PENHELIG ARMS	90.37
4	RSJ	84.05
5	THE WILDEBEEST ARMS	82.45
6	THE GRANGE BRAMPTON	76.98
7	SANGSTER'S	76.67
8	DARROCH LEARG	73.73
9	YE OLDE BULL'S HEAD	72.32
10	KILLIECRANKIE HOUSE	71.27
11	LE CAFÉ DU JARDIN	57.05
12	CROWN AT WHITEBROOK	56.25
13	PENMAENUCHAF HALL	50.66
14	LUMIERE	49.00
15	FISHERS IN THE CITY	48.23
16	FIRENZE	46.75
17	THE STAR INN HAROME	46.29
18	CHERWELL BOATHOUSE	43.34
19	THE ALBANNACH	42.33
20	THE WEAVER'S SHED	41.67
21	TYDDYN LLAN	41.13
22	THE LIME TREE	40.74
23	CHAMPIGNON SAUVAGE	38.91
24	WHITE MOSS HOUSE	38.86
25	OPERA HOUSE LEICESTER	38.81

WINE LISTS

Details of Top 20 Overall

1 THE DEVONSHIRE ARMS - BURLINGTON RESTAURANT
Bolton Abbey, North Yorkshire, BD23 6AJ
Tel. 01756 710441   www.devonshirehotels.co.uk

This is one of the most serious and imposing wine lists we have ever come across. Over 2,000 wines listed, with over 1,300 being of at least 4 star quality and almost another 400 of 3 star quality, making it an impressive tome. The sheer volume of the list can be daunting, and there is an attempt to channel a selection of the less expensive wines at the beginning of the list as a shortcut. But it would be a pity to stop there, as there are many hidden gems within the main body of the list, some of which are at quite affordable prices. Although there are literally hundreds of wines at stratospheric prices, there are 63 four and five star wines at £50 or less (including 5 at under £30) and 57 three star wines at £30 or less (including 4 at under £20), so you have got 120 quality wines to play with which is more than some establishment's entire list. What we like, too, are the 128 choices in small formats (half bottles or 50cl.), of which almost 100 are of three star quality or more. There are only 13 dry wines by the glass, but even 5 of these are quality wines, whereas in most establishments you would be lucky to get even one. Best buy: Cline Cellars Small Berry Vineyard Mourvèdre 1998 at £29.50

Rankings: Quality 2   Value 78   Impression 2   Overall 1

2 TATE BRITAIN RESTAURANT   Millbank, London SW1 4RG
Tel. (020) 7887 8902   www.tate.org.uk

30-odd years ago, you might have been surprised, as you slipped into the restaurant at the Tate Gallery to take a break from all those Turner's you have been viewing, to find the place absolutely heaving with members of the wine trade guzzling down several bottles of smart Clarets at extraordinarily cheap prices to accompany the pretty ordinaire food on offer. Sadly, all that wine has gone and whilst it is still the policy of the Tate to cellar their wines for many years, prices have inevitably crept up, but then so has the quality of the food! Nevertheless, you will be hard pressed to find better drinking value in the centre of London, the only drawback being that the restaurant is only open for lunch, which poses a terrible dilemma for those who actually have to return to work in the afternoon! This is one of the finest lists that you will come across - it has moved away from the traditional Tate stronghold of fine Clarets and Burgundies, with much more exciting offerings elsewhere, particularly from Australia and the USA. It's hard to pick out a best buy, but if we have to come down to it, we suppose that the 5 star Ridge Geyserville Zinfandel 1999 at £37 would just about take the prize, with half a dozen others close behind.

Rankings: Quality 3   Value 29   Impression 21=   Overall 2

3 RSJ   33 Coin Street, London SE1 9NR
Tel (020) 7928 4554   www.rsj.uk.com

This restaurant has been a long time specialist in wines from the Loire Valley and whilst there is a tiny selection from elsewhere, you will have to content yourself in mainly furthering your knowledge of the wines from this remarkably diverse region of France. There is a detailed explanation at the beginning of the list about grape varieties, vintages and peculiarities of each part of the region, so that you will be fully familiar with what the Loire Valley has to offer. Vintage information is particularly important, since there are enormous variations in quality between one year and the next and even between one part of the region and another, so you should read this section carefully. And even if you find that Loire wines don't exactly turn you on, you do have the certain knowledge that by and large, these wines offer exceptional value for money. All in all, this is an intriguing wine list - you can make many new discoveries at prices that won't break the bank. Best Buy: Patrick Baudouin's Côteaux du Layon "Aprés Minuit" 1997 at £69.95 for 50cl.

336   *Rankings:* Quality 43   Value 4   Impression 34=   Overall 3

WINE LISTS

4 SHARROW BAY HOTEL   Ullswater, Cumbria CA10 2LZ
Tel. (01768) 486301   www.sharrow-bay.com

This is a terrific list with over 60% of the entries rating 3 stars or more. Nicolas Chièze, the Head Sommelier, has built on the solid foundations begun by his predecessor, to produce one of the most intriguing wine lists in the country. Prices are pretty much up to London levels, but certainly not outrageous, and whilst there are many fine establishments in the land where you could find some of the wines at a considerably cheaper price, there are few which could beat this list for sheer balance. This is a very comprehensive list - well worth the effort and a complementary asset to the rest of the services offered by this establishment. Best buy - Ch. Rieussec 1988 (a great Sauternes vintage and a super 5 star wine), which catches the eye at £75.

Rankings: Quality 7   Value 43   Impression 4   Overall 4

5 GORDON RAMSAY   68-69 Royal Hospital Road, London SW3 4HP
Tel. (020) 7352 4441   www.gordonramsay.com

This is a wine list of the highest quality, as befits a restaurant with three Michelin stars. There are over 900 wines to choose from, with around a quarter of the wines rated 3 star or more, and a further half rated 4 stars or more. As a model quality wine list, this rates second to none in the UK, but of course, there is a hefty price to pay for this. There are only six wines rated 4 star or more that sell for £50 or less and only nine 3 star wines selling for £30 or less. For example, Leeuwin Estate "Prelude" Chardonnay is £42 a bottle here, but at Sycamore House (q.v.) it is a mere £21. But you may feel it's worth the splash to find a great rare wine, and there are plenty of those, whatever the price. This is a fascinating list with many wines of the highest quality. If only the management could be persuaded to lower their prices by 20% or so, this would be the clear overall winner. Best buy: Cline Cellars Contra Costa County Ancient Vines Mourvèdre 2002 at £36.

Rankings: Quality 1   Value 100   Impression 28=   Overall 5

6 RANSOME'S DOCK   35 - 37 Parkgate Road, London SW11 4NP
Tel. (020) 7924 2614   www.ransomesdock.co.uk

Why is it that so many wine merchants are seen eating at Ransome's Dock? Is it because that they know that there they will find one of the most exciting wine lists in London (in the whole country, even), or is it because they hope that Martin Lam's ever expanding cellar will accommodate even more of their wines! Whatever it is, this is a list that is in the vanguard of modernity - it has pzazz, buzz, beat - a pot pourri of all that's new in the wine world and that's probably why this has taken over from the Tate Gallery as the wine merchant's favourite watering hole. Martin was one of the first in the country to list his wines by style rather than by region and his innovative approach still continues to this day. Well over half the wines on the 300 plus strong list qualify on our quality criteria, but of those, less that a quarter qualify on our price criteria, so prices are not that cheap, but for London, they are pretty fair. There is a better quality/price ratio on the halves and it is very refreshing to see such an outstanding proportion of dry wines by the glass of real quality rather than being the lowest common denominator. There is a "feel good" factor about this list, but it is not as cheap as you might think, but if you pick your way through it carefully enough, there are some good price/quality wines to be had. Best Buy: Joseph 'Moda Amarone' Cabernet Sauvignon/Merlot 1998 from Primo Estate in South Australia at £30.

Rankings: Quality 6   Value 40   Impression 15=   Overall 6

7 DYLANWAD DA   2 Ffôs-y-Felin, Dolgellau LL40 1BS
Tel (01341) 422870   www. dylanwad.co.uk

Compared with most of the lists we have reviewed, this is a small operation, but we are sure that the undoubted enthusiasm for wine that Dylan Rowlands shows in his introduction to the list will ensure that it will grow in size over the next few years. Let's hope that he will continue to pursue his extraordinarily fair pricing policy (at least, fair for the customer), because this is one of the places where you can drink some real quality wines at a very, very reasonable price. Only about 25% of the list falls into our quality criteria of 3 stars or above, but of those wines, practically all meet our price criteria, so you can happily drink away with confidence, knowing that it won't break the bank. There is also a fair proportion of half bottles in the list, a quarter of which rank 3 stars or more, but none of the wines by the glass available meet our quality criteria. Nevertheless, this is a minor criticism of this customer friendly list with its informative tasting notes for each wine. It's a pity Dylan doesn't have any accommodation where we could sleep it all off! Best Buy: Vouvray 'Le Mont' Demi-Sec 2000 from Huët at £19.20.

Rankings: Quality 85   Value 2   Impression 73=   Overall 7

8 YE OLDE BULL'S HEAD INN   Castle Street, Beaumaris, Isle of Anglesey, LL58 8AP
Tel. (01248) 810329   www.bullsheadinn.co.uk

If you are getting the ferry from Holyhead to Dublin, this is an ideal stopover, barely a half an hour from the ferry terminal, and a very civilised stopover it is. The wine list is fairly short (121 bins) with pretty much half the wines of 3 star quality or more. Out of this half, more than half the wines meet our price criteria which accounts for the pretty high score that this establishment has achieved. The list is conventionally divided into regions and there isn't even a concession to dessert wines which are listed under whichever region they come from, together with the dry wines. There are some hidden gems in this list at extraordinarily reasonable prices and a decent amount of wines with some bottle age to make a most enjoyable drinking experience. Best Buy: Joseph Phelps Napa Valley Syrah 1995 at £28.50.

Rankings: Quality 40   Value 9   Impression 80=   Overall 8

9 PENHELIG ARMS HOTEL AND RESTAURANT   Terrace Road, Aberdovey, Gwynedd LL35 OLT
Tel. (01654) 767215   www.penheligarms.com

The enthusiasm of Robert Hughes for his wines at this seaside oasis of gastronomy shines through the list, but what is most remarkable is the gentleness of the prices, which have people coming from many miles away. Bearing in mind the remoteness from the major distribution centres, it must certainly cost him more to get his wine delivered than any flunky restaurant in London, which must surely eat into the already modest mark ups on his wines. Still, that's his business and any apparent loss foreseen is to the customers' gain. In fact, the prices are so gentle that it pays to go upmarket here, where you can still drink real quality at very reasonable prices. This is a wine list of outstanding value with a good selection of quality wines. Beat a path to the door! Best buy: Quinto do Vale Dona Maria 2000 from the Douro in Portugal at £16.

Rankings: Quality 71   Value 3   Impression 34=   Overall 9

10 THE CROOKED BILLET   2 Westbrook End, Newton Longville, Bucks MK17 ODF
Tel.(01908) 373936   www.thebillet.co.uk

This is one of the most remarkably impressive wine lists we have seen. Not because of its size (at 342 bins, it's one of the middle ranking in length), nor for its overall quality (there are other lists with a greater percentage of quality wines), but for the remarkable fact that 97% of the wines listed are available by the glass. What a fantastic way of exploring your way through the list! The only downside, however, is that the prices are pretty stiff, both for wines by the glass, as well as full bottles, so whatever you do, it's going to be a pretty expensive night out. The wines by flavour list is very well compartmentalised and described and is a very useful adjunct to the list by country. All in all, John Gilchrist has put together a very user-friendly list - it's a pity that the enormous wastage that must occur by serving so many wines by the glass means that the prices are inevitably very high - a 10% or 15% reduction in the prices might have made him the overall winner. Best buy: Marcel Guigal's Côte-Rôtie La Turque 1997 at £180 (£50 the glass).

Rankings: Quality 42   Value 98   Impression 1   Overall 10

11 CHERWELL BOATHOUSE   50 Bardwell Road, Oxford OX2 6ST
Tel. (01865) 552746

The wine list at Tony Verdin's (literally) converted boathouse in donnish Oxford has impressed under- and post-graduates for many years, for both quality and value. No doubt his partnership with Jasper Morris MW, in forming one of the best wine merchant's in the country has more than something to do with it. Although the list is dominated by Morris & Verdin wines (now FMV), there is a lot of good kit bought elsewhere to enhance the quality. All in all, this is a good list, full of high quality offerings with many at exceptionally low prices. The layout of the list is a bit confusing and although there are some tasting notes, we could probably have done with a bit clearer information all round. Nevertheless, it's certainly worth a punt into this Boathouse at any time! Best Buy: Morris and Verdin's own vineyard Beaune Les Pertuisots 2001 at £7.50 the glass, £25 the bottle - surely something to swig down with impunity (or better still, "le patron"!)

Rankings: Quality 12   Value 18   Impression 87=   Overall 11

12 SYCAMORE HOUSE   1 Church Street, Little Shelford, Cambridgeshire CG2 5HG
Tel. (01223) 843396

This is the shortest wine list we have had to consider in our quest for the Top 100, but certainly one of the most agreeable. Why? Well the prices are unbelievable. Nearly half the wines on the list cost £20 or less, but that is not the prime reason why you should be beating a path to Michael Sharpe's door. Just set your sights a little higher and you will realise that everything on the list costs less than £30. Then realise that 21 of the 57 wines listed are wines of 3 star ranking and above. All in all, this is a great place for inexpensive imbibement, especially when you realise that you have a reasonable choice of quality wines for less than £30 - it's a shame Sycamore House has no accommodation to crawl upstairs to after such delights! Best Buy - Ridge Geyserville Zinfandel 2001, 5 star quality at £29.50.

Rankings: Quality 83   Value 1   Impression 100   Overall 12

13 DARROCH LEARG   Braemar Road, Ballater, Scotland AB35 5UX
Tel. (013397) 55443   info@darach-learg.demon.co.uk

This is a VERY civilised wine list, with helpful tasting notes and a good spread of wines from around the world at very reasonable prices indeed. The only criticism is the poor selection of Californian wines, when there are so many world class wines from that area, but no doubt this will be rectified in due course. There are over 200 bins on the list with almost half being of 3 star quality or more, and of those, over 60% meet our value criteria, so there are plenty of good value wines to choose from. There is also a goodly number of half bottles on the list, although the price/quality ratio here is less apparent. The 5 dry House wines by the glass are sound, but not exciting. Nigel Franks has put a lot of effort into producing this very user-friendly list - one of the best in the country. Best Buy: the super 5 star Châteauneuf-du-Pape, Domaine du Vieux Télégraph 1999 at a remarkable £28.

Rankings: Quality 62   Value 8   Impression 15=   Overall 13

14 LA TROMPETTE   5-7 Devonshire Road, Chiswick, London W4 2EU
Tel. (020) 8747 1836

Another super London suburban restaurant wine list from Nigel Platts-Martin, this time in Chiswick. Wine has been important in all his restaurants and this one is no exception. There over 500 bins here, of which over 60% are of 3 star quality or more. Prices, are of course the issue here, although they are not overtly excessive for London, like its sister restaurant, The Glasshouse, in Kew (q.v.). The wine list, apart from the Champagne and Sparkling Wine section at the beginning and pages of half bottles, magnums, sweet wines and Sherry, Port and Madeira at the end, is divided into colour sections and then conventionally arranged by country and region, so you may have to rely heavily on advice from the sommelier team in making your choices. A page of wines by the glass precedes everything with three Champagnes and one French cider offered in 150ml. glasses and 15 other dry wines offered in either 175ml. or 250ml. glasses. There aren't many places in Britain that can boast of a wine list better than this and the residents of Chiswick are lucky to find such a gem on their doorstep. Best buy: Dean Hewitson's Old Garden Mourvèdre 2001, from vines planted in 1853, at £35.50.

Rankings: Quality 9   Value 42   Impression 43=   Overall 14

15 THE OLD BRIDGE AT HUNTINGDON 1 High Street, Huntingdon, Cambridgeshire PE29 3TQ
Tel. (01480) 424 300   www.huntsbridge.co.uk

This is a mature wine list of around 300 different wines expertly put together over the years by John Hoskins MW. It has much to be desired - a good selection of first class wines, plenty of choice at all prices, a goodly number of half bottles and a price/quality ratio on most of the wines, which should be an example to others. This is a grand list - enough to cater for all kinds of pockets and palates, with some very, very serious offerings. If there is to be any criticism, the choice appears to be a bit lightweight in the best of wines from California (particularly reds) and Italy, but that's really nit-picking. Best Buy; Kistler Sonoma Coast Chardonnay 1998 - a snip at £55, around a third of the price you would see it in some top London restaurants,

Rankings: Quality 25   Value 27   Impression 13=   Overall 15

16 THE GLASSHOUSE   14 Station Parade, Kew TW9 3PZ
Tel. (020) 8940 6777

Not quite what you would expect from a local restaurant in Kew, but then all of the restaurants that Nigel Platts-Martin ever had a hand in were out of the ordinary. Wine has been important in all his restaurants and this one is no exception. There are nearly 600 bins here, of which around two-thirds are of 3 star quality or more. Prices, are of course the issue here, although they are not overtly excessive for London, but expect to pay around half as much again for the same bottle you can drink at the Penhelig Arms in Aberdovey (q.v.). This list has been very well thought out, with an eye to quality - it is very long and it is not a run-of-the-mill list, but the absence of tasting notes makes it hard for the customer to make decisions, so reliance on the sommeliers is essential. Nevertheless, it is certainly worth the voyage for the wine list alone and if you choose carefully, you won't come away too light in the pocket. Best buy: Roberto Voerzio's Barolo Cerequio 1998 at £95.

Rankings: Quality 10   Value 50   Impression 21=   Overall 16

17 TYDDYN LLAN HOTEL   Llandrillo, Denbighshire, Ll21 OST
Tel. (01490) 440414   www.tyddynllan.co.uk

There are a growing number of establishments in rural Wales with exciting wine lists and this is the latest of them. What is really impressive is the gentleness of the prices, although it is certainly not the cheapest in the area, but nevertheless, you do come away with the feeling that you have had a good choice of quality wines without being ripped off. There are over 200 bins on the wine list, which is divided quite comprehensively into style, with 17 different style sections to choose from. Within the style sections, the wines are grouped by country, rather than price. Additionally, there is a reasonable selection of half bottles and 18 wines by the glass. Comprehensive tasting notes for all but the most famous producers is a useful adjunct to the listing arrangement by style and obviates the need to employ a sommelier. The savings in this respect have obviously been passed on to the consumer to the benefit of all concerned. Best Buy: Alban Vineyards "Lorraine" Syrah 1997 at £43.50.

Rankings: Quality 32   Value 21   Impression 11=   Overall 17

18 LOCANDA LOCATELLI 8 Seymour Street, London WlH 7JZ
Tel. (020) 7935 1149 www.locandalocatelli.com

This list has one of the greatest percentages of 4 and 5 star wines (over 50% of the list) with a further 25% of 3 star quality. With the exception of a few Champagnes and fortified wines, all the wines come from Italy, which might cause some commentators to downgrade the list, but this, after all, is an Italian restaurant, and there are enough quality wines from Italy to justify in having over three hundred of them on its wine list. Head sommelier Max Salli has put together one of the most exciting Italian lists in the UK and it is mainly the usual problem of London prices that prevents this list from obtaining an even higher score. A small selection of dry wines by the glass and the practical absence of half bottles has further reduced the score. A complete absence of tasting notes doesn't help either. Despite the prices, this is a model list, containing much of the best of Italy and much to be commended. Best buy: the 5 star Serpico (Irpinia Aglianico) 1999 from Feudi di San Gregorio at £65.

Rankings: Quality 4 Value 93 Impression 74= Overall 18

19 THE BENTLEY KEMPINSKI 1880 RESTAURANT 27-33 Harrington Gardens, London SW7 4JX
Tel. (020) 7244 5566 www.thebentley-hotel.com

This list has been created for the up market restaurant of this relatively new hotel by head sommelier, Deborah Kemp. The emphasis is on having available wines with a number of different grape varieties as well as a large selection of wines by the glass, currently 43, of which 25 are of 3 star quality or more. The list is conventionally arranged by country and region and of the 262 bins on the list, over 70% meet our quality criteria, but alas, only 7 wines of the 262 meet our value criteria. Nevertheless, this is a very good list and as long as you are not too worried about price, you should have an enjoyable time with it. It's a pity, really, because the list is full of quality wines, but it's like treading over eggshells to carefully find the value wines. Best Buy: Pagos de Posada Reserva Tilenus 2000 from Bodegas Estafania at £65.

Rankings: Quality 5 Value 95 Impression 21= Overall 19

20 THE SIR CHARLES NAPIER INN Sprigg's Alley, Chinnor, Oxfordshire OX39 4BX
Tel. (01494) 483011 www.sircharlesnapier.co.uk

Another long running establishment, which has seen their wine list mature and move with the times. There are a lot of New World up and coming producers featured on the list, but alas, no tasting notes to help and to guide the uninitiated. Still, there is a philosophy statement at the front of the list with some useful pointers and if you are not sure, we assume you can always ask any of the front of house team. About 50% of the list is of 3 star quality or more and there are a number which meet our quality/price criteria. There are a fair number of quality half bottles of dry wines but not a lot by the glass. Nevertheless, this is a very fine list with reasonable prices for Home Counties fine dining. As they state on their introduction to the list, they are working hard on improving it - they have come a long way so far, and if it keeps going this way, it won 't be long before it reaches the top ten in the country. Best buy: Côtes du Soleil Mourvèdre/Syrah 1997 from Jade Mountain in California at £18.50

Rankings: Quality 22 Value 32 Impression 43= Overall 20

Aglianico Important late ripening, southern Italy grape of considerable potential. Ageworthy with a noble structure, its smoky, minerally, berry-fruited character gains greater complexity and refined texture with keeping. The best wines come from Campania (Taurasi and various IGTs) and Basilicata (Aglianico del Vulture) but good examples are also made in Puglia.

Albariño Galicia's (north-west Spain) great white hope, Albariño is often compared to Viognier. It not only shares some of Viognier's perfume and succulent peachiness but also the wide disparity in quality levels. Needs to come from low yields. As Alvarinho, Portugal's best examples appear as varietal Vinho Verdes.

Arneis Leading Piedmont white grape, also making a minor foray into California and Australia. Light, dry, enticing perfumed examples usually need to be drunk very young; lightly oaked versions will keep a little longer but aren't necessarily superior.

Barbera Marvellous Piedmont grape which comes in any number of styles and quality levels. The greatest acclaim comes for rich, modern oaked-aged versions but some unoaked versions can also be stunning. There are many good examples as both Barbera d'Alba and Barbera d'Asti and occasionally convincing versions from Emilia. Simple, supple, fruity, quaffing Barbera can be good too. Also good examples from California. Its potential in Australia and Argentina remains largely unrealised.

Blaufränkisch Important red variety in Austria's Burgenland giving some of Austria's best reds. Sometimes blended with other varieties to moderate its relatively high acidity and tannin. Of minor importance in Washington State and Germany where it is known as Lemberger. One and the same as Hungary's Kékfrankos.

Cabernet Franc Parent variety of the more famous Cabernet Sauvignon it is more successful in cooler soils. Only in the Anjou and Touraine in the Loire Valley does it thrive as a varietal as despite its importance on Bordeaux's Right Bank it is almost invariably blended with Merlot and some Cabernet Sauvignon. Its importance as a component in Bordeaux style blends both at home and around the world is undeniable. Though it can emulate the flavours of its off-spring, it can miss its extra richness and depth and also show more of a raspberry-like fruit and a more leafy, herbal or even floral, component.

Cabernet Sauvignon Grown almost everywhere, a grape of forceful and easily recognisable personality, it is much more fussy in showing at its best. Though capable of great richness, depth and structure, a lack of full ripeness in both fruit and tannin tends to detract from so many examples. A long growing season and well-drained soils are two prerequisites to producing the greatest elegance and classic telltale blackcurrant but also black cherry or blackberry flavours that mesh so well with new French oak. Though Cabernet Sauvignon

dominates blends, the majority of top examples many do include a percentage of complementary varietals such as Merlot or Cabernet Franc which complement it in both flavour and structure. Many countries have identified at least one region where it really excels with the greatest riches from the Médoc, Napa Valley, Tuscany, Coonawarra and Margaret River. A significant number of world class examples have also come from Washington State, New Zealand, Chile, Argentina as well as a few from Spain and South Africa.

Cannonau Sardinian version of Grenache, for long produced as an inexpensive quaffing red, Cannonau di Sardegna. One of two committed growers are beginning to realize its true potential. Rare good fortified versions are also made from late-harvested or dried grapes.

Carignan Infamous red grape of the Languedoc-Roussillon still widely planted and often very high-yielding resulting in dilute, astringent wine. However from low yields and fully ripe fruit its a different beast. Deeply coloured, robust but characterful reds are possible not only in the Midi but also occasionally in Spain (as Cariñena), Sardinia (as Carignano) and California (as Carignane).

Carmenère Old Bordeaux variety of increasing importance in Chile where much of it continues to be sold as Merlot. As they are often planted in a field blend together the disparity in ripening times further compromises the quality of fruit from high-yielding vines. Once isolated and made from well-established low-yielding vines it has excellent potential with a characterful wild berry and spice character. Also thought to be confused with other grapes in regions where plantings were established from Bordeaux cuttings in the 19th century.

Chardonnay Ironically the only significant wine regions where this grape is not grown are found in France. The great white grape of Burgundy has a great affinity for oak and can produce whites of marvellous texture, depth and richness but will also render a wonderful expression of its origins where yields are low. High quality grapes allied to winemaking sophistication is essential – too many examples, wherever they are made, show a clumsy winemaking fingerprint (excessive leesy, skin contact or oak flavours) or inferior fruit (under-ripe, over-ripe) or are simply unclean, acidified or lacking balance. Chardonnay forms a part of almost all top quality sparkling wines, especially Champagne. When varietal and sparkling it is known as Blanc de Blancs. Rich botrytised versions are unusual but have been made to a high standard in the Mâconnais, Austria and New Zealand.

Chenin Blanc High quality white grape of Touraine and Anjou in the Loire Valley. Outstanding long-lived wines ranging from dry to sweet are made and owe much to the grape's high acidity. Apple and citrus flavours within a firm, demanding texture are usually complemented by floral, honey and mineral characters with quince, peach even apricot in sweeter styles. Despite there being more extensive plantings in California and South Africa, good examples from outside the Loire remain few. Washington State and New Zealand also provide one or two. Also an important base for some good quality sparkling wines.

Cinsaut/Cinsault Characterful Rhône variety where taken seriously. Can add perfume and complexity both to southern Rhône blends and wines from the Languedoc and Corsica, especially when yields are low.

Corvina Leading red variety in Italy's Veneto for Valpolicella, Amarone and Recioto della Valpolicella. Though only giving moderate colour and tannin its thickish skins help it to resist rot during the drying process or *appassimento*. The related Corvinone can bring more colour, concentration and structure to a blend.

Dolcetto Piedmont grape capable of wonderful fruit intensity yet lively acidity and moderate tannin. Most are unoaked with a mineral or herbal streak to black cherry/black plum fruit; best with 1-3 years' age. More ageworthy examples come from old low-yielding vines in Dogliani or Alba zones. Known as Ormeasco in Liguria.

Falanghina Another potential star grape from southern Italy set to rival Fiano and Greco. An increasing number of good examples, showing imp-ressive texture and flavour with a couple of years' age.

Fiano White variety mostly confined to Campania for perfumed spicy, dry wines with fullish peachy, slightly nutty fruit. Also late-harvested and botrytised versions.

Furmint Top quality Hungarian grape giving its greatest expression as the basis of the sweet wines of the Tokaj region thanks to its high acidity, susceptibility to noble rot and refined flavours. Also occasionally made in good dry versions and used by some producers in Austria's Burgenland for sweet Ausbruch wines.

Gamay The grape of the Beaujolais region and well-suited to its granitic soils. Examples range from the dilute and insipid to the impressively deep and fruity. Most but not all of it is produced by semi- carbonic maceration producing a supple texture but partly compromising its cherry fruit perfume and flavour. Plantings extend into the Mâconnais to the north where it performs poorly; mercifully, some at least, is being replaced by Chardonnay. The only really significant other area where the true Gamay grape is planted is in Touraine in the Loire Valley.

Garganega 'Good' grape of Soave giving intense, sleek whites when yields are low. Equally impressive from late-harvested or dried grapes (for Recioto di Soave).

Gewürztraminer / Traminer Both names are used to describe a remarkably aromatic distinctive grape variety giving good varietal examples from around the world. As a versatile grapy white it is redolent in scents from floral and musky to rose petal, lychee and spices. Styles range from the light and fresh to rich, oily textured wines and from dry to off-dry through late-harvested to sweet, botrytised wines. Weaker efforts lack definition and can show a certain coarseness on the finish. The greatest range of styles and highest quality comes from Alsace which is followed by Italy's Alto Adige and Germany. Though fewer in number the best new world examples arguably come from New Zealand but there is good quality too in Australia, California, Oregon and Canada and in Chile's Casablanca Valley.

Greco Specifically Greco di Tufo (as distinct from other similar names), and originally from Greece. Does well in volcanic soils in Campania in southern Italy; scented with citrus, peachy fruit and a firm texture and slightly nutty finish.

Grenache Leading variety in the southern Rhône as the backbone for reds from leading appellations such as Châteauneuf-du-Pape and Gigondas. Quality and style vary enormously but is capable of great longevity when produced from low-yielding fruit. Grenache also forms a component of many of Languedoc-Roussillon's reds including Banyuls and Collioure near the border with Spain. As Garnacha it is the base for top Spanish reds from small but dynamic region of Priorat as well as the leading variety in several other appellations in the north-east of the country. It is also a significant component in many reds from Navarra and Rioja. Known as Cannonau in Sardinia. In South Australia it is often combined with Shiraz and Mourvèdre.

Grenache Blanc Previously undistinguished grape, important in southern Rhône and Languedoc whites. Low yields and better winemaking have given it much more personality and it is sometimes made varietally.

Grüner Veltliner Leading and widely planted Austrian variety. Excels on terraces above the Danube in the Wachau. Similarly full-bodied whites from elsewhere in Lower Austria also reveal peppery, citrus, yellow plum character that becomes gently honeyed and complex with age. Tends to high alcohol, needing to be balanced by good acidity and fruit richness. Cheaper examples can be dilute and lack charm.

Inzolia Important in Sicily for fresh dry whites with good perfume and flavour; also a component of some of the best Marsala. Known in Tuscany as Ansonica.

Lagrein A leading variety in Trentino-Alto Adige (North-East Italy) for both supple, fruity everyday reds and deep coloured, concentrated, often oak-aged versions full of bramble, dark plum and cherry fruit. Has the fruit intensity of other native North-East varieties but more moderate tannin and acidity levels.

Macabeo/Viura Widely used if relatively unexciting variety of greatest importance in northern Spain. Its chief manifestations are white Rioja and Cava (usually with Parellada and Xarel-lo). Also widely planted in Roussillon as Maccabéo or Maccabeu.

Malbec Essentially another of Bordeaux's rejects, the peppery, black-fruited Malbec has found favour as the major constituent of Cahors in South-West France but has become even more strongly associated with Argentina. The latter examples tend to be softer and more approachable but can want for structure but there is high quality from both sources. Good quality is also obtained from a limited amount of old vine plantings in South Australia while it is on the increase in Chile and performs well in New Zealand. Of minor importance in Loire Valley where it is known as Cot.

Malvasia This name covers a great many closely related varieties from Italy, Spain and Portugal. In North-East Italy Malvasia Istriana can be a characterful dry white. In Tuscany dried Malvasia grapes bring more quality when added to Trebbiano for Vin Santo while in Lazio Malvasia can rescue the whites of the Colli Albani, such as Frascati, from blandness. In the south it turns sweet when made from *passito* grapes on the volcanic island of Lipari. In Spain it can add substance to some white Rioja while in Portugal's Douro Malvasia grapes could end up in White Port or as a dry white. As Malvasia Fina occasional good varietal white Dão are made. On Madeira it is responsible for the richest, sweetish style, Malmsey.

Malvasia Nera A black version of Malvasia of most importance in southern Italy, especially Puglia. Its aromatic, distinctive black plum fruit adds character to Negroamaro, Primitivo or Sangiovese-based reds.

Marsanne At its best this is an intensely flavoured white with succulent peach and apricot fruit and often a tell-tale honeysuckle character. It is particularly important in northern Rhône whites, sometimes in partnership with Roussanne. It is also produced in Hermitage as *Vin de Paille*. It crops up again in blends in Côtes du Rhône whites (but not white Châteauneuf-du-Pape), Languedoc-Roussillon and even in Provence. It is grown too in Switzerland's Valais (as Ermitage) and makes a rare appearance (or two) in Italy. Its use in California is likely to increase while the best examples in Australia come from the Goulburn Valley in Victoria.

Merlot Planted in almost all leading wine producing countries. Its home is Bordeaux where it ranges from a few per cent of a blend to almost varietal. Much Merlot is lean, weedy and under-ripe. In fact few Merlot-dominated wines in fact come close to those of Bordeaux's Right Bank. Although good ripe, lush reds have been produced from Australia, New Zealand, Chile, Argentina, South Africa, California, Washington State and Italy, relatively few combine richness with the classic berry plumminess and fruitcake, spice, fig or clove character that make it so enticing. Tuscany and California do it most often.

344

Montepulciano Gutsy peppery red variety that dominates the adriatic seaboard in central Italy. Most examples are fruity with good extract and colour; a mere handful develop the breadth, refinement and complexity of which it is also capable.

Mourvèdre High quality grape found in southern France at the very limits of ripening. It is most important incarnation is as powerful, tannic and ageworthy Bandol but some in Châteauneuf-du-Pape use it for blending as do producers in the Languedoc-Roussillon. In Spain (as Monastrell) it has been rather neglected in terms of producing high quality but a handful of producers in Jumilla and elsewhere are starting to realize its potential there. In Australia and California it is sometimes called Mataro but in both places it can also excel both varietally and in blends.

Muscadelle Relatively unsung grape of Bordeaux where it is used sparingly in sweet wines (including Sauternes) and in some of the dry whites. Its true potential however, where it can achieve extraordinary complexity (as Tokay), is seen in Victoria, Australia - mostly in and around Rutherglen in the North-East of the state.

Muscat A whole family of grapes of 3 principal forms: Muscat Blanc à Petits Grains, Muscat of Alexandria and Muscat Ottonel. It can be dry, medium-dry or sweet – whether from dried grapes or fortified or a combination of the two. It is also made sparkling. Common to the best is an intense, heady grapiness – that taste of the grape itself. Only occasionally is it a wine for ageing. Alsace makes it both dry and intensely sweet, in southern France there are the *Vins Doux Naturel* of Beaumes de Venises and Rivesaltes (amongst others). Spain makes light sweet versions of Moscatel while Portugal has the sweet fortified Moscatel de Setúbal. In Italy there's Asti or the better Moscato d'Asti and there's also yellow and pink forms of it (Moscato Giallo and Moscato Rosa) in the North-East – usually made off-dry or medium-sweet. Off-shore from Sicily the grapes Zibibbo are dried for raisiny, apricotty Passito di Pantelleria. In Germany (called Muskateller) it ranges from dry to sweet and Austria's best examples are also sweet. Gelber Muskateller is for the yellow/gold-skinned variant, Roter Muskateller for the red-skinned version. In Greece, Samos Muscat is produced. In North-East Victoria the intense raisiny Rutherglen Muscat is produced while in the US dry, medium-dry and sweet examples are produced by a few (but including Black Muscat and Orange Muscat). From South Africa comes rich, sweet Vin de Constance. In fact there seemly no end to it.

Nebbiolo The classic variety of Piedmont that remains almost exclusively the source of high quality examples of the grape. Capable of exquisite aroma and flavour its youthful austerity and tannin, while less formidable than in the past, can still present a challenge to some palates. Its dark raspberry, cherry or blackberry fruit, herb and floral aromas take on increasing complexity with age and the best examples give a wonderful expression of their *terroir*. Oak needs to be used with care in order not to overwhelm its unique perfumes and flavour. Lighter, fragrant but fruity examples of the grape can be a bit hit and miss, often being produced from less good sites. The only source of Nebbiolo-based wines in any significant quantity outside Piedmont is as Valtellina Superiore in Lombardy where it is called Chiavennasca.

Negroamaro Previously formed the core of rustic, raisiny reds from Italy's Puglia, including Salice Salentino. It can show dark, bitter flavours but subject to better winemaking recently there are now exciting varietal examples.

Nerello Mascalese Once seen only as a high-yielding blending variety, now emerging as quality rival to highly-regarded Nero d'Avola with which it is often blended. From volcanic soils on the slopes of Mount Etna, it can show remarkble texture and perfume. Also often blended with the related Nerello Cappuccio.

Nero d'Avola Widely planted Sicilian native. It produces rich, intense, deep-coloured reds with a peppery black-fruited character and adding more depth and complexity with age. Character varies with altitude, location and vine age.

Petit Manseng Quality grape producing sometimes exquisite dry and sweet wines of Jurançon in South-West France. Increasingly used by growers in the Languedoc for its exotic, floral and spice character that is supported by good acidity. Also gaining a foothold in California.

Petit Verdot Sometimes an important minor component in Bordeaux, especially the Médoc but increasingly too in similar blends made in other regions where Cabernet Sauvignon is successful. Late ripening, it can show more than hint of violet in aroma as well as intense blackberry fruit. Varietal examples are rare.

Petite Sirah The name given to Durif in California which produces powerful, robust tannic varietal wines with dense spicy, brambly fruit. Also used to add complexity to some leading examples of Zinfandel.

Pinot Blanc Most associated with Alsace and Italy's Alto Adige and Friuli. In Alsace old low yielding vines give it good character though often blended with the delightfully scented Auxerrois which can make the better wine. Also the basis of most Crémant d'Alsace. Fine Italian examples come in both oaked and unoaked styles. Increasingly, the best German examples are unoaked, intense and mineral. Also some decent examples from California, Oregon and Canada.

Pinot Gris Excellent white grape most associated with Alsace where it produces distinctively flavoured whites of intense spice, pear and quince flavours. Late-harvested it takes on an almost exotic, honeyed richness and nobly-rotted *Sélection des Grains Nobles* can be superb. In Germany as Grauburgunder or Ruländer

good examples are made in warmer regions. Beyond simple Italian Pinot Grigio, there are some fine concentrated, delicately creamy examples from Friuli and Alto Adige. Oregon has made something of a speciality of it to complement its Pinot Noir while despite its proven potential in New Zealand it has only recently captured the imagination of a wider number of wine producers. Good examples are also made in Victoria and Canada.

Pinot Meunier Very important component in most Champagne blends if rarely used for anything else. Early ripening and as a wine, early developing, it complements both Chardonnay and Pinot Noir. Ignored by many New World producers of premium sparkling wines but some have significant plantings.

Pinot Noir Success with Pinot Noir beyond Burgundy has been slow coming but there are now many regions in the world at least emulating the fabulous flavour complexity if not the structure and supreme texture of the top Burgundies. Flavours include cherry, raspberry, strawberry but can also include sappy, undergrowth characters or become more gamey in response to both origin and wine making. The expressions of *terroir* and differing winemaking interpretations in Burgundy are almost endless. Outside of Burgundy those regions or countries emerging with the greatest potential for Pinot Noir are California, Oregon, New Zealand, Tasmania but also cool parts of Victoria, South Australia and Western Australia. Success in Italy, Germany, Austria, Chile and South Africa is considerably more limited yet further potential exists. Pinot Noir is also very important as a component of most of the world's best sparkling wines.

Pinotage Characterful yet tainted South African variety due to its tendency to produce unattractive paint-like aromas (isoamyl acetate). A crossing of Cinsaut and Pinot Noir, from old bush vines in particular it can produce deep, concentrated reds with spicy, plum and berry fruit flavours uncompromised by any volatile esters. The occasional adequate example is produced in New Zealand.

Primitivo DNA fingerprinted as one and the same as Zinfandel, though debate continues about where in Europe they originated from. As Primitivo it is increasingly important in southern Italy, particularly in Puglia where old *alberello*-trained vines produce robust, characterful reds with moderate ageing potential.

Riesling An outstanding variety with an almost infinite number of expressions. Styles vary from bone dry to intensely sweet, from low alcohol to powerful and full-bodied. Its impressive range of flavours including apple, citrus, peach and apricot, are complemented by a minerality that subtle differences of place or *terroir* bring. It is nearly almost made varietally and aged in stainless steel or large old wood. Obtaining full ripeness and the right balance between sugar and acidity is crucial to quality. The most delicate, exquisite Riesling comes from Germany though there are many different expressions there while Alsace provides the fullest, most powerful examples. Austria's Wachau is closer to this style than Germany but with purity and minerality of its own. Australia also produces high quality Riesling, showing different expressions from Western Australia to the Clare, Eden Valley and Tasmania. Some of the best New Zealand Riesling comes from Marlborough and Central Otago. Also good in North America, including Washington State and the Fingers Lakes region of New York State. Some examples of Canadian Icewine are based on Riesling.

Roussette Fine white grape of Savoie in eastern France (also known as Altesse). Best wines have good structure and weight with a mineral, herb and citrus intensit; adding more exotic nuances if from low yielding vines on the best steep slopes.

Roussanne High quality white grape that is difficult to grow. Roussanne's impressive texture and depth can be seen in wines from both the northern and southern Rhône, sometimes on its own but other times complementing Marsanne. It is also favoured by some of the leading quality producers in Languedoc-Roussillon and Provence, if mostly in blends. Also the grape used for fine perfumed Chignin-Bergeron whites in Savoie. Outside France, California and Australia have a few high quality whites based, at least partly, on Roussanne.

Sagrantino Central Italian variety localized at Montefalco in Umbria. Potentially rich in extract, tannin and with high acidity its true potential as an outstanding dry red has long been realized by Caprai. Recently a wave of promising new examples thanks to better viticulture and winemaking. Rarer are good sweet *passito* versions, from dried grapes.

Sangiovese Leading variety in Italy, dominating production in Tuscany. All the classic Tuscan appellations are based on it and the improvement in quality is on-going as the revolution in winemaking is being followed by one in the vineyard. Styles range from the light and fruity to oaky, powerful and tannic but the best are pure, refined and individual. It is made to a very high standard both varietally and in blends with Cabernet Sauvignon and Merlot yet some of the most distinctive expressions include a small percentage of minor native varieties such as Canaiolo or Colorino. The most important area for its production outside Tuscany is Romagna but it also plays an important role in Umbria. Good if not great examples have been produced in California – both varietally or in blends with Cabernet or other varieties. Adequate examples from Australia if mostly in attractive everyday mould.

Sauvignon Blanc Aromatic white grape capable of a wide range of expression and quality. The most

structured and ageworthy examples come from France whether the classic mineral-laced wines of Sancerre and Pouilly-Fumé (now richer and riper than previously) or the more oak-influenced, peachy examples from Bordeaux (some blended with Sémillon) that will age for more than a decade. The most overt fruit expression is seen in examples from Marlborough in New Zealand but most of these need to be drunk within a year of the vintage. Bright gooseberryish Sauvignon for immediate drinking is also made in Chile's Casablanca Valley and good vibrant, nettly Sauvignon Blanc from South Africa is on the increase. Some of the best Australian examples of Sauvignon Blanc have very ripe gooseberry fruit with a hint of tropical flavours; it is also sometimes blended with Sémillon. California offers both fresh, more herbaceous examples and riper ,melon and fig versions capable of some age. North-East Italy provides high quality Sauvignon with good structure but more restraint. Good examples come from Spain and Austria (Südsteiermark) too though the latter are usually best when unoaked. Sauvignon Blanc is also important in combination with Sémillon for Bordeaux's sweet wines.

Savagnin Best known for the production of Vin Jaune, the speciality of the Jura. It can also form a part of some of the region's best dry whites and impresses too when produced varietally. A naturally firm structure can be enhanced by oak, cradling intense citrus and mineral fruit that becomes more nutty with age.

Sémillon Great Sémillon comes from either of two sources: France or Australia. In Bordeaux Sémillon is made both dry, in usually oak-aged blends with Sauvignon Blanc (as it is in Bergerac), or sweet where it is typically the dominant component in all its great sweet wines. Botrytis enrichment is the key to the power, flavour richness and complexity of the best long-lived Sauternes and Barsac. Lesser appellations can also make attractive sweet wines and some good examples come from neighbouring Monbazillac. The classic Australian Sémillon comes from the Hunter Valley. Though increasing rare, unoaked wines become remarkably toasty and honeyed with a decades' age or more. Oaked-aged examples are made to give more immediate pleasure; those from the Margaret River are usually combined with Sauvignon Blanc. Relatively few rich, sweet Australian examples are also made. New Zealand and South Africa have had some success with dry examples of the grape.

Shiraz Australian name for Syrah but also favoured by some South African producers. Australia produces a galaxy of styles from the powerful, American-oaked blockbuster to more elegant, more Rhône-like expressions aged in French oak. Every region produces a different stamp whether Hunter Valley, Clare, Barossa, Eden Valley, McLaren Vale, Grampians, Heathcote, Great Southern or one of many other exciting areas. Sparkling Shiraz is an Australian speciality and high quality from a limited number of producers. Also see Syrah.

Silvaner/Sylvaner The best Silvaner comes from Germany's Franken region while that given the French spelling (Sylvaner) comes from Alsace. Although a relatively neutral grape, from old vines in Alsace it can take on real richness and a smoky, spicy flavour. In Franken it shows more of a minerally, nuanced subtlety – an intriguing earthy, appley character. Also occasional good examples from other German regions, Italy's Alto Adige, and Switzerland's Valais (as Johannisberg).

Syrah The home of Syrah is in the northern Rhône where a range of appellations give the most classic expression to one of the most exciting red grapes in the world. Those showing the most aromatic, smoky, white pepper and herbs expression come from Côte Rôtie (where they often include a little Viognier); broader, more powerful, minerally versions come from the hill of Hermitage. Many good examples also come from the surrounding appellations of Crozes-Hermitage, Cornas and Saint-Joseph. Syrah is also made varietally in the southern Rhône but more often is used to complement Grenache. As well as being important in Provence many of the best wines from the Languedoc-Roussillon are either based on it or include a significant percentage. Some very good varietal Syrah also comes from Italy where it is also added in small amounts to an increasing number of reds. Spain and Portugal also have good quality interpretations of the grape but Australia apart (also see Shiraz) the best Syrah outside of France comes from the US, primarily California but also Washington State. A few good examples of Syrah come from Chile and Argentina.

Tannat Vine from France's basque country, most important in Madiran where its powerful tannins need to be softened. Also widely grown in Uruguay.

Tempranillo Spain's leading red grape and a first class one though that has not always been apparent going by the quality from the most famous appellation based on it – Rioja. The grapes need to be concentrated and retain acidity, something more often achieved in Ribera del Duero where the best powerful blackberry and black plum reds are among Spain's very best. Tempranillo is also important in many other appellations including Toro and Costers del Segre — both varietally or as blends. As **Tinta Roriz** it is extremely important both in the production of Port but also as a component in Douro where its splendid aromatic complexity is sometimes fully realised. It is also important both varietally and in blends in several other Portuguese regions where there has recently been a massive increase in planting. In Alentejo in southern Portugal (as Aragonês) it is usually combined with Trincadeira and can develop into deep, savoury reds with age.

Tempranillo also has potential in Australia and Argentina.

Touriga Franca Backbone of much Port and usually blended with Tinta Roriz and Touriga Nacional. Also important in table wines from the Douro, occasionally varietally. From old vines it can show great class and complexity.

Touriga Nacional Fashionable high quality Portuguese grape, important both in the Douro and most other Portuguese regions. It is characterised by deep colour, floral even violet aromas and dark damson plum, mulberry or blackberry fruit and a dash of pepper. Deep, fleshy varietal reds are made but works best with Tinta Roriz, Touriga Franca and other grapes (similarly as an integral part of most Port).

Verdelho One of the noble varieties of Madeira that arguably produces the best style of all. A lightly honeyed and preserved citrus character togther with its vibrancy, refinement and general versatility secure its appeal. Known in the Douro as Gouveio. Significant in Australia for attractive relatively inexpensive dry whites.

Verdicchio Leading variety in Marche (Central Italy). Both oaked and unoaked it can produce moderately ageworthy whites of good texture and depth.

Vermentino Lemony, herb-scented Italian grape, best from Tuscan/Ligurian coast and north of Sardinia. Can be extremely stylish and a delight to drink young.

Viognier The best Viognier comes from Condrieu (Northern Rhône). Here the wine is opulent, lush and superbly aromatic – rich in apricot and peach with floral, blossom, honeysuckle and spice. Most are dry and best drunk young though a few age quite well, especially when they have acquired an enhanced structure from delicate oak treatment. One or two examples are made from late-harvested grapes. Also increasingly important in the southern Rhône, Languedoc-Roussillon and Provence, sometimes made varietally but as often injecting some perfume and fruit into a blend. There's a little in Italy, Austria and Greece. In California and Australia there are a fair number of good examples but only handful of these have the concentration and balance to suffice as a substitute for Condrieu.

Zinfandel The grape California made its own. From a rich resource of old free-standing vines, rich, powerful and concentrated wines are produced – most typically full of peppery, blackberry fruit and sometimes a riper raisiny, pruny character. Great examples come from Dry Creek, Russian River, Sonoma Valley, even Napa but also the Sierra Foothills and the Central Coast. It also grown successfully in Arizona and Washington State and there's also a little Zinfandel in New Zealand, Australia, Chile and South Africa. Also see Primitivo.

Glossary

AC Appellation Controlée is the top category of French wine regulations and guarantees origin, grape varieties and style.

Acidification Addition of acid to must or wine if the wine has either naturally low acidity or is from a particularly warm grown climate. Usually in the form of tartaric acid.

Assemblage This is the final blend of a wine prior to its bottling. Many fine wines are assembled from different components after ageing.This process will determine the final selection for wines such as those from top Bordeaux Châteaux.

Autolysis Enzymatic process in sparkling wine whereby dead yeast cells add increased flavour to wine. The longer the period the richer and more complex the characteristic becomes. Sparkling wines with less than 18 months on their yeast sediment will have little or no autolysis character.

Bâtonnage Stirring of a wines fine lees to provide additional flavour and texture. Commonplace among top white Burgundies and other premium barrel fermented whites and also now lesser whites as well. Lees also need stirring to provide limited aeration and to avoid the development of off smelling sulphides.

Barriques The most well-known barrel type of 225 litre capacity. The Burgundian Pièce is fractionally larger with thicker staves than the classic Bordeaux barrique.

Biodynamic Method of organic farming that seeks to promote the natural balance of the land.This includes both soil and plants. Natural treatments are used to protect the vineyard and applications carried out in line with lunar and planetary activity. Many first class wine producers now farm biodynamically.

Botrytis Botrytis or Botrytis Cinerea is a fungal infection of the vine which is particularly harmful to red grapes. In certain unique conditions though it provides for the development of Noble Rot in areas such as Sauternes, the Mosel and the Loire Valleys Coteaux du Layon. In late warm harvests with early morning humidity and sunny days the grapes will dehydrate concentrating their sugar and flavour. Wines produced from such grapes have a uniquely intense, peachy character.

Canopy Management Vineyard management techniques designed to improve yield and quality as well as minimizing risk of vine disease. Utilises a number of trellising/training systems to better expose the vines foliage and fruit to sunlight, resulting in improved photosynthesis and grape ripening.

Carbonic maceration Method used prior to conventional fermentation of red wine whereby colour rather than tannin is extracted.This occurs during a limited fermentation which takes place within grapes kept in anaerobic conditions.The berries will gradually split and fermentation will proceed as normal. Red winemaking particularly of Pinot Noir but also other varieties may involve using whole uncrushed grape bunches and partial carbonic maceration will occur. Greater colour and flavour complexity can be achieved.The flavours are forward and vibrant often resembling bubble gum and can have a hint of green pepper from the grape stems.The process has long been used in Beaujolais but increasingly elsewhere.

Cépage ameliorateurs This means an improving variety. The term has been widely used in Languedoc-Roussillon where there have been increasing amounts of Syrah, Grenache and Mourvedre planted in addition to the widely distributed Carignan.

Champagne method Method for the production of sparkling wine originating in Champagne. A secondary fermentation takes place in bottle and the wine is left on the resulting yeast lees.The finest sparkling wine is all made in this way.

Chaptalisation The addition of sugar to grape must to increase its alcoholic strength. If added during fermentation has the added effect of prolonging the process. Some winemakers feel this can add complexity.

Clones Vines reproduced by clonal selection provide for uniformity of yield and flavour but wines produced from whole vineyards of the same clone can lack complexity. Many fine winegrowers instead use mass selection establishing vineyards from a range of original vinecuttings.

Cold maceration Period prior to fermentation where crushed red grapes are kept in solution with the juice at a cool temperature to extract both colour and primary fruit flavours.

Crossing The result of a cross between two different grape varieties of the same vine species, almost always Vinifera. While some crossings have been commercially and qualitatively successful they rarely approach the best of what nature has produced (i.e all the most highly regarded varieties).

Cru Classé (CC) Classification of Bordeaux wines. Those from the Médoc (from 1er to 5ème Cru Classé/ first to fifth growth) and Barsac/Sauternes (1er or 2ème Cru Classé/ first and second growths) are covered by a famous classification of 1855. Graves (1959) and Saint-Emilion (Grand Cru Classé or Premier Grand Cru Classé) are also classified, the latter is now subject to revision every ten years (the last in 1996).

Cryo-Extraction Process used during sweet wine production where a must is frozen in order to concentrate the wine. Used in particular in Sauternes in poorer vintages with low botrytis levels. (also see Must Concentration).

Cuvaison This is the period during red wine vinification where the grape skins and other solid matter are kept in solution in the grape juice and then finished wine. This may include a period cold maceration to extract more colour, followed by fermentation and in some cases continued contact post-fermentation to round the wines tannins and provide greater harmony.

Débourbage Period where white grape juice or wine is left in order for solid matter to settle. Lighter aromatic and fruity whites will require all solids settling whereas a top white Burgundy or Chardonnay is more likely to be vinified from only partially settled must. Straightforward commercial whites may also be fined and even filtered as well prior to fermentation.

De-stemmed Most wine must is crushed and de-stemmed prior to fermentation. Some whites however, particularly Chardonnay may be whole bunch pressed and reds may include whole bunches added to the fermentation vat. Wine produced by carbonic maceration will also retain its stems. Traditionally made reds may also be vinified with some of their stems in order to add additional tannin and structure. In the case of the latter aggressive green tannins can be extracted if the stems as well as the grapes are not fully ripe.

DO Denominación de Origen is Spain's main regulatory category which defines both origin and methods of production. It is not however it the highest – Priorat and Rioja have DOC status.

DOC The Italian Denominazione di Origine Controllata is the main category for that country's protection of wine names and styles. Regulations cover origin, grape varieties and both the type and length of ageing permitted. Many have been revised or at least modified in response to progress to higher quality but there is much debate as to how best protect tradition while accomodating those committed to higher quality. There are well over 300 and many of these include sub-categories. While some DOCs boast numerous quality wines, others fail to deliver even a single premium wine. Also see DOCG. In Portugal Denominação de Origem Controlada is the highest regulated category recently extended to include broad regional areas (with sub-zones) to make for easier identification as Portuguese wines increase in popularity.

DOCG The top level of Italian wine appellations, Denominazione di Origine Controllata e Garantita includes a guarantee of origin and stipulates grape varieties but like the French AC it does not ensure top quality.

Dosage Sparkling wine produced from the Champagne method will be topped up after disgorging with a mix of wine and sugar and this dosage determines the style and sweetness of the final wine.

En Primeur Sale of wine while still in barrel. Commonplace now in Bordeaux and becoming so in Burgundy and other regions.

Filtration The removal of solid particles by means of a filter prior to bottling. While it saves the time required for a natural settling it may also rob a wine of flavour and character. Where the wine is healthy both filtration and fining (see below) have proved to be unnecessary.

Fining Process used to clarify grape juice or wine by removing the smallest (soluble) microscopic particles which attach themselves to the fining agents added. Great care should be used to avoid stripping the must or wine of flavour.

Flor The thin yeast film found on dry Fino and Manzanilla sherries after fermentation. It is unstable and dissolves when exposed to high alcohol. Amontillado sherries will have started life as Finos but will have been unable to sustain their Flor cover. The salty taste it provides is unique.

Foudres French term for large wooden vats used to age wine in.

Guyot Old and very well established French vine training system. One or two fruiting canes are trained along wires

with the new seasons shoots trained above on a second wire.

Hybrid Vine variety produced by crossing two different vine species. It should not be confused with a Crossing which is produced from two varieties of the same species. Hybrids of Vinifera formed with the more hardy American vine species are generally held in low regard but a few such as Seyval Blanc can yield good quality wine without any trace of a so-called 'foxy' quality.(also see Crossing, Vinifera)

Lees The sediment left after fermentation, including the dead yeast cells. White wine will often be racked off the gross lees but some sediment will remain which is known as the fine lees. This is important in providing additional flavour and texture as well as acting as an anti-oxidant during early barrel maturation. Lees stirring (see Bâtonnage) is regularly practiced at the same time. An increasing number of top quality reds are also now being aged on lees, some with micro-oxygenation.

Maceration The period during which flavour, colour, tannins and other components are leeched from the grape skins before, during and after fermentation. Temperature plays an important role with primary fruit aromas and colour extracted at cooler temperatures whereas more tannin is released with heat. The cap of grape skins formed during fermentation needs to be kept in solution with the fermenting must and various methods are used which also aid extraction (see Pigeage). Pre-fermentation maceration (see Cold maceration) is regularly practiced as well as extended post fermentation maceration which helps to polymerise the wines tannins, making them rounder and softer in texture. Some skin contact prior to fermentation is also practiced by a number of producers of white wines (see Macération Pelliculaire).

Macération pelliculaire French expression meaning skin contact. In effect it refers to the period of just a few hours where white wine must is macerated with its skins prior to fermentation. Semillon and Sauvignon Blanc in Bordeaux and Chenin Blanc in the Loire as well as more aromatic varieties like Muscat have all successfully been vinified using this technique. Excessive skin contact will result in coarseness and very early oxidation.

Malolactic fermentation Chemical process whereby malic acid is transferred into softer lactic acid. All red wine is put through malolactic but for whites it depends on the variety and style. For aromatic varieties such as Sauvignon Blanc and Riesling the process is avoided. For cool climate top quality Chardonnay it will add weight and texture. It may often be blocked with warmer grown Chardonnay to preserve acidity. Top reds including Cabernet Sauvignon and similarly structured and tannic blends are increasingly having the malolactic conducted in new oak. The wines are lusher and more softly textured, particularly in their youth but long term development remains a questionmark.

Meritage Term used in the United States to describe a Bordeaux style blend either red or white.

Mesoclimate The localised climate found generally within a vineyard or small specific area and responsible for particular characteristics found in the resulting wines. Often

349

incorrectly referred to as a microclimate. The latter is in fact the very specific climate of the vine canopy.

Micro-oxygenation Cellar operation devised by Patrick Ducournau in Madiran to assist in softening the often aggressively tannic wines produced from the local Tannat. Now increasingly practiced around the globe, small quantities of oxygen are regularly pumped into the ageing wine avoiding the need to rack the wine from one container to another, minimising handling and providing better balanced, finer tannins.

Monopole French for a solely owned vineyard site, particularly relevant in Burgundy.

Must concentration Any of a series of techniques for removing water from grape juice in order to make more concentrated wine. As well as evaporation under vacuum, freeze concentration (see Cyro-Extraction), which simu-lates eiswein/icewine production, can be used to remove water. Reverse Osmosis is a sophisticated process that allows the water content in finished wine to be reduced.

Oxidation Exposure of must or wine to air. Controlled oxidation is important in the maturation of wine before bottling and can add complexity to fortified wines aiding the production of rancio character. Oxidation of grape juice is also popular in producing barrel fermented white wine particularly premium Chardonnay. Reduction is the opposite of oxidation.

Phenolics Compounds found in grapes and extracted during vinification. These include tannins, flavour compounds and anthocyanins (responsible for the colour in red wines). See also Cuvaison, Extraction and Maceration.

Phylloxera Vine aphid which was the great scourge of the worlds vineyards in the 19th century. It can be resisted by planting vinifera varieties on resistant American species rootstocks.

Pigeage Method of plunging down the cap produced during red wine fermentation. This can be done by hand plunging with a number of devices or even by foot. A number of specialist automatic machine driven methods have also been developed. Particularly common and successful among the latter is the Rotofermenter. Pigeage can be gentler and less aggressively extractive than remontage or pumping the must back over itself.

Racked Winery procedure where must or wine is pumped or transferred under gravity from one container to another. This is both to remove the wine from solids but also to provide adequate aeration during maturation.

Rancio Maderised character with burnt, toffee like aromas produced in the development of aged fortified wines through a combination of controlled oxidation and exposure to heat. Banyuls, Maury and Rivesaltes in the Roussillon as well as the fortified Muscats and Tokays of Rutherglen all show classic rancio character.

Reduced This is the opposite of oxidised. Excessive reduction can result in the development foul smelling sulphides during cask ageing and so wines need to be exposed to controlled aeration during this phase, this can be achieved by either racking or more recently the use of micro-oxygenation.

Residual Sugar There is always a small portion of unfermentable sugar in wine even those that are technically classified as dry. It is commonplace in some whites particularly straightforward fruit driven styles to purposely leave a hint of residual sugar. More serious wines from cooler regions like Alsace and the Mosel may well be completed with some sugar left naturally. Late harvested wines are deliberately left on the vine to accumulate sufficient sugar to ensure considerable sweetness after vinification. (also see Botrytis)

Rootstock The plant formed from the root system of the vine to which the scion (fruiting part) is grafted. Most vinifera vines (the european species to which most quality grape varieties belong) are grafted on to rootstocks of American vines (or hybrids of them) due to its resistance to phylloxera.

Solera A system of fractional blending used in Jerez in the production of sherry to provide consistency and enrichment. It is also used to some extent in other fortified production such as Rutherglen or Madeira. The name is derived from the bottom rung of a series of barrels containing the oldest wine. Only a small part of the wine is drawn from this bottom level at one time. Successive levels are then replenished by younger wines from the level above.

Terroir French concept which considers the unique physical environment of a site or vineyard. Also refers to the character in a wine that is derived from its origins rather than the grape variety.

Traditional method The classic method of Champagne production (see Champagne method) as it is referred to in other regions for sparkling wines made in this way. Known as méthode traditionelle or méthode classique in other parts of France, as metodo classico in Italy.

Vin Doux Naturels French term for fortified wines. These are sweet, achieved by adding fortifying spirit part way through fermentation in much the same way as is practiced in producing Port.

Vin de Pays French category of regional identification for wines that fall outside either the boundaries or regulations of an AC.

Volatile Acidity The volatile acids in wine are those that are unstable and chief among these is acetic acid. Excessive exposure of a wine with high volatile acidity to air will encourage a bacterial reaction that causes off volatile aromas (similar to nail varnish) and will eventually convert wine to vinegar.

Yield The size of crop yielded from a vineyard. Yield is fundamental to wine quality. In general the smaller the yield the greater the wine quality. There are though many additional influences. If yield is reduced too much then the vines balance and equilibrium will be disturbed and quality will suffer. Increasingly yields are measured per vine rather than per acre or hectare because of the variable conditions within a vineyard and the density of planting. Older vines are naturally less productive and when their crop is reduced the resulting grapes can be of exceptional quality. In all cases the yield of a vine should be sufficiently restricted in order to achieve complete physiological ripeness.

Buying guide

A code is provided in most A-Z producer entries and these can be found listed alphabetically on the pages that follow. In the first instance these are intended to give the most direct link with that producer in the UK. When the first code given appears in bold this indicates the agent or direct importer of the wines. In some instances such an agent sells only to the trade or acts purely a producers representative in the UK but all should still be able to suggest retail stockists of a given wine. Additional codes (not in bold) indicate a retailer (or regional agent) who are regular stockists of these wines. In a few cases where we have found there to be no UK agent or retailer we have suggested a broker who has traded some vintages of the wine. Where there is no code at all we hope that producers inclusion will prompt someone in the UK to sell these wines. We have already been able to fill in many of the gaps since our first 3 editions. Many of these codes refer to a leading independent merchant/retailer who sell much of the best or most interesting wine in this country – often very competitively priced against the bigger, better known brands. While we haven't profiled individual merchants, a glance through the codes within any regional section is likely to give a good idea as to which ones have a particular strength there.

In Bordeaux most wine from the leading châteaux is sold through a Bordeaux broker (*courtier*) or agent and then to retailers and merchants in different countries. While the system is elaborate it is not so difficult to obtain many of the wines. Both independent UK merchants, such as one of 'The Bunch' (a group of six leading merchants - Adm, Tan, JAr, C&B, L&W, Yap) and leading broker/shippers (such as Farr Vintners - Far) are the best place to start. These contacts also provide the opportunity to buy wine en primeur or ex-cellars. This requires paying for the cost of the wine before it is shipped with the additional costs (freight, VAT and duty) paid on its arrival in the UK. Purchasing wine in this way was once seen as an investment opportunity for would be speculators, but it is now increasingly important as the only means of obtaining the best, not only from Bordeaux but also from Burgundy, the

Rhône, or some Vintage Port. It also usually means that the wine hasn't changed hands several times already. Leading merchants will also prove useful when buying older vintages as will auction houses and brokers (additional contacts have been provided at the end of the list of codes). Bordeaux wines stocked by a large number of merchants have been coded AAA.

This same code (AAA) is also used for wines that are that are easily found in supermarkets or on the high street. Supermarkets account for the bulk of wine sold in the UK. To an extent their ranges tend to be dominated by the ubiquitous big volume brands – much of it outside of the scope of this book. The small production of many high quality estates remains outside their reach whether as part of a deliberate decision on the part of the producer or due to logistical reasons. Nonetheless the best supermarkets include those producers who combine quality and quantity. In addition there is an increasing trend toward the inclusion of a selection of fine wines of more limited availability in their flagship stores or through an on-line facility. Although the national supermarkets chains have not been included as agents or leading stockists, a search on their internet sites can be used as a quick check for availability. There are also an increasing number of Internet-only retailers whose search engines provide a further aid to tracking down a hard to find wine, the best known being www.everywine.co.uk.

It is also worth noting that a growing number of producers now sell their wine direct via a mailing list or over the internet. Such is the demand for their wines there is no need for them to use an agent and the cost saving is effectively passed on to the wine drinker. This applies particularly to leading new world producers who often have oversubscribed lists composed entirely of consumers in their local market – yet some choose to retain a small percentage of their production for export via a foreign merchant. Individual producers websites are worth checking for information about buying their wines.

AAA
Widely available
In supermarkets or the high street
OR
in the case of Bordeaux or Port
available through any number of
wine merchants.
also see Buying Guide

A&B – A & B Vintners
Tel 01892 724977
Fax 01892 722673
info@abvintners.co.uk
www.abvintners.co.uk

ABy – Anthony Byrne
Tel 01487 814555
Fax 01487 814962
admin@abfw.co.Uk
www.abfw.co.uk

ACh – Andrew Chapman Fine Wines
Tel 01235 550707
Fax 0870 136 6335
info@surf4wine.co.uk
www.surf4wine.co.uk

Acy – Alchemy Wines Ltd
Tel 01934 460750
Fax 01934 460970
www.alchemywines.co.uk

Add – Addison Wines
Tel 020 7924 2416
Fax 020 7924 2417
sales@addisonwines.co.uk
www.addisonwines.co.uk

Adm – Adnams
Tel 01502 727222
Fax 01502 727223
wines@adnams.co.uk
www.adnams.co.uk

ADo – Allied Domecq Wine UK
Tel 020 8323 8196
Fax 020 8323 8313
www.allieddomecqplc.com

AHW – AH Wines
Tel 01935 850166
Fax 01935 851264

Ala – La Alacena
Tel 01604 784159
Fax 01604 784159
info@alacena.co.uk
www.alacena.co.uk

AlF – Alfie Fiandaca
Tel 020 8752 1222
Fax 020 8752 1218

All – Alliance Wine Co
Tel 01505 506060
Fax 01505 506066
sales@alliancewine.co.uk
www.alliancewine.co.uk

Alo – Alouette Wines
Tel 0151 6089900
Fax 0151 608 8844
info@alouettewines.co.uk
www.alouettewines.co.uk

Alv – Alivini
Tel 020 8880 2526
Fax 020 8880 2708
enquiries@alivini.com

Amp – Amps Fine Wines
Tel 01832 273502
Fax 01832 273611
info@ampsfinewines.co.uk
www.ampsfinewines.co.uk

AMW - American Wine Merchants
Tel 07793 816672
sales@americanwinemerchants.co.uk
www.americanwinemerchants.co.uk

AnI – Anglo International Wine Shippers
Tel 01372 469841
Fax 01372 469816

AoW – Architects of Wine
Tel 0870 121 3610
Fax 0870 121 3655
sales@aow-uk.com
www.aow-uk.com

ARe – Arthur Rackham Emporia
Tel 0870 870 1110
Fax 0870 870 1120
cellars@ar-emporia.com
www.ar-emporia.com

Ast – Astrum Wine Cellars
Tel 020 8870 5252
Fax 020 8870 2244
sales@astrumwinecellars.com
www.astrumwinecellars.com

AVD – Australian Vineyards Direct
Tel 020 7259 8520
Fax 020 7259 8501
info@austvine.com
www.austvine.com

AVn – Allez Vins!
Tel 01926 811969
Fax 01926 815840
wine@allezvins.co.uk
www.allezvins.co.uk

AWA – Australian Wine Agencies
Tel 01753 544546
Fax 01753 591369
info@australian–wine.co.uk
www.austwineagencies.com

AWs – Australian Wineries
Tel 01780 755810
Fax 01780 766063
admin@australianwineries.co.uk
www.australianwineries.co.uk

AWW – Andrew Wilson Wines
Tel 01782 791798
Fax 01782 791787
andrew@awwines.co.uk
www.awwines.co.uk

B&B – Barrels & Bottles
Tel 0114 255 6611
Fax 0114 255 1010
sales@barrelsandbottles.co.uk
www.barrelsandbottles.co.uk

B&T – C G Bull & Taylor
Tel 020 7498 8022
Fax 020 7498 7851
info@cgbull.co.uk
www.cgbull.co.uk

Bac – Bacchus Fine Wines
Tel 01234 711140
Fax 01234 711199
wine@bacchus.co.uk
www.bacchus.co.uk

Bal – Ballantynes of Cowbridge
Tel 01446 774840
Fax 01446 775253
sales@ballantynes.co.uk
www.ballantynes.co.uk

Bat – Bat & Bottle
Tel 0845 108 4407
Fax 0870 458 2505
post@batwine.co.uk
www.batwine.co.uk

BBl – Beringer Blass UK
Tel 020 8843 8411
Fax 020 8843 8422
info@beringerblass.co.uk
www.beringerblass.com

BBR – Berry Bros & Rudd
Tel 020 7396 9600
Fax 020 7396 9611
orders@bbr.com
www.bbr.com

Bel – Bella Wines Limited
Tel 01638 604899
Fax 01638 604901
sales@bellawines.co.uk
www.bellawines.co.uk

Ben – Bennetts
Tel 01386 840392
Fax 01386 840974
enquiries@bennettsfinewines.com
www.bennettsfinewines.com

BFs – Bonhote Foster
Tel 01440 730779
Fax 01440 730789
info@bonhotefoster.co.uk
www.bonhotefoster.co.uk
BFW – Brown-Forman Wines
Tel 020 7478 1300
Fax 020 7287 4661
BGL – Bottle Green Ltd
Tel 0113 2054500
Fax 0113 2054501
info@bottlegreen.com
www.bottlegreen.com
Bib – Bibendum
Tel 020 7449 4120
Fax 020 7722 7354
sales@bibendum-wine.co.uk
www.bibendum-wine.co.uk
Bir – Birchwood Agencies
Tel 01322 627500
Fax 01322 627488
info@birchwoodagencies.co.uk
Bli – Belloni
Tel 020 7700 7760
Fax 020 7700 7767
office@belloni.co.uk
www.belloni.co.uk
Blx – Bordeaux Index
Tel 020 7253 2110
Fax 020 7490 1955
sales@bordeauxindex.com
www.bordeauxindex.com
Box – Boxford Wine Co
Tel 01787 210187
Fax 01787 211391
boxfordwine@aol.com
BRW – Big Red Wine Company
Tel 01638 510803
Fax 01638 510803
sales@bigredwine.co.uk
www.bigredwine.co.uk
B-S – Billecart-Salmon UK
Tel 020 8405 6345
Fax 020 8405 6346
info@billecart-salmon.co.uk
www.billecart-salmon.co.uk
BSh – Burgundy Shuttle
Tel 020 7341 4053
Fax 020 7244 0618
mail@burgundyshuttle.ltd.uk
www.burgundyshuttle.co.uk
Bur – Burridges of Arlington St
Tel 01293 530151
Fax 01293 530104
sales@burridgewine.com
www.burridgewine.com

But – Butler's Wine Cellar
Tel 01273 698724
Fax 01273 622761
henry@butlers-winecellar.co.uk
www.butlers-winecellar.co.uk
BWC – Berkmann Wine Cellars
Tel 020 7609 4711
Fax 020 7607 0018
info@berkmann.co.uk
www.berkmann.co.uk
C&B – Corney & Barrow
Tel 020 7265 2400
Fax 020 7265 2539
wine@corbar.co.uk
www.corneyandbarrow.com
C&C – Champagnes & Châteaux
Tel 020 7326 9655
Fax 020 7326 9656
info@champagnesandchâteaux.co.uk
C&D – C & D Wines
Tel 020 8778 1711
Fax 020 8778 1710
info@canddwines.co.uk
www.canddwines.co.uk
C&O – C & O Wines
Tel 0161 976 3696
Fax 0161 962 4525
info@cowines.com
C&R – Classic & Rare
Tel 01293 525777
Fax 01293 528144
sales@classicrarewines.com
www.classicrarewines.com
Cac – Cachet Wine
Tel 01482 581792
Fax 01482 587042
sales@cachetwines.co.uk
Cad – Cadman Fine Wines
Tel 0845 121 4011
Fax 0845 121 4014
sales@cadmanfinewines.co.uk
www.cadmanfinewines.co.uk
Cam – Cambridge Wine Merchants
Tel 01223 568991
Fax 01223 568992
info@cambridgewine.com
www.cambridgewine.com
Cap – Capricorn
Tel 0161 908 1360
Fax 0161 908 1365
sales@capricornwines.co.uk
www.capricornwines.co.uk
Car – Carringtons
Tel 0161 832 5646
Fax 0161 832 5626
carringtons@winebeerandspirits.co.uk

Cas – Castang Wine Shippers
Tel 01503 220359
Fax 01503 220650
sales@castang-wines.co.uk
www.castang-wines.co.uk
Cav – Cavavin/Le Bon Vin
Tel 0114 256 0090
Fax 0114 256 0092
cavavin@lebonvin.co.uk
www.lebonvin.co.uk
CBg – Charles Blagden
Tel 0033 4 90 20 07 07
Fax 0033 4 90 20 05 77
blagwin@aol.com
CCC – Cave Cru Classé
Tel 020 7378 8579
Fax 020 7378 8544
enquiries@ccc.co.uk
www.cave-cru-classe.com
Cco – Champagne Company
Tel 020 7373 5578
Fax 020 7373 4777
ukchampagne@aol.com
www.champagnecompany.co.uk
CdP – Les Caves de Pyrene
Tel 01483 538820
Fax 01483 455068
sales@lescaves.co.uk
www.lescaves.co.uk
CeB – Croque-en-Bouche
Tel 01684 540011
Fax 0870 706 6282
mail@croque.co.uk
www.croque-en-bouche.co.uk
Che – Cheviot UK / WM Morton
Tel 0141 649 9881
Fax 0141 649 7074
cheviot@w-m.co.uk
CHk – Charles Hawkins
Tel 01572 823030
Fax 01572 823040
info@charleshawkinsandpartners.com
www.charleshawkins-wines.com
Cht– Charterhouse Wine Co Ltd
Tel 01775 720300
Fax 01775 722271
info@charterhousewine.co.uk
www.charterhousewine.co.uk
ChV – Château Vintners
Tel 020 7376 8828
Fax 020 7376 8818
châteauvintners@yahoo.com
Cib – Ciborio
Tel 020 8578 4388
Fax 020 8575 2758
www.ciborio.com

Coe – Coe Vintners
Tel 020 8551 4966
Fax 020 8550 6312
enquiries@coevintners.com
www.coevintners.com

Col - Colombier Vins Fins
Tel 01283 552552
Fax 01283 550675
colombier@colombierwines.co.uk
www.colombierwines.co.uk

Con – Connolly's Wine Merchants
Tel 0121 236 9269
Fax 0121 233 2339
sales@connollyswine.co.uk
www.connollyswine.co.uk

CPp – Christopher Piper Wines
Tel 01404 814139
Fax 01404 812100
sales@christopherpiperwines.co.uk

CPW – Cornish Point Wines
Tel 01803 712860
Fax 01803 712870
nigel@cornishpoint.com
www.cornishpoint.com

CRs – Chalié Richards
Tel 01403 250500
Fax 01403 250123
admin@chalie-richards.co.uk

Cst – Constellation Wines
Tel 01483 690000
Fax 01483 690140
www.cbrands.eu.com

CTy – Charles Taylor / Montrachet Fine Wine
Tel 020 7928 1990
Fax 020 7928 3415

CWF – CWF Ltd (Continental Wine & Food)
Tel 01484 538333
Fax 01484 544734
info@continental-wine.co.uk
www.continental-wine.co.uk

CyT – Concha y Toro UK
Tel 01865 338013
Fax 01865 338100
enquiries@conchaytoro.cl
www.conchaytoro.com

D&D – D & D Wines
Tel 01565 650952
Fax 01565 755295
ddwi@ddwinesint.com

D&F – D & F Wines
Tel 020 8838 4399
Fax 020 8838 4500
inquiry@dandfwines.co.uk

Dan – Danmar International
Tel 01784 477812
Fax 01784 477813
sales@danmarinternational.co.uk
www.danmarinternational.co.uk

DAy – Dreyfus Ashby & Co
Tel 01732 361639
Fax 01732 367834
office@dreyfusashby.co.uk

DDr – Domaine Direct
Tel 020 7837 1142
Fax 020 7837 8605
mail@domainedirect.co.uk
www.domainedirect.co.uk

DeB – De Bortoli Wines UK
Tel 01725 516467
Fax 01725 516403
debortoli@talk21.com
www.debortoli.com.au

Dec – Decorum Vintners
Tel 020 8969 6581
Fax 020 8960 7693
admin@decvin.com
www.decvin.com

Dis – Discover Wine
Tel 0870 3300267
Fax 0870 3307910
www.discover-wine.co.uk

DLW – Daniel Lambert Wines Ltd
Tel 01656 661010
Fax 01656 668088
www.daniellambertwines.co.uk
info@daniellambertwines.co.uk

DMT – DMT Wine Importers/The Cellar Door
Tel 01256 770397
Fax 01256 770944
info@thecellardoor.co.uk
www.thecellardoor.co.uk

Dou – Dourthe UK
Tel 020 7720 6611
Fax 020 7720 2670
uk@cvbg.com
www.cvbg.com

DWS – Direct Wine Shipments (NI)
Tel 028 9050 8000
Fax 028 9050 8004
enquiry@directwine.co.uk
www.directwine.co.uk

E&T – Elliot & Tatham
Tel 0870 762 0900
Fax 0870 762 0901
wine@elliot-tatham.com

Ear – Earle Wines
Tel 01765 677296
Fax 01765 677839
sales@earlewines.com
www.earlewines.com

Ecl – Eclectic Wines
Tel 020 7736 3733
Fax 020 7736 3733
mary@eclecticwines.com
www.eclecticwines.com

EdV – Eaux de Vie
Tel 020 7724 5009
Fax 020 7723 7053
info@eauxdevie.co.uk

EGe – Ernst Gorge
Tel 01865 341817
Fax 01865 343184

Ehr – Ehrmanns
Tel 020 7418 1800
Fax 020 7359 7788

EJG – E & J Gallo
Tel 01895 813444
Fax 01895 818048
www.gallo.com

ElV – El Vino
Tel 020 7353 5384
Fax 020 7936 2367
all@elvino.co.uk
www.elvino.co.uk

Eno – Enotria Winecellars
Tel 020 8961 4411
Fax 020 8961 8773
info@winecellars.co.uk
www.winecellars.co.uk

EoR – Ellis of Richmond
Tel 020 8744 5550
Fax 020 8744 5581
www.ellisofrichmond.co.uk

Eur – Eurowines
Tel 020 8747 2100
Fax 020 8994 8054
enquiries@eurowines.co.uk
www.eurowines.co.uk

Eve – Evertons
Tel 01299 890113
Fax 01299 890114
sales@evertonswines.co.uk
www.evertonswines.co.uk

Evg – Evington's Wines
Tel 0116 254 2702
Fax 0116 254 2702
info@evingtons-wines.com
www.evingtons-wines.com

EWG – EWGA (European Wine Growers Associates)
Tel 01524 701723
Fax 01524 701189
sales@ewga.net

ExC – Ex Cellar
Tel 01372 275247
Fax 01372 813937
charles@excellar.co.uk
www.excellar.net

F&R – Fine & Rare Wines Ltd
Tel 020 8960 1995
Fax 020 8960 1911
wine@frw.co.uk
www.frw.co.uk
F&M – Fortnum & Mason
Tel 020 7734 8040
Fax 020 7437 3278
info@fortnumandmason.co.uk
www.fortnumandmason.com
Fal – Falcon Vintners
Tel 020 8516 7780
Fax 020 8516 7781
info@falconvintners.co.uk
Far – Farr Vintners
Tel 020 7821 2000
Fax 020 7821 2020
sales@farr-vintners.com
www.farr-vintners.com
FCA – Fraser Crameri Associates
Tel 01580 200304
Fax 01580 200308
fraser@frasercrameri.com
www.frasercrameri.com
FDB – First Drinks Brands
Tel 023 8031 2000
Fax 023 8031 1111
contact@first-drinks-brands.co.uk
FEM – F & E May Ltd
Tel 020 7843 1600
Fax 020 7843 1601
sales@fandemay.com
www.fandemay.com
FFW – Food & Fine Wine
Tel 01142 668747
Fax 0870 8912376
www.foodandfinewine.com
Fin – The Fine Wine Company Ltd
Tel 0131 665 0088
Fax 0131 665 0098
mail@thefinewinecompany.co.uk
www.thefinewinecompany.co.uk
FMV – Fields, Morris & Verdin
Tel 020 7921 5300
Fax 020 7921 5333
info@fmvwines.com
www.fmvwines.com
Fol – Folio Wines
Tel 01305 751300
Fax 01305 751302
www.foliowines.com
For – Forth Wines
Tel 01577 866001
Fax 01577 866020
enquiries@forthwines.com
www.forthwines.com

Frt – Freixenet UK
Tel 01344 758500
Fax 01344 758510
enquiries@freixenet.co.uk
www.freixenet.co.uk
Frw – Friarwood
Tel 020 7736 2628
Fax 020 7731 0411
sales@friarwood.com
www.friarwood.com
Fsp – Flagship Wines Ltd
Tel 01727 841968
Fax 01727 841968
info@flagshipwines.co.uk
www.flagshipwines.co.uk
FSt – Frank Stainton Wines
Tel 01539 731886
Fax 01539 730396
admin@stainton-wines.co.uk
www.stainton-wines.co.uk
Fte – Fortitude Wines Ltd
Tel 020 8660 8456
Fax 020 8660 6686
info@fortitudewines.com
www.fortitudewines.com
FWC – Fareham Wine Cellar
Tel 01329 822733
Fax 01329 282355
dominic@farehamwinecellar.co.uk
www.farehamwinecellar.co.uk
FWW – FWW Wines UK Ltd
Tel 020 8567 1589
Fax 020 8567 3731
sales@fwwwines.demon.co.uk
G&C – Growers & Château
Tel 01372 374239
Fax 01372 377610
info@winesite.net
www.winesite.net
Gar – Garrigue Wines
Tel 0845 8886677
Fax 0845 8886678
themacaloneys@garriguewines.com
www.garriguewines.com
Gau – Gauntleys
Tel 0115 911 0555
Fax 0115 911 0557
rhône@gauntleywine.com
www.gauntleywine.com
GBa – Georges Barbier
Tel 020 8852 5801
Fax 020 8463 0398
georgesbarbier@f2s.com
GBr – G Bravo & Son Ltd
Tel 020 8648 8555
Fax 020 8648 2686
gbravo@gbravo.co.uk

GCW – Grand Cru Wines
Tel 0871 474 0635
Fax 0033 49047 13 12
gcw@wanadoo.fr
www.grandcruwinesltd.net
Gel – Gelston Castle Fine Wines
Tel 01556 503012
Gen – Genesis Wines
Tel 020 7963 9060
Fax 020 7963 9069
sales@genesiswines.com
www.genesiswines.com
GFy – Folly Wines
Tel 01453 731509
Fax 01453 731134
info@follywines.co.uk
www.follywines.co.uk
GGW – Great Gaddesden Wines/The Flying Corkscrew
Tel 01442 412312
Fax 01442 412313
info@flyingcorkscrew.com
GGg – Great Grog
Tel 0131 662 4777
Fax 0131 662 4983
richard@greatgrog.co.uk
www.greatgrog.co.uk
GID – GIDA (Gruppo Italiano Distribuzione Alimentari Ltd)
Tel 020 7224 0060
Fax 020 7224 0010
info@gida.co.uk
Goe – Goedhuis & Co
Tel 020 7793 7900
Fax 020 7793 7170
enquiries@goedhuis.com
www.goedhuis.com
GPW – GP Wines
Tel 01403 891163
Fax 01403 892590
info@gpwines.com
www.gpwines.com
GrD – Winegrowers Direct
Tel 01954 230176
Fax 01954 231822
GSe – Gerrard Seel
Tel 01925 819695
Fax 01925 818192
wine@gerrardseel.co.uk
www.gerrardseel.co.uk
Gun – Gunson Fine Wines
Tel 07979 861026
Fax 01342 843955
dion@gunsonfinewines.co.uk
GVF – Grand Vins de France
Tel 020 8442 1088
Fax 020 8444 4288

GVS – GVSN Imports/ LENZ Wine
Tel 0870 609 1185
help@lenzwine.co.uk
www.lenzwine.co.uk
GWW – Great Western Wine
Tel 01225 322800
Fax 01225 442139
post@greatwesternwine.co.uk
www.greatwesternwine.co.uk
Hal – Hallgarten
Tel 01582 722538
Fax 01582 723240
sales@hallgarten.co,uk
www.hallgarten.co.uk
Ham – Hamer Wine
Tel 020 8549 9119
Fax 020 8549 9119
info@hamer-wine.co.uk
www.hamer-wine.co.uk
Han – Handford Fine Wine
Tel 020 7221 9614
Fax 020 7221 9613
wine@handford.net
www.handford.net
Har – Harris Fine Wine
Tel 01355 571157
Fax 01355 571158
Has – Haslemere Cellar
Tel 01428 645081
Fax 01428 645108
info@haslemerecellar.co.uk
www.haslemerecellar.co.uk
Hay – Hayward Bros Ltd
Tel 020 7237 0576
Fax 020 7237 6212
wine@haybrowine.co.uk
www.haybrowine.co.uk
HBJ – Hayman Barwell Jones Ltd
Tel 01473 232322
Fax 01473 280381
www.hbjwines.co.uk
Hel – Hellion Wines
Tel 07765 472263
Fax 01257 423157
email@hellionwines.com
www.hellionwines.com
Hfx – Halifax Wine Company
Tel 01422 256333
andy@halifaxwinecompany.com
www.halifaxwinecompany.com
HHB – H & H Bancroft
Tel 020 7232 5440
Fax 020 7232 5451
sales@handhbancroftwines.com
www.bancroftwines.com

HHC – Haynes, Hanson & Clark
Tel 020 7259 0102
Fax 020 7259 0103
london@hhandc.co.uk
www.hhandc.co.uk
His – Hispa Merchants Ltd
Tel 020 7370 4449
Fax 020 7370 5086
sales@hispamerchants.com
www.hispamerchants.com
HMA – Hatch Mansfield Agencies
Tel 01344 871800
Fax 01344 871871
sales@hatch.co.uk
www.hatchmansfield.co.uk
HMW – Harvey-Miller Wine Agencies
Tel 01360 860012
Fax 01360 860148
info@hmwa.net
www.hmwa.net
HoK – Hammonds of Knutsford
Tel 01565 872872
Fax 01565 872900
wine@hammondsofknutsford.co.uk
HoM – House of Menzies
Tel 01887 829666
Fax 01887 829666
info@houseofmenzies.com
www.houseofmenzies.com
Hrd – Harrods
Tel 020 7730 1234
Fax 020 7225 5872
www.harrods.com
HRp – Howard Ripley
Tel 020 8877 3065
Fax 020 8877 0029
info@howardripley.com
www.howardripley.com
HrV – Harrison Vintners
Tel 020 8752 1400
Fax 020 8993 9720
sales@harrisonvintners.co.uk
www.harrisonvintners.co.uk
HSA – HS Wine Agencies
Tel 01223 234604
Fax 01223 234604
hswineagencies@ntlworld.com
HWC – HWCG
Tel 01279 873500
Fax 01279 873501
wine@hwcg.co.uk
www.hwcg.co.uk

Idg – Indigo Wine
Tel 020 7733 8391
Fax 020 7733 8391
info@indigowine.com
www.indigowine.com
IGH – Ian G Howe
Tel 01636 704366
Fax 01636 610502
howe@chablis-burgundy.co.uk
www.chablis-burgundy.co.uk
IRW – Irvine Robertson Wines
Tel 0131 553 3521
Fax 0131 553 5465
irviner@nildram.co.uk
www.irwines.co.uk
Itv / IWS – Italvini / International Wine Services
Tel 01442 29300
Fax 01442 293006
iws@intwine.co.uk
www.wine-info.co.uk
IVi – I Vini
Tel 01285 655595
Fax 01285 650684
enquiries@ivini.co.uk
www.ivini.co.uk
IVV – In Vino Veritas
Tel 01827 899449
Fax 01827 899936
webmaster@ivvltd.com
www.ivvltd.com
J&B – Justerini & Brooks
Tel 020 7484 6400
Fax 020 7484 6499
www.justerinis.com
JAr – John Armit
Tel 020 7908 0600
Fax 020 7908 0601
info@armit.co.uk
www.armit.co.uk
Jas – Jascots Wine Merchants Ltd
Tel 020 8965 2000
Fax 020 8965 9500
team@jascots.co.uk
www.jascots.co.uk
JBa – Julian Baker
Tel 01206 262538
Fax 01206 263574
julianbaker@supranet.com
JEF – John E Fells
Tel 01442 870900
Fax 01442 878555
info@fells.co.uk
www.fells.co.uk

JFW – James Fearon Wines
Tel 01407 765200
Fax 01407 765620
enquiries@jamesfearonwines.co.uk
www.jamesfearonwines.co.uk

JIC – Just In Case
Tel 01489 892969
Fax 01489 892969

JNi – James Nicholson
Tel 028 4483 0091
Fax 028 4483 0028
info@jnwine.com
www.jnwine.com

JNV – Jackson Nugent Vintners
Tel 020 8947 9722
Fax 020 8944 1048
www.jnv.co.uk

JTD – J T Davies & Son
Tel 020 8681 3222
Fax 020 8681 5931
postbox@jtdavies.co.uk
www.jtdavies.co.uk

KJn – Kendall Jackson UK
Tel 020 8747 2840
Fax 020 8987 6160
kjsales@kjmail.com

L&S – Lea & Sandeman
Tel 020 7244 0522
Fax 020 7244 0533
info@leaandsandeman.co.uk
www.londonfinewine.co.uk

L&T – Lane & Tatham
Tel 01380 720123
Fax 01380 720111
wines@lanetat.demon.co.uk

L&W – Lay & Wheeler
Tel 0845 330 1855
Fax 0845 330 4095
sales@laywheeler.com
www.laywheeler.com

LaC – La Caneva
Tel 020 8888 0535
Fax 020 8888 2965
lacaneva@lacaneva.com
www.lacaneva.com

Las – L'Assemblage
Tel 01243 537775
Fax 01243 538644
sales@lassemblage.co.uk
www.lassemblage.co.uk

Lay – Jeroboams / Laytons
Tel 020 7259 6716
Fax 020 7495 3314
sales@jeroboams.co.uk
www.jeroboams.co.uk

Lib – Liberty Wines
Tel 020 7720 5350
Fax 020 7720 6158
info@libertywine.co.uk
www.libertywine.co.uk

LLt – Louis Latour UK
Tel 020 7409 7276
Fax 020 7409 7092
enquiries@louislatour.co.uk
www.louislatour.com

LNa – Lion Nathan UK
Tel 020 7449 4060
Fax 020 7449 4105
www.lnwg.com.au

LoW – For the Love of Wine
Tel 01359 270377
Fax 01359 271483
www.i-love-wine.co.uk

L-P – Laurent Perrier UK
Tel 01628 475404
Fax 01628 471891
enquiries@laurent-perrier.co.uk
www.laurent-perrier.co.uk

Luv – Luvians Bottleshop
Tel 01334 654820
Fax 01334 654820
info@luvians.com
www.luvians.com

Lwt – Laithwaites / Direct Wines Ltd
Tel 0870 444 8282
Fax 0870 444 8182
www.laithwaites.co.uk

LyS – Laymont & Shaw
Tel 01872 270545
Fax 01872 223005
info@laymont-shaw.co.uk
www.laymont-shaw.co.uk

Mag – Magellan Wine
Tel 020 8520 0630
info@magellanwine.co.uk
www.magellanwine.co.uk

Maj – Majestic Wine Warehouses
Tel 01923 298200
Fax 01923 819105
info@majestic.co.uk
www.majestic.co.uk

Mar – Martinez Wines
Tel 01943 603241
Fax 0870 9223940
julian@martinez.co.uk
www.martinez.co.uk

Max – Maxxium
Tel 01786 430500
Fax 01786 430600

May – Mayfair Cellars
Tel 020 7386 7999
Fax 020 7386 0202
sales@mayfaircellars.co.uk
www.mayfaircellars.co.uk

MCD – Marne & Champagne Diffusion
Tel 020 7499 0070
Fax 020 7408 0841
sales@mcduk.com

McK – McKinley Vintners
Tel 020 7928 7300
Fax 020 7928 4447
info@mckinleyvintners.co.uk
www.mckinleyvintners.co.uk

MCl – Matthew Clark
Tel 01275 891400
Fax 01275 890595
www.mclark.co.uk

MCW – Morgan Classic Wines
Tel 01273 487000
Fax 01273 487700
sales@morganclassics.com
www.morganclassicwines.com

Mdl – Mondial Wine Ltd
Tel 020 8335 3455
Fax 020 8335 3587
info@mondialwine.co.uk
www.mondialwine.co.uk

Men – Mentzendorff
Tel 020 7840 3600
Fax 020 7840 3601
www.mentzendorff.co.uk

Mer – Meridian
Tel 0161 908 1351
Fax 0161 908 1355
www.meridianwines.co.uk

MGF – MG Fine Wines Ltd
Tel 01925 650931
Fax 01925 650931
markgoucher@netscape.net

Mgi – Mille Gusti
Tel 020 8997 3932
Fax 020 8566 8480
millegusti@hotmail.com

MHn – Moët Hennessey UK
Tel 020 7235 9411
Fax 020 7235 6937

MHv – Margaret Harvey / Fine Wines of New Zealand
Tel 020 7482 0093
Fax 020 7267 8400
info@fwnz.co.uk
www.fwnz.co.uk

Mis – Mistral Wines
Tel 020 7262 5437
Fax 020 7402 7957
info@mistralwines.co.uk

UK stockists

MMD – Maison Marques & Domaines
Tel 020 8812 3380
Fax 020 8812 3390
maison@mmdltd.co.uk
www.mmdltd.com

Mor – Moreno Wines
Tel 020 8960 7161
Fax 020 8960 7165
sales@moreno-wines.co.uk

MPe – Michael Peace MW
Tel 020 7937 9345
Fax 020 7937 7884

MSd – Milton Sandford
Tel 01628 829449
Fax 01628 829424
sales@milton-sandford.demon.co.uk

Msp – Masterpiece Wines
Tel 01634 293141
Fax 01634 719109
simon@masterpiecewines.com
www.masterpiecewines.com

Mst – Must Wines
Tel 01848 200677
Fax 01848 200677
service@mustwines.com
www.mustwines.com

MtC – Morgenrot-Chevaliers
Tel 01204 573093
Fax 01204 466259
sales@morgenrot.co.uk
www.morgenrot-chevaliers.co.uk

MVs – Merchant Vintners
Tel 01482 329443
Fax 01482 213616
sam@merchantvintners.co.uk

N&P – Nickolls & Perks
Tel 01384 394518
Fax 01384 440786
sales@nickollsandperks.co.uk
www.nickollsandperks.co.uk

NDb – Nick Dobson Wines
Tel 0800 849 3078
Fax: 0870 460 2358
sales@nickdobsonwines.co.uk
www.nickdobsonwines.co.uk

Neg – Negociants UK
Tel 01582 462859
Fax 01582 462867
neguk@negociants.com
www.negociantsuk.com

Nid – Nidderdale Fine Wines
Tel 01423 711703
Fax 01423 712239
info@southaustralianwines.com
www.southaustralianwines.com

NoG – Noble Grape
Tel 0131 556 3133
Fax 0131 556 8766
info@thenoble-grape.co.uk
www.thenoble-grape.co.uk

Nov – Novum Wines
Tel 020 7820 6720
Fax 020 7091 0878
info@novumwines.com
www.novumwines.com

NWW – New World Wines
Tel 020 8877 3555
Fax 020 8877 1476
info@newworldwines.co.uk
www.newworldwines.co.uk

NYg – Noel Young Wines
Tel 01223 844744
Fax 01223 844736
admin@nywines.co.uk
www.nywines.co.uk

NZH – New Zealand House of Wine
Tel 0800 085 6273
Fax 01428 648945
www.nzhouseofwine.com

O & L – Osborne & Lynch
Fax 01625 252175
ciaran@osbornelynch.com

Oak – Oakley Wine Agencies
Tel 01787 220070
Fax 01787 224734
oakleywine@btconnect.com

Ock – Ockse Wines
Tel 020 8858 8636
Fax 020 8333 8889
office@ocksewines.net
www.ocksewines.net

Odd – Oddbins
Tel 0800 328 2323
Fax 0800 328 3848
customer.services@oddbinsmail.com
www.oddbins.com

Orb – Orbital Wines
Tel 020 7802 5415
Fax 020 7976 5376
nick@orbitalwines.co.uk

OWL – O W Loeb
Tel 020 7234 0385
Fax 020 7357 0440
finewine@owloeb.com
www.owloeb.com

OxW – Oxford Wine Company
Tel 01865 301144
Fax 01865 301155
info@oxfordwine.co.uk
www.oxfordwine.co.uk

OzW – Oz Wines
Tel 0845 4501261
Fax 020 8870 8839
sales@ozwines.co.uk
www.ozwines.co.uk

P&S – Philglas & Swiggot
Tel 020 7924 4494
Fax 020 7924 4736
info@philglas-swiggot.co.uk
www.philglas-swiggot.co.uk

Par – Paragon Vintners
Tel 020 7887 1800
Fax 020 7887 1810
welcome@paragonvintners.co.uk

Pat – Patriarche Wine Agencies
Tel 020 7381 4016
Fax 020 7381 2023
sales@patriarchewines.com

PaV – Passione Vino
Tel 020 7720 1600
Fax 020 7720 4885
info@passionevino.co.uk
www.passionevino.co.uk

PBW – Paul Boutinot Agencies
Tel 0161 908 1371
Fax 0161 908 1375
marketing@boutinot.com
www.boutinot.com

PDn – Pimlico Dozen / Vintage Cellars
Tel 020 7834 3647
Fax 020 7233 7536
pimlico@winecellarsales.co.uk
www.winecellarsales.co.uk

PFx – Percy Fox & Co
Tel 01279 756200
Fax 01279 757022
percyfoxmarketing@diageo.com

PLB – PLB Group Ltd
Tel 01342 318282
Fax 01342 314023
general@plb.co.uk
www.plb.co.uk

PLh – Peter Lehmann Wines UK
Tel 01227 731353
Fax 01227 738538
admin@lehmannwines.com
www.peterlehmannwines.com.au

Pic – Pic Wines
Tel 0033 499 62 09 27
Fax 0033 467 55 81 28
contact@picwines.co.uk
www.picwines.co.uk

Pol – Pol Roger Ltd
Tel 01432 262800
Fax 01432 262806
wineshops@polroger.co.uk
www.polroger.co.uk

Por – Portland Wine
Tel 0161 928 0357
Fax 0161 905 1291
portwineco@aol.com
www.portlandwine.co.uk

POs – Peter Osborne & Co
Tel 01491 612311
Fax 01491 613322
info@peterosbornewine.co.uk
www.peterosbornewine.co.uk

PRc – Pernod Ricard UK
Tel 020 8538 4484
Fax 020 8538 4488
general@pernodricard-uk.com

Pre – Premier Vintners
Tel 020 7978 4047
Fax 020 7978 4053
info@premiervintners.co.uk
www.premiervintners.co.uk

**PVF – Producteurs et
Vignerons de France**
Tel 01273 730277
Fax 01273 328691
admin@vigneronsdefrance.co.uk

PWa – Peter Watkins Wine
Tel 01604 882370
Fax 01604 889465
sales@peterwatkinswine.co.uk
www.peterwatkinswine.co.uk

PWt – Peter Watts Wines
Tel 01376 561130
Fax 01376 562925
sales@peterwattswines.co.uk
www.peterwattswines.co.uk

**PWy – Peter Wylie Fine
Wines**
Tel 01884 277555
Fax 01884 277557
peter@wylie-fine wines.demon.co.uk
www.wyliefinewines.co.uk

Rae – Raeburn Fine Wines
Tel 0131 343 1159
Fax 0131 332 5166
sales@raeburnfinewines.com
www.raeburnfinewines.com

Rec – Recount Wines
Tel 020 7730 6377
Fax 020 7730 6377

Ren – Renvic Wines
Tel 01763 852470
Fax 01763 852470

Rev – Revelstoke Wine Co
Tel 020 8545 0077
Fax 020 8545 0044
info@revelstoke.co.uk
www.revelstoke.co.uk

**RGr – Richard Granger
Fine Wine**
Tel 0191 281 5000
Fax 0191 281 8141
sales@richardgrangerwines.co.uk
www.richardgrangerwines.co.uk

RHW – Roger Harris Wines
Tel 01603 880171
Fax 01603 880291
sales@rogerharriswines.co.uk
www.rogerharriswines.co.uk

RMe – Richard Marlowe
Tel 01285 770401
Fax 01285 771211

RRl – Robert Rolls
Tel 020 7606 1166
Fax 020 7606 1144
mail@rollswine.com
www.rollswine.com

RSJ – RSJ Wine
Tel 020 7928 4554
Fax 020 7928 9768
tom.king@rsj.uk.com
www.rsj.uk.com

RSL – RS Wines Ltd
Tel 01275 331444
Fax 01275 332444
info@rswines.co.uk
www.rswines.co.uk

RSo – Raisin Social
Tel 01883 731173
Fax 01883 731174
info@raisin-social.com
www.raisin-social.com

RsW – Richards Walford
Tel 01780 460451
Fax 01780 460276
sales@r-w.co.uk

RTo – Royal Tokaji Wine Co
Tel 020 7495 3010
Fax 020 7493 3973
sales@royal-tokaji.com

Rui – Ruinart UK
Tel 020 7416 0592
Fax 020 7416 0593
www.ruinart.com

RWs – Reid Wines
Tel 01761 452645
Fax 01761 452642

RyR – Raymond Reynolds
Tel 01663 742230
Fax 01663 742233
info@raymondreynolds.co.uk
www.raymondreynolds.co.uk

Sav – Savage Selection
Tel 01451 860896
Fax 01451 860996
wine@savageselection.co.uk
www.savageselection.co.uk

ScE – Southcorp Europe
Tel 020 8917 4600
Fax 020 8917 4646
www.southcorp.com

SCh – Sommeliers Choice
Tel 020 8689 9643
Fax 020 8684 3340
tim@sommelierschoice.com

Sec – Seckford Wines
Tel 01394 446622
Fax 01394 446633
sales@seckfordwines.co.uk
www.seckfordwines.co.uk

Sel – Selfridges & Co
Tel 020 7318 3730
Fax 020 7491 1880
www.selfridges.co.uk

SFW – Stokes Fine Wines
Tel 020 8944 5979
Fax 020 8944 5935
sales@stokesfinewines.com

**SsG – Stevens Garnier
& FSA**
Tel 01865 263300
Fax 01865 791594
info@stevensgarnier.co.uk
www.stevensgarnier.co.uk

**Str – Stratford's Wine
Agencies**
Tel 01628 810606
Fax 01628 810605
sales@stratfordwine.co.uk
www.stratfordwine.co.uk

SVS – Stone, Vine & Sun
Tel 01962 712351
Fax 01962 717545
sales@stonevine.co.uk
www.stonevine.co.uk

SWB – Southern Vintners
Tel 01484 608898
Fax 01484 609495
info@southernvintners.com

Swg – Swig
Tel 08000 272 272
Fax 020 8995 7069
imbibe@swig.co.uk
www.swig.co.uk

T&W – T & W Wines
Tel 01842 814414
Fax 01842 819967
contact@tw-wines.com
www.tw-wines.com

**Tan – Tanners Wine
Merchants**
Tel 01743 234500
Fax 01743 234501
sales@tanners-wines.co.uk
www.tanners-wines.co.uk

Ter – Terroir Limited
Tel 01756 700512
Fax 01756 797856
enquiries@terroirlanguedoc.co.uk
www.terroirlanguedoc.co.uk
The – Theatre of Wine
Tel 020 8858 6363
Fax 020 8305 1936
info@theatreofwine.com
www.theatreofwine.com
ThP – Thomas Panton
Tel 01666 503088
Fax 01666 503113
sales@wineimporter.co.uk
www.wineimporter.co.uk
THt – Thorman Hunt
Tel 020 7735 6511
Fax 020 7735 9779
info@thormanhunt.co.uk
TPg – Thos Peatling
Tel 01284 755948
Fax 01284 714483
sales@thospeatling.co.uk
www.thospeatling.co.uk
TPt – Terry Platt
Tel 01492 874099
Fax 01492 874722
Tra – Transatlantic Wines
Tel 01664 565013
Fax 01664 564938
patrick@transatlantic-wines.co.uk
Tri – Tria Wines Limited
Tel 020 8878 1236
Fax 020 8878 1151
sales@triawines.co.uk
www.triawines.co.uk
Tur – Turville Valley Wines
Tel 01494 868818
Fax 01494 868832
info@turville-valley-wines.com
www.turville-valley-wines.com
TWS – Thierry's Wine Services
Tel 01794 507100
Fax 01794 516856
info@thierrys.co.uk
www.thierrys.co.uk
UnC – Uncorked
Tel 020 7638 5998
Fax 020 7638 6028
drink@uncorked.co.uk
www.uncorked.co.uk
V&C – Valvona & Crolla
Tel 0131 556 6066
Fax 0131 556 1668
wine@valvonacrolla.co.uk
www.valvonacrolla.co.uk

Vbr – Vickbar
Tel 020 7267 3324
gjdlemos@btinternet.com
VCq – Veuve Clicquot
Tel 020 7408 7430
Fax 020 7408 7457
yellow@veuve-clicquot.co.uk
www.veuveclicquot.fr
Vcs – Vinceremos Organic Wines
Tel 0113 244 0002
Fax 0113 288 4566
info@vinceremos.co.uk
www.vinceremos.co.uk
VDu – Van Duuren Wines Ltd
Tel 020 8567 4428
Fax 020 8567 4428
svanduuren@aol.com
VdV – Vin du Van
Tel 01233 758727
Fax 01233 758389
Ver - Veritaus & Co
Tel 0870 7704112
Fax 0870 7704113
info@veritaus.com
www.veritaus.com
Vex - Vinexcel Ltd
Tel 0161 485 4592
Fax 0161 485 4892
Vic - Vickery Wines
Tel 01582 469930
Fax 01582 462039
info@vickerywines.co.uk
www.vickerywines.co.uk
Vim – Vinum
Tel 020 8847 4699
Fax 020 8847 4771
vinum@vinum.co.uk
www.vinum.co.uk
Vin – Vineyard Cellars
Tel 01488 681313
Fax 01488 681411
jameshocking@vineyardcellars.com
www.vineyardcellars.com
Vir – Virgin Wines Online Ltd
Tel 0870 164 9593
Fax 01603 619277
help@virginwines.com
www.virginwines.com
ViV – Vitis Vinifera
Tel 01371 873383
Fax 01371 873383
VKg - The Vine King
Tel 020 8879 3030
Fax 020 8946 6474
erik@thevineking.com
www.thevineking.com

vLw - von Loewensprung
Tel 01603 890058
Fax 01603 890521
finewine@vlwines.com
www.vlwines.com
Vne - Villeneuve Wines Ltd
Tel 01721 722500
Fax 01721 729922
wines@villeneuvewines.com
www.villeneuvewines.com
Vnf - Vin Neuf
Tel 01789 261747
Fax 01789 261749
info@vinneuf.co.uk
www.vinneuf.co.uk
Vni – Vinites UK
Tel 020 7924 4974
Fax 020 7228 6109
Vns – Vinoceros
Tel 01209 314711
Fax 01209 314712
enquiries@vinoceros.com
www.vinoceros.com
Vnt – The Vintner Ltd
Tel 01483 458700
Fax 01483 454677
info@thevintner.co.uk
www.thevintner.co.uk
VRt – Vintage Roots
Tel 0118 976 1999
Fax 0118 976 1998
info@vintageroots.co.uk
www.vintageroots.co.uk
VsV – Vinus Vita UK Ltd
Tel 0771 160977
Fax 01225 743077
vinusvita@aol.com
www.vinusvita.com
VTr – Vine Trail
Tel 0117 921 1770
Fax 0117 921 1772
enquiries@vinetrail.co.uk
www.vinetrail.co.uk
Vts – Veritas Wines
Tel 01223 212500
info@veritaswines.co.uk
www.veritaswines.co.uk
VWs – Vinifera Wines
Tel 020 8880 2526
Fax 020 8442 8215
vinifera@alvini.com
www.alivini.com
Vxs – Vinexus
Tel 020 7704 6313
Fax 020 7704 6318
vinexus.ltd@virgin.net
WAe – WineAlive.com
Tel 01905 731730
Fax 01905 731443
info@winealive.com
www.winealive.com

Wai – Waitrose/John Lewis
Tel 01344 424680
Fax 01344 825255
www.waitrose.com
Wat – Waterloo Wine Co.
Tel 020 7403 7967
Fax 020 7357 6976
sales@waterloowine.co.uk
www.waterloowine.co.uk
Wav – Waverley TBS
Tel 01442 293000
Fax 01442 293006
iws@intwine.co.uk
www.waverley-group.co.uk
WBn – Wine Barn
Tel 01962 774102
Fax 01962 774102
info@thewinebarn.co.uk
www.thewinebarn.co.uk
WhW – Whittaker Wines
Tel 01663 764497
Fax 01663 765910
sales@whittakerwines.com
www.whittakerwines.com
**WIE – Wine Importers
Edinburgh**
Tel 0131 556 3601
Fax 0131 557 8493
www.wine-importers.net
Win – The Winery
Tel 020 7286 6475
Fax 020 7286 2733
Wit – Withers Agencies
Tel 01273 477132
Fax 01273 476612
WKe – The Wine Keller
Tel 01628 620143
Fax 01628 620143
info@thewinekeller.co.uk
www.thewinekeller.co.uk
WRk – Wine Raks
Tel 01224 311460
Fax 01224 312186
enq@wineraks.com
www.wineraks.com
WsB – Wills-Burgundy
Tel 0845 057 3218
Fax 0870 755 9722
will@wills-burgundy.com
www.wills-burgundy.com
WSc – The Wine Society
Tel 01483 741177
Fax 01483 741392
memberservices@thewinesociety.com
www.thewinesociety.com
WSe – Wineservice
Tel 01342 837333
Fax 01342 837444
sales@wineservice.co.uk

**WSH – Wine Select
Handels GMBH**
Tel 0043 1 4060445
Fax 0043 1 4060455
www.wineselect.at
WSo – Winesource
Tel 01225 783007
Fax 01225 783152
winesource@saqnet.co.uk
WSS – Siegel Wine Agencies
Tel 01256 701101
Fax 01256 701518
wine@walter-siegel.co.uk
www.walter-siegel.co.uk
Wtr – Winetraders
Tel 01993 848777
Fax 01993 848778
winetraders@winetraders.org.uk
www.winetraders.org.uk
WTs – The Wine Treasury
Tel 020 7793 9999
Fax 020 7793 8080
www.winetreasury.com
**Wvr – Weavers of
Nottingham**
Tel 0115 958 0922
Fax 0115 950 8076
weavers@weaverswines.com
www.weaverswines.com
**WWC – Wimbledon Wine
Cellar**
Tel 020 8540 9979
Fax 020 8540 9399
enquiries@wimbledonwinecellar.com
www.wimbledonwinecellar.com
WWs – Western Wines
Tel 01952 235700
Fax 01952 235711
manager@western-wines.com
www.western-wines.com
Yap – Yapp Brothers
Tel 01747 860423
Fax 01747 860929
sales@yapp.co.uk
www.yapp.co.uk
Yng – Young and Company
Tel 020 8875 7007
Fax 020 8875 7197
winedirect@youngs.co.uk
www.youngswinedirect.co.uk
Zon – Zonin UK Ltd
Tel 020 8538 9009
Fax 020 8538 9119
info@zonin.co.uk
www.zonin.co.uk
3DW – 3D Wines Ltd
Tel 01205 820745
Fax 01205 821042
info@3dwines.com
www.3dwines.com

Other wine traders of note

Bonhams
Tel 020 7447 7447
Fax 020 7447 7400
wine@bonhams.com
www.bonhams.com
Christie's
Tel 020 7752 3295
Fax 020 7752 3023
delswood@christies.com
www.christies.com
LIV-ex
Tel 020 7228 2233
admin@live-ex.co.uk
www.liv-ex.com
Sotheby's
Tel 020 7293 6423
Fax 020 7293 5961
wine.london@sothebys.com
www.sothebys.com
**Uvine (Universal Wine
Exchange)**
Tel 020 7089 2200
Fax 020 7089 2211
enquiries@uvine.com
www.uvine.com
Wilkinson Vintners
Tel 020 7616 0404
Fax 020 7616 0400
wine@wilkinsonvintners.com

Vintage Charts

Bordeaux vintage chart

	Northern Médoc inc Saint-Èstephe, Paulliac, Saint-Julien	Southern Médoc inc Margaux	Red Graves	White Graves
2004	★★★★ A	★★★★ A	★★★/★★★★ A	★★★★ A
2003	★★★★ A	★★★★ A	★★★★ A	★★★★ A
2002	★★★★ A	★★★/★★★★ A	★★★★ A	★★★★ A
2001	★★★/★★★★ A	★★★/★★★★ A	★★★/★★★★ A	★★★★/★★★★★ A
2000	★★★★★ A	★★★★★ A	★★★★★ A	★★★★ B
1999	★★★/★★★★ B	★★★/★★★★ B	★★★/★★★★ B	★★★★ B
1998	★★★/★★★★ A	★★★/★★★★ A	★★★★ A	★★★★/★★★★★ B
1997	★★★ B	★★★ B	★★★ B	★★★★ C
1996	★★★★/★★★★★ A	★★★★ A	★★★★ B	★★★★ C
1995	★★★★ A	★★★★ B	★★★★ B	★★★/★★★★ C
1990	★★★★★ B	★★★★★ B	★★★★ C	★★★★/★★★★★ C
1989	★★★★ C	★★★★ C	★★★★ C	★★★/★★★★ C
1988	★★★★ B	★★★/★★★★ C	★★★★ C	★★★★ D
1986	★★★★/★★★★★ C	★★★★ C	★★★★ C	★★★ D
1985	★★★★ C	★★★★ C	★★★★ C	-
1982	★★★★★ C	★★★★/★★★★★ C	★★★★★ C	-

	Saint-Emilion	Pomerol	Sauternes
2004	★★★★ A	★★★★ A	★★★/★★★★ A
2003	★★★★ A	★★★★ A	★★★★/★★★★★ A
2002	★★★/★★★★ A	★★★/★★★★ A	★★★★/★★★★★ A
2001	★★★★ A	★★★★ A	★★★★/★★★★★ A
2000	★★★★★ A	★★★★★ A	★★ B
1999	★★★/★★★★ B	★★★/★★★★ BA	★★★★ A
1998	★★★★ A	★★★★/★★★★★ A	★★★★ A
1997	★★★ B	★★★ B	★★★★ A
1996	★★★/★★★★ B	★★★/★★★★ B	★★★★/★★★★★ B
1995	★★★★ B	★★★★ B	★★★/★★★★ B
1990	★★★★★ C	★★★★★ C	★★★★ C
1989	★★★★/★★★★★ C	★★★★/★★★★★ C	★★★★ C
1988	★★★★ C	★★★★ C	★★★★★ C
1986	★★★/★★★★ C	★★★/★★★★ C	★★★★/★★★★★ C
1985	★★★★ C	★★★★ C	★★★★ C
1982	★★★★★ C	★★★★★ C	★★★ D

Côte d'Or & Côte Chalonnaise vintage chart

	Côte de Nuits Red	Côte de Beaune Red	Côte Chalonnaise Red	Côte de Beaune White
2004	★★★ A	★★/★★★ A	★★/★★★ A	★★★★A
2003	★★★/★★★★ A	★★★/★★★★ A	★★/★★★★ A	★/★★★ B
2002	★★★★/★★★★★★ A	★★★★/★★★★★★ A	★★★★B	★★★★/★★★★★ A
2001	★★★ B	★★★ B	★★/★★★ B	★★★ B
2000	★★★ B	★★ B	★★ C	★★★★/★★★★★ B
1999	★★★★ B	★★★★/★★★★★★ A	★★★★/★★★★★ B	★★★★/★★★★★ B
1998	★★★/★★★★ B	★★★ B	★★★ C	★★/★★★ C
1997	★★★ C	★★/★★★ C	★★/★★★ C	★★★/★★★★ B
1996	★★★/★★★★★ B	★★★/★★★★★ B	★★★★ C	★★★★/★★★★★ B
1995	★★★★ C	★★★★ C	★★★/★★★★ D	★★★★/★★★★★ B
1994	★/★★ C	★/★★ C		★★★ C
1993	★★★★ B	★★★★ C		★★ D
1992	★★ C	★★ C		★★★★ C
1991	★★★/★★★★ C	★★★/★★★★ C		★★/★★★ D
1990	★★★★★ C	★★★★★ C	★★★★/★★★★★★ C	★★★/★★★★ C
1989	★★★★ C	★★★★ C		★★★★/★★★★★ C
1988	★★★★ C	★★★★ C		★★★/★★★★ D

Alsace vintage chart

	Riesling Grand or Top Cru	Pinot Gris Grand or Top Cru	Gewürztraminer Wines Grand or Top Cru	Late-Harvest Vendange Tardive or SGN
2004	★★★/★★★★ A	★★★/★★★★ A	★★★/★★★★ A	★★★ A
2003	★★★★ A	★★★★ A	★★★★ A	★★★/★★★★ A
2002	★★★★ A	★★★★/★★★★★ A	★★★★/★★★★★ A	★★★★ A
2001	★★★★ A	★★★★ A	★★★★ A	★★★★ A
2000	★★★★ A	★★★★ A	★★★★ A	★★★★ A
1999	★★★★ A	★★★/★★★★ B	★★★/★★★★ B	★★★★ A
1998	★★★★/★★★★★ B	★★★★ B	★★★★ B	★★★★/★★★★★ A
1997	★★★★ B	★★★★/★★★★★ B	★★★★/★★★★★ B	★★★★/★★★★★ B
1996	★★★★/★★★★★ B	★★★★/★★★★★ B	★★★★ B	★★★★/★★★★★ B
1995	★★★★/★★★★★ B	★★★★/★★★★★ B	★★★★ C	★★★★/★★★★★ B
1994	★★★ C	★★★ C	★★★ C	★★★★ B
1990	★★★★/★★★★★ C	★★★★/★★★★★ C	★★★★/★★★★★ C	★★★★/★★★★★ B
1989	★★★★ C	★★★★/★★★★★ C	★★★★/★★★★★ C	★★★★/★★★★★ B
1988	★★★★/★★★★★ C	★★★★ C	★★★★ C	★★★★ C
1985	★★★★ C	★★★★/★★★★★ C	★★★★ C	★★★★ C

Loire Valley vintage chart

	Anjou & Touraine Top Dry Whites inc Savennières	Anjou & Touraine Sweet Whites	Saumur & Touraine Top Red Cuvées	Sancerre & Pouilly- Fume Whites
2004	★★★★ A	★★★★ A	★★★★ A	★★★★ A
2003	★★★★/★★★★★ A	★★★★★ A	★★★★/★★★★★ A	★★★ C
2002	★★★★ A	★★★★ A	★★★/★★★★ A	★★★★/★★★★★ B
2001	★★★ A	★★★/★★★★ A	★★★/★★★★ A	★★★ C
2000	★★★/★★★★ B	★★★ B	★★★ A	★★★★/★★★★★ B
1999	★★★ B	★★★ B	★★★ A	★★★★/★★★★★ B
1998	★★★ B	★★★ B	★★★ B	★★★★/★★★★★ C
1997	★★★/★★★★ B	★★★★/★★★★★ B	★★★★ B	★★★★ C
1996	★★★★/★★★★★ B	★★★★/★★★★★ B	★★★★/★★★★★ B	★★★★ C
1995	★★★★ B	★★★★ B	★★★★/★★★★★ B	★★★★ C
1993	★★★ C	★★/★★★ C	★★★ D	★★★ D
1990	★★★★/★★★★★ B	★★★★/★★★★★ B	★★★★/★★★★★ C	★★★★/★★★★★ D
1989	★★★★/★★★★★ C	★★★★★ C	★★★★/★★★★★ C	–
1988	★★★★ C	★★★★ C	★★★★ C	–

Rhône Valley vintage chart

	Côte-Rôtie	Red Hermitage	White Hermitage	Châteauneuf -du-Pape
2004	★★★★ A	★★★★ A	★★★★ A	★★★★ A
2003	★★★/★★★★ A	★★★/★★★★ A	★★★★ A	★★★/★★★★ A
2002	★★ B	★★ A	★★/★★★★ A	★★ A
2001	★★★★ A	★★★★ A	★★★★/★★★★★ A	★★★★ A
2000	★★★★/★★★★★ A	★★★★ A	★★★★ A	★★★★/★★★★★ A
1999	★★★★/★★★★★ A	★★★★/★★★★★ A	★★★★/★★★★★ A	★★★★ B
1998	★★★★ A	★★★★ A	★★★★ A	★★★★★ B
1997	★★★/★★★★ B	★★★/★★★★ A	★★★/★★★★ A	★★★ C
1996	★★★ C	★★★ C	★★★/★★★★ B	★★/★★★ C
1995	★★★★CB	★★★★ B	★★★/★★★★ C	★★★★ C
1994	★★★/★★★★ C	★★★/★★★★ C	★★★/★★★★ C	★★★ C
1991	★★★★★ B	★★★★ C	★★★★ C	★/★★ D
1990	★★★★ C	★★★★★ B	★★★★/★★★★★ C	★★★★/★★★★★ C
1989	★★★★ C	★★★★/★★★★★ C	★★★★ C	★★★★/★★★★★ C
1988	★★★★ C	★★★★ C	★★★★/★★★★★ C	★★★★ C

Languedoc & Roussillon vintage chart

	Corbieres & Minervois	Coteaux du Languedoc	Côtes duRoussillon-Villages including Collioure
2004	★★★★ A	★★★★ A	★★★★ A
2003	★★★★ A	★★★★ A	★★★★ A
2003	★★★/★★★★ A	★★★/★★★★ A	★★★★ A
2002	★★★ B	★★★ A	★★★/★★★★ A
2001	★★★★/★★★★★ B	★★★★/★★★★★ A	★★★★/★★★★★ A
2000	★★★★/★★★★★ B	★★★★/★★★★★ B	★★★★ B
1999	★★★/★★★★ B	★★★/★★★★ B	★★★★ B
1998	★★★★/★★★★★ B	★★★★/★★★★★ B	★★★★★ B
1997	★★/★★★ D	★★/★★★C	★★★ C
1996	★★★ C	★★★ C	★★★ C
1995	★★★★ C	★★★★ C	★★★★ C
1994	★★★ D	★★★ D	★★★/★★★★ C
1993	★★★/★★★★ D	★★★/★★★★ C	★★★/★★★★ C
1991	★★/★★★ D	★★/★★★ D	★★/★★★ D
1990	★★★★★ D	★★★★ D	★★★★ C

Provence vintage chart

	Bandol	Côtes de Provence Top Reds	Les Baux de Provence Top Reds
2004	★★★/★★★★ A	★★★/★★★★ A	★★★/★★★★ A
2003	★★★★ A	★★★/★★★★ A	★★★/★★★★ A
2002	★★★ A	★★★ A	★★★ A
2001	★★★★ A	★★★★ A	★★★★ A
2000	★★★★/★★★★★ A	★★★★/★★★★★ B	★★★★/★★★★★ A
1999	★★★★ A	★★★★ B	★★★★ B
1998	★★★★/★★★★★ A	★★★★/★★★★★ B	★★★★/★★★★★ B
1997	★★★/★★★★ B	★★★ C	★★★C
1996	★★★/★★★★ B	★★★/★★★★ C	★★★/★★★★ C
1995	★★★/★★★★ C	★★★/★★★★ C	★★★/★★★★ C
1994	★★★ C	★★★ D	★★★ C
1993	★★★/★★★★ C	★★/★★★ D	★★/★★★ D
1991	★★★/★★★★ C	★★★ D	★★★ D
1990	★★★★★ B	★★★★★ D	★★★★★ C

Piedmont vintage chart

	Barolo	Barbaresco	Barbera (premium)
2004	NYR	NYR	NYR
2003	NYR	★★/★★★★ A	★★★/★★★★ B
2002	★/★★★ B	★/★★★ B	★/★★ C
2001	★★★★/★★★★★ A	★★★★/★★★★★ A	★★★★ B
2000	★★★/★★★★★ A	★★★/★★★★★ A	★★★★/★★★★★ B
1999	★★★★/★★★★★ A	★★★★/★★★★★ A	★★★/★★★★ C
1998	★★★★ B	★★★★ B	★★★★ C
1997	★★★★/★★★★★ B	★★★★/★★★★★ B	★★★★ /★★★★★ C
1996	★★★★/★★★★★ B	★★★★/★★★★★ B	★★★ C
1995	★★★/★★★★ C	★★★/★★★★ B	★★★/★★★★ C
1994	★★/★★★ C	★★/★★★ C	★★/★★★ D
1993	★★★ C	★★★ C	★★★ C
1992	★/★★ C	★/★★ C	★/★★ D
1991	★★/★★★ C	★★ C	★★★ D
1990	★★★★/★★★★★ C	★★★★/★★★★★ C	★★★★/★★★★★ D
1989	★★★★/★★★★★ C	★★★★/★★★★★ C	★★★★/★★★★★ D
1988	★★★/★★★★ C	★★★/★★★★ C	★★★/★★★★ D

Tuscany vintage chart

	Chianti Classico (Riserva)	Vino Nobile di Montepulciano	Brunello di di Montalcino	Bolgheri/Suvereto
2004	NYR	NYR	NYR	NYR
2003	★★★/★★★★ A	★★★/★★★★ A	NYR	★★★/★★★★ A
2002	★★ A	★/★★ A	NYR	★/★★★ A
2001	★★★★ A	★★★/★★★★ A	★★★★/★★★★★ A	★★★★ A
2000	★★★/★★★★ B	★★★ B	★★★ A	★★★★ A
1999	★★★★/★★★★★★ B	★★★★/★★★★★ B	★★★★/★★★★★ A	★★★★/★★★★★ B
1998	★★★ B	★★★/★★★★ B	★★★/★★★★ B	★★★/★★★★ B
1997	★★★★★ B	★★★★★ B	★★★★★ B	★★★★/★★★★★ B
1996	★★★ C	★★★ C	★★ C	★★★★ B
1995	★★★★ B	★★★/★★★★ C	★★★★ B	★★★/★★★★ C
1994	★★★ C	★★★ C	★★★ C	★★★ C
1993	★★★/★★★★ C	★★★ C	★★★★ B	★★★/★★★★ C
1992	★★ D	★/★★ D	★/★★ C	★★ C
1991	★★★ C	★★★ C	★★★/★★★★ C	★★★ C
1990	★★★★/★★★★★ C	★★★★/★★★★★ C	★★★★/★★★★★ B	★★★★/★★★★★ C
1989	★★/★★★ D	★★/★★★ D	★★★/★★★★ C	★★★ C
1988	★★★★ C	★★★★ C	★★★★ C	★★★★ C

Spanish vintage chart

	Rioja	Ribera del Duero	Priorat
2004	★★★★ A	★★★★ A	★★★★ A
2003	★★★★ A	★★★★/★★★★★ A	★★★★ A
2002	★★★/★★★★ A	★★★/★★★★ A	★★★/★★★★ A
2001	★★★★/★★★★★ B	★★★★/★★★★★ A	★★★★ A
2000	★★★ B	★★★ A	★★★/★★★★ A
1999	★★★/★★★★ B	★★★/★★★★ B	★★★/★★★★ B
1998	★★★ B	★★★/★★★★ B	★★★★/★★★★★ A
1997	★★★ B	★★★ B	★★★ B
1996	★★★ C	★★★★ B	★★★★ B
1995	★★★★ C	★★★★ B	★★★★ B
1994	★★★★/★★★★★ C	★★★★ C	★★★★/★★★★★ B
1993	★★★ C	★★/★★★ C	★★★/★★★★ C
1990	★★★/★★★★ C	★★★★ C	★★★★ C

Port vintage chart Portuguese red vintage chart

			Douro	Dão	Alentejo
2004	NYR	2004	★★★/★★★★ A	★★★/★★★★ A	★★★/★★★★ A
2003	★★★★/★★★★★ A	2003	★★★★/★★★★★ A	★★★/★★★★★ A	★★★/★★★★★ A
2000	★★★★/★★★★★ A	2002	★★/★★★★ B	★★/★★★ B	★★★/★★★★ B
1997	★★★/★★★★ A	2001	★★★★/★★★★★ A	★★★★ A	★★★★ B
1995	★★★ B	2000	★★★★/★★★★★ A	★★★★ B	★★★★ B
1994	★★★★★ A	1999	★★★/★★★★ B	★★★ B	★★★/★★★★ B
1992	★★★★ B	1998	★★/★★★ B	★★ C	★★/★★★ B
1991	★★★/★★★★ B	1997	★★★★ B	★★★★/★★★★★ B	★★★★ C
1987	★★/★★★ C	1996	★★/★★★ B	★★★★ B	★★/★★★ C
1985	★★/★★★★ A	1995	★★★/★★★★ B	★★★/★★★★ C	★★★★ C
1983	★★★★ C	1994	★★★★/★★★★★ C	★★★/★★★★ C	★★★ C
1980	★★★ C	1992	★★★★ C	★★★/★★★★ C	★★/★★★ D
1977	★★★★/★★★★★ C	1991	★★★★ C	★★★/★★★★ C	★★★/★★★★ C
1970	★★★★ C	1990	★★★ D	★★/★★★ D	★★★★ D
1966	★★★★/★★★★★ C				
1963	★★★★★ C				

VINTAGE CHARTS

VINTAGE CHARTS

German vintage chart

	Mosel Riesling	Rhine Riesling	Pfalz Riesling
2004	★★★★ A	★★★★ A	★★★★ A
2003	★★★★/★★★★★ A	★★★★/★★★★★ A	★★★★/★★★★★ A
2002	★★★★/★★★★★ A	★★★★/★★★★★ A	★★★★/★★★★★ A
2001	★★★★★ B	★★★★★ B	★★★★★ B
2000	★★★/★★★★ B	★★★ B	★★/★★★ B
1999	★★★/★★★★ B	★★★/★★★★ B	★★★★ B
1998	★★★★ B	★★★★ B	★★★★/★★★★★ B
1997	★★★★ B	★★★/★★★★ C	★★★/★★★★ C
1996	★★★/★★★★ C	★★★★ C	★★★★/★★★★★ B
1995	★★★★/★★★★★ B	★★★/★★★★ B	★★/★★★ C
1994	★★★★ C	★★★★ C	★★★/★★★★ C
1993	★★★★ C	★★★★ C	★★★★ C
1992	★★★/★★★★ C	★★★/★★★★ C	★★★/★★★★ C
1991	★★★/★★★★ C	★★/★★★ D	★★/★★★ D
1990	★★★★★ C	★★★★★ C	★★★★★ C

Austrian vintage chart

	Wachau/Kremstal/Kamptal Riesling	Wachau/Kremstal/Kamptal Grüner Veltliner	Neusiedlersee/N-Hügelland Sweet whites
2004	★★★★ A	★★★★ A	NYR
2003	★★/★★★★ B	★★/★★★★ B	★★★★/★★★★★ A
2002	★★★/★★★★ B	★★★/★★★★ B	★★★★ B
2001	★★★★/★★★★★ B	★★★★/★★★★★ B	★★★/★★★★ B
2000	★★★★ B	★★★★ B	★★★★/★★★★★ B
1999	★★★★★ B	★★★★★ B	★★★★ B
1998	★★★/★★★★ C	★★★/★★★★ C	★★★★ B
1997	★★★★★ B	★★★★★ C	★★★★ B*
1996	★★ C	★★ D	★★★ C
1995	★★★★ B	★★★★ C	★★★★★ B
1994	★★★ C	★★★ D	★★/★★★ C
1993	★★★/★★★★ C	★★★/★★★★ C	★★★★ C
1992	★★★ C	★★★ D	★★/★★★ D
1991	★★/★★★ D	★★★ C	★★★★ C
1990	★★★★/★★★★★ C	★★★★/★★★★★ C	

368

* little produced

California North Coast vintage chart

	Pinot Noir	Chardonnay	Zinfandel	Cabernet Sauvignon
2004	★★★/★★★★ A	★★★/★★★★ B	★★★/★★★★ A	★★★/★★★★ A
2003	★★★★ A	★★★★ B	★★★★/★★★★★★ A	★★★★/★★★★★★ A
2002	★★★★ B	★★★★ B	★★★★ A	★★★★A
2001	★★★★ B	★★★★ B	★★★★ B	★★★★/★★★★★★ A
2000	★★★/★★★★B	★★★ B	★★/★★★ B	★★★ B
1999	★★★★ B	★★★/★★★★ B	★★★★ B	★★★/★★★★ B
1998	★★★/★★★★ B	★★★/★★★★ C	★★/★★★ C	★★★ B
1997	★★★★ C	★★★★ C	★★★/★★★★ C	★★★★ B
1996	★★★/★★★★ C	★★★ C	★★★/★★★★ C	★★★/★★★★ B
1995	★★★/★★★★ C	★★★★ C	★★★/★★★★ C	★★★★ B
1994	★★★★ D	★★★/★★★★ D	★★★★ C	★★★★ B
1993	★★★/★★★★ D	★★★★ D	★★★/★★★★ C	★★★/★★★★ B
1992	★★★/★★★★ D		★★★/★★★★ C	★★★★ C
1991		–	★★★★ D	★★★★ C
1990	–	–	★★★★ D	★★★★ C

California Napa & Carneros vintage chart

	Cabernet and Meritage Blends	Zinfandel	Pinot Noir	Chardonnay
2004	★★★/★★★★ A	★★★/★★★★ A	★★★★ A	★★★★ A
2003	★★★★/★★★★★★ A	★★★★/★★★★★ A	★★★★ A	★★★★ B
2002	★★★★ A	★★★★ A	★★★★ B	★★★★ B
2001	★★★★/★★★★★★ A	★★★★ A	★★★★ B	★★★★ B
2000	★★/★★★ A	★★/★★★ B	★★★/★★★★ B	★★★/★★★★ B
1999	★★★/★★★★ A	★★★★ B	★★★★ B	★★★/★★★★ C
1998	★★★ B	★★/★★★ C	★★★/★★★★ C	★★★ C
1997	★★★★ A	★★★/★★★★ B	★★★★ C	★★★★ C
1996	★★★/★★★★ B	★★★/★★★★ C	★★★/★★★★ C	★★★ C
1995	★★★★ B	★★★/★★★★ C	★★★/★★★★ C	★★★★ D
1994	★★★★/★★★★★★ B	★★★★ C	★★★★ C	★★★/★★★★ D
1993	★★★★ B	★★★/★★★★ C	★★★ D	★★★★ D
1992	★★★★ C	★★★/★★★★ C	★★★/★★★★ D	
1991	★★★★ C	★★★★ C		–

California Central Coast vintage chart

	Pinot Noir South Central Coast	Syrah South Central Coast	Cabernet Sauvignon Santa Cruz Area	Zinfandel Amador County
2004	★★★★ A	★★★/★★★★ A	★★★/★★★★ A	★★★/★★★★ A
2003	★★★★ A	★★★★ A	★★★★ A	★★★★ A
2002	★★★★ B	★★★★ A	★★★★ A	★★★★ A
2001	★★★/★★★★ B	★★★★ B	★★★★ A	★★★★ B
2000	★★★★ B	★★★/★★★★ B	★★★★ A	★★★★ B
1999	★★★★ C	★★★/★★★★ B	★★★/★★★★ B	★★★/★★★★ B
1998	★★★/★★★★ C	★★★/★★★★ B	★★★★ B	★★★/★★★★ B
1997	★★★★ C	★★★★ C	★★★★ B	★★★★ C
1996	★★★★ C	★★★/★★★★ C	★★★★ B	★★★/★★★★ C
1995	★★★★ C	★★★/★★★★ C	★★★/★★★★ B	★★★/★★★★ C
1994	★★★/★★★★ D	★★★/★★★★ C	★★★★ B	★★★/★★★★ C
1993	★★★/★★★★ D	★★★/★★★★ C	★★★★/★★★★★ B	★★★★ C
1992	★★★/★★★★ D	★★★★ C	★★★★ C	★★★/★★★★ D
1991		★★★★ D	★★★★/★★★★★ C	★★★/★★★★ D
1990	–	★★★★ D	★★★★ C	–

South Australia vintage chart

	Barossa/Clare Shiraz	Coonawarra Cabernet	Clare/Eden Valley Riesling	Adelaide Hills Chardonnay
2005	★★★★/★★★★★★ A	★★★★ A	★★★★/★★★★★★ A	★★★★/★★★★★ A
2004	★★★/★★★★ A	★★★★/★★★★★ A	★★★ B	★★★★/★★★★★ B
2003	★★/★★★ A	★★★★ A	★★★/★★★★ B	★★★★ B
2002	★★★★/★★★★★ A	★★★★/★★★★★ A	★★★★★ B	★★★★★ B
2001	★★★★ B	★★★/★★★★ B	★★★/★★★★B	★★★ B
2000	★★★ B	★★★★/★★★★★★ A	★★★/★★★★ C	★★★ C
1999	★★★/★★★★ B	★★★★ B	★★★/★★★★ C	★★★/★★★★ C
1998	★★★★★ A	★★★★★ B	★★★★ C	★★★/★★★★★ C
1997	★★★★ B	★★★/★★★★ B	★★★★★ C	★★★★ C
1996	★★★★/★★★★★ B	★★★★ B	★★★★/★★★★★ C	★★★★/★★★★★ C
1995	★★★/★★★★ B	★★ C	★★★★ C	★★★★/★★★★★ D
1994	★★★★/★★★★★ B	★★★★ B	★★★★ C	★★★/★★★★ D
1993	★★★/★★★★ C	★★★/★★★★ C	★★★/★★★★ D	
1991	★★★★/★★★★★ C	★★★★/★★★★★ C	★★★★ C	
1990	★★★★/★★★★★ C	★★★★★ C	★★★★★ C	

Victoria & Tasmania vintage chart

	Bendigo/Heathcote Shiraz	Grampians/Pyrenees Shiraz	Yarra Valley Pinot Noir	Tasmanian Pinot Noir
2005	★★★★/★★★★★ A	★★★★/★★★★★ A	★★★★/★★★★★ A	★★★★/★★★★★ A
2004	★★★★ A	★★★★ A	★★★ A	★★/★★★★ A
2003	★★★★/★★★★★ A	★★★★ A	★★★★/★★★★★ B	★★★★ B
2002	★★★★★ A	★★★★/★★★★★ A	★★★★★ B	★★★★/★★★★★ B
2001	★★★★★ B	★★★★/★★★★★ B	★★★★ B	★★★/★★★★ B
2000	★★★★ B	★★★/★★★★ B	★★★★/★★★★★ B	★★★★ B
1999	★★★★ B	★★★★ B	★★★/★★★★ C	★★★/★★★★ C
1998	★★★★★ B	★★★★/★★★★★ B	★★★★/★★★★★ C	★★★★/★★★★★ C
1997	★★★★/★★★★★ B	★★★★ B	★★★★/★★★★★ C	★★★★ C
1996	★★★★ B	★★★★/★★★★★ B		
1995	★★★ C	★★★/★★★★ C		
1994	★★★★ C	★★★★ C		
1993	★★★ D	★★/★★★ D		
1992	★★★/★★★★ C	★★★/★★★★ C		
1991	★★★★/★★★★★ C	★★★★/★★★★★ C		
1990	★★★★★ C	★★★★/★★★★★ C		

New South Wales vintage chart

	Hunter Valley Shiraz	Central Ranges Shiraz	Hunter Valley Semillon
2005	★★★★ A	★★★★ A	★★★★/★★★★★ A
2004	★★/★★★★ A	★★★★ A	★★★ A
2003	★★★★★ A	★★★/★★★★ A	★★★★★ A
2002	★★★/★★★★ A	★★★★/★★★★★ A	★★★★ A
2001	★★★/★★★★ B	★★/★★★ B	★★★/★★★★ B
2000	★★★★/★★★★★ B	★★/★★★ B	★★★★/★★★★★ B
1999	★★★★ B	★★★/★★★★ B	★★★★ B
1998	★★★★★ B	★★★★ B	★★★★★ B
1997	★★★ C	★★/★★★ C	★★★/★★★★ C
1996	★★★★/★★★★★ B	★★★★ B	★★★★/★★★★★ B
1995	★★★/★★★★ C	★★★★/★★★★★ C	★★★/★★★★ C
1994	★★★/★★★★ C	★★★★ C	★★★★ C
1993	★★★/★★★★ C	★★/★★★ C	★★★/★★★★ C
1992	★★★ D	★★/★★★ C	★★★/★★★★ C
1991	★★★★★ C	★★★/★★★★ C	★★★★/★★★★★ C

VINTAGE CHARTS

Western Australia vintage chart

	Margaret River Cabernet	Great Southern Shiraz	Margaret River Chardonnay
2005	★★★★/★★★★★★ A	★★★★/★★★★★ A	★★★★/★★★★★ A
2004	★★★/★★★★★★ A	★★★★/★★★★★ A	★★★★/★★★★★ B
2003	★★★/★★★★ A	★★★ A	★★★/★★★★ B
2002	★★★★ A	★★★★ B	★★★★/★★★★★★ B
2001	★★★★★ B	★★★★★ B	★★★★★ C
2000	★★★/★★★★ B	★★★ B	★★★/★★★★ C
1999	★★★★/★★★★★★ B	★★★ B	★★★★ C
1998	★★★ C	★★★ C	★★★ D
1997	★★★★ C	★★★★ C	★★★★/★★★★★ C
1996	★★★★/★★★★★ C	★★★★/★★★★★ C	★★★★ C
1995	★★★★/★★★★★ C	★★★★/★★★★★ C	★★★★★ C
1994	★★★★★ C	★★★★/★★★★★★ C	★★★★/★★★★★ D
1993	★★★★ C	★★/★★★ D	
1992	★★★/★★★★ C	★★★★ C	
1991	★★★★/★★★★★ C	★★★/★★★★ D	

New Zealand vintage chart

	Hawkes Bay reds	Martinborough Pinot Noir	Central Otago Pinot Noir
2005	★★★/★★★★ A	★★★/★★★★ A	★★★/★★★★ A
2004	★★★★/★★★★★★ A	★★★★ A	★★/★★★ A
2003	★★★ B	★★★ B	★★★★/★★★★★★ B
2002	★★★★/★★★★★★ B	★★★★/★★★★★ C	★★★★★ C
2001	★★★ B	★★★/★★★★ C	★★★★/★★★★★ C
2000	★★★★/★★★★★★ B	★★★★ C	★★★★/★★★★★ C
1999	★★★/★★★★ C	★★★★ C	★★★★ C
1998	★★★★★ C	★★★★★ C	★★★★/★★★★★ C
1997	★★★★ C	★★★★/★★★★★★ D	
1996	★★/★★★ C	★★★★/★★★★★ D	
1995	★★★ D		
1994	★★★★ C		

Index

This producer index is ordered by the name to which an estate is most commonly referred. There is priority to surnames but otherwise they appear as they are written. 'Domaine' is ignored but 'Château', 'Castello', 'Quinta' etc are respected as is the definite article when implicitly part of the name (eg Il Poggione appears under 'I'). The only exception is in Bordeaux where 'Château' is also ignored and the name of the château or estate takes precedent.

Index

INDEX

Index